Technology Transfer and Strategic Applications for Commercial Human-AI Interaction

Muhammad Abdus Salam
https://orcid.org/0000-0001-9599-632X
Universiti Brunei Darussalam, Brunei

Vai Shiem Leong
Universiti Brunei Darussalam, Brunei

Nazlida Muhamad
https://orcid.org/0000-0003-2790-8900
Prince Sultan University, Saudi Arabia

IGI Global
Scientific Publishing
Publishing Tomorrow's Research Today

Vice President of Editorial	Melissa Wagner
Director of Acquisitions	Mikaela Felty
Director of Book Development	Jocelynn Hessler
Production Manager	Mike Brehm
Cover Design	Jose Rosado

Published in the United States of America by
IGI Global Scientific Publishing
701 East Chocolate Avenue
Hershey, PA, 17033, USA
Tel: 717-533-8845 | Fax: 717-533-7115
Website: https://www.igi-global.com E-mail: cust@igi-global.com

Library of Congress Cataloging-in-Publication Data

LCCN: 2026012238 (CIP Data Pending)
ISBN13: 9798337393254
Isbn13Softcover: 9798337393261
EISBN13: 9798337393278
British Cataloguing in Publication Data
A Cataloguing in Publication record for this book is available from the British Library.

Editorial Advisory Board

Table of Contents

Detailed Table of Contents

Md. Sobhan Ali, Begum Rokeya University, Bangladesh
Sadia Akter, International American University, USA
Afsana Mimi, Begum Rokeya University, Bangladesh
Md Ferdaus Ahmed Pranto, The People's University of Bangladesh, Bangladesh
Promit Roy, Rangamati Science and Technology University, Bangladesh

The development of commercial human-AI interactions commercializes human-AI interactions because it transforms how consumers and companies and platforms engage with each other as well as how they choose which products or services to buy and how they create market value. The chapter conducts a systematic review which uses PRISMA 2020 to analyze empirical and review literature from 2020 to 2026 until February 1 2026 through Scopus and Web of Science. The investigated publications present comprehensive evaluations of the primary results which stem from human-AI interactions including market efficiency and various benefits and customer experience and trust and transparency and decision making quality. The chapter shows how AI systems create unfair results because of their design and operational features which affect different consumer groups in various market sectors. The framework creates an integrative conceptual model which connects all evidence from the chapter with the interaction design features of AI systems.

This chapter is a systematic review of 73 Scopus-indexed articles (2019-2026) on the human-AI interaction transforming marketing by providing personalization, automation, and conversational interface. It combines fragmented knowledge about human-computer interaction, marketing, and consumer psychology to describe why augmentation and not complete automation provide the best results: a 47 percent increase in engagement and a 31 percent increase in conversion upon combining human creativity and AI analytics. A Tripartite Interaction Framework presented in the chapter connects AI design cues, user psychology, and marketing context via propositions testable through research. The analysis of qualitative themes indicates that there exist opportunities (hyper-personalization, scalable service, richer engagement) and challenges such as algorithm aversion, privacy issues, issues with the quality of the data, and organizational resistance to implement human-in-the-loop, emotionally intelligent, transparent AI to realize ethical, high-performance human -AI marketing systems.

The chapter discusses how Artificial Intelligence (AI) is commercialized in the marketing, healthcare, financial, and logistics industries, which illustrates the disjointed technology transfer processes. It identifies phases of AI commercialization, such as finding, intellectual property protection, validation, scaling, and governance, concentrating on intellectual property management, university-industry collaboration, and startup ecosystems. The chapter combines findings about two critical areas transfer object and process enabler through a PRISMA-based systematic literature review (3,645 studies). The TOE-DCV framework has combined Technologies and Organization Environment settings and dynamic capabilities, focusing on AI-related enablers such as data governance and regulatory compliance. The chapter represents TTO capabilities, obstacles, and geopolitical variations with some solutions such

Preface

INTRODUCTION

Artificial Intelligence (AI) has rapidly evolved from a specialized technological innovation into a transformative force shaping nearly every sector of the global economy and business. As AI systems become increasingly integrated into commercial environments, organizations are confronted with both unprecedented opportunities and complex challenges associated with technology adoption, market deployment, governance, and human interaction. The commercialization of AI is no longer solely a technical endeavor; rather, it requires a multidisciplinary understanding of technology transfer, organizational readiness, consumer behavior, ethical considerations, and strategic implementation. This volume, *Technology Transfer and Strategic Applications for Commercial Human-AI Interaction*, was conceived to address these interconnected dimensions and provide a comprehensive examination of how AI technologies move from innovation ecosystems into practical commercial applications.

The growing prominence of human-AI interaction has fundamentally reshaped the ways businesses engage with customers, employees, and stakeholders. AI-powered systems increasingly influence decision-making processes, personalize consumer experiences, optimize operational performance, and redefine organizational structures. Yet, alongside these advancements emerge concerns surrounding transparency, trust, privacy, bias, workforce transformation, and regulatory oversight. Successfully navigating these challenges requires a balanced understanding of both technological capabilities and human-centered design principles. This book seeks to bridge these perspectives by bringing together contributions from scholars across disciplines including marketing, management, information systems, supply chain management, tourism, human resource management, and technology transfer studies.

A central theme running throughout this volume is the process of technology transfer—the mechanisms through which AI innovations are transformed from research outputs into scalable commercial solutions. While substantial attention has been devoted to AI development, comparatively less focus has been placed on the pathways that facilitate successful commercialization and sustainable adoption. The chapters collected here explore these pathways from multiple angles, examining institutional structures, governance frameworks, innovation ecosystems, national readiness, and sector-specific applications. Together, they provide valuable insights into how organizations can effectively translate AI capabilities into meaningful economic and societal value.

As editors, we believe this volume arrives at a particularly important moment. The rapid acceleration of AI deployment across industries has created a pressing need for research that integrates technological innovation with practical implementation and responsible governance. The contributions in this book offer both theoretical advancements and practical guidance for researchers, practitioners, policymakers, technology transfer professionals, and organizational leaders seeking to understand and shape the future of commercial human-AI interaction. Through diverse perspectives and international case studies, this volume contributes to ongoing conversations regarding the responsible commercialization of AI technologies in a rapidly changing global landscape.

OVERVIEW OF THE CHAPTERS

The volume opens with Chapter 1, which provides a systematic review of commercial human-AI interaction within digital markets. The authors examine opportunities, risks, and policy challenges associated with AI-enabled consumer engagement while proposing an integrative conceptual framework linking AI design characteristics with market outcomes and consumer experiences.

Chapter 2 extends the discussion into the marketing domain by synthesizing theoretical and empirical evidence regarding human-AI interaction in marketing environments. The chapter introduces a Tripartite Interaction Framework that connects AI design, consumer psychology, and marketing contexts while highlighting opportunities and barriers associated with AI-enabled marketing strategies.

In Chapter 3, attention shifts toward technology commercialization processes. The author investigates pathways through which AI innovations move from research environments into market applications and develops the TOE-DCV framework to explain how technological, organizational, environmental, and dynamic capability factors influence successful technology transfer.

Chapter 4 addresses one of the most persistent challenges in innovation ecosystems—the "Valley of Death" between technological development and market adoption. The authors propose an integrated framework that combines technology readiness, consumer readiness, ethical legitimacy, and governance considerations to improve the commercialization success of AI-driven personalization technologies.

Chapter 5 offers a comparative international perspective by examining technology transfer readiness across the United States, Germany, Japan, and India. Through benchmarking and cross-national analysis, the chapter highlights how differing innovation systems, policy environments, and commercialization infrastructures shape AI adoption and scalability.

Chapter 6 explores the strategic implications of AI adoption within Human Resource Management. The authors investigate how AI technologies transform recruitment, performance management, learning and development, and job design while emphasizing the importance of human-centered technology transfer and responsible organizational integration.

Chapter 7 examines AI-driven decision support systems within supply chain and logistics management. The chapter demonstrates how machine learning, predictive analytics, and optimization technologies enhance forecasting, inventory management, operational efficiency, and organizational resilience while addressing implementation challenges and ethical concerns.

Chapter 8 focuses on AI as an enabler of Integrated Brand Communication. The authors discuss how AI technologies support personalized communication, content creation, predictive analytics, and stakeholder engagement while emphasizing the importance of governance, transparency, and human oversight in branding strategies.

Chapter 9 investigates the transformative role of augmented reality and virtual reality technologies in commercial environments. Through a structured review of AI-enhanced immersive technologies, the chapter examines their impact on consumer experiences, e-commerce, healthcare, tourism, and educational applications.

Chapter 10 presents an innovative application of Graph Neural Networks for tourism analytics. By integrating machine learning and graph-based approaches, the authors develop predictive models for rating Indian tourist destinations and demonstrate the growing potential of AI-enabled recommendation systems within tourism ecosystems.

Chapter 11 provides a case study examining AI-based user experience enhancement in online book retail platforms. Using the MyBookOne platform as an example, the authors propose a systematic framework for improving search capabilities, personalization, customer service, and platform usability through AI integration.

The volume concludes with Chapter 12, which introduces Generative Engine Optimization (GEO) as a strategic capability for digital marketing communication in the era of generative AI and large language models. The chapter develops a capability-based framework that positions GEO as a critical mechanism for visibility, relevance, and engagement within AI-mediated digital ecosystems.

Collectively, these chapters provide a multidimensional examination of commercial human-AI interaction, highlighting both foundational theories and practical applications across diverse industries and organizational contexts.

CONCLUSION

The accelerating convergence of artificial intelligence, technology transfer, and commercial innovation is transforming the way organizations create value, interact with stakeholders, and compete in increasingly digital markets. As demonstrated throughout this volume, the successful deployment of AI technologies depends not only on technical sophistication but also on the effectiveness of commercialization pathways, governance structures, organizational capabilities, and human-centered implementation strategies. The chapters presented herein collectively reinforce the notion that technological advancement alone is insufficient without thoughtful consideration of ethical, social, and managerial dimensions.

A recurring insight emerging from this collection is the importance of balancing automation with human oversight. Whether examining marketing systems, supply chain optimization, human resource management, immersive technologies, tourism analytics, or digital commerce, the contributors consistently emphasize that sustainable AI adoption requires collaboration between human expertise and intelligent systems. Human-AI interaction is therefore best understood not as a replacement paradigm but as a partnership model capable of enhancing decision-making, innovation, and organizational performance.

This volume also underscores the growing significance of technology transfer ecosystems in determining the success of AI commercialization efforts. Universities, research institutions, industry partners, startups, policymakers, and regulatory bodies each play critical roles in facilitating innovation diffusion and market adoption. Effective collaboration among these stakeholders will be essential for overcoming barriers to commercialization, reducing implementation risks, and ensuring that AI innovations generate broad societal and economic benefits.

As editors, we hope this book serves as both a scholarly resource and a practical guide for understanding the evolving landscape of commercial human-AI interaction. The insights presented throughout these chapters offer valuable directions for future research, policy development, and organizational practice. While AI technologies will undoubtedly continue to evolve, the fundamental challenges surrounding trust, ethics, governance, and human engagement will remain central to their success. It is our expectation that this volume will contribute meaningfully to ongoing discussions and inspire future investigations into the responsible, effective, and sustainable commercialization of artificial intelligence in a rapidly changing world.

Muhammad Abdus Salam

Universiti Brunei Darussalam, Brunei & Noakhali Science and Technology University, Bangladesh

Vai Shiem Leong

Universiti Brunei Darussalam, Brunei

Nazlida Muhamad

Prince Sultan University, Saudi Arabia

Acknowledgment

The editors sincerely thank all authors and reviewers whose dedication, expertise, and valuable contributions made this book possible. We are especially grateful to the chapter authors for sharing their knowledge and to the reviewers for their thoughtful evaluations, which significantly enhanced the quality and coherence of the manuscript. We also express our appreciation to the UBD School of Business and Economics, Universiti Brunei Darussalam, Brunei Darussalam; Prince Sultan University, Saudi Arabia; and Noakhali Science and Technology University, Bangladesh, for providing a supportive research environment and institutional assistance throughout this project. Finally, we extend our heartfelt thanks to the entire IGI Global publishing team for their guidance and professional support from the proposal stage through publication, with special appreciation to Jocelynn Hessler, Mikaela Vargo, Melissa Wagner, Puja Phuyel, Daniel Kreiss, and Caitlin Meehan for their invaluable contributions.

Muhammad Abdus Salam
Universiti Brunei Darussalam, Brunei & Noakhali Science and Technology University, Bangladesh

Vai Shiem Leong
Universiti Brunei Darussalam, Brunei

Nazlida Muhamad
Prince Sultan University, Saudi Arabia

Chapter 1
Commercial Human-Artificial Intelligence Interaction in Digital Markets: Opportunities, Risks, and Policy Challenges

Md. Sobhan Ali
Begum Rokeya University, Bangladesh

Sadia Akter
http://orcid.org/0009-0003-8262-7076
International American University, USA

Afsana Mimi
http://orcid.org/0000-0003-1055-9919
Begum Rokeya University, Bangladesh

Md Ferdaus Ahmed Pranto
http://orcid.org/0009-0009-8750-6795
The People's University of Bangladesh, Bangladesh

Promit Roy
http://orcid.org/0009-0008-9354-0626
Rangamati Science and Technology University, Bangladesh

DOI: 10.4018/979-8-3373-9325-4.ch001

ABSTRACT

The development of commercial human-AI interactions commercializes human-AI interactions because it transforms how consumers and companies and platforms engage with each other as well as how they choose which products or services to buy and how they create market value. The chapter conducts a systematic review which uses PRISMA 2020 to analyze empirical and review literature from 2020 to 2026 until February 1 2026 through Scopus and Web of Science. The investigated publications present comprehensive evaluations of the primary results which stem from human-AI interactions including market efficiency and various benefits and customer experience and trust and transparency and decision making quality. The chapter shows how AI systems create unfair results because of their design and operational features which affect different consumer groups in various market sectors. The framework creates an integrative conceptual model which connects all evidence from the chapter with the interaction design features of AI systems.

INTRODUCTION

The swift multiplication of artificial intelligence (AI) technologies has fundamentally altered business environments, especially by means of human-AI interactions in the marketing, logistics, supply chains, and digital platforms (Sahut & Laroche, 2025). This chapter is called Commercial Human Artificial Interaction and investigates theoretical perspectives, evidence based on empirical data and future agendas on these dynamics using a systematic literature review (SLR) in accordance with PRISMA standards of rigor and replicability (Anam et al., 2026). The interaction between the human and the AI has historically become complex due to the progression of the simplistic human-computer interfaces to the advanced symbiotic relationships, where AI not only automates the operations, but also mediates communication and decision-making in the business (Abdul et al., 2018; Guzman and Lewis, 2020). This occurs in business contexts through AI-based virtual influencers, deepfake marketing and customized consumer experience, where traditional marketing is converting into an active, data-driven experience (Salam et al., 2026).

Moreover, the major platforms like Amazon and Alibaba Group use AI-based recommendation systems and dynamic pricing strategies to provide personalized services and maximize the efficiency of the market, thus providing a real-life example of the application of theoretical concepts. Similarly, the use of AI-based customer service tools by platforms like ChatGPT is an example of the application of theoretical concepts related to the use of human involvement and the capabilities of AI systems (Abdul et al., 2018; Virvou, 2022; Bhuiyan et al., 2026). Moreover, the use of algorithmic pricing strategies by companies like Uber is an example of the application of theoretical concepts related to the use of AI and its impact on the market. However, the application of AI-based tools by the aforementioned platforms also poses various challenges related to the privacy of the data and the biasness of the algorithm, as observed by the use of AI-based tools by major technology-based companies like Meta Platforms (Guzman and Lewis, 2020; Obrenovic et al., 2025).

BACKGROUND

The development of Industry 4.0, where human-AI cooperation represents a smart factory or automated logistics (Benotsmane et al., 2019; Klumpp, 2018). Such works as the one by Loureiro et al. (2021) summarize AI business research as the impacts that it has in society, the effect on organizations, systems, and methods, and identify marketing and regulations among the key areas. An example is that generative AI and human-robot interaction involves ethical business challenges, which require user agendas (Obrenovic et al., 2025; Jiang et al., 2024). The extended TAM models in Bangladesh and other emerging economies emphasize the aspects of adoption of AI platforms, with education being connected to commercial digitalization (Anam et al., 2026; Islam et al., 2026).

This is further placed into context by cybersecurity and big data analytics, in which machine learning mediates supply chain resilience and information security (Bhuiyan et al., 2024; Bhuiyan et al., 2025). Bibliometric analysis through sustainable development frameworks highlights the digitalized concept of green entrepreneurship where AI is integrated in the development of eco-commercial strategies (Faisal-E-Alam et al., 2025). Earlier studies such as Kitchenham et al. (2007) recommend use of empirical evidence rather than opinion in software engineering just the way a strong SLR is required in human-AI research. HRI architectures based on emotional intelligence facilitate cooperative relations in retail banking, and the degree of resistance in the logistics can indicate human factors (Erol et al., 2019; Klumpp, 2018).

The interplay of policies stands out, with AI influencing behavior through design and control (Charisi, 2025; Hancock et al., 2020). AI enables digital transformation and changes the value is created and delivered within the interactive marketing domain, often through machines mimicking intelligent human behavior (Peltier et al., 2024). Ethical attitudes of human-machine partnership are discussed at organizational symposia (Bahmani et al., 2024). Standard, substitute, superiority, synthesis affective computing and synthesis models conceptualize commercial posts and interplays, as firms focus on hybrid intelligence (Lichtenthaler, 2018; Lopes da Costa et al., 2019). The background of this chapter therefore cuts across the HCI agendas of explainability (Abdul et al., 2018; Virvou, 2022), ethical terrain (Gachayeva et al.,

2025), and PRISMA-synthesized gaps of 73 Scopus studies (2019-2026), including the e-commerce, platforms, and governance (file methodology details). All these factors put commercial human-AI interaction in the role of a multidisciplinary nexus, requiring joint analysis to make business viable.

The chapter brings together the multidisciplinary approach on marketing, logistics, supply chain management and policy models and provides a holistic perspective on this subject which has been sorely wanted in the literature (Krakowski et al., 2026). This is particularly applicable because the consumer experience and business processes are being redefined with increased speed by AI systems, such as personalization algorithms and engine-based recommendations (Moro-Visconti, 2026). The ethical, legal, and policy issues of human autonomy and decision-making impact by AI are also highlighted in the chapter and are getting more urgent as AI finds its way into daily consumer-focused exchanges (Jalilvand & Ataei, 2026). It is an important contribution to a reasoned debate around the regulation of such technologies, as by considering the overlap of AI functions and the industry of consumer protection, data privacy and fairness, this work will show that innovation may not be optimally aligned with moral principles and the well-being of society (Yu et al., 2025a; Ntoutsi et al., 2020). The chapter presents a substantiated basis of future research and policy making in this domain due to its stringent methodology, including a PRISMA-based systematic literature review.

Rationale of the Book Chapter

The justification of this chapter is based on the fact that there is a pressing need to integrate existing disjointed literature on commercial human-AI interaction in the face of the rapid uptake of AI in business. The classical reviews tend to ignore commercial specificity, e.g., the role of AI in marketing personalization and digitalization of supply chain, and a PRISMA-based SLR must be done to facilitate transparency (Riaj et al., 2025; Kitchenham et al., 2007). The gap in the synthesis of theoretical frameworks, such as TAM extensions and ISM-HBM hybrids of adoption and security, is filled in this chapter since the initial records found in Scopus were narrowed down to 73 relevant studies (Anam et al., 2026).

This is motivated by business needs: AI influencers and deepfakes transform consumer interaction, but the absence of ethical and policy frameworks (Salam et al., 2024). There are organizational effects, such as cybersecurity methods, BDAC mediation across healthcare-supply chains, which need to be thematically analyzed (Bhuiyan et al., 2025). Special attention is also based on the sustainability of digital transformation in the field of entrepreneurship (Khatun et al., 2025; Riaj et al., 2025). The HCI agendas focus on collaboration and solicit a multidisciplinary integration (Jiang et al., 2024; Abdul et al., 2018).

The socio-economic dynamics of smart factories require AI-robot relationships to operate socio-economically (Benotsmane et al., 2019), and human resistance to automation in logistics underlines the need to collaborate (Klumpp, 2018). Synthesis interplay -the added value of replacement- will help to create value because firms will shift towards hybrid forms (Lichtenthaler, 2018). Viable commerciality is ready by the emotional HRI and HHI tendencies (Gentile et al., 2011). The policy-research nexus addresses the influence of behaviour (Charisi, 2025; Hancock et al., 2020).

The SLR justification of this chapter is that PRISMA is reproducible and has screened 2,149 records after subtracting them (to map recurrent constructs, such as trust, bias, and symbiosis) (Obrenovic et al., 2025; Guzman and Lewis, 2020). It reacts to explainable AI and generative ethics agenda requests (Virvou, 2022; Gachayeva et al., 2025). The thematization of 73 studies offers practical implications to managers, policymakers, and researchers but closes the gap between the expert opinion and the evidence (Kitchenham et al., 2007; Loureiro et al., 2021). Finally, in the context of AI becoming a commercial reality, this chapter justifies a comprehensive approach to opportunities and risks exploration.

Significance of the Book Chapter

The chapter is relevant and contributed to the field of knowledge on commercial human-AI interaction, where synthesized knowledge is provided to practitioners, academics, and policymakers. It has enlightened the behavioral consequences of marketing personalization by PRISMA-analyzing 73 studies and informs practice in the light of virtual influencers (Salam et al., 2026). It is also important to supply chain resilience, whereby BDAC intermediates innovation through AI-human synergy (Bhuiyan et al., 2025).

In theory, it enhances HCI with user-based agendas, incorporating TAM to be adopted in new markets (Jiang et al., 2024). In practice, it directs the practices of cybersecurity and green digitalization. In Industry 4.0, it highlights the smart factory productivity through the cooperation of robots (Benotsmane et al., 2019). Morally, it deals with AI-MC and generative risks, which encourages responsible designs (Hancock et al., 2020; Obrenovic et al., 2025). Integration of behavioral policies eliminates impacts (Charisi, 2025). The exploration of human-AI partnerships benefits organizational behavior (Bahmani et al., 2024).

Synthesis models allow new value paradigms to be created commercially (Lichtenthaler, 2018; Lopes da Costa et al., 2019). The strategies of logistics resistance improve teamwork (Klumpp, 2018). Emotional architectures enhance the efficiency of retail (Erol et al., 2019). It secures sustainable development and digital entrepreneurship globally (Riaj et al., 2025). It leads to research, prepares managers to work with AI, and informs regulations, making sure that commercial evolution is fair (Abdul et al., 2018; Virvou, 2022; Guzman and Lewis, 2020; Gachayeva et al., 2025).

The multidisciplinary nature of this chapter is one of the greatest contributions to the study because it is a complex and multifaceted field of study in the digital economy that requires the synthesis of various disciplines, such as marketing, behavioral economics, information systems, and legal studies, to clarify human-AI interactions (Raman et al., 2026). Such a holistic approach is particularly relevant in a time when AI-powered systems, such as chatbots, recommendation engines, and dynamic pricing algorithms, are changing how businesses engage with consumers, providing hyper-personalized experiences that are both more enjoyable and more challenging to businesses-customer relationships. Besides, the chapter presents crucial ethical and policy issues, especially the dangers of algorithmic bias, data privacy breach, and loss of consumer control. It emphasizes the need to have regulatory frameworks that are able to strike a balance between innovation and consumer protection, to make sure that AI technologies are developed in a transparent, fair, and responsible manner (Hajiyeva et al., 2026). Such an approach to the responsible development of AI contributes not only to the scholarly relevance of the chapter but also to its practical usefulness, offering practical information to those who have to address the issue of introducing AI in a business environment without violating ethical norms (Petropoulos, 2022).

Research Gap

In spite of the swelling literature, there are critical gaps in the interaction between humans and AI. SLR demonstrates conceptual emphasis over the practical one without incorporating TAM-ISM-HBM as the concept of security-adoption (Islam et al., 2026; Anam et al., 2026). The commercial specificity is slow; marketing AI does not have behavioral data over time (Salam et al., 2024). Different users and symbiosis research are required by HCI agendas, but commercial applications, such as banking HRI, are not investigated properly (Jiang et al., 2024; Abdul et al., 2018). BDAC Supply chain BDAC mediation ignores contextual moderators (Bhuiyan et al., 2025). There should be more AI-human collaboration structures in areas of cybersecurity. Sustainable digitalization reviews disregard gaps in policy.

The level of logistics resistance requires an empirical validation that is not model based (Klumpp, 2018). The smart factories demand socio-economic impact metrics (Benotsmane et al., 2019). Generative AI and ethical HMC do not have business-related morality (Guzman and Lewis, 2020; Obrenovic et al., 2025). Causal evidence is required when it comes to behavioral policy interaction (Charisi, 2025; Hancock et al., 2020). In business, synthesis is theoretical as opposed to being experimented in organizations (Lichtenthaler, 2018). PRISMA based on 73 studies emphasizes the lack of representation of emerging markets and multi-level studies (file methodology). Affective HRI commercialises datasets yet scalability gaps still exist (Erol et al., 2019).

Objectives of the Book Chapter

The objectives of this book chapter are multifaceted, aiming to provide a comprehensive framework for understanding and integrating human-AI interactions in commercial settings.

Formulate Conceptual Framework: Build a multi-dimensional model which incorporates human-AI interactions (collaboration, substitution, synthesis) where applied to commercial settings such as marketing and logistics.

PRISMA-Based Methodology: Use PRISMA principles to conduct a systematic literature review to filter Scopus data (2019-2026) to include/ exclude and extract keywords (e.g., Human-AI Interaction, AI Marketing) and suggest a conceptual framework based on thematic clusters.

Break-Down Research Agendas: Summarize agendas in user diversity gaps, symbiosis, explainable AI, and multi-disciplinary strategies.

Analyze Policy Implications: Assess the governance policies of biases, ethics, and resistance to commercial AI use.

Recommendation: Present actionable advice of integrating human and AI in business, policy, and sustainability.

LITERATURE REVIEW

Human-artificial intelligence (AI) interaction in the business world symbolizes a major change in business processes whereby the AI systems complement, replace, or synthesize human capabilities to boost productivity, decision making, and value creation. The literature review will provide major research findings in the area of affective architectures, cognitive issues, industry implementation, and synthesis and outline its commercial implications in retail, logistics, smart factories, and management. Based on various fields such as human-robot interaction (HRI) and adoption of AI in business, the review sees the trends towards collaborative synthesis alongside overcoming resistance and ethical issues (Lichtenthaler, 2018; Lopes da Costa et al., 2019). In business, HRI research is quickly becoming commercialized, which highlights the financial feasibility of emotional and cognitive AI interfaces (Erol et al., 2019). The schemes of common work in the banking sector and in logistics also demonstrate the real applications, where emotional intelligence and multi-dimensional working together are essential (Benotsmane et al., 2019; Klumpp, 2018).

Commercial interactions between humans and artificial intelligence rely on affective and cognitive structures of natural and cooperative interactions. Erol et al. (2020) propose a new affection-based perception architecture of HRI, which will allow agents to perceive human emotional conditions and develop bonds with humans in the social context of retail services. This is vital in banking areas (Molla et al., 2026), where cognitive robots will be required to negotiate issues of decision making to share space and tasks in a manner that justifies frameworks using case studies of individual and collaborative skills (Gentile et al., 2011). This is extended through speech technology, which is an AI-driven technology that enables natural language interaction with applications, which are essential in customer-facing commercial tools (Mohapatra, 2021). Elsewhere, a new type of interaction, the human-to-human interface (HHI), is being developed through the needs of the videogame market to have affordable interaction technologies, a move that bodes a larger commercial opportunity (Gentile et al., 2011).

In logistics and smart factories, human and AI collaboration stimulates productivity in the age of automation. Klumpp (2018) presents obstacles to automation, with four growing levels of resistance, skepticism to complete rejection, which humans have towards AI, requiring trusted cooperation within the business logistics system, such as automated truck driving. Investment decisions involving collaboration are differentiated into multi-dimensional types that are ex ante to be tested using extensive case studies that show practical implications of human-AI task-sharing (Klumpp, 2018). The article by Benotsmane et al. (2019) discusses the economic and social benefits of smart factories, in which intelligent robots communicate with humans, machines, and other intelligent robots to improve quality and productivity. Partnering between robots and humans or among robots becomes central to unmanned works, and the simulation and AI increase the viability of Industry 4.0 (Benotsmane et al., 2019). The data of such works are frequently commercialized after publication, which throws up the possibilities of monetization of collaborative robots in supply chains.

AI can transform human functions and replace them with synthesizing, which is the contribution to the commercial management. Lopes da Costa et al. (2019) issue on the application of AI to business and conclude that managers can use it to develop functions, which allows them to spend time on complex problems, not on their replacement. AI is helpful in terms of data analysis and decision support, enhancing the role of humans in dynamic markets (Mohapatra, 2021). Lichtenthaler (2018) suggests that four interplays Standard (routine AI), Substitute (AI replacement), Superiority (AI dominance), and Synthesis (integrated intelligence) exist and that synthesis generates value by pooled, sequential, or reciprocal dependencies. This change is reflected in major companies, which are coming up with variations of hybrid models regarding innovative solutions (Lichtenthaler, 2018; Khatun et al., 2025).

Effective HRI systems have potential of being a good natural bond, yet have to be verified in different industries such as banking and logistics (Erol et al., 2019). Socio-economic analyzes are needed to ensure there are fair human-robot teams in the smart factories. The policymakers are encouraged to create structures that overcome the levels of resistance, so that AI supplements and not replaces humans (Klumpp, 2018; Lichtenthaler, 2018). Finally, commercial human-AI interaction is effective because it is synthesis, the combination of human intuition and AI efficiency to build a robust business model in table 1(Lopes da Costa et al., 2019).

Table 1. A List of Previous Studies to Identify the Research Gap on this Chapter

Title	Summary	Main Findings	Source
Artificial intelligence and communication: A Human–Machine Communication research agenda	A research agenda for human–machine communication is proposed, focusing on functional dimensions, relational dynamics, and metaphysical implications of AI interactions, to address gaps in communication theory. Theoretical framework rather than empirical evidence. No specific findings or evidence provided.	The main findings include the introduction of a theoretical basis for human–machine communication (HMC) and a research agenda focusing on three key aspects: functional dimensions, relational dynamics, and metaphysical implications of communicative AI technologies.	(Guzman & Lewis, 2020)
AI-Mediated Communication: Definition, Research Agenda, and Ethical Considerations	Artificial Intelligence-Mediated Communication (AI-MC) involves AI modifying or generating messages in interpersonal communication; a research agenda should consider design, psychological, linguistic, relational, policy, and ethical implications.	Not mentioned (the abstract does not provide specific findings but rather outlines a research agenda)	(Hancock et al., 2020)
Human-AI interaction research agenda: A user-centered perspective	Human-AI Interaction research themes include collaboration, competition, conflict, and symbiosis; future research should focus on diverse user groups and integrate multi-disciplinary theories and methods.	The study reviewed research themes, theoretical foundations, and methodological frameworks in the HAII field. HAII research themes include human-AI collaboration, competition, conflict, and symbiosis. Theories from communication, psychology, and sociology support HAII studies. Methods include self-reporting and observational approaches. Future research should focus on diverse user groups, AI roles, and tasks. There is a need to develop multi-disciplinary theories and integrate multi-level research methods. The study provides theoretical and practical insights for future research and catalyzes seamless human-AI interaction.	(Jiang et al., 2024)

continued on following page

Table 1. Continued

Title	Summary	Main Findings	Source
Artificial intelligence in business: State of the art and future research agenda	A comprehensive analysis of AI research in business identifies 18 topics across four clusters, including societal impact, and proposes a future research agenda addressing trends and challenges relevant to commercial human-AI interaction, based on 404 articles.	The main findings are categorized into four clusters: societal impact of AI, organizational impact of AI, AI systems, and AI methodologies. Societal impact includes topics like robots in society, law and regulations, marketing, and social and digital impacts. Organizational impact covers AI's impact on work, manufacturing, knowledge management, decision support, fuzzy logic approach, and risk management. AI systems include expert systems, systems design, and information infrastructure. AI methodologies focus on methods, forecasting, data analysis, neural networks, learning, and problem solving. Implications of a hybrid working environment and potential for a super intelligent society are discussed.	(Loureiro et al., 2021)
Charting the Ethical and Moral Landscapes of Human-AI Interactions	Human-AI interactions have profound ethical and moral implications, transforming societal norms and professional practices, with a focus on understanding agency, identity, and ethical responsibility in hybrid systems.	Profound ethical and moral implications for individual subjectivity, professional identity, and societal norms. Reshaping of individual perceptions of skills, autonomy, and value in professional settings. Transformation of societal norms, professional practices, and fairness and accountability. Exploration of multi-level dynamics from individual to societal levels. Rich understanding of ethical, professional, and societal transformations driven by human-AI interaction.	(Gachayeva et al., 2025)

continued on following page

Table 1. Continued

Title	Summary	Main Findings	Source
Humans + AI: Organizational Behavior Research on Human-Machine Interactions	The symposium explores critical aspects of human-AI interactions, focusing on ethical considerations, individual attitudes, and partnerships, contributing to the growing body of knowledge on AI and human behavior, with implications for organizational behavior and societal impact.	The main findings of the symposium are related to the exploration of human-AI interactions within organizational behavior, focusing on ethical considerations, impact on attitudes and behaviors, and the evolution of human-AI partnerships, offering insights into challenges and opportunities in an increasingly artificial workplace.	(Bahmani et al., 2024)
The Emerging Era Of Human-Ai Interaction: Keynote Address	Human-AI interaction is shifting towards autonomous decision-making, affecting daily lives with potential benefits in cognitive overload alleviation and insights, but challenges include uncertainty and the need for trustworthy and explainable AI, emphasizing human needs and understanding as key research areas.	A major paradigm shift is occurring where AI systems are becoming more autonomous and decision-making. AI is increasingly affecting daily life and work, with broad societal impact. AI alleviates human cognitive overload and assists in various applications. There are challenges related to uncertainty and errors in AI results. There is a need for more research on trustworthy and explainable AI.	(Virvou, 2022)

CONCEPTUAL FOUNDATIONS OF AI IN DIGITAL MARKETS

Artificial intelligence is applied in commerce to facilitate conversational commerce in which a customer can query products by Virtual assistants and make a purchase without any human intervention. Hybrid intelligence as a combination of human judgment and machine abilities, is a developing trend in AI contact that can redefine the future of work by uniting the advantages of humans and intelligent systems (Alt, 2021). Interaction tools (chatbots, voice assistants, recommendation engines, etc.) based on AI are changing the way consumers interact with online stores, making online shopping experiences more seamless, personalized, and satisfying. The development of digital marketplaces is transforming how interactions between AI and customer choices are reshaping the ways in which businesses interact and react to their audiences (Wang, 2025). The AI systems help e-commerce to improve customer engagement by having chatbots and messaging applications to respond to the queries of customers quickly, automatically, and consistently. Simultaneously,

AI allows customer data to be gathered and analyzed on a platform, thus making business more informed about customer purchasing behavior and helping determine what to expect when new and old customers purchase the product (Khrais, 2020).

AI-based interactions with customers in terms of personalization, omnichannel, and recommendations systems improve the user experience, satisfaction, and loyalty to a considerable extent, facilitating the sustainable development of the business. It also analyzes the level of AI utilization in B2C and B2B relations as a measure of AI adoption levels within medium and large-sized companies (Jankovic and Curovic, 2023). A continuum of human AI hybrid arrangements on digital platforms, consisting of task substitution, where AI replaces human labor, to task augmentation and task assemblage, where human and AI interactively complement and integrate. It also treats digital labor platforms as digital spaces where services are created and managed by human and AI agents working jointly to deliver them to the recipient or customer at no fee (Rai et al, 2019). Artificial empathy can be used to increase customer and firm value by reducing the divide between AI-based and human-oriented interaction in emotional and social customer experiences. It further describes which circumstances AI empathy is suitable, and which situations can make its implementation redundant or even counterproductive in the marketing domain (Liu-Thompkins et al, 2022).

AI Agents and Chatbots in Commercial Settings

AI is transforming the trends in the e-commerce market with the help of chatbots, virtual assistants, and predictive analytics, which make customer interaction more engaging and predict customer preferences. It also mentions major ethical issues of AI-based personalization, such as the threat of data privacy, and algorithm bias, which are the leading points in commercial human AI interaction (Raji et al, 2024). The value creation through AI is changing the face of industries globally, including manufacturing, transportation, retail, healthcare, and financial services, and it opens new venues of commercial human-AI interaction. It also singles out digital personal helpers which are AI-based services that replicate human interaction to complete such tasks as responding to queries, schedule management, and product purchase (Du and Xie, 2021). The collaboration between AI systems and e-commerce professionals is one of the main areas in successful commercial human-AI interaction. The need for a balance between automation and human interaction to achieve success and sustainability of AI applications in business processes. AI-based content personalization has a huge impact on customer satisfaction, interaction, and conversion rates in e-commerce. It also indicates that the AI can be used to make behavioral data on a large scale to improve personalization beyond the level of transactional interaction, generating more emotional customer experiences (Vashishth et al, 2024).

Trust, Transparency, and Explainability

Trust–risk dual-way in AIGC commerce has been identified whereby the quality of AI-generated content decreases perceived risk, increases trust but negatively and positively affects purchase intention, respectively. The perceived platform responsibility has a moderating effect by increasing the negative effects of perceived risk and the positive effects of trust on consumer purchase intentions (Yu et al, 2025b). The range of ethical issues includes bias, privacy, cybersecurity, and threats to the autonomy of human beings as a result of the mass use of AI-enabled products and services in digital markets. It also offers a multi-layered socio-technical examination of the ethical concerns regarding the product, consumer, and society and demonstrates the dangers as well as chances of the interaction between human beings and AI in consumer markets (Du and Xie 2021). Foreseeability of human-AI contact is highlighted as one of the most important elements in the liability determination in case of AI-related harm. The companies should consider and address the potential risks that can be predicted during the implementation of AI systems to diminish the liability and guarantee safe application in human-focused environments (Kowert, 2017; Ienca, 2023).

The danger of AI-driven market grooming is that just enough of an algorithm can encourage consumers to make a decision that would not be in their best interests. Strong regulatory structures are essential to guarantee that digital activities are ethical and that users are not exploited by markets that are run through AI (Oshadi Karunanayaka et al, 2024). AI-based manipulation exploits human bias, customized addictive methods, and emotional susceptibility to sell commercially based products, which tend to harm the welfare of the users. The profit-seeking AI systems can influence consumer behaviour in a manner that contradicts that of the user, and it is therefore imperative that certain policies can protect human autonomy (Petropoulos, 2022). The major consumer risk areas in the electronic marketplaces include threats to security and privacy, AI bias, and threats to personal autonomy and well-being. Global ethical and moral issues related to AI-powered systems, including cybersecurity threats, joblessness, and consequences of algorithmic decision-making (Thamik and Wu, 2022).

The DMA has an effect on AI models and data disclosure requirements, training data regulation, access rules, and equitable ranking regimes, with its fairness provisions going beyond traditional non-discrimination law by using competition law and the FRAND principles as a means of ensuring fair rankings (Hacker et al, 2024; Fassiaux, 2023). Although legal measures have increased consumer trust, e-commerce fraud has increased three times, and it demonstrates how legally strict measures have limited effects and the necessity of adopting an alternative between the two methods of policy-making: strict legal measures and AI-enhanced fraud detection tools to combat emerging cyber threats (Spulbar, 2025). The quality of AI-generated content (AIGCQ) affects the purchase intention of users on e-commerce sites by trust and perceived risk, with an ethical concern and perceived platform responsibility mediating the effects, underscoring the importance of governance frameworks and ethical labelling to handle the two-sided effects of platform accountability (Yu et al, 2025b).

REGULATORY AND POLICY CHALLENGES

Digital technologies, big data, and AI provoke social, economic, legal, and ethical issues, as such tools should be accompanied by legal regulations that would balance autonomy and responsibility, and manipulative tools such as nudging are more and more actively used by the states through digital devices to control behavior. The current EU consumer legislation is confronted with the difficulty of dealing with AI, whether employed internally by firms or offered as a contractual object that the trader will be liable, dark patterns, information asymmetry, algorithmic choices, flawed systems, and the lack of a set of objective conformity criteria (Ebers, 2021). There are legal and regulatory implications that the introduction of AI, machine learning, autonomous systems, and similar technologies have brought, such as the effects on labour, social inequality, and physical risks, which raise the call to be more cautious, coupled with the need to create a policy framework that suggests caution and a policy of permissionless innovation, only regulating in the case of demonstrable harm (Thierer et al, 2017). Consumer protection poses a legal and regulatory problem when applying AI to transactions, especially in the financial markets, posing a threat to consumers and necessitating the need to change the consumer protection laws to combat the risk of AI category (Nizioł, 2021).

METHODOLOGY OF THE STUDY

The method of conducting a systematic literature review (SLR) was applied by the researchers in the chapter to analyze theoretical frameworks as well as the practical findings on the topic of human-AI interactions in marketing settings (Abdul et al., 2018; Anam et al., 2026). The researchers used the Scopus database to host the studies in the chapter due to the worldwide access to the academic literature on this issue.

Methods

The authors applied several methods in order to assess the study regarding the role of AI technology in helping businesses interact with customers via online platforms. These three aspects that the researchers concentrated on involved developing definitions of new business opportunities and finding the existing problems as well as their risk factors and policy implications (Faisal-E-Alam et al., 2025). The methodology of the study employed by its authors to describe the research was the PRISMA (Preferred Reporting Items to Systematic Reviews and Meta-Analyses) framework, which presupposed search and evaluation of the relevant studies concerning the effect of AI technology on business relationships in terms of fairness and accountability (Khatun et al., 2025). The authors have developed a holistic evaluation of various dimensions of commercial AI systems by employing the framework that they developed based on their research methodology.

Research Design

The researchers applied the PRISMA framework in Figure 1 to implement a systematic review that determines the impact of human-AI interaction on businesses within digital marketplaces. PRISMA protocol offers a mechanism of undertaking the procedure of reviewing since it sets standards that allow the researcher to carry out his work using the same techniques starting with searching databases to ultimate synthesis. The digital markets paradigm is suitable to investigate since AI-based applications, such as algorithm pricing and recommendation systems or conversational agents, have become a critical part that drives consumer behavior and defines market forces. The review gathers the scientific work of various scholarly disciplines to assemble an evidence base that assists policymakers wishing to learn more about the economic positive aspects of AI and the threats it presents to fairness and consumer protection and the shifting guidelines regarding governance and accountability.

The review gains practical importance because it uses quasi-experimental evidence from field studies which examined actual AI-based business interactions to build its research framework. The approach enables researchers to study how machine-based systems affect decision-making processes and trust development and competition dynamics. The literature review focuses on studies published between 2020 and February 1 2026 because researchers believe that digitalization efforts reached their peak after the pandemic. The framework enables researchers to study new sustainability trends which emerge from human-AI partnership market practices that focus on human-machine interaction.

Figure 1. PRISMA Based Methodology

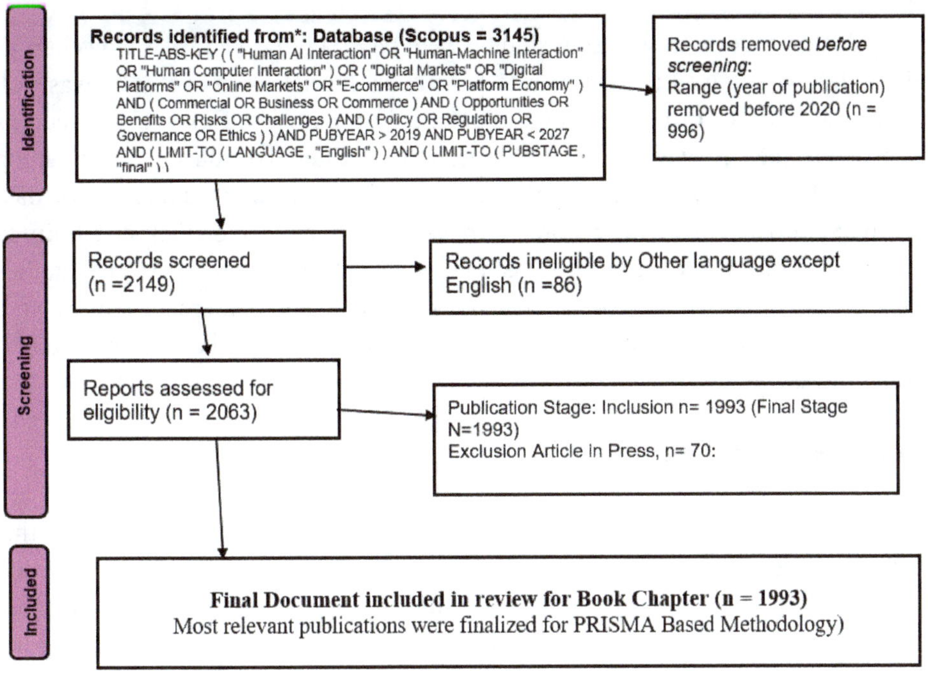

Source: Scopus Database (February 1, 2026)

Searching Technique

Scopus serves as the primary database for our literature review because it provides complete access to high-quality academic research materials that span multiple academic fields (Salam et al., 2024). The database enables users to obtain superior bibliographic records which include peer-reviewed journals and conference proceedings and scholarly publications. Scopus meets the requirement of having an established academic index which contains high-quality research materials and will function as an essential resource for this project.

Figure 1 illustrates the search query combined Boolean operators: TITLE-ABS-KEY ((“Human AI Interaction” OR “Human-Machine Interaction” OR “Human Computer Interaction”) OR (“Digital Markets” OR “Digital Platforms” OR “Online Markets” OR “E-commerce” OR “Platform Economy”) AND (Commercial OR Business OR Commerce) AND (Opportunities OR Benefits OR Risks OR Challenges) AND (Policy OR Regulation OR Governance OR Ethics)) AND PUBYEAR > 2019 AND PUBYEAR < 2027 AND (LIMIT-TO (LANGUAGE, “English”)) AND (LIMIT-TO (PUBSTAGE, “final”))

Selection Technique

Inclusion criteria in selecting studies were based on the PRISMA flowchart as highlighted in Figure 1 and this was to ensure that the selection of studies was well structured in terms of the inclusion of studies in the review. Firstly, 3145 records were determined, however, some of them have been filtered out during the screening stage according to such criteria as the non-English language or the publication date before 2020. The other 2146 records were carefully evaluated on their eligibility to the research questions in Figure 1 basing on their relevancy, and only 1993 studies were included. Peer-reviewed articles, book chapters, and conference papers were included in this research to filter through the most relevant and quality research to use in the analysis.

Analysis Technique

The qualitative synthesis method is the review one, and will be applied in this review, whereby the findings of the used studies will be compared and contrasted to establish the common themes, trends, and insights of the studies. The approach applied to draw nuanced insights regarding how AI technologies are changing the manner in which marketing is conducted and how consumers experience it (Bhuiyan et al., 2025). The overview section will include a synthesis of the results of various studies and will present a holistic picture of the situation in this sphere with regard to successful usage and the need for further analysis. The repetitive concepts that support this qualitative synthesis by means of thematic analysis include theoretical approaches and trends, and situational aspects that affect the adoption of AI use by marketers.

CONCEPTUAL FRAMEWORK/THEORETICAL FRAMEWORK

Scope of the Framework

The framework defines the relationship between commercial AI technologies and consumers as a part of the virtual market system. The model is based on its three interactive layers: Market Drivers, Interaction Dynamics, and Regulated Outcomes.

The Conceptual Structure

Layer A-Market Drivers (Inputs): The fundamental market drivers which create artificial intelligence to function in all business operations are established through Layer A. Data liquidity which enables constant access to substantial consumer behavior data for digital interactions serves as one of the vital market drivers. The existence of data constitutes a fundamental requirement that enables artificial intelligence systems to acquire knowledge and generate relevant insights. The second vital driver of artificial intelligence systems operates through their capacity to execute tasks which users and organizations define through independent and semi-independent decision processes. Business organizations require artificial intelligence systems to achieve operational efficiency because market competition drives them to implement such systems for maintaining their competitive advantage (Janiesch et al., 2021).

Layer B-The Interaction Core (Process): The Interaction Core (Process) serves as the human-AI interaction component of Layer B. The layer demonstrates how AI systems interact with their human users through active engagement, which results from decision-making structures that organize options in ways that drive human users to make choices. The system enables human-AI interaction through its dynamic exchange mechanisms, which allow AI to adjust product features and costs based on human actions and different environmental conditions according to Nam et al. (2021). The layer relies on feedback loops because AI systems use human feedback to develop better interactive skills for future use.

Layer C-The Tension (Outcomes): The opportunity vector demonstrates how consumer welfare increases when businesses provide hyper-personalized products which enable customers to easily find products while artificial intelligence-powered systems create new market opportunities. The systems enable consumers to make rapid choices because they will receive personalized solutions which meet their specific requirements (Zhang et al., 2025). The risk vector identifies significant problems which AI-driven systems create through their use of dark patterns and their implementation of discriminatory pricing practices which reduce consumer choice. The risks will create consumer trust problems because virtual markets require customers to make choices without giving them full control over their personal information.

Layer D-Policy & Governance (Control): The “Policy and Governance” or “Control” Layer focuses on regulating artificial intelligent system operations through authorized access. To achieve transparency the development of explainable algorithmic logic needs to be established. The process of establishing accountability for individuals and systems requires the creation of frameworks which establish unambiguous legal responsibility for damages resulting from artificial intelligent system usage in business and consumer relationships. The “Policy and Governance” or “Control” Layer will incorporate the “ethics by design” principle through its requirement that artificial intelligent systems must protect consumers as a fundamental design element which designers must implement from their initial programming stage.

Conceptual Table for Research Alignment

Table 2. Conceptual Table for Research Alignment

Framework Pillar	Key Variables	Theoretical Lens
Technological	Complexity, Autonomy, Speed	Actor-Network Theory (ANT)
Behavioral	Trust, Manipulation, Nudge	Behavioral Economics
Legal/Policy	Privacy, Antitrust, Fairness	Regulatory Governance

Source: Author's Contribution

A summary of the main pillars and corresponding variables and theories is given in Table 2 . The framework integrates technological, behavioral, and legal/policy dimensions to provide a comprehensive foundation for understanding AI-driven digital market competition, as presented in Table 2.

Conceptual Framework Analysis

Figure 2. Conceptual Framework Analysis

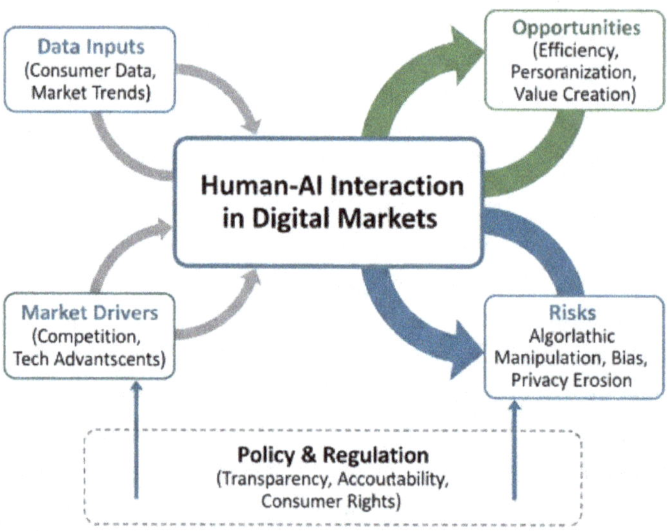

Source: *Author's Contribution*

THEORETICAL FOUNDATIONS

The framework of figure 2 contains three primary academic theories which demonstrate how consumers interact with AI technologies in digital marketplaces. The research demonstrates that AI systems use consumer cognitive limitations to process digital content which results in their decision-making patterns (Petrescu, & Krishen, 2023). Information asymmetry examines how consumer-AI interactions create an increasing power imbalance because AI systems rely on extensive consumer behavioral data which most consumers find difficult to comprehend (Du, & Xie, 2020). Nudge theory demonstrates that AI systems create consumer decision frameworks which systematically steer users toward specific outcome paths.

The Dynamic Feedback Loop

This interaction between users and systems driven by AI is, however, not a one-off occurrence but rather one that creates a feedback loop that continually manifests itself over a period, helping shape the markets, as shown in figure 2 . Users interact with the AI interface, like a chatbot or a recommender system, and initiate a new dialogue that continually creates a chain reaction on the responses generated by the systems (Banh & Strobel, 2023). In all this, behavioral data is continually collected from users on actions such as clicking, scrolling, and even hesitation, all of which is sought to be understood better (Hofmann et al., 2024). Using such data, users' willingness-to-pay is predicted, as is emotional trigger use that may impact decision-making processes (Krarup & Horst, 2023). Using all this data, a feedback loop is initiated so that a digital interface is continually adjusted by the AI system in real-time that seeks to optimize the chances of a transaction succeeding (Janiesch et al., 2021).

Dimensions of Risk and Vulnerability

Figure 2 presents the framework recognizes commercial risks based on three interconnected dimensions of risks and vulnerabilities. First, cognitive exploitation is defined as a situation where there is a use of dark patterns that exploit consumers by taking advantage of common cognitive biases, such as a false sense of urgency and continuity, with the aim of affecting consumer decision-making processes (Nalbant & Aydin, 2022). Algorithmic discrimination pricing is a situation that arises when prices are adjusted on the basis of certain factors, such as consumers' device type and location that may cause a loss of consumer surplus. Lastly, there is erosion of autonomy when artificial intelligence automatically moves from serving a supportive role, enabling consumers to make their own choices, to a situation where it primarily serves organizational interests and becomes responsible for making consumer choices on their own behaves.

Integrated Policy Pillars

Accordingly, in line with addressing these challenges, the research proposes a three-pronged approach in figure 2 that combines elements of transparency, accountability, and empowerment. On one note, the transparency pillar of the approach focuses on the need for the management of autonomous commercial agents to adopt the Explainable Artificial Intelligence technology so that consumers can understand the reasons for being presented with certain prices or virtual communications (Maedche et al., 2019). The second stage requires establishing accountability as the primary responsibility which commercial agents need to prove as they conduct their autonomous market activities. This particular method helps to resolve problems which arise from biased lending practices that are conducted through credit scoring systems (Bormane & Blaus, 2024). The third dimension of the approach is centered on the need for the rights of consumers to be protected through measures such as data portability as well as the "right to object" to data profiling activities. This process confirms that human beings maintain their status as the primary participants in all digital transactional processes.

The Psychological Architecture of Human-AI Interaction

This section will examine how "Choice Architects" like AI are subtly impacting human decision-making processes through behavioral science , as presented in Figure 3.

Cognitive Bias Exploitation

The term cognitive bias exploitation refers to methods which enable AI systems to take advantage of human psychological biases during digital marketplace interactions. The methods used by these systems track inventory levels and customer indecision to create urgent "limited time offer" alerts which induce consumers to make unplanned purchases according to their FOMO (fear of missing out). Moreover, digital market interactions involving AI algorithms also involve what is called hyper-personalized nudging, which can be differentiated from advertisements due to its dynamic nature of changing over time. Hyper-personalized nudging can involve inferring consumers' psychological biases, such as loss aversion, based on past buying behavior and structuring messages around possible gain or possible loss, thereby increasing persuasion and entering consumers' decision-making minds (Sidlauskiene et al., 2023).

The Trust-Automation Paradox

The critical pillar of this framework is Trust Calibration.

Figure 3 shows that trust calibration is a basic critical pillar in the Trust-Automation framework. It is identified that a challenge in trust calibration is automation bias, in which consumers trust recommendation systems based entirely on "mathematically certain" technologies, without using any other intuition. Figure 3 illustrates that consumers rely entirely on technology's recommendation and ignore their intuition, according to Zhang et al. (2025). The next identified challenge in trust calibration is the black box tension, in which a conflict may exist between transaction efficiency and a consumers need to be informed, according to Abrardi et al. (2021).

Figure 3. The Trust-Automation Paradox

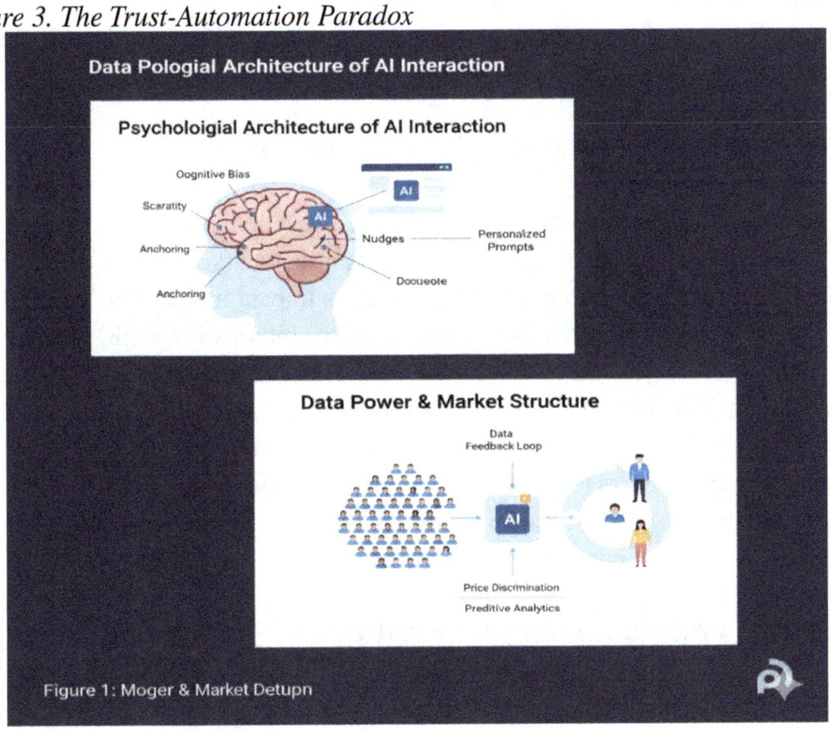

Source: *Author's Contribution*

Algorithmic Market Power and Data Asymmetry

This section shifts from individual psychology to the structural impact of AI on market fairness and competition.

Data as the Feedback Engine (The Value Loop)

The interaction between humans and AI establishes a self-sustaining value loop wherein every "event" or interaction, such as every click, hover, and cart abandonment, becomes a form of input for a machine-learning model (Nam et al., 2021). Such an interaction lends significant predictive strength to firms, enabling them not merely to respond to, but even anticipate, consumer demand, thus providing a significant information advantage for AI-driven firms over their traditional peers.

This process is a contributing factor to the phenomenon of "surveillance capitalism" in digital markets, wherein the product being sold is, ultimately, knowledge about consumers' future behavior (Bawack et al., 2022). Such data enables firms to increasingly fine tune their models of price discrimination, ultimately determining the amount a person is "willing" to pay for a good, a discovery attainable by AI systems.

Barriers to Entry and Algorithmic Monopolies

The interaction between humanity and AI has resulted in what economists refer to as a "data moat" or rather high entry barriers into a market. One of the effects of AI in this context is seen in how network effects impact interactions with AI systems. As the number of people seeking services or interactions with, say, Amazon or Google AI, the intelligence of AI increases. This has generated entry barriers in that new firms may have difficulties competing, as they will not have had multiple interactions to offer a personalized experience, as their rivals have. Moreover, AI technology enables firms to create what can be considered as a "market of one." As such, firms can reap optimal consumer surplus, potentially leading to an unbalanced transfer of funds from consumers to firms (Krarup & Horst, 2023).

Synthesis and Regulatory Implications

The last component of the framework focuses on a transition towards Autonomous AI and then to Human-Centric AI. Therefore, policies should focus on prioritizing a sense of transparency by design, providing a right to understanding for consumers why they have been targeted for a specific price or product (Hofmann et al., 2024). Moreover, there should always be a human-in-the-loop within high-stakes commercial interactions involving AI systems, such as credit scoring and insurance, to prevent bias and protect consumers against predatory behaviors.

DISCUSSION

The objective of this part is to discuss human-AI interaction to show the contemporary evidence in digital marketing, focusing on opportunities, risks, and governance challenges. Applying PRISMA-driven analysis of both empirical and conceptual studies, the findings show that AI is expanding beyond operations automation to market-changing autonomy, whereby systems of algorithms directly affect the strategies of businesses, consumer choices, and marketplace dynamics. The rest of the discussion integrates ideas from the conceptual framework, literature, and policy-related debate.

Integration of the prospects of Commercial Human and AI

The previous sections illustrate the way commercial human and AI relationships have emerged from general tools to sophisticated socio-technical networks that strongly impact the consumer organizational strategies and customers' choices. The emergence of AI to enhance the capacity of output and client service at this time is one of the significant opportunities (Rahman et al., 2025). With the integration of voice assistants, chatbots, and recommender systems, enterprises can provide consistent, instant, and fixable consumer engagement. These networks give very personalized relationships driven by data mining, reduce the operating cost, and extend accessibility of service above the human capacity (Alt, 2021). Notably, the studies indicate that mixed intelligence designs resulting in machine learning not entirely taking over human intuition to provide the most economic value (Raisch & Krakowski, 2021). In digital marketing, one of the major scopes is personalization of commercialization. AI-driven customization leverages contextualized and behavioral information to personalize offerings, pricing, and products for each client (Patil, 2024). Empirical investigations constantly demonstrate this sort of personalized shopping, which minimizes the abandonment of carts, increases ties among loyal customers, and retains firm performance in the long run. In addition to transactional effectiveness, AI-powered tools will facilitate a sense of empowerment and emotional attachment with the business. In this perspective, AI redefines the relationship between the firm and consumers, interacting as a mediation link compared to a mere mechanical tool of communication. In the macroeconomic perspective, AI involves transforming the ecosystems of entrepreneurial and business models as well (Acemoglu & Restrepo, 2020). Machine learning, data-based sources of revenue, and varied offerings of values have become increasingly significant to digital services, offering diverse opportunities for creativity and competitive edge. The changes are aligned with wider environmentally sustainable and economically viable goals by the allocation of resources and reducing waste and providing real-time responses to the demand of markets. Digital platforms increasingly rely on predictive analytics, data-driven revenue streams, and dynamic value propositions, enabling new forms of competition and innovation. These developments align with broader sustainability and efficiency goals by optimizing resource allocation, reducing waste, and enabling real-time responsiveness to market demand (OECD, 2022).

Table 3. Thematic Analysis

Study (Author, Year)	Core Claim	Key Insights / Evidence	Thematic Section
Raisch & Krakowski, 2021	Personalization improves commercial outcomes	AI-driven recommendation systems reduce cart abandonment, increase cross-selling, enhance loyalty, and improve long-term marketing performance by leveraging behavioral and contextual data.	Integration (Prospects)
Patil, 2024	Hybrid AI-human service models optimize customer interactions	Emphasizes the need for combining AI automation with human judgment in banking, finance, and service sectors to manage complex or emotionally sensitive customer interactions.	Integration (Prospects)
Rai et al., 2019	Balance between automation and human interaction is crucial	Successful commercial human-AI interactions (HAI) require human oversight to complement AI efficiency, ensuring ethical decision-making, innovation, and sustainable performance.	Integration (Prospects)
Vashishth et al., 2024d	AI enhances emotional customer experiences	AI enables personalization beyond transactional efficiency by analyzing large-scale behavioral data, fostering emotional engagement and higher conversion rates.	Integration (Prospects)
Patil, 2024	Dynamic AI pricing systems maximize revenue	Predictive AI analytics allow firms to offer personalized pricing, real-time adjustments, and competitive advantages, improving online sales, revenue streams, and customer satisfaction.	Integration (Prospects)

Risks and Tensions in Human–AI Commercial Environments

Despite having huge potentialities, commercialized human-AI connection presents significant risks, which render its adoption and management more challenging. The risk-trust dichotomy associated with AI-generated content and AI-mediated chosen contexts are major issues in studies (Lankton et al., 2015; Helberger et al., 2020; Rai et al., 2021). While effective AI platforms may improve confidence and reduce risk perception, if their activities are obscure and poorly operated, they may also induce over-reliance, manipulation, or uncertainty (Rai et al., 2019; Følstad et al., 2021). Customer's freedom is one of the most critical risks. While these tactics are helpful for shaping consumer buying patterns, modern personalization approaches and excessive pushing raise questions on moral boundaries and agency of consumers. Customers might not fully understand how AI-powered recommendation mechanisms may gradually affect their choices and way of decision-making, creating ethical dilemmas and inequity in distribution (Morozovaite, 2023; Turki, 2025). By exploiting the advantages of cognitive perceptions, symmetry of information, and vulnerabilities of emotion, the application of dark trends, the marketplace of algorithm marketing, and behavior targeting could result in buyers taking poor decisions (Turki, 2025; Oshadi Karunanayaka et al., 2024).

The privacy and security of data are also becoming matters of tension. AI-based systems are highly susceptible to improper use, unauthorized access, and surveillance, as they depend on huge datasets that contain transactional, personal, and behavioral data (Arunasalam, 2025; Oshadi Karunanayaka et al., 2024). The imbalance of power between companies and their customers has become worse by the centralization of information and decision-making authority in most platforms, which raises the potentiality of misuse (Ntoutsi et al., 2025). The blended nature of AI systems and human presence makes accountability and liability difficult to maintain. It may be hard to separate accountability among platform operators, end users and developers whenever damage takes place because of automatic decisions, misleading content, and discriminatory prices (Yu et al., 2025a; Arunasalam, 2025). Organizational disputes and labor disagreements are also prevalent. As the adoption of AI worsens the gap of skill and challenges common jobs, it forces continuous reskilling and organizational adjustment while it creates additional highly skilled professionals in the Table 4.

Table 4. Thematic Analysis

Study (Author, Year)	Core Claim	Key Insights / Evidence	Thematic Section
Yu et al., 2025a	Trust-risk duality affects purchase intention	Highlights how AI content quality reduces perceived risks and builds consumer trust, while platform accountability moderates negative effects and reinforces confidence in AI-mediated decisions.	Risks
Arunasalam, 2025	Security and privacy in human-AI systems are critical	Demonstrates that large language models can provide guidance on security/privacy but also raises ethical concerns about misuse of sensitive data in commercial AI systems.	Risks
Oshadi Karunanayaka et al., 2024	Strong regulation is needed to curb digital manipulation	Stresses that AI algorithms can exploit cognitive biases and behavioral vulnerabilities, requiring robust policy frameworks to safeguard consumer autonomy and welfare.	Risks

Human–AI Commercial Environments: The Policy and Regulatory Challenges

The existing customer protections and competition laws are often insufficient to cope with the adaptive, autonomous, and data-based nature of AI, and the regulatory setting for business Human-AI remains volatile and fragmented (Morozovaite, 2023; Krarup & Horst, 2023). Reactive regulation is shown by current frameworks, including the Digital Markets Act (DMA), the EU AI Act, and the Digital Services Act (DSA), which each place a high priority on fairness, ethical governance, transparency, and accountability in AI-powered markets (Hacker et al., 2024; Fassiaux, 2023).

However, the challenges still exist. Because of AI's statistical and predictive nature, risk evaluation and forecasting are naturally complicated. In an attempt to reconcile the dispute between regulation and innovation, enterprises must take into account possible harm while developing and executing systems (Turki, 2025). Highly rigid rules may impede innovation in technology, while insufficient management may undermine customers' trust and welfare (Turki, 2025). International dealings make adherence much harder since various laws in the EU, US, and China introduce legal uncertainty and require standards (Spulbar, 2025; Pakuhinezhad & Afsham, 2025).

The research consistently stresses the importance of multidisciplinary methods that combine legal, ethical, and behavioral standards. To safeguard customers' liberty and ensure just outcomes, AI platforms ought to be designed having accountability, transparency, and fairness, backed by governmental and institutional protections (Krarup & Horst, 2023; Ntoutsi et al., 2025). In order to guarantee international electronic markets remain reliable and viable, efficient governance demands global cooperation, moral principles, and international principles in the Table 5.

Table 5. Thematic Analysis

Study (Author, Year)	Core Claim	Key Insights / Evidence	Thematic Section
Morozovaite, 2023	AI-driven hypernudging challenges digital market regulation	Highlights how EU frameworks (AI Act, Digital Markets Act, Digital Services Act) aim to regulate AI personalization and behavioral influence, addressing ethical and market manipulation concerns.	Policy & Regulation
Hacker et al., 2024	Fairness in AI rankings requires regulation	Highlights DMA provisions enforcing transparency, equitable ranking, and FRAND principles to prevent algorithmic bias and promote fair competition in digital markets.	Policy & Regulation
Fassiaux, 2023	EU law must integrate behavioral risks	Suggests interdisciplinary regulatory strategies to address dark patterns, behavioral advertising, and AI personalization, ensuring protection against manipulation in commercial AI.	Policy & Regulation
Celestin, 2024	Legal measures alone are insufficient	Indicates that strict e-commerce laws alone do not prevent fraud; recommends integrating AI-enhanced fraud detection and proactive measures alongside legal frameworks.	Policy & Regulation
Krarup & Horst, 2023	Ethical AI regulation complements competition	Shows the EU's integrated approach, combining competition law with AI ethics, which contrasts with more fragmented US and Chinese regulatory frameworks.	Policy & Regulation
Spulbar, 2025	AI requires novel economic regulations	Argues that responsibility, bias, intellectual property, and competition challenges require new economic and legal regulations tailored to AI-driven commercial markets.	Policy & Regulation
Pakuhinezhad & Afsham, 2025	Cross-border AI governance is complex	Emphasizes the need for international coordination to harmonize AI regulations on data protection, IP, bias mitigation, and liability in multinational digital commerce.	Policy & Regulation
Ntoutsi et al., 2025	Anti-discrimination laws are insufficient	Existing laws primarily act after-the-fact; ethical, moral, and inclusive design principles in AI are necessary to prevent discrimination and promote fairness proactively.	Policy & Regulation
Turki, 2025	Personalization creates governance gaps	Highlights that highly personalized AI interventions expose gaps in governance, calling for interdisciplinary strategies combining behavioral science, ethics, and responsible AI regulation to manage risks effectively.	Policy & Regulation

Policy Responses and Responsible AI Design

The rapid integration of Artificial Intelligence (AI) in the digital market calls for a comprehensive policy response that ensures the benefits of AI are maximized while, at the same time, mitigating the risks involved. A comprehensive policy response, therefore, entails the development of a comprehensive framework that sets the ethical standards for the use of AI in the market. This framework should address issues related to data privacy, bias, consumer protection, and market competitiveness, among others. For example, a comprehensive policy framework should be established that ensures transparency in the decision-making process of AI, thus allowing consumers to understand how their information is used, collected, and processed. Another policy response, therefore, entails the development of a comprehensive framework that promotes the use of a standardized auditing process for AI systems, ensuring that these systems are fair and non-discriminatory against certain classes of consumers or market players. Audits can be conducted to identify biases in algorithms, especially where these biases are against certain classes of consumers, particularly the marginalized in society.

In this regard, AI design plays a vital role in supplementing the interventions of policies. It is of paramount importance for organizations to follow a "human-centered AI" approach, which means AI systems are designed in such a manner that they can complement human decision-making. This also entails incorporating ethical considerations into AI systems, from their development to their use. The major principles of responsible AI design are fairness, accountability, transparency, and explainability, also known as the FATE framework.

In addition, it is also important for organizations to follow privacy-by-design and security-by-design approaches, which can ensure the security of users' data and prevent their exploitation. This can be done by ensuring minimum data collection, using proper encryption, and empowering users regarding their data. Another significant aspect of AI is ensuring diversity in data sets and teams during AI system development, which can also play a significant role in making AI systems more reliable. Lastly, it is also important for organizations to ensure proper monitoring of AI systems, which can ensure their alignment with ethical standards. This can be done by establishing proper governance systems, including AI ethics committees, within organizations.

RECOMMENDATIONS

Recommendations for Responsible and Sustainable Human–AI Commerce

Given the above-presented synthesis of opportunities, risks, and regulatory challenges, the following section will provide the key recommendations that firms, policymakers, and researchers should implement to make the commercial human-AI interactions responsible.

Firm and Platform Operators Recommendations

Firms should emphasize more on the hybrid type of intelligence with both AI capabilities and human intuition rather than seeking to fully automate as an objective. The tools of artificial intelligence are more efficient in carrying out repetitive, data-driven, and predictive tasks, whereas people have their own unique benefits in the aspects of empathy, context-based analysis, moral judgment, and addressing complex problem situations (Raisch and Krakowski, 2021). Human-in-the-loop or human-on-the-loop models are essential in all commercial engagements and interactions that are emotionally sensitive, high-risk, or complex to determine the best way to promote decision-making and reduce risks. Such designs create trust, bring less ambiguity to accountability, and improve the quality of services in such sectors as finance, retail, and platform-based services.

Ethical considerations should be incorporated throughout the AI lifecycle, including the process of system design and implementation and its maintenance. The ethical-by-design approaches, which include explainable AI, the identification and resolution of biases, and transparent data governance should also be implemented by the companies, which can help them align business objectives with societal expectations and reduce legal and reputational risks (Ntoutsi et al., 2025).Regular efforts to assess AI algorithms and establish internal oversight systems, including interdisciplinary AI ethics committees, should help reduce legal and reputational risks.

AI-led personalization should be developed as a helping service rather than a fraudulent instrument. Personalization results in a higher conversion rate and customer loyalty, but excessive and careless personalization may pose a threat to consumer autonomy through subtle manipulation and guidance (Susser, Roessler, and Nissenbaum, 2019; Mathur et al., 2021). Companies should adopt limited forms of personalization, such as providing meaningful opt-out options, access to information about AI-generated content, and provide end-users with the ability to control how their data is used. The protection of autonomy does not only address ethical concerns but also builds long-lasting trust and long-term relationships between customers and companies.

Policymaker and Regulator Recommendations

The traditional post-facto regulations are inadequate to address the systemic risks as well as the cumulative risks of the AI-driven markets. The governance approaches that should be adopted by policymakers are risk-based and proactive, which means that companies must anticipate and mitigate potential harms before implementing the AI-based application and actively monitor it once it is already implemented (OECD, 2022).

Human and AI interaction is mixed, which blurs traditional lines of responsibility and complicates the pursuit of justice in the event of damage. The regulatory frameworks have to clearly specify the different duties of the developers, deployers, and operators of the platforms. Traceability can be enhanced by a set of requirements on training data documentation, model updates, and decision-making processes, whereas well-structured liability distribution mechanisms can reduce uncertainty in companies and enhance consumer protection when cross-border digital markets are involved. The policymakers should aim to achieve better coordination by developing shared ethical standards, minimum standards of commercial AI, and compliance frameworks that can collaborate with each other (OECD, 2022). International co-operation in law enforcement and data management is essential in addressing the global nature of the digital platform and AI-based trading (Bradford, 2020).

The involvement of AI in the business environment requires continuous human resource investment. The business and government institutions should encourage AI studies, constant reskilling, and human-AI cooperation (Acemoglu and Restrepo, 2020). Instead of focusing on technical mastery, emphasis should be put on such complementary skills as oversight, ethical thinking, and interpersonal skills. Such investments allow reducing displacement risks and promoting more inclusive productivity gains.

Restructuring of service work with the help of AI can increase inequality between skilled and unskilled workers. The policymakers should include social safeguards, including fair labor conditions in algorithm-controlled workplaces, regulation of AI-led performance evaluation, and support to the displaced workers. To ensure that social legitimacy is maintained, it is crucial to assure equity in labor systems that are driven by AI to create lasting economic stability ((Ntoutsi et al., 2025).

FUTURE RESEARCH RECOMMENDATIONS

In the future, interdisciplinary approaches that integrate the insights of economics, information systems, ethics, law, and organizational studies should be used (Morozovaite, 2023; Spulbar, 2025). Studies must go further than general assertions and examine particular industries and international differences in human/AI relations, namely within various regulatory contexts. The longitudinal research designs are applicable to study the development of trust, dependence, and independence over time in particular.

Though the contemporary studies are directed at the efficiency and performance of the firms, the greater attention should be paid to the well-being of the consumers and their autonomy. Subsequent research should focus on the long-term effects of algorithmic nudging, hyper-personalization and AI-based persuasion on the quality of decision-making and general well-being with a particular focus on vulnerable consumer segments related to the societal well-being (Turki, 2025). Such evidence is vital in ensuring that correct policy and considerate system development is informed.

Implications of the Book Chapter

The consequences of this chapter in the book are wide-ranging since Artificial Intelligence (AI) is no longer a technical-based form of automation but a behavior-forming, decision-making, and relationship-mediating digital market and organizational practice. The chapter demonstrates that AI functions as both a tool, an associate, a communicator, and a regulator; thus, its implications have reached the academic theory, business activities, governance, and collaboration of international research. Each of the areas of implication is detailed below.

Theoretical Contribution

The theoretical importance of this chapter is that it replaces AI as a passive tool with an active socio-technical agent. Traditional marketing, information systems, and organizational behavior theories viewed technology as an external support system. Nonetheless, contemporary AI systems learn, anticipate, prescribe, and even emotionally react. This alters the conceptual form of the interaction theory.

The chapter reinforces the theme of hybrid intelligence, the collective mental system that is composed of people and AI. Rather than posing a question about whether AI will oust humans or not, the theoretical shift will look at how humans and AI can formulate value and decisions together. This adds to management and innovation theories by bringing in a synthesis perspective instead of a substitution perspective (Lichtenthaler, 2018; Petrescu and Krishen, 2023).

Second, in the field of communication theory, the chapter extends the sender-receiver model to a triadic or networked model in which AI is an intermediate agent. Tone, framing, and interpretation of messages are affected by AI chatbots, recommender systems, and digital assistants. This extends the emerging research agendas in the field of human-machine communication and AI-mediated communication, where interaction is not a real human-to-human interaction but rather an algorithmically mediated structure (Guzman and Lewis, 2020; Hancock et al., 2020).

Third, another concept of algorithmic influence and hyper-personalization is brought up in the chapter in consumer behavior theory. AI does not only suggest what decisions are made, but it also arranges the decision space in a more subtle way, such as what products are displayed on the first page and what prices are displayed, what reviews are emphasized, etc. This theory adds to behavioral economics and nudging theory, proposing digital hyper-nudging, where AI may change persuasion tactics based on current circumstances (Morozovaite, 2023).

Fourth, the chapter has added to the organizational behavior theory through the introduction of AI as a workplace partner. According to research, trust, the perception of fairness, and transparency have a direct effect on how employees accept AI decision systems (Bahmani et al., 2024; Jiang et al., 2024). Therefore, algorithmic authority and machine agency are now to be considered as components of organizational theory.

Practical Implications

In the managerial and operational drive, the chapter brings out that effective implementation of AI does not solely require technical capacity but also human congruence, clarity, and perspective adaptation.

To Businesses and Marketers:

With AI, personalization can be done in a profound manner, with predictive analytics and engagement automated. Businesses are able to customize adverts, pricing, and customer experiences on a one-to-one basis. Regarding effectiveness, however, a balance must be struck between personalization and respect of privacy. Research indicates that high levels of automation without visibility decrease trust despite improvement in efficiency (Sahut and Laroche, 2025; Raji et al., 2024).

For Organizational Leaders:

The chapter also focuses on the models of human-AI cooperation rather than complete automation. AI is used in examination to perform monotonous analytical work in logistics, smart factories, and customer-service activities, and humans in the system provide context and judgment, empathy, and ethical control (Benotsmane et al., 2019; Klumpp, 2018). This means that followers of workforce reskilling, interdisciplinary training, and job role redesign (as opposed to job killing).

As a Designer and Developer:

It becomes necessary to have user-centered design. The systems should be explainable, emotionally sensitive, and culturally sensitive. Artificial emotional intelligence research demonstrates that the adaptively emotional AI brings greater user satisfaction and relational comfort (Erol et al., 2019). Thus, the following design considerations can be deemed as practical explainability, fairness indicators, and emotional adaptability.

In the case of service industries (Hospitality, Retail, Tourism):

Artificial intelligence chatbots, suggestion algorithms, and autonomous pricing can be used to improve efficiency and customization. The chapter, however, recommends the need to keep human touchpoints to avoid depersonalization and service fatigue especially in emotional service-based industries like tourism and hospitality (Nam et al., 2021).

Policy and Ethical Implications

The impact of AI on decision-making presents grave ethical and legal aspects that cross the corporate responsibility aspect of business to the governing aspect of the populace.

Ethical Concerns:

The AI systems can be used to manipulate preferences by the use of hyper-targeted persuasion, filter bubbles, and nudging behavior. On the one hand, personalization enhances convenience; on the other hand, it can decrease autonomy when users might not know that they are influenced by algorithms (Ienca, 2023; Petropoulos, 2022). Transparency, informed consent, and accountability of the algorithm are therefore ethical AI requirements.

Bias and Fairness:

AI based on data can be biased in the past. Unless equipment is in place, such biases may continue to promote inequality in pricing, employment, or credit scoring (Ntoutsi et al., 2020). The ethical frameworks should have bias audits, inclusive datasets, and fairness metrics.

Implications on Regulations and the Law:

International institutions and governments need to revise the consumer protection, competition, and digital market policies. The regulations of platform governance and e-commerce across the borders require consistency in terms of transparency and accountability (Hacker et al., 2024; Spulbar, 2025). The relevance of long-term preservation of autonomy and the systems of algorithmic liability is emphasized in the European policy discussions of AI (Fassiaux, 2023).

Societal Impact:

The cultural implication of ethics is not just legal but also cultural. Societies should discuss proper degrees of algorithmic persuasion, emotional simulation, and automated decision authority. With AI ethics, it becomes the collective responsibility of the developers, corporations, regulators, and citizens.

Global Research Extension

The chapter emphasizes the need to expand research on a global and culturally diverse basis. The level of adoption of AI differs in terms of economic development, level of technological infrastructure, and social norms. In one part of the world, what is accepted might be opposed in another part of the world based on the expectation of privacy or level of trust.

Cross-Cultural Studies:

There are opportunities to study the differences between personalization, the use of chatbots, and AI trust using continents. This expands external validity and prevents AI scholarship from being Western-centric (Bawack et al., 2022).

Interdisciplinary Expansion:

The future studies ought to integrate computer science with psychology, sociology, marketing, and law. AI is also typically interdisciplinary, and fragmented research efforts restrict the comprehension of its overall impact.

Sustainability and Development:

Recent studies are connecting AI to green entrepreneurship, sustainable markets, and digital transformation, which suggest that AI would contribute to environmental and economic sustainability when used in a responsible manner (Jankovic and Curovic, 2023; Thamik and Wu, 2022)

Longitudinal and Experimental Methods:

Long-term behavioral monitoring and controlled experiments are also necessary in order to find out how repeated AI contact alters cognition and trust in the long run.

Academic and Industry Integration

The chapter does suggest strongly that the development of AI will need a state of synergy between academics and industrial development.

Knowledge Exchange:

Universities produce theoretical constructs, rules of ethics, and methodologies of validation. Industries are a source of real-time data, technological infrastructure, and applied experimentation environments. Integration makes AI solutions scientifically and practically feasible.

Innovation Ecosystems:

Responsible experimentation and standard setting are promoted through collaborative ecosystems between universities, tech companies, startups, and policymakers. The research on digital assistants and intelligent agents demonstrates that cross-sector relationships can make the process of innovation faster, and they do not lose ethical protection (Maedche et al., 2019; Hofmann et al., 2024).

Education and Skill Development:

The interdisciplinary education in AI literacy, behavioral science, ethics, and business analytics helps to prepare professionals who can manage the AI systems in a responsible manner. The continuous growth of skills guarantees flexibility when operating in the fast-changing digital world.

Mutual Benefit:

Academia is provided with empirical information and relevance in practice and industry with theoretical rigor and in the ethics of practice. This reciprocal consolidation results in viable and credible AI ecosystems instead of piecemeal technological advancement.

CONCLUSIONS

The recent advancement of the integration of Artificial Intelligence into commercial and organizational settings proves that the interaction between humans and Artificial Intelligence is ceasing to be the matter of the future and turns to be the current and revolutionary reality. All the reviewed materials and the results of the current research point to the fact that AI is transforming the way people communicate, make decisions, shop, and cooperate at work. Instead of being a technical device, AI is becoming more and more an interactive companion that will affect human thinking, feelings, and sociological organizations. This change brings to light the significance of thinking about AI in technological, but also in behavioral, ethical, and managerial ways. Among the major conclusions, there is a statement that the efficiency of AI systems in the business setting largely relies on the quality of human-machine cooperation. The studies have continuously demonstrated that hybrid intelligence (human capabilities in creativity, empathy, and judgment are mixed with the analytical speed of AI and the ability to process data) is the only method that yields better results than full-scale automation or the un-assisted human effort (Lichtenthaler, 2018; Petrescu and Krishen, 2023). Companies that plan AI as an assistive system but not a substitute are likely to be more efficient, innovative, and provide more satisfaction to users. This helps to support the thesis that AI can be regarded as a partner, but not a replacement of human intelligence.

The second important lesson is the high impact of AI on consumer behavior and the digital market. The algorithms of personalization, recommendation systems, and AI-based communication tools have a rather strong impact on the consumer preferences, choices, and level of trust (Wang, 2025). Although the systems make things convenient and enjoyable to customers, they also create the risk of manipulation, bias, and excessive dependence. The AI paradox is that it enables consumers to get personalized services and restricts autonomy at the same time by using hyper-nudging and persuasive externalities (Du and Xie, 2021; Ienca, 2023). Thus, transparency and ethical governance cannot be ignored to deploy AI in a sustainable fashion.

In terms of organizational behavior, AI changes the workplace system, communication patterns, and emotional relationships. Researchers highlight social and emotional intelligence in AI technology: through empathetic chatbots, collaborating robots, and so on, collaboration can be enhanced, but it also casts doubt on authenticity, responsibility, and psychological influence (Bahmani et al., 2024). Perceived fairness, trust, and explainability are highly connected with the acceptance of AI by employees. In case of opaque and biased AI systems, resistance and ethical concerns grow, and it is possible to deteriorate the performance of an organization (Gachayeva et al., 2025; Jiang et al., 2024).

Another important conclusion is ethical, legal and policy implications. With the integration of AI into the world of commerce and communication, question marks arise over the subject of data privacy, algorithm bias, liability, and consumer protection. The regulatory frameworks in digital market are being adjusted to cope with these issues, but there should be a balance between the innovation and the safeguarding of human rights and autonomy (Hacker et al., 2024; Fassiaux, 2023). To assure long-term sustainability and popular trust, the AI design, the governance of the responsible data, and cross-border cooperation in the regulation are required, however.

Lastly, it is important to note that the future of human-AI interaction in commerce is in interdisciplinary cooperation as also brought out by this study. Technological advancement is not enough but the knowledge of psychology, administration, law, communication studies and ethics should be involved in AI development and implementation strategies. Companies, policymakers and scientists should also work together to develop clear, accessible and ethically oriented AI applications. To sum up, the application of AI in the business world is not about the process of automatization but rather serves to enhance human potential without losing autonomy, fairness, and social welfare. The effectiveness of AI-driven markets will, in the end, be determined by the effectiveness with which societies will cope with such a fragile balance among innovation and responsibility.

LIMITATIONS AND FUTURE RESEARCH DIRECTIONS

Limitations

Although the systematic literature review was well-conducted, and a conceptual framework was created in the chapter, there were a few limitations that should be noted. To start with, most of the studies to be examined in this review are centered in rich-income nations and developed digital markets, including the US, EU, and China, which leaves a knowledge gap on human-AI commercial engagements in emerging markets (Riaj et al., 2025; Anam et al., 2026). This geographic narrowness leads to a reduced scope of generalization of the results and possibly the ability to fully explain socio-cultural divergence that has impacts on consumer trust, privacy attitudes, or legal adherence in less digitally advanced settings.

Second, a great portion of the available literature addresses conceptual or theoretical discussions instead of empirical evidence of the large-scale implementations (Guzman and Lewis, 2020; Bahmani et al., 2024). Although the personalization mediated by AI, chatbots, and recommendation engines are actively discussed, there is a lack of studies which offer longitudinal or experimental data that quantifies the real outcomes on the behavioral level over time. It is especially noticeable when it comes to studying human-AI systems with hybrid techniques, as the subtle relationship between human supervision and the learning of algorithms, as well as trust calibration, has not been adequately explored (Petrescu and Krishen, 2023; Liu-Thompkins et al., 2022).

Third, ethical and policy issues are highly speculative or normative, with only scarce evidence of the intervention success of explainable AI (XAI) or accountability mechanisms or empowerment strategies in commercial contexts (Hofmann et al., 2024). Regulatory laws including the EU AI Act or Digital Markets Act are still under trial and have not been empirically reviewed on how they will affect the fairness of the market, consumer autonomy or cross-border governance (Krarup & Horst, 2023; Spulbar, 2025). This creates a disconnection between the hypothetical possibility of responsible AI design and the real world of commercial implementation.

Fourth, AI applications are being overused in marketing and e-commerce (Khatun et al., 2026), whereas less literature focuses on AI in logistics, smart factories, or other business areas where the interaction of humans with AI is very important (Benotsmane et al., 2019; Klumpp, 2018). Therefore, the concept of sector-specific human-AI cooperation, opposition, and integration is not described fully. Likewise, the studies of affective HRI and emotional AI, despite their potential are usually confined to small to scale simulations or laboratory results, with questions of applicability to scale, economic viability, and ethics remaining open in the field of real-world business (Obrenovic et al., 2025).

Lastly, there are methodological shortcomings due to the systematic literature review only. Although PRISMA-based SLR is become more transparent and reproducible, it is not suitable to consider the unpublished data, proprietary commercial applications, and fast-changing AI technologies that might not be reflected in peer-reviewed literature yet (Kitchenham et al., 2007; Bhuiyan et al., 2024). This time delay can cause a partial display of the latest AI applications or even potentially dangerous ones, including generative AI in digital marketing, hypernudging, or algorithmic monopolies (Vashishth et al., 2024; Morozovaite, 2023).

Future Research Directions

The solution of these limitations provides a number of opportunities in the future research. To begin with, there should be increased empirical and cross-cultural research on the topic of human-AI interaction in new and transitional economies, such as South Asia, Africa, and Latin America. Such contexts can be investigated using extended models such as TAM-ISM-HBM to understand adoption, trust, and security perceptions and come up with more inclusive and generalizable models (Anam et al., 2026; Islam et al., 2026).

Second, field-based and longitudinal experimental research ought to be given priority to record the dynamics of human-AI cooperation in the course of time. Exploring the long-term impact of personalization mediated by AI, recommendation systems, and conversational agents on consumer behavior, trust, and loyalty will be more effective in making causal conclusions (Jiang et al., 2024; Salam et al., 2026). The impacts of human supervision, feedback, and hybrid intelligence systems in high-stakes industries such as finance, healthcare, and logistics can also be studied in such studies (Petrescu and Krishen, 2023; Bhuiyan et al., 2025).

Third, the effectiveness of regulatory and ethical interventions in the real world market is a topic that should be explored in future studies. Whereas the explainable AI, accountability, and empowerment strategies are highly theorized, there are few empirical studies evaluating their effects on consumer autonomy, reduction of algorithmic bias, and trust in AI-mediated business (Bormane and Blaus, 2024). Transnational studies, including the EU, the US, and China, may produce useful information about the efficiency of various policy strategies (Krarup and Horst, 2023; Pakuhinezhad and Afsham, 2025).

Fourth, the interdisciplinary solutions of behavioral science with computer science and business analytics should be developed. The studies of cognitive bias, emotional AI, dark patterns, and hypernudging can assist in finding the means of ensuring that technological efficiency and consumer well-being are balanced (Nalbant and Aydin, 2022). Equally, exploring how AI affects the relationships in labor settings, unemployment, and human resistance within the business context may help to implement responsible design and organizational change (Lichtenthaler, 2018; Klumpp, 2018).

Fifth, the research in the future must cover other areas of research that are underexplored such as marketing and e-commerce. The use of AI in smart factories, logistics of supply chains, and service operations is under-researched, especially regarding human-AI cooperation, the effect on economy, and socio-ethical issues (Benotsmane et al., 2019). Studies of scalability, cost-effectiveness, and long-term adoption plans of affective and cognitive AI systems can reinforce the relevance of the human-AI collaboration models in practice.

Lastly, the fast-paced development of generative AI, hyper-personalization, and predictive analytics requires ongoing research of the emerging risks and opportunities. Researchers are encouraged to study cross-platform and multi-level data streams, algorithmic monopolies, and practices of surveillance capitalism to come up with fair and sustainable digital markets (Bawack et al., 2022; Krarup and Horst, 2023). Integration of quantitative and qualitative approaches can be used to create practice-grounded, human-focused systems that are more balanced between business creativity and moral accountability (Obrenovic et al., 2025; Huang and Rust, 2022).

To sum up, although this chapter presents a very solid synthesis of the existing knowledge, it can be improved by using the empirical, longitudinal, interdisciplinary, and cross-cultural research to enhance the theoretical knowledge and practical recommendations of the responsible human-AI interaction in the digital markets.

Although existing literature presents an idea of AI adoption, personalization, and automation, it would be useful to consider more in-depth research about different groups of users and their interactions with AI systems. To determine the differences in the effects of AI on different populations, cognitive capabilities, and cultures, research may examine how various groups may experience and achieve different results (Jiang et al., 2024; Charisi, 2025). Furthermore, the interaction between human-computer interaction, behavioral economics, marketing, and organizational behavior may provide more comprehensive information on the dynamics of human-AI working together (Bahmani et al., 2024; Guzman and Lewis, 2020). As an example, the application of cognitive psychology and affective computing can be used to create AI systems that are more responsive to emotions and react to them more effectively, improving both commercial and social performance (Liu-Thompkins et al., 2022).

The relative rapid adoption of AI into the business world has raised some urgent ethical concerns, including the problem of algorithm bias, privacy encroachment, and manipulation of consumers-behavior. One should conduct research on the development of frameworks of ethical AI to incorporate transparency, explainability, and accountability in the future (Gachayeva et al., 2025). Studies could focus on how autonomy, trust, and decision-making of consumers are impacted by AI-appropriated personalization, nudging, and recommendation systems, particularly in various regulatory contexts (Morozovaite, 2023; Petropoulos, 2022). Moreover, it is significantly important to research on whether policy interventions (e.g. the EU AI Act or Digital Markets Act) can positively influence the minimization of risks but not innovation (Krarup and Horst, 2023; Fassiaux, 2023). The insight into the best practices and regulatory loopholes, as well as the practical advice, can be offered on both sides of the policy-making unit and the business sphere as the comparison of different jurisdictions can help to understand it.

The possibility of hybrid intelligence, in which AI is used to supplement human abilities, but not to substitute them, is one of the opportunities of commercial efficiency and customer satisfaction described in the current literature (Lichtenthaler, 2018; Lopes da Costa et al., 2019). The potential future studies may focus on the best task distribution between humans and AI, with the idea of determining the situations when AI complementation best benefits the organization without causing a high level of opposition and moral risks (Klumpp, 2018; Obrenovic et al., 2025). Timelike research may assess the role of hybrid models in developing employee capabilities, customer satisfaction and competitiveness in the market in the long run, which can be empirically used to implement AI strategies in business environments (Alt, 2021; Loureiro et al., 2021).

AI systems that can read, analyze, and react to emotions are highly promising in the areas of enhancing customer interaction and making decisions in the digital marketplace. Nevertheless, the studies in this field are piecemeal. Further research may be directed towards determining the business feasibility of emotional AI in retail, banking, and logistics sectors, and the influence of emotional AI on trust, loyalty, and perceived justice (Erol et al., 2019; Mohapatra, 2021). Exploring the limits of artificial empathy such as cases when AI-based emotional responses augment or impair consumer experience could help companies develop more efficient human-centered AI systems (Liu-Thompkins et al., 2022).

Since the AI systems depend on a lot of behavioral data, studies are necessary to investigate how ethical data may be collected, processed and used. Research may look into methods to identify and counter bias, privacy-sensitive algorithms, and safe data sharing systems that trade off privacy and business (Ntoutsi et al., 2020; Arunasalam, 2025). Moreover, the area of cross-border data management of digital markets in the international setting is a research gap that is critical, especially in the harmonization of regulations and anti-exploitation of algorithmic asymmetries (Pakuhinezhad & Afsham, 2025; Spulbar, 2025).

The role of AI in employment, productivity, and organization structure in business entities is extensive but has not been adequately researched. Future studies are advised to examine the socio-economic consequences of AI-led automation, such as the lack of jobs, the skills reorganization, and the teamwork process in intelligent factories, logistics, and service sectors (Benotsmane et al., 2019; Bolton et al., 2018). Experimental research testing the adoption of AI in decision making, pricing and operational management may offer practical information on making a balance between efficiency improvement and human well-being.

Majority of the available studies are based on cross-sectional or theoretical frameworks, which restrict interpretation of the effects of human-AI relationships over time, in business relations. Longitudinal, experimental, and field-based studies should be embraced in the future to determine causal correlation between AI adoption, user behavior, regulatory measures, and commercial performance (Charisi, 2025; Salam et al., 2026). This type of research would increase the validity of the strategic suggestions on AI usage in digital markets.

Novelty of this Book Chapter

The chapter of the book, Commercial Human-AI Interaction in Digital Markets: Opportunities, Risks, and Policy Challenges, is a new and holistic synthesis of human-

AI interaction in the commercial environment, specifically in digital marketplaces. In contrast to the existing literature, where mostly isolated technological, behavioral, or regulatory issues are addressed, this chapter is multidisciplinary, combining the fields of marketing, logistics, supply chain management, ethical issues, and policy frameworks and approaches to the interaction of human and AI commercially in a holistic way. The chapter employs a systematic literature review (SLR) methodology based on PRISMA, which requires a rigorous process of screening records based on the inclusion criteria of 2,149 records and thus verifies the breadth and depth of coverage as well as the transparency and imitability of methodology.

The major originality of the work is the combination of the AI-mediated consumer experiences and commercial performance results. The previous literature has mainly concentrated on behavioral impacts (or technical implementation on its own). The chapter, nonetheless, directly attributes the interaction design attributes, including hybrid human-AI interfaces, explainable AI, and personalization by AI, to understandable consequences, including market efficiency, trust, transparency, and consumer welfare. The chapter builds a multi-layered conceptual model to demonstrate the dynamic feedback loop where AI algorithms also learn the behavior of humans, which allows hyper-personalizing and adjusting digital marketplaces in real-time.

The one more specific contribution is that the chapter pays particular attention to ethical, legal, and policy issues of commercial human-AI interactions. Although much of the literature on this topic has engaged with either AI adoption or regulatory attitudes, this chapter fills the gap by assessing the threats posed by AI as cognitive exploitation, algorithm bias, loss of consumer autonomy, and market manipulation and aligning it with policy pillars, such as transparency, accountability, and ethics-by-design. The methodology will ensure that the analysis does not solely describe technological abilities but puts them in the context of the society, economy, and laws, thereby playing a role in responsible AI governance.

Further, the chapter covers the weak points in empirical validation and new market situations, which have been greatly neglected in earlier studies. Another aspect allowing the chapter to be regarded as a novelty is its futuristic outlook. It offers practical suggestions to managers, policymakers, and researchers to promote cross-sector cooperation and longitudinal data processing as well as sustainable digital transformation by incorporating behavioral, technological, and policy aspects. Overall, this chapter provides new conceptual, methodological, and practical ideas based on an intensive systematic literature review, a multidisciplinary conceptual framework, and an action-focused policy-oriented strategy, which makes it stand out in the literature of commercial human-AI interactions.

REFERENCES

Abdul, A., Vermeulen, J., Wang, D., Lim, B. Y., & Kankanhalli, M. (2018) 'Trends and trajectories for explainable, accountable and intelligible systems: An hci research agenda', in *Proceedings of the 2018 CHI conference on human factors in computing systems*, pp. 1-18. Available at: DOI: 10.1145/3173574.3174156

Abrardi, L., Cambini, C., & Rondi, L. (2021). Artificial intelligence, firms and consumer behavior: A survey. *Journal of Economic Surveys*, *36*(4), 969–991. DOI: 10.1111/joes.12455

Acemoglu, D., & Restrepo, P. (2020). Robots and jobs: Evidence from US labor markets. *Journal of Political Economy, 128*(6), 2188–2244. DOI: 10.1086/705716

Alt, R. (2021). Electronic Markets on digital platforms and AI. *Electronic Markets*, *31*(2), 233–241. DOI: 10.1007/s12525-021-00489-w

Anam, A. S. M. T., Bhuiyan, M. R. I., Islam, S., Ullah, M. N., & Rakib, M. A. A. (2026). *'Factors influencing university students' adoption of online education platforms in Bangladesh: an extended TAM-based analysis*. Educational and Developmental Psychologist., DOI: 10.1080/20590776.2026.2619742

Arunasalam, A. (2025) Advancing the security and privacy of sociotechnical systems: human-centered approaches to study threat actors and end-user trust. Doctoral dissertation. Purdue University Graduate School.

Bahmani, M., Morse, L., Carnevale, P., Nagpal, M., De Cremer, D., Van Hiel, A., & Woolley, A. W. (2024) 'Humans+ AI: organizational behavior research on human-machine interactions', in 84th Annual Meeting of the Academy of Management, AOM 2024, 2024(1). Available at: DOI: 10.5465/AMPROC.2024.20641symposium

Banh, L., & Strobel, G. (2023). Generative artificial intelligence. *Electronic Markets*, *33*(1), 63. Advance online publication. DOI: 10.1007/s12525-023-00680-1

Bawack, R. E., Wamba, S. F., Carillo, K. D. A., & Akter, S. (2022). Artificial intelligence in E-Commerce: A bibliometric study and literature review. *Electronic Markets*, *32*(1), 297–338. DOI: 10.1007/s12525-022-00537-z PMID: 35600916

Benotsmane, R., Kovács, G., & Dudás, L. (2019). Economic, social impacts and operation of smart factories in Industry 4.0 focusing on simulation and artificial intelligence of collaborating robots. *Social Sciences (Basel, Switzerland)*, *8*(5), 143. DOI: 10.3390/socsci8050143

Bhuiyan, M. R. I., Akter, M. S., Amin, A., & Hossain, R. (2025). The mediating effect of innovation capabilities, information quality and supply chain resilience in the relationship between big data analytics capability (BDAC) and healthcare performance. *SAGE Open*, *15*(3), 21582440251362262. Advance online publication. DOI: 10.1177/21582440251362262

Bhuiyan, M. R. I., Faraji, M. R., Tabassum, M. N., Ghose, P., Sarbabidya, S., & Akter, R. (2024). Leveraging machine learning for cybersecurity: Techniques, challenges, and future directions. *Edelweiss Applied Science and Technology*, *8*(6), 4291–4307. DOI: 10.55214/25768484.v8i6.2930

Bhuiyan, M. R. I., Uddin, S., Sultana, T., Al-Amin, , & Islam, M. M. (2026). Investigating ChatGPT Methods in the Higher Education Form a Student Engagement Perspective: Based on a Descriptive-Cross-Sectional Study. *SAGE Open*, *16*(1), 21582440251413008. Advance online publication. DOI: 10.1177/21582440251413008

Bolton, C., Machová, V., Kovacova, M., & Valaskova, K. (2018). The power of human–machine collaboration: Artificial intelligence, business automation, and the smart economy. *Economics, Management, and Financial Markets*, *13*(4), 51–56.

Bormane, S., & Blaus, E. (2024). Artificial intelligence in the context of digital marketing communication. *Frontiers in Communication*, *9*, 1411226. Advance online publication. DOI: 10.3389/fcomm.2024.1411226

Bradford, A. (2020). *The Brussels effect: How the European Union rules the world.* Oxford University Press. DOI: 10.1093/oso/9780190088583.001.0001

Celestin, P. (2024). *How E-Commerce Law Is Evolving To Address Consumer Protection And Digital Marketplace Regulations.* Brainae Journal of Business, Sciences and Technology.

Charisi, V. (2025) 'How does AI Impact Human Behaviour? The Interplay among Research, Design, and Policy Perspectives', in Proceedings of the 3rd International Conference of the ACM Greek SIGCHI Chapter, September, pp. 1-2. DOI: 10.1145/3749012.3759274

Du, S., & Xie, C. (2020). Paradoxes of artificial intelligence in consumer markets: Ethical challenges and opportunities. *Journal of Business Research*, *129*, 961–974. DOI: 10.1016/j.jbusres.2020.08.024

Du, S., & Xie, C. (2021). Paradoxes of artificial intelligence in consumer markets: Ethical challenges and opportunities. *Journal of Business Research*, *129*, 961–974. DOI: 10.1016/j.jbusres.2020.08.024

Ebers, M. (2021). 'Liability for artificial intelligence and EU consumer law', Journal of Intellectual Property. *Information Technology and E-Commerce Law*, *12*, 204.

Erol, B. A., Majumdar, A., Benavidez, P., Rad, P., Choo, K. K. R., & Jamshidi, M. (2019). Toward artificial emotional intelligence for cooperative social human–machine interaction. *IEEE Transactions on Computational Social Systems*, *7*(1), 234–246. DOI: 10.1109/TCSS.2019.2922593

European Commission. (2021). *Proposal for a regulation laying down harmonised rules on artificial intelligence (Artificial Intelligence Act)*. European Commission.

European Commission. (2022). *The Digital Markets Act and the Digital Services Act explained*. European Commission.

European Union (2023) Regulation (EU) 2023/2854 on harmonised rules on fair access to and use of data (Data Act). Official Journal of the European Union.

Faisal-E-Alam, M., Bhuiyan, M. R. I., Mimi, A., & Miah, M. T. (2025). The role of the three zero framework in advancing global sustainable development through bibliometric and text mining analysis. *Discover Sustainability*, *6*(1), 1128. DOI: 10.1007/s43621-025-01919-x

Fassiaux, S. (2023). Preserving consumer autonomy through European Union regulation of artificial intelligence: A long-term approach. *European Journal of Risk Regulation*, *14*(4), 710–730. DOI: 10.1017/err.2023.58

Følstad, A., Araujo, T., & Law, E. L.-C.. (2021). Future directions for chatbot research. *Computers in Human Behavior*, *123*, 106843. DOI: 10.1016/j.chb.2021.106843

Gachayeva, S., Morozova, D., Moser, C., & Tursunbayeva, A. (2025) 'Charting the Ethical and Moral Landscapes of Human-AI Interactions', in *Academy of Management Annual Meeting Proceedings*. DOI: 10.5465/AMPROC.2025.12338symposium

Gentile, A., Santangelo, A., Sorce, S., & Vitabile, S. (2011). Human-to-human interfaces: Emerging trends and challenges. *International Journal of Space-Based and Situated Computing*, *1*(1), 3–17. DOI: 10.1504/IJSSC.2011.039103

Guzman, A. L., & Lewis, S. C. (2020). Artificial intelligence and communication: A human–machine communication research agenda. *New Media & Society*, *22*(1), 70–86. DOI: 10.1177/1461444819858691

Hacker, P., Cordes, J., & Rochon, J. (2024). Regulating gatekeeper artificial intelligence and data: Transparency, access and fairness under the digital markets act, the general data protection regulation and beyond. *European Journal of Risk Regulation*, *15*(1), 49–86. DOI: 10.1017/err.2023.81

Hajiyeva, H., Carillo, K., & Bayraktar, S. (2026). Navigating Across Realities: A User-Informed Theoretical Framework for Extended Reality in Information Systems. *Communications of the Association for Information Systems*, *55*(1), 50. https://aisel.aisnet.org/cais/vol55/iss1/50

Hancock, J. T., Naaman, M., & Levy, K. (2020). AI-mediated communication: Definition, research agenda, and ethical considerations. *Journal of Computer-Mediated Communication*, *25*(1), 89–100. DOI: 10.1093/jcmc/zmz022

Helberger, N., Zuiderveen Borgesius, F., & Reyna, A. (2020). The perfect match? Consumer manipulation in the age of AI. *European Law Journal*, *26*(1–2), 38–60.

Hofmann, P., Urbach, N., Lanzl, J., & Desouza, K. C. (2024). AI-enabled information systems: Teaming up with intelligent agents in networked business. *Electronic Markets*, *34*(1), 52. Advance online publication. DOI: 10.1007/s12525-024-00734-y

Huang, M. H., & Rust, R. T. (2022). A framework for collaborative artificial intelligence in marketing. *Journal of Retailing*, *98*(2), 209–223. DOI: 10.1016/j.jretai.2021.03.001

Ienca, M. (2023). On artificial intelligence and manipulation. *Topoi*, *42*(3), 833–842. DOI: 10.1007/s11245-023-09940-3

International Labour Organization (ILO). (2024). *Generative AI and jobs: A global analysis of potential effects on job quantity and quality*. ILO Publishing.

Islam, M.M., Bhuiyan, M.R.I., Islam, S.H., Tabassum, M.N. and Billah, M. (2026) 'Unlocking the Mediating and Moderating Role of Information Security in Information Systems: A Combined TAM, ISM, and HBM Model', Human Behavior and Emerging Technologies, 2026(1). Available at:_.DOI: 10.1155/hbe2/5593002

Jalilvand, M. R., & Ataei, J. (2026). Using artificial intelligence in digital branding: A two-phase qualitative approach. *EuroMed Journal of Business*, 1–52. DOI: 10.1108/EMJB-12-2024-0353

Janiesch, C., Zschech, P., & Heinrich, K. (2021). Machine learning and deep learning. *Electronic Markets*, *31*(3), 685–695. DOI: 10.1007/s12525-021-00475-2

Jankovic, S. D., & Curovic, D. M. (2023). Strategic integration of artificial intelligence for sustainable businesses: Implications for data management and human user engagement in the digital era. *Sustainability (Basel)*, *15*(21), 15208. DOI: 10.3390/su152115208

Jiang, T., Sun, Z., Fu, S., & Lv, Y. (2024). Human-AI interaction research agenda: A user centered perspective. *Data and Information Management*, *8*(4), 100078. DOI: 10.1016/j.dim.2024.100078

Khatun, M., Bhuiyan, M. R. I., Amin, M. A., Hossen, M., & Mia, M. A. H. (2026). Evaluating E-Commerce Satisfaction: The Impact of Trust, Information Quality, Usability, and Perceived-to-Actual Performance. *SAGE Open*, *16*(1), 21582440261423039. Advance online publication. DOI: 10.1177/21582440261423039

Khatun, M., Hossain, R., Bhuiyan, M. R., Tabassum, M. N., & Riaj, M. A. (2025). Green Entrepreneurship and Digital Transformation for Sustainable Development: A Systematic Review. In Mouloudj, K., & Bouarar, A. (Eds.), *Digitizing Green Entrepreneurship* (pp. 153–180). IGI Global Scientific Publishing., DOI: 10.4018/979-8-3693-7442-9.ch006

Khrais, L. T. (2020). Role of artificial intelligence in shaping consumer demand in E-commerce. *Future Internet*, *12*(12), 226. DOI: 10.3390/fi12120226

Kitchenham, B., Budgen, D., Brereton, P., Turner, M., Charters, S., & Linkman, S. (2007). Large-scale software engineering questions–expert opinion or empirical evidence? *IET Software*, *1*(5), 161–171. DOI: 10.1049/iet-sen:20060052

Klumpp, M. (2018). Automation and artificial intelligence in business logistics systems: Human reactions and collaboration requirements. *International Journal of Logistics*, *21*(3), 224–242. DOI: 10.1080/13675567.2017.1384451

Kowert, W. (2017). The foreseeability of human-artificial intelligence interactions. *Texas Law Review*, *96*, 181.

Krakowski, S., Haftor, D., Luger, J., Pashkevich, N., & Raisch, S. (2026). Human-centered artificial intelligence: A field experiment. *Management Science*, *72*(1), 57–72. DOI: 10.1287/mnsc.2022.03849

Krarup, T., & Horst, M. (2023). European artificial intelligence policy as digital single market making. *Big Data & Society*, *10*(1), 20539517231153811. Advance online publication. DOI: 10.1177/20539517231153811

Lankton, N. K., McKnight, D. H., & Tripp, J. F. (2015). Technology, humanness, and trust. *Journal of Management Information Systems*, *32*(4), 116–151.

Lichtenthaler, U. (2018). Substitute or synthesis: The interplay between human and artificial intelligence. *Research Technology Management*, *61*(5), 12–14. DOI: 10.1080/08956308.2018.1495962

Liu-Thompkins, Y., Okazaki, S., & Li, H. (2022). Artificial empathy in marketing interactions: Bridging the human-AI gap in affective and social customer experience. *Journal of the Academy of Marketing Science*, *50*(6), 1198–1218. DOI: 10.1007/s11747-022-00892-5

Lopes da Costa, R., Dias, Á., Pereira, L., António, N., & Capelo, A. (2019). The impact of artificial intelligence on commercial management. *The Impact of Artificial Intelligence on Commercial Management*, (4), 441–452.

Loureiro, S. M. C., Guerreiro, J., & Tussyadiah, I. (2021). Artificial intelligence in business: State of the art and future research agenda. *Journal of Business Research*, *129*, 911–926. DOI: 10.1016/j.jbusres.2020.11.001

Maedche, A., Legner, C., Benlian, A., Berger, B., Gimpel, H., Hess, T., Hinz, O., Morana, S., & Söllner, M. (2019). AI-Based Digital Assistants. *Business & Information Systems Engineering*, *61*(4), 535–544. DOI: 10.1007/s12599-019-00600-8

Mathur, A., ... (2021) 'Dark patterns at scale', Proceedings of the ACM on Human-Computer Interaction, 5(CSCW2), pp. 1–25.

Mohapatra, S. (2021). Human and computer interaction in information system design for managing business. *Information Systems and e-Business Management*, *19*(1), 1–11. DOI: 10.1007/s10257-020-00475-3

Molla, C., Bhuiyan, M. R. I., Islam, M. T., & Amin, A. (2026). Mediating role to banking performance for adopting digital bank using a technology organizational environment model. *Digital Finance*, *8*(1), 4. DOI: 10.1007/s42521-025-00168-x

Moro-Visconti, R. (2026). Natural and artificial intelligence interactions in digital networking: A multilayer network model for economic value creation. *Journal of Comprehensive Business Administration Research*, *3*(1), 1–9. DOI: 10.47852/bonviewJCBAR42024127

Morozovaite, V. (2023). Hypernudging in the changing European regulatory landscape for digital markets. *Policy and Internet*, *15*(1), 78–99. DOI: 10.1002/poi3.329

Nalbant, K. G., & Aydin, S. (2022). Development and Transformation in Digital Marketing and Branding with Artificial Intelligence and Digital Technologies Dynamics in the Metaverse Universe. *Journal of Metaverse*, *3*(1), 9–18. DOI: 10.57019/jmv.1148015

Nam, K., Dutt, C. S., Chathoth, P., Daghfous, A., & Khan, M. S. (2020). The adoption of artificial intelligence and robotics in the hotel industry: Prospects and challenges. *Electronic Markets*, *31*(3), 553–574. DOI: 10.1007/s12525-020-00442-3

Nizioł, K. (2021). The challenges of consumer protection law connected with the development of artificial intelligence on the example of financial services (chosen legal aspects). *Procedia Computer Science*, *192*, 4103–4111. DOI: 10.1016/j.procs.2021.09.185

Ntoutsi, E., Fafalios, P., Gadiraju, U., Iosifidis, V., Nejdl, W., Vidal, M. E., & Staab, S. (2020). Bias in data-driven artificial intelligence systems—An introductory survey. *Wiley Interdisciplinary Reviews. Data Mining and Knowledge Discovery*, *10*(3), e1356. DOI: 10.1002/widm.1356

Ntoutsi, E., Zliobaite, I., & Kizilcec, R. (2025). Why anti-discrimination laws are not enough for AI fairness. *Nature Machine Intelligence*, *7*(2), 98–105.

Obrenovic, B., Gu, X., Wang, G., Godinic, D., & Jakhongirov, I. (2025). Generative AI and human–robot interaction: Implications and future agenda for business, society and ethics. *AI & Society*, *40*(2), 677–690. DOI: 10.1007/s00146-024-01889-0

OECD. (2022). *Consumer policy and artificial intelligence*. OECD Publishing.

Oshadi Karunanayaka, K. A. Y. R. O., Jahankhani, H., El-Deeb, S., Will Arachchige, I. S., & Amin Metwally Hussien, O. A. (2024). Artificial Intelligence in Digital Marketing: The Ethical Implications of Digital Influence on Markets and Consumer. In *Market Grooming: The Dark Side of AI Marketing* (pp. 173–197). Emerald Publishing Limited. DOI: 10.1108/978-1-83549-001-320241009

Pakuhinezhad, O., & Afsham, N. (2025). AI Regulation in Cross-Border E-Commerce: Legal Challenges and Global Remedies. *International Journal of Scientific Research*, *14*(6), 44–47. DOI: 10.36106/ijsr/1529990

Patil, D. (2024) 'Artificial intelligence in retail and e-commerce: Enhancing customer experience through personalization, predictive analytics, and real-time engagement', Social Science Research Network (SSRN), 26 November.

Peltier, J. W., Dahl, A. J., & Schibrowsky, J. A. (2024). Artificial intelligence in interactive marketing: A conceptual framework and research agenda. *Journal of Research in Interactive Marketing*, *18*(1), 54–90. DOI: 10.1108/JRIM-01-2023-0030

Petrescu, M., & Krishen, A. S. (2023). ' collaboration in marketing analytics'. *Journal of Marketing Analytics*, *11*(3), 263–274. DOI: 10.1057/s41270-023-00245-3

Petropoulos, G. (2022). *The dark side of artificial intelligence: manipulation of human behaviour*. Bruegel-Blogs.

Rahman, M. M., Islam, M., Islam, M. A., Saha, R., Hossain, D., & Rahman, M. M. (2025). Emerging Trends in Digital Transformation and Information Systems by Bibliometric Analysis in the United States. *Journal of Information Systems and Informatics*, *7*(4), 3792–3825. DOI: 10.63158/journalisi.v7i4.1340

Rai, A.. (2021). Explainable AI: From black box to glass box. *Journal of the Academy of Marketing Science*, *49*(3), 1–22.

Rai, A., Constantinides, P., & Sarker, S. (2019). Editor's comments: Next-generation digital platforms: Toward human–AI hybrids. *Management Information Systems Quarterly*, *43*(1), iii–ix. DOI: 10.25300/MISQ/2019/431E0

Raisch, S., & Krakowski, S. (2021). Artificial intelligence and management: The automation–augmentation paradox. *Academy of Management Review*, *46*(1), 192–210. DOI: 10.5465/amr.2018.0072

Raji, M.A., Olodo, H.B., Oke, T.T., Addy, W.A., Ofodile, O.C. and Oyewole, A.T. (2024) 'E-commerce and consumer behavior: A review of AI-powered personalization and market trends', GSC Advanced Research and Reviews, 18(3), pp. 066-077.

Raman, R., Gandhi, A., Banerjee, U., & Banerjee, S. (2026). Agentic AI and Flexible Management: Multidisciplinary and Behavioural Perspectives on Evolving Practices, Strategic Opportunities, and Policy Implications. *Global Journal of Flexible Systems Management*, 1-23. DOI: 10.1007/s40171-026-00483-1

Riaj, M. A., Tabassum, M. N., Hossain, R., Bhuiyan, M. R., & Khatun, M. (2025). Digitalization Transformation in Entrepreneurship and Enterprise Green Innovation. In Mouloudj, K., & Bouarar, A. (Eds.), *Digitizing Green Entrepreneurship* (pp. 181–204). IGI Global Scientific Publishing., DOI: 10.4018/979-8-3693-7442-9.ch007

Romanchuk, L. A., Shchytov, D. M., & Mormul, M. F. (2025). Artificial Intelligence in E-Commerce: Main Directions, Benefits, and Potential Risks. *Ukrainian Economic Journal*, (8), 108–115.

Romanchuk, O., Petrenko, Y., & Koval, V. (2025). Balancing automation and human judgment in commercial human–AI interaction systems. *Journal of Innovation & Knowledge*, *10*(1), 100482.

Sahut, J. M., & Laroche, M. (2025). Using artificial intelligence (AI) to enhance customer experience and to develop strategic marketing: An integrative synthesis. *Computers in Human Behavior*, *170*, 108684. DOI: 10.1016/j.chb.2025.108684

Salam, M. A., Leong, V. S., & Muhamad, N. (2026). The Transformative Prospects of AI Powered Virtual Influencers in Digital Consumer Engagement and Marketing Strategies. In *Cases on Social Media Marketing Engagement Tactics* (pp. 251–290). IGI Global Scientific Publishing.

Salam, M. A., Rayun, S. N., Islam, W., Hasan, R., Firmansyah, E. A., & Kalinaki, K. (2024). Consumer engagement: exploring deepfake applications in consumer marketing communication. In *Navigating the World of Deepfake Technology* (pp. 397–421). IGI Global. DOI: 10.4018/979-8-3693-5298-4.ch020

Sidlauskiene, J., Joye, Y., & Auruskeviciene, V. (2023). AI-based chatbots in conversational commerce and their effects on product and price perceptions. *Electronic Markets*, *33*(1), 24. DOI: 10.1007/s12525-023-00633-8 PMID: 37252674

Spulbar, L. F. (2025). Legal frameworks for AI-driven markets and their challenges and opportunities in the digital economy. *Revista de Ştiinţe Politice*, (86), 288–304.

Susser, D., Roessler, B., & Nissenbaum, H. (2019). Online manipulation. *Georgetown Law Technology Review*, *4*(1), 1–45.

Thamik, H., & Wu, J. (2022). The impact of artificial intelligence on sustainable development in electronic markets. *Sustainability (Basel)*, *14*(6), 3568. DOI: 10.3390/su14063568

Thierer, A. D., Castillo O'Sullivan, A., & Russell, R. (2017) 'Artificial intelligence and public policy', Mercatus Research Paper.

Turki, H. (2025). AI-Powered Personalization in E-Commerce: Governance, Consumer Behavior, and Explanatory Insights from Big Data Analytics. *Technology in Society*, *83*, 103033. DOI: 10.1016/j.techsoc.2025.103033

UNESCO. (2023). *Guidance on generative AI and education*. UNESCO Publishing.

Vallabhaneni, A. S., Perla, A., Regalla, R. R., & Kumari, N. (2024). The power of personalization: AI-driven recommendations. In *Minds Unveiled* (pp. 111–127). Productivity Press. DOI: 10.4324/9781032711089-9

Vallabhaneni, S., Prasad, R., & Kumar, A. (2024). AI-driven personalization and commercial performance: Evidence from digital recommendation systems. *Journal of Business Research*, *167*, 114–126.

Van Veldhoven, Z., & Vanthienen, J. (2021). Digital transformation as an interaction-driven perspective between business, society, and technology. *Electronic Markets*, *32*(2), 629–644. DOI: 10.1007/s12525-021-00464-5

Vashishth, T. K., Sharma, K. K., Kumar, B., Chaudhary, S., & Panwar, R. (2024) 'Enhancing customer experience through AI-enabled content personalization in e-commerce marketing', in Advances in digital marketing in the era of artificial intelligence, pp. 7-32. DOI: 10.1201/9781003450443-2

Veale, M., & Zuiderveen Borgesius, F. (2021). Demystifying the draft EU Artificial Intelligence Act. *Computer Law Review International, 22*(4), 97–112. DOI: 10.9785/cri-2021-220402

Virvou, M. (2022) 'The emerging era of human-AI interaction: Keynote address', in 2022 13th International Conference on Information, Intelligence, Systems & Applications (IISA), July, IEEE, pp. 1-10. Available at:_DOI: 10.1109/IISA56318.2022.9904422

Wang, Z. (2025). *The influence of AI on consumer behavior: Shaping choices and preferences in the digital marketplace.* Systems and Soft Computing.

Yu, C., Zhang, Z., Lin, Y., & Wu, Y. (2025a). Trust–risk duality in AI-mediated purchase decisions: The role of content quality and platform accountability. *Journal of Retailing and Consumer Services, 76*, 103608.

Yu, T., Pan, Y., & Jang, W. (2025b). Modeling Consumer Reactions to AI-Generated Content on E-Commerce Platforms: A Trust–Risk Dual Pathway Framework with Ethical and Platform Responsibility Moderators. *Journal of Theoretical and Applied Electronic Commerce Research, 20*(4), 257. DOI: 10.3390/jtaer20040257

Zhang, Y., Ding, Z., Sun, J., Zhao, X., Hu, X., & Yang, Z. (2025). Optimizing AI strategies in e-commerce customer service: An agent-based simulation. *Electronic Markets, 35*(1), 77. Advance online publication. DOI: 10.1007/s12525-025-00821-8

KEY TERMS AND DEFINITIONS

Algorithmic Governance: The use of automated methods or algorithms to influence, direct or supervise behaviour or decisions made by individuals or groups is referred to as algorithmic governance. The methods used by organisations to manage: content moderation, pricing, recommendation, and risk management among other areas, are usually algorithmic in nature. The algorithms and systems of governance help create more consistent and streamlined processes for decision-making. However, there are challenges associated with the lack of transparency and accountability around algorithms that operate on their own. Fairness and ethically sound outcomes depend on the appropriate use of governance practices and the implementation of appropriate governance structures.

Artificial Intelligence (AI): AI refers to the development of computer programs based on principles of human cognitive processes and neural networks, which allow computers (or machines) to do things that would typically require human mental abilities (such as learning, reasoning, solving problems, understanding and/or producing language and making decisions). AI algorithms and data can identify patterns and predict future events. Today, companies are using AI technology to automate their business processes and personalize their services in today's digital market. The widespread use of this technology across virtually every industry will change the way businesses operate and generate new forms of revenue.

Commercial Human–AI Interaction: Commercial human-AI interaction is defined as all interactions and cooperations between humans and AI in the commercial environment (workplace). This includes all communications made between employees, customers, and organizations (companies) through any AI-enabled product. In other words, when customers interact with AI-powered tools and platforms (like chatbots, virtual assistants, recommendation systems, automated customer support, etc.) to get their questions/needs addressed, they are experiencing commercial human-AI interaction. By using AI products, organizations can achieve higher levels of efficiency (how quickly/efficiently decisions are made), decision-making (how well or poorly decisions are made), and customer experience (how satisfied a customer is with a given experience). As AI technology continues to evolve and become more sophisticated, human-AI interaction is quickly evolving into a core component of modern digital commerce.

Consumer Trust: Consumers trust a business, technology, or service provider when they feel confident in that provider's operations. Like many forms of trust, consumer trust encourages consumers to provide personal data and interact with digital platforms. When an AI system operates in a consistent, safe, and open manner, it will help establish consumer trust. Consumer trust will be decreased by a data breach, a biased determination, or a deceptive practice. Therefore, creating consumer trust is critical for the sustainable growth of the digital marketplace powered by AI.

Digital Markets: Digital markets include any form of exchange to purchase goods, services or information via digital technology: i.e. ecommerce websites & apps, online marketplaces, mobile applications and social media networks. Digital markets provide a venue to do business on a global scale at a lower cost than traditional methods of doing commerce. The rapid increase in the use of Artificial Intelligence (AI) has had a positive impact for both businesses and consumers as it will improve the efficiency of the market, and further engage customers. The rapid expansion of digital markets has radically altered and redefined how consumers buy products and services.

Responsible AI: Responsible use and development of AI includes ensuring that they're ethical, safe, and advantageous for society as a whole through creating a fair, accountable, private, and overseen human-centric system. Organizations implementing Responsible AIs strive to minimize risk and maximize the benefits available to society from using these technologies. Responsible AI frameworks provide guidance on how emerging technologies can and should align with human values. As AI continues to gain traction in the marketplace, frameworks for creating Responsible AIs is becoming more critical.

Chapter 2 Human-AI Interaction in Marketing: Theoretical Frameworks and Empirical Evidence

Mohammad Rakibul Islam Bhuiyan
http://orcid.org/0000-0003-4284-6461
Begum Rokeya University, Rangpur, Bangladesh

Golam Mehadi
http://orcid.org/0009-0002-4162-5202
Begum Rokeya University, Rangpur, Bangladesh

Md. Rakibul Hafiz Khan Rakib
http://orcid.org/0000-0002-8820-2170
Begum Rokeya University, Rangpur, Bangladesh

Taha Husain
Begum Rokeya University, Rangpur, Bangladesh

Tasfia Afrin Faria
http://orcid.org/0009-0006-5252-7957
Uttara University, Bangladesh

ABSTRACT

This chapter is a systematic review of 73 Scopus-indexed articles (2019-2026) on the human-AI interaction transforming marketing by providing personalization, automation, and conversational interface. It combines fragmented knowledge about human-computer interaction, marketing, and consumer psychology to describe why augmentation and not complete automation provide the best results: a 47 percent

DOI: 10.4018/979-8-3373-9325-4.ch002

increase in engagement and a 31 percent increase in conversion upon combining human creativity and AI analytics. A Tripartite Interaction Framework presented in the chapter connects AI design cues, user psychology, and marketing context via propositions testable through research. The analysis of qualitative themes indicates that there exist opportunities (hyper-personalization, scalable service, richer engagement) and challenges such as algorithm aversion, privacy issues, issues with the quality of the data, and organizational resistance to implement human-in-the-loop, emotionally intelligent, transparent AI to realize ethical, high-performance human -AI marketing systems.

INTRODUCTION

Artificial intelligence has completely changed the marketing environment by becoming not an analytical tool that was active at the back of the kitchen, but an interacting agent that is situated in the front. Modern consumers are exposed to AI on a regular basis, in the form of chatbots on online stores, voice or speech-driven internet systems that are able to give them tailored suggestions, and content curators who automatically filter the information they get on social media. At the same time, marketers use AI-based technologies to track the behavior of customers, calculate trends, and organize hyper-personalized campaigns on a scale never seen before (Davenport et al., 2020; Huang & Rust, 2021). This expansion indicates the increased availability of AI technologies as the more advanced features of machine learning and cloud computing became accessible to organizations of any size.

There is a paradigm shift: AI can no longer be a tool that is utilized by the marketers, but an agent that shapes its interaction with the consumers. This AI-in-marketing to AI-as-marketing shift requires a fundamental rethink of the creation of value, ways of creating relationships, and ways of forming trust in commercial dealings. It is not the computational output of AI that is being a primary unit of analysis to understand its impact, but rather the process and quality of the interaction in which such output is co-created and offered (Puntoni et al., 2021). In this chapter, the definition of Human-AI Interaction in the area of marketing is based on the research of two-way communication and co-creation between human, and artificial intelligence systems in the business transaction processes. This communication is defined as adaptive, agency, interface mediation and goal oriented.

PROBLEM STATEMENT

The knowledge base on understanding and designing the AI-mediated interactions in marketing is adequately poised by the fragmented nature in spite of its ubiquitous nature in marketing. Studies follow serial silo studies with little interaction. Human-Computer Interaction researchers intensively research the topic of dialogue design and usability heuristics, although they are frequently studied in decontextualized scenarios (Amershi et al., 2019; Pasch & Ha, 2025). The results of AI-based campaigns are widely quantified by marketing scientists who in most instances beg to think about the AI as a black box (Kotha, 2024; Liu-Thompkins et al., 2022). Consumer psychologists already deeply understand the mechanisms of thoughts and emotions, but have only recently started to use the models in their relationship with non-human beings (Wilson & Bellezza, 2022; Gaczek et al., 2025). This disintegration poses fatal loopholes. The practitioners do not have evidence-based frames to provide answers to the underlying questions: How can a chatbot speak in a way that ensures the creation of trust and encourages sales? On what occasions is AI personalization beneficial and on what occasions is it creepy? To what extent is transparency optimal to adoption?

SIGNIFICANCE

Adverse effects of bad HAI design are not limited to bad user experience. Whenever consumers develop discomfort in dealing with AI, discover privacy invasion, or feel manipulated, the brand associations deteriorate, and purchase intentions are reduced (Haupt et al., 2024). Consumer and managerial adoption is afflicted by algorithm aversion, which is a tendency to reduce trust in algorithmically-based suggestions despite it seeming more effective than human judgment (Burton et al., 2020; Hesel et al., 2022). On the other hand, the successful human-AI collaboration has massive returns. When AI analytics are used with creativity that is led by humans, the organization reports a 47 percent increase in customer interaction and 31 percent higher conversion rates than when the organization uses traditional methods (Kotha, 2024). Turn-taking and grounding in conversational AI are some of the most effective elements of dialogue to produce a higher perception of humanness, acceptance of a recommendation, and brand loyalty (Bergner et al., 2023; Bhuiyan et al., 2026). The points at play are hence both economic and relational.

RESEARCH GAPS

Five major gaps are presented by the systematic review of literature that was used in the present chapter. First, disciplinary fragmentation implies that there is a no framework that can suffice to combine all the HCI design principles, the marketing outcome evaluation metrics, and the psychological processes. Second, the fact that the mediating processes linking specific interaction cues and business outcomes are under-explored is because the micro-macro disconnect has been not taken into account. Third, the relational void is due to the fact that most empirical studies model one-off interaction instead of longitudinal effects.Fourth, theories are usually tested in vacuums, given that they overlook contingent product involvement, channel and relationship stage effects. Fifth, under-specification of the ethics and governance implies that the guidance on compliance with regulations and cross-cultural considerations is not developed yet.

CHAPTER OBJECTIVES

These gaps have been covered in this chapter by seven interrelated purposes: to synthesize interdisciplinary literature on HAI in marketing; to determine and critically evaluate major theoretical theories and limitations; to synthesize the evidence on HAI effectiveness; to consider a conceptual framework integrating AI design cues, user psychology, and marketing contexts; to discuss fundamental tensions in marketing HAI and suggest their solution strategies; to write evidence-based recommendations to practitioners, policymakers, and scholars; and to formulate a research agenda in the future that inquiries into longitudinal dynamics, cross-cultural.

LITERATURE REVIEW

The Human-AI Interaction Conceptualization

Human-AI Interaction in marketing is defined as a two-way, changing interrelation between human-oriented participants and AI-oriented systems in the marketing interactions. As opposed to conventional human-computer interaction, HAI is defined by the AI adaptivity, agency, learning, and social presence capability (Auernhammer, 2020; Margetis et al., 2021). The presented conceptualization represents a great shift compared to the views of AI as a passive analytical instrument in the past. Modern AI systems are interactive actors and are involved in the process of value creation, decision-making, and relationship interactions (Huang & Rust, 2021). A chatbot does not just provide information, it is in the form of a conversation, it listens to user tones, and can also affect purchase choices. This obstruction between the impacts of AI as a tool and AI as an agent has significant consequences on marketing theory and practice whereby frameworks must consider the social, psychological and relational aspects of interactions with non-human agents.

Theoretical Foundations

Technology Acceptance Model and its variants have been adopted extensively to describe adoption of AI-based marketing technologies (Bhuiyan et al., 2025). TAM assumes that perceived ease of use and perceived usefulness are the major determinants that affect technology acceptance. The literature indicates that these constructs are predictors of the adoption of chatbots, recommendation systems, and voice assistants applied in the marketing settings (Cloarec, 2020; Gupta and Mukherjee, 2025; Sharma et al., 2022). The involvement of the Personalization-Privacy Paradox research builds on the concept of TAM, in that consumer attitudes towards AI-oriented personalization are split between those who appreciate such services and those who are fearful of surveillance, abuse of information, and absence of control over their personal data (Puntoni et al., 2021; Kronemann et al., 2023). Research indicates that perceived usefulness tends to determine this correlation between personalization and adoption, yet privacy issues moderate the mediacy at all levels of involvement exceptionally high personalities such as finance or healthcare (Peltier et al., 2024; Qiu et al., 2025).

The challenge of algorithm aversion, which is the disposition to mistrust or rebuff algorithmic suggestion even when it is objectively of a superior quality, is an obstacle to HAI adoption (Haupt et al., 2024; Burton et al., 2020). This is seen at the consumer level and the management level. It has been explained psychologically on the Compensatory Control Theory: when people feel discomposed by external systems affecting their feeling of control, they defend themselves by rejecting autonomous algorithms (Burton et al., 2020). Since human-in-the-loop algorithms constantly give users the override disable option, research proves that these algorithms have a significantly lower chance of aversion than their un-in-the-loop counterparts due to restored autonomy by the human subject (Davenport et al., 2020; Li et al., 2025). Trust comes in as a mediating variable, which includes competence, benevolence, integrity, and transparency (Puntoni et al., 2021). Research findings are always identified to conclude that opaque black-box AI causes a lack of trust, and explainable AI properties increase acceptance and satisfaction (Auernhammer, 2020; Margetis et al., 2021).

Although TAM models (Anam et al., 2026) have strong pillars, their shortcomings can be realized when they are used in an HAI setting. To begin with, TAM fails to include emotional and relational dimensions. Emotions of discomfort, euphoria, or deceit are ultimately the main factors influencing consumer attitudes toward AI, which cannot be forecasted by the perceived usefulness alone (Puntoni et al., 2021). Second, TAM disregards the dynamic reciprocity.In contrast to traditional technologies, AI systems improve the feedback mechanism in response to user input and represent loops of trust, in which previous experiences influence the progression of the next interaction (Jones et al., 2022). Third, the contextual contingency is not theorized enough. The identical AI development can produce acceptance in low involvement entertainment scenarios, but create opposition in high involvement financial choices.

Anthropomorphism and Interaction Design

The Anthropomorphism concept of giving human-like traits to AI systems has become a serious design variable. Anthropomorphic behaviors involve the use of conversational language, avatars or human-like, the expression of emotions and social dialogue pattern. The meta-analysis results prove that moderate anthropomorphism increases social presence, enjoyment, and perceived warmth and results in higher levels of satisfaction and engagement (Yanxia et al., 2024; Li et al., 2025; Liu et al., 2023). Nevertheless, the correlation is disproportional. When the levels of human-likeness are high, the uncanny valley effect may take place, spreading the feeling of unease that reduces the levels of trust, especially in the event that AI performance is not delivered to human-like standards (Kumar, 2025; Liu et al., 2025). In addition to the visual clues at the surface level, the style of an interaction has a significant influence on the perceptions of the users. Turn taking, turn taking, turn-initiation, grounding behaviours, and mistake recovery strategies are important elements to bring improved perceived intelligence and social presence and relational quality in both chatbot and voice assistant experiences (Bergner et al., 2023; Liu et al., 2023; Oliveira, 2025).

User Psychology

The Elaboration Likelihood Model is an effective tool in examining the process of information processing of AI-generated data by users. In low-involvement situations or when there are poor cognitive resources, users make use of peripheral cues like friendliness and anthropomorphism. In high-involvement or high-stakes situations, central route processing is the dominant experience, and the user will examine the transparency, logic, and reasons AI advice (Petrescu and Krishen, 2023). It is based on the assumption of Self-Determination Theory which holds that human beings tend to be more constructive with systems that meet their needs in relation to autonomy, competence, and relatedness. The studies prove that AI systems leading to meaningful decision making, recommendations that can be explained, and ensuring a feeling of connection lead to increasing intrinsic motivation and engagement in the long run (Gupta and Mukherjee, 2025; Sharma et al., 2022). Cognitive Absorption Theory refers to profound engagement and flow experiences, and it was demonstrated that immersive AI experiences have the ability of causing more cognitive absorption to be produced when compared to human-to-human interactions (Balakrishnan et al., 2021, 2024). Responses to AI systems are strongly mediated by the individual differences such as AI literacy, personality factors, cultural orientation, background in the field of technology, and so forth (Yanxia et al., 2024; Liu et al., 2025; Jin and Eastin, 2022).

Marketing Context

Marketing context has a systemic effect on HAI effectiveness. Raising transactional and relational tasks, task type helps differentiate between the tasks that are highly prioritized in terms of efficiency (and benefits of efficiency), and the ones that are satisfied with warmth and relationship (Huang and Rust, 2021; Wirtz et al., 2018). The requirements are determined by the product involvement: the high-involvement decisions are the ones that can be done more openly and with more human factors, whereas the low-involvement ones allow more playful and free-to-the-house interactions with AI (Cloarec, 2020; Peltier et al., 2024). Attributes of the channels are important: voice-based and immersive AR/VR interfaces experience greater emotional reactions and privacy issues compared to text-based interactions (Huang and Rust, 2018; Song et al., 2020; Islam et al., 2026). Relationship stage is a distinction between starting the interaction and continuing, with conventional relationships giving an opportunity to access more data but expect more as well (Gao and Liu, 2023).

Empirical Evidence

The effectiveness of human-AI integration is invested in empirical research. Companies that merge AI analytics and people-driven creativity are 47 and 31 times more likely to engage customers and increase their conversion (Kotha, 2024).On the interactivity level, AI systems that embrace the principles of a human conversation make not only perceived humanness, trust, and relational outcomes such as recommendation acceptance and loyalty much higher but also associated adverse emotions such as surprise and even disgust (Bergner et al., 2023; Liu et al., 2023). Important visiting conditions are however found out to exist. The disclosure of AI would backfire in the cases where the user realizes that he or she is communicating with AI, not with human beings (Luo et al., 2019; Odeibat, 2024). These adverse impacts are reduced by human-AI collaboration which indicates perceived human control to retain credibility (Haupt et al., 2024). Privacy calculus is one of the primary intermediaries: consumers consider the positive aspect of the personalization and the negative aspect of the privacy and control tools shift the balance (Thomaz et al., 2019; Kronemann et al., 2023).

Table 1. Literature Comparison - AI in Marketing & Consumer Psychology

Paper (Year)	Journal (Citations)	AI Marketing Application Area	AI Technology Focus	Key Consumer Psychological Constructs
Jin et al. (2022).	International Journal of Human-Computer Interaction (119)	Fashion & tourism product/service promotion	AI-powered chatbots	Social presence, imagery processing, and psychological ownership
Song et al. (2024).	Journal of Theoretical and Applied Electronic Commerce Research (11)	Interactive marketing, personalized shopping, virtual try-ons, recommendations, and customer service	AI-powered try-on technology (AR/VR)	Customer satisfaction
Kronemann et al. (2023).	Spanish Journal of Marketing - ESIC (47)	Consumer information disclosure	Digital assistant (AI)	Information disclosure behavior, privacy calculus
(Liu et al. 2025; Khatun et al., 2026)	Frontiers in Psychology (1)	E-commerce product recommendations	Product recommendation chatbots	Purchase intention, personal innovativeness, Big Five personality traits
Huh et al. (2023).	Journal of Research in Interactive Marketing (34)	Customer-brand relationships	AI-powered voice assistants	Perceived control, flow, consumer happiness, brand loyalty
Thomaz et al. (2019).	Journal of the Academy of Marketing Science (154)	Customer engagement, personalization, and eliciting self-disclosure	Conversational agents (chatbots)	Privacy concerns, information disclosure

Collaboration Models

This is a recurrent observation that successful HAI comes about through augmentation rather than replacement. AI works best in the case of complimenting human abilities (Davenport et al., 2020). The human-in-the-loop models enable the user to preserve override control, limiting the fear of the algorithm (Hesel et al., 2022).

Figure 1. Evolution of Human-AI Collaboration Models in Marketing

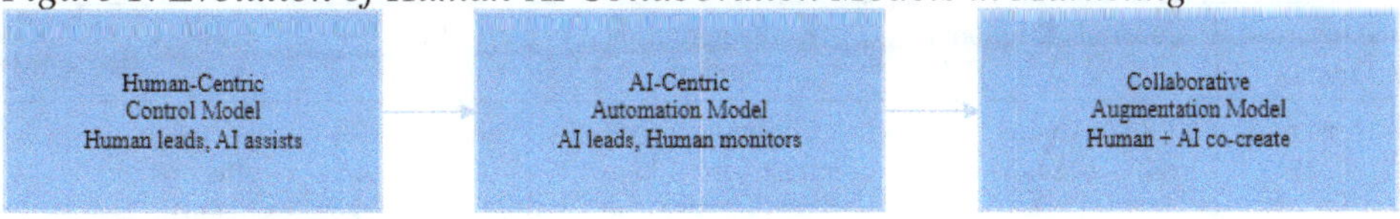

Human authorship with the help of AI offers the advantage of preserving human voice and using AI efficiency, whereas human directed AI offer greater quantity of content to be produced and keeping the quality under human control (Haupt et al., 2024). New types of team model with shared control, interoperability, and mutual learning are focused on humans and AI as equal participants of a team (Li et al., 2025; Tsamados et al., 2024).

Implementation Challenges

Algorithms aversion among managers and cross-functional differences between data science and marketing departments are the elements that facilitate organizational resistance (Hesel et al., 2022; Noranee et al., 2023). Consumer mistrust and privacy risks occur when artificial intelligence operates in undocumented manners and where contextual integrity breaches may evoke a very strong negative emotional response (Puntoni et al., 2021; Odeibat, 2024). Such psychological obstacles as anticipatory anxiety and mistrust of AI-generated content (Li et al., 2025; Frenkenberg and Hochman, 2025) exist. Technical issues include problem of data quality described as well as integration problems (Noranee et al., 2023).Regulation laws such as the EU AI Act mandate a level of transparency and human control and companies do not have a clearly defined roadmap to follow. Overall, failures in the use of AI such as Microsoft chatbot called Tay or biased facial recognition technologies are documented, highlighting the danger of implementation without sufficient risk measures (Liu-Thompkins et al., 2022).

Synthesis

Previous findings including the literature show that the results of HAIs are subject to the coordination of design attributes, user-based preferences, and the situational elements and not on individual factors. The same insight drives the Tripartite Interaction-framework provided in Section 4.

Table 2. Literature Comparison - AI Implementation Challenges and Human-AI Issues

Paper (Year)	Journal (Citations)	Implementation Challenges	Focus Level of AI	Human-AI Issue
Hesel et al. (2022).	NIM Marketing Intelligence Review (2)	Insufficient budgets, lack of infrastructure, know-how, skilled staff, and data-related issues	Strategic-level AI in marketing decision-making	Synergetic collaboration of humans and algorithms
Keegan et al. (2022).	Information Systems Frontiers (43)	Culturally or politically challenging contradictions	A broader spectrum of AI applications	Socio-technical aspects of AI use, contradictions
Davenport et al. (2019).	Journal of the Academy of Marketing Science (1532)	Privacy, bias, and ethics	Strategic and customer behaviors	AI augments (rather than replaces) human managers
Odeibat (2024)	Cross-Cultural Management Journal (2)	Ethical and societal concerns	Broader spectrum of AI applications in marketing	Ethical and societal concerns about AI adoption
Haupt et al. (2024).	Reviews of Management Sciences (30)	Negative consumer perceptions and ethical concerns	Strategic and operational applications	Human-AI collaboration to preserve consumer message credibility
Noranee et al. (2023).	JMM17: JurnalIlmuEkonomi dan Manajemen (3)	Privacy, ethical concerns, data quality, integration, and upskilling marketers	Operational and strategic applications in marketing	Balancing AI automation with human judgment and expertise

METHODOLOGY

Research Design

In this chapter, a systematic review of literature methodology is used to combine theoretical viewpoints and facts concerning HAI in marketing. The approach is based on PRISMA principles, which provide the transparency, rigour, and reproducibility (Page et al., 2021). The fundamental research question that will inform this synthesis is how theoretical insights and empirical research in the field of HCI, marketing, and consumer psychology can be used in conjunction to inform the processes and results of HAI in business settings. Systematic literature review is like a search method that allows thorough discovery, access, and synthesis of studies that transcends across disciplines (Kitchenham and Charters, 2007). It is an integrative kind of review integrating the findings of quantitative experiments and qualitative studies, concept papers, and industry reports to create the total picture.

Search Strategy

Scopus has been chosen because it is the best database; it covers numerous subjects in computer science, business, and psychology. The search strategy was based on keyword combinations such as artificial intelligence, AI, chatbot, conversational agent, recommendation agent, voice assistant, algorithm, human-AI interaction, human-computer interaction, HAI, user experience, trust, anthropomorphism, transparency, marketing, consumer, customer, personalization, brand, service, and adoption. AI terms were associated with interaction terms and marketing context terms through the use of the Boolean combinations. Only publications in English language published in 2019-2026 were searched, which covers the current years of machine learning-based AI. The types of documents used were peer-reviewed articles, conference proceedings and book chapters.

Selection Criteria

Research papers were also incorporated provided that they explicitly studied human interaction with AI systems, and it used commercial or marketing settings and investigated psychological or marketing outcome variables and it had to be peer-reviewed.

Figure 2. PRISMA Based Methodology

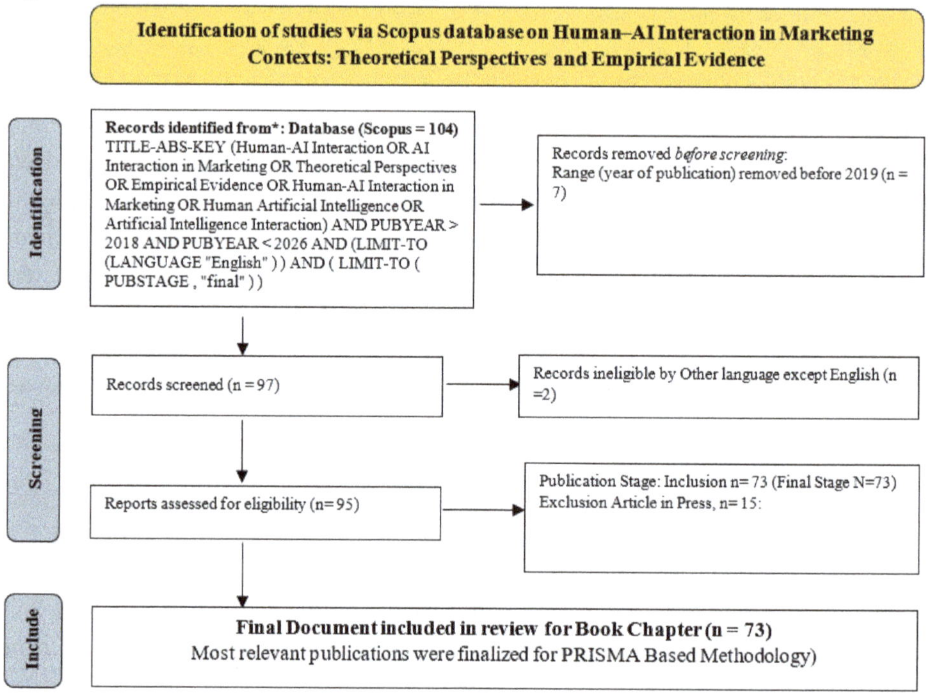

Source: Scopus Database (January, 2026)

It has excluded studies that were interested in the technical architecture of AI alone, without human contact measures, studies that investigated AI outside of the commercial environment with no implications to be applied, and non-scholarly studies. Selection was done according to the PRISMA guidelines in four stages. Scopus and citation snowballing identification yielded 416 and 28 records respectively. Following the elimination of duplicity 387 records were filtered by title and abstract, and 267 rejected mostly because technical focus. The analysis of 120 articles was carried out in full text and led to the inclusion of 73 articles in the qualitative synthesis.

ANALYSIS

The process of analysis was performed in three steps. Descriptive coding was used to organize studies by discipline origin and found common themes. Cross-disciplinary comparison was looking at convergence, contradiction, and gaps between disciplines. The Tripartite Interaction Framework served as the organizing heuristic of integrative synthesis and was developed and refined progressively by the data instead of being applied a priori. Quality was also maintained by focusing on peer-reviewed materials, triangulating assertions of assorted research, including quantitative and qualitative data, cross-embedding scholarly outcomes with reliable grey literature.

CONCEPTUAL FRAMEWORK

Tripartite Interaction Framework of Marketing HAI

In this part, the Tripartite Interaction Framework is presented, a new conceptual model that explains Human -AI Interaction results in marketing to apply the active interaction of three major aspects: AI Agent Design and Cues, Human User Psychology, and Marketing Context and Task Characteristics. The framework solves the issue of disintegration in the field of discipline by incorporating the application of HCI, marketing science, and consumer psychology to respond to a given coherent and testable framework. The essence of the argument is that the HAI outcomes cannot be attributed to a particular factor acting in isolation, but to the harmony or disharmony of all three three-dimensional aspects. This contingency-driven reasoning takes the field out of the issue of whether a feature works to the more specific issue of in what circumstances to users and in what aspects of marketing a feature will yield what should happen.

THEORETICAL FOUNDATION

There are four premises the Tripartite Framework is based on. Firstly, AI as interactive agent implies that modern AI is a social agent that provokes human-like reactions and needs the frameworks that consider the relational and psychological processes (Auernhammer, 2020; Huang and Rust, 2021). Second, disciplinary complement has it that HCI can provide design principles, marketing can provide outcome measures, and psychology can provide explanatory mechanisms, and no individual discipline can fully explain (Petrescu and Krishen, 2023). Third, contingency not universality admits that the effectiveness of HAI is context-specific, and in this case, frameworks that indicate the conditions of boundaries are required (Dwivedi et al., 2023). Fourth, dynamic two-way interaction acknowledges that HAI is a long-term relationship during which each interaction influences the expectations and responses of the other party (Jones et al., 2022).

Framework Components

The element A that is referred to as AI Agent Design and Cues includes the attributes and perceived characteristics of the AI system that are designed in four dimensions. The human-like features of the anthropomorphism and social cues are visual representation, verbal style, emotional expression, and patterns of social dialogue (Yanxia et al., 2024; Kumar, 2025; Liu et al., 2025). Transparency and explainability principle implies revealing AI nature, logic of the work, and justifying the decision in the form of upfront and on-demand explanations (Auernhammer, 2020; Margetis et al., 2021). The agency and control architecture can be described as the autonomy of AI and control by its users, which contain the actions of override, correction, and customization (Davenport et al., 2020; Li et al., 2025). This interaction style and communication involves language and behavior patterns such as formality, warmth, flexibility, turn-taking, and recovery of errors (Bergner et al., 2023; Liu et al., 2023)

Figure 3. The Tripartite Interaction Framework for Marketing HAI

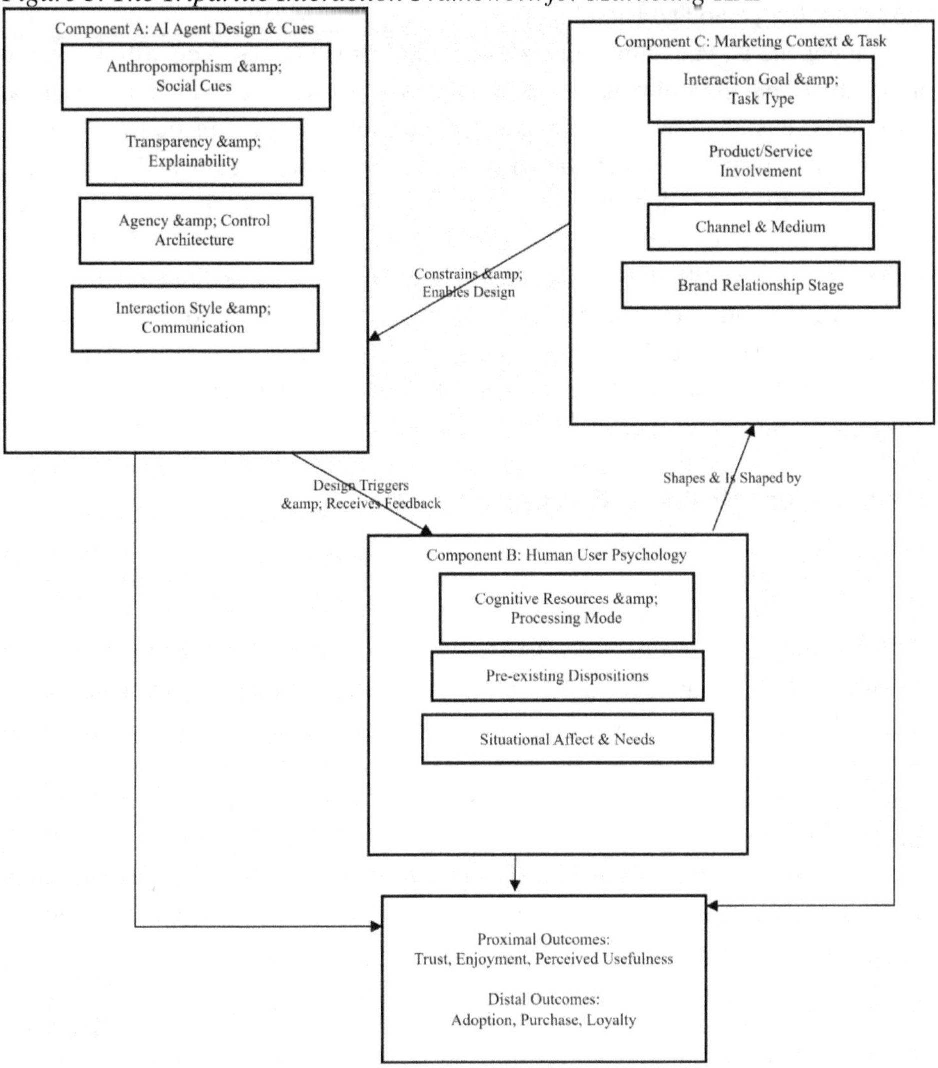

Source: Author's Work

Component B, Human User Psychology, is a dynamic which reflects the inner state of the user at the point of interaction along three dimensions. Cognitive-affective state contains processing mode, such as frustrations or curiosity affective state and psychological needs, such as autonomy, competence, and relatedness (Petrescu and Krishen, 2023; Gupta and Mukherjee, 2025). Such pre-existing orientations are technology trust propensity, AI literacy, cultural orientation, domain expertise, and personality traits (Yanxia et al., 2024; Jin and Eastin, 2022; Liu et al., 2025). Goal orientation is characterized by a judgement of dominance such as utilitarian task achievement, hedonic exploration, social bond and relational maintenance (Huang and Rust, 2021; Gao and Liu, 2023).

Components C, Marketing Context and Task Characteristics, declare the backdrop of the situation in four dimensions. Kind of task and objective involves commercial purpose, i.e. customer service, sales persuasion, relationship interaction, and content delivery, and form i.e. conversational versus transactional (Huang and Rust, 2021; Wirtz et al., 2018). Product and service involvement may be defined as a perceived relevance, risk, and cost the differentiation between high- and low-involvement decisions (Cloarec, 2020; Peltier et al., 2024). Channel and medium embrace text, voice, AR, VR and graphical interfaces that have different levels of constraints and affordances (Huang and Rust, 2018; Song et al., 2020). The acquisition and retention differ in brand relationship stage as brand relationship established at the point of acquisition provides more data access but demands high pressure (Gao and Liu, 2023).

Active Interactions and Propositions.

The explanatory ability of the framework lies in targeted relationships among the elements. There are four testable propositions that are formalised.

Propositions 1, Context-Dependent Efficacy of Design Cues, according to which the influence of certain AI design cues on user perceptions and behaviors is dependent on the marketing context. Transparency is more important in high-involvement situations where playful designs are allowed in low-involvement situations (Cloarec, 2020; Peltier et al., 2024). The interaction between the design and context are important predictors of trust and adoption.

Proposition 2, Psychological State as Filter, is the statement that the cognitive-affective processing makes the user react to the same AI design cue with different outcomes according to their psychological being. Anthropomorphic warmth is positively received by hedonic users and the same warmth is inefficiently felt by stressed utilitarian users (Kull et al., 2025; Yanxia et al., 2024). Design and psychology interaction are major predictors of the enjoyment and competence perceptions.

Proposition 3, Context Activates Psychological Processing, is asserting that the marketing context captures the achievement of the activation of particular user psychological states that pre-empt particular processing modes and needs. Without default processing, high-risk purchase circumstances cause both systematic processing and an increase in risk assessment despite the style of default processing (Petrescu and Krishen, 2023). The mode of processing is highly predicted by context.

According to proposition number three Three-Way Congruence Principle, the best HAI performance will occur when the design of AI is consistent with both the psychological state activated by the user and the marketing environment. Failure to align on any of the dimensions slows down effectiveness. Three-way congruence establishes much more trust, satisfaction, and loyalty compared to all other types of miss alignment (Gao and Liu, 2023; Jones et al., 2022).

Outcome Variables

The model identifies proximal psychological, distal behavioral and commercial outcomes. The identified proximal outcomes are cognitive beliefs, including perceived usefulness, ease of use and quality, affective beliefs, including enjoyment, social presence and perceived creepiness, relational beliefs, including trust in competence, benevolence and integrity, perceived fairness and perceived autonomy. Distal measures consist of behavioral intentions like adoption, continued use and purchase intent; actual behavior like conversion, spending and compliance with recommendations and relational measures like satisfaction, loyalty and customer lifetime value.

Theoretical Contributions

The Tripartite Interaction Framework has four contributions. Integrative precision shifts scholarly inquiry off descriptive questions onto contingent questions that allow more accurate hypothesis generation. Disciplinary bridge offers vernacular and framework in interdisciplinary study by clearly interrelating the variables of HCI design, the psychological processes, and the marketing effects. The diagnostic utility provides the practitioners with a structured checklist in order to diagnose systematically HAI failures. Dynamic perspective is more receptive to time-dynamics and mutual effects, providing possibilities to do longitudinal investigations on the relationships of HAI. The framework offers a contingent logic of designing, evaluating and researching marketing HAI that acknowledges complexity and context-dependence as unveiled by the literature.

Illustrations of Live Application

Practical 1: E-commerce Customer Support AI Chatbot

To address the customer queries like order tracking and returns, an e-commerce company introduces an AI chatbot to respond to the customer inquiries. The chatbot has conversational turn-taking and grounding techniques, which enhance perceived responsiveness and user satisfaction. Nevertheless, in case of complicated problems by the customers (e.g. refunds), the system refers to human agents, which guarantees relational authenticity. This is an opinion of the human-in-the-loop model that minimizes the aversion towards algorithms and maximizes trust (Davenport et al.,

2020; Hesel et al., 2022). Research indicates that AI that talks to customers in the style of a human being enhances their interest and retention (Bergner et al., 2023).

Practical Application 2: Recommendation System in Streaming platform-personalized

Artificial intelligence is implemented as streaming sites such as Netflix or Spotify use algorithms to suggest content to users based on their behavior. These systems are based on the data of behavior and predictive analytics and provide hyper-personalized experiences. Although personalization brings greater user satisfaction and engagement, excessive personalization can cause the privacy personalization paradox, where users experience uneasiness regarding the use of data (Kronemann et al., 2023; Puntoni et al., 2021). Balance between trust and usefulness is provided with the help of transparency (e.g., Because you watched...).

Practical example 3: Voice Assistants in Smart Retail

Retailers use voice prompts (e.g., Alexa in smart stores) to help customers with search and recommendation of products. Such systems are useful since they increase convenience and save search effort, which is appropriate in TAM to the perceived ease of use factor and usefulness. Nevertheless, voice interfaces also create privacy issues and emotional reactions, particularly when it comes to high-involvement decisions (Huang and Rust, 2021; Song et al., 2020). This means that retailers include user control mechanisms and opt-in systems in an attempt to preserve trust.

Case Illustrations

Case Illustration 1: Sephora Beauty Recommendations AI Chatbot

Sephora launched an AI chatbot, which gives the personalized advice on beauty. The chatbot employs anthropomorphic indicators and conversational communication, enhancing interaction and the sense of social presence.

Anthropomorphism is, however, not heavily applied by Sephora in order to avoid the uncanny valley effect, and the AI is not made overly human-like (Kumar, 2025; Liu et al., 2025). This coincides with the Tripartite Framework where the design cues should be in accordance with the user expectation and context.

Case Study 2: The Recommendation Engine of Amazon

The recommendation system developed by Amazon is one of the primary examples of AI-based personalization. It interprets the history of browsing, purchases, and preferences to make suggestions on the products, which highly boosts the conversion rates.

The system shows that AI analytics and human-developed strategies could be used to achieve better performance (Kotha, 2024). Nevertheless, Amazon is also transparent (e.g., "Customers also bought) and it covers the trust aspect and perceived manipulation (Puntoni et al., 2021).

Case Illustration 3: Erica (AI Financial Assistant) of bank of America

Bank of America introduced the financial assistant Erica, which is an AI-based system that assists its users in financial matters, spending monitoring, and financial advice.

Considering the high-involvement environment (finance), Erica accentuates:

- Openness (describing recommendations)
- User control (manual overrides)
- Security assurances

This is in line with studies that have found that high-risk decisions need explainable decisions and trust-building processes (Peltier et al., 2024; Auernhammer, 2020). Erica shows how the context-sensitive design of AI can enhance adoption and satisfaction.

DISCUSSION

Openness versus Secretiveness

One of the fundamental issues in the design of HAI is the conflict between the principles of transparency and the wish to feel one's independence. The argument in favor of transparency is that reliability and trust of AI decisions should be described in highly involved situations to reduce the black box problem and address the need of users to understand (Auernhammer, 2020; Margetis et al., 2021). Nevertheless, being overly transparent may be an antithesis to users in need of a fast solution as they interpret a thorough explanation as something burdensome, diminishing the ease of use and perceived freedom (Balakrishnan et al., 2021). The optimum aspect on this trade-off would be based on the interplay of the three elements. High transparency is important to trust when a novice investor employs robo-advisors to plan his or her retirement. Transparency is a burden to an expert user when one needs voice assistants to perform routine tasks. The progressive transparency resolution strategy is basic identity disclosure required and explanatory detail available on-demand, so that, depending on their current psychological condition and task requirement, an individual can choose their preferred form of disclosure (Davenport et al., 2020).

The Paradox of Anthropomorphism

The application of anthropomorphic prompt is a two-sided sword. The relationship value is that the anthropomorphism may meet the relational requirement of users who need to socialize and establish fun interactions, especially where the relationship-building and brand narrative are the focus (Yanxia et al., 2024; Li et al., 2025). The competence trap however arises due to the fact that human like cue increases expectations towards human like cognitive and emotional intelligence. In case of a complex complaint about the customer service recovery handled by an anthropomorphic chatbot, negative disconfirmation is worse than when the interface is mechanical, and it harms the trust even more deeply (Kumar, 2025; Liu et al., 2025). The anthropomorphism and outcome relationship is not linear but situation-specific. In interactive relations with people who are interested in becoming motivated, warm anthropomorphism increases interactivity. In transactional settings, where consumers are time-pressed, non-social interaction which is efficiency oriented is more effective. The solution to this dilemma is calibrated anthropomorphism, balancing warmth to functional anthropomorphism with high anthropomorphism to provide emotional support and low anthropomorphism to be efficient with express capability cues to the world so it doesn't get over-scheduled.

Privacy and Personalization

Consumers have the ability to customize their digital devices to meet their individual needs and preferences (Sonicor, 2019). The hyper-personalization offered by AI is projected as the marketing promise of the technology, though this promise must be perceived through the calculus of privacy and deeming suitability of the scenarios by the users. The value-creating aspect is that personalization based on explicit preferences or identifying signals of a clear situation is considered useful and relevant, leading to the increased user experience and conversion (Kotha, 2024; Gao and Liu, 2023). The creepiness trigger happens with personalization that may manifest on mysterious, guessed, or intimate information, particularly, in a sudden revelation that instigates reactance and being watched. This effect breaks the contextual integrity, where users are unable to comprehend how the AI comprehended something (Puntoni et al., 2021, Kronemann et al., 2023). The boundary between useful and creepy is based on the alignment of the source of data to the user expectations and contextual norms. Explicit user input is assumed to be beneficial, intra-context acting is thought to be an acceptable behavior, cross-context acting may be creepy, and inference of emotion or voice acting without any consent is very creepy. The resolution strategy is the contextual integrity and the transparent use of data and inclination to personalization according to an explicit input and understandable intra-contextual behavior, transparent disclosure of inference logic, meaningful control, and non-application of data with intimate contexts without granular permission.

The Relational Authenticity versus Efficiency

The AI systems are more efficient, but relational authenticity in the marketing outcomes more and more relies on the appearance of real and caring interactions. Its efficiency advantage makes it possible to process thousands of active interactions in real-time and with perfect consistency, which is worth transactional (Wirtz et al., 2018). The authenticity condition entails that the bond of brand relationships be based on the apparent concern, contextual awareness, and valuable emotional reactions, which AI can hardly convincingly replicate (Huang and Rust, 2023). Transactional contexts are less anthropomorphic with quick lastingness. The type of relationship necessitates moderate anthropomorphism, emotional intelligence, and human escalation sequences. The complexity of the solution of the problem needs efficiency in the initial triage and genuine nature in the resolution with smooth human transition. The hybrid one is where AI should be used to manage those cases when a routine is applicable, whereas the human must be used to address instances, in which an actual feeling is necessary, with handoffs between contexts to retain the perception of sincerity (Haupt et al., 2024).

Cross-Cultural Issues

The literature reviewed includes mostly western individualistic settings but cultural dimensions moderately systematically moderate HAI responses. The cultures of individualism values personal freedom and face-to-face communication, and the AI systems focus on user control and detailed explanations, which are partners of these qualities. The Focus on collectivism cultures put much emphasis on group harmony and relational context, the AI systems with the focus on social presence and warmth are more effective, and the anthropomorphism is more easily accepted (Jin et al., 2022; Yanxia et al., 2024). The high power distance cultures tolerate hierarchical relations and might be satisfied with authoritative AI, whereas the low power distance cultures anticipate partnering framing. This culture has high uncertainty avoidance which requires high levels of transparency and human control and low uncertainty which can tolerate ambiguity. In the case of global brands, it means that they should not adopt the one-size-fits-all HAI design models, cross-cultural testing of response to these models, and taking into consideration culturally-aware versions where anthropomorphism, communication style, and various norms may be different.

Implications on Regulatory and Governance

The Tripartite Framework casts some light on why regulatory methods should be context sensitive. The transparency needs can not be universal, though the explainability focused on the EU AI Act is suitable to high-stakes, the same can not be said about the low-stakes interaction; such a standard prevents increased user experience by introducing unwarranted mental load (Dwivedi et al., 2023). Protections to consumer autonomy must also challenge AI design which aims to manipulate cognitive weakness of the consumer, like anthropomorphic stimuli with the aim of by-passing consumer persuasion knowledge in vulnerable consumers. In addition to data privacy, interactive manipulation, patterns of design that systematically behave in a manner that deceives or exploits people psychologically should be regulated. The issue of cross-border governance by cultural difference in privacy expectations can be challenging, and there is scope of principle-based regulation that allows such differences the liberty to adapt to context, but leaves essential principles intact.

Recommendations

For Designers and Marketers

The anthropomorphism should be implemented calmly by designers and marketers in fitting cues that correspond to the task context and the desires of users instead of relying on the human-like modeling. Relational High warmth is more appropriate when coaching wellness and brand stories, and transactional Low warmth is more appropriate when tracking orders and recovering services. Explicit capability signaling should be used when anthropomorphic cues are present to help deal with expectations and prevent competence trap. Gradual disclosure of AI identity through tiers of definitions should be introduced where basic AI identity disclosure at the front side is the default setting with optional explanatory information, aided by clicking on links, that the user has the opportunity to self-determine his or her needed level of transparency regarding current psychological condition and task requirements. The user control and override systems are to be designed with overt, simple to locate controls on correcting errors, controlling preferences and overriding AI recommendations, which perceived control decreases the aversion to algorithms and promotes trust despite being rarely used (Burton et al., 2020; Hesel et al., 2022).

The designers need to come up with solid failure and escalation plans, recognizing that AI will fail and pre-planning such events as crucial moments of trust-building with empathetic preemptive grace and easy routes to human support. Empathic recovery plans, which are written, can reduce adverse reactions and improve the perceived care (Liu et al., 2025; Wirtz et al., 2018). Personalization logic Creepiness audits are to be developed and operated on prior to deployment, interrogating data sources and inference logic in the light of contextual integrity by inquiring whether data is volunteered, observed or gleaned elsewhere, whether users would anticipate data to be treated thus, and whether there is a relationship between the sensitivity of data and the extent of personalization benefits. Prefer personalization using definite input and definite intra context action and do not utilize data on intimate contexts unless explicitly granted with granular authorization.

The performance measured by marketers should go beyond conversion metrics with interaction-quality metrics predicting the effectiveness of HAI. The survey to be conducted after the interaction is over must be done on the perceived usefulness, ease of use, enjoyment and trust. Escalation rates, frequency of correction and abandonment are supposed to be trailed in the interaction logs. Longitudinal tracking must follow up satisfaction, intention to be loyal, and customer lifetime value.When initiatives are performing poorly, the Tripartite Framework would be applicable as a diagnostic tool to assess systematically whether AI design did not match the context, design did not match the user psychology, they did not assess the right user psychology, or that all three dimensions are out of line.

For Leaders and Strategists

The leaders can develop cross-functional HAI governance to have specific committees that represent marketing, UX, data science, legal, and ethics to submit significant HAI initiatives to avoid downstream issues and focus on organizational values alignment (Noranee et al., 2023). The machine behind trust infrastructure must devote substantial resources to explainability interfaces and user control panels, ethical auditing tools, and smooth human versions pathways, as trust brings about returns by achieving faster adoption and a tarnished brand reputation (Davenport et al., 2020; Puntoni et al., 2021). The new performance metrics must also be adjusted to feature transactional efficiency alongside relational quality, experiential quality to create balanced scorecards that will measure financial performance (conversion and CLV), operational performance (resolution rate), customer experience performance

(CSAT and trust score) and innovation performance (AI improvement rate). The definition of AI must be presented as augmentation rather than replacement, the terms of the partnership and collaboration are to be used to minimize the internal opposition and consumer anxiety, and the examples of how AI can allow humans to devote more attention to more valuable tasks should be mentioned (Davenport et al., 2020; Haupt et al., 2024). Marketers should be trained on emotional intelligence to be able to work with AI-generated content because when creating emotional backgrounds to AI-responses, emotional intelligence will improve the level of creative performance (Tsakalerou et al., 2025).

For Policymakers

In place of a uniform set of rules, policy makers ought to come up with context-sensitive standards of transparency that adjust the requirements need to risk and severity of involvement instead of the rule itself. Recent and high-risk applications like credit decisions and health advice should be subject to detailed explainability, and access to clarifications, medium-risk applications including major purchases should be subject to disclose AI use clearly and on demand, and low risk applications like content recommendations do not need identity disclosure. High-risk applications are necessary to have algorithmic impact assessment of potential manipulation, discrimination, and psychological harm threats, prior to deployment, and the vulnerable population or group that is likely to face the system should be assessed (Liu-Thompkins et al., 2022). The industry would need to create benchmarks and icons of transparency, which would be designed as standard cues contributing to the understanding of the level of AI involvement, personalization activity, and the degree of explainability to allow consumer education and informed choice. The effects of the longitudinality and society effects should be funded by independent research, which should explore the effects of the long-term on the well-being of the consumer, decision-making independence, and fairness of the market place especially to the vulnerable populations and democracy.

IMPLICATIONS

Theoretical Implications

The main implication of the theoretical concepts is that consilience approaches and methods that strategically combine constructs across multiple disciplines are needed. The Tripartite Framework proves the fact that to come up with a genuine understanding, the principles of HCI design, psychological processes, and marketing effects need to be considered at the same time, so academic institutions must promote the work of truly interdisciplinary character (Dwivedi et al., 2023). Interaction design should be made a central marketing construct, which may be a fifth P or pillar of relationship management, because the quality of the interactive interface is the key aspect of value co-creation in AI-mediated markets (Huang and Rust, 2021). AI needs to be re-conceptualized as agentic, not as a tool, and new theoretical frames of brand agency need to be discovered, persuasive communication must require non-human persuasers, and the provision of services must involve co-creator AI agents, not a channel (Aaraujo et al., 2023). The framework connects micro-macro by precisely relating micro-level design of interaction decisions with macro level marketing performance gains in regard to defined psychologically mediating mechanisms, bridging the critically important gap between HCI design principles and business performance metrics (Jones et al., 2022).

Practical Implications

New functions of organization such as Conversation Architects to design a dialogue flow and personality, AI Interaction Designers, to create a transparency mechanism and control interface, HAI Ethics Officers, to audit interactions in search of manipulative patterns, and Human-AI Collaboration Leads to design work processes to team in a seamless way, will arise. The copywriting needs to become like dialogue scripting, UX design needs the addition of psychological contingency, and interaction governance should be a part of marketing strategy (Rayun et al., 2026). To invest strategically in trust infrastructure, it is essential to devote a serious amount of resources to the explainability interfaces, user controls, ethical auditing tools, and human escalation avenues, and it is worth noting that it is the infrastructure of trust that needs to be invested in deliberately (Davenport et al., 2020). Data strategy turns into experience strategy, when data practices are the prospective sources of competitive advantage founded on trust. In certain respects, brands whose signals about transparent data usage can be credibly communicated in a manner predicted to be transparent will be preferred over those considered surveillance engine (Puntoni et al., 2021). The performance management will need to develop with balanced scorecards that monitor efficiency measures with the experience measures of perceived effort and trust score, and relationship measures of trust evolution and emotional attachment.

Policy and Ethical implications

The existing data-centric regulation lacks the interactional aspect of the AI harm. Even a system that completely adheres to the rules of data might be faulty based on manipulating conversation patterns built from the sphere of cognitive biases, anthropomorphic structures that lie to poor users, or personalization building filter bubbles. The regulation has to be modified to deal with interactional manipulation, design principles that systematically defraud (or exploit) users in a psychological manner (Liu-Thompkins et al., 2022). Governance must be risk-sensitive that faces high levels of risk control with high transparency conditions in high-risk situations, transparent disclosure in medium risk situations, and simple identity disclosure in low-risk situations. To safeguard consumer agency and online well-being, the standards that make AI systems adhere and amplify instead of manipulate the psychological frailty of humans should be established (Frenkenberg and Hochman, 2025). Mechanisms to be executed include HAI review boards, high-risk application algorithmic impact assessment, documentation of design decisions through audit trails, and redress mechanisms to customers who were harmed as a result of AI interactions.

Cross Cultural and Sectoral Implications

Existing research has a biased presentation of the research problem: the preponderance of the WEIRD restricts generalizability because culture dimensions selectively moderate HAI responses. Autonomy and relationship warmth are supported by collectivist and individualist cultures respectively, authoritative AI is tolerated in high power distance cultures, where partnership are preferred in low power distance cultures, transparency is desired in high uncertainty avoidance cultures and ambiguity is accepted in low uncertainty avoidance cultures. International brands cannot afford generalized HAI, should invest in cross-cultural user study and view to culturally-modified alternative with different degrees of warmth, directness, and autonomy depending on the local culture. Industry-specific implication is the difference between B2C marketing that is chiefly characterized by consumer psychology and B2B marketing that needs to be transparent and needs human-in-the-loop designs owing to the presence of multiple stakeholders. No negotiable transparency, human supervision and explainability are regulatory demands in the high-involvement industries, including finance, and healthcare. Low-involvement customer services like entertainment and retail are more concerned with efficiency and fun with anthropomorphism that is task-oriented. Guidelines and audit tools should be accessible to small and medium enterprises as AI democratization has solutions available on sophisticated HAI without enough resources on governance.

CONCLUSIONS

The chapter has created a logical comprehension of the Human-AI Interaction in marketing through the synthesis of the historically alienated disciplines of Human-Computer Interaction, Marketing Science and Consumer Psychology. We have shown that algorithmic power is not the competitive edge in the AI era through the systematic PRISMA-based review of 73 studies and the creation of the new Tripartite Interaction Framework, and the skill to create the interaction design. This synthesis has three fundamental contributions. The Tripartite Interaction Framework offers an integrative conceptual framework specifically connecting AI design cues, user psychology, and marketing context, via four propositional hypotheses that are testable, putting the field beyond descriptive questions to contingent ones that allow specific hypothesis generating and diagnostic application. Essentially, the examination of the core tensions (as transparency versus autonomy, the anthropomorphism paradox, personalization-privacy trade-offs, efficiency versus authenticity, and cross-cultural variation) use shows that HAI is effective because using context-specific strategies and not rules governs it (Rayun et al., 2025). The Principle of Congruent Interaction summarises this observation; effective HAI must be balanced between what the AI indicates, what the user is experiencing, and what the context is asking. The stratified recommendations are the evidence-based recommendations given to designers, leaders, policymakers, and researchers based on empirical evidence as opposed to speculation.

It is haplessly a human experience as the journey between algorithms and market impact is undertaken. With AI systems becoming the main point of connection between brands and consumers, the quality of interactions they provide will rise to set brand perception, loyalty and value. The way forward should be to go past technocentric opinions that better algorithms will be sufficient and humanistic opinion that AI diminishes genuine connection. The facts have indicated a conscious evidence-based interaction design by capitalizing on the capabilities of AI with its superiority in volume and pattern recognition, but not by sacrificing or undermining human capabilities in their empathy, judgment, and the sensitivity of contexts. The relationships that prosper will not only comprehend the science of algorithms but also the art and morals of dealing with each other, creating AI agents that understand when to talk and when to listen, when to clarify and when to do, when to guide and when to be guided. The future of marketing does not lie with the best data, or the quickest algorithm, but rather with the most able and upright to carry out the dialogue between human and artificial intelligence. The call of interaction requires the greatest interest of interdisciplinary methodology, the most rigorous empirical research and the utmost dedication to human values.

FUTURE RESEARCH AND LIMITATIONS

There are a number of limitations existing in this work. The narrative integrative review methodology, which is suitable in terms of interdisciplinary ideas synthesis, lacks quantitative meta-analysis summaries of effect sizes, and the conclusion is based on the interpretive prism of the authors, regardless of the systematic searching. The current rate of AI development implies that large language models and generative AI are establishing new paradigms of interaction not sufficiently represented in the 2019 to 2026 literature, despite the chapter revolving around long-term psychological themes. The production is mainly aimed at to B2C dynamics in Western, Educated, Industrialized, Rich, and Democratic cultures, and B2B environments as well as cultural non-WEIRD settings might involve different dynamics that should be validated by a framework (Salam et al., 2026). The domination of the WEIRD prevents cross-cultural generalization since collectivism, power distance, and high-contextual communication are known to mediate HAI responses in a systematic way but are under-researched. There is little longitudinal research available on dynamics of trust and attachment interactions at repeated contact despite the strategic significance, as most empirical research studies only capture a particular interaction once. Conceptual and psychological mapping, as opposed to algorithmic architecture or software development protocols, is offered in the chapter, instead of technical design manuals.

The dynamics of the relationships and dynamics of the user reliance on the marketing AI agents will have to be investigated with regard to how trust, attachment, and reliance on marketing AI agents develop with repeated interactions (across months or years). Longitudinal field research monitoring the interactions of the same users with particular AI agents and regular surveys of the trust and relational outcomes would guide the design of the long-term relationship management instead of initial adoption. The cross-cultural validation and adaptation should test the moderating effect of cultural dimensions, such as, individualism-collectivism, power distance, uncertainty avoidance, and the high-low context in responding to AI design cues and the moderating effect of the Tripartite Framework propositions. Comparative experimental studies at scale and manipulation of AI designs in various cultural settings during standardized tasks would facilitate culturally-adjusted HAI design of international brands and test structure boundary conditions.

The dark side of manipulation, addiction, and vulnerability needs to be studied of terms, according to which AI-mediated persuasion is manipulative or exploitative; and psychological implications of long-term interaction with AI that is intended to deliver as many interactions or as much money as possible. Ethical guidelines: studies involving EE, and their influence on vulnerable populations, would be learned through experimental research on effects of manipulative design patterns such as false urgency, emotional leveraging, and deceptive anthropomorphism on user welfare, and neuropsychological outcome measures and efforts to study vulnerable groups in qualitative research would guide the development of protective design principles. Contingencies in the sector concern the need to explore the proposals in the framework in various manifestations in B2B versus B2C, high-involvement finance versus healthcare versus low-involvement entertainment and retail, and various stages of relationships. Sector-specific proposals would be facilitated by comparative case studies across sectors and sector specific surveys analysing either a sector-specific framework proposal.

The regulatory influence and regulation should be investigated in the form of how new frameworks such as the EU AI Act affect the design of HAI, consumer trust, and organizational processes, and what regulation would promote responsible HAI without inhibiting innovation. Evidence-based policy would be informed through comparative policy analysis, organization case studies on implementation of compliance through organizational context, and experimentation of consumer about repercussion of varied transparency regimes on trust. The Multimodal and embodied interaction involves studying the change in HAI when the interaction is extended to include more than a text and voice. The framework would be extended in the case of new modalities in the form of lab experiments in regulated VR and AR environments and field studies with social robots. The human AI teaming in organizations necessitates the exploration of the ways in which marketing managers relate to the AI decision making systems including algorithm aversion, over-reliance and complementary intelligence in strategic decision making. Ethnographic research in marketing departments involving the use of AI tools and experiments of the impacts of diverse AI explanation styles on manager confidence and the quality of decisions would guide the integration of AI within the organization.The development and validation of measurement would need exploration of the psychophysiological and behavioral proxies of trust-in-interaction, and perceived autonomy in developing valid measurement of HAI experience beyond satisfaction and usability. Methodological measures of methodological tools to develop HAI research Scale development and validation studies that cross to behavioral and physiological measures would be useful in the triangulation of an HAI study.

REFERENCES

Amershi, S., Weld, D. S., Vorvoreanu, M., Fourney, A., Nushi, B., Collisson, P., Suh, J., Iqbal, S. T., Bennett, P. N., Quinn, K., Teevan, J., Kikin-Gil, R., & Horvitz, E. (2019). Guidelines for human-AI interaction. *International Conference on Human Factors in Computing Systems*. https://doi.org/DOI: 10.1145/3290605.3300233

Anam, A. S. M. T., Bhuiyan, M. R. I., Islam, S., Ullah, M. N., & Rakib, M. A. A. (2026). Factors influencing university students' adoption of online education platforms in Bangladesh: an extended TAM-based analysis. Educational and Developmental Psychologist, 1–17. DOI: 10.1080/20590776.2026.2619742

Auernhammer, J. (2020). Human-centered AI: The role of human-centered design research in the development of AI. In S. Boess, M. Cheung, & R. Cain (Eds.), *Synergy: Proceedings of the DRS International Conference 2020*.https://doi.org/DOI: 10.21606/drs.2020.282

Balakrishnan, J., & Dwivedi, Y. K. (2021). Role of cognitive absorption in building user trust and experience. *Psychology and Marketing*, *38*(4), 643–668. Advance online publication. DOI: 10.1002/mar.21462

Balakrishnan, J., Dwivedi, Y. K., Hughes, L., & Boy, F. (2024). Enablers and inhibitors of AI-powered voice assistants: A dual-factor approach by integrating the status quo bias and technology acceptance model. *Information Systems Frontiers*, *26*(3), 921–942. DOI: 10.1007/s10796-021-10203-y

Bergner, A. S., Hildebrand, C., & Häubl, G. (2023). Machine talk: How verbal embodiment in conversational AI shapes consumer-brand relationships. *The Journal of Consumer Research*, *50*(4), 742–764. DOI: 10.1093/jcr/ucad014

Bhuiyan, M. R. I., Akter, M. S., Amin, A., & Hossain, R. (2025). The mediating effect of innovation capabilities, information quality and supply chain resilience in the relationship between big data analytics capability (BDAC) and healthcare performance. *SAGE Open*, *15*(3), 21582440251362262. DOI: 10.1177/21582440251362262

Bhuiyan, M. R. I., Uddin, S., Sultana, T., Al-Amin, , & Islam, M. M. (2026). Investigating ChatGPT Methods in the Higher Education Form a Student Engagement Perspective: Based on a Descriptive-Cross-Sectional Study. *SAGE Open*, *16*(1), 21582440251413008. Advance online publication. DOI: 10.1177/21582440251413008

Burton, J. W., Stein, M. K., & Jensen, T. B. (2020). A systematic review of algorithm aversion in augmented decision making. *Journal of Behavioral Decision Making*, *33*(2), 220–239. DOI: 10.1002/bdm.2155

Cloarec, J. (2020). The personalization–privacy paradox in the attention economy. *Technological Forecasting and Social Change, 161*, 120299. DOI: 10.1016/j.techfore.2020.120299

Davenport, T., Guha, A., Grewal, D., & Breßgott, T. (2020). How artificial intelligence will change the future of marketing—. *Journal of the Academy of Marketing Science, 48*(1), 24–42. Advance online publication. DOI: 10.1007/s11747-019-00696-0

Dwivedi, Y. K., Kshetri, N., Hughes, L., Slade, E. L., Jeyaraj, A., Kar, A. K., Baabdullah, A. M., Koohang, A., Raghavan, V., Ahuja, M., Albanna, H., Albashrawi, M. A., Al-Busaidi, A. S., Balakrishnan, J., Barlette, Y., Basu, S., Bose, I., Brooks, L., Buhalis, D., & Wright, R. (2023). Opinion Paper: "So what if ChatGPT wrote it?" Multidisciplinary perspectives on opportunities, challenges and implications of generative conversational AI for research, practice and policy. *International Journal of Information Management, 71*, 102642. DOI: 10.1016/j.ijinfomgt.2023.102642

Esmark Jones, C. L., Hancock, T., Kazandjian, B., & Voorhees, C. M. (2022). Engaging the avatar: The effects of authenticity signals during chat-based service recoveries. *Journal of Business Research, 144*, 703–716. DOI: 10.1016/j.jbusres.2022.01.012

Frenkenberg, A., & Hochman, G. (2025). *It's scary to use it, it's scary to refuse it: The psychological dimensions of AI adoption - anxiety, motives, and dependency.* Syst., DOI: 10.3390/systems13020082

Gaczek, P., Leszczyński, G., Kot, M., & Pozharliev, R. (2025). How locus of causality shapes human-AI decision-making. *Management Decision, 63*(13), 522–544. Advance online publication. DOI: 10.1108/MD-07-2024-1635

Gao, Y., & Liu, H. (2023). Artificial intelligence-enabled personalization in interactive marketing: A customer journey perspective. *Journal of Research in Interactive Marketing, 17*(5), 663–680. DOI: 10.1108/JRIM-01-2022-0023

Gupta, A. S., & Mukherjee, J. (2025). Framework for adoption of generative AI for information search of retail products and services. *International Journal of Retail & Distribution Management, 53*(2), 165–181. DOI: 10.1108/IJRDM-05-2024-0203

Haupt, M., Freidank, J., & Haas, A. (2024). Consumer responses to human-AI collaboration at organizational frontlines: Strategies to escape algorithm aversion in content creation. *Review of Managerial Science, 19*(2), 377–413. https://hdl.handle.net/10419/318868. DOI: 10.1007/s11846-024-00748-y

Hesel, N., Buder, F., & Unfried, M. (2022). *The next frontier in intelligent augmentation: Human-machine collaboration in strategic marketing decision-making*. NIM Marketing Intelligence Review., DOI: 10.2478/nimmir-2022-0017

Huang, M.-H., & Rust, R. (2023). The caring machine: Feeling AI for customer care. *Journal of Marketing*. Advance online publication. DOI: 10.1177/00222429231224748

Huang, M. H., & Rust, R. T. (2018). Artificial intelligence in service. *Journal of Service Research*, *21*(2), 155–172. DOI: 10.1177/1094670517752459

Huang, M. H., & Rust, R. T. (2021). A strategic framework for artificial intelligence in marketing. *Journal of the Academy of Marketing Science*, *49*(1), 30–50. DOI: 10.1007/s11747-020-00749-9

Huh, J., Kim, H.-Y., & Lee, G. (2023). "Oh, happy day!" Examining the role of AI-powered voice assistants as a positive technology in the formation of brand loyalty. *Journal of Research in Interactive Marketing*, *17*(5), 794–812. Advance online publication. DOI: 10.1108/JRIM-10-2022-0328

Islam, M. M., Bhuiyan, M. R. I., Islam, S. H., Tabassum, M. N., & Billah, M. (2026). Unlocking the Mediating and Moderating Role of Information Security in Information Systems: A Combined TAM, ISM, and HBM Model. *Human Behavior and Emerging Technologies*, *2026*(1), 5593002. DOI: 10.1155/hbe2/5593002

Jin, E., & Eastin, M. (2022). Birds of a feather flock together: Matched personality effects of product recommendation chatbots and users. *Journal of Research in Interactive Marketing*. Advance online publication. DOI: 10.1108/JRIM-03-2022-0089

Jin, S. V., & Youn, S. (2022). Social presence and imagery processing as predictors of chatbot continuance intention in human-AI-interaction. *International Journal of Human-Computer Interaction*. Advance online publication. DOI: 10.1080/10447318.2022.2129277

Keegan, B., Dennehy, D., & Naudé, P. (2022). Implementing artificial intelligence in traditional B2B marketing practices: An activity theory perspective. *Information Systems Frontiers*. Advance online publication. DOI: 10.1007/s10796-022-10294-1 PMID: 35637917

Khatun, M., Bhuiyan, M. R. I., Amin, M. A., Hossen, M., & Mia, M. A. H. (2026). Evaluating E-Commerce Satisfaction: The Impact of Trust, Information Quality, Usability, and Perceived-to-Actual Performance. *SAGE Open*, *16*(1), 21582440261423039. Advance online publication. DOI: 10.1177/21582440261423039

Kotha, S. (2024). *The convergence of artificial intelligence and human marketing: A framework for enhanced customer insights and personalization.* International Journal For Multidisciplinary Research., DOI: 10.36948/ijfmr.2024.v06i06.30266

Kronemann, B., Kizgin, H., Rana, N. P., & Dwivedi, Y. K. (2023). How AI encourages consumers to share their secrets? The role of anthropomorphism, personalisation, and privacy concerns, and avenues for future research. *Spanish Journal of Marketing - ESIC*, *27*(1), 3–19. DOI: 10.1108/SJME-10-2022-0213

Kumar, A., & Kumari, N. (2025). The future of tourism: the metaverse as a tool for promoting sustainable tourism. Asia Pacific Journal of Tourism Research, 0(0), Article 2574038. https://doi.org/10.1080/10941665.2025.2574038, DOI: 10.1080/10941665.2025.2574038

Li, J., Qu, L., Cai, T., Zhao, Z., Haldar, N. A. H., Krishna, A., Kong, X., Macau, F., Chakraborty, T., Deroy, A., Lin, B., Blackmore, K., Noman, N., Cheng, J., Cui, N., & Xu, J. (2025). AI-generated content in cross-domain applications: Research trends, challenges, and propositions. *Knowledge-Based Systems*, *330*, 114634. Advance online publication. DOI: 10.1016/j.knosys.2025.114634

Li, J., Zhu, Z., Zhang, R., & Lee, Y. C. (2025). Exploring the effects of chatbot anthropomorphism and human empathy on human prosocial behavior toward chatbots. *Proceedings of the ACM on Human-Computer Interaction*, *9*(7), 1–29. DOI: 10.1145/3757596

Liu, R., Hao, J.-X., Yu, Y., & Shan, W. (2025). Helpful or harmful? A curvilinear perspective on AI agent anthropomorphism in service failure tolerance. *Journal of Retailing and Consumer Services*, *85*, 104299. DOI: 10.1016/j.jretconser.2025.104299

Liu, Z., Wang, X., Luo, X. R., Song, X., Liu, N., & Zhang, Y. (2023). Be together, run more: Enhancing group participation in fitness technology. *Journal of the Association for Information Systems*, *24*(2), 530–554. DOI: 10.17705/1jais.00779

Liu-Thompkins, Y., Okazaki, S., & Li, H. (2022). Artificial empathy in marketing interactions: Bridging the human-AI gap in affective and social customer experience. *Journal of the Academy of Marketing Science*, *50*(6), 1198–1218. Advance online publication. DOI: 10.1007/s11747-022-00892-5

Luo, X., Tong, S., Fang, Z., & Qu, Z. (2019). Frontiers: Machines vs. Humans: The impact of artificial intelligence chatbot disclosure on customer purchases. *Marketing Science*, mksc.2019.1192. Advance online publication. DOI: 10.1287/mksc.2019.1192

Margetis, G., Ntoa, S., Antona, M., & Stephanidis, C. (2021). Human-centered design of artificial intelligence. *Handbook of human factors and ergonomics*, 1085-1106.

Noranee, S., & Othman, A. K. B. (2023). Understanding consumer sentiments: Exploring the role of artificial intelligence in marketing. *JMM17: JurnalIlmuEkonomi dan Manajemen*. https://doi.org/DOI: 10.30996/jmm17.v10i1.8690

Odeibat, A. (2024). *The impacts of artificial intelligence on the future of marketing and customer behaviour*. Cross-Cultural Management Journal., DOI: 10.70147/c261934

Oliveira, F. S. (2025). From commands to connections: how voice assistants shape and are shaped by consumer–brand relationships.

Pasch, S., & Ha, S.-Y. (2025). Human-AI interaction and user satisfaction: Empirical evidence from online reviews of AI products. *International Journal of Human-Computer Interaction*. Advance online publication. DOI: 10.1080/10447318.2025.2545463

Peltier, J. W., Dahl, A. J., & Schibrowsky, J. A. (2024). Artificial intelligence in interactive marketing: A conceptual framework and research agenda. *Journal of Research in Interactive Marketing*, *18*(1), 54–90. DOI: 10.1108/JRIM-01-2023-0030

Petrescu, M., & Krishen, A. S. (2023). Hybrid intelligence: Human–AI collaboration in marketing analytics. *Journal of Marketing Analytics*, *11*(3), 263–274. DOI: 10.1057/s41270-023-00245-3

Puntoni, S., Reczek, R. W., Giesler, M., & Botti, S. (2021). Consumers and artificial intelligence: An experiential perspective. *Journal of Marketing*, *85*(1), 131–151. DOI: 10.1177/0022242920953847

Qiu, X., Wang, Y., Zeng, Y., & Cong, R. (2025). Artificial intelligence disclosure in cause-related marketing: A persuasion knowledge perspective. *Journal of Theoretical and Applied Electronic Commerce Research*, *20*(3), 193. DOI: 10.3390/jtaer20030193

Rayun, S. N., Salam, M. A., Islam, W., Firmansyah, E. A., & Kalinaki, K. (2025). Unraveling the dynamics of mobile wallets in promoting cashless tourism in Bangladesh: Implementation of UTAUT2 model. *Journal of Hospitality and Tourism Technology*, *16*(5), 1046–1065. DOI: 10.1108/JHTT-04-2024-0222

Rayun, S. N., Salam, M. A., Islam, W., & Leong, V. S. (2026). Green FinTech Innovations: Empowering Inclusive Development and Advancing Towards the Sustainable Economy. In *Promoting Inclusivity and Accessibility With FinTech* (pp. 245-278). IGI Global Scientific Publishing.

Salam, M. A., Leong, V. S., & Muhamad, N. (2026). The Transformative Prospects of AI Powered Virtual Influencers in Digital Consumer Engagement and Marketing Strategies. In *Cases on Social Media Marketing Engagement Tactics* (pp. 251–290). IGI Global Scientific Publishing.

Sharma, S., Islam, N., Singh, G., & Dhir, A. (2022). Why do retail customers adopt artificial intelligence (AI) based autonomous decision-making systems? *IEEE Transactions on Engineering Management*, *71*, 1846–1861. DOI: 10.1109/TEM.2022.3157976

Song, X., &BonaSidaoui, K., Jaakkola, M., & Burton, J. (2020). AI feel you: customer experience assessment via chatbot interviews. https://doi.org/DOI: 10.1108/JOSM-11-2019-0341

Thomaz, F., Salge, C., Karahanna, E., & Hulland, J. (2019). Learning from the Dark Web: Leveraging conversational agents in the era of hyper-privacy to enhance marketing. *Journal of the Academy of Marketing Science*. Advance online publication. DOI: 10.1007/s11747-019-00704-3

Tsakalerou, M., Tynybayeva, N., & Abil, A. S. (2025). Bridging minds and machines: Emotional intelligence as intellectual capital for human-AI collaboration. *European Conference on Knowledge Management*. https://doi.org/DOI: 10.34190/eckm.26.2.4006

Tsamados, A., Floridi, L., & Taddeo, M. (2024). Human control of AI systems: From supervision to teaming. *AI and Ethics*. Advance online publication. DOI: 10.1007/s43681-024-00489-4 PMID: 40352578

Wilson, A. V., & Bellezza, S. (2022). Consumer Minimalism. *The Journal of Consumer Research*, *48*(5), 796–816. DOI: 10.1093/jcr/ucab038

Wirtz, J., Patterson, P., Kunz, W., Gruber, T., Lu, V., Paluch, S., & Martins, A. (2018). Brave new world: Service robots in the frontline. *Journal of Service Management*, *29*(5), 907–931. Advance online publication. DOI: 10.1108/JOSM-04-2018-0119

Yanxia, C., Shijia, Z., & Yuyang, X. (2024). A meta-analysis of the effect of chatbot anthropomorphism on the customer journey. *Marketing Intelligence & Planning*, *42*(1), 1–22. DOI: 10.1108/MIP-03-2023-0103

Yau, K., Saad, N., & Chong, Y.-W. (2021). Artificial Intelligence Marketing (AIM) for enhancing customer relationships. *Applied Sciences (Basel, Switzerland)*, *11*(18), 8562. Advance online publication. DOI: 10.3390/app11188562

KEY TERMS AND DEFINITIONS

Algorithm Aversion: A disconnect that makes consumers or managers cease to trust or accept the recommendations made by algorithms although these recommendations are better, even given human sensibilities. The phenomenon of algorithm aversion in marketing environments occurs when the users feel they lack control when interacting with the algorithm or when the algorithm implies a threat to their autonomy, and can be addressed by automated designs with opportunities to override the algorithm.

Anthropomorphism: Giving AI systems anthropomorphic characteristics, actions, and feelings, such as employing conversational language, using avatars, emojis and describing social dialogue styles. For marketing applications of human-AI interactions, moderate anthropomorphism has a positive effect on social presence, the fun of the experience and the level of trust, while excessive human likeness may create the "uncanny valley" effect where trust and satisfaction is decreased.

Augmentation (vs. Automation): A cooperation model that does not replace human skills and abilities, retaining human creativity, empathy and context-based judgment, while taking advantage of AI's efficiency and pattern recognition. Results of the empirical analysis in this chapter reveal an augmentation boost of 47% of customer engagement and 31% of the conversion rate over conventional approaches.

Human-AI Interaction (HAI) in Marketing: A dialogue and co-creation between people (Consumer or Marketer) and artificial or intelligent systems in business transactions, which includes exchanging information and takes two forms adaptive: listening and speaking, goal-oriented: listening and generation. In contrast to traditional HCI, HAI is characterised by the fact that AI is: agents, learning entities, a social presence and endowed with dynamic reciprocity, meaning every step stimulates expectations and reactions in the other.

Personalization-Privacy Paradox: The tension consumers feel between the advantages of using AI for personalisation, making things easier and more useful, and on one hand, and the fear that their data is being used for tracking, surveillance, inappropriate use, or losing control of their personal data. Paradox is reduced through the involvement in the products, the transparency of the products, and the congruence between the data sources and the normative understandings in the context.

PRISMA Methodology: This chapter follows the Preferred Reporting Items for Systematic Reviews and Meta-Analyses (PRISMAS) guidelines for this systematic literature review in order to ensure transparency, rigor and reproducibility. Methodology/groundwork for the study consisted of staging the methodology for screening (identifying, screening, eligibility, including compilation) of 387 records and a compilation of 73 peer-reviewed articles for qualitative synthesis.

Tripartite Interaction Framework: A conceptual model was developed within the context of this chapter that explains outcomes of human-AI interaction in marketing, by engaging the three core components: (A) AI Agent Design and Cues (anthropomorphism, transparency, agency, interaction style); (B) Human User Psychology (cognitive-affective state, pre-existing orientations, goal orientation); and (C) Marketing Context and Task Characteristics (task type, product involvement, channel, relationship stage). The framework assumes when all three dimensions are congruent optimal performance will result.

Transparency (Explainability): The design principle of 'making an AI system transparent' in terms of its nature, intended mechanism and the reasons for its decisions. For marketing HAI, transparency receives a positive response and boosts trust – especially in high-involvement, high-risk situations (such as financial or healthcare). But there is a "too transparent" level, too, in non-critically oriented communications, which would need progressive or on-demand disclosure strategies.

Chapter 3
Algorithms to Markets: Towards Pathways for Commercializing AI Systems in Technology Transfer

Mohammad Rakibul Islam Bhuiyan
http://orcid.org/0000-0003-4284-6461
Begum Rokeya University, Rangpur, Bangladesh

ABSTRACT

The chapter discusses how Artificial Intelligence (AI) is commercialized in the marketing, healthcare, financial, and logistics industries, which illustrates the disjointed technology transfer processes. It identifies phases of AI commercialization, such as finding, intellectual property protection, validation, scaling, and governance, concentrating on intellectual property management, university-industry collaboration, and startup ecosystems. The chapter combines findings about two critical areas transfer object and process enabler through a PRISMA-based systematic literature review (3,645 studies). The TOE-DCV framework has combined Technologies and Organization Environment settings and dynamic capabilities, focusing on AI-related enablers such as data governance and regulatory compliance. The chapter represents TTO capabilities, obstacles, and geopolitical variations with some solutions such as AI literacy training and regulatory actions. The policy implications focus on equity, advancing sustainable development targets and overcoming the issue of IP ownership and social hazards.

DOI: 10.4018/979-8-3373-9325-4.ch003

1.0 INTRODUCTION

AI is a technology applicable in commercial settings in custom marketing, predictive maintenance, clinical decision support, and optimization of the supply chain (Bhimavarapu, 2025). Models of technology transfer, which were initially developed to transfer pharmaceuticals and engineering inventions, are stretched to address data intensive and software intensive AI inventions that are continually developed even after they come to the market (Mohammed et al., 2022; Fangyu et al., 2024). In this respect, university research, business R&D laboratories, and AI startups are co-producers of knowledge, which are liable to IP regimes, financing, and regulatory control before they can to find end-users recommended by (Renz & Hilbig, 2020).

Rodgers and Nguyen (2022) argued that it has become more and more apparent that to conceptualize the peculiarities of AI, including its dependence on large amounts of data and constant retraining, as well as its ability to overstep ethical and legal boundaries, one will need to look to traditional conceptions of technology transfer. The proactive exploration of AI-specific transfer routes will bridge the major gap in the knowledge of scholars and practitioners concerned with understanding how AI-driven innovation can be implemented between prototypes and systems that are already available in the market (Ma & Wang, 2024; Renz and Hilbig, 2020). The chapter carries the greatest significance to the fields of marketing and management where AI-driven analytics and decision-support systems are changing the customer strategy and value generation (Tyukin et al., 2018; Rodgers and Nguyen, 2022; Lazaroiu et al., 2024).

1.1 Background

Wan et al. (2025) stated that artificial intelligence (AI) has become one of the powerful general-purpose technologies of the Fourth Industrial Revolution. The notion of the Fourth Industrial Revolution provides a broader context in which artificial intelligence has emerged as a powerful general-purpose technology reshaping production, services, and innovation systems (Wan et al., 2025). AI has transitioned beyond the symbolic reasoning systems to data-rich, learning-based architectures that can make autonomous decisions, predict and optimize in a wide range of areas (Tsolakis et al., 2023). Nowadays, AI does not fulfill the role of a laboratory experiment anymore; instead, it is becoming the object and the means of the technology transfer processes, redefining the process of creating, valorising and commercialisation of knowledge (Alkhazaleh et al., 2022).

Traditionally, technology transfer is the process where scientific knowledge, inventions, or technologies created in research institutions are converted into commercial products, services or processes that can bring economic and societal value

(Kingsley et al., 1996). The classical models of technology transfer were originally created in the view of tangible, discrete innovations as pharmaceuticals, mechanical devices or industrial processes. These models are often based on the linear or phase models that entail the invention disclosure, intellectual property (IP) protection, licensing, and commercialization with the help of the industry partnerships or spin-offs (National Academies of Sciences, Engineering, and Medicine, 2021).

Figure 1. Technology transfer performance factors.

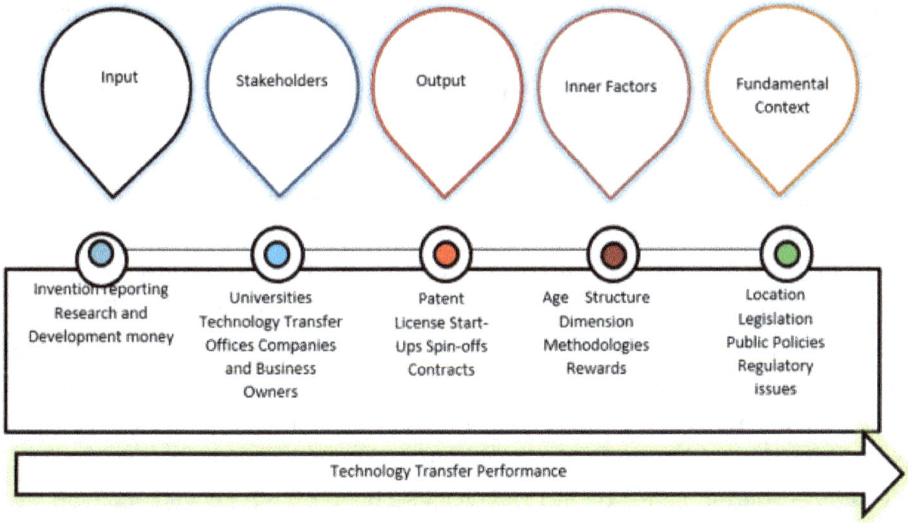

Source: Author's Contribution

The figure 1 illustrates the different internal and external variables that define the success and effectiveness of technology transfer, especially with the AI systems. The internal forces, including structure, methodology and rewards of an organization, have direct impact on the effectiveness of an organization in adapting and implementing technology transfer. Age and size of organization are also contributing factors towards its capacity to control the effective use and adoption of technology. These factors are indications of the internal strengths of the organization to manage the dynamics of transferring innovative technologies.

The external factors are the factors that cause the technology transfer to be facilitated or hindered by the location, legislation, public policies and regulation issues. These are the macro-factors in which the technology transfer process takes place and influence commercialization greatly. The presence of strategic stakeholders like universities, technology transfer offices (TTOs), and businesses augers well in the transfer of technology in the research environment to the market practices.

The figure 1 highlights the significance of systematic approach, when the input of resources and research data is channeled by the stakeholders to produce output in the form of commercialization and market integration, which entails the necessity of coordination on the level of various areas.

Ojha et al. (2025) state that outside academia, the AI-based innovation has infiltrated several industries, such as agriculture, finance, manufacturing, and strategic decisions in SMEs. The agri-food sector is one of the sectors where AI has been demonstrated to increase productivity, efficiency in logistics, risk reduction, and decision support, but there is an uneven adoption because of organizational and institutional barriers. In the same way, studies on SMEs show that AI can be of great benefit to the speed and quality of international strategic decision-making but resource limitations and cultural opposition still prevent its mass adoption (Aiudi et al., 2025).

The studies about the industry highlight a more general phenomenon: AI is altering not only how operations are carried out but the process of transferring and commercialising knowledge (Chen et al., 2022). AI systems are even integrated with the technology transfer processes themselves, which allows automated IP analytics, recommendation-based partner search, valuation modeling, and due diligence (De Bruyn et al., 2020). Simultaneously, AI technologies bring new risks on the basis of algorithmic bias, explainability, market power, and unintended coordination effects as illustrated in the financial markets research on algorithmic collusion and price efficiency. It is against this background that that the subject of AI-specific technology transfer pathways has emerged as a timely scholarly and practical issue (Paschen et al., 2019; Huang and Rust, 2021).

1.2 Significance

The relevance of studying artificial intelligence in technology transfer is its potential to transform the economy as well as institutional disruption (Malthouse and Copulsky, 2023). The innovation powered by AI is considered to be one of the sources of productivity growth, competitiveness, and sustainability in all industries (Gao et al., 2025). Successful commercialization however is determined by the strength of the transfer mechanism which matches technical capability in the market need, in morality and regulative frameworks. Conventional structures tend to presuppose the stability of technologies, where ownership lines are known and there is very little evolution after transfer (Alkhazaleh et al., 2022).

In practice, universities and research institutions are under growing pressure to show what societal and economic impact AI research funded by the public can have (Satornino et al., 2024). Responsible AI deployment, digital sovereignty, and ethical governance are key aspects of policymaking by policymakers in national and supranational governments and organizations, notably in the European Union. The CESAER report specifically investigates the use of clearer IP guidance, common infrastructures, and regulatory sandboxes as the means of allowing safe experimentation with AI in the context of technology transfer (Davenport et al., 2020; Chintalapati and Pandey, 2022; Eriksson et al., 2020).

The relevance of this chapter is further increased by the fact that AI has a dual role in technology transfer. To start with, AI is a transferable technology, and it needs dedicated channels in order to be commercialized. Second, AI is an enabling infrastructure that transforms the processes of transfers through enhancing efficiency, transparency, and quality of decisions (Lee and Chen, 2022; Agrawal et al., 2019). The studies on AI-assisted trading show how autonomous learning frameworks might make unforeseen market phenomena, including tacit collusion, occur even in the absence of direct coordination (Tapalova and Zhiyenbayeva, 2022). Technology transfer markets should be similarly vulnerable to such risks in case AI-based matchmaking or valuation systems strengthen or increase biases or dominant actors (Rayun et al., 2025). Thus, it is crucial to learn the AI transfer pathway not only to achieve innovation performance but also to protect the competition, trust, and social good (Singh et al., 2024; Soliman et al., 2024). The chapter has provided an addition to the interdisciplinary arguments in the field of technology transfer, AI governance, and innovation studies to academics. It builds on the systematic literature reviews that indicate the increasing yet disjointed body of research on AI and technology transfer (Etzkorn et al., 2025) and addresses the calls of conceptual frameworks that incorporate AI-specific enablers in existing transfer theories (Arya et al., 2025).

AI systems are data-driven, software intensive, and evolutionary in nature, and may keep on learning and evolving when deployed. In the recent policy and academic publications, AI innovations are not just conditioned by the presence of an algorithm, but the availability of quality data, computing capability, human capital, and regulatory compliance systems (Etzkorn et al., 2025). This makes it difficult to own and govern structures in technology transfer processes.

Universities and government-funded research organizations are central participants in AI innovation ecosystems, which serve as centers of fundamental research, talent development, and early experimentation (Gao et al., 2025; Cetindamar et al., 2020; ALLAN et al., 2019). Technology Transfer Offices (TTOs) have therefore emerged as central institutional players in the mediation of AI commercialization as a step-out of academia research. However, there is manifesto evidence that the use of AI in TTOs is in its infancy (Kingsley et al., 1996; Khan et al., 2024). According to the report by CESAER on AI pathways to technology transfer, it is reported that less than fifty percent of TTOs surveyed in Europe actively employ AI tools, with most mainly using tools to support patent analytics, document drafting, and partner matching, whereas many are still limited by lack of expertise, funding, and data protection and IP leakage (Dean, 1988).

To professionals in technology transfer and university administrators, the chapter discusses the practical issues related to the commercialization of AI, including IP management, data governance, talent limitations, and the choice of partners (Yu et al., 2023; Bock et al., 2020). The experience of European TTOs shows that there is great need to have practical recommendations on how to use AI responsibly, train and develop infrastructure. Practitioners and SMEs in the industry have an interest in how they can avail AI-based technology, adapt it, and scale it by working together with universities and research institutions (Tsolakis et al., 2023; Bednar and Welch, 2020). Research of AI in SMEs indicates that AI has the potential to democratize strategic decisions and increase the international competitiveness, however, the advantages of applying AI rely on the transfer-supporting mechanisms and the alignment between institutions (Aiudi et al., 2025; Khan et al., 2024).

1.3 Research Gaps

Although there are increased research interests, there are still a number of gaps in research that are critical at the boundary of artificial intelligence and technology transfer.

First, a large part of the current literature discusses the implementation of AI in companies or industries, but there is no explicit discussion on the routes of transfer between research and market. Although the sectoral analyses of the agri-food, finance, and manufacturing are very helpful, they frequently do not realize the institutional processes that facilitate or limit commercialization (Bednar and Welch, 2020).

Second, technology transfer theory and research on AI governance have very little integration. Along with the transparency of algorithms and their ownership and ethical responsibility, they are often debated separately, without references to commercialization process, which leads to a lack of an integrated view of the analysis (Rayun et al., 2026).

Third, there is still little empirical evidence regarding the use of AI as a tool in TTOs. The CESAER report offers one of the most systematic evaluations of AI implementation in European TTOs, which indicate initial experimentation and a huge gap in capabilities.

1.4 Objectives

To address the above gaps, this chapter of the book seeks four connected objectives:

Follow AI-Specific Technology Transfer Pathways: The chapter will follow the path of AI systems through research to market, highlighting such stages as discovery, protection of IP, validation, scaling and governance, based on the PRISMA approach.

Determine Key Actors and Institutional Arrangements: It aims to realize the central stakeholders, including universities, TTOs, startups, investors, and regulators, that determine the results of AI commercialization, on the basis of the conceptual framework.

Expand Classical Technology Transfer Models: This is aimed at extending traditional technology transfer models by incorporating AI-specific enablers including data governance, computational infrastructure, and ethical compliance.

Present Applied AI Transfer Advice: The chapter provides practical advice to universities, TTOs, industry, and policymakers at implementing AI commercialization using AI literacy, governance frameworks, and regulatory sandboxes.

Research gaps and Future directions: The chapter indicates the gaps in empirical studies about AI transfer, especially in emerging economies and TTO acceptance, and presents future research directions to confirm AI transfer mechanisms in sectors.

With these goals, the chapter aims at promoting not only theoretical knowledge but also practical application of AI channels in modern technology transfer in the context of innovation ecosystems.

2.0 LITERATURE REVIEW

The existing studies show that AI is reshaping capital markets, industrial operations, TTO practices, and SME decision-making, yet they rarely conceptualise AI-specific technology transfer as a coherent process from algorithms to market-ready systems. Research on algorithmic trading and symbolic regression focuses mainly on technical performance and emergent risks such as collusion or opacity, while work on Industry 4.0, SMEs, and TTOs tends to emphasise adoption conditions and organisational readiness rather than the transfer mechanisms linking university research, intermediaries, and markets. Governance and ethical perspectives are often discussed separately from technology transfer, which leads to a fragmented understanding of how IP management, data governance, and responsible AI practices interact during commercialization. These gaps justify our PRISMA-based systematic review and the development of an integrated conceptual framework that traces AI-specific transfer pathways, identifies key actors and institutional arrangements, and incorporates AI-related enablers into classical technology transfer theories. Based on the documents provided, here is the comprehensive background and context for each study.

2.1 Trading with AI Power, Algorithms Collusion and Efficiency of Price

Market Environment and Regulation: AI-based trading strategies are now much more common in capital markets and major investment firms such as BlackRock and JPMorgan have invested in these technologies (Bednar and Welch, 2020; Tsvetovatyy et al., 1997; Grundner and Neuhofer, 2021). Such a common use of AI has led to a great regulatory interest among the SEC and financial supervisors in all parts of the world that consider AI a priority to be regulated because it may cause systemic risks (Renz & Hilbig, 2020).

Core Research Problem: The research question is a critical problem in the area of algorithmic trading: the regulators might admit that algorithms can minimize human biases, however, the process of reinforcement learning in such systems has its own biases called artificial stupidity, which might strengthen the existing biases of the designers and lead to poor market performance (Allal-Chérif et al., 2021; Tschang and Almirall, 2021; Ledro et al., 2022). The study examines the effects of AI-based trading algorithms on informed trader market power as well as the efficiency of the prices in general.

Theoretical Framework Extension: The article builds on the powerful framework by Kyle in the three new dimensions; Multiple informed speculators in a repeated-game setup, a representative preferred-habitat investor, and a market maker that takes into account both inventory and pricing error (Kulshrestha and Kapoor, 2025; Di Vaio et al., 2020; Mahboub and Ghanem, 2024). The study provides evidence that, with Q-learning algorithms serving as an example of proof-of-concept, knowledgeable AI speculators are capable of learning collusive trading strategies without having to engage in explicit coordination.

Mechanisms Important to note: There are two mechanisms of algorithmic collusion that are distinguished: collusion by price-trigger strategies (artificial intelligence) and collusion by learning biases (artificial stupidity). The article is an original theory on the infeasibility of collusion in the presence of information asymmetry and it shows that tacit collusion can be maintained under price-triggered strategy when the preferred-habitat investors have a significant impact on defining the price (Raisch and Krakowski, 2021).

2.2 Technology Transfer and Artificial Intelligence

Industrial Revolution Background: Industry 4.0 introduced disruptive technologies such as AI and robotics to transform society in the social, economic, and environmental aspects (Samtani et al., 2021; Karunakaran et al., 2025). The goals of these technologies are to improve human lives and well-being by making human work more productive and efficient due to robots as well as AI-based tools that supplement human work.

Technology Overview: AI technologies have the ability to perceive environments, learn through previous experience, and solve certain programmed tasks. Machine learning helps algorithms to detect patterns and propose decisions. The most available type of AI implementation is introduced as Robot Process Automation (RPA) that provides quick payback and is especially helpful when precise tasks are involved and human beings are error prone (Balakrishnan and Dwivedi, 2024; Jiménez-Luna et al., 2021).

Historical Development: The history of AI development can be traced back to 1943 when people first suggested the use of artificial neural networks, then the Dartmouth Conference took place in 1956 when the name of artificial intelligence was officially coined, which included several fields of study, such as logic, computer science, and philosophy (Menzies et al., 2024; Jiang et al., 2022).

Societal Implications: Although AI could be considered an answer to better living standards and the introduction of new categories of jobs, it endangers people with low and medium quality in their repetitive jobs and may result in the increase of inequality (Di Guardo et al., 2025; Paramesha et al., 2024). Technology transfer is a means of knowledge, innovations, and developments dissemination to the populace of a given country, through science, education, and state intervention.

2.3 AI Applications to technology transfer

Strategic Significance: AI has become a general-purpose technology that stands to transform research, education, and innovation. It also poses both chances to hasten the innovation and burdens to universities and their Technology Transfer Offices (TTOs) to guarantee open, fair, and gainful AI implementation (Samara et al., 2020).

Xia et al. (2026) state that role of Technology Transfer offices: TTOs are particularly important bridges between research and application because they are uniquely placed to test and deploy AI tools in knowledge valorization, whether in patent analysis, contract management, partner search, and spinout support.

European Policy Framework The work is located in the context of European policy where AI has become a key priority after the passing of the AI Act. The European Commission is currently developing actions to steer the responsible AI use in research, education, and innovation with special focus on the AI in Science Strategy that speeds up the scientific advancement without sacrificing trust, transparency, and accountability (Xia et al., 2025).

Survey Scope: The CESAER Task Force, in turn, held a survey and expert consultations to investigate the current use of AI, the opportunities to provide value, risks, and support requirements in TTOs, making AI a possible facilitator of knowledge valorization by searching prior art, analyzing patents, matchmaking between partners, and collaborating with universities (Anayat and Rasool, 2024).

2.4 Trends in Trend Regressions and Pathways using Symbolic Regressions

Scientific Paradigm Shift: AI and big data are placed as the disruptive force in all scientific disciplines, and the fourth paradigm of science currently uses AI to promote research in bioinformatics, particle physics, space research, medical imaging and construction applications (Riaj et al., 2025).

Machine Learning in Science: Machine Learning is also mentioned as one of the techniques of AI with significant interest in data analysis, which shapes the possibility of learning through experience and submitting correct approximations and predictions about the underlying patterns (Faisal-E-Alam et al., 2025). Nevertheless, the use of traditional ML is different with what statistical analysis gives: ML offers data classification and prediction algorithms, whereas statistics aims at precise description of observations (Khatun et al., 2025).

The Black-Box Problem: This issue is considered among the most important because it is the black-box problem with neural networks when the outputs are preset, yet cannot be understood by people, and the issue of explainability and generalizability of the AI systems becomes a problem (Bhimavarapu, 2025).

Symbolic Regression Solution: Symbolic Regression (SR) is marketed as a solution- an ML-based technique that explicitly generates symbolic expressions (analytical equations) without any pre-constrained information, as well as offers physics-inspired interpretation (Mohammed et al., 2022; Fangyu et al., 2024). The swift increase in the literature on SR proves its new significance in physics-related computations.

2.5 The Artificial Intelligence in International Strategic Decision-Making among SMEs

Digital Transformation Impact: Digital transformation has a profound impact on the activity, business model, decision-making processes, boundaries, cultures, and value chain of firms and AI is central to it (Renz and Hilbig, 2020). According to the OECD, AI is a machine-based system that makes predictions, recommendations, or decisions that have an impact on real or virtual environments with a relative degree of autonomy.

AI Capabilities: The key capabilities of AI can be considered adaptive learning, relational inference and dynamic evolution. Its disruptive nature is its ability to solve multi-faceted issues that human intelligence used to handle and automate work, use data to determine the essence, and forecast analytics to enhance decision-making and competitive positioning.

Strategic Advantages of AI in International Operations: Rodgers and Nguyen (2022) provide an overview of the strategic advantages of AI, which is improved demand predictions, risk addressing, better supply chain coordination, and more support of international operations. Such abilities deal with complex issues and offer sustainable and cost efficient solutions to businesses.

SME Adoption Challenges: SMEs have a high number of challenges in adopting AI based on structural limitations such as limited financial power and lack of technical expertise. The study is based on Strategic Decision-Making Process (SDMP) theory, which theorizes that the use of AI technologies changes SDMP dimensions in resource-constrained global companies (Ma and Wang, 2024; Renz and Hilbig, 2020; Alkhazaleh et al., 2022).

Research Methodology: The research will be a multiple case study comprising of six small manufacturing firms in central Italy that will extend SDMP theory to AI-based decisions in SMEs and introduce AI as a mediating factor that influences the structure, pace, and decentralization of the decision-making process in resource-constrained firms (Ma and Wang, 2024).

2.6 Human–AI interaction in AI technology transfer

AI technology transfer cannot be considered complete at the moment of licensing or commercialization; it only fully materializes when AI systems are embedded in organizational workflows and used by human decision-makers who interpret, override, or operationalize their outputs (Rajagopal et al., 2022). Recent work on AI in management and marketing shows that transparency, explainability, and perceived reliability strongly shape professionals' trust in, and actual use of, AI tools, and that the allocation of decision authority between humans and AI (automation versus augmentation) is a central design choice rather than a technical detail (Shabankareh et al., 2025). At the same time, empirical studies on AI adoption in organizations emphasize how such tools reconfigure work practices and skill requirements, and how user behavior and feedback in real contexts feed back into model updating, governance mechanisms, and subsequent cycles of technology transfer, suggesting that "deployment and interaction" should be treated as an explicit additional stage in AI-specific transfer pathways beyond IP protection and commercialization (Oliveira et al., 2025).

2.7 AI in capital markets

AI has transformed capital markets trading, price discovery, and market structure at both high-frequency and algorithmic trading, as well as reinforcement-learning-based strategies, which outperform human reaction time and pattern-recognition abilities. Research indicates that automatic artificially intelligent trading can enhance liquidity and informational efficiency but also can create novel systemic risks, such as tacit algorithmic collusion, flash crashes, and opaque feedback paths between models and market states (Paschen et al., 2019; Huang and Rust, 2021). This literature highlights that AI systems are design-based instruments and the choice of design options related to aim, data and restraint is a significant determinant of how an algorithm learns, coordinates, or competes and that these choices are relevant to regulation, competition policy and technology transfer points between academic laboratories and financial establishments (Tyukin et al., 2018).

2.8 AI in Industry 4.0 and SMEs

In Industry 4.0, AI is closely connected to cyber-physical systems, the IoT, and sophisticated analytics to streamline production, maintenance, and logistics in manufacturing and agri-food value chains (Tsolakis et al., 2023). Empirical studies of the SMEs emphasize the productivity increases as well as high obstacles: resource scarcity, skills mismatch, cultural resistance, and fractured data infrastructures frequently hinder the implementation of AI, especially not in large multinationals (Aiudi et al., 2025; Chen et al., 2022). These papers indicate that the idea of AI commercialization in smaller companies relies not only on the technical preparedness but also on the institutional support, ecosystem alliances, and custom transfer schemes that will embrace incremental experimentation, shared infrastructures, and risk-sharing among universities, vendors, and SME consumers (Bednar and Welch, 2020).

2.9 AI among TTOs and intermediaries.

Studies of technology transfer offices (TTOs) and innovation intermediaries have found that AI is starting to reshape their inner operations, but its use is not widespread and remains experimental. The opportunities of automated IP analytics, partner recommendation, and valuation modeling, mentioned in market-based approaches to AI services, can decrease information asymmetries and accelerate deal-flow (Mohammed et al., 2022). Simultaneously, according to the evidence provided by European TTOs, fewer than half of them actively use AI tools, and the majority of the use cases involve patent searches and document drafting because of the differences in capabilities, financial resources, and the fear of information protection and confidentiality (National Academies of Sciences, Engineering, and Medicine, 2021; Kingsley et al., 1996). This new body of literature makes TTOs users and brokers of AI, and theoretical research on AI-specific transfer models remains immature (Renz & Hilbig, 2020).

2.10 AI governance and ethics

The literature on governance and ethics highlights that the diffusion of AI also has some questions concerning transparency, accountability, and long-term responsibility, which do not receive a full response in traditional technology transfer models. According to the policy and management scholars, design of the commercialization pathways would need the incorporation of data governance, explainability of the algorithms, and human oversight, rather than the latter as the downstream compliance add-ons (Agrawal et al., 2019; Malthouse and Copulsky, 2023). Contributions to the discourse of European higher-education and research ecosystems highlight the importance of better IP guidance, common infrastructures, and regulatory sandboxes to facilitate safe experimentation with AI, as well as to alleviate risks of bias, market concentration, and unplanned coordination behaviour in practical applications (Davenport et al., 2020; Eriksson et al., 2020; Satornino et al., 2024).

3.0 METHODOLOGY

In order to be transparent, replicable, and methodologically sound in investigating the existence of AI-specific technology transfer pathways, the chapter has chosen a systematic literature review (SLR) approach in accordance with the PRISMA (Preferred Reporting Items to Systematic Reviews and Meta-Analyses) guidelines (Renz and Hilbig, 2020). The study brings together literature of peer-reviewed empirical and conceptual studies that directly deal with the movements in algorithms and AI systems between research and commercial marketplaces, especially with respect to the functions of intellectual property (IP) management, university-industry relationships, start-up ecosystems, and AI-based technology transfer instruments (Raji et al., 2026).

3.1 Research Design

This chapter adopts a systematic literature review design, following the PRISMA 2020 guidelines for transparent reporting of the identification, screening, eligibility assessment, and inclusion of studies. The review synthesises peer-reviewed empirical and conceptual work that explicitly addresses AI-specific technology transfer pathways, from algorithms and research prototypes to market-ready commercial system (Ma and Wang, 2024; Renz and Hilbig, 2020; Alkhazaleh et al., 2022).

The given approach is especially suitable to investigate the case of AI technology transfer since:

Interdisciplinary Integration: AI transfer happens at the convergence of technology transfer theory: It involves the systematic incorporation of knowledge across fields through innovation studies, AI governance, and organizational management.

Emerging Field Consolidation: The body of empirical research explicitly considering AI-mediated technology transfer processes are still scarce with most empirical research emphasising adoption as opposed to a transfer process. A systematic review brings together piecemeal evidence.

Development of Conceptual Frameworks: The research will integrate the findings to create a consistent system building upon the classical technology transfer models incorporating AI-specific facilitating factors, such as data resources, computational platforms, regulatory adherence, and responsible AI governance (Bhimavarapu, 2025).

Dual Role of AI: Unlike other innovations of the past, AI is not only a transfer object but also a tool that facilitates transfer processes. This duality is holistically captured by a systematic approach.

The search strategy used to select and search databases was as follows: 3.2 Database Selection and Search Strategy.

3.2 Database Selection

The databases selected are essential in assuring completeness and reliability of a systematic review. Scopus was selected as the main database since it has:

Diverse databases encompassing broad academic sources within the broad-based knowledge fields such as computer science, management, economics, engineering and public policy.

Citation of quality peer journal articles, conference papers and book chapters.

Among Web of Science, Google Scholar, and other databases, Scopus is chosen as the most appropriate solution due to its coverage of interdisciplinary literature on AI and technology transfer, as well as in terms of rigour founded on the ability to index by peer review and track citations.

The query and philosophy of the search and selection will be developed as follows: 3.2.2 Search Strategy and Query Development.

The search strategy was created to include all the studies that were relevant to the topic and contained AI-driven technology transfer by combining several sets of keywords and using Boolean operators. The overall Scopus search query is:

TI-ABS-KEY ((“Commercial Artificial Intelligence” OR “Technology transfer” OR Artificial intelligence OR TOE framework OR Technology Transfer Offices AND PUBYEAR > 2020 AND PUBYEAR < 2026 AND (LIMIT-TO (PUBSTAGE, final)) OR (LIMIT-TO (DOctype, ch) or (LIMIT-TO (DOctype, ar) or (LIMIT-TO (DOctype, re)) AND (LIMIT-TO (Language, English))

The logic behind the choice of the keywords in this systematic review is based on the fact that it is necessary to consider the most significant concepts that are directly related to the AI commercialization and technology transfer. The name Commercial Artificial Intelligence or Commercial AI is selected to consider AI systems that are market-ready, i.e. not academic or research. This will make the research represent the practical and real-world uses of AI. The terms of Technology transfer and Technology Transfer offices are also listed as necessary terms to define the process of transferring novelty between the research centers and the market. These are key ideas to be considered in the context of commercialization of technologies, such as AI.

The term Artificial intelligence is used as an overall term in AI technologies and includes such domains as machine learning, deep learning, and autonomous systems that are significant in the current technology transfer processes. The framework of TOE (Technology-Organization-Environment) is enclosed because it is one of the fundamental models of technology adoption and diffusion, which offers a systematic angle through which AI implementation in different organizational and environmental situations can be interpreted. The so-called AI-specific enablers are denoted as data governance and dynamic capabilities, which are considered organizational structures and governance mechanisms that are necessary to ensure successful technology transfer. The book “Algorithms to Markets” specifically describes how AI innovations can be transferred between their algorithmic origin to commercial application.

To make the research applicable and up-to-date, the search is confined to those studies published between 2021 and 2025. This updated temporal limit will make sure that the review is as up-to-date as possible in terms of the latest trends in AI commercialization and technology transfer, as well as in correspondence with current policy frameworks, such as the EU AI Act (2024). The search filters are also restricted to exclude the way-too-young conceptual work and only peer-reviewed studies that convey empirical evidence and expert opinions are included. The article, review, and book chapter are all limited to document types, which will guarantee that only well-established sources of high quality are used. Finally, the search is limited to English-language publications to ensure the consistency and availability of interpretation.

Figure 2. PRISMA Based Methodology

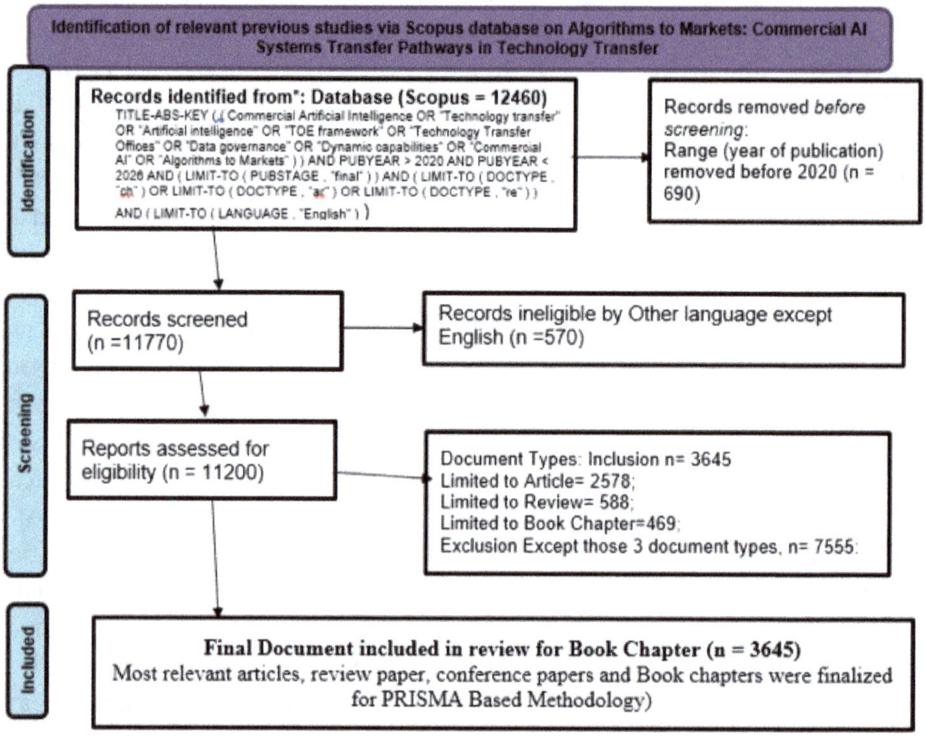

Source: Scopus Database (2026)

3.3 Identification of Search Results and Preliminary Filters.

During the identification step of the search query, 12,460 records had been identified in the Scopus database. This vast amount of records reminds of an increasing academic focus of the AI technology transfer as it is related to numerous disciplines such as computer science, business management, innovation studies, public policy, and engineering. Prior to screening, 1,260 records were filtered out, having been published prior to the year 2021 (690) and non-English language (570). This reduced the number of records to be screened further to 11,200 records, thus only relevant and up-to-date English studies would be taken into account during the review.

The technique of selection and the screening process will be 3.4.

In the selection, PRISMA flowchart was used in systematic reviews which is a generally recognized tool of assessing and sorting studies to be included. It involved several steps in which the initial step was the screening stage whereby 11,200 records who were to be developed in the identification phase were screened against predetermined eligibility criteria using the title and the abstract.

The inclusion criteria targeted the presence of articles that made an explicit reference to AI or machine learning applications, was discussing transfer of technology, commercialisation or innovation pathway and was discussing organisational, institutional or policy mechanisms that made transfer possible. Such articles were required to be peer-reviewed publications, review papers, or book chapters, and may comprise empirical data, conceptual analysis, or synthesis. The exclusion criteria eliminated merely technical accounts of AI algorithms, broad discourse of AI implementation not focusing on transfer, non-peer-reviewed articles, and studies that do not investigate AI in non-transfer settings. A total of 3,645 documents passed the screening process and 7,555 documents were rejected, which constituted 67.5 percent of the total population. This exclusion rate is indicative of the fact that this review is very strict in its focus on transfer-specific literature.

3.5 Analysis Method and Pre-screening Level.

This review uses a mixed-method approach, synthesis and conceptual mapping, to analyze the relevant studies and uncover major themes, trends, enablers, and barriers in the studies. 3,645 documents represent the screened and broadly eligible pool, not the set used for full thematic analysis. A subsequent purposive sampling step, in which a smaller subset of 120 core studies would be selected for in-depth thematic analysis and conceptual framework development, based on their relevance to AI-specific transfer pathways, institutional mechanisms, and governance issues. It also analyses the critical actors and institutional structures, including universities, technology transfer offices (TTOs), AI startups, industry partners, and investors, and regulators, that enable the commercialization of AI. The analysis identifies AI-specific enabling factors such as data assets, computational infrastructure, regulatory compliance, human capital, responsible AI governance, and management of intellectual property. Moreover, contextual moderators including the Technology-Organization-Environment (TOE) framework and dynamic capabilities are also looked into in order to know the factors that influence the organizational readiness as well as the effects of sector, geographic, and economic situation.

Table 1. A steps of Data Screening in Scopus Database

Stage	Details
Records Identified from Database	Scopus = 12,460
Records Removed by Publication Year (pre-2021)	690
Records Removed by Language (non-English)	570
Records Proceeding to Screening	11,200
Document Type Inclusion	3,645 (Article, Review, Book Chapter)
Document Type Exclusion	7,555 (Other types)
Final Included Documents	3,645
Articles	2,578
Reviews	588
Book Chapters	469

Source: Author's Work

Synthesis method combines the findings using narrative synthesis, a summary of the way different researchers answers the essential questions regarding the currency of transfer mechanism of AI technology and institutional configurations. It aligns such themes with the TOE framework and Dynamic Capabilities View (DCV), taking into account AI-specific traits and needs in governance. Comparative analysis is also used to compare the results between sectors and geographies to find out the principles that can be transferred and those that should be local. Some of the research gaps also mentioned in the review comprise the long-term results of AI transfer programs, the efficiency of transfer schemes (license versus spin-offs), the place of AI inside TTOs, and the dynamics of AI transfer in emerging economies. Moreover, it deals with undesirable or secondary effects, including algorithmic collusion and market concentration that are poorly investigated in the literature.

Author then conducted a narrative thematic synthesis, clustering studies around key themes: AI-specific transfer pathways, institutional arrangements, AI-enabled tools within TTOs and transfer systems, ethical and lifecycle risks, and emerging-economy and geopolitical dynamics. These themes informed the conceptual framework presented in Section 4.0 and the subsequent discussion of implications.

4.0 CONCEPTUAL FRAMEWORK

The conceptual model describes the application of algorithms into market-ready commercial AI systems via pathways of technology transfer in the figure 3. It is based on the Technology Organization Environment (TOE) paradigm and the Dynamic

Capabilities View (DCV) and theorizes AI commercialization as a dynamic and capability-focused process instead of a technology handover (Alkhazaleh et al., 2022).

At the technology context level, the underlying algorithms are advanced AI tools, including expert systems and digital twins, which can be used in making predictive, adaptive, and automated decisions (Tyukin et al., 2018; Rodgers and Nguyen, 2022; Lazaroiu et al., 2024). Such technologies identify the technical feasibility, scalability, and interoperability of AI systems when transferring.

Figure 3. Conceptual Framework

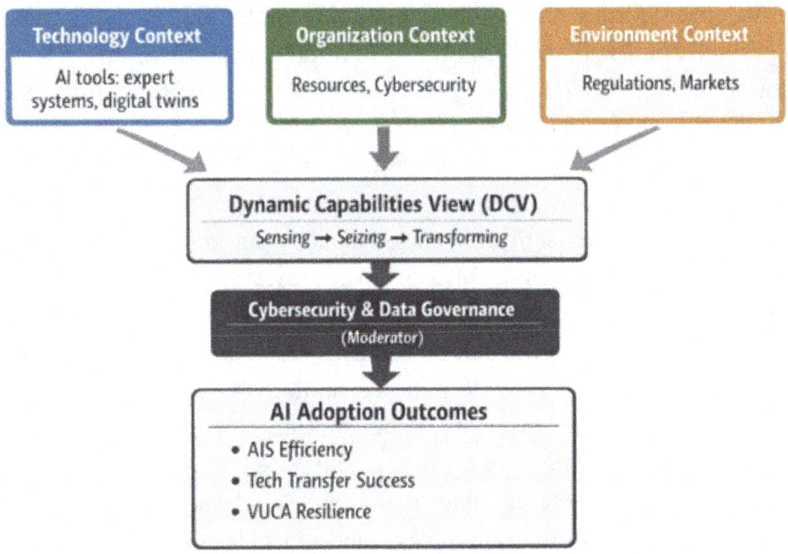

Source: *Author's Work*

Organizational environment entraps in-house firm capacity, such as resources, absorptive capacity and cybersecurity preparedness. Organizations need to have not only the technical infrastructure but also the governance systems that will help hack AI into the current information systems safely and efficiently (Alkhazaleh et al., 2022). The environmental environment gives an indicator of the outside forces like regulatory systems, market demand, and rivalry. They create the incentive to commercialize, alter requirements related to compliance, and the pace and extent of AI penetration into markets (Bhuiyan et al., 2025a).

The combination of the three contexts gives rise to the Dynamic Capabilities View that serves as the main process of the framework in the figure 3 (Rodgers & Nguyen, 2022). Organizations sense AI opportunities that are commercially viable;

seize them to mobilize investments, partners and business models; and transform them to reorganize processes and structures to make AI part of operational and market offerings (Lazaroiu et al., 2024).

Cybersecurity and data governance play a significant role as a moderating mechanism enhancing or diminishing the effectiveness of the dynamic capabilities throughout the transfer process. Strong governance improves trust, compliance with regulations, and reliability of systems, which decrease the risk of commercialization (Tyukin et al., 2018).

AI commercialization in emerging markets and ethical/regulatory frameworks, and they do so in current, peer-reviewed outlets consistent with up-to-date and high-quality evidence. Studies such as Güner Gültekin et al. (2025) and Moharrak et al. (2024) provide empirical analyses of how entrepreneurial firms and new ventures in emerging markets commercialize AI under context-specific constraints, while Strusani and Houngbonon (2019) offer a development oriented perspective on the role of AI in supporting growth in emerging economies. These works strengthen your claims about structural barriers, business-environment conditions, and opportunities for AI-driven internationalisation beyond advanced economies, and therefore should be integrated where you discuss SMEs, start-ups, dynamic capabilities, and Global South dynamics. Similarly, Islam et al. (2026) and Khatun et al. (2026) justify your focus on data governance, information security, trust, and perceived performance as critical AI-specific enablers within the Technology–Organization–Environment and Dynamic Capabilities lenses, by demonstrating how these factors mediate or moderate outcomes in contemporary digital and AI-enabled systems.

On the ethical and regulatory side, Wani et al. (2025) and El Arab et al. (2025) offer recent, sector-specific analyses of legal and ethical frameworks for AI in finance and healthcare, directly supporting your arguments about balancing innovation with responsibility, protection, and economic viability in high-stakes domains. Hurmuzlu (2024) extends this with a broader examination of the ethical implications of AI commercialization, aligning with your discussion of long-term societal risks, bias, and responsible innovation pathways. Strusani and Houngbonon (2019) by connecting AI transfer pathways to sustainable development and governance concerns in both advanced and emerging markets.

The framework ends in the results of AI adoption, successful algorithm-to-market movement. Such results are increased efficiency of AI-enabled information systems (AIS), increased technology transfer performance, and greater organizational resilience in volatile, uncertain, complex, and ambiguous (VUCA) condition (Bhuiyan et al., 2025b). On the whole, the framework shows that the business commercialization of AI requires the interplay of contextual factors, dynamic organizational resources, and governance protection and provides a full trajectory of commercial AI systems transfer between development and market impact (Arya et al., 2025).

4.1 Technology Transfer Conceptual Foundations

4.1.1 Classical Technology Transfer Models

The conventional understanding of technology transfer (TT) has always been the process by which the knowledge, technologies, or inventions created in research institutions can be converted into commercially viable product or service. The initial models focused on linear and stage processes, with the initial one being research and development (R&D), invention disclosure, intellectual property protection, licensing, and market diffusion (Kingsley et al., 1996; Dean, 1988). These models focused mostly on physical and capital-intensive technologies, including energy systems, nanotechnology and industrial manufacturing (ALLAN et al., 2019).

Kingsley et al. (1996) proposed the R&D value-mapping approach, which was an extension of the previous linear models, which included absorptive capacity, institutional preparedness and industry demand as determinants of transfer success. On the same note, systems-based approaches stressed on the congruence between commercial goals, technological maturity and policy environments (Dean, 1988). Although these strategies offered some ground work, they also assumed a fairly stable technology and clearly defined ownership arrangements.

4.1.2. Limitations of the Traditional Models in the Digital Age

As digital and data-driven technologies emerged and became prevalent, researchers started doubting the effectiveness of classical TT frameworks. Digital products have a fundamental difference than physical innovations because of their scalability, the modular nature of an innovation, and reliance on complementary resources like data, platforms, and user communities (National Academies of Sciences, Engineering, and Medicine, 2021). These restrictions are further heightened in the case of artificial intelligence, where the technologies keep developing once they are transferred and the creation of values requires constant learning and adaptation.

4.2 Artificial Intelligence as a General-Purpose Technology

4.2.1 Artificial Intelligence definition in the Innovation Systems

The concept of artificial intelligence has become a highly popularized overall-purpose technology that can transform the dynamic of the economic system, organizational processes, and innovation (Agrawal et al., 2019; Jiang et al., 2022). Artificial intelligence systems are a combination of machine learning, data analytics and automation to fulfill the functions that have been traditionally linked with human intelligence including prediction, decision making and pattern recognition.

The fact that AI is a general-purpose system enables it to spread across industries, including manufacturing, marketing, finance, education, and energy systems (Huang and Rust, 2021; Gao et al., 2025). The cross sectoral applicability maximizes its usefulness in transferring technologies since AI innovations can be used in academia and commercial use in a variety of industry contexts.

4.2.2 AI Diffusion and Adoption Dynamics

Competition in the market, policy incentives, and network effects affect the diffusion of AI technologies. Ma and Wang (2024) prove that the evolutionary game models help to show that AI diffusion is faster when supportive policies and competitive forces are present simultaneously. Nevertheless, access disparities in data, infrastructure, and skills may slow down adoption, especially in low-income nations and resource-limited settings (Khan et al., 2024). These results also point out that AI transfer is not only a technical procedure but a process that is rooted in the socio-economic and institutional situations.

4.3 Artificial Intelligence-Technology Transfer Interface

4.3.1 AI-Specific Characteristics that Influence Technology Transfer

According to recent literature, an AI is challenging established assumptions of TT because it depends on data, algorithms, and continuous retraining. In their systematic literature review, Etzkorn et al. (2025) recognize the following AI-specific enablers, which need to be incorporated into TT models: data governance, ethical accountability, and computational infrastructure. In contrast to stagnant technologies, AI systems continue to develop after transfer, and it is difficult to value, own, and be responsible (Salam et al., 2026).

In the same tone, Bhimavarapu (2025) states that the process of AI transfer must have sustainable models based on long-term university-industry cooperation, in which the trust, joint data ecosystems, and the building of capabilities are essential.

4.3.2 AI as an Object and A Tool of Technology Transfer

One of the peculiarities of AI is its duality in TT processes. On the one hand, AI systems are the thing that is transferred out of research to the market. Conversely,

AI tools are also becoming more helpful in TT activities by improving matching partners, IP analytics, and speed of decision-making (Fangyu et al., 2024).

It is possible to enhance the effectiveness of technology matchmaking by using recommendation algorithms that can help to match inventions with the needs of the industry, minimizing transaction costs and information asymmetries (Fangyu et al., 2024). This twofold role puts AI as a product and a facilitator of innovation systems.

4.4. Sharing of knowledge and knowledge transfer in AI situations

4.4.1 Transparency of Human to AI Knowledge

The idea of knowledge transfer in the context of AI is not a human-to-human setting only as it can also be applied to intelligent systems. Tyukin et al. (2018) consider knowledge transfer between AI systems, and it focuses on learning, adapting, and interoperability of the system. This idea broadens the scope of the conventional TT approach as it acknowledges the AI systems as the agents of knowledge sharing.

4.4.2 Organizational and Knowledge sharing - Sharing based on market

Mohammed et al. (2022) suggest a market-based knowledge sharing in AI services and emphasize the importance of incentives, price structures, and trust in knowledge sharing based on AI services. TT requires proper coordination of economic incentives with the norms of data sharing and collaboration in the context of AI.

The interaction between universities and industries becomes an important source of AI knowledge transfer. Arya et al. (2025) present the idea of so-called AI-enhanced competency transfer hubs, in which universities can be viewed as the mediators of skills development, access to data, and collaborative innovation.

4.5 Industrial 4.0 and Digital Ecosystems Technology Transfer

4.5.1 Artificial Intelligence-Based Innovation and Industry 4.0

Industry 4.0 involves the combination of AI and cyber-physical systems, digital twins, and Internet of things (IoT) to provide the opportunity to make smart manufacturing and make decisions based on the data (Lazaroiu et al., 2024). In that regard, TT processes should support complex system integration and not isolated technologies. Alkhazaleh et al. (2022) note that the success of TT in Industry 4.0 relies on the level of coordination in the ecosystem, digital preparedness, and the ability to learn in an organization. These results support the fact that holistic TT frameworks are required in order to tackle interdependencies between technologies.

4.5.2 Sector-Specific Applications and Spillovers

AI-based TT has been reported in various industries like energy sustainability (Gao et al., 2025), agri-food systems (Di Vaio et al., 2020), and microbial fuel cell technologies (Ojha et al., 2025). Cetindamar et al. (2020) show the potential of AI knowledge spillovers in entrepreneurial ecosystem to drive regional innovation with localized networks and institutional support.

4.6.1 Ethical, social, and Governance Dimensions

The responsibility of responsible transfer and ethical AI lies in the fourth section. The aspects of AI commercialization are becoming more ethically-oriented. In their research, Rodgers and Nguyen (2022) demonstrate that ethical AI algorithms increase the value creation and trust in advertising settings to imply the same in TT processes. Accountable transfer of AI must have transparency, fairness and responsibility at all stages of the innovation process.

4.6.2 Social-Technical and Labor Implications

The use of AI brings the issue of labor displacement, inequality, and changing the workplace. Agrawal et al. (2019) and Raisch and Krakowski (2021) talk about the automation-augmentation paradox according to which AI replaces and enriches the human work at the same time. These processes affect TT performance by determining the acceptance of the organization and policy reactions. Karunakaran et al. (2025) also describe how AI can contribute to workplace disparities when there is no governance, which should demonstrate the social accountability in TT decisions.

4.7 AI Implementation in Business Functions and Markets

4.7.1 AI in Customer Engagement and Marketing

There is a large body of literature that describes AI as a transformative force in marketing, such as customer relationship management, decision systems, and conversational commerce (Davenport et al., 2020; Ledro et al., 2022; Balakrishnan and Dwivedi, 2024). The B2B marketing AI adoption frameworks focus on the readiness of the organization, data quality, and alignment (Chen et al., 2022). These papers are applicable to TT since they demonstrate how AI technologies that began in research contexts are downstream commercialized.

4.7.2 Transfer of AI Ecosystems and Platform Based

Malthouse and Copulsky (2023) view AI ecosystems as networks of firms, platforms, and data providers, which are interconnected. This redefines TT because it allows platform-mediated diffusion instead of bilateral licensing agreements. Although the scholarship has expanded, there are still a number of gaps. To start with, empirical investigation involving direct exploration of AI-facilitated TT mechanisms is still scarce, and most studies are conducted on adoption but not transfer processes (Etzkorn et al., 2025). Second, commercialization frameworks are frequently considered independently of ethical and governance issues. Third, there is a lack of research on TT in low-income and emerging economies, where there are structural limitations to the diffusion of AI (Khan et al., 2024).

5.0 DISCUSSION

The chapter begins with the argument that AI puts stress on classical, linear models of technology transfer previously created to focus on discrete, tangible inventions, including pharmaceuticals and mechanical devices (Kingsley et al., 1996; National Academies of Sciences, Engineering, and Medicine, 2021). Conventional channels of invention disclosure, IP protection, licensing, and diffusion are incapable of fully defining data-driven, constantly learning AI systems whose performance is post-deployment and relies on availability of data, computational resources, and expertise talent. Such reframing makes AI a general-purpose technology and a moving target where technology transfer theories need to incorporate the notions of data governance, algorithmic transparency, and long-term responsibility of the consequences (Alkhazaleh et al., 2022).

Conversely, AI tools are integrated into technology transfer offices (TTOs) and innovation intermediaries, which facilitate patent analytics, prior-art search, matchmaking of partners, deal-flow and valuation modeling, and information asymmetries (Fangyu et al., 2024). This duality implies that AI does not just follow the existing channels but it also remodels them as it diffuses (Mohammed et al., 2022).

The chapter is based on the Technology-Organization-Environment (TOE) framework and the Dynamic Capabilities View, creating a conceptual model of AI commercialization, where the context, capabilities, and governance play a central role (Davenport et al., 2020). Feasibility, scalability, and interoperability in the technological context are characterized by the use of AI tools, including expert systems and digital twins, whereas absorptive capacity, governance mechanisms, and cybersecurity preparedness are the factors that define the level of success of firms in integrating AI into the current information systems in the organizational context (Lazaroiu et al., 2024; Balakrishnan and Dwivedi, 2024).

The chapter identifies a few research gaps in the intersection of AI and technology transfer that occurrence drives its contribution (Etzkorn et al., 2025). Another aspect of technology transfer theory, limited integration of technology transfer theory with AI governance arguments on transparency, data ownership, and ethical accountability is also largely treated independently of commercialization dynamics (Ledro et al., 2022).

To demonstrate the scope of AI-related transfer, the chapter presents the results of numerous areas, such as agri-food, finance, energy, manufacturing, and the foreignization of SMEs (Aiudi et al., 2025; Gao et al., 2025). These literature reviews indicate that AI has the potential to increase productivity, risk, and quality of decisions and that its implementation is not uniform because of financial, technical, and cultural factors, especially among SMEs and players in low-income nations (Khan et al., 2024). The complexity of transfer in Industry 4.0 and digital ecosystems increases further because AI is interconnected with cyber-physical systems, digital twins, and IoT, where ecosystem-level coordination, digital readiness, and regional innovation systems are the key to successful AI knowledge spillovers and commercialization (Cetindamar et al., 2020).

Lastly, the chapter makes its practical relevance as an academician, TTO practitioner, industry practitioner, SME, and policymaker clear, and formulates four principal goals: mapping AI-specific pathways of transfer, defining key actors and resources, expanding classical models with AI-specific enablers, and providing concrete suggestions (Arya et al., 2025). It highlights the importance of regulatory systems, funding tools, and tracks of experimentation (Bhimavarapu, 2025). In total, the chapter progresses to a unified viewpoint that ties conceptual backgrounds, empirical patterns, and ethical issues to clarify how algorithms become AI-ready market solutions and the effectiveness and quality of the technology transfer processes can be reinforced by AI itself (Tyukin et al., 2018).

Figure 4 describes the course of technology in global context with the particular emphasis on the commercialization of AI systems. The fundamental component of this flow is the technology transfer of the research institutions to the companies, which incorporates such important processes as licensing, patents, and spin-offs that are indispensable in introducing the innovations to the market.

Figure 4. Operating flow of international technology transfer.

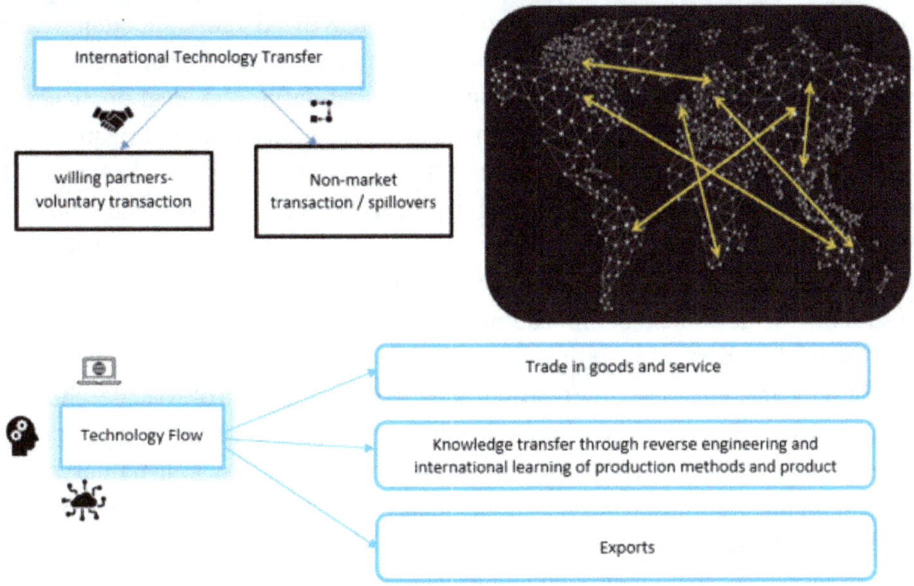

Source: Author's Contribution

The chapter begins with the argument that AI puts stress on classical, linear models of technology transfer previously created to focus on discrete, tangible inventions, including pharmaceuticals and mechanical devices (Kingsley et al., 1996; National Academies of Sciences, Engineering, and Medicine, 2021). Conventional channels of invention disclosure, IP protection, licensing, and diffusion are incapable of fully defining data-driven, constantly learning AI systems whose performance is post-deployment and relies on availability of data, computational resources, and expertise talent. Such reframing makes AI a general-purpose technology and a moving target where technology transfer theories need to incorporate the notions of data governance, algorithmic transparency, and long-term responsibility of the consequences (Alkhazaleh et al., 2022). Conversely, AI tools are integrated into technology transfer offices (TTOs) and innovation intermediaries, which facilitate patent analytics, prior-art search, matchmaking of partners, deal-flow and valuation modeling, and information asymmetries (Fangyu et al., 2024). This duality implies that AI does not just follow the existing channels but it also remodels them as it diffuses (Mohammed et al., 2022).

The chapter is based on the Technology-Organization-Environment (TOE) framework and the Dynamic Capabilities View, creating a conceptual model of AI commercialization, where the context, capabilities, and governance play a central role (Davenport et al., 2020). Feasibility, scalability, and interoperability in the technological context are characterized by the use of AI tools, including expert systems and digital twins, whereas absorptive capacity, governance mechanisms, and cybersecurity preparedness are the factors that define the level of success of firms in integrating AI into the current information systems in the organizational context (Lazaroiu et al., 2024). The incentives and constraints are determined by the environmental context, which includes regulation, market demand, and competitive pressure, and dynamic capabilities (sensing, seizing, and transforming) mediate the way organizations recognize AI opportunities, mobilize resources, and restructure in the context of embedding AI in products and processes (Balakrishnan and Dwivedi, 2024).

The chapter identifies a few research gaps in the intersection of AI and technology transfer that occurrence drives its contribution (Etzkorn et al., 2025). Another aspect of technology transfer theory, limited integration of technology transfer theory with AI governance arguments on transparency, data ownership, and ethical accountability is also largely treated independently of commercialization dynamics (Ledro et al., 2022). Moreover, there is limited empirical evidence regarding AI as a tool within TTOs, surveys (e.g., CESAER) show that there is early-stage experimentation, capability gaps, and worries on data protection and IP leakage.

To demonstrate the scope of AI-related transfer, the chapter presents the results of numerous areas, such as agri-food, finance, energy, manufacturing, and the foreignization of SMEs (Aiudi et al., 2025; Gao et al., 2025). These literature reviews indicate that AI has the potential to increase productivity, risk, and quality of decisions and that its implementation is not uniform because of financial, technical, and cultural factors, especially among SMEs and players in low-income nations (Khan et al., 2024). The complexity of transfer in Industry 4.0 and digital ecosystems increases further because AI is interconnected with cyber-physical systems, digital twins, and IoT, where ecosystem-level coordination, digital readiness, and regional innovation systems are the key to successful AI knowledge spillovers and commercialization (Cetindamar et al., 2020).

The three dimensions of ethics, social, and governance constitute an important layer within the discussion of the transfer pathways of AI in the chapter (Rodgers and Nguyen, 2022). Finally, the chapter makes its practical relevance as an academician, TTO practitioner, industry practitioner, SME, and policymaker clear, and formulates four principal goals: mapping AI-specific pathways of transfer, defining key actors and resources, expanding classical models with AI-specific enablers, and providing concrete suggestions (Arya et al., 2025). To universities and TTOs, it is a matter of investing in AI literacy, shared infrastructures, and data governance systems; to firms and startups, it is a matter of development of dynamic capabilities and governance systems to bring AI responsible and ethical and resiliency in lab-to-market routes; and to policymakers, it highlights the importance of regulatory systems, funding tools, and tracks of experimentation (Bhimavarapu, 2025). In total, the chapter progresses to a unified viewpoint that ties conceptual backgrounds, empirical patterns, and ethical issues to clarify how algorithms become AI-ready market solutions and the effectiveness and quality of the technology transfer processes can be reinforced by AI itself (Tyukin et al., 2018).

Figure 4 describes the course of technology in global context with the particular emphasis on the commercialization of AI systems. The fundamental component of this flow is the technology transfer of the research institutions to the companies, which incorporates such important processes as licensing, patents, and spin-offs that are indispensable in introducing the innovations to the market. This flow of technology can guarantee that the AI technologies can be appropriately commercialized and distributed across industries once they are created so that the organizations could take advantage of the value such innovations bring.

Table 2. Comparative Stages in Pathway

Trend / issue	Stage(s) in pathway	TOE-DCV element	Typical context / example
Algorithmic collusion & market power	Scaling, postâ€‘deployment	Environment, sensing capability	AI trading, platform deals
Data governance & privacy	Discovery, validation	Technology/organization, seizing	Health, agriâ€‘food
Limited TTO AI capabilities	IP, validation, matchmaking	Organization, learning	European TTO survey
Emergingâ€‘market transfer barriers	All stages	Environment, reconfiguring	SMEs in Global South

6.2 Limitations and Future Directions

This table 3 systematically addresses the chapter's identified research gaps while acknowledging methodological limitations of current evidence (predominantly conceptual/theoretical, limited longitudinal data, Western-centric focus) and proposes concrete, feasible future research directions with clear methodological approaches for advancing AI technology transfer.

Table 3. A list of Studies on Studies Gaps of Limitations and Future Directions

Name of Gaps	Limitations	Future Directions
Empirical scarcity on AI-enabled TTO mechanisms	Current research focuses primarily on AI adoption within firms rather than transfer processes themselves (Etzkorn et al., 2025). Limited quantitative data on TTO AI tool effectiveness.	Longitudinal studies tracking AI platform implementation in TTOs measuring time-to-market reduction, deal closure rates, and ROI from automated matching systems.
Limited integration of technology transfer theory with AI governance	Ethical, transparency, and accountability issues treated separately from commercialization frameworks, creating fragmented perspectives.	Develop integrated theoretical models combining TT lifecycle stages with responsible AI principles, testing through mixed-methods studies across sectors.
Underexplored transfer dynamics in emerging economies	Most evidence from developed contexts; structural barriers in low-income countries remain understudied (Khan et al., 2024).	Comparative case studies examining AI transfer success factors across Global North-South contexts, focusing on infrastructure, talent, and policy constraints.
Lack of long-term outcome data	Studies capture initial commercialization but not sustained performance, model evolution, or lifecycle governance.	Multi-year cohort studies tracking AI spin-offs and licensed technologies through scaling, adaptation phases, measuring survival rates and value creation.
Insufficient sectoral deep dives	General frameworks dominate; healthcare, finance, agriculture-specific transfer dynamics under-researched (Bhuiyan et al., 2026).	Sector-specific research programs examining unique validation, regulatory, and scaling requirements for AI applications in high-stakes domains.
Limited evidence on dual-role AI platforms	AI as transfer tool (matching, analytics) documented conceptually but lacking operational impact data.	Field experiments testing AI-enabled TTO platforms against traditional processes, measuring efficiency gains, matching quality, and commercialization acceleration.
Gap in dynamic capabilities measurement	TOE-DCV framework proposed but lacks validated scales for AI-specific sensing, seizing, transforming capabilities.	Instrument development and validation studies creating psychometrics for AI transfer dynamic capabilities, tested across organizational types and sectors.
Underdeveloped data governance frameworks	Data treated as byproduct rather than core IP asset; governance models for collaborative AI development lacking.	Action research developing and testing data governance protocols for university-industry AI consortia, evaluating impact on trust and transfer success.
Absence of transfer success taxonomies	No standardized metrics or classification systems for measuring AI commercialization outcomes beyond patents/revenue.	Delphi studies with transfer practitioners developing comprehensive AI transfer success KPIs encompassing technical, economic, and societal dimensions.

continued on following page

Table 3. Continued

Name of Gaps	Limitations	Future Directions
Limited comparative mechanism analysis	Little evidence comparing licensing vs spin-offs vs partnerships for AI technologies across contexts.	Matched-pair analyses comparing transfer mechanisms effectiveness for similar AI technologies, controlling for organizational and market factors.
Neglected platform economics in transfer	AI marketplaces and ecosystem effects on transaction costs, network formation understudied.	Economic modeling and empirical studies of AI transfer platforms analyzing pricing, matching efficiency, and competition dynamics.
Ethical risk amplification in transfer chains	Potential for bias propagation, collusion risks through successive AI transfers underexamined.	Simulation studies modeling ethical risk transmission through multi-stage transfer processes, developing mitigation protocols.
Policy impact evaluation missing	Regulatory sandboxes, funding programs proposed but lacking rigorous outcome evaluation.	Quasi-experimental designs evaluating policy interventions (sandboxes, grants) on AI commercialization rates and quality.
Talent pipeline assessment gap	University-industry skill alignment for AI transfer specialists unmeasured.	Labor market analysis identifying transfer-specific competency gaps, developing targeted training programs with outcome tracking.
Cybersecurity integration deficiency	Data protection, model security considerations absent from most transfer frameworks.	Risk assessment frameworks incorporating cybersecurity requirements throughout the AI transfer lifecycle, tested in high-stakes sectors.

7.0 CONCLUSION AND IMPLICATIONS

algorithms move out of research laboratories to commercial markets in organized phases of discovery, IP protection, validation, scaling and governance (Allal-Chérif et al., 2021; Tschang and Almirall, 2021; Ledro et al., 2022). Based on a combination of a TOE-DCV framework, it demonstrates the duality of AI as a transfer object and an enabling tool, which disrupts the linear paradigm of models of inactive technologies. The major conclusions include lack of TTO capabilities, data governance necessities, dynamic capabilities necessities, and regulatory innovation necessities to achieve successful commercialization (Samtani et al., 2021; Karunakaran et al., 2025).Such theoretical novelty is in the spread of classical theory of technology transfer with AI-specific enablers (data assets, compute infrastructure, responsible governance) to formulate a complex model that has been experimented in multiple sectors (Xia et al., 2025). Some practical contributions involve TOE readiness assessments, AI literacy roadmaps, competency hubs, and dual-role platforms that paradigm transfer processes.

Regulatory sandboxes, focused investment, and ecosystem-building are also among the policy recommendations to hasten ethical AI commercialization (Mohammed et al., 2022; Fangyu et al., 2024). The framework deals with the fragmentation between transfer theory and AI governance, providing the stakeholders in the domain of universities, TTOs, industry, and policymakers with practical action in a way that maximizes the use of the research by the populace. Longitudinal outcome and emerging economy setting studies, as well as the testing of proposed mechanisms on empirical platforms, should be the focus of future research. These ways will help to achieve the potential of the economy and society that laboratory algorithms can reach international markets at a responsible and efficient rate by eliminating institutional gaps and capitalizing on the transformative power of AI (Faisal-E-Alam et al., 2025).

7.1 Implications

7.1.1 Theoretical implications

This chapter advances technology transfer theory by conceptualising AI commercialization not as a linear handover but as a dynamic, capability-driven pathway from algorithms to market-ready systems. By embedding AI-specific enablers such as data governance, computational infrastructure, and responsible AI governance into the Technology–Organization–Environment and Dynamic Capabilities frameworks, we extend classical models that were developed for stable, tangible technologies. The review also bridges previously separate literatures on technology transfer and AI governance, showing how issues of explainability, bias, and regulatory compliance must be analysed together with IP strategy, value appropriation, and long-term responsibility for evolving AI systems.

Technology transfer offices (TTOs) and innovation intermediaries should explicitly factor human–AI interaction into licensing negotiations and collaborative project design, rather than focusing solely on IP terms and technical performance. This includes embedding requirements for user training, intuitive and context-appropriate interface design, meaningful explainability, and clear protocols for monitoring real-world use (e.g., logging errors, overrides, and near-misses). Such provisions would help ensure that transferred AI systems are not only legally and technically sound but also usable, trustworthy, and safe for the professionals who rely on them in practice.

7.1.2 Practical implications

For universities and TTOs, the chapter highlights the need to treat AI as both a transfer object and an enabling infrastructure, investing in AI literacy, secure data infrastructures, and staff capabilities to use AI tools in patent analytics, partner matchmaking, and valuation. For SMEs and industry partners, our pathways underscore that successful AI commercialization depends not only on technical performance but also on alignment between partners, clear data-sharing arrangements, and governance mechanisms that manage ongoing model updates and risks. For policy makers, the framework points to concrete levers—such as regulatory sandboxes, targeted funding instruments, and harmonised IP guidance—that can support ethical and effective AI transfer while safeguarding competition, trust, and societal objectives.

Table 4. Mapping issues to SDGs and framework elements

Issue / risk	SDG link	TOE context	DCV emphasis
Algorithmic collusion & market power	8, 10, 16	Environment (regulation)	Sensing, monitoring
Bias & exclusion in AI transfer	10, 16	Technology, organization	Seizing, governance
Emerging-economy infrastructure gaps	9, 10	Technology, environment	Reconfiguring
Data governance & sovereignty	9, 16	Environment	Sensing, seizing

7.2 Future Research Directions

Responsible AI transfer should also extend beyond pre-deployment due diligence to include robust post-deployment monitoring and user support mechanisms. Agreements between universities, TTOs, and commercial partners can specify shared responsibilities for tracking performance drift, handling user-reported issues, and updating models or interfaces in response to emerging risks. Building structured feedback loops—through training, helpdesks, and governance committees—would allow institutions to detect unintended consequences early and to adapt both the AI systems and the transfer arrangements over time. Future empirical research should compare how different transfer models—such as licensing to large platforms, creating university spin-offs, or forming public–private partnerships—shape the quality of human–AI interaction and downstream outcomes like trust, error rates, and productivity.

8.0 NOVELTY OF THE CHAPTER

Table 5. A list of Novelty of the Chapter

Section	Description
Bridges AI Commercialization with Sustainable Development Goals (SDGs)	This chapter introduces AI technology transfer as a solution to attainment of UN SDGs, in particular, scaled AI-based renewable energy (SDG 7), AI-based diagnostics in healthcare (SDG 3), AI-based agricultural optimization (SDG 2), and AI-based climate modeling (SDG 13). It also introduces fair access to emerging economies, which is SDG 9 (innovation infrastructure) and SDG 17 (partnerships).
Addresses Geopolitical Dimensions of AI Transfer	TOE-DCV framework includes such aspects of geopolitical factors as the digital sovereignty, the inequality of technological access, and inconsistency in regulatory aspects. It looks at how AI core transfer relationships change between Global North and South, suggesting policy sandboxes and competency hubs to prevent monopolies on technology, and enabling technologies-dependent countries to become involved in innovation systems.
Operationalizes Sustainable Innovation through Dual-Role AI	In this section, AI is introduced as a sustainable technology object (green AI applications) and facilitator of transfer processes (AI-powered TTO platforms). The AI operationalization generates positive feedback loops of successful technology transfer due to the acceleration in green technology implementation, and effective commercialization financing new sustainable R&D. TTO AI literacy and data governance models would generate responsible scaling.
Provides Equitable Development Framework for Emerging Markets	The chapter extrapolates Western-based models of technology transfer to contexts with resource constraints and finds obstacles facing SMEs, and suggests regional centres that integrate university research with regional industry demands. It focuses on the development of dynamic capabilities, which focuses the commercialization of AI on a broader range of institutions than elite ones.
Integrates Ethical AI Governance with Economic Development	Development objectives are combined with the ethical principles of AI governance, including transparency and mitigating bias. This develops governing models that weigh the pace of innovation and the management of risks in the society that is vital to a stable and sustainable dispersion of AI technologies in the global contexts.
Empirical TTO Roadmap for Innovation Infrastructure	On this section, the CESAER report findings are collected along with the rest of the literature, and actionable recommendations on how the TTOs could be transformed (e.g., AI platforms and IP models). These measures are directly linked to SDG 9 (capacity building towards innovation) and this is particularly true in the various geopolitical settings.

REFERENCES

Agrawal, A., Gans, J. S., & Goldfarb, A. (2019). Artificial intelligence: The ambiguous labor market impact of automating prediction. *The Journal of Economic Perspectives*, *33*(2), 31–50. DOI: 10.1257/jep.33.2.31

Alkhazaleh, R., Mykoniatis, K., & Alahmer, A. (2022). The success of technology transfer in the industry 4.0 era: A systematic literature review. *Journal of Open Innovation*, *8*(4), 202. DOI: 10.3390/joitmc8040202

Allal-Chérif, O., Simón-Moya, V., & Ballester, A. C. C. (2021). Intelligent purchasing: How artificial intelligence can redefine the purchasing function. *Journal of Business Research*, *124*, 69–76. DOI: 10.1016/j.jbusres.2020.11.050

ALLAN, J., Ferreri, A., Grande, S., Giannantonio, R., & Matteucci, F. (2019). *Technology transfer in nanotechnology*. DOI: 10.2760/183529

Anayat, S., & Rasool, G. (2024). Artificial intelligence marketing (AIM): Connecting-the-dots using bibliometrics. *Journal of Marketing Theory and Practice*, *32*(1), 114–135. DOI: 10.1080/10696679.2022.2103435

Arya, V., Saraf, A., Chichkanov, N., et al. (2025). AI-enhanced competency transfer hubs: A conceptual framework for university-industry engagement and knowledge sharing. The Journal of Technology Transfer, 51, 682–712. https://doi.org/10.1007/s10961-025-10233-7, DOI: 10.1007/s10961-025-10233-7

Balakrishnan, J., & Dwivedi, Y. K. (2024). Conversational commerce: Entering the next stage of AI-powered digital assistants. *Annals of Operations Research*, *333*(2), 653–687. DOI: 10.1007/s10479-021-04049-5

Bednar, P. M., & Welch, C. (2020). Socio-technical perspectives on smart working: Creating meaningful and sustainable systems. *Information Systems Frontiers*, *22*(2), 281–298. DOI: 10.1007/s10796-019-09921-1

Bhimavarapu, U. (2025). AI in Technology Transfer Developing Sustainable Models Through University-Industry Collaboration. In *Bridging Technology and Development for Sustainable Innovation and Geopolitical Dynamics* (pp. 67–86). IGI Global Scientific Publishing., DOI: 10.4018/979-8-3693-9072-6.ch004

Bhuiyan, M. R. I., Akter, M. S., Amin, A., & Hossain, R. (2025a). The mediating effect of innovation capabilities, information quality and supply chain resilience in the relationship between big data analytics capability (BDAC) and healthcare performance. *SAGE Open*, *15*(3), 21582440251362262. DOI: 10.1177/21582440251362262

Bhuiyan, M. R. I., Husain, T., Islam, S., & Amin, A. (2025b). Exploring the prospective influence of artificial intelligence on the health sector in Bangladesh: A study on awareness, perception and adoption. *Health Education, 125*(3), 279–297. DOI: 10.1108/HE-10-2024-0125

Bhuiyan, M. R. I., Uddin, S., Sultana, T., Al-Amin, , & Islam, M. M. (2026). Investigating ChatGPT Methods in the Higher Education Form a Student Engagement Perspective: Based on a Descriptive-Cross-Sectional Study. *SAGE Open, 16*(1), 21582440251413008. DOI: 10.1177/21582440251413008

Bock, D. E., Wolter, J. S., & Ferrell, O. C. (2020). Artificial intelligence: Disrupting what we know about services. *Journal of Services Marketing, 34*(3), 317–334. DOI: 10.1108/JSM-01-2019-0047

Cetindamar, D., Lammers, T., & Zhang, Y. (2020). Exploring the knowledge spillovers of a technology in an entrepreneurial ecosystem—The case of artificial intelligence in Sydney. *Thunderbird International Business Review, 62*(5), 457–474. DOI: 10.1002/tie.22158

Chen, L., Jiang, M., Jia, F., & Liu, G. (2022). Artificial intelligence adoption in business-to-business marketing: Toward a conceptual framework. *Journal of Business and Industrial Marketing, 37*(5), 1025–1044. DOI: 10.1108/JBIM-09-2020-0448

Chintalapati, S., & Pandey, S. K. (2022). Artificial intelligence in marketing: A systematic literature review. *International Journal of Market Research, 64*(1), 38–68. DOI: 10.1177/14707853211018428

Davenport, T., Guha, A., Grewal, D., & Bressgott, T. (2020). How artificial intelligence will change the future of marketing. *Journal of the Academy of Marketing Science, 48*(1), 24–42. DOI: 10.1007/s11747-019-00696-0

De Bruyn, A., Viswanathan, V., Beh, Y. S., Brock, J. K. U., & Von Wangenheim, F. (2020). Artificial intelligence and marketing: Pitfalls and opportunities. *Journal of Interactive Marketing, 51*(1), 91–105. DOI: 10.1016/j.intmar.2020.04.007

Dean, S. O. (1988). Commercial objectives, technology transfer, and systems analysis for fusion power development. *Journal of Fusion Energy, 7*(1), 25–47. DOI: 10.1007/BF01108257

Di Guardo, A., Trovato, F., Cantisani, C., Dattola, A., Nisticò, S. P., Pellacani, G., & Paganelli, A. (2025). Artificial Intelligence in Cosmetic Formulation: Predictive Modeling for Safety, Tolerability, and Regulatory Perspectives. *Cosmetics, 12*(4), 157. DOI: 10.3390/cosmetics12040157

Di Vaio, A., Boccia, F., Landriani, L., & Palladino, R. (2020). Artificial intelligence in the agri-food system: Rethinking sustainable business models in the COVID-19 scenario. *Sustainability (Basel), 12*(12), 4851. DOI: 10.3390/su12124851

El Arab, R. A., Al Moosa, O. A., & Sagbakken, M. (2025). Economic, ethical, and regulatory dimensions of artificial intelligence in healthcare: An integrative review. *Frontiers in Public Health, 13*, 1617138. DOI: 10.3389/fpubh.2025.1617138 PMID: 40951387

Eriksson, T., Bigi, A., & Bonera, M. (2020). Think with me, or think for me? On the future role of artificial intelligence in marketing strategy formulation. *The TQM Journal, 32*(4), 795–814. DOI: 10.1108/TQM-12-2019-0303

Etzkorn, M., Römer, Y., Tavakoligargari, M., Lumiere, M. M., Lamdaghri, N., & von Korflesch, H. (2025). The Interface Between Technology Transfer and Artificial Intelligence: A Systematic Literature Review. In *International Scientific-Practical Conference* (pp. 476-489). Springer, Cham. https://doi.org/DOI: 10.1007/978-3-031-88052-0_38

Faisal-E-Alam, M., Bhuiyan, M. R. I., Mimi, A., & Miah, M. T. (2025). The role of the three zero framework in advancing global sustainable development through bibliometric and text mining analysis. *Discover Sustainability, 6*(1), 1128.[REMOVED HYPERLINK FIELD]DOI: 10.1007/s43621-025-01919-x

Fangyu, G., Di, C., Shuai, Y., Zhenghu, H., Qiong, W., & Xu, Z. (2024, October). Research on Enhancing Technology Transfer Efficiency through Artificial Intelligence and Recommendation Algorithms. In *2024 3rd International Conference on Data Analytics, Computing and Artificial Intelligence (ICDACAI)* (pp. 770-773). IEEE. https://doi.org/DOI: 10.1109/ICDACAI65086.2024.00145

Gao, Z., Hua, M., Jia, Z., Li, L., & Hao, Y. (2025). Intelligent Pathway: Artificial Intelligence and the Path to Energy Sustainability. *Growth and Change, 56*(4), e70050. DOI: 10.1111/grow.70050

Grundner, L., & Neuhofer, B. (2021). The bright and dark sides of artificial intelligence: A futures perspective on tourist destination experiences. *Journal of Destination Marketing & Management, 19*, 100511. DOI: 10.1016/j.jdmm.2020.100511

Güner Gültekin, D., Pinarbasi, F., Yazici, M., & Adiguzel, Z. (2025). Commercialisation of artificial intelligence: A research on entrepreneurial companies with challenges and opportunities. *Business Process Management Journal, 31*(2), 605–630. DOI: 10.1108/BPMJ-10-2023-0836

Huang, M. H., & Rust, R. T. (2021). A strategic framework for artificial intelligence in marketing. *Journal of the Academy of Marketing Science*, *49*(1), 30–50. DOI: 10.1007/s11747-020-00749-9

Hurmuzlu, O. (2024). Ethical implications of the commercialization of artificial intelligence (AI). In *Innovative and Intelligent Digital Technologies; Towards an Increased Efficiency* (Vol. 1, pp. 321–333). Springer Nature Switzerland. DOI: 10.1007/978-3-031-70399-7_23

Islam, M. M., Bhuiyan, M. R. I., Islam, S. H., Tabassum, M. N., & Billah, M. (2026). Unlocking the Mediating and Moderating Role of Information Security in Information Systems: A Combined TAM, ISM, and HBM Model. *Human Behavior and Emerging Technologies*, *2026*(1), 5593002. DOI: 10.1155/hbe2/5593002

Jiang, Y., Li, X., Luo, H., Yin, S., & Kaynak, O. (2022). Quo vadis artificial intelligence? *Discover Artificial Intelligence*, *2*(1), 4. DOI: 10.1007/s44163-022-00022-8

Jiménez-Luna, J., Grisoni, F., Weskamp, N., & Schneider, G. (2021). Artificial intelligence in drug discovery: Recent advances and future perspectives. *Expert Opinion on Drug Discovery*, *16*(9), 949–959. DOI: 10.1080/17460441.2021.1909567 PMID: 33779453

Karunakaran, A., Lebovitz, S., Narayanan, D., & Rahman, H. A. (2025). Artificial Intelligence at Work: An Integrative Perspective on the Impact of AI on Workplace Inequality. *Academy of Management Annals*, (ja), annals-2023. https://doi.org/DOI: 10.5465/annals.2023.0230

Khan, M. S., Umer, H., & Faruqe, F. (2024). Artificial intelligence for low income countries. *Humanities & Social Sciences Communications*, *11*(1), 1–13. DOI: 10.1057/s41599-024-03947-w

Khatun, M., Bhuiyan, M. R. I., Amin, M. A., Hossen, M. D., & Mia, M. A. H. (2026). Evaluating E-Commerce Satisfaction: The Impact of Trust, Information Quality, Usability, and Perceived-to-Actual Performance. *SAGE Open*, *16*(1), 21582440261423039. DOI: 10.1177/21582440261423039

Khatun, M., Hossain, R., Bhuiyan, M. R., Tabassum, M. N., & Riaj, M. A. (2025). Green Entrepreneurship and Digital Transformation for Sustainable Development: A Systematic Review. In Mouloudj, K., & Bouarar, A. (Eds.), *Digitizing Green Entrepreneurship* (pp. 153–180). IGI Global Scientific Publishing., DOI: 10.4018/979-8-3693-7442-9.ch006

Kingsley, G., Bozeman, B., & Coker, K. (1996). Technology transfer and absorption: An 'R & D value-mapping' approach to evaluation. *Research Policy*, *25*(6), 967–995. DOI: 10.1016/0048-7333(96)00890-6

Kulshrestha, C., & Kapoor, A. (2025). Conversational AI and Consumer Decision Pathways: A Comparative Analysis of Impulsive versus Deliberate Buying in Voice Commerce. *Advances in Consumer Research. Association for Consumer Research (U. S.)*, *2*(5).

Lazaroiu, G., Gedeon, T., Rogalska, E., Valaskova, K., Nagy, M., Musa, H., Zvarikova, K., Poliak, M., Horak, J., Cre oiu, R. I., Krulicky, T., Ionescu, L., Popa, C., Hurloiu, L. R., Nistor, F., Avram, L. G., & Braga, V. (2024). Digital twin-based cyber-physical manufacturing systems, extended reality metaverse enterprise and production management algorithms, and Internet of Things financial and labor market technologies in generative artificial intelligence economics. *Oeconomia Copernicana*, *15*(3), 837–870. DOI: 10.24136/oc.3183

Ledro, C., Nosella, A., & Vinelli, A. (2022). Artificial intelligence in customer relationship management: Literature review and future research directions. *Journal of Business and Industrial Marketing*, *37*(13), 48–63. DOI: 10.1108/JBIM-07-2021-0332

Lee, J. C., & Chen, X. (2022). Exploring users' adoption intentions in the evolution of artificial intelligence mobile banking applications: The intelligent and anthropomorphic perspectives. *International Journal of Bank Marketing*, *40*(4), 631–658. DOI: 10.1108/IJBM-08-2021-0394

Ma, X., & Wang, J. (2024). Simulation analysis of artificial intelligence technology diffusion under market competition and policy incentives based on complex network evolutionary game models. *Systems*, *12*(7), 242. DOI: 10.3390/systems12070242

Mahboub, R., & Ghanem, M. G. (2024). The mediating role of knowledge management practices and balanced scorecard in the association between artificial intelligence and organization performance: Evidence from MENA region commercial banks. *Cogent Business & Management*, *11*(1), 2404484. DOI: 10.1080/23311975.2024.2404484

Malthouse, E., & Copulsky, J. (2023). Artificial intelligence ecosystems for marketing communications. *International Journal of Advertising*, *42*(1), 128–140. DOI: 10.1080/02650487.2022.2122249

Menzies, J., Sabert, B., Hassan, R., & Mensah, P. K. (2024). Artificial intelligence for international business: Its use, challenges, and suggestions for future research and practice. *Thunderbird International Business Review*, *66*(2), 185–200. DOI: 10.1002/tie.22370

Mohammed, T., Naas, S. A., Sigg, S., & Di Francesco, M. (2022). Knowledge sharing in ai services: A market-based approach. *IEEE Internet of Things Journal, 10*(2), 1320–1331. DOI: 10.1109/JIOT.2022.3206585

Moharrak, M., Nguyen, N. P., & Mogaji, E. (2024). Business environment and adoption of AI: Navigation for internationalization by new ventures in emerging markets. *Thunderbird International Business Review, 66*(4), 355–372. DOI: 10.1002/tie.22384

National Academies of Sciences, Engineering, and Medicine. (2021). Technology Transfer Pathways for Digital Products. In *Advancing Commercialization of Digital Products from Federal Laboratories.* National Academies Press (US).https://doi.org/DOI: 10.17226/26006

Ojha, R., Dash, J., Satpathy, S. S., Ojha, P. C., & Pradhan, D. (2025). A brief review on factors affecting the performance of microbial fuel cell and integration of artificial intelligence. *Discover Sustainability, 6*(1), 702. DOI: 10.1007/s43621-025-01619-6

Oliveira, P., Carvalho, J. M., & Faria, S. (2025). AI integration in organisational workflows: A case study on job reconfiguration, efficiency, and workforce adaptation. *Information (Basel), 16*(9), 764. DOI: 10.3390/info16090764

Paramesha, M., Rane, N., & Rane, J. (2024). Artificial intelligence, machine learning, deep learning, and blockchain in financial and banking services: A comprehensive review. DOI: 10.2139/ssrn.4855893

Paschen, J., Kietzmann, J., & Kietzmann, T. C. (2019). Artificial intelligence (AI) and its implications for market knowledge in B2B marketing. *Journal of Business and Industrial Marketing, 34*(7), 1410–1419. DOI: 10.1108/JBIM-10-2018-0295

Raisch, S., & Krakowski, S. (2021). Artificial intelligence and management: The automation–augmentation paradox. *Academy of Management Review, 46*(1), 192–210. DOI: 10.5465/amr.2018.0072

Rajagopal, N. K., Qureshi, N. I., Durga, S., Ramirez Asis, E. H., Huerta Soto, R. M., Gupta, S. K., & Deepak, S. (2022). Future of business culture: An artificial intelligence-driven digital framework for organization decision-making process. *Complexity, 2022*(1), 7796507. DOI: 10.1155/2022/7796507

Raji, I. A., Ismail, A. I., & Salam, M. A. (2026). High-performance work systems, organizational identification, trust in leader, perceived organizational support and healthcare professionals' turnover intention. Journal of Health Organization and Management, 40(4), 785-810. https://doi.org/10.1108/JHOM-06-2025-0366, PMID: 41171870

Rayun, S. N., Salam, M. A., Islam, W., Firmansyah, E. A., & Kalinaki, K. (2025). Unraveling the dynamics of mobile wallets in promoting cashless tourism in Bangladesh: Implementation of UTAUT2 model. *Journal of Hospitality and Tourism Technology*, *16*(5), 1046–1065. DOI: 10.1108/JHTT-04-2024-0222

Rayun, S. N., Salam, M. A., Islam, W., & Leong, V. S. (2026). Green FinTech Innovations: Empowering Inclusive Development and Advancing Towards the Sustainable Economy. In *Promoting Inclusivity and Accessibility With FinTech* (pp. 245-278). IGI Global Scientific Publishing.

Renz, A., & Hilbig, R. (2020). Prerequisites for artificial intelligence in further education: Identification of drivers, barriers, and business models of educational technology companies. *International Journal of Educational Technology in Higher Education*, *17*(1), 14. DOI: 10.1186/s41239-020-00193-3

Riaj, M. A., Tabassum, M. N., Hossain, R., Bhuiyan, M. R., & Khatun, M. (2025). Digitalization Transformation in Entrepreneurship and Enterprise Green Innovation. In Mouloudj, K., & Bouarar, A. (Eds.), *Digitizing Green Entrepreneurship* (pp. 181–204). IGI Global Scientific Publishing., DOI: 10.4018/979-8-3693-7442-9.ch007

Rodgers, W., & Nguyen, T. (2022). Advertising benefits from ethical artificial intelligence algorithmic purchase decision pathways. *Journal of Business Ethics*, *178*(4), 1043–1061. DOI: 10.1007/s10551-022-05048-7

Salam, M. A., Leong, V. S., & Muhamad, N. (2026). The Transformative Prospects of AI-Powered Virtual Influencers in Digital Consumer Engagement and Marketing Strategies. In *Cases on Social Media Marketing Engagement Tactics* (pp. 251–290). IGI Global Scientific Publishing.

Samara, D., Magnisalis, I., & Peristeras, V. (2020). Artificial intelligence and big data in tourism: A systematic literature review. *Journal of Hospitality and Tourism Technology*, *11*(2), 343–367. DOI: 10.1108/JHTT-12-2018-0118

Samtani, S., Kantarcioglu, M., & Chen, H. (2021). A multi-disciplinary perspective for conducting artificial intelligence-enabled privacy analytics: Connecting data, algorithms, and systems. [TMIS]. *ACM Transactions on Management Information Systems*, *12*(1), 1–18. DOI: 10.1145/3447507

Satornino, C. B., Du, S., & Grewal, D. (2024). Using artificial intelligence to advance sustainable development in industrial markets: A complex adaptive systems perspective. *Industrial Marketing Management*, *116*, 145–157. DOI: 10.1016/j.indmarman.2023.11.011

Shabankareh, M., Khamoushi Sahne, S. S., Nazarian, A., & Foroudi, P. (2025). The impact of AI perceived transparency on trust in AI recommendations in healthcare applications. *Asia-Pacific Journal of Business Administration*. Advance online publication. DOI: 10.1108/APJBA-12-2024-0690

Singh, H., Arora, M., & Singh, A. (2024). ChatGPT in marketing: Innovative pathways, decision systems, and forward perspectives. *Journal of Decision Systems*, •••, 1–28. DOI: 10.1080/12460125.2024.2438615

Soliman, M. M., Ahmed, E., Darwish, A., & Hassanien, A. E. (2024). Artificial intelligence powered Metaverse: Analysis, challenges and future perspectives. *Artificial Intelligence Review*, *57*(2), 36. DOI: 10.1007/s10462-023-10641-x

Strusani, D., & Houngbonon, G. V. (2019). *The role of artificial intelligence in supporting development in emerging markets*. International Finance Corporation. DOI: 10.1596/32365

Tapalova, O., & Zhiyenbayeva, N. (2022). Artificial intelligence in education: AIEd for personalised learning pathways. *Electronic Journal of e-Learning*, *20*(5), 639–653. https://eric.ed.gov/?id=EJ1373006. DOI: 10.34190/ejel.20.5.2597

Tschang, F. T., & Almirall, E. (2021). Artificial intelligence as augmenting automation: Implications for employment. *The Academy of Management Perspectives*, *35*(4), 642–659. DOI: 10.5465/amp.2019.0062

Tsolakis, N., Schumacher, R., Dora, M., & Kumar, M. (2023). Artificial intelligence and blockchain implementation in supply chains: A pathway to sustainability and data monetisation? *Annals of Operations Research*, *327*(1), 157–210. DOI: 10.1007/s10479-022-04785-2 PMID: 35755830

Tsvetovatyy, M., Gini, M., Mobasher, B., Ski, Z. W., & Ski, W. (1997). Magma an agent based virtual market for electronic commerce. *Applied Artificial Intelligence*, *11*(6), 501–523. DOI: 10.1080/088395197118046

Tyukin, I. Y., Gorban, A. N., Sofeykov, K. I., & Romanenko, I. (2018). Knowledge transfer between artificial intelligence systems. *Frontiers in Neurorobotics*, *12*, 49. DOI: 10.3389/fnbot.2018.00049 PMID: 30150929

Wan, Y., Tao, H., Zhao, Y., & Huang, L. (2025). The economic impact of artificial intelligence as a general purpose technology and its innovations in economic research. *International Journal of Computer Science and Information Technologies*, *5*(1), 22–34. DOI: 10.62051/ijcsit.v5n1.03

Wani, N. U. H., Hamza, N., & Saboori, B. (2025). Legal and Ethical Frameworks for AI in Financial Services: Balancing the Innovation with Responsibility and Effective Protection. In *Green Horizons: Role of AI in Sustainable Finance* (pp. 177–196). Springer Nature Singapore. DOI: 10.1007/978-981-96-6495-5_10

Xia, S., Zhou, Y., Wang, Z., He, Q., & Parry, G. (2026). Enhancing green innovation through university–industry collaboration and artificial intelligence: Insights from regional innovation systems in China. The Journal of technology transfer, 51(2), 653-681. https://doi.org/10.1007/s10961-025-10232-8, DOI: 10.1007/s10961-025-10232-8

Yu, X., Xu, S., & Ashton, M. (2023). Antecedents and outcomes of artificial intelligence adoption and application in the workplace: The socio-technical system theory perspective. *Information Technology & People*, *36*(1), 454–474. DOI: 10.1108/ITP-04-2021-0254

KEY TERMS AND DEFINITIONS

Algorithms to Markets: The phrase "algorithms to markets" describes the end-to-end pathway through which AI models or algorithms are developed, validated, transferred, and scaled into market-ready products, services, or systems that create economic and societal value.

Artificial Intelligence: Artificial intelligence is the field of developing computer systems that can perform tasks usually requiring human intelligence, such as learning from data, recognizing patterns, and making predictions or decisions.

Data governance: Data governance is the set of policies, roles, standards, and processes that ensure an organization's data is accurate, secure, ethically used, and compliant with legal and regulatory requirements.

Dynamic capabilities: Dynamic capabilities are an organization's higher-level abilities to sense opportunities and threats, seize them through investments and decisions, and reconfigure resources and processes to adapt and innovate over time.

Technology Transfer Office (TTOs): Technology Transfer Offices are specialized units, usually within universities or public research organizations that manage intellectual property and facilitate the commercialization of research outputs through licensing, spin-offs, and partnerships.

Technology transfer: Technology transfer is the process of moving knowledge, inventions, or technologies from research settings into organizations or markets where they are commercialized or applied in practice.

Technology-Organization-Environment (TOE) framework: The TOE framework explains how a firm's technological characteristics, internal organizational factors, and external environmental conditions jointly influence its adoption and implementation of innovations.

Chapter 4
Bridging the "Valley of Death": An Integrated Technology Transfer Framework for AI-Driven Personalization in Commercial Ecosystems

Kundan Sagar Bedmutha
http://orcid.org/0009-0000-4391-3107
Vishwakarma University, India

Rajkumar Sadashiv Jagdale
http://orcid.org/0000-0002-4074-1095
Vishwakarma University, India

ABSTRACT

The commercialization of artificial intelligence (AI) innovations continues to face high failure rates despite rapid technological progress. In personalization-driven markets, the challenge is greater because AI systems must align not only with technical performance but also with consumer trust, ethical legitimacy, and governance structures. The gap between laboratory validation and scalable adoption—often called the "Valley of Death"—is intensified by the socio-technical nature of personalization systems, which actively shape consumer journeys and influence decisions. This chapter proposes an integrated technology transfer framework that bridges technology-push innovation with market-pull validation. Extending traditional Technology Readiness Level (TRL) models, it incorporates consumer readiness and

DOI: 10.4018/979-8-3373-9325-4.ch004

ethical legibility as parallel determinants of success. The framework identifies key risks—algorithmic bias, privacy concerns, intrusiveness, and trust erosion—and outlines governance-oriented principles for responsible AI commercialization.

INTRODUCTION

Artificial intelligence (AI) is reshaping commercial ecosystems by embedding predictive analytics, recommendation systems, automation, and hyper-personalized marketing into core business functions (Davenport et al., 2020; Huang & Rust, 2018). Among these applications, AI-driven personalization has emerged as a strategically disruptive capability, enabling firms to tailor products, pricing, and communication in real time based on behavioral data and adaptive learning models (Arora et al., 2008; Paschen et al., 2020). Yet despite strong technical performance in pilot settings, many personalization initiatives fail to achieve sustainable commercialization. This persistent gap between laboratory validation and scalable adoption—commonly described as the "Valley of Death" (Auerswald & Branscomb, 2003; Markman et al., 2008)—reflects more than financial or operational constraints.

In personalization contexts, failure often arises from socio-technical misalignment: AI systems directly mediate consumer experiences, shaping recommendations, pricing, and interactions through algorithmic agents (Abd-Alrazaq et al., 2019; Loureiro et al., 2021). Consequently, adoption depends not only on predictive accuracy but also on trust, perceived fairness, transparency, and ethical governance (Glikson & Woolley, 2020; Shneiderman, 2022). While firms pursue personalization to enhance engagement and conversion, consumers frequently express privacy concerns and skepticism toward profiling practices, reflecting the privacy paradox and heightened sensitivity to bias and opacity (Norberg et al., 2007; Mittelstadt et al., 2016). Traditional technology transfer models, focused on research maturity and intellectual property pathways (Etzkowitz & Leydesdorff, 2000; Teece, 1986), insufficiently capture these relational and governance dynamics.

This chapter argues that bridging the Valley of Death in AI-driven personalization requires an integrated socio-technical framework that aligns technical robustness with consumer readiness, ethical legibility, and ecosystem coordination. Drawing on innovation management, human–AI interaction, and AI governance scholarship (Barney, 1991; Floridi et al., 2018; Dignum, 2019), it reconceptualizes commercialization as a process of alignment rather than linear scaling. Specifically, the chapter reframes the Valley of Death as a socio-technical misalignment problem, integrates technology-push and market-pull dynamics within AI-mediated markets, and positions ethical legibility and human–AI interaction as strategic determinants of adoption.

The following sections develop the theoretical foundations, review relevant literature, present the integrated framework, outline the conceptual methodology, analyze commercialization risks, and discuss managerial, policy, regulatory, and research implications for sustainable AI-driven personalization.

THEORETICAL FOUNDATIONS

This chapter advances several interrelated theoretical contributions to the study of AI commercialization, technology transfer, and socio-technical innovation governance.

It first reconceptualizes the "Valley of Death" in AI-driven personalization as a socio-technical misalignment rather than a purely financial or technological gap. Commercialization failure is reframed not as a resource deficiency or scaling inefficiency, but as a breakdown in alignment among algorithmic capability, consumer trust, ethical legitimacy, and ecosystem coordination.

In doing so, the chapter expands innovation management theory by embedding relational and governance-based determinants within commercialization models. It further integrates technology-push and market-pull dynamics in a manner specific to AI-mediated markets, arguing that algorithmic advancement and consumer, regulatory, and institutional readiness must co-evolve rather than unfold sequentially. Commercialization is thus conceptualized as a process of dynamic synchronization rather than linear transfer.

The chapter also introduces ethical legibility as a distinct commercialization variable, defined as the extent to which AI systems are perceived as fair, transparent, and normatively aligned. By positioning ethical perception as a mediator between technical readiness and adoption, the analysis connects AI governance scholarship with strategic management and consumer trust theory, reframing legitimacy as a strategic asset rather than a compliance obligation.

Finally, the chapter elevates Human–AI Interaction (HAII) from an interface concern to a foundational element of commercialization infrastructure, demonstrating that explainability, autonomy-preserving controls, and transparency cues directly shape scaling trajectories. Through this integration, interaction design is repositioned as a structural enabler of sustainable AI commercialization rather than a post-deployment refinement.

Figure 1. Socio-Technical Valley of Death in AI-Driven Personalization

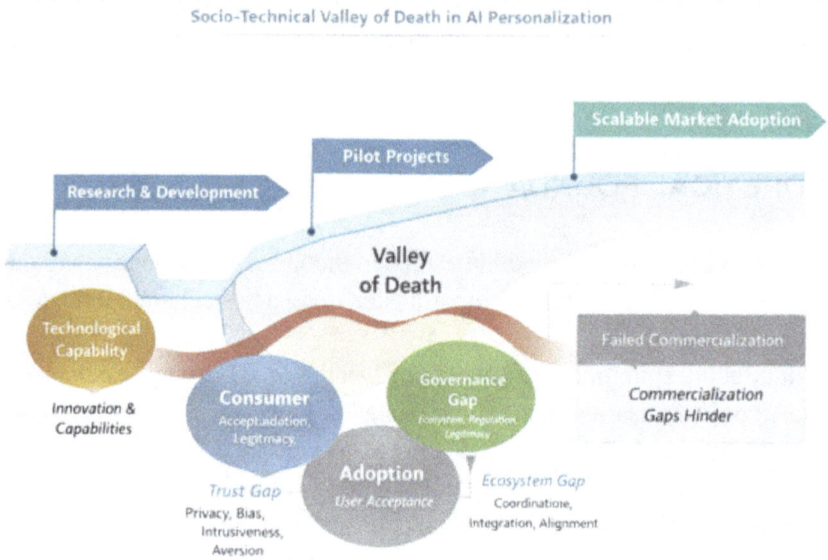

Figure 1 reconceptualizes the Valley of Death in the context of AI-driven personalization as a socio-technical misalignment gap rather than solely a financial or technological transition barrier. The diagram demonstrates how commercialization breakdown can occur between research and scalable market adoption when trust gaps, governance deficiencies, consumer resistance, or ecosystem misalignment undermine deployment. The model highlights that bridging the Valley requires synchronization between technological capability, consumer legitimacy, and institutional governance structures.

Finally, the chapter contributes to innovation ecosystem theory by emphasizing ecosystem alignment as a core determinant of AI personalization scaling. Commercial success is shown to depend not only on internal firm capabilities but also on coordinated governance structures, regulatory compatibility, cross-functional integration, and stakeholder collaboration. By synthesizing resource-based theory, dynamic capabilities, open innovation, and socio-technical systems perspectives, the chapter advances an integrated model in which technical performance, consumer perception, ethical governance, and institutional coordination are mutually constitutive. Together, these contributions provide a theoretically grounded and interdisciplinary foundation for understanding how AI-driven personalization technologies can transition from experimental innovation to sustainable commercial infrastructure.

LITERATURE REVIEW

AI Commercialization: From Technical Feasibility to Market Viability

Research on artificial intelligence in business has expanded rapidly, with much of the literature emphasizing performance gains, automation efficiency, and competitive advantage (Davenport et al., 2020; Ghasemaghaei & Calic, 2023). Although empirical evidence suggests that AI adoption can enhance predictive accuracy and operational effectiveness, outcomes vary significantly across firms and industries, indicating that technical implementation alone does not guarantee value creation. Commercialization depends on complementary assets, strategic alignment, and institutional legitimacy (Markman et al., 2008; Teece, 1986), yet many organizations struggle to scale AI pilots beyond experimental contexts due to data silos, regulatory uncertainty, coordination gaps, and user resistance. Existing research often treats AI as an internal optimization tool rather than as a consumer-facing system embedded within relational and institutional environments, an omission that becomes especially salient in personalization contexts where AI directly shapes user experiences.

AI-Driven Personalization and Consumer Psychology

AI-driven personalization extends traditional marketing capabilities by enabling real-time adaptation and predictive targeting at scale (Arora et al., 2008; Paschen et al., 2020). However, personalization generates psychological ambivalence. The personalization paradox demonstrates that consumers value relevance while resisting opaque data collection and profiling practices (Aguirre et al., 2015; Norberg et al., 2007). Trust plays a mediating role: transparency enhances acceptance, whereas perceived intrusiveness provokes resistance. Research on algorithm aversion further shows that users judge algorithmic errors more harshly than human mistakes (Dietvorst et al., 2015), heightening sensitivity to fairness and accountability concerns. Despite these insights, personalization scholarship largely frames AI as a performance-enhancing marketing instrument rather than as a governance-sensitive system whose legitimacy shapes commercialization outcomes..

Human–AI Interaction (HAII) and Explainability

Human–AI Interaction (HAII) research emphasizes that perceived competence, transparency, and value alignment are central to trust formation (Glikson & Woolley, 2020). Explainability mechanisms can strengthen perceived legitimacy (Rai, 2020; Ribeiro et al., 2016), though they introduce trade-offs between interpretability and predictive accuracy. Human-centered AI principles advocate preserving user agency through oversight features, opt-out controls, and transparent data practices (Shneiderman, 2022). However, HAII studies typically concentrate on micro-level interaction design rather than integrating these insights into broader technology transfer and commercialization frameworks, leaving relational determinants of scaling insufficiently theorized

Ethical AI, Bias, and Regulatory Legitimacy

Ethical AI research underscores risks related to bias, fairness, accountability, and transparency (Floridi et al., 2018; Mittelstadt et al., 2016). Empirical studies demonstrate that algorithmic systems can reproduce structural inequities when trained on biased datasets (Obermeyer et al., 2019). In personalization contexts, such bias may manifest through discriminatory pricing or unequal recommendation visibility.

Responsible AI frameworks advocate integrating fairness auditing and governance mechanisms into system design (Dignum, 2019), and regulatory regimes increasingly demand transparency in automated decision-making. Yet ethics is often treated as post-deployment risk management rather than as a determinant of commercialization success. The perceptual dimension of legitimacy—how users interpret fairness and accountability—remains under-theorized within commercialization scholarship.

Innovation Ecosystems and Platform Dependencies

AI-driven personalization systems operate within digital ecosystems involving platforms, data providers, vendors, and regulators. Innovation ecosystem theory emphasizes coordinated value creation across actors (Etzkowitz & Leydesdorff, 2000), while open innovation research highlights cross-organizational collaboration (Chesbrough, 2003). However, ecosystem dependencies also introduce governance complexity through fragmented data ownership, privacy standards, and cross-border compliance requirements.

Existing literature does not offer an integrated framework that simultaneously addresses ecosystem coordination, consumer trust, ethical governance, and technical maturity in AI personalization commercialization.

Identified Gaps in the Literature

Synthesizing across these streams reveals persistent fragmentation. AI commercialization research emphasizes internal capabilities while underestimating consumer legitimacy dynamics. Personalization studies prioritize marketing effectiveness without systematically integrating ethical governance considerations. HAII scholarship focuses on interaction-level trust but rarely connects these insights to strategic technology transfer. Ethical AI research advances fairness principles yet seldom links them to competitive positioning and scaling outcomes.

Collectively, these gaps leave unresolved how firms can transition AI-driven personalization technologies from research environments to scalable, trusted, and institutionally legitimate commercial ecosystems. Addressing this challenge requires a socio-technical framework that integrates technical readiness, consumer readiness, ethical legibility, and ecosystem alignment. The following section introduces such a framework.

Integrated Technology Transfer Framework

Bridging the Valley of Death in AI-driven personalization requires rethinking technology transfer as a socio-technical alignment process rather than a linear deployment sequence. Existing commercialization models often focus on research maturity, intellectual property protection, licensing, and financial scaling mechanisms (Auerswald & Branscomb, 2003; Markman et al., 2008). While these remain relevant, AI personalization systems introduce relational, psychological, and governance complexities that demand a broader conceptual lens.

This chapter proposes an **Integrated Technology-Push and Market-Pull Framework for AI-Driven Personalization Transfer**, built upon four interdependent dimensions: (1) Technical Readiness, (2) Consumer Readiness, (3) Ethical Legibility, and (4) Ecosystem Alignment. The framework argues that sustainable commercialization occurs only when these four dimensions are strategically aligned.

Dimension I: Technical Readiness and Deployment Feasibility

Technical readiness refers to the maturity, reliability, and scalability of AI systems within operational environments. Although innovation management literature often evaluates readiness through development stages and proof-of-concept validation (Dosi, 1982), personalization systems require robustness that extends beyond predictive accuracy. Effective commercialization depends on stable and integrated data pipelines capable of continuous ingestion, preprocessing, and updating; fragmented or low-quality data undermines both performance and scalability. Model robustness is equally critical, as AI systems degrade over time in response to behavioral shifts, seasonal changes, and evolving market dynamics, necessitating ongoing retraining, performance monitoring, and bias auditing. Interoperability with existing digital infrastructures—such as customer relationship management systems, e-commerce platforms, and analytics architectures—further determines integration feasibility. Finally, scalability across markets and demographic segments underpins economic viability. Yet even highly sophisticated systems may fail commercially if technical excellence is not aligned with user expectations, ethical governance, and institutional coordination. Technical readiness is therefore a necessary but insufficient condition for successful AI-driven personalization transfer.

Beyond predictive accuracy, operational deployment introduces additional technical challenges. Organizations must establish reliable data pipelines capable of ingesting heterogeneous data sources, implement monitoring systems to detect model drift and performance degradation, and ensure interoperability with existing enterprise systems such as CRM platforms, analytics infrastructures, and marketing automation tools. Without these operational capabilities, technically promising personalization models may fail during large-scale deployment.

Amazon's recommendation system illustrates the importance of technical readiness in personalization commercialization. The system continuously retrains models using large-scale behavioral data and integrates them with e-commerce infrastructure, logistics systems, and user interaction signals, enabling scalable and adaptive personalization.

Figure 2. Integrated Technology Transfer Framework for AI-Driven Personalization

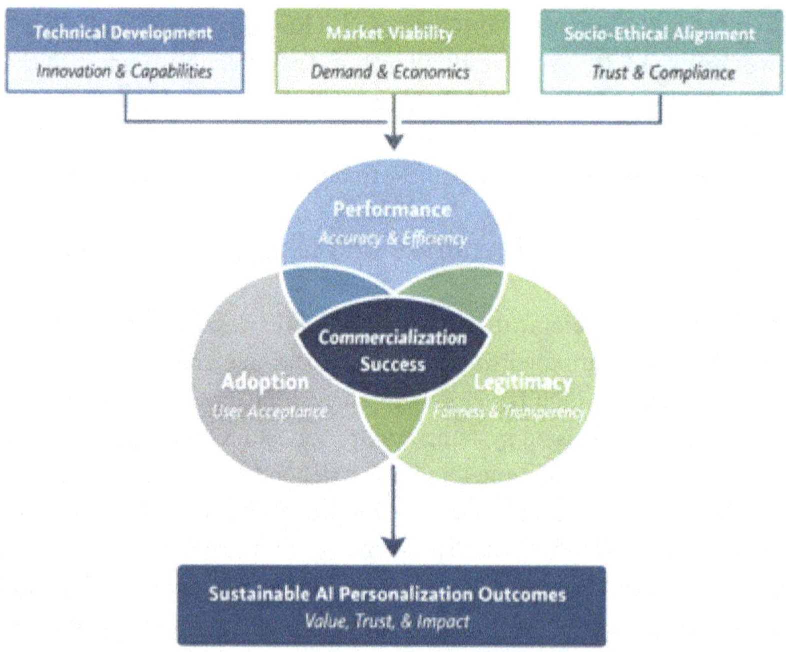

Figure 2 illustrates the proposed integrated technology transfer framework for AI-driven personalization. The model conceptualizes sustainable commercialization as the outcome of alignment across four interdependent dimensions: technical readiness, consumer readiness, ethical legibility, and ecosystem alignment. These dimensions converge to shape performance, legitimacy, and adoption, collectively determining commercialization success and long-term sustainability in personalization-driven ecosystems. The framework emphasizes that commercialization viability emerges not from technical capability alone, but from coordinated socio-technical integration.

Dimension II: Consumer Readiness and Experience Legibility

Consumer readiness emphasizes that individuals do not adopt algorithms in isolation; they adopt the experiences those algorithms create. It refers to the psychological and perceptual conditions that enable acceptance of AI-mediated personalization. While technology acceptance models highlight perceived usefulness and ease of use as drivers of adoption (Davis, 1989; Venkatesh et al., 2003), personalization systems introduce additional evaluative criteria, including perceived fairness, transparency, and autonomy. Research on the personalization paradox shows that consumers value relevance yet resist intrusive or opaque profiling practices (Aguirre et al., 2015; Norberg et al., 2007). Commercial success therefore depends on calibrating personalization intensity to users' sense of control. Consumer readiness is strengthened when value is clearly visible, when users can adjust or opt out of personalization features, and when recommendation processes are communicated transparently. Without such experience legibility—where users understand and accept how personalization functions—even technically advanced systems may provoke skepticism and resistance.

Dimension III: Ethical Legibility and Trust Assurance

Ethical legibility extends this logic by focusing on whether AI systems are perceived as fair, accountable, and aligned with societal norms. Although ethical AI scholarship emphasizes fairness and non-discrimination (Floridi et al., 2018; Mittelstadt et al., 2016), commercialization research has rarely treated ethical perception as central to scaling. Evidence shows that biased or discriminatory outcomes can damage reputation and trigger regulatory scrutiny (Obermeyer et al., 2019), particularly in personalization contexts involving pricing or recommendation visibility. Ethical legibility therefore encompasses fairness auditing, explainability mechanisms, transparent data governance, and regulatory alignment. Because trust in algorithmic systems is fragile and errors are judged more harshly than human mistakes (Dietvorst et al., 2015), firms must embed visible governance structures that reinforce institutional integrity. In this way, ethical legibility shifts from reactive compliance to a strategic asset that supports sustained adoption and competitive differentiation.

Dimension IV: Ecosystem Alignment and Commercial Governance

Ecosystem alignment recognizes that AI-driven personalization operates within interconnected digital environments involving platforms, data providers, regulators, and organizational stakeholders. Innovation ecosystem theory underscores that value creation depends on coordinated multi-actor interaction rather than isolated firm capabilities (Etzkowitz & Leydesdorff, 2000), and open innovation research highlights the importance of cross-organizational collaboration (Chesbrough, 2003). Effective commercialization therefore requires coherent data stewardship agreements, regulatory coordination, cross-functional integration, and partnership governance. When alignment breaks down—through fragmented oversight, regulatory misfit, or weak organizational coordination—scaling can stall even if technical systems and consumer-facing features perform effectively. Sustainable AI-driven personalization commercialization thus depends on the synchronized development of technical robustness, consumer acceptance, ethical legitimacy, and ecosystem governance, as summarized in Table 1.

Table 1. Core Dimensions of the Integrated Technology Transfer Framework for AI-Driven Personalization

Dimension	Core Focus	Key Barriers	Commercial Risk if Weak
Technical Readiness	Model robustness, scalability, system interoperability	Data instability, model drift, integration failures	Deployment breakdown
Consumer Readiness	Trust, usability, perceived fairness	Privacy concerns, uncanny effect, resistance	Low adoption
Ethical Legibility	Transparency, fairness, explainability	Bias, opacity, manipulation concerns	Reputational damage
Ecosystem Alignment	Regulatory compliance, stakeholder coordination	Governance gaps, legal uncertainty	Scaling delays

Table 1 provides a consolidated overview of the Integrated Technology Transfer Framework by organizing its four dimensions—Technical Readiness, Consumer Readiness, Ethical Legibility, and Ecosystem Alignment—into analytically distinct but interdependent components. For each dimension, the table identifies the central strategic focus, common implementation barriers, and the commercial consequences of underdevelopment. By synthesizing these elements, the table demonstrates that commercialization failure is rarely attributable to technical weakness alone; rather, it emerges from imbalances across socio-technical and institutional domains. This structured summary reinforces the argument that bridging the Valley of Death requires coordinated alignment rather than isolated optimization.

Collectively, these research streams highlight the multidimensional nature of AI commercialization. AI commercialization literature emphasizes technological capability and complementary assets, aligning with the technical readiness dimension of the framework. Consumer psychology and personalization research highlight trust, privacy concerns, and algorithm acceptance, which inform the consumer readiness dimension. Human–AI interaction studies emphasize explainability and transparency mechanisms that shape user perceptions, supporting the ethical legibility component. Finally, innovation ecosystem research underscores the importance of stakeholder coordination, regulatory alignment, and platform dependencies, corresponding to the ecosystem alignment dimension. Integrating these insights reveals that successful commercialization depends on simultaneous alignment across technological, psychological, ethical, and institutional domains.

Interdependence of the Four Dimensions

The framework treats these dimensions as mutually reinforcing rather than sequential. Technical sophistication without consumer trust generates resistance, while consumer acceptance without ethical governance exposes firms to reputational and regulatory risk. Ethical transparency unsupported by technical robustness undermines performance credibility, and ecosystem coordination without user legitimacy fails to produce meaningful adoption. Sustainable AI-driven personalization commercialization therefore arises at the intersection of technical maturity, consumer acceptance, ethical integrity, and institutional alignment. Overcoming the Valley of Death requires these dimensions to evolve in parallel, ensuring that technological capability, user trust, governance structures, and collaborative coordination are synchronized.

Strategic Implications of the Framework

Strategically, the framework reframes technology transfer from a linear research-to-market pipeline into a dynamic process of socio-technical alignment. It positions human–AI interaction design and ethical governance as central commercialization enablers rather than peripheral considerations. At a practical level, the framework functions as a diagnostic tool, enabling firms and technology transfer offices to identify whether commercialization barriers stem from technical instability, weak consumer legitimacy, insufficient governance, or ecosystem misalignment. By integrating technical, relational, and institutional determinants within a unified model, the framework advances a more comprehensive approach to AI commercialization in personalization-driven ecosystems.

METHODOLOGY

This chapter employs a conceptual and integrative research design suited to interdisciplinary theory development. Because AI-driven personalization commercialization spans innovation management, consumer psychology, human–AI interaction, and ethical governance, no single empirical method can adequately capture its complexity. Accordingly, the methodology relies on systematic literature synthesis, conceptual integration, and theory-driven model construction to develop the Integrated Technology Transfer Framework. Rather than generating new empirical data, the analysis synthesizes established scholarship to clarify key constructs, identify relationships, and integrate fragmented theoretical perspectives into a coherent explanatory model.

Conceptual and Theoretical Synthesis

The synthesis followed a structured process in which foundational concepts were first drawn from technology transfer research, the Valley of Death literature, dynamic capabilities theory, human–AI interaction studies, personalization psychology, and ethical AI governance. Cross-domain tensions and complementarities were then examined to identify recurring commercialization barriers, which were subsequently organized into technical, consumer, ethical, and ecosystem-level constraints. These categories were integrated into four interdependent dimensions—technical readiness, consumer readiness, ethical legibility, and ecosystem alignment—forming the basis of the proposed framework. This approach ensures theoretical rigor while advancing interdisciplinary coherence.

Interdisciplinary Integration Strategy

The literature informing the framework spans five streams: innovation management, AI adoption and performance, personalization and consumer trust, human–AI interaction, and ethical AI governance. Rather than reviewing these traditions independently, the analysis focused on their intersections—particularly where commercialization failures emerge.

For example, personalization research emphasizes the privacy paradox, while ethical AI scholarship highlights fairness and accountability. Both ultimately shape consumer trust. Similarly, dynamic capabilities theory intersects with regulatory compliance and ecosystem coordination in AI deployment. Mapping these overlaps enabled the development of a unified socio-technical perspective that integrates relational, institutional, and technical determinants of commercialization outcomes.

Framework Construction

The framework is grounded in a socio-technical analytical lens that recognizes AI systems as embedded within interconnected technical, organizational, regulatory, and behavioral environments. Technological performance and social acceptance are treated as mutually constitutive, such that commercialization success depends on alignment among algorithmic robustness, consumer trust, governance integrity, and institutional coordination. To illustrate practical relevance, the chapter incorporates analytically constructed scenarios based on documented industry patterns, demonstrating how misalignment across framework dimensions contributes to commercialization failure in real-world contexts. As a conceptual synthesis, the framework does not offer empirical validation; however, it establishes a foundation for future research employing surveys, case studies, or experimental designs. Conceptual model development remains particularly valuable in rapidly evolving domains where theoretical integration has not yet kept pace with technological advancement.

Strategic Commercialization Risks and Failure Modes

AI-driven personalization technologies frequently demonstrate strong technical potential yet struggle to achieve sustainable market integration. Drawing on the Integrated Technology Transfer Framework, this section identifies recurring commercialization failure modes that emerge when misalignment occurs across technical readiness, consumer readiness, ethical legibility, and ecosystem coordination. These risks are not isolated operational challenges; they represent systemic socio-technical breakdowns that contribute to the Valley of Death in AI commercialization.

Technical Overconfidence and Deployment Fragility

A common failure mode arises when firms overestimate technical maturity. AI systems that perform well in controlled environments may degrade when exposed to real-world variability. Data drift, incomplete data pipelines, and inadequate monitoring mechanisms can lead to declining model accuracy and inconsistent user experiences.

In personalization systems, technical fragility manifests through irrelevant recommendations, incorrect targeting, or poorly timed promotions. Such failures not only reduce performance but also erode consumer trust. Because AI operates invisibly, users often interpret inconsistent outputs as incompetence or manipulation rather than technical instability.

This failure mode reflects an imbalance between technological sophistication and operational governance. Firms that prioritize predictive accuracy without establishing continuous auditing and retraining infrastructures risk early-stage credibility loss.

The Personalization–Intrusion Threshold

AI-driven personalization operates within a delicate psychological boundary. While relevance enhances perceived value, excessive precision can trigger discomfort or "creepiness." Consumers may feel surveilled when recommendations appear overly intimate or predictive.

This personalization–intrusion threshold represents a commercialization tipping point. When personalization intensity surpasses perceived legitimacy, user resistance increases, leading to reduced engagement or opt-out behavior. The privacy paradox literature suggests that users tolerate data use when benefits are transparent and controllable, but resist when data practices appear opaque. Failure to manage this threshold reflects weak consumer readiness alignment. Organizations that optimize algorithmic targeting without embedding control mechanisms or transparency signals risk backlash and reputational damage.

A widely discussed example involves Target's predictive analytics system, which inferred pregnancy status based on purchasing behavior and sent targeted advertisements to consumers before they had publicly disclosed the information. Although technically effective, the system generated consumer discomfort and public criticism, illustrating how excessive personalization can cross the intrusion threshold and undermine trust.

Algorithmic Bias and Reputational Risk

Algorithmic bias constitutes one of the most significant strategic risks in AI commercialization. Bias may arise from skewed training datasets, proxy variables, or feedback loops that reinforce historical inequalities. In personalization contexts, bias can produce differential pricing, exclusionary recommendation patterns, or underrepresentation of certain demographic groups.

Such outcomes have legal, ethical, and reputational consequences. Even when unintentional, discriminatory patterns undermine brand legitimacy and invite regulatory scrutiny. Public exposure of biased algorithms can rapidly erode trust and stall adoption.

This failure mode reflects insufficient ethical legibility. Firms that treat fairness auditing as an afterthought rather than a core governance process are particularly vulnerable. Ethical governance must be embedded at the design stage to prevent reactive crisis management.

Trust Erosion Through Opacity

Many AI personalization systems function as "black boxes," offering optimized outputs without explanation. While opaque models may achieve high predictive accuracy, they reduce user comprehension and perceived control.

Research on algorithm aversion indicates that users are more forgiving of human error than algorithmic error. When systems provide no explanation for unexpected recommendations or decisions, consumers may attribute negative intent or manipulation to the firm.

Opacity undermines ethical legibility and consumer readiness simultaneously. Without explainability features—such as contextual recommendation cues or transparent data usage disclosures—AI systems struggle to maintain long-term trust.

Ecosystem Misalignment and Scaling Barriers

AI-driven personalization systems rarely function as standalone technologies. Instead, they are embedded within broader ecosystems that include cloud infrastructure providers, data-sharing agreements, regulatory compliance frameworks, and internal cross-functional coordination mechanisms. Even when technical performance is robust and consumer acceptance is strong, misalignment within this ecosystem can significantly hinder or completely stall scaling efforts.

At the ecosystem level, common barriers include regulatory uncertainty across jurisdictions, inconsistent privacy standards, fragmented data ownership structures, and insufficient coordination between marketing and technical teams. These challenges create friction not because the technology itself is inadequate, but because institutional and organizational systems are not synchronized. When ecosystem governance is weak, firms may face deployment delays, compliance penalties, or operational inefficiencies that undermine commercialization momentum. In such cases, failure reflects insufficient institutional alignment rather than technological deficiency, highlighting the critical importance of coordinated governance structures in AI deployment.

Performance–Legitimacy Trade-Offs

A deeper structural tension in AI commercialization involves the trade-off between optimization performance and social legitimacy. Highly complex models may deliver superior personalization accuracy but reduce transparency. Simplified models may enhance explainability but sacrifice performance.

Firms must strategically navigate this trade-off. Over-prioritizing optimization may produce short-term gains but long-term resistance if users perceive unfairness or opacity. Conversely, over-simplification may reduce competitive advantage.

Successful commercialization requires balancing performance with legitimacy, aligning technical and ethical considerations rather than treating them as competing objectives.

Figure 3 presents the conceptual trade-off between algorithmic optimization and perceived legitimacy in AI-driven personalization systems. The model illustrates how over-optimization may generate consumer backlash due to perceived intrusiveness or opacity, while under-optimization may reduce commercial value. Sustainable commercialization is achieved within a balanced zone where performance efficiency and ethical legitimacy are strategically aligned. The figure emphasizes the importance of managing optimization intensity in relation to consumer trust and social acceptance.

Figure 3. Performance–Legitimacy Trade-Off in AI-Driven Personalization

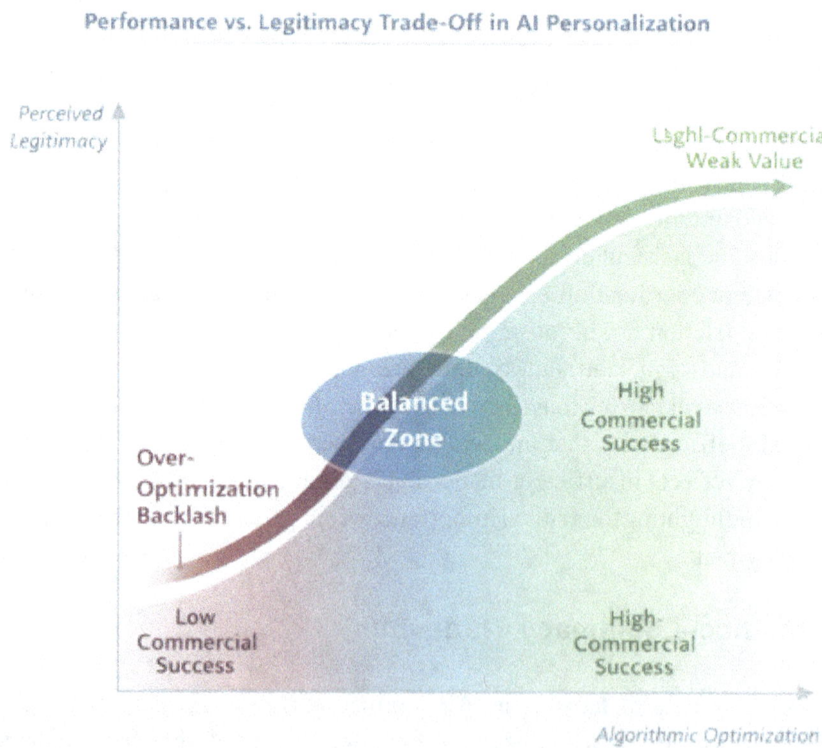

The Cumulative Risk Effect

Importantly, these failure modes rarely occur in isolation. Commercialization breakdown often results from cumulative misalignment across multiple dimensions. For example, a technically robust system may fail due to consumer distrust, while a trusted system may collapse under regulatory pressure.

The Integrated Technology Transfer Framework allows firms to diagnose where misalignment occurs and implement corrective measures. Rather than attributing failure solely to funding shortages or insufficient marketing, organizations can evaluate structural weaknesses across technical readiness, consumer trust, ethical governance, and ecosystem coordination.

For example, Netflix's recommendation engine demonstrates how large-scale AI personalization can successfully balance relevance and transparency. The platform provides users with explanations such as "Because you watched…", which function as lightweight explainability cues that increase perceived transparency and trust while maintaining high recommendation accuracy.

Strategic Insight

AI commercialization failure is rarely about algorithmic inadequacy alone. It emerges when socio-technical alignment is incomplete. Bridging the Valley of Death therefore requires proactive risk identification across relational, institutional, and governance domains—not merely technological refinement.

Implications for Practice, Education, and Policy

The Integrated Technology Transfer Framework developed in this chapter has implications that extend beyond theoretical contribution. AI-driven personalization operates at the intersection of business strategy, technological innovation, consumer psychology, and regulatory governance. Accordingly, its successful commercialization requires coordinated action across firms, educational institutions, and policy bodies. This section outlines implications for practitioners, educators, and policymakers seeking to bridge the Valley of Death in AI-driven personalization.

IMPLICATIONS FOR BUSINESS PRACTICE

Reframing Commercialization as Socio-Technical Alignment

For business leaders, the central implication is clear: AI commercialization cannot be reduced to model accuracy, system efficiency, or return-on-investment metrics alone. While performance indicators remain important, they represent only one dimension of a broader socio-technical equation. Firms must evaluate AI initiatives holistically across four interdependent domains—technical readiness, consumer readiness, ethical legibility, and ecosystem alignment. Achieving this broader evaluation requires structured cross-functional collaboration among data scientists, marketing teams, legal advisors, compliance officers, and governance specialists.

Organizations should institutionalize diagnostic assessments before full-scale deployment. Instead of asking solely, "Does the model work?", decision-makers should examine deeper alignment questions: Is the personalization experience understandable and meaningful to users? Does the system provide clear control and transparency mechanisms? Are fairness audits embedded within deployment and monitoring processes? Are ecosystem partners aligned with shared governance and compliance standards? By shifting from an optimization-centric mindset to an alignment-centric strategy, firms can reduce the risk of premature scaling failures and strengthen the long-term sustainability of AI-driven personalization initiatives.

Human–AI Interaction as a Competitive Asset

Firms should treat Human–AI Interaction (HAII) design as a strategic capability rather than a peripheral interface issue. Explainability features, adaptive personalization controls, and visible transparency cues can differentiate brands in increasingly algorithm-mediated markets.

Trust-building design elements—such as "Why am I seeing this?" prompts, personalization dashboards, and adjustable recommendation intensity—can convert potential resistance into engagement. In markets where algorithmic mistrust is rising, legitimacy may become a primary source of competitive advantage.

Governance Capabilities and Dynamic Adaptation

Sustained AI commercialization requires dynamic capabilities in monitoring, auditing, and adapting algorithmic systems. Firms must invest in ongoing bias detection, performance recalibration, and regulatory compliance monitoring. Governance cannot be static; it must evolve alongside model updates and changing legal environments.

Organizations that proactively integrate ethical governance may reduce reputational risk and strengthen stakeholder trust. In this sense, responsible AI practices should be reframed as long-term strategic investments rather than compliance costs.

Implications for Technology Transfer Offices (TTOs) and Startups

The Integrated Technology Transfer Framework carries implications beyond theory, as AI-driven personalization sits at the intersection of strategy, technology, consumer psychology, and regulation. For firms, commercialization cannot be evaluated solely through model accuracy or return on investment. Sustainable scaling requires coordinated alignment across technical readiness, consumer readiness, ethical legibility, and ecosystem integration. This demands cross-functional collaboration among data science, marketing, legal, and governance teams, along with structured pre-deployment diagnostics that assess not only performance but also user comprehension, transparency mechanisms, fairness auditing, and partner alignment. Human–AI interaction design should be treated as a strategic capability rather than a peripheral interface concern, as explainability features, personalization controls, and visible transparency cues can strengthen trust and differentiate firms in increasingly algorithm-mediated markets. Likewise, governance must be dynamic; continuous monitoring, bias detection, and regulatory adaptation are essential to sustaining legitimacy and minimizing reputational risk.

For technology transfer offices and startups, commercialization criteria should extend beyond intellectual property strength and projected market size to include ethical impact assessment, consumer perception testing, regulatory foresight, and ecosystem feasibility. Embedding transparency and governance mechanisms early in product development reduces scaling barriers and strengthens institutional trust. Educational institutions must similarly adopt interdisciplinary approaches, integrating AI governance, consumer psychology, and human-centered design into business and data science curricula to prepare leaders capable of managing socio-technical alignment. Policymakers, meanwhile, should encourage proactive governance integration, proportionate explainability standards, and international regulatory coordination while avoiding excessive rigidity that could deter innovation. Ultimately, sustainable AI personalization commercialization depends on coherent alignment among organizational capability, consumer trust, ethical accountability, and regulatory stability. When these dimensions are synchronized, firms can generate value while maintaining legitimacy; when they diverge, even technically robust systems risk stalling within the Valley of Death.

Table 2. Strategic Commercialization Failure Modes in AI-Driven Personalization

Failure Mode	Underlying Cause	Affected Dimension	Strategic Consequence
Privacy Backlash	Opaque data practices	Ethical Legibility	Consumer churn
Algorithmic Bias	Skewed training data	Technical + Ethical	Regulatory penalties
Uncanny Effect	Over-personalization	Consumer Readiness	Trust erosion
Governance Breakdown	Lack of monitoring	Ecosystem Alignment	Compliance risk

Table 2 consolidates the principal failure modes associated with AI-driven personalization commercialization. Each risk—such as privacy backlash, algorithmic bias, uncanny user reactions, or governance breakdown—is linked to the underlying structural cause and the specific framework dimension most affected. By connecting operational weaknesses to strategic outcomes, the table demonstrates how localized design flaws can escalate into systemic commercialization barriers. This synthesis highlights that successful AI transfer requires anticipatory governance and proactive alignment mechanisms across technical, consumer, ethical, and ecosystem domains.

Firms evaluating AI-driven personalization initiatives often rely on a combination of operational and behavioral metrics, including click-through rates, conversion rates, recommendation accuracy, consumer engagement duration, retention rates, and incremental revenue attributable to personalization. At a strategic level, organizations may also assess customer lifetime value improvements and return on investment from personalization-driven campaigns.

DISCUSSION

This chapter reframes AI-driven personalization commercialization as a socio-technical alignment challenge rather than a linear diffusion process. Whereas traditional models emphasize adoption stages, resource advantages, or financial constraints, the analysis here shows that scaling in personalization markets is legitimacy-dependent and structurally nonlinear. The "Valley of Death" is therefore not simply a funding or maturity gap, but a misalignment between algorithmic capability and stakeholder acceptance. Technical performance does not automatically produce trust, scalability does not ensure ethical legitimacy, and predictive accuracy does not guarantee regulatory compliance. In this sense, the Valley represents a trust and governance gap as much as an economic one.

The chapter further extends technology-push and market-pull theory by arguing that AI personalization requires their simultaneous co-evolution. Algorithmic breakthroughs generate new capabilities, but sustainable scaling depends on consumer readiness, regulatory clarity, and ethical alignment. When technological advancement outpaces societal acceptance, backlash emerges; when expectations exceed technical maturity, disillusionment follows. Commercialization success therefore rests on synchronization rather than dominance of either force. Within this logic, ethical legibility becomes a central commercialization variable, moderating the relationship between technical readiness and adoption. Even highly accurate systems may fail if perceived as opaque or manipulative, making legitimacy part of the value proposition and linking governance directly to competitive advantage.

The chapter also repositions Human–AI Interaction as commercialization infrastructure rather than interface refinement. Explainability, adjustable personalization controls, and transparency mechanisms shape how systems are interpreted and trusted, transforming user experience design into an adoption enabler. Similarly, governance is reconceptualized as a dynamic capability involving continuous monitoring, recalibration, and institutional adaptation. Firms able to detect bias drift, respond to regulatory change, and maintain transparency are better positioned to overcome commercialization barriers. Collectively, these insights support a broader socio-technical commercialization paradigm in which technological performance, consumer perception, ethical evaluation, and regulatory coordination are mutually constitutive. Sustainable scaling emerges not from acceleration alone, but from deliberate alignment across these interdependent domains.

For instance, successful personalization deployment often requires coordination among cloud infrastructure providers, data partners, marketing teams, and regulatory compliance units to ensure that data flows, governance practices, and deployment architectures remain aligned.

Regulatory and Ethical Considerations

AI-driven personalization operates within increasingly complex regulatory and ethical landscapes. As personalization engines move from experimental pilots into large-scale commercial ecosystems, firms must navigate evolving legal standards, societal expectations, and normative debates surrounding fairness, transparency, and data governance. Unlike traditional digital tools, AI personalization systems continuously adapt, infer behavioral patterns, and influence consumer decision-making. This dynamic and persuasive capacity intensifies ethical risk and regulatory scrutiny. Bridging the Valley of Death therefore requires not only technical and market alignment, but regulatory and ethical integration as core components of commercialization strategy.

Regulatory Landscape and Institutional Constraints

Across jurisdictions, regulatory frameworks are evolving rapidly to address the risks associated with AI deployment. Although legal regimes vary in scope and enforcement intensity, several recurring themes directly affect AI-driven personalization systems: data protection and consent requirements, algorithmic transparency obligations, anti-discrimination and fairness standards, safeguards for automated decision-making, and clearly defined accountability and liability structures. These regulatory developments reflect growing concern over how algorithmic systems shape consumer behavior and allocate opportunities.

In many regions, privacy laws restrict how personal data may be collected, processed, and repurposed for personalization. Practices such as consumer profiling, behavioral inference, and predictive targeting may trigger obligations related to explicit consent, explainability rights, data minimization, and opt-out mechanisms. For firms operating across borders, fragmented regulatory standards can complicate system design and deployment strategies.

From a commercialization standpoint, regulatory uncertainty can widen the Valley of Death by increasing compliance costs, delaying scaling decisions, and creating strategic hesitation—particularly for startups with limited legal and governance resources. However, proactive regulatory alignment can also serve as a competitive advantage. Organizations that embed compliance architecture and governance safeguards early in product development reduce costly retrofitting, mitigate reputational risk, and strengthen institutional legitimacy.

The framework advanced in this chapter therefore conceptualizes regulatory integration not as an external constraint, but as a core component of ecosystem alignment. By treating compliance as an embedded dimension of socio-technical coordination, firms can transform regulatory complexity into strategic resilience.

Ethical Risks in AI-Driven Personalization

Beyond formal legal compliance, AI-driven personalization raises deeper ethical concerns because such systems infer preferences, predict vulnerabilities, and subtly shape consumer behavior. The privacy paradox illustrates this tension: consumers express concern about data collection yet continue to use personalized services, creating ambiguity around what constitutes meaningful consent. Formal consent mechanisms often fail to address asymmetries in knowledge and bargaining power, meaning that regulatory compliance alone does not guarantee informed choice. Ethically responsible personalization therefore requires substantive transparency and user empowerment, including clear explanations of data use, accessible privacy controls, adjustable personalization settings, and understandable accounts of recommendation logic. Without these safeguards, personalization risks being perceived as surveillance rather than service, undermining long-term legitimacy.

Algorithmic bias further complicates commercialization. Systems trained on historical data can reproduce or amplify embedded inequalities, leading to discriminatory pricing, exclusionary targeting, or unequal recommendation visibility. Such outcomes may arise unintentionally from skewed datasets or optimization goals, yet they carry reputational and regulatory consequences. Fairness, therefore, cannot be reduced to technical metrics alone; it must engage broader questions of distributive impact and social responsibility. Operationalizing fairness requires systematic bias auditing, representative training data, and continuous oversight of algorithmic outputs. Crucially, ethical legibility—the perception that systems operate fairly and responsibly—matters as much as statistical parity. Even technically balanced systems may face resistance if users perceive opacity or discrimination.

AI personalization also raises concerns about manipulation and autonomy. By optimizing for engagement or conversion, algorithms may exploit behavioral biases such as scarcity effects or social proof, blurring the line between helpful guidance and coercive persuasion. Strategies that prioritize short-term behavioral capture at the expense of user trust risk reputational harm and regulatory scrutiny. Responsible deployment therefore requires preserving autonomy through the avoidance of dark patterns, transparent recommendation logic, user override options, and limits on exploitative micro-targeting. Embedding such safeguards strengthens legitimacy and brand equity, underscoring that sustainable AI commercialization depends not only on optimization performance but also on the preservation of trust and agency.

Explainability and Ethical Legibility

Explainability has become a cornerstone of contemporary AI governance debates. In AI-driven personalization systems, explainability serves several interconnected functions: it enhances user trust by clarifying why certain recommendations appear, enables accountability by making algorithmic reasoning open to scrutiny, supports regulatory compliance where explanation rights are mandated, and reduces the perceived opacity often associated with automated decision-making. In commercial environments, these functions directly influence adoption and long-term legitimacy.

However, explainability must be carefully calibrated. Overly technical explanations—such as references to model architecture or probabilistic weighting—may overwhelm or alienate consumers. Conversely, overly simplistic justifications (e.g., "because you liked this") may appear superficial or evasive, potentially undermining credibility. Effective explainability therefore requires translating algorithmic reasoning into contextually meaningful narratives that align with user expectations.

Figure 4. Ethical Legibility Mechanisms in AI Personalization Commercialization

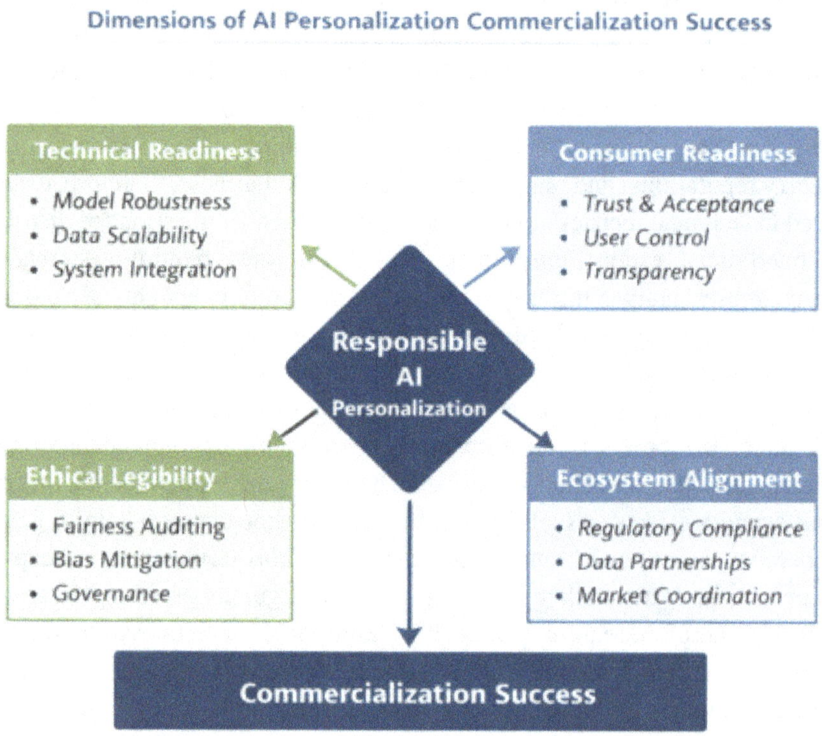

Figure 4 depicts the mechanisms through which ethical legibility contributes to trust formation and commercialization success in AI-driven personalization. The model highlights fairness auditing, transparency, bias mitigation, user control mechanisms, and governance integration as core components that enhance perceived legitimacy. These mechanisms strengthen consumer trust and support scalable market adoption, positioning ethical governance as a strategic enabler rather than a compliance constraint.

The concept of ethical legibility advanced in this chapter extends beyond technical explainability. Ethical legibility concerns whether a system is perceived as fair, understandable, and normatively appropriate. A system may be technically explainable yet still fail if its outcomes conflict with societal values or distributive expectations. Thus, perception and legitimacy are as critical as transparency itself.

Design strategies that enhance ethical legibility include incorporating visual cues that clarify personalization logic, transparently disclosing ranking or recommendation criteria, articulating explicit fairness commitments, and allowing users to adjust personalization intensity according to their preferences. When AI systems are perceived as transparent, bounded, and responsive to user control, resistance to adoption diminishes and trust becomes more sustainable.

Governance Models for Responsible Commercialization

Embedding ethics into AI commercialization requires structured governance architectures rather than ad hoc or reactive decision-making. As personalization systems scale, informal oversight becomes insufficient to manage ethical complexity, regulatory scrutiny, and reputational exposure. Organizations should therefore adopt multi-layer governance models that institutionalize accountability and oversight across the AI lifecycle.

Such models may include internal AI ethics committees responsible for reviewing high-impact deployments; independent audit mechanisms that provide objective evaluation of fairness and compliance; ongoing fairness monitoring dashboards to track model performance across demographic and behavioral segments; cross-functional oversight structures that integrate marketing, data science, and legal expertise; and clearly defined accountability hierarchies specifying responsibility for algorithmic decisions and outcomes. These mechanisms ensure that ethical considerations are embedded systematically rather than treated as peripheral concerns.

Governance processes must also remain adaptive. As AI models evolve through retraining and environmental changes, organizations should implement drift detection systems and bias recalibration procedures as routine operational practices. Continuous monitoring reduces long-term exposure to regulatory penalties, litigation risk, and reputational damage by identifying issues before they escalate.

Importantly, governance should not be framed solely as a defensive or compliance-driven function. When properly designed, governance structures can support innovation by clarifying acceptable operational boundaries, reducing uncertainty, and enabling responsible scaling. In this sense, ethical governance becomes an enabler of sustainable commercialization rather than merely a constraint on experimentation.

Global and Cross-Cultural Regulatory Complexity

AI-driven personalization systems increasingly operate across national and cultural boundaries, yet expectations regarding privacy, transparency, and fairness vary substantially across regions. Practices that are perceived as convenient and value-enhancing in one market may be interpreted as intrusive or manipulative in another. Cultural norms shape how consumers interpret data collection practices, automated recommendations, and algorithmic decision-making, directly influencing trust and adoption.

Firms pursuing international commercialization must therefore conduct contextual assessments before scaling personalization systems globally. These assessments should examine cultural tolerance for data collection and behavioral profiling, prevailing levels of trust in digital platforms and institutions, regional regulatory standards governing AI and privacy, and societal norms surrounding algorithmic transparency and fairness. Understanding these contextual variables enables firms to calibrate personalization intensity and governance mechanisms appropriately.

Localization strategies must integrate both regulatory compliance and cultural alignment. Merely satisfying legal requirements may be insufficient if personalization practices conflict with social expectations. Conversely, culturally sensitive design without regulatory alignment risks compliance violations. When organizations fail to account for these contextual dynamics, systems that perform successfully in one market may encounter resistance, reputational backlash, or slowed adoption in another—thereby widening the Valley of Death in cross-border commercialization efforts.

From Compliance to Strategic Legitimacy

The central insight of this section is that regulatory compliance, while necessary, is not sufficient to ensure sustainable AI commercialization. Minimal adherence to legal standards may protect firms from immediate sanctions, but it does not automatically generate trust, credibility, or long-term acceptance. Sustainable scaling requires legitimacy rather than mere compliance.

Legitimacy emerges when consumers perceive personalization systems as fair and respectful of their autonomy; when regulators observe structured, responsible governance practices; when external stakeholders recognize clear accountability mechanisms; and when employees themselves trust the integrity of internal processes. These perceptions collectively shape whether AI deployment is viewed as socially acceptable and institutionally responsible.

Organizations that position ethical governance as strategic infrastructure—embedded within product design, operational processes, and leadership accountability—are better positioned to scale AI-driven personalization effectively. By moving beyond a compliance mindset toward legitimacy-oriented governance, firms can strengthen resilience, reduce reputational risk, and build durable trust within complex commercial ecosystems.

Ethical Integration as Valley-of-Death Mitigation

Bridging the Valley of Death ultimately depends on reducing multiple forms of uncertainty—technological feasibility, market acceptance, and institutional stability. While firms often focus on technical validation and revenue projections, ethical and regulatory misalignment can introduce equally significant risks. When governance structures are weak or poorly integrated, organizations become vulnerable to consumer backlash, legal penalties, platform restrictions, and reputational crises. These uncertainties can stall scaling decisions, deter investment, and undermine long-term viability.

Integrating regulatory foresight and ethical governance early in the commercialization process reduces these uncertainties and strengthens stakeholder confidence. Proactive fairness auditing, autonomy-preserving design choices, and visible accountability mechanisms enhance what this chapter terms ethical legibility—the perception that AI systems operate fairly and responsibly. These elements are not peripheral safeguards; they are foundational determinants of commercialization viability in AI-driven personalization ecosystems.

The following section therefore examines the limitations of the proposed framework and identifies directions for future research, particularly regarding empirical validation, cross-cultural applicability, and evolving governance models in AI personalization commercialization.

LIMITATIONS AND FUTURE RESEARCH DIRECTIONS

While this chapter advances an integrated framework for bridging the Valley of Death in AI-driven personalization, several limitations warrant acknowledgment and point toward future research. The framework is conceptual and has not yet been empirically validated; its core dimensions—technical readiness, consumer readiness, ethical legibility, and ecosystem alignment—require operationalization into measurable constructs. Future studies should develop validated scales and examine their predictive power for outcomes such as adoption rates, scaling speed, trust development, and long-term performance. In addition, industry-specific dynamics may moderate the framework's applicability, as personalization in sectors such as fintech or healthcare operates under different regulatory pressures and risk profiles than retail or media. Comparative sectoral research could clarify whether certain dimensions, particularly ethical legibility, carry greater weight in high-risk environments.

Geographic and cultural variation also remains underexplored. Consumer tolerance for data-driven inference, transparency practices, and persuasive design differs across institutional contexts, suggesting the need for cross-regional studies examining how culture and regulatory maturity shape consumer readiness. The construct of ethical legibility itself requires deeper empirical refinement, particularly regarding how users interpret algorithmic explanations and whether perceived transparency aligns with objective fairness metrics. Experimental and longitudinal research could investigate how explainability design, visible fairness audits, and autonomy-enhancing controls influence trust trajectories over time. Furthermore, the framework does not explicitly model algorithmic drift or governance evolution, leaving open questions about how organizations adapt oversight mechanisms in response to performance decay, regulatory shifts, or competitive pressures. Longitudinal case studies could illuminate governance as a dynamic capability supporting socio-technical resilience.

Additional research should compare commercialization pathways between startups and established firms, examine the ethical boundaries of behavioral optimization through the lens of behavioral economics, and clarify when personalization shifts from assistance to manipulation. Finally, future work could operationalize the Valley of Death quantitatively by modeling indicators such as time-to-scale, adoption decay, regulatory delays, and consumer churn, thereby transforming it from a metaphor into a measurable strategic risk variable. Advancing this agenda requires interdisciplinary integration across marketing analytics, innovation theory, AI ethics, and institutional analysis. Only through systematic empirical validation can the proposed socio-technical framework evolve from conceptual synthesis into an evidence-based foundation for sustainable AI-driven personalization commercialization.

CONCLUSION

The rapid diffusion of artificial intelligence into commercial ecosystems has generated extraordinary expectations. AI-driven personalization, in particular, promises to transform how firms understand consumers, design experiences, and generate value. Yet the persistent failure of many AI initiatives to scale beyond pilot phases reveals a structural gap between technical innovation and sustainable commercialization. This gap—conceptualized as the Valley of Death—is not simply a funding problem or a performance issue. It is a socio-technical alignment challenge.

This chapter has argued that AI-driven personalization cannot be commercialized successfully through technical readiness alone. While robust models, scalable data pipelines, and interoperable architectures are necessary conditions, they are insufficient. Consumer readiness, ethical legibility, and ecosystem alignment are equally critical determinants of adoption, legitimacy, and long-term viability.

By integrating innovation management theory, market adoption frameworks, human–AI interaction research, and AI governance principles, this chapter introduced an Integrated Technology-Push and Market-Pull Framework for AI personalization transfer. The framework repositions commercialization as a multi-dimensional process in which algorithmic performance, user perception, ethical accountability, and institutional compliance must converge.

A central insight emerging from this analysis is that AI personalization systems function not merely as computational tools, but as active market actors. They shape consumer journeys, influence decision architectures, and participate in value co-creation. As a result, commercialization success depends not only on predictive accuracy, but on perceived fairness, transparency, and autonomy preservation. When personalization systems lack ethical legibility, consumer trust erodes. When ecosystem governance is weak, regulatory risk intensifies. When socio-technical alignment fails, innovations stagnate.

The implications are clear: bridging the Valley of Death requires reframing AI commercialization from an engineering problem to a strategic governance problem.

For firms, this means embedding fairness auditing, transparency mechanisms, and human-centered design into early development stages rather than retrofitting them after reputational crises. For startups and technology transfer offices, it means expanding commercialization criteria to include consumer legitimacy and regulatory foresight. For educators, it demands interdisciplinary training that prepares future leaders to integrate technical, psychological, and ethical reasoning. For policymakers, it underscores the need to design regulatory environments that protect consumers while enabling responsible innovation.

Importantly, this chapter does not position governance and ethics as constraints on innovation. Instead, it demonstrates that responsible integration is a pathway to scalability. Ethical legibility, consumer trust, and institutional alignment reduce uncertainty, mitigate risk, and enhance adoption. In this sense, legitimacy is not peripheral to commercialization—it is its foundation.

Looking forward, AI-driven personalization will continue to evolve toward increasingly autonomous and adaptive systems. As algorithmic systems become more embedded in everyday consumer environments, the boundary between service enhancement and behavioral influence will blur further. Organizations that treat AI as purely a performance optimization mechanism may achieve short-term gains but risk long-term erosion of trust. Those that integrate governance, transparency, and human–AI interaction as strategic assets will be better positioned to sustain competitive advantage.

Ultimately, the Valley of Death in AI commercialization is not inevitable. It reflects misalignment—between technology and market, innovation and trust, optimization and legitimacy. By adopting an integrated socio-technical perspective, firms can transform personalization from experimental capability into sustainable commercial infrastructure.

The future of AI-driven personalization will not be determined solely by algorithmic sophistication. It will be shaped by the capacity of organizations to align innovation with human values, regulatory expectations, and ecosystem coordination. Bridging this alignment is the strategic task ahead.

REFERENCES

Abd-Alrazaq, A. A., Alajlani, M., Alalwan, A. A., Bewick, B. M., Gardner, P., & Househ, M. (2019). An overview of the features of chatbots in mental health: A scoping review. *International Journal of Medical Informatics*, *132*, 103978. DOI: 10.1016/j.ijmedinf.2019.103978 PMID: 31622850

Aguirre, E., Mahr, D., Grewal, D., De Ruyter, K., & Wetzels, M. (2015). Unraveling the personalization paradox: The effect of information collection and trust-building strategies on online advertisement effectiveness. *Journal of Retailing*, *91*(1), 34–49. DOI: 10.1016/j.jretai.2014.09.005

Arora, N., Dreze, X., Ghose, A., Hess, J., Iyengar, R., Jing, B., & Zhang, Z. J. (2008). Putting one-to-one marketing to work: Personalization, customization, and choice. *Marketing Science*, *27*(3), 305–321. DOI: 10.1287/mksc.1070.0316

Auerswald, P. E., & Branscomb, L. M. (2003). Valleys of death and Darwinian seas. *The Journal of Technology Transfer*, *28*(3–4), 227–239. DOI: 10.1023/A:1024980525678

Barney, J. (1991). Firm resources and sustained competitive advantage. *Journal of Management*, *17*(1), 99–120. DOI: 10.1177/014920639101700108

Chesbrough, H. (2003). *Open innovation*. Harvard Business School Press.

Davenport, T. H., Guha, A., Grewal, D., & Bressgott, T. (2020). How artificial intelligence will change the future of marketing. *Journal of the Academy of Marketing Science*, *48*(1), 24–42. DOI: 10.1007/s11747-019-00696-0

Davis, F. D. (1989). Perceived usefulness, perceived ease of use, and user acceptance of information technology. *Management Information Systems Quarterly*, *13*(3), 319–340. DOI: 10.2307/249008

Dietvorst, B. J., Simmons, J. P., & Massey, C. (2015). Algorithm aversion. *Journal of Experimental Psychology. General*, *144*(1), 114–126. DOI: 10.1037/xge0000033 PMID: 25401381

Dignum, V. (2019). *Responsible artificial intelligence*. Springer., DOI: 10.1007/978-3-030-30371-6

Dosi, G. (1982). Technological paradigms and technological trajectories. *Research Policy*, *11*(3), 147–162. DOI: 10.1016/0048-7333(82)90016-6

Etzkowitz, H., & Leydesdorff, L. (2000). The dynamics of innovation. *Research Policy*, *29*(2), 109–123. DOI: 10.1016/S0048-7333(99)00055-4

Floridi, L., Cowls, J., Beltrametti, M., Chatila, R., Chazerand, P., Dignum, V., Luetge, C., Madelin, R., Pagallo, U., Rossi, F., Schafer, B., Valcke, P., & Vayena, E. (2018). AI4People—An ethical framework. *Minds and Machines, 28*(4), 689–707. DOI: 10.1007/s11023-018-9482-5 PMID: 30930541

Ghasemaghaei, M., & Calic, G. (2023). Artificial intelligence adoption and firm performance. *Journal of Business Research, 155*, 113391. DOI: 10.1016/j.jbusres.2022.113391

Glikson, E., & Woolley, A. W. (2020). Human trust in artificial intelligence. *Academy of Management Review, 45*(3), 627–660. DOI: 10.5465/amr.2018.0196

Huang, M.-H., & Rust, R. T. (2018). Artificial intelligence in service. *Journal of Service Research, 21*(2), 155–172. DOI: 10.1177/1094670517752459

Loureiro, S. M. C., Guerreiro, J., & Tussyadiah, I. (2021). Artificial intelligence in business. *Journal of Business Research, 129*, 911–926. DOI: 10.1016/j.jbusres.2020.11.001

Markman, G. D., Siegel, D. S., & Wright, M. (2008). Research and technology commercialization. *Journal of Management Studies, 45*(8), 1401–1423. DOI: 10.1111/j.1467-6486.2008.00803.x

Mittelstadt, B. D., Allo, P., Taddeo, M., Wachter, S., & Floridi, L. (2016). The ethics of algorithms. *Big Data & Society, 3*(2), 2053951716679679. Advance online publication. DOI: 10.1177/2053951716679679

Norberg, P. A., Horne, D. R., & Horne, D. A. (2007). The privacy paradox. *The Journal of Consumer Affairs, 41*(1), 100–126. DOI: 10.1111/j.1745-6606.2006.00070.x

Obermeyer, Z., Powers, B., Vogeli, C., & Mullainathan, S. (2019). Dissecting racial bias in an algorithm. *Science, 366*(6464), 447–453. DOI: 10.1126/science.aax2342 PMID: 31649194

Paschen, J., Pitt, C., & Kietzmann, J. (2020). Artificial intelligence in marketing. *Journal of Business Research, 124*, 404–414. DOI: 10.1016/j.jbusres.2020.10.016

Rai, A. (2020). Explainable AI. *Journal of the Academy of Marketing Science, 48*(1), 137–141. DOI: 10.1007/s11747-019-00710-5

Ribeiro, M. T., Singh, S., & Guestrin, C. (2016). "Why should I trust you?" Explaining the predictions of any classifier. *Proceedings of the ACM SIGKDD*, 1135–1144. https://doi.org/DOI: 10.1145/2939672.2939778

Shneiderman, B. (2022). Human-centered AI. *International Journal of Human-Computer Interaction, 38*(16), 1472–1492. DOI: 10.1080/10447318.2022.2071257

Teece, D. J. (1986). Profiting from technological innovation. *Research Policy*, *15*(6), 285–305. DOI: 10.1016/0048-7333(86)90027-2

Venkatesh, V., Morris, M. G., Davis, G. B., & Davis, F. D. (2003). User acceptance of information technology. *Management Information Systems Quarterly*, *27*(3), 425–478. DOI: 10.2307/30036540

KEY TERMS AND DEFINITIONS

AI-Driven Personalization: The use of artificial intelligence systems, including machine learning and predictive analytics, to dynamically tailor content, recommendations, pricing, or user experiences based on individual behavioral data, preferences, and contextual signals.

Algorithmic Bias: Systematic and repeatable distortions in AI outputs resulting from skewed training data, flawed model design, or contextual misalignment, leading to unequal or discriminatory outcomes across demographic or behavioral groups.

Commercial Governance Architecture: The formal structures, oversight mechanisms, compliance processes, and accountability systems established within organizations to manage AI risks and ensure ethical deployment.

Consumer Readiness: The extent to which target users understand, trust, and accept AI-driven systems, including their perceived usefulness, fairness, and transparency.

Dynamic Capability (AI Governance Context): An organizational capability that enables firms to continuously monitor, adapt, and recalibrate AI systems in response to regulatory shifts, performance drift, and stakeholder expectations.

Ecosystem Alignment: The coordination between innovation producers, platform operators, regulators, and complementary stakeholders to ensure interoperability, compliance, governance integration, and market scalability.

Ethical Legibility: The degree to which AI systems are perceived as fair, transparent, accountable, and aligned with normative expectations. Ethical legibility emphasizes stakeholder interpretation of algorithmic legitimacy rather than technical fairness metrics alone.

Explainability: The capacity of an AI system to provide understandable and interpretable justifications for its outputs, enabling users and stakeholders to assess its reasoning processes.

Fairness Auditing: The systematic evaluation of AI systems to detect and mitigate discriminatory patterns, performance disparities, or unintended exclusion effects across user segments.

Human–AI Interaction (HAII): The design and experience layer through which users engage with AI systems. HAII includes interface transparency, explainability features, control mechanisms, and communication cues that influence trust and adoption.

Market-Pull Strategy: A commercialization approach driven by consumer demand, market needs, and user expectations, shaping innovation design and deployment decisions.

Privacy Paradox: The phenomenon in which consumers express concern about data privacy while simultaneously engaging with personalized digital services that require data sharing.

Responsible AI: An approach to AI development and deployment that prioritizes fairness, transparency, accountability, privacy protection, and alignment with societal values.

Socio-Technical Alignment: The coordinated integration of technological performance, consumer perception, ethical standards, and institutional governance necessary for sustainable AI commercialization.

Technical Readiness: The degree to which an AI system demonstrates robustness, scalability, interoperability, and operational reliability within production environments. Often associated with Technology Readiness Levels (TRLs).

Technology Transfer: The structured process through which innovations developed in research institutions, laboratories, or startups are translated into commercially viable products, services, or platforms within market ecosystems.

Technology-Push Strategy: A commercialization approach driven primarily by technological advancement and R&D breakthroughs, where innovation supply precedes clear market demand.

Uncanny Effect (AI Context): A psychological discomfort experienced when AI systems appear overly predictive, intrusive, or human-like, reducing trust and increasing resistance.

Valley of Death (Innovation Commercialization): The critical transition gap between research and development (R&D) and large-scale market deployment, where innovations demonstrate technical feasibility but fail to achieve sustainable commercialization due to financial, institutional, market, or legitimacy barriers.

Chapter 5 Comparative Assessment of Technology Transfer Readiness for Commercial Human–AI Interaction: Evidence From the USA, Germany, Japan, and India

Jayeshkumar Pathak
http://orcid.org/0000-0003-4584-3506
Parul University, India

Satish Kumar
http://orcid.org/0000-0001-6071-0109
G.L. Bajaj Institute of Technology and Management, India

Sakshi Narula
http://orcid.org/0009-0000-8302-1250
Chandigarh University, India

Pardeep Bawa Sharma
http://orcid.org/0000-0003-2703-1600
Chandigarh University, India

ABSTRACT

This paper aimed at comparing readiness to transfer technology to commercial human-AI interaction in the United States, Germany, Japan, and India. This work

DOI: 10.4018/979-8-3373-9325-4.ch005

explains how the differences in national systems of innovation and policy environments are critically important in determining the capability of scaling AI-based interaction technologies. The study followed descriptive and comparative research design based solely on secondary quantitative data. Thematically synthesized standardized indicators concerning global innovation performance, digital readiness, AI governance and commercialization capacity are measured using descriptive benchmarking to determine cross-national similarities and differences. The results indicate that national models of technology transfer preparedness are distinct: the United States is characterized by the market-driven and fast commercialization path; Germany and Japan are characterized by the coordinated, institutionally based, and human-centered models; and India is an emerging and state-controlled, diffusion-oriented model.

1. INTRODUCTION

1.1 AI and Human-AI Interaction

The rapid development of artificial intelligence has radically changed the ways how people and organizations can communicate with digital systems and has created commercially viable ways of human-AI interaction in the marketing, customer service, healthcare, manufacturing, and many other such sectors. These interactions have moved beyond the experimental and research environments and have become an inseparable part of the everyday business operations using applications such as AI-enabled customer engagement systems, virtual assistants, recommendation algorithms, and intelligent branding solutions (Khanal, Zhang, & Taeihagh, 2025). With the maturation of AI technologies, the strategic challenge facing the firms and nations is not only in the creation of innovation, but also in the successful transfer of AI knowledge, capabilities, and research outputs into scalable commercial applications. Technology transfer therefore takes a leading role in filling the research-market deployment gap which includes a network of institutional, regulatory, infrastructural and organizational processes which brings about commercialization of innovation (Scantamburlo et al., 2025).

1.2 Technology Transfer and Commercialization Readiness in AI

Technology transfer preparedness in human-AI interaction context refers to the degree to which countries are able to transform AI-related research, data resources, and human capital into commercially viable solutions that can be utilized to improve productivity, user experience, and competitive advantage. The more developed transfer ecosystems a country has, the better it is placed to realize the rapid diffusion and stronger penetration of the AI-based interaction technologies into the business settings (Pande, Khanal, & Taeihagh, 2025; Rowe et al., 2024). Even more complicated is the commercialization of human-AI interaction as it requires the incorporation of the principles of technological sophistication with human-centered design, ethical considerations, and user trust (Flew, 2024). The readiness of national innovation systems to facilitate responsible, scalable, and market-oriented application has become a decisive factor as organizations are starting to make an increased use of AI-mediated interfaces. Major facilitating factors are the digital infrastructure, the level of innovation, regulatory coherence, industry-academia cooperation, and effective AI governance systems (Hartley & Aldag, 2024; Sharma & Kumar, 2024). Based on this, the evaluation of technology transfer preparedness should follow a holistic approach which goes beyond the technical measures to the institutional and socio-economic aspects (Khanal, Zhang, & Taeihagh, 2024; Sharma, Kaur, and Pathak, 2025). Although the literature concerning AI adoption and commercialization is increasing, the available literature is primarily based on firm or industry-specific analysis without much consideration on cross-national comparative analysis of technology transfer systems. In addition, most of the available literature is based on qualitative methods or survey research, which, although valuable, might not have the power to provide macro-level readiness trends in detail. Conversely, secondary data based on world indices and policy reports report standardized and comparable indicators of national capability in the areas of innovation, digital infrastructure, quality of governance and commercialization potential. These clues do not only inform the policy discourse, but also define the overall commercial ecosystem in which the interaction between humans and AI develops.

1.3 Framing the Study: Scope and Focus

The research is set on technology transfer preparedness, which is used as the analytical prism capable of comprehending the manner in which artificial intelligence technologies transform into scalable and economically viable ones. In this context, the field of human-AI interaction is analyzed as a practical area to consider the results of commercialization, but it is not considered a unique phenomenon. Instead, it can be viewed as a contextual prism in terms of which the ability of national systems to transform AI capabilities into market-ready, user-oriented solutions can be assessed critically. Moreover, the research takes a cross-national comparative approach, which allows making systematic benchmarking in different institutional and economic contexts. This would help move out of the purely descriptive explanations of AI adoption and toward a more sophisticated analysis of the structural and systemic factors of business preparedness. The focus on the readiness to transfer technologies is especially crucial since the successful commercialization of AI, in particular, in the context of human-AI interaction, is not only technologically advanced but also the capacity of the national ecosystems to facilitate diffusion, scalability, and acceptance by the users. The existing literature has mostly focused on the technical aspects or micro-level adoption behaviours of AI systems that do not necessarily consider the larger commercialization processes happening at the micro and macro levels. The current study aims to overcome this shortcoming and provide a more integrated view of the interplay of innovation systems, governance structures, and market dynamics to influence the creation and introduction of AI-based business applications with technology transfer as the main constrcut.

1.4 Country Selection and Comparative Context

The choice of the United States, Germany, Japan, and India is based on the fact that they represent different developmental paths and institutional structures in the field of AI commercialization: the market-driven model, industry-coordinated model, the human-centered and robotics-focused model, and an emerging, digitally growing economy, respectively. This comparative prism allows gaining a subtle insight into the differences in preparedness in the world and their consequences in terms of human-AI interaction in a commercial environment.

2. LITERATURE REVIEW

2.1 Technology Transfer and AI Commercialization

The growing significance of artificial intelligence in business ecosystems has, in turn, triggered an academic interest in the processes that occur to deliver AI innovations to the market as viable solutions (Lockey & Gillespie, 2024). The main idea of this discussion is the technology transfer readiness as the ability of national and institutional systems to successfully transfer the technological know-how in research fields to the business worlds. This preparedness is especially essential in the field of human-AI interaction, since the commercialization success does not rely solely on the technical excellence, but also on the user-centered design, ethical management, and alignment with the ecosystem (Novozhilova, Mays, & Katz, 2024; Bawa, 2016). The literature continues to describe technology transfer as a multi-dimensional construct that is influenced by the innovation systems, digital infrastructures, institutional settings, and market forces (Pande & Taeihagh, 2024; Scantamburlo et al., 2025). Countries that have well-developed research systems, high-quality intellectual property frameworks, and well-organized industry-academic connections are likely to enjoy high commercialization rates of high-tech technology, such as the AI-powered interaction systems like conversational agents and smart-decision systems.

2.2 Innovation Systems, Digital Infrastructure, and Governance

The innovativeness and digital infrastructure is generally known as the cornerstone prerequisites of AI commercialization (Liang, Zhang & Zhou, 2025; Sharma & Sarmah, 2020). A large amount of research and development capital leading to high digital connectivity, data availability, and computational assets contributes to increase the scale of human-AI interaction technologies in the country. Digital readiness enables a smooth incorporation of AI-based applications into consumer-facing settings, whereas a long-term innovation potential guarantees constant improvement and adjustment (Cukurova, 2025; Rožman, Oreški, & Tominc, 2023). According to comparative evidence, the differences in these areas lead to inequalities in the dissemination of AI across the countries and support the relevance of cross-national benchmarking. Institutional and governance considerations also influence the outcome of technology transfer by creating a regulatory and policy environment through which AI commercialization is occurring (McDaniel, 2025). Leadership structures that create a balance between incentive and ethical aspects of innovation; data protection and accountability are critical towards establishing user confidence and acceptance in the market. Regulatory clarity and institutional coordination are key indicators of countries whose success in investment attraction and AI-driven business models is more prevalent (Costa, & Marques, 2025; Bawa and Bathurutheen, 2016). The importance of commercialization ecosystems such as the environment of startups, the presence of venture capital, and networks of people in the industry, as the pathways of interactions between research and commercialization, is also important (Laux, Wachter, & Mittelstadt, 2024). Effective entrepreneurial ecosystems can be seen as enhancing the rate of diffusion of AI technologies because they provide opportunities to experiment, scale, and innovate. Such ecosystems are especially favourable in terms of the fast development and deployment of user-oriented applications in the context of human-AI interaction (Hongladarom & Bandasak, 2024; Jarrahi et al., 2023). Comparative insights indicate that there is a significant difference in the number of nations that fund AI startups and transfer technology by use of incubators, accelerators, and public-private connections.

2.3 Commercialization Ecosystems and Cross-National Perspectives

More often, researchers have applied comparative benchmarking techniques based on secondary data of world indices to measure macro-level technology transfer preparedness (Jiyoung, Woo, & Kim, 2024; Gołąb-Andrzejak, 2023). Through these approaches, the identification of the national strengths and weaknesses in various dimensions can be done and the insights can be provided which otherwise would not be easily noticed in the studies at the micro level. Such methodological orientation is particularly suitable to the study of human-AI interaction, where the systemic factors, as opposed to isolated factors, determine the outcomes (Ancillai et al., 2023; Bawa, 2017).

Even beyond the countries that have been chosen to be analyzed, the global path of artificial intelligence commercialization is highly heterogeneous in terms of regions. Though, this research focuses on the United States, Germany, Japan, and India as examples of the developed and developing technology transfer regimes, the process of AI technologies diffusion and commercialization is far broader than national settings. In the emerging parts of the world like Southeast Asia, Africa, and South America, the interaction between humans and AI is being embraced in different structural, institutional, and developmental contexts. Singapore and Indonesia are two economies in Southeast Asia that are developing and applying AI in areas like financial technology, education, and smart urban systems, with the development of digital infrastructures and an active state-driven innovation agenda. The African background, in turn, indicates a more development-focused direction, with the applications of AI being tightly interconnected with the urgent needs of society, especially in agriculture, healthcare diagnostics, and financial inclusion, although within the frames of insufficient infrastructure and regulatory changes. On the same note, South American countries are exploring AI-related solutions in the field of the state administration, retail, and natural resources management, which suggests a slow but inconsistent trend of digitalization. Such regional differences highlight the degree to which the commercialization of AI is socialized by the differences in the socio-economic realities, institutional capacities, and policy ecosystems. In this regard, although the current research uses a narrow comparative prism, conceptual framework it pursues. has a wider applicability, as it presents an opportunity to understand how technology transfer preparedness can determine AI implementation and commercialization in different global settings.

Despite the increasing interest in the commercialization of AI, there are still many gaps in literature, specifically in integrated transnational evaluation of readiness to transfer technology in humans-AI interaction. The existing literature explored the adoption of AI in broad areas or dwelled upon the technical and ethical aspects of it but does not explicitly connect this interpretation to the technological transfer processes. Moreover, the use of qualitative case studies or primary data restricts comparability and generalizability. A significant lack of such research that proves indicators of innovation, infrastructure, governance, and commercialization into a single comparative framework is apparent. Different national strategies toward AI technology transfer are also reflected in the literature: market-based systems are based on the dominance of the leadership of the private sector and venture capital; coordinated models are based on the collaboration of institutions and state backing; human-centric models are based on the dominance of the usability and social acceptance; and emerging economy models are based on the dominance of the scalability and digital inclusion. These differences are essential in interpreting differences in business performance and in making strategic decisions. In general, the available literature supports the necessity of a systematic, comparative analysis of technology transfer readiness based on secondary data and, therefore, allows understanding the role of national ecosystems in influencing the commercialization of technologies of human-AI interaction more comprehensively.

Building on the above review, which highlights the critical role of technology transfer readiness, institutional enablers, and cross-national differences in shaping AI commercialization, the following objectives are formulated to systematically examine these dimensions through a comparative framework.

3. OBJECTIVES

1. To assess technology transfer readiness for commercial human-AI interaction in the United States, Germany, Japan, and India using secondary indicators.
2. To compare national innovation and digital infrastructure capabilities supporting commercial human-AI interaction across the selected countries.
3. To examine institutional and governance-related factors influencing AI technology transfer and commercialization in the selected countries.
4. To benchmark the selected countries on key human-AI interaction commercialization readiness dimensions using descriptive analysis.
5. To identify cross-country similarities and differences in technology transfer pathways for commercial human-AI interaction.

The next section explains the methodology to achieve these objectives in a systematic and structured way.

4. RESEARCH METHODOLOGY

This research used a cross country qualitative comparative research design based on secondary data supported with descriptive statistics. This method is especially appropriate since the readiness of technology transfer and commercialization of the human-AI interaction is a macro-level phenomenon that is affected by the institutional, technological, and policy-related factors. These dimensions can be measured with the help of globally accepted indices and international data sets. The data were collected based on the credible and authoritative reports, such as global innovation and competitiveness reports, national and international AI readiness reports, ICT development indicators, intellectual property and patent databases, and policy analyses of AI governance. All indicators were harmonized with consistent definitions, measurement units, and data periods so that the indicators were consistent across countries. In cases where there were different sources that were measured differently or on a different scale, they were normalized to a comparable scale so that meaningful comparisons could be made. As an example, the measurements of indices that were expressed on varying numeric scales were transformed into a standardized range of 0-100, and qualitative scores were pegged to international standards. This standardization of the approach allowed the comparative analysis of real differences in readiness as opposed to measurement or reporting differences among countries. The latest figures of each country were condensed and harmonized so that they could be compared directly across countries. The similarities and differences were compared and contrasted through descriptive statistical techniques, such as comparative index scores, rankings and relative positions. The data are shown through comparative tables to promote benchmarking, interpretation, and transparency. Inferential statistics was not used since the study was exploratory and comparative. The analysis aims at detecting trends and making significant conclusions based on quantitative indicators. The study guarantees the methodological transparency, reliability, and rigor by incorporating several credible secondary data sources, analytical framework, and harmonization, which offers a systematic methodology to evaluate national preparedness to transfer technology in human-AI interaction. The implementation of this methodological framework allows to conduct a systematic assessment of the level of technology transfer preparedness in the chosen countries, the findings of which are presented and discussed in the next section.

5. ANALYSIS

The analysis part of the paper offers a comparative assessment of the readiness to transfer technology on the basis of commercial human-AI interaction in the four chosen countries. Arranged according to the objectives of the study, the analysis utilizes the comparative benchmarking to explore convergences and divergences of national capabilities. The study is multidimensional because it organizes the indicators into major dimensions: technology transfer preparedness, innovation and digital infrastructure, institutional and governance support, commercialization preparedness, and technology transfer pathways. The standardized quantitative measures allow the use of strong cross-national comparison and reduce subjectivity. The analysis does not focus on the identification of causal relationships; instead, the structural patterns, the relative strengths, and gaps in the system that affect the translation of AI innovation into commercial human-AI interaction are identified. The findings are tabulated and explained in the framework of the national innovation systems and institutional perspectives.

Table 1. Technology Transfer Readiness Indicators for Commercial Human-AI Interaction

Metric (Secondary Indicator)	United States	Germany	Japan	India
Global Innovation Index Score (0-100)	61.8	57.3	54.7	40.6
R&D Expenditure (% of GDP)	3.45	3.13	3.26	0.77
AI Readiness Index Score (0-100)	85.2	79.1	78.3	60.2
University–Industry Collaboration Index (0-100)	82.4	76.8	74.5	55.6
High-Tech Patent Applications (per million population)	285	190	210	32
Digital Infrastructure Index (0-100)	88.6	84.9	86.1	62.7
Venture Capital Investment in AI (USD billion)	67.2	12.4	15.1	8.3
Technology Transfer Efficiency Score (0-100)	81.5	75.2	73.6	56.8

Source: Author compilation

Table 1 results indicate that there are strong cross-country differences in the general preparedness of technology transfer. US is on the top of the list in most of the indicators, which boasts of high innovation environment and better commercialization preparedness. The scores of the Global Innovation Index are high, and the proportion of research and development investments to GDP is large, highlighting the strong background to the implementation of AI research in the market. The high degree of university-industry partnership and a huge presence of venture capital in AI also boosts the ability of the country to successfully transfer human-AI interaction technology between research and commercialization. The fact that there is high technology transfer efficiency reveals that the institutional and market mechanisms are well functioning to ensure that commercialization acts fast. Germany and Japan exhibit a relatively similar level of preparedness, although because of structural peculiarities.

The advantages Germany has are in its highly established innovation system, a large investment in industrial R&D, and in high coordination of academia and industry, which would allow making the AI technologies incremental and industry-focused in terms of commercialization. Japan has competitive scores on R&D intensity, digital infrastructure, and high-tech patenting, which is indicative of its focus on human-centered AI, robotics, and applied innovation. The two nations are highly rated in the preparedness of AI and digital infrastructure, which means that the conditions are favorable to scale commercial human-AI interaction, but the country has lower venture capital ecosystems in comparison with the United States. Conversely, though India scores poorly on various indicators when compared to developed economies, it shows a developing preparedness. Weaker R&D investment, patent intensity, and collaboration are indicative of structural constraints; but moderate AI preparedness and augmented digital infrastructure is a sign of rising foundational capabilities, through the increasing connectivity digitally and an emerging AI startup ecosystem.

The numbers in table 1 indicate that foundational readiness is not uniformly distributed as there are obvious asymmetries in digital capacity and access among countries. These distinctions are not a sign of overall ability, but rather a difference in the amount of readiness to consume and expand AI applications. Interestingly, the increase in the infrastructure scores seems to be associated with the increase in the consistency of the performance across indicators, which reflects the systemic stability. On the contrary, the new systems are characterized by areas of progress and structural gaps, signifying partial but not integrated preparedness. This divergence points out to the fact that infrastructure is not sufficient to guarantee smooth commercialization, rather it delineates the conditions under which innovation can take place. The results therefore highlight the significance of consistency between technological capacity and institutional underpinning structures. In sum, table 1 defines the conditions of the base that determines the further dimensions of technology transfer preparedness. (Refer to table 1 the results)

In table 2, the comparative evaluation of innovation capacity and digital infrastructure is presented, which are the key enablers of commercial human-AI interaction.

Table 2. Innovation and Digital Infrastructure Capabilities Supporting Commercial Human-AI Interaction

Metric (Secondary Indicator)	United States	Germany	Japan	India
Digital Competitiveness Index Score (0-100)	89.3	82.7	84.1	61.5
ICT Development Index Score (0-10)	8.9	8.6	8.7	6.1
Broadband Penetration (subscriptions per 100 people)	92.4	90.1	88.6	67.3
Cloud Computing Adoption Rate (%)	74.5	66.2	68.9	52.6

continued on following page

Table 2. Continued

Metric (Secondary Indicator)	United States	Germany	Japan	India
Data Center Capacity (MW per million population)	38.7	22.4	26.1	8.9
AI Research Publications (per million population)	412	285	301	94
Availability of Skilled AI Workforce (Index 0-100)	86.7	78.9	80.3	58.4
Digital Public Infrastructure Maturity Score (0-100)	83.5	79.6	81.2	74.8

Source: Author compilation

United States shows better results, especially in digital competencies, cloud computing usage, capacities of data centers and output of AI research. Further broadband penetration and developed cloud computing supports easy implementation of AI-based interfaces like conversational agents, recommendation systems and forms of customer engagement. An extremely talented workforce of AI also contributes to the creation of an innovation base by constantly enhancing and polishing technologies of human-AI interaction. The capability profiles in Germany and Japan are advanced, which are characteristics of mature and differentiated innovation systems. Germany has good ICT development, broadband coverage and is characterized by good human capital which facilitates AI application on industries and enterprises. Similarly equipped with relatively more mature digital infrastructure, Japan ranks among the nations with a relatively higher level of AI research, matching robotics, embedded AI, and human-centered design capabilities. The cloud adoption and the presence of the digital public infrastructure is also strong in both countries, which allows the effective implementation of AI systems in the business and government spheres. India is such a different though changing profile. Despite low rates of broadband penetration, data center capacity, intensity of AI research, and workforce availability, it is very strong in digital public infrastructure, which is a strategic focus on scalability and digital inclusion. Mediocre scores in cloud adoption and ICT development show an increased willingness to embrace cost-effective high-volume human-AI interaction application.

Results show that not only the intensity of investment is an important factor in innovation capacity, but also the interconnectedness of knowledge systems. Nations that have developed ecosystems are not only more productive, but also more efficient in transforming research into usable innovations. By contrast, new systems are characterized by indications of growth, but these frequently are fragmented and diffused unevenly. The difference between indicators implies that the level of innovation performance can be affected by not only the depth of structures but also the level of coordination between key actors. Notably, the statistics show that robust research abilities do not necessarily result in commercialization without facilitating ecosystems. It highlights the difference between innovation generation and innovation utilization. (Refer to table 2 for results)

Table 3 focuses on institutional and governance aspects affecting transferring and commercializing AI technologies.

Table 3. Institutional and Governance Factors Influencing AI Technology Transfer and Commercialization

Metric (Secondary Indicator)	United States	Germany	Japan	India
Government AI Strategy Implementation Score (0-100)	82.6	79.4	81.1	70.3
Regulatory Quality Index (–2.5 to +2.5)	1.58	1.63	1.47	0.12
Rule of Law Index (0-1)	0.74	0.83	0.81	0.55
Data Protection and Privacy Enforcement Score (0–100)	78.9	85.6	82.4	67.2
Ease of Doing Business Score (0-100)	84.1	79.8	78.5	71
Intellectual Property Protection Index (0-100)	86.5	88.2	84.7	63.9
Public–Private Partnership Intensity Index (0-100)	81.3	83.7	80.2	65.4
AI Governance Maturity Score (0-100)	80.7	82.9	81.6	69.1

Source: Author compilation

Germany and the United States become the leaders in the quality of the governance, though they are differently institutional. Germany is the best in terms of quality regulation, rule of law, intellectual property protection, and government-business cooperation as it demonstrates a well-coordinated and predictable system of governance, which promotes the stable and industry-oriented transfer of technology. The presence of robust data protection protocols also increases the level of trust within the user, which is an essential aspect of commercialization of AI-mediated interactions. United States also scores well on indicators of governance, especially ease of doing business, intellectual property protection and implementation of AI strategies. It has a relatively lenient regulatory regime and a strong IP protection regime which enables quick commercialization by the relatively private sector, but data protection regulations are relatively weaker than in Germany. Japan has a fairly integrated institutional structure, which is indicated by a high score in such dimensions as AI governance maturity, rule of law, data protection, and productive interaction between governmental and non-governmental participants. It has an orientation towards governance, with a specific focus on ethical factors and a humanistic approach to AI, which leads to the creation of more trust and acceptance of AI in the business. The quality of its regulatory framework is slightly lower than the one witnessed in Germany and the United States, but the general quality of its institutional framework enables stable and predictable technology transfer procedures. India, on the other hand, is more moderate in terms of governance preparedness. The fact that the scores are low in the categories like regulatory quality, rule of law, and intellectual property protection is indicative of structural limitations that can hinder the effectiveness of the technology transfer mechanism. Simultaneously, comparatively high scores on the AI strategy implementation and the collaboration between the public and the private indicate the growing policy focus and involvement of the institution in the field of AI. Combined, the evidence in Table 3 highlights the importance of the quality of governance, the clarity of regulations, and the coordination of the institutions to facilitate the responsible and effective commercialization of technologies based on human-AI interaction.

The data in table 3 also indicate that governance as a phenomenon is rather a stabilizing factor rather than a direct driver of technological development. Cross-country differences denote that differences in the clarity of the regulations, institutional trust, and policy stability have an impact on the larger setting, in which AI systems are designed and implemented. These situations, where there are strong governance mechanisms, are more likely to provide predictability and increased ability to reduce the risk, which means that there will be more systematic uptake of new technologies. These results suggest that although governance does not necessarily suggest that it can speed up innovation, it is decisive in maintaining and legitimizing innovation. The situation of the institution, then, takes centre stage in the minimization of frictions in the process of transferring the technology. In this respect, table 3 gives a synthesized perspective of the effects of institutional environments in the progression of technological capability to credible and scalable commercialization.

Table 4 assesses the level of commercialization preparedness, and it shows that there is a significant difference in the capacity of countries to transform AI capabilities into large scale commercial uses.

Table 4. Benchmarking Human-AI Interaction Commercialization Readiness

Metric (Commercialization Readiness Indicator)	United States	Germany	Japan	India
AI Startup Density (startups per million population)	58.4	24.7	27.9	12.6
AI Market Size (USD billion)	165.3	38.6	42.1	21.4
Commercial AI Adoption Rate (% of firms)	62.8	54.2	56.7	38.9
Human-AI Interaction Deployment Index (0-100)	84.6	76.3	78.9	63.1
Availability of AI Commercial Platforms (Index 0-100)	88.2	79.4	81.6	66.8
Industry Digital Transformation Index (0-100)	86.9	80.2	82.4	68.7
AI Scale-Up Success Rate (%)	41.3	29.6	31.8	18.5
Cross-Sector AI Integration Score (0-100)	85.1	78.7	80.9	65.2

Source: Author compilation

The US has the high levels of readiness in all the indicators, which is backed by an extensive network of AI startups, responsive and large market size, and participation of venture capital. The level of commercialization is evident in high AI implementation rates especially in marketing, finance, and digital platform which is further enhanced by the established scaling mechanisms. Germany and Japan are at the middle, with the proven and well-financed systems of commercialization in place. The advantages of Germany are in the digital transformation of industrial sectors and a high cross-sector integration, in particular, manufacturing and logistics, whereas Japan has the comparatively better deployment of human-AI interaction technologies in accordance with its user-centric and service-oriented strategy. Despite the fact that both nations have less startup base and market size as compared to the United States, their commercialization performance is maintained through strong institutional and industrial demand. India, in its turn, is a developing ecosystem, with a weaker base of startups and a weaker scaling, but with a slow improvement in platform accessibility, digitalization, and integration of sectors, specifically fintech and e-commerce. Comprehensively, Table 4 indicates that the results of commercialization do not solely rely on the technological capability, but also on the depth of the market, the dynamism of the entrepreneur and the efficiency of the scaling processes.

The cross-country difference as seen in table 4 demonstrates that there are differences in the degree of translating the technological capabilities into market results. The good performance on commercialization is highly related with active market connection, availability of capital and entrepreneurial ability. Simultaneously, the results have shown that commercialization is formed as a result of the interplay of different system elements, as opposed to being a terminal innovation in isolation. Integrated ecosystems are more likely to enable a smoother development to deployment, compared to fragmented systems, which have bottlenecks to underlying capabilities. This indicates the significance of coordination between research institutions and the industry players and financial systems.

Table 5 presents a comparative analysis of national technology transfer pathways, highlighting distinct institutional approaches to AI commercialization.

Table 5. Cross-Country Comparison of Technology Transfer Pathways for Commercial Human-AI Interaction

Metric (Comparative Pathway Indicator)	United States	Germany	Japan	India
Public R&D Share in Total AI R&D (%)	28.6	41.9	38.7	54.2
Private Sector Contribution to AI Commercialization (%)	71.4	58.1	61.3	45.8
Industry-Oriented AI Transfer Index (0-100)	76.5	84.2	80.1	62.7

continued on following page

Table 5. Continued

Metric (Comparative Pathway Indicator)	United States	Germany	Japan	India
Market-Driven AI Commercialization Score (0-100)	88.7	72.4	74.9	65.3
Human-Centric AI Deployment Index (0-100)	79.6	77.8	83.5	70.2
Government-Led AI Diffusion Score (0-100)	68.4	75.9	73.6	82.1
SME Participation in AI Transfer (%)	46.8	58.2	54.7	63.4
Speed of AI Commercialization (years from lab to market)	2.1	3.4	3.1	4.6

Source: Author compilation

The United States is a market-based channel whereby private enterprise, venture capital and startup ecosystem has been at the core of commercialization acceleration. This model is linked with high efficiency and reduced commercialization time with the larger part of the enablers being the public sector. In Germany, by contrast, there is a more organized approach to the industrial policy, with high levels of government spending on R&D, involvement of SMEs, and industry networks. This makes technology transfer more gradual and systematic with longer timelines but more stability and quality, especially in the industrial applications. Japan represents a hybrid direction which incorporates the aspects of industrial coordination and high priority given to the human-centric deployment. Its emphasis on usability, trust and social acceptance contributes to stable and socially entrenched commercialization although at a comparatively slower rate. India in its turn follows a diffusion-based and policy-oriented strategy, with the prospectives of technology transfer determined by the governmental initiatives, programs of development of digital infrastructure, and involvement of SME in the process. Even though commercialization is a slower process, it is a more accessible and scalable route, especially in cost-sensitive situations. On the whole, Table 5 shows that the preparedness of technology transfer depends on both the national opportunities and the institutional channels through which AI innovations can be converted into market deliverables, with their own advantages and disadvantages.

The results indicate that the performance is not decided by the excellence in one of the dimensions, but by the extent of the compatibility of infrastructure, the ability to be innovative, the governance and the market structures. Systems that are coherent in all these aspects are more likely to have consistent commercialization results, and lack of balance in each dimension can hamper performance in spite of strengths in particular domains. This supports the scholarship that technology transfer preparedness is naturally multidimensional and cannot be properly evaluated separately. Differences between countries also indicate the difference in the level of systemic maturity, where some countries are fully integrated and some are in the transitional development stages. In this regard, table 5 gives a holistic view of the systemic coherence of AI commercialization effectiveness and scalability.

The results presented above give a comparative approach towards national preparedness of AI commercialization. These results are discussed in the following discussion section to interpret them in terms of available theoretical frameworks and to point out their general implications.

6. DISCUSSION

6.1 Key Findings and Comparative Insights

The current research paper reviews the readiness of technology transfer in terms of commercial interaction between humans and AI by comparing the United States, Germany, Japan, and India with regard to various indicators. Transcending a very limited perspective on AI commercialization as an entirely technological product, the analysis includes the aspects of innovation capacity, the presence of digital infrastructure, the system of governance, and the commercialization avenues as the explanations of the cross-national differences. The results continuously indicate that the preparedness of technology transfer is preconditioned by the extent of alignment between the research ecosystems, institutional structures, and market forces, which supports the available body of literature about the centrality of the national innovation systems and technology transfer models (Mihai, Aleca, and Gheorghe, 2023; Khanom, 2023; Perifanis and Kitsios, 2023 In the countries under consideration, the United States stands out as the most developed in the context of technology transfer preparedness, which is largely due to good innovation performance, well-developed digital infrastructure, and a rather market-oriented model of commercialization. Abundant access to private capital, vibrant startup culture, and comparatively lenient regulatory frameworks enable the commercial application of artificial intelligence research to be translated into commercial outcomes at an exceptionally rapid pace. These results are consistent with the existing literature on the value of venture capital intensity and entrepreneurial ecosystems in enhancing the AI commercialization process (Aldoseri et al., 2023; Karkošková, 2023; Grebe, Franke, and Heinzl, 2023). Simultaneously, the findings show that whereas market-driven models are efficient in facilitating speed and scalability, they can be relatively less intensive on the long-term institutional coordination. This brings up significant questions concerning the concept of sustainability, governance, and ethical responsibility, especially in the field of human-AI interaction, where the questions of trust and user-centeredness are in the main focus.

6.2 Implications for Technology Transfer Models and Commercialization Pathways

Alternative, but equally educative models of technology transfer preparedness are found in Germany and Japan. The industry-based strategy in Germany supports a more systematic cooperation of the governmental research institutions, the small and medium size industry and large industry participants. The comparatively slow speed of commercialization that was used in the analysis is not to be seen as inefficiency, but as a conscious focus on reliability, quality assurance, and compatibility with the traditional industrial systems. This finding is in line with the literature that argues that coordinated innovative systems are effective in increasing long-term competitiveness and reducing the risks associated with adoption in complex technological sectors (Neumann, Guirguis, & Steiner, 2023; Bharadiya, 2023). Such coordination is used in human-AI interaction, where it has been applied to enable a stable, context-sensitive deployment, especially in the case of enterprise and industrial applications. The technology transfer channel of Japan also illuminates the importance of humanism as a governance style and social acceptance in the commercialization of AI. Its moderately good results in the fields of innovation, infrastructure, and governance indicators indicate that the preparedness is not only a matter of volume and pace, but also consistency with the social norms, user expectations, and ethics. This confirms that the effective commercialization of technologies of human-AI interaction needs not just technical maturity but also the development of trust, usability, and ethical integration. The hybrid form of Japan is therefore an example of how the maturity of governance can supplement innovation capacity to achieve good results of technology transfer. India proposes a unique approach to development, prioritizing the contribution of the state-led diffusion and digital public infrastructure to technology transfer. Though the country still falls behind developed economies in the intensity of R&D and depth of commercialization, its comparatively good results in digital infrastructure development and development of public-private cooperation suggest one more way to the commercialization of AI. This is in line with the current literature that indicates that emerging economies can follow non-linear or leapfrog paths, especially in the use of human-AI interaction in large-scale and cost-sensitive applications (Li et al., 2023; Rawashdeh, 2023; Seenivasan, 2023). Such contexts have better preparedness conceptualized through scalability and inclusiveness than direct commercialization efficiency. Taken together, the comparative analysis shows that there is no single indicator or dimension that would be an adequate measure of technology transfer being ready to engage in commercial interaction between humans and AI. Instead, readiness is the result of the dynamic interaction of inputs of innovation, institutional quality, the coherence of governance and commercialization ecosystems. This multidimensional understanding aligns with more extensive academic criticism of single-metric approaches to innovation measurement and supports the necessity of combined analytical approaches. Although there is a certain convergence in such fields as AI governance maturity and digital infrastructure development, there is still a high level of divergence in commercialization paths. Notably, the analysis shows that there are trade-offs between speed and scalability inherent to market-driven systems and stability and inclusiveness in coordinated and state-led models, though these models have slower commercialization paths. The consequences of these trade-offs are especially important in the context of human-AI interaction, as the ethical considerations, the trust of the users, and social acceptance are part and parcel of the commercial success.

6.3 Ethical and Social Dimensions of Human–AI Interaction

Human-AI interaction technologies commercialization does not simply limit itself to technical performance and financial feasibility but also includes ethical issues and social acceptance. The most important part of this process is user trust which is essential to mass adoption. The lack of transparency in most of the AI systems however creates an issue of bias, explainability and reliability therefore creating the need to design more transparent and interpretable systems. The principle of inclusiveness is also important. The human-AI systems should take into account the differences in language, digital literacy, socio-economic status, and accessibility to allow fair and meaningful interaction between different groups of users. The inability to respond to these issues can contribute to prevailing inequalities particularly in the developing economies. Moreover, the issues of data privacy, displacement of jobs, and loss of human autonomy make the commercialization process more difficult. Good governance structures, ethical responsibility, and responsible innovation are needed in order to adequately tackle these issues. It is possible to incorporate ethical protection into the technology transmission policies in order to establish trust-based ecosystems and facilitate a sustainable, inclusive, and socially responsible use of AI technologies.

6.4 Sector-Specific Applications of Human-AI Interaction

The sectoral dispersion of human-AI interaction technologies offers more information about how the national technology transfer preparedness is translated into the effective commercialization results. The comparative evidences indicate that all nations exhibit adoption in the major sectors although the nature, magnitude and complexity of applications differ substantially depending on institutional capacity and strategic priorities. The United States is representative of a market-oriented model in the healthcare industry with a high rate of implementation of AI-driven diagnostics, telemedicine, and patient interaction platforms financed by robust private investment and innovation environments. On the other hand, the German model is more regulation-based, focusing on clinical validation, data protection, and system integration, which is more reliable but can slow down the adoption process. The emphasis on assistive technologies and elderly care in Japan shows that human-centred is the primary way of using AI, which can be explained by the demographic pressures, in contrast to India, which is on accessibility needs, where a gap in healthcare delivery is being filled by AI-enabled telehealth and diagnostic technologies. It is also reflected in the education sector, with the United States at the forefront of adaptive learning technologies and AI-based analytics, which is an indication of a well-established edtech ecosystem commercially. Germany focuses AI implementation on occupational training and industrial skills acquisition, and Japan focuses on it to supplement formal learning settings. India has a strategy that is focused on scalability and access, which takes advantage of AI platforms to increase access to education in resource-constrained environments. The forefront of Industry 4.0 in Germany is seen to be in the manufacturing industry which proves the significance of combined innovation systems and good industry-academia connections in facilitating enhanced human-machine interaction. The human-centric design philosophy of Japan is further supported by its focus on the precision automation and the collaborative robotics. The US still relies on the innovation of the private sector, whereas India is experiencing a slow, policy-assisted shift to the introduction of AI. The United States leads in retail and customer service by personalization using data and AI-driven customer engagement and Japan by experiential interaction using service robotics. The conservative nature of Germany is based on regulatory priorities, whereas India demonstrates high growth rates through the use of digital platforms and a high number of consumers. Altogether, these sectoral differences underscore the fact that the commercialization of human-AI does not take place in a uniform manner, but rather is influenced by national trajectories, technology transfer-readiness defines the extent and the inclusiveness of adoption.

6.5 Emerging Trends and Future Directions in AI Commercialization

The further evolution of artificial intelligence is being predetermined by the new directions of artificial intelligence, including generative AI, edge AI, and advancing technologies based on quantum computing, which have significant consequences to the field of technology transfer and commercialization. Large language models and generative AI, in general, are radically transforming human-AI interaction by allowing more natural, contextually aware and scalable interaction in fields including healthcare, education and customer support. The need to implement agile innovation and regulatory frameworks that can tackle emerging issues regarding the governance of data, intellectual property, and ethical use is highlighted by its blistering spread. Meanwhile, the emergence of edge AI is considered an important technological change, with the computations becoming more and more proximate to the end users and devices. Such a shift allows improving the real-time responsiveness, reinforcing data privacy, and increasing operational efficiency. These developments are particularly important in such areas as manufacturing, healthcare, and intelligent infrastructure, where strong data security and low latency are the most important elements. Simultaneously, edge AI adoption is closely connected to the presence of robust digital infrastructure and system interoperability, and it indicates the persistence of the significance of institutional and technological preparedness in general. Although in the early phase of development, quantum computing developments are also of long-term importance. Their potential to solve complex optimization tasks in areas like logistics, pharmaceuticals and financial modelling implies that initial research investments might have an implication on future trends of technology transfer despite the lack of commercialization to date. Combined, these trends indicate that the commercialization of AI is getting more complicated and multifaceted and needs policy frameworks that can be adapted, innovation systems that constantly change, and institutions that can respond to the changes in technologies in the future. The comparative analysis results also indicate that the context should be approached in the policy responses, which are elaborated in the next section.

7. POLICY IMPLICATIONS

7.1 Strengthening Technology Transfer Ecosystems

There are also significant policy implications of the study to governments who are interested in enhancing technology transfer to facilitate commercial interaction between humans and AI. The results indicate that the integrated AI policy frameworks are required that would coordinate the investments into the innovation, the development of the digital infrastructure, the governance system, and the commercialization support. Instead of disjointed or isolated interventions, policymakers ought to implement coordinated interventions that bridge the research and market implementation gap. It is specifically critical in the area of human-AI interaction technologies where the constant adoption is not only predetermined by the technical performance but also the continuous interaction with the users, their trust, and proper ethical management.

7.2 Enhancing Institutional and Regulatory Frameworks

The results also highlight the significance of the institutional quality of a particular institution and regulatory transparency in the successful transfer of technology. The countries that are typified by a good legal system, good intellectual property laws and rule of law would realise a better commercialization results. It is in this respect that the policymakers must focus on how to create clear, foreseeable and dynamic regulatory conditions that ease the uncertainty of firm and protect the rights of the users. This necessitates the reinforcement of data protection systems, the improvement of AI accountability procedures, and the regulation by the current risks posed by AI. The research highlights that R&D investment is not enough but there are other complementary measures to effective commercialization like availability of venture capital, scale-up facilities and well-established market connections. Governments ought to thus encourage AI entrepreneurship through providing startups, industry-academia partnership, and the wider proliferation of human-AI technologies, complemented by demand-side interventions, including government procurement and pilot projects. The opportunities of technology transfer are quite situational and require specific policy strategies. The market-based systems have a propensity to have good governance and ethical control systems, and industry-based models might need more incentives to take risks. Innovation in the use of digital public infrastructure and public-private collaborations is vital in emerging economies and should be used as the key to realizing inclusive and scalable adoption, as opposed to directly copying models out of developed economies. Lastly, human-centric thinking of AI is a key to commercialization preparedness. The policies ought to focus on the usability, transparency, and trust through establishment of standards, certification and capacity-building programs. It is also important to strengthen AI capabilities and encourage interdisciplinary learning to make innovation sustainable, competitive, and inclusive.

Building on these policy insights, the final section summarizes the key limitations of the study and outlines directions for future research.

8. LIMITATIONS AND SCOPE FOR FUTURE RESEARCH

Although this research presents a structured and comparative evaluation of technology transfer preparedness within the framework of human-AI interaction, it is constrained by some factors, which leaves certain opportunities to advance research into this field. To begin with, the analysis is founded mostly on the secondary quantitative indicators, which, although contribute to the possibility to cross-country compare the processes of technology transfer, can be quite unhelpful in terms of describing the complexity of events and processes that are highly specific to each specific context. Organizational culture, stakeholder interactions, informal institutional practices, and user perceptions (especially critical in human-AI interaction) are qualitative factors that cannot be explored in the current framework. This limitation of this study could be overcome by the inclusion of qualitative methods, such as case studies, interviews with experts, and field research, in future studies to get a more in-depth understanding of the mechanisms behind AI commercialization.

Second, the research concentrates on four countries, namely, the United States, Germany, Japan, and India, which are a mix of advanced and developing technology ecosystems. Although such a choice makes it possible to meaningfully compare the different models of development, it will necessarily restrict the generalizability of the results across the world. The omission of various regions like Africa, South America and Southeast Asia implies that various institutional settings, developmental imperatives and innovation directions are not entirely included. Future research ought to consider the expansion of the analytical framework to a larger number of countries to gain a clearer insight into the working of technology transfer readiness in diverse socio-economic and policy settings.

Third, the research has a macro-level of focus and have focused on the national-level readiness indicators. Despite the fact that this method is helpful to determine the systemic trends, it fails to provide an adequate consideration of the sector-specific differences in the adoption and commercialization of human-AI interaction technologies. As indicated in the discussion, the various industries including healthcare, education, manufacturing, and retail have different dynamics, regulation, and patterns of user engagement. Further studies may take a more detailed design by carrying out sector analysis studies to understand the mechanisms of technology transfer within a particular industry.

Lastly, the research followed a fixed evaluation, using the available data, which might not be fully relevant to the dynamically changing environment of AI technologies and policy. The longitudinal studies that can track the changes in technology transfer readiness would be of great help in the directions AI commercialization has followed and effects of policy interventions.

9. CONCLUSION

As found in this research, commercialization of technologies of human-AI interaction is closely associated with the willingness of the national systems to successfully transfer the technology. The results show that the nations with high coherence among the digital infrastructure, the innovation capacity, the governance frameworks, and the market ecosystems are likely to have more successful commercialization results.

Meanwhile, the national strategies vary greatly. The US model is a dynamic and market-driven model that allows quicker innovation and implementation, compared to Germany and Japan which have more organized institutional structures that facilitate predictable and stable commercialization. India is an emerging ecosystem with structural constraints, but it is showing a significant progress due to policy-based programs that are boosting adoption rates. These differences imply that the effectiveness of the commercialization of AI is not based on individual capabilities, but the interdependence and consistency of system-level elements. The other important lesson is that sectoral use of human-AI interaction is determined by underlying national circumstances, which have an effect on the scope and diversity of adoption. Ethical issues, especially trust, transparency, and accessibility are very significant to long-term acceptance and sustainability. In general, the results indicate the significance of the balanced and combined approach to AI commercialization where the institutional quality, regulatory clarity, and market preparedness are all aimed at the technological progress. This offers a more subtle concept of how countries may build their systems of technology transfer to allow adopting human-AI interaction technologies in a way that is effective, reliable, and inclusive.

REFERENCES

Aldoseri, A., Khalifa, M., Al-Khalifa, N., & Hamouda, A. M. (2023). Re-thinking data strategy and integration for artificial intelligence: Concepts, opportunities, and challenges. *Applied Sciences (Basel, Switzerland), 13*(12), 7082. DOI: 10.3390/app13127082

Ancillai, C., Sabatini, A., Gatti, M., & Perna, A. (2023). Digital technology and business model innovation: A systematic literature review and future research agenda. *Technological Forecasting and Social Change, 188*, 122307. DOI: 10.1016/j.techfore.2022.122307

Bawa, P. (2016). How value congruence affects customer focus and survival of business. *International Journal of Applied Business and Economic Research, 14*(7), 5085–5096.

Bawa, P. (2017). Evidence based classroom management practices: An analysis through kano's model. *Indian Journal of Marketing, 47*(6), 35–49. DOI: 10.17010/ijom/2017/v47/i6/115368

Bawa, P., & Bathurutheen, F. (2016). Effect of extrinsic cues on perception of private label quality and customer satisfaction. *Indian Journal of Marketing, 46*(7), 55–66. DOI: 10.17010/ijom/2016/v46/i7/97127

Bharadiya, J. P. (2023). A comparative study of business intelligence and artificial intelligence with big data analytics. *American Journal of Artificial Intelligence, 7*(1), 24. DOI: 10.11648/j.ajai.20230701.14

Costa, A. F., & Marques, R. P. (2025). Research trends in artificial intelligence in education and the ethics of privacy. In *2025 IEEE International Conference on Advances in Data-Driven Analytics and Intelligent Systems (ADACIS)* (pp. 1–6). IEEE. https://doi.org/DOI: 10.1109/ADACIS65663.2025.11436431

Cukurova, M. (2025). The interplay of learning, analytics and artificial intelligence in education: A vision for hybrid intelligence. *British Journal of Educational Technology, 56*(2), 469–488. DOI: 10.1111/bjet.13514

Flew, T. (2024). Mediated trust, the internet and artificial intelligence: Ideas, interests, institutions and futures. *Policy and Internet, 16*(2), 443–457. DOI: 10.1002/poi3.390

Gołąb-Andrzejak, E. (2023). AI-powered digital transformation: Tools, benefits and challenges for marketers-Case study of LPP. *Procedia Computer Science, 219*, 397–404. DOI: 10.1016/j.procs.2023.01.305

Grebe, M., Franke, M. R., & Heinzl, A. (2023). Artificial intelligence: How leading companies define use cases, scale-up utilization, and realize value. *Informatik Spektrum.*, *46*(4), 197–209. DOI: 10.1007/s00287-023-01548-6

Hartley, K., & Aldag, A. (2024). Public trust and support for government technology: Survey insights about Singapore's smart city policies. *Cities (London, England)*, *154*, 105368. DOI: 10.1016/j.cities.2024.105368

Hongladarom, S., & Bandasak, J. (2024). Non-western AI ethics guidelines: Implications for intercultural ethics of technology. *AI & Society*, *39*(4), 2019–2032. DOI: 10.1007/s00146-023-01665-6

Jarrahi, M. H., Kenyon, S., Brown, A., Donahue, C., & Wicher, C. (2023). Artificial intelligence: A strategy to harness its power through organizational learning. *The Journal of Business Strategy*, *44*(2), 126–135. DOI: 10.1108/JBS-11-2021-0182

Jiyoung, P., Woo, S. E., & Kim, J. J. (2024). Attitudes towards artificial intelligence at work: Scale development and validation. *Journal of Occupational and Organizational Psychology*, *97*(3), 920–951. DOI: 10.1111/joop.12502

Karkošková, S. (2023). Data governance model to enhance data quality in financial institutions. *Information Systems Management*, *40*(1), 90–110. DOI: 10.1080/10580530.2022.2042628

Khanal, S., Zhang, H., & Taeihagh, A. (2024). Building an AI ecosystem in a small nation: Lessons from Singapore's journey to the forefront of AI. *Humanities & Social Sciences Communications*, *11*(1), 1–12. DOI: 10.1057/s41599-024-03289-7

Khanal, S., Zhang, H., & Taeihagh, A. (2025). Why and how is the power of Big Tech increasing in the policy process? The case of generative AI. *Policy and Society*, *44*(1), 52–69. DOI: 10.1093/polsoc/puae012

Khanom, M. T. (2023). Business strategies in the age of digital transformation. *The Journal of Business*, *8*, 28–35.

Laux, J., Wachter, S., & Mittelstadt, B. (2024). Trustworthy artificial intelligence and the European Union AI Act: On the conflation of trustworthiness and acceptability of risk. *Regulation & Governance*, *18*(1), 3–32. DOI: 10.1111/rego.12512 PMID: 38435808

Li, B., Qi, P., Liu, B., Di, S., Liu, J., Pei, J., Yi, J., & Zhou, B. (2023). Trustworthy AI: From principles to practices. *arXiv*. https://doi.org//arXiv.2110.01167DOI: 10.48550

Liang, Z., Zhang, F., & Zhou, T. (2025). Generative AI in LEGO education: Opportunities and ethical challenges in digital learning development. In *2025 5th International Conference on Artificial Intelligence and Education (ICAIE)* (pp. 779–784). IEEE. https://doi.org/DOI: 10.1109/ICAIE64856.2025.11158547

Lockey, S., & Gillespie, N. (2024). Understanding trust in artificial intelligence: A research agenda. In Mayer, R. C., & Mayer, B. M. (Eds.), *A research agenda for trust: Interdisciplinary perspectives* (pp. 11–24). Edward Elgar Publishing., DOI: 10.4337/9781802200942.00009

McDaniel, A. (2025). Integrating artificial intelligence in STEM education: Enhancing learning through smart technologies. *American Journal of STEM Education*, *7*, 1–10. DOI: 10.32674/6s0qz548

Mihai, F., Aleca, O. E., & Gheorghe, M. (2023). Digital transformation based on AI technologies in European Union organizations. *Electronics (Basel)*, *12*(10), 2386. DOI: 10.3390/electronics12112386

Neumann, O., Guirguis, K., & Steiner, R. (2023). Exploring artificial intelligence adoption in public organizations: A comparative case study. *Public Management Review*. Advance online publication. DOI: 10.1080/14719037.2023.2182901

Novozhilova, E., Mays, K., & Katz, J. E. (2024). Looking towards an automated future: U.S. attitudes towards future artificial intelligence instantiations and their effect. *Humanities & Social Sciences Communications*, *11*(1), 1–11. DOI: 10.1057/s41599-024-02625-1

Pande, D., Khanal, S., & Taeihagh, A. (2025). Conceptualising public trust in high-risk AI policymaking: A comparative analysis of three Asian cities. *Journal of Comparative Policy Analysis*, *27*(5–6), 578–602. DOI: 10.1080/13876988.2025.2543546

Pande, D., & Taeihagh, A. (2024). A governance perspective on user acceptance of autonomous systems in Singapore. *Technology in Society*, *77*, 102580. DOI: 10.1016/j.techsoc.2024.102580

Perifanis, N.-A., & Kitsios, F. (2023). Investigating the influence of artificial intelligence on business value in the digital era of strategy: A literature review. *Information (Basel)*, *14*(2), 85. DOI: 10.3390/info14020085

Rawashdeh, A. (2023). The consequences of artificial intelligence: An investigation into the impact of AI on job displacement in accounting. *Journal of Science and Technology Policy Management*. DOI: 10.1108/JSTPM-02-2023-0030

Rowe, F., Jeanneret Medina, M., Journé, B., Coëtard, E., & Myers, M. (2024). Understanding responsibility under uncertainty: A critical and scoping review of autonomous driving systems. *Journal of Information Technology*, *39*(3), 587–615. DOI: 10.1177/02683962231207108

Rožman, M., Oreški, D., & Tominc, P. (2023). Artificial intelligence-supported reduction of employees' workload to increase company performance in today's VUCA environment. *Sustainability (Basel)*, *15*(6), 5019. DOI: 10.3390/su15065019

Scantamburlo, T., Cortés, A., Foffano, F., Barrué, C., Distefano, V., Pham, L., & Fabris, A. (2025). Artificial intelligence across Europe: A study on awareness, attitude and trust. *IEEE Transactions on Artificial Intelligence*, *6*(2), 477–490. DOI: 10.1109/TAI.2024.3461633

Seenivasan, D. (2023). ETL (extract, transform, load) best practices. *International Journal of Computer Trends and Technology*, *71*(1), 40–44. DOI: 10.14445/22312803/IJCTT-V71I1P106

Sharma, P., Kaur, G., & Pathak, R. (2025). The effect of COVID-19 induced work stressors on life satisfaction of university teachers in India: An empirical study. *International Journal of Business and Globalisation*, *40*(1), 130–150. DOI: 10.1504/IJBG.2025.146219

Sharma, P., & Sarmah, R. (2020). Perception and awareness of youth towards digital India campaign [IJM]. *International Journal of Management (Kolkata)*, *11*(6), 1381–1393.

Sharma, P. B., & Kumar, A. (2024). Interventions of organizational identification and job satisfaction on person-environment perceptions and work engagement: Insights for K12 school administrators in India. *International Journal of Public Administration*, *47*(10), 690–703. DOI: 10.1080/01900692.2023.2175852

Chapter 6
A Strategic Synthesis of Technology Transfer, Job Design, and Human-AI Interaction in HRM

Sherzodbek Murodilla Ugli Dadaboyev
http://orcid.org/0000-0002-2842-4177
Central Asian University, Uzbekistan

Yasmina Akbarova
Central Asian University, Uzbekistan

Farangiz Baxtiyorova
Central Asian University, Uzbekistan

Guljakhon Gulomova
Central Asian University, Uzbekistan

Samira Hojimurodova
Central Asian University, Uzbekistan

ABSTRACT

Artificial intelligence (AI) is fundamentally restructuring the landscape of Human Resource Management (HRM), shifting from an administrative tool to an active commercial market actor that directly influences workforce dynamics. This chapter provides a strategic synthesis of how AI technologies are transferred from commercial developers into organizational ecosystems, and how this integration reshapes job design and Human-AI Interaction (HAII), and explores the functional applications

DOI: 10.4018/979-8-3373-9325-4.ch006

of AI in automated recruitment, predictive performance management, and personalized learning and development (L&D). The chapter argues that the successful commercialization and implementation of AI in HRM depend on a human-centric approach to technology transfer. Ultimately, this chapter outlines the ethical, legal, and social implications (ELSI) of AI adoption and provides actionable recommendations for managers to balance database precision with human values, ensuring sustainable, equitable, and legally compliant human-machine integration in the modern workplace.

1. INTRODUCTION

The evolution of Human Resource Management (HRM) has undergone a deep paradigm shift in the 21st century, transitioning from purely administrative personnel management to strategic human capital management, and now, to algorithmic, data-driven HR. Contemporary artificial intelligence (AI) is at the epicenter of this revolution, fundamentally restructuring global business practices and influencing how organizations interact with the labor market. AI is transforming the HR environment by integrating traditional, human-centric management practices with advanced database analytics, machine learning, and automated processes (Bositkhanova & Dadaboyev, 2025; Dadaboyev, Abdullayeva, et al., 2025). This integration allows organizations to diversify their internal services, enhance workplace productivity, and maintain agility across diverse sectors, ranging from IT to healthcare (Cavanagh et al., 2023; Trocin et al., 2021).

However, the current wave of technological integration represents more than just a software upgrade. Moving beyond early, tool-centric discussions—where technology was viewed merely as passive software requiring constant human input—modern commercial AI has emerged as an *active market actor* within the workplace. Today, AI manifests through predictive analytical engines, virtual HR chatbots, automated screening algorithms, and autonomous decision-support technologies that directly influence how employees are hired, evaluated, managed, and developed. As AI assumes these quasi-managerial roles, it creates a complex triad of Human-AI Interaction (HAII), fundamentally altering traditional job designs and requiring a strategic synthesis of technology transfer mechanisms to ensure sustainable commercial application.

1.1 The Rise of the Commercial HR-Tech Ecosystem

The rapid commercialization of AI-driven HR analytics has created a booming, multi-billion-dollar HR-Tech ecosystem. Third-party vendors and technology developers are continuously bringing new algorithmic products to market, promising extraordinary operational efficiency, cost reduction, and objective decision-making. AI enables organizations to differentiate their internal employee services and external talent acquisition strategies, thereby gaining distinct competitive advantages in tight labor markets (Trocin et al., 2021).

Through increased efficiency, AI offers robust opportunities to streamline historically labor-intensive operations. Research demonstrates that AI and HR analytics serve as vital instruments for business alignment, helping organizations predict workforce outcomes, optimize daily operations, and create highly efficient HR processes. This is particularly evident in fast-paced environments such as the IT sector, where agility is paramount (Sharma et al., 2025). Furthermore, AI is increasingly utilized to automate repetitive, administrative processes in talent acquisition. By automating resume screening, parsing unstructured candidate data, and conducting initial algorithmic evaluations, AI boosts overall productivity and significantly reduces workforce expenses. These automated mechanisms free up HR professionals' time, ideally allowing them to pivot their focus toward high-level strategic initiatives, relationship building, and organizational development (Madancian & Taherdoost, 2023).

Beyond administrative efficiency, the commercial HR-tech ecosystem is enabling highly personalized Learning and Development (L&D) interventions. AI systems can now adapt training content and delivery methods dynamically, basing their recommendations on an individual employee's existing skills, historical performance data, and unique learning preferences. Concurrently, predictive analytics can forecast future organizational skill gaps based on broader market trends (Dadaboyev, Hojimurodova et al., 2025; Huang et al., 2023). This dual capacity allows organizations to deliver personalized learning programs tailored to each employee's needs while aligning with the firm's strategic goals (Sharma et al., 2025). In broader strategic HR planning, AI-enabled analytics demonstrate strong potential for predicting employee turnover (flight risk) and optimizing talent development, ultimately positively impacting organizational resilience and workforce sustainability (Venugopal et al., 2024; Xiao et al., 2025).

1.2 Defining AI as an Active Market Actor in the Workplace

To understand the full impact of AI in HRM, it is necessary to conceptualize AI not just as a tool but as a *market actor* with agency that actively shapes the organizational environment. In commercial settings, AI algorithms shape the labor market by deciding which candidates are visible to recruiters, and they shape internal talent markets by recommending which employees receive promotions, training, or corrective interventions.

As AI transitions from a background utility to a frontline decision-maker, its role as a market actor sparks considerable debate, particularly regarding performance feedback and job design. On the one hand, advanced data analytics enable AI to comprehensively track employee behavior, assess productivity in real time, and generate personalized recommendations for job improvement (Heaven, 2020). Supporters argue that this continuous, data-rich monitoring leads to more objective performance evaluations, potentially reducing the cognitive biases and prejudices inherent in human managerial reviews. However, the heavy reliance on AI-generated feedback raises profound concerns regarding algorithmic transparency, workplace surveillance, and employee trust (Huang et al., 2023; Tong et al., 2021).

This tension is particularly evident in fields requiring high cognitive input, emotional intelligence, and creative problem-solving. In creative industries, the balance between algorithmic automation and human creativity remains a central concern. Research by Öztaş and Arda (2025) observes that AI necessitates design technologies that carefully consider users' perceptions of creative agency. Employees place high value on the creative aspects of their work, asserting that the opportunity to utilize their creative potential and exercise independent judgment is a primary intrinsic motivator for their occupations. This underscores the critical importance of designing AI systems that augment, rather than replace, human imagination. If commercial AI tools are implemented with an overemphasis on standardization and efficiency—without considering workers' specific psychological needs and values—there is a significant risk that AI will suppress creative expression, diminish meaningful work, and damage the overall employee experience (Perez et al., 2022).

1.3 The Challenge of Technology Transfer and Job Design

The successful integration of AI into commercial HRM is not simply a transactional matter of purchasing off-the-shelf software; it is a complex, multi-stage process of *technology transfer*. In this context, technology transfer refers to the movement of algorithmic innovations from technology developers and commercial platforms into practical, market-facing HR applications within an organization. This transfer fundamentally reshapes the relationship between human workers, management, and the organizational structure.

A major friction point in this technology transfer is the gap between the algorithmic capabilities designed by vendors and the actual technological readiness of the organizations adopting them. While technological advances offer vast opportunities to improve performance, human-machine integration frequently creates socio-organizational challenges that affect workplace skill development (Chuang et al.,

2024; Dadaboyev, Baxtiyorova et al., 2025). Furthermore, commercial algorithms often operate as "black boxes," using proprietary data optimization methods that obscure how decisions are made. When organizations scale these cloudy systems to establish legitimacy and efficiency, they risk unintentionally scaling systemic biases at an industrial level.

Consequently, introducing AI can lead to severe disparities in workforce capabilities, particularly threatening the autonomy of middle-skilled workers. To prevent technological displacement, organizations must invest heavily in upskilling programs and continuing education to ensure their workforce remains competitive in AI-driven sectors. To ensure long-term professional viability, management must implement proactive career development programs that enable employees to progress alongside these new technologies, transforming the human-AI relationship from competition to collaboration (Chuang et al., 2024).

Ultimately, building a culture for the human-centric adoption of AI requires organizations to successfully blend technological deployment with an environment that equally values human expertise (Berretta et al., 2023). This necessitates robust change management programs, adaptive implementation strategies, and inclusive policies that promote employee engagement. AI in HR should not be viewed merely as a mechanism for cost reduction; its ultimate value lies in its potential to balance database precision with human values. The future of HRM will be defined by this alliance: technology-expanded human potential guided by human ethics to ensure sustainable, commercially viable AI adoption.

1.4 Chapter Objectives and Structure

While existing literature extensively covers the technical capabilities of AI in HRM, many review-based studies remain limited. They tend to focus either purely on the algorithmic efficiency of HR-Tech or exclusively on isolated ethical dilemmas, frequently overlooking the transitional conflict that occurs when these technologies are actually implemented. A significant research gap exists regarding the holistic, socio-technical journey of AI—specifically, how the mechanics of technology transfer directly alter job design and the psychological HAII experience. This chapter uniquely contributes to the literature by bridging this gap, differentiating itself from prior studies by offering a multi-disciplinary theoretical synthesis that connects capabilities with human-centric workplace outcomes.

To achieve this, the chapter employs an *integrative conceptual review* methodology. Literature sources were systematically selected and synthesized across multiple disciplines—including human resource management, information systems, organizational psychology, and technology governance—focusing on peer-reviewed articles and conceptual frameworks published predominantly within the last five years. By integrating Socio-Technical Systems (STS) Theory, the Job Demands-Resources (JD-R) model, Technology Acceptance, and Self-Determination Theory (SDT), this integrative review provides a comprehensive conceptual framework for understanding AI not merely as a software tool, but as an active market actor.

To explore these dynamics, the remainder of this chapter is structured as follows. Section 2, "Theoretical Frameworks," establishes the guiding principles of technology acceptance and human-machine interaction in the workplace. Section 3, "The Mechanics of Technology Transfer in HRM," examines the processes by which algorithmic innovations move into HR departments, highlighting the critical analytical skill gaps and implementation barriers organizations face. Section 4, "Commercial AI Techniques and Functional Applications," explores the most prominent commercial uses of AI in HR today, specifically detailing automated recruitment, predictive performance management, and personalized L&D. Section 5, "The Human-AI Interaction (HAII) Experience," critically analyzes the job design outcomes of automation versus human augmentation, addressing psychological consequences such as technostress and person-tool fit. Section 6, "Ethical, Legal, and Social Implications (ELSI)," outlines the pressing concerns of algorithmic HR, particularly regarding data privacy, bias, and algorithmic opacity. Finally, Section 7, "Recommendations for Managers," provides actionable, strategic guidance to navigate these complexities, followed by concluding remarks and directions for further study in Section 8, "Future Research Directions and Conclusion."

2. THEORETICAL FRAMEWORKS

To critically analyze the transfer of AI technologies into HRM and their subsequent impact on job design, it is essential to ground the discussion in robust theoretical frameworks. The rapid deployment of commercial AI within organizations often outpaces empirical research, leading to a reliance on vendor-driven narratives that emphasize technological determinism—the assumption that implementing advanced software will automatically yield organizational efficiency. However, human-AI interaction (HAII) is a deeply complex phenomenon. To understand how AI acts as a market actor that reshapes human behavior, alters job characteristics, and triggers psychological responses, this chapter utilizes four interconnected theoretical lenses: Socio-Technical Systems (STS) Theory, the Job Demands-Resources (JD-R) Model, Technology Acceptance and Algorithmic Aversion, and Self-Determination Theory (SDT).

2.1 Socio-Technical Systems (STS) Theory and Technology Transfer

Socio-Technical Systems (STS) theory posits that an organization comprises two interdependent subsystems: the technical system (the tools, technologies, and procedures used to complete tasks) and the social system (the employees, their relationships, organizational culture, and human values). Originally developed in the mid-20th century to explain the friction caused by the mechanization of labor, STS theory is highly applicable to the modern commercialization of AI. According to STS principles, introducing a new technology will only succeed if there is a "joint optimization" of both the social and technical systems. If an organization optimizes only the technical system—such as deploying a highly accurate, automated recruitment algorithm—without considering the social system (e.g., recruiter workflows, candidate perceptions, and ethical norms), the implementation will yield sub-optimal or even destructive organizational outcomes.

In the context of technology transfer in HRM, commercial AI vendors frequently focus exclusively on technical optimization. They market predictive analytics and automated tracking systems based on their statistical accuracy and processing speed. However, as these technologies transition from the developer's platform into the live HR environment, they disrupt established social systems. For example, when an applicant tracking system (ATS) takes over the initial screening of resumes, it fundamentally alters the recruiter's role, stripping away certain social judgments and replacing them with standardized algorithmic scoring (Madancian & Taherdoost, 2023).

STS theory highlights that the successful transfer of AI into HRM requires organizations to actively redesign the social system to accommodate the new technical reality. This means upskilling HR professionals to critically assess algorithmic outputs rather than blindly accepting them, redesigning job roles to focus on empathy and strategic negotiation, and establishing governance frameworks that align AI operations with the organization's cultural values (Berretta et al., 2023). By viewing AI integration through the STS lens, organizations can move away from viewing AI merely as a "plug-and-play" tool and recognize it as a structural intervention that requires holistic, socio-technical alignment.

2.2 The Job Demands-Resources (JD-R) Model in Algorithmic Management

To understand the psychological outcomes of AI adoption—specifically the dichotomy between employee satisfaction and technostress—the JD-R model serves as a vital framework. The JD-R model classifies working conditions into two broad categories: job demands and job resources. Job demands refer to the physical, psychological, social, or organizational aspects of the job that require sustained physical or mental effort and are therefore associated with physiological and psychological costs (e.g., high workload, emotional labor, role ambiguity). Conversely, job resources are aspects of the job that facilitate achieving work goals, reduce job demands, or stimulate personal growth and development (e.g., autonomy, performance feedback, social support).

When commercial AI is introduced into the workplace, it can function as either a powerful job resource or a burdensome job demand, depending entirely on its design and implementation (Tong et al., 2021). When AI is deployed with an *augmentation-oriented design*, it acts as a job resource. For instance, an AI-powered HR analytics dashboard that quickly synthesizes complex data allows HR managers to make faster, more informed decisions. By automating ordinary, repetitive administrative tasks, AI frees up cognitive bandwidth, reducing workload and allowing employees to engage in higher-value, meaningful work. In this scenario, AI enhances employees' capabilities, leading to higher job satisfaction, increased engagement, and improved retention (O'Callaghan, 2023).

Conversely, when AI is deployed with a strict *automation-oriented or surveillance-oriented design*, it frequently operates as a job demand. Commercial AI systems utilized for continuous performance monitoring—where algorithms track employee keystrokes, communication patterns, and active hours—drastically increase psychological pressure. This continuous monitoring strips away human discretion and generates intense “technostress” (Ragu-Nathan et al., 2008; Vuori et al., 2019). The JD-R model clarifies why employees experience burnout and high turnover rates under such algorithmic management: the introduction of AI has increased their cognitive and emotional demands (the pressure of constant surveillance and navigating complex, “black box” algorithms) without providing corresponding job resources (transparency, autonomy, or human support).

2.3 Technology Acceptance and Algorithmic Aversion

The success of AI as a commercial application in HR is entirely dependent on user adoption. Even the most mathematically sophisticated predictive model will fail to deliver return on investment if human workers refuse to utilize its insights. To examine this dynamic, we draw upon theories of technology adoption, notably the Technology Acceptance Model (TAM) and the Unified Theory of Acceptance and Use of Technology (UTAUT). These models traditionally suggest that an individual's behavioral intention to use a technology is driven primarily by two factors: *perceived usefulness* (the degree to which a person believes the system will enhance their job performance) and *perceived ease of use* (the degree to which a person believes using the system will be free of effort).

However, commercial AI introduces a unique psychological barrier not present in traditional software adoption: the concept of *algorithmic aversion*. Algorithmic aversion occurs when human users reject an algorithmic forecast or decision, even when they know the algorithm consistently outperforms human judgment. In HRM, this is frequently observed when seasoned managers dismiss AI-generated hiring recommendations or predictive turnover alerts because they trust their own "gut feeling" or intuition over a machine's calculation. This aversion is often triggered by the impenetrability of machine learning models. Because deep learning networks operate as a "black box," HR professionals cannot clearly see *how* the AI arrived at its conclusion (Huang et al., 2023). When human users cannot comprehend a system's logic, their trust plummets, negating any perceived usefulness.

Furthermore, literature indicates that employees judge AI mistakes far more harshly than human mistakes. If a human recruiter makes a bad hire, it is written off as human error; if an AI recommends a bad hire, users rapidly lose faith in the entire system. Therefore, from a technology transfer perspective, bridging the gap between algorithmic capability and human acceptance requires building "Explainable AI" (XAI) and ensuring high "person-tool fit" (Perez et al., 2022). By allowing employees to question AI decisions, contest algorithmic feedback, and customize the interface to their working style, organizations can mitigate algorithmic aversion and foster a culture of algorithmic appreciation.

2.4 Self-Determination Theory (SDT) and Job Crafting

Finally, to understand how AI impacts the fundamental nature of employee motivation and creative agency, this chapter applies Self-Determination Theory (SDT). SDT posits that high-quality human motivation and well-being are achieved when three innate psychological needs are satisfied: *autonomy* (the need to feel in control of one's own behaviors and goals), *competence* (the need to feel effective and master one's environment), and *relatedness* (the need to feel connected to and cared for by others).

The deployment of commercial AI in HR environments directly interacts with all three of these basic needs, creating what Perez et al. (2022) refer to as the "autonomy tussle." When an organization implements an algorithmic system that dictates task allocation—telling an employee exactly what to do, how to do it, and how long it should take—the employee's sense of autonomy is severely compromised. This loss of agency is particularly detrimental in creative industries, where professional identity is deeply tied to independent thought and creative execution (Öztaş & Arda, 2025). If AI systems are perceived as authoritative planners rather than supportive tools, they undermine intrinsic motivation, leading to passive compliance or active resistance.

Figure 1. A Conceptual Framework for AI Integration in HRM. This model illustrates the sequential relationship from the mechanics of technology transfer to ultimate employee outcomes, mediated by job design and the HAII experience, all firmly grounded in transparent, ethical AI governance.

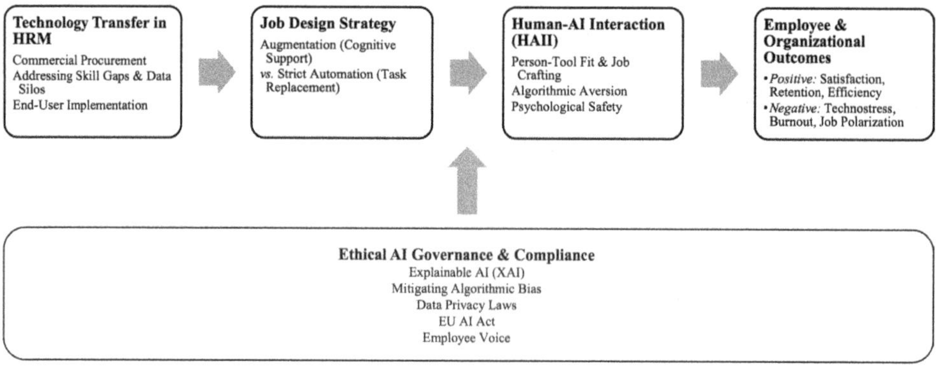

Conversely, when AI is used to support job crafting, it can enhance SDT outcomes. L&D platforms exemplify this positive interaction. When an AI career coach provides an employee with personalized insights into their skill gaps and suggests tailored training pathways—while leaving the ultimate decision to participate to the employee—it fulfills the need for competence without violating autonomy (Chuang et al., 2024). The employee feels empowered to master new skills using AI as a supportive guide. By applying SDT to human-AI interaction, it becomes clear that HR technologies must be designed to empower human agency rather than overpower it. Commercial AI systems must be calibrated to respect human autonomy, foster professional competence, and maintain the relatedness inherent in human-to-human workplace relationships.

Together, these four theoretical frameworks—STS, JD-R, Technology Acceptance, and SDT—provide a comprehensive analytical foundation. They demonstrate that the successful transfer of AI into commercial HRM extends far beyond software installation; it requires a strategic, ethically driven redesign of the socio-technical workplace environment.

3. THE MECHANICS OF TECHNOLOGY TRANSFER IN HRM

In the context of HRM, "technology transfer" is not merely the physical installation of new software; it is the complex, multi-stage process of moving algorithmic innovations from commercial developers, tech vendors, and data science laboratories into practical, everyday use within an HR department. This process is inherently fraught with friction. While commercial vendors market their AI solutions as seamless, "plug-and-play" platforms that instantly optimize workforce management, the reality of implementing these systems demands profound organizational adaptation. The mechanics of this transfer rely heavily on developing new technical competencies, reconfiguring HR jobs, and navigating significant systemic barriers.

3.1 The Commercial Technology Transfer Pipeline

The transfer of AI into HRM generally follows a three-stage commercial pipeline. The first stage is *innovation and development*, in which third-party technology firms (ranging from major enterprise resource planning vendors such as SAP and Workday to specialized AI start-ups) develop machine learning algorithms. These algorithms are trained on vast, generalized datasets to recognize patterns in candidate resumes, employee performance metrics, or retention data.

The second stage is *organizational procurement and alignment*. This is frequently where technology transfer faces its first major hurdle. Organizations purchase commercial AI systems expecting immediate return on investment (ROI) through heightened efficiency. However, there is often a severe misalignment between the vendor's generalized models and the specific, highly contextualized culture and data architecture of the adopting organization. If an organization's historical HR data is fragmented, stored in siloed legacy systems, or riddled with historical human biases, the AI cannot function as advertised.

The third and final stage is *end-user implementation*. This stage dictates the ultimate success or failure of the technology transfer. It involves the actual HR professionals and front-line managers who must interact with the AI interface daily. For the technology to be successfully transferred and commercialized, these end-users must not only accept the technology but possess the requisite skills to operate it, interpret its outputs, and integrate its recommendations into their workflow.

3.2 The Analytical Skill Gap and Upskilling Requirements

A primary mechanical requirement for the successful transfer of AI into HRM is the drastic evolution of the HR professional's skill set. Historically, the HR profession has been anchored in "soft skills"—such as interpersonal communication, conflict resolution, empathy, and organizational psychology. However, integrating algorithmic management requires a pivot toward "hard" quantitative competency.

Research by Sharma et al. (2025) indicates that adopting HR Analytics and AI requires HR professionals to acquire foundational technical skills, including basic coding, advanced data analysis, and design thinking. To effectively implement and manage commercial AI systems, proficiency in data manipulation and visualization tools such as Excel, SPSS, Tableau, and Power BI is now a baseline expectation. Furthermore, as organizations seek to customize commercial AI models to their specific workforce needs, there is an increasing demand for HR professionals to develop competencies in programming languages such as Python and R (Böhmer & Schinnenburg, 2023).

Beyond mere technical operation, the critical mechanism of technology transfer lies in the development of *analytical data literacy*. Training in R, Python, and data analysis platforms is essential to bridge the current gap in analytical capabilities among HR practitioners (Oswald et al., 2020). However, technical skills are insufficient without analytical and critical thinking skills. As Sharma et al. (2025) emphasize, analytical thinking is paramount for evaluating the context behind the numbers. Data visualization plays a crucial role in this process; HR professionals must leverage visual analytics to effectively interpret complex behavioral patterns within massive datasets (Oswald et al., 2020).

Crucially, HR personnel must possess the quantitative literacy required to critically assess the validity of AI algorithms. When an automated system produces a predictive score—for example, flagging a specific employee as a "high flight risk"—the HR professional cannot simply accept the output as absolute truth. They must understand the underlying variables the algorithm weighed, identify meaningful patterns, and determine if the recommendation aligns with the nuanced reality of the workplace. Without this critical data literacy, the technology transfer fails, as HR departments become overly dependent on vendor algorithms, surrendering their strategic judgment to automated systems.

3.3 Job Reconfiguration and Task Displacement

As analytical capabilities are introduced into the HR department, the daily mechanics of HR work are fundamentally altered. The productive use of AI can massively enhance departmental productivity by automating highly routinized, mechanistic tasks. For instance, tasks that once consumed hours of human labor—such as manually screening thousands of applicant resumes, scheduling interviews, answering basic employee payroll queries, and aggregating performance review scores—are now rapidly executed by AI agents and natural language processing (NLP) chatbots.

This automation facilitates significant job redesign. The current literature demonstrates that jobs are being reconfigured to allow employees to focus on high-value cognitive tasks, thereby reducing routine work and creating robust opportunities for increased productivity and strategic impact (Callari & Puppione, 2025). In this newly reconfigured landscape, the HR professional shifts from an administrative processor to a strategic consultant. Instead of spending time gathering data, they interpret AI-generated insights to advise executive leadership on workforce planning, organizational culture, and talent development.

However, this transition is not without friction. The integration of advanced analytics raises valid concerns about worker domination, skill displacement, and a decline in employee satisfaction (Tong et al., 2021). As AI systems become more sophisticated, they begin to perform tasks previously considered to require human judgment, such as assessing candidate cultural fit or evaluating employee performance. If technology transfer is poorly managed, HR professionals may feel their expertise is being marginalized or displaced by the algorithm. To counteract this, organizations must consciously design HR roles around *augmentation*, ensuring that AI serves as a decision-support mechanism that amplifies human capability, rather than a total replacement that dominates the workflow.

3.4 Systemic Barriers to Successful Transfer

Despite the compelling commercial benefits of AI in HRM, the mechanics of technology transfer are frequently stalled by several systemic barriers inherent to diverse organizational cultures.

A foundational barrier to technology transfer is the quality and accessibility of organizational data. Commercial AI algorithms require massive, continuous streams of high-quality data to train predictive models and generate accurate insights. However, many organizations suffer from fragmented technological infrastructures where payroll data, performance metrics, and recruitment records are stored in disparate, unconnected legacy systems. Without a unified data warehouse or a seamlessly integrated HR Information System (HRIS), the AI cannot generate holistic insights. The saying “garbage in, garbage out” is acutely relevant here; if an organization's historical data is incomplete or inaccurate, the AI's predictive outputs will be inherently flawed, stalling the transfer process and eroding trust in the system.

Another significant barrier arises from the commercial nature of HR-Tech vendors. Many vendors utilize proprietary, closed-source machine learning models to protect their intellectual property. This creates a “black box” environment where the inputs and outputs are visible, but the algorithm's internal logic for decision-making is entirely hidden from the organization using it. From a technology transfer perspective, this proprietary opacity prevents HR professionals from auditing or validating the vendor's models, stalling organizational procurement and integration.

Finally, the transfer of AI technology must navigate the complex barrier of organizational culture. Integrating AI alters the power dynamics within a firm. Middle managers may resist the implementation of predictive performance analytics if they feel the system undermines their traditional managerial authority or reduces their subjective discretion in evaluating their teams. Overcoming this barrier requires comprehensive change management programs. As organizations transition toward a data-driven paradigm, leadership must transparently communicate the purpose, capabilities, and limitations of AI systems, and actively involve employees and HR staff in the implementation process to foster a culture of technological collaboration rather than apprehension.

3.4.1 Cross-Cultural Contexts and the Global South

Furthermore, technology transfer frequently encounters severe cross-cultural barriers, particularly concerning adoption in the Global South. The vast majority of commercial AI models are developed and trained on datasets originating from the Global North (primarily the US and Europe). When these models are exported to emerging markets, they often fail to account for local cultural nuances, informal labor market dynamics, or non-Western educational credentials. For instance, algorithmic personality assessments trained on Western communication styles may inaccurately flag candidates from high-context cultures in Asia or Africa as "unfit." Successful AI adoption therefore requires localized model recalibration to ensure cultural inclusivity and relevance.

4. COMMERCIAL AI TECHNIQUES AND FUNCTIONAL APPLICATIONS

As AI transitions from a theoretical concept into an active commercial market actor, its impact is most visibly realized through specific, functional applications within the HR lifecycle. Organizations today utilize an array of commercial AI software suites to fundamentally alter how they attract, evaluate, and develop human capital. This section critically examines the three most prominent areas of commercial AI integration in HRM: automated recruitment, predictive performance management, and personalized L&D. By analyzing these functional applications, we can observe the direct tension between commercial efficiency, algorithmic bias, and human-centric job design.

4.1 Automated Recruitment and the Search for "Unbiased" Hiring

Recruitment represents the most heavily commercialized entry point for AI in HRM. The talent acquisition field offers highly measurable, quantitative metrics—such as time-to-hire, cost-per-hire, and screening volume—making it highly susceptible to automation. Organizations are under constant pressure to hire staff faster, operating at maximum efficiency while maintaining consistent decision-making standards across multiple staffing categories. Consequently, automated recruitment systems have become the primary means of implementing artificial intelligence in HR operations (Sharma et al., 2025; Trocin et al., 2021).

4.1.1 The Mechanics of Algorithmic Screening

Commercial Applicant Tracking Systems (ATS) and online hiring platforms (e.g., LinkedIn Recruiter, HireVue) serve as the central ecosystems where organizations deploy AI-powered recruitment tools. These systems leverage a combination of machine learning algorithms, NLP, and predictive modeling to evaluate massive volumes of resumes, extract both structured and unstructured data, and generate standardized applicant data points. The algorithm assesses candidates against established competency frameworks, historical hiring records, and success prediction factors. Ultimately, it produces a numerical "algorithmic fit score" that directs human recruiters toward a narrow pool of shortlisted candidates.

Organizations achieve three distinct commercial benefits through this automation: a drastic reduction in manual labor for recruiters, exponentially quicker hiring intervals, and improved procedural consistency throughout the selection process (Madancian & Taherdoost, 2023). By converting candidate characteristics into numerical data, these systems construct job-suitability models based on statistical links to past performance, fundamentally altering how companies define talent and assess suitability for employment.

For empirical illustration, multinational corporations like Unilever have successfully utilized AI-powered platforms such as HireVue to analyze candidates' video interviews, employing natural language processing to evaluate language complexity and facial expressions. Similarly, IBM's use of Watson for recruitment has significantly shortened their time-to-hire by automatically matching candidate profiles against historically successful employee traits.

4.1.2 The Illusion of Unbiased Hiring and Algorithmic Discrimination

A primary selling point utilized by commercial AI vendors is the promise of "unbiased" hiring. Supporters of algorithmic recruitment argue that software reduces human bias by standardizing evaluation methods and assessing all applicants strictly according to measurable criteria such as educational background, practical skills, and historical performance indicators. Theoretically, this minimizes the cognitive biases, fatigue, and stereotypes that inevitably affect human recruiters during repetitive screening tasks. Furthermore, organizations often perceive AI-supported recruitment systems as a highly efficient mechanism for meeting legal compliance requirements, believing that data-driven software protects their recruitment practices from external audits and discrimination lawsuits (Sharma et al., 2025).

However, academic and practitioner literature strongly disputes the assumption that AI technology inherently produces unbiased results. Because machine learning algorithms are trained on historical organizational data, they frequently absorb and replicate persistent historical biases regarding gender, ethnicity, age, and disability. If an organization has historically favored hiring a specific demographic for a particular role, the AI model will learn to replicate those exact exclusionary patterns, penalizing candidates whose profiles do not match the historical norm.

O'Neil (2017) famously argues that such algorithmic systems can quickly turn into "weapons of math destruction." When automated decision-making processes utilize biased datasets, organizations inadvertently scale discrimination to an industrial level, using the veneer of mathematical objectivity to establish legitimacy. Similarly, Williams (2020) demonstrates that commercial AI recruitment systems develop bias through their reliance on data optimization methods that operate within existing social inequalities. A critical failure in the technology transfer process occurs when organizations treat vendor-supplied algorithmic results as scientifically validated, neutral facts, rather than recognizing them as probabilistic recommendations dependent on highly specific, historically flawed datasets.

As technical systems increasingly replace human decision-makers, a hidden form of accountability emerges. If an AI discriminates, it is difficult to pinpoint liability, yet the direct pathways to employment and economic benefits are severely compromised. To mitigate major ethical, legal, and reputational risks, organizations must establish stringent governance systems. This includes mandating commercial vendors to conduct rigorous bias audits, ensuring balanced training datasets, providing complete model documentation, and establishing explainability protocols so that both recruiters and candidates can understand the specific factors influencing algorithmic recommendations.

4.2 Predictive Analytics in Performance Management

Beyond talent acquisition, the commercialization of AI has profoundly transformed performance management. Historically, performance evaluations were retrospective, relying on annual or bi-annual reviews characterized by subjective human judgment and recency bias. Today, organizations increasingly utilize predictive analytics to conduct continuous, real-time evaluations of employee performance.

4.2.1 The Architecture of Algorithmic Management

Commercial AI-powered performance management systems (such as Microsoft Viva or highly customized enterprise platforms) aggregate organizational data from a vast array of digital sources. These data streams include task achievement metrics, workflow management software, digital communication tools (email and chat metadata), customer evaluations, and instant productivity measurements. Machine learning models analyze this continuous influx of data to generate predictive insights that directly drive critical HR decisions on employee evaluation, promotion, targeted development, and retention strategies (Madancian & Taherdoost, 2023).

The capabilities of predictive analytics enable businesses to deliver highly responsive operational solutions. By using continuous feedback systems, organizations can detect shifts in employee performance in real time. This allows HR and management to identify potential burnout, flight risk, or disengagement issues weeks or months before they become critical problems, enabling proactive coaching or training interventions. When implemented transparently—establishing clear performance expectations and direct links between behavioral metrics and organizational objectives—predictive analytics can significantly enhance role clarity and alignment (Tong et al., 2021).

4.2.2 Surveillance, Transparency, and the Trust Deficit

Despite the operational advantages, the introduction of continuous predictive performance systems fundamentally alters the psychological contract between employees and the organization. Performance management is a highly sensitive area within HRM; it shapes how employees develop their professional identity, influences their motivation, and forms the basis of their perception of workplace fairness.

The use of AI-powered performance monitoring systems creates significant social, psychological, and ethical friction because commercial platforms often extend tracking beyond direct work-related tasks to encompass broader behavioral patterns. Employees often perceive predictive systems as highly disruptive and invasive, especially when data collection encompasses their communication frequencies, collaboration networks, and active screen time (Huang et al., 2023). This level of granular monitoring rapidly shifts the perception of AI from a supportive management tool to a mechanism of corporate surveillance.

Furthermore, the lack of transparency in complex, multi-layered AI models creates significant difficulties regarding accountability. When a "black box" algorithm dictates essential matters that impact salaries, promotions, and employee terminations, employees feel robbed of their agency (Huang et al., 2023). The development of predictive assessments can also create self-reinforcing, deterministic systems. If an algorithm forecasts that an employee has low advancement potential, management may withhold development opportunities, thereby guaranteeing the employee's stagnation and fulfilling the algorithm's prophecy (Tong et al., 2021).

Research demonstrates that employee acceptance of predictive performance systems is driven far more by the transparency of the evaluation methods than by the mathematical accuracy of the system itself. Employees tend to trust AI-generated feedback only when assessment standards are clear, stable, and contestable. To maintain perceptions of fairness, the algorithm must account for contextual human variables—such as workload limitations, resource scarcity, and dynamic task difficulty. Consequently, predictive analytics should only be deployed commercially as a *decision-support system* that enhances, rather than replaces, managerial judgment. If organizations rely on AI as their primary evaluation method, they simply replace visible human managerial bias with invisible algorithmic bias.

4.3 Personalized Learning & Development (L&D): AI as a Career Coach

While automated recruitment focuses on organizational efficiency and predictive performance management focuses on operational evaluation, the integration of AI into L&D represents a shift toward employee-centric augmentation. AI-enabled L&D platforms demonstrate a novel approach to human capital development by prioritizing long-term employee value creation over short-term, efficiency-based automation.

4.3.1 Dynamic Content Adaptation and Skill Mapping

Commercial AI-driven L&D platforms (such as Cornerstone OnDemand or EdCast) operate by processing comprehensive employee profiles—which include historical training records, current performance data, self-reported career aspirations, and broader labor market trends. Utilizing predictive analytics, these systems detect specific individual skill deficiencies and generate highly targeted learning recommendations designed to bridge the gap between an employee's current capabilities, future competency needs, and the organization's overarching strategic objectives (Huang et al., 2023).

The primary functional advantage of AI in this space is dynamic content adaptation. Unlike traditional, one-size-fits-all corporate training programs, AI systems tailor educational content delivery to the specific learning preferences and career development needs of each user. For instance, if the algorithm detects that middle-skilled employees are at risk of technological displacement due to automation, the L&D platform can automatically curate upskilling and reskilling modules to help them transition into higher-value, technology-adjacent roles (Chuang et al., 2024).

In practice, industry leaders such as IBM have demonstrated the effectiveness of this through their internal "Your Learning" platform, which operates much like a Netflix algorithm for education. By tracking an employee's role, search history, and organizational skill shortages, the AI pushes highly personalized, bite-sized training modules to the user, grounding the theoretical benefits of AI-driven L&D in tangible, daily workflows.

4.3.2 The Tension Between Organizational Control and Operational Independence

In this context, AI effectively serves as an autonomous career coach, providing individuals with ongoing information on shifting skill requirements, diverse career options, and professional growth paths. Research indicates that personalized learning programs vastly improve perceived organizational support when employees view AI technology as a dedicated resource for their professional growth rather than a covert means to monitor their compliance. Learning analytics afford users a degree of operational independence because their fundamental capabilities differ from recruitment and performance systems. While performance algorithms monitor and evaluate, L&D algorithms empower and develop, shifting some control over career trajectory back to the individual worker.

However, a commercial and ethical tension remains. The organization requires specific, strategically aligned skills, and the AI is fundamentally programmed to recommend content that serves the firm's bottom line. Conversely, the system must allow users the autonomy to choose their preferred developmental options to maintain motivation. This creates a conflict between corporate workforce planning and the employee's right to make independent career decisions.

To maintain trust in personalized L&D programs, organizations must adhere to two critical design elements: absolute transparency into how algorithmic recommendations are generated and the preservation of employee choice about whether they wish to participate in the suggested pathways. When the technology transfer of L&D programs prioritizes employee agency, organizations achieve exceptional operational effectiveness. By using AI as a supportive, personalized guide rather than an authoritative, top-down planner, employees maintain higher baseline engagement, commit to continuous learning, and consistently deliver greater value to the organization.

4.4 Generative AI and Large Language Models in Employee Communication and Support

While predictive analytics dominate performance and recruitment evaluations, the recent explosion of Generative AI and Large Language Models (LLMs)—such as OpenAI's ChatGPT or enterprise-grade co-pilots—introduces an entirely new dimension to HRM. Unlike predictive models that classify and score, generative models create new content, fundamentally transforming employee communication and automated HR support.

In talent acquisition, LLMs are increasingly used to instantly draft optimized job descriptions, generate personalized candidate outreach emails, and simulate interview scenarios. Internally, Generative AI powers sophisticated conversational agents (HR chatbots) capable of answering complex employee queries regarding benefits, labor policies, and onboarding protocols in natural, conversational language.

However, Generative AI introduces unique socio-technical risks. A primary concern is "algorithmic hallucination," where LLMs generate plausible but factually incorrect HR policy information, potentially creating legal liabilities. Furthermore, because LLMs are trained on vast, uncurated internet datasets, they can inadvertently generate biased or culturally insensitive communications. Therefore, the implementation of Generative AI in HR requires a "human-in-the-loop" safeguard, where HR professionals edit and verify AI-generated content before it is disseminated to the workforce, ensuring that communication remains accurate, empathetic, and legally compliant.

5. THE HUMAN–AI INTERACTION (HAII) EXPERIENCE

As artificial intelligence is commercialized and integrated into the daily operations of Human Resource Management, the focal point of organizational success shifts from the technology itself to the interface between the machine and the worker. The Human-AI Interaction (HAII) experience encompasses the cognitive, emotional, and behavioral dynamics that occur when human employees are required to collaborate with, manage, or be managed by algorithmic systems. HAII is not merely a matter of user interface design; it is a profound socio-technical phenomenon that fundamentally alters job architecture, professional identity, and workplace well-being. By examining the impact of AI on job design, the psychological outcomes of algorithmic exposure, and the critical concept of person-tool fit, we can understand how HAII dictates the ultimate success or failure of AI integration in HRM.

5.1 Impact on Job Design: The Dichotomy of Automation vs. Augmentation

The implementation of commercial AI in HRM acts as a massive catalyst for job redesign. It dictates how organizations distribute tasks, the degree of autonomy afforded to workers, and the cognitive demands placed upon them. Within the HAII literature, there is a fundamental, structural dichotomy regarding how AI systems are deployed in relation to human labor: the choice between a*utomation-* and *augmentation-oriented designs* (Perez et al., 2022).

5.1.1 Automation-Oriented Job Design: Deskilling and Disconnection

Automation-oriented job designs view the human worker as a source of friction, bias, and inefficiency. Consequently, these designs seek to replace human decision-making by implementing algorithm-based systems to achieve maximum operational efficiency and standardization. In this paradigm, commercial AI is deployed to take over entire processes—such as automated resume screening, algorithmically generated employee schedules, or automated payroll dispute resolutions.

While these systems effectively decrease baseline work demands and operational inconsistencies, they carry severe negative consequences for human job design. When AI is utilized strictly to automate, it restricts employees from performing diverse tasks and exercising independent judgment. This echoes the historical principles of Taylorism (scientific management), where complex work is broken down into highly simplified, mechanistic steps. When applied via AI, this leads to the "deskilling" of the HR workforce. Instead of utilizing their complex social and analytical skills, human workers are reduced to simply clicking "approve" or "deny" on algorithmic outputs.

When organizations follow an exclusively automation-driven approach, they create environments characterized by excessive control. This results in employees losing their innate sense of independence, leading to a phenomenon known as "cognitive offloading," where workers stop thinking critically about their tasks because they assume the machine is always correct. Furthermore, when AI operations primarily monitor employees rather than assist them, workers become increasingly disconnected and alienated from the core purpose and meaning of their work (O'Callaghan, 2023).

5.1.2 Augmentation-Oriented Job Design: Amplifying Human Capability

Conversely, an augmentation-oriented design approach to AI as a cognitive prosthesis—an extra asset explicitly designed to improve and elevate human skills. In this framework, the AI does not replace the human decision-maker; rather, it handles high-volume data processing and delivers sophisticated analytical information, empowering the human to make superior, contextually aware decisions (Tong et al., 2021).

Employees operating within an augmented HAII environment gain access to powerful operational leverage. Because the AI handles basic administrative tasks through automated background processes, employees can devote their cognitive energy and time to intricate, high-value work that requires emotional intelligence, strategic negotiation, and creative problem-solving. For an HR professional, an augmented job design means spending less time formatting spreadsheets and more time providing deep, empathetic career coaching to employees.

Empirical HAII studies demonstrate that organizations observe a direct, positive relationship between augmentation-based AI adoption and three critical outcomes: a marked increase in job satisfaction, greater acceptance of technological changes, and the proliferation of positive attitudes toward organizational changes. While the technical capabilities of a commercial AI system may be fixed, the actual HAII outcomes depend entirely on how leadership chooses to distribute work responsibilities between their staff members and the algorithms. Organizations that proactively emphasize human augmentation over algorithmic substitution are vastly more likely to achieve positive psychological and performance outcomes (Tong et al., 2021).

5.2 Psychological Outcomes: Technostress, Burnout, and Algorithmic Exhaustion

The psychological consequences of AI adoption constitute the most sensitive and critical dimension of the HAII experience. While the commercial narrative surrounding AI emphasizes seamless efficiency, the reality of working alongside advanced algorithms often creates significant psychological friction. A growing body of research identifies *technostress* as the primary mechanism linking AI implementation to negative changes in employee attitudes, behaviors, and well-being (Ragu-Nathan et al., 2008; Vuori et al., 2019).

Technostress arises when employees interact with AI systems they perceive as overly complex, unpredictable, and uncontrollable. Drawing on the JD-R model, when commercial AI is introduced without adequate training or transparency, it creates a massive workload, rapidly depleting an employee's mental and emotional resources. The HAII literature identifies several distinct dimensions of technostress exacerbated by algorithmic management.

- *Techno-Overload:* While AI processes data at lightning speed, it often creates an expectation that human workers must match this machine-like pace. AI systems can generate hundreds of predictive insights, alerts, and recommendations daily, overwhelming the cognitive capacity of HR professionals tasked with acting on them.
- *Techno-Invasion:* The use of AI for continuous performance monitoring blurs the boundaries between work and personal life. Because predictive algorithms track digital footprints in real time, employees feel they are always "on the clock," making it difficult to psychologically detach from work.
- *Techno-Complexity:* The "black box" nature of machine learning algorithms leaves employees feeling inadequate. When a manager cannot explain how an AI system generated a specific performance score, they experience deep frustration and a loss of professional competence.
- *Techno-Insecurity:* The constant, looming threat that an algorithm is capable of performing a human's job better, faster, and cheaper generates profound job insecurity, paralyzing innovation and risk-taking.

Employees experience chronically elevated stress levels, burnout, and higher turnover when organizations use continuous monitoring alongside unclear decision-making processes and opaque algorithmic performance assessments (Vuori et al., 2019). These detrimental effects are most acute when employees have no control or input over the implementation and operation of the AI system. The resulting phenomenon, often termed "algorithmic exhaustion," occurs when the mental toll of navigating complex, untrustworthy systems drains the workforce of its vitality and organizational commitment.

5.3 Determinants of Satisfaction, Retention, and Psychological Safety

Despite the severe risks of technostress, the HAII experience can be highly positive if governed by human-centric principles. Empirical findings consistently show that positive psychological effects in an AI-driven workplace are not derived from the algorithm's technological sophistication; rather, they stem from human perceptions of *usefulness, fairness, and transparency* (Jianchun, 2024). In the HAII equation, advanced technology serves merely as a secondary factor. Employee perceptions act as the primary intermediaries that determine how different systemic elements affect outcomes.

Job satisfaction and employee retention improve significantly when AI systems are used to provide clearer role definitions and reduce mental workload. For instance, when AI handles scheduling conflicts or automates compliance reporting, it effectively removes highly frustrating administrative bottlenecks. This allows the employee to successfully complete their core, meaningful responsibilities, thereby enhancing their intrinsic motivation and happiness at work (Jianchun, 2024; Moin & Zhang, 2025).

Furthermore, the concept of *psychological safety* is paramount in HAII. Psychological safety refers to an employee's belief that they will not be punished or humiliated for speaking up, making mistakes, or challenging the status quo. In an algorithmic workplace, psychological safety is maintained only when employees possess the right to contest AI-generated decisions. If an AI performance system flags an employee as underperforming based on an anomaly in their digital workflow, the employee must feel safe challenging that algorithmic assumption without fear of retaliation. When organizations establish clear, human-in-the-loop appeal processes, they foster a culture of fairness. This transparent, flexible approach to algorithmic governance directly reduces technostress and builds the trust necessary to retain top talent in a highly digitized environment.

5.4 The Crucial Role of "Person–Tool Fit" in Technology Adoption

A central determinant of success in technology transfer is the concept of "person-tool fit." Evolving from the broader organizational psychology theory of Person-Environment (P-E) fit, person-tool fit describes the degree of alignment between an individual employee's characteristics—including their technical skills, moral values, and professional expectations—and the specific design and function of the AI systems they are required to operate. Research strongly indicates that when individuals achieve a high state of person-tool fit, they exhibit significantly higher trust in AI technologies and utilize them far more effectively to generate organizational value (Perez et al., 2022).

5.4.1 Professional Identity and Algorithmic Friction

Person-tool fit is deeply intertwined with a worker's professional identity. Employees are vastly more likely to accept and leverage algorithmic insights in their daily work when they view the commercial AI tools as seamlessly matching their personal work styles and complementing their professional self-concept. For example, if an HR manager views their professional identity as an "analytical strategist," an AI dashboard that provides deep workforce analytics creates a high person-tool fit, affirming their identity and amplifying their capabilities.

However, when human capabilities, values, and identities clash with algorithmic requirements, severe operational friction occurs. This is particularly pronounced in creative industries and roles that demand high emotional intelligence (Öztaş & Arda, 2025). If a seasoned corporate recruiter perceives their core value as their empathetic ability to understand the nuanced, unspoken potential of a human candidate, being forced to rely on a rigid, automated AI screening system violates their professional identity. When human values conflict with technological constraints, workers will actively resist the system. They may create "workarounds" (alternative, non-sanctioned solutions), ignore the AI entirely, or engage in malicious compliance, rendering the system unproductive and drastically reducing the return on AI investments.

5.4.2 Job Crafting and Participatory Implementation

From a technology transfer perspective, establishing high person-tool fit operates as a mandatory, necessary condition for commercial success because it represents the critical bridge connecting system design with actual organizational results. Organizations cannot dictate person-tool fit from the top down; it must be cultivated through user autonomy.

One of the most effective mechanisms for achieving this fit is empowering employees to engage in *AI-based job crafting* (Xiao et al., 2025). Job crafting refers to the proactive steps employees take to redesign their own jobs—altering task, relational, and cognitive boundaries to make their work more meaningful. When organizations provide adaptive AI interfaces and allow employees the autonomy to customize how, when, and where they interact with the algorithms, employees can craft their HAII experience to maximize person-tool fit.

Furthermore, the combination of comprehensive training and participatory implementation is vital (Callari & Puppione, 2025). Rather than imposing commercial AI systems unilaterally, organizations must involve end-users in the procurement, testing, and implementation phases. Involving employees in the co-design of their algorithmic workflows creates a system that naturally aligns with their needs. It enables employees to develop the necessary technical skills and psychological confidence required to manage complex AI systems without feeling subjugated by them.

Ultimately, the success of AI in human resource management is determined by the harmonious intersection of two factors: the mathematical and processing abilities of the algorithms, and their sociotechnical compatibility with human users.

6. ETHICAL, LEGAL, AND SOCIAL IMPLICATIONS (ELSI)

The rapid proliferation of commercial AI within HRM does not merely present technical and operational challenges; it introduces a profound array of ethical, legal, and social implications (ELSI). Because HR fundamentally deals with human livelihoods—governing who is hired, how they are compensated, and when they are terminated—the delegation of these decisions to algorithmic systems carries immense moral weight. As AI assumes the role of an active market actor and quasi-manager, it operates at the sensitive intersection of corporate efficiency and human rights. Consequently, the commercial deployment of AI in HRM must be critically scrutinized regarding algorithmic impenetrability, systemic discrimination, data privacy, and the broader social polarization of the workforce.

6.1 Algorithmic Opacity and the "Black Box" Dilemma

One of the most pervasive ethical challenges in the commercial HR-Tech ecosystem is the "black box" nature of advanced machine learning algorithms. Deep learning networks and predictive models frequently operate with a level of mathematical complexity that defies human interpretation. While commercial vendors can explain the initial data inputs and the final predictive outputs, the internal, hidden layers of computational logic used to weigh variables and reach a conclusion remain entirely opaque.

From an ethical standpoint, this algorithmic opacity is highly problematic because it fundamentally undermines due process and employee confidence in decision-making transparency (Huang et al., 2023). In a traditional, human-managed HR environment, if an employee is denied a promotion or a candidate is rejected for a role, they possess the right to ask *why*, and the human manager is obligated to provide a reasoned justification. However, when an AI system generates a low performance score or rejects an applicant, HR professionals are often unable to explain the exact rationale behind the algorithmic decision. This inability to provide understandable, human-readable reasons for AI-generated decisions severely impairs employee perceptions of fairness and workplace equity (Zhou et al., 2023).

Establishing a transparent AI governance structure is crucial to counteract this ethical deficit. Given that a lack of transparency can rob employees of trust and provoke fierce organizational resistance (Bankins et al., 2024), organizations must prioritize "Explainable AI" (XAI). Effective governance means explicitly communicating how the AI system affects job evaluations and task assignments, and providing clear, logical reasons for AI-generated decisions to promote procedural fairness. Without this transparency, the psychological contract between the employer and the employee is fundamentally broken, replacing mutual trust with suspicion and algorithmic determinism.

6.2 Data Privacy, Surveillance Capitalism, and Legal Compliance

Data privacy and security represent major, ongoing concerns in the adoption of AI-driven HR platforms. Commercial AI algorithms are voracious; their predictive accuracy depends entirely on the continuous ingestion of massive datasets. To feed these algorithms, organizations rely on the continuous incorporation of the massive behavioral datasets harvested during daily operations. This intensive data analysis shapes the line between legitimate workforce management and invasive corporate surveillance.

Confirming the severity of this issue, recent studies highlight that the increasing privacy risks associated with data collection constitute a key negative effect of AI in HRM (Zhou et al., 2023). The ethical boundary between legitimate workforce management and corporate surveillance capitalism is rapidly blurring. This intensive data analysis can lead to a profound loss of privacy, with employees frequently viewing such pervasive tracking as highly unethical and invasive (Hamilton & Davison, 2022).

From a legal perspective, HR professionals face immense challenges in navigating the complex web of global data protection laws (such as the General Data Protection Regulation (GDPR) in Europe or the California Consumer Privacy Act (CCPA) in the United States). These legal frameworks mandate strict data minimization, require informed employee consent, and grant workers the "right to be forgotten." However, commercial machine learning models are designed to retain and learn from historical data indefinitely, creating a direct conflict between algorithmic architecture and legal compliance. As AI raises serious legal and ethical concerns, HR professionals must proactively develop a deep understanding of these issues. HR must take the lead in addressing these challenges, with thorough knowledge of data privacy laws and active identification and mitigation of potential risks before commercial systems are fully deployed (Madancian & Taherdoost, 2023).

6.3 Bias, Discrimination, and the Perpetuation of Inequality

While commercial vendors market their recruitment systems as neutral, algorithmic bias remains a pervasive ethical and legal threat in HRM (Huang et al., 2023). When algorithms are trained on historically skewed data, they codify those inequalities into automated decisions, shifting the discussion from technical error to systemic legal liability.

A critical research paper by Hamilton and Davison (2022) explores the severe legal and ethical challenges HR managers face with machine learning, specifically focusing on systemic discrimination. Under many labor laws, organizations can be held legally liable for "disparate impact"—practices that are outwardly neutral but disproportionately harm protected classes of people. Because AI systems optimize for the majority of data, they frequently penalize outliers, leading to the systemic exclusion of minority candidates, individuals with non-traditional career paths, or neurodivergent applicants who do not conform to the algorithm's normalized parameters.

Disturbingly, research demonstrates that racial equity and anti-discrimination measures are not a priority for most commercial HR analytics providers (Williams, 2020). Because vendors are primarily incentivized by commercial market forces to deliver speed and efficiency, the rigorous, time-consuming process of auditing training data for intersectional biases is often bypassed. These findings strongly suggest that immense, critical attention must be paid to the specific data sets used to train AI algorithms to ensure fairness and avoid discriminatory outcomes. HR professionals play a vital, non-delegable role in shaping AI systems by scrutinizing vendor screening criteria, conducting continuous bias audits, and ensuring strict ethical and legal compliance (Madancian & Taherdoost, 2023).

6.4 Social Implications: Job Polarization and Workplace Inequality

Beyond individual privacy and bias, the integration of AI carries broad, structural social implications regarding job restructuring and workplace inequality. The commercial deployment of AI has the potential to render the workplace fundamentally more unequal without clear, human-centric governance.

A primary societal concern is the threat of AI-induced job polarization. As organizations implement AI to automate mechanistic and administrative tasks, the workforce is increasingly divided into two distinct extremes. On one end are the highly skilled workers who manage, design, and strategically leverage the AI (experiencing job augmentation, increased autonomy, and higher compensation). On the other end are the lower-skilled workers who are managed *by* the AI (experiencing job deskilling, algorithmic surveillance, and stagnant wages). Middle-skilled jobs are the most vulnerable to complete technological displacement, creating a hollowed-out organizational structure.

This polarization leads to an unfair distribution of workload and promotion opportunities (Jianchun, 2024). If AI systems are used as authoritative surveillance tools to squeeze the maximum productivity out of frontline workers, they exacerbate existing workplace inequalities and degrade the dignity of labor (Perez et al., 2022). Furthermore, the psychological toll of this dynamic creates a socially toxic environment characterized by hyper-competition and algorithmic exhaustion. Managers must address these ethical and psychological concerns by responsibly deploying AI to ensure the workplace is free of inequalities (Perez et al., 2022). This requires actively equalizing workloads to prevent job polarization due to AI use, and explicitly fostering psychological safety by defining AI as an assisting rather than an observing tool (Bankins et al., 2024; Jianchun, 2024).

Addressing this polarization also requires active consideration of labor relations and employee voice. The introduction of algorithmic management often disrupts traditional collective bargaining structures. In highly unionized environments, workers and labor unions are increasingly demanding 'algorithmic transparency' as a core collective bargaining right, pushing back against independent, black-box monitoring. To maintain industrial harmony, organizations must provide employees with a formalized voice in the design and deployment of AI systems, ensuring that technology acts as a negotiated tool for shared prosperity rather than an imposed instrument of top-down control.

6.5 Building Transparent AI Governance Frameworks

To navigate this complex web of ethical, legal, and social implications, companies must transition from ad-hoc technological adoption to formalized AI governance. AI integration in HR presents both immense opportunities and severe challenges, but realizing its potential depends entirely on how the workplace considers and mitigates these ethical, legal, and cultural barriers. The black box nature of AI will continually undermine trust and human relationships unless it is actively managed.

From a pragmatic point of view, organizations must adopt AI deployment strategies that fundamentally empower employees rather than merely extract value from them. Transparent AI governance processes, employee-driven customization of AI interfaces, and continuous retraining programs can help bridge the widening gap created between AI automation and human expertise (Moin & Zhang, 2025).

Transparency and ethics are central to supporting a healthy, sustainable AI-driven workplace. Globally, regulatory landscapes are rapidly shifting to enforce these ethical boundaries. A primary example is the European Union's Artificial Intelligence Act (EU AI Act), which represents the world's first comprehensive legal framework for AI. Crucially, the EU AI Act classifies AI systems used in employment, worker management, and access to self-employment—such as automated CV screening and algorithmic performance evaluation—as "high-risk."

For global organizations, this mandates strict compliance mechanisms, including rigorous pre-market conformity assessments, high-quality data governance, and the implementation of Explainable AI (XAI). XAI ensures that the outputs of machine learning models can be understood and traced by human users, directly countering the "black box" dilemma. Organizations must establish clear ethical policies regarding AI surveillance, explicitly detailing what data is collected, how long it is stored, and who has access to it. Furthermore, bias, discrimination, and legal risks highlight the urgent need for a comprehensive Code of Ethics to manage and guide AI use. For successful AI automation to take root, organizations must maintain a delicate, unwavering balance between technological efficiency and human workforce-oriented ethics.

7. RECOMMENDATIONS FOR MANAGERS

To effectively navigate the immense complexities of AI implementation in commercial HRM, organizational leaders and HR managers must transition from passive consumers of technology to active architects of the human-AI workplace. Realizing the substantial benefits of AI—including increased efficiency, improved decision-making, and enhanced strategic HR planning—requires careful planning, targeted resource investment, and an unwavering commitment to ethical implementation. Based on the synthesis of technology transfer mechanics, job design, and human-AI interaction dynamics, the following strategic recommendations are provided for managers.

The most critical decision a manager makes during AI implementation is how the technology interacts with human labor. Managers must prioritize balancing automation with human oversight. This means explicitly utilizing AI to support human capabilities rather than strictly seeking to replace them. Organizations should deploy AI to automate mundane, mechanistic, and highly routinized administrative tasks—such as initial data parsing, scheduling, and compliance reporting. However, managers must ensure that AI strictly *assists* human decision-making in complex areas, allowing employees the autonomy to exercise subjective judgment, empathy, and creativity (Öztaş & Arda, 2025; Tong et al., 2021). By maintaining a "human-in-the-loop" architecture, managers can leverage computational efficiency while safeguarding against the rigid determinism of algorithms.

Enhancing employee satisfaction and retention through AI requires that job redesign is conducted in a highly participatory, democratic manner (Callari & Puppione, 2025). Managers should actively involve employees in co-designing AI applications and mapping out new workflows to ensure the technology aligns with actual user needs. By establishing timely, anonymous mechanisms for employee feedback, managers can continuously monitor the effects of AI on job satisfaction. Furthermore, allowing employees to customize their AI interfaces and personalize their digital work experiences will significantly alleviate job clarity stress and mitigate the feeling of being overwhelmed by increased technological workloads (O'Callaghan, 2023).

Given the severe reliance on reskilling to avert technological job displacement—especially for vulnerable, middle-skilled employees—fostering continuous skill development is critical (Chuang et al., 2024). Managers must aggressively support training programs focused on AI data literacy, enabling HR professionals to critically interpret algorithmic outputs. Furthermore, leadership must promote healthy human-AI partnerships by actively teaching employees to collaborate effectively with AI tools (Jianchun, 2024). To prevent job polarization, managers must establish clear, accessible career pathways that facilitate employees' adaptation to AI-driven transformations within their specific job roles (Moin & Zhang, 2025).

Finally, managers must tackle the ethical and mental concerns associated with algorithmic management by governing AI responsibly. It is imperative to keep the workplace free from technologically induced inequalities (Perez et al., 2022). Managers must establish and enforce clear ethical policies regarding AI surveillance and data privacy, strictly limiting the scope of behavioral data collection to what is explicitly necessary for work performance. To prevent burnout, managers must purposefully equalize workloads, ensuring that AI-generated efficiency does not simply translate into higher production quotas for human workers (Jianchun, 2024). Most importantly, managers must create psychological safety by officially defining and deploying AI as an assisting, developmental tool rather than a punitive, observing tool (Bankins et al., 2024).

8. FUTURE RESEARCH DIRECTIONS AND CONCLUSION

8.1 Future Research Directions

As artificial intelligence continues to evolve as a commercial market actor, the academic and practitioner literature must keep pace with the rapid technological shifts occurring in HRM. The current intersection of AI and job design showcases vast opportunities for proactive implementation that align with human work needs; however, significant empirical gaps remain. Future research should prioritize the following directions.

First, more longitudinal research is needed to understand the long-term impact of AI on critical employee outcomes, such as job satisfaction, intrinsic engagement, and holistic well-being. Long-term studies should explore the association between positive initial perceptions toward AI and sustained willingness to learn new skills, while also mapping how negative views may give rise to systemic resistance, decreased productivity, and prolonged job insecurity.

Second, applied research is urgently needed to develop robust best practices for mitigating bias in AI algorithms. Future studies should focus on creating standardized, cross-industry auditing frameworks to ensure fairness and intersectional equity in AI-driven HR decisions.

Third, more research is needed to explore the evolving ethical implications of AI in HR, particularly concerning the deployment of newer Generative AI models (e.g., Large Language Models) in the workplace. Research must address how Generative AI exacerbates issues of data privacy, algorithmic transparency, and intellectual property within commercial HR ecosystems.

Finally, in approaching human creativity and autonomous creative technologies, the AI turn must be understood not just as a technological update, but as a societal reformulation of values. Future qualitative research should employ Interpretative Phenomenological Analysis (IPA) in combination with Critical Discourse Analysis (CDA) to develop a critical, theory-based conceptualization of creative workers' experiences with AI. Such research is vital for identifying the grassroots terms of genuine co-creative engagements and for developing socially intelligible, ethical AI technologies that protect creative agency.

8.2 Conclusion

Artificial intelligence has unequivocally transitioned from a passive administrative tool to a powerful, active market actor, fundamentally restructuring the HRM landscape. As demonstrated throughout this chapter, the commercial integration of AI—ranging from automated recruitment platforms to predictive performance algorithms and personalized career coaches—offers unprecedented opportunities to optimize talent acquisition, streamline organizational efficiency, and personalize the employee lifecycle.

However, realizing these benefits requires navigating highly complex socio-technical challenges. The mechanics of technology transfer dictate that AI cannot simply be installed; it must be carefully woven into the organization's social fabric. If implemented poorly, commercial AI risks perpetuating historical biases, eroding workplace privacy through surveillance capitalism, and triggering severe technostress and job polarization among the workforce. Conversely, when organizations prioritize "person-tool fit" and purposefully design jobs around human augmentation rather than strict automation, AI serves as a powerful catalyst for professional growth and strategic alignment.

Ultimately, the future of HR will not be defined by the mathematical superiority of machine learning models, but by the strategic alliance between technology and human ethics. By investing in transparent governance, prioritizing data privacy, and fostering a culture that values human-centric AI adoption, organizations can harness the power of algorithmic management to create a more efficient, effective, and equitable workplace. The successful integration of AI in HRM relies on the unwavering recognition that while algorithms can process the data, human beings must remain the ultimate architects of the work experience.

REFERENCES

Bankins, S., Ocampo, A. C., Marrone, M., Restubog, S. L. D., & Woo, S. E. (2024). A multilevel review of artificial intelligence in organizations: Implications for organizational behavior research and practice. *Journal of Organizational Behavior, 45*(2), 159–182. DOI: 10.1002/job.2735

Berretta, S., Tausch, A., Peifer, C., & Kluge, A. (2023). The Job Perception Inventory: Considering human factors and needs in the design of human–AI work. *Frontiers in Psychology, 14*, 1128945. DOI: 10.3389/fpsyg.2023.1128945 PMID: 37287772

Böhmer, N., & Schinnenburg, H. (2023). Critical exploration of AI-driven HRM to build up organizational capabilities. *Employee Relations, 45*(5), 1057–1082. DOI: 10.1108/ER-04-2022-0202

Bositkhanova, N., & Dadaboyev, S. M. U. (2025). Revolutionizing workforce planning: The strategic role of AI in HR strategy. *Discover Global Society, 3*(1), 100. DOI: 10.1007/s44282-025-00252-y

Callari, T. C., & Puppione, L. (2025). Can generative artificial intelligence productivity tools support workplace learning? A qualitative study on employee perceptions in a multinational corporation. *Journal of Workplace Learning, 37*(3), 266–283. DOI: 10.1108/JWL-11-2024-0258

Cavanagh, J., Pariona-Cabrera, P., & Halvorsen, B. (2023). In what ways are HR analytics and artificial intelligence transforming the healthcare sector? *Asia Pacific Journal of Human Resources, 61*(4), 785–793. DOI: 10.1111/1744-7941.12392

Chuang, S., Shahhosseini, M., Javaid, M., & Wang, G. G. (2024). Machine learning and AI technology-induced skill gaps and opportunities for continuous development of middle-skilled employees. *Journal of Work-Applied Management*. Advance online publication. DOI: 10.1108/JWAM-08-2024-0111

Dadaboyev, S., Hojimurodova, S., & Gulomova, G. (2025). AI in HR analytics: A synthesis of current research and future directions. In *Proceedings of the AAAI Symposium Series* (Vol. 6, No. 1, p. 60). DOI: 10.1609/aaaiss.v6i1.36026

Dadaboyev, S. M. U., Abdullayeva, J., Abbosova, N., Suleymenova, A., & Mamadjanova, K. (2025). Role of artificial intelligence in employee recruitment: Systematic review and future research directions. *Discover Global Society, 3*(1), 99. DOI: 10.1007/s44282-025-00246-w

Dadaboyev, S. M. U., Baxtiyorova, F., & Akbarova, Y. (2025). AI and the Future of Work: How Can We Design Jobs That Benefit Both Organizations and Employees. In *Proceedings of the AAAI Symposium Series* (Vol. 6, No. 1, p. 59). DOI: 10.1609/aaaiss.v6i1.36025

Hamilton, R. H., & Davison, H. K. (2022). Legal and ethical challenges for HR in machine learning. *Employee Responsibilities and Rights Journal, 34*(1), 19–39. DOI: 10.1007/s10672-021-09377-z

Heaven, D. (2020). Why faces don't always tell the truth about feelings. *Nature, 578*(7796), 502–505. DOI: 10.1038/d41586-020-00507-5 PMID: 32103200

Huang, X., Yang, F., Zheng, J., Feng, C., & Zhang, L. (2023). Personalized human resource management via HR analytics and artificial intelligence: Theory and implications. *Asia Pacific Management Review, 28*(4), 598–610. DOI: 10.1016/j.apmrv.2023.04.004

Jianchun, Y. (2024). Enhancing employee job satisfaction through organizational climate and employee happiness at work: A mediated–moderated model. *BMC Psychology, 12*(744), 744. Advance online publication. DOI: 10.1186/s40359-024-02269-5 PMID: 39696658

Madancian, M., & Taherdoost, H. (2023, October). The impact of artificial intelligence on human resource management: opportunities and challenges. In *International Conference on Interdisciplinarity in Engineering* (pp. 406-424). Cham: Springer Nature Switzerland.

Moin, M. F., & Zhang, J. (2025). Stemming the tide: Linking AI technology with worker retention. *International Journal of Managing Projects in Business, 18*(4-5), 721–732. DOI: 10.1108/IJMPB-01-2024-0015

O'Callaghan, M. (2023). Can decision intelligence help organizations retain employees? Serial multiple mediation of job characteristics and meaningful work. *Cogent Psychology, 10*(1), 2258475. Advance online publication. DOI: 10.1080/23311908.2023.2258475

O'Neil, C. (2017). *Weapons of math destruction: How big data increases inequality and threatens democracy.* Crown Publishing Group.

Oswald, F. L., Behrend, T. S., Putka, D. J., & Sinar, E. (2020). Big data in industrial-organizational psychology and human resource management: Forward progress for organizational research and practice. *Annual Review of Organizational Psychology and Organizational Behavior, 7*(1), 505–533. DOI: 10.1146/annurev-orgpsych-032117-104553

Öztaş, Y. E., & Arda, B. (2025). Re-evaluating creative labor in the age of artificial intelligence: A qualitative case study of creative workers' perspectives on technological transformation in creative industries. *AI & Society*, *40*(5), 4119–4130. DOI: 10.1007/s00146-025-02180-6

Perez, F., Conway, N., & Roques, O. (2022). The autonomy tussle: AI technology and employee job crafting responses. *Relations Industrielles. Relations Industrielles*, *77*(3), 1–25. DOI: 10.7202/1094209ar

Ragu-Nathan, T. S., Tarafdar, M., Ragu-Nathan, B. S., & Tu, Q. (2008). The consequences of technostress for end users in organizations: Conceptual development and empirical validation. *Information Systems Research*, *19*(4), 417–433. DOI: 10.1287/isre.1070.0165

Sharma, P., Bhattacharya, S., & Bhattacharya, S. (2025). HR analytics and AI adoption in IT sector: Reflections from practitioners. *Journal of Work-Applied Management*. Advance online publication. DOI: 10.1108/JWAM-12-2024-0179

Tong, S., Jia, N., Luo, X., & Fang, Z. (2021). The Janus face of artificial intelligence feedback: Deployment versus disclosure effects employee performance. *Strategic Management Journal*, *42*(9), 1600–1631. DOI: 10.1002/smj.3322

Trocin, C., Hovland, I. V., Mikalef, P., & Dremel, C. (2021). How artificial intelligence affords digital innovation: A cross-case analysis of Scandinavian companies. *Technological Forecasting and Social Change*, *173*, 121081. Advance online publication. DOI: 10.1016/j.techfore.2021.121081

Venugopal, M., Madhavan, V., Prasad, R., & Raman, R. (2024). Transformative AI in human resource management: Enhancing workforce planning with topic modeling. *Cogent Business & Management*, *11*(1), 2432550. Advance online publication. DOI: 10.1080/23311975.2024.2432550

Vuori, V., Helander, N., & Okkonen, J. (2019). Digitalization in knowledge work: The dream of enhanced performance. *Cognition Technology and Work*, *21*(2), 237–252. DOI: 10.1007/s10111-018-0501-3

Williams, S. D. (2020). A textual analysis of racial considerations in human resource analytics vendors' marketing. *Management Research and Practice*, *12*(4), 49–63.

Xiao, Q., Yan, J., & Bamber, G. J. (2025). How does AI-enabled HR analytics influence employee resilience: Job crafting as a mediator and HRM system strength as a moderator. *Personnel Review*, *54*(3), 824–843. DOI: 10.1108/PR-03-2023-0198

Zhou, Y., Wang, L. J., & Chen, W. S. (2023). The dark side of AI enabled HRM on employees based on AI algorithmic features. *Journal of Organizational Change Management*, *36*(7), 1222–1241. DOI: 10.1108/JOCM-10-2022-0308

Chapter 7
Artificial Intelligence-Driven Decision Support for Supply Chain and Logistics Optimization

Abdullah Sheikh
http://orcid.org/0009-0009-0044-7383
Wright State University, USA

Susmitha Sajja
http://orcid.org/0009-0008-9536-0936
University of Missouri–Kansas City, USA

Sadath Ali Syed
http://orcid.org/0009-0009-6605-3782
McNeese State University, USA

Jannatul Ferdousi
http://orcid.org/0009-0001-8651-1375
Indiana Wesleyan University, USA

ABSTRACT

Artificial intelligence (AI) is increasingly transforming how organizations make operational and strategic decisions. In supply chain and logistics environments, decision makers must evaluate large volumes of operational data while responding to uncertainty, demand volatility, and global disruptions. This chapter examines how AI-driven decision support systems enhance business optimization across supply chain operations. We analyze the integration of machine learning, predictive analytics, and optimization models within decision support frameworks and discuss

DOI: 10.4018/979-8-3373-9325-4.ch007

their impact on forecasting, inventory management, logistics planning, and supply chain resilience. Drawing on recent academic literature and industry practices, this chapter illustrates how AI technologies improve operational efficiency and decision accuracy in complex supply networks. We further discuss implementation challenges, ethical considerations, and future research opportunities related to AI adoption in supply chain management.

1. INTRODUCTION

Modern supply chains operate in an increasingly complex and uncertain environment characterized by demand volatility, global disruptions, and rising customer expectations. Organizations are required to make rapid and accurate decisions across procurement, production, transportation, and distribution processes. However, traditional decision-making approaches, which rely heavily on historical data and managerial intuition, are often insufficient for addressing the scale and complexity of contemporary supply chain systems.

Decision support systems (DSS) have long been used to assist managers in analyzing structured data and improving operational decision making. While early DSS platforms provided valuable analytical capabilities, their functionality was largely limited to descriptive and diagnostic analysis. As supply chains became more data-intensive and interconnected, the limitations of traditional DSS became increasingly evident, particularly in their ability to process large volumes of real-time data and generate predictive insights.

Artificial intelligence (AI) has emerged as a transformative technology that enhances the capabilities of decision support systems by enabling predictive and prescriptive analytics. AI technologies, including machine learning, deep learning, and optimization algorithms, allow organizations to identify complex patterns in data, forecast future outcomes, and recommend optimal decisions (Davenport & Ronanki, 2018). The integration of AI into DSS frameworks enables a shift from reactive decision making toward proactive and data-driven strategies.

Despite the growing adoption of AI technologies in business operations, there remains a significant gap in understanding how AI-driven decision support systems can be systematically applied to achieve end-to-end business optimization within supply chain and logistics contexts. Existing studies often focus on isolated applications of AI, such as demand forecasting or route optimization, without examining how these technologies can be integrated within a comprehensive decision support framework. Recent studies highlight that the integration of artificial intelligence in supply chain environments also requires new leadership approaches that balance algorithmic insights with managerial judgment (Sheikh, 2025).

This chapter addresses this gap by examining the role of AI-driven decision support systems in enhancing supply chain and logistics performance. We argue that the integration of AI technologies within DSS frameworks enables organizations to improve decision accuracy, enhance operational efficiency, and build more resilient supply chains.

Specifically, this chapter makes the following contributions:

- It provides a comprehensive overview of the evolution of decision support systems in business analytics.
- It analyzes the role of artificial intelligence technologies in supply chain decision making.
- It examines key applications of AI in logistics and supply chain operations.
- It discusses implementation challenges, managerial implications, and future research directions.

By synthesizing academic literature and industry practices, this chapter contributes to the growing body of knowledge on AI-enabled business optimization and provides practical insights for managers seeking to leverage AI in supply chain decision making.

Research Gap

Although artificial intelligence has attracted growing attention in supply chain management research, much of the existing literature focuses on isolated applications of specific technologies such as machine learning forecasting models, warehouse robotics, or predictive analytics tools. While these studies provide valuable insights, they often examine individual technological solutions rather than analyzing how artificial intelligence functions as part of an integrated decision support framework within supply chain systems. As a result, there remains a limited understanding of how multiple AI technologies interact to support strategic and operational decision-making across different supply chain functions.

Furthermore, many studies emphasize technical model development while giving comparatively less attention to the managerial, organizational, and governance implications associated with implementing AI-driven decision support systems. Issues such as data governance, human–AI collaboration, and supply chain resilience require further exploration in order to understand how organizations can successfully integrate artificial intelligence into real-world logistics operations.

To address these gaps, this chapter examines artificial intelligence–driven decision support systems from a holistic perspective. Rather than focusing solely on algorithmic techniques, we analyze how AI technologies can be integrated into supply chain decision processes, how they influence managerial practices, and how organizations can overcome implementation challenges when adopting AI-enabled logistics systems.

Chapter Contribution and Structure

This chapter contributes to the growing literature on artificial intelligence–enabled supply chain management by examining how AI-driven decision support systems can improve operational efficiency and strategic decision-making in complex logistics environments. While previous studies have examined individual AI technologies such as machine learning or predictive analytics, this chapter provides an integrated perspective on how these technologies function within modern decision support frameworks across multiple supply chain activities.

Specifically, this chapter makes three contributions. First, we synthesize existing research on artificial intelligence, business analytics, and decision support systems to establish a conceptual foundation for AI-driven supply chain decision-making. Second, we analyze key operational applications of AI technologies, including demand forecasting, inventory optimization, warehouse automation, and transportation planning. Third, we examine managerial and governance implications associated with implementing AI-enabled decision systems within large-scale logistics networks.

The remainder of the chapter is organized as follows. Section 2 discusses the evolution of decision support systems and business analytics within supply chain management. Section 3 examines key artificial intelligence technologies that enable modern decision support systems. Section 4 analyzes major applications of AI within supply chain and logistics operations. Section 5 presents an industry case study illustrating the practical implementation of AI-driven logistics systems. Sections 6 and 7 discuss implementation challenges and ethical considerations associated with AI adoption. Section 8 identifies future research directions, while Section 9 examines managerial implications. Finally, Section 10 concludes the chapter.

2. BACKGROUND: DECISION SUPPORT SYSTEMS AND BUSINESS ANALYTICS

Decision support systems (DSS) have long been recognized as important tools for assisting managers in making complex organizational decisions. These systems emerged in the 1970s as computer-based information systems designed to support decision-making activities that involve large amounts of data and analytical models. Early DSS platforms primarily focused on structured data processing and statistical analysis, enabling managers to analyze operational information and generate reports to support planning and resource allocation.

Over time, DSS evolved significantly alongside advancements in information technology and data management. The introduction of enterprise resource planning (ERP) systems and large-scale databases allowed organizations to integrate operational data from multiple business functions, including finance, logistics, procurement, and manufacturing. As a result, DSS platforms became increasingly capable of providing more comprehensive insights into organizational performance and operational trends.

In the early stages of DSS development, decision support tools were primarily designed to assist managers in solving structured problems. These systems relied on predefined analytical models and rule-based algorithms that processed historical data to generate reports or perform scenario analysis. While these approaches provided valuable insights, they often lacked the flexibility required to address complex and dynamic decision environments.

The development of business intelligence (BI) systems during the late 1990s and early 2000s significantly expanded the capabilities of decision support technologies. BI platforms introduced advanced data visualization tools, dashboards, and reporting systems that enabled managers to monitor organizational performance in real time. According to Waller and Fawcett (2013), business intelligence systems played a crucial role in transforming raw operational data into meaningful insights that could support strategic and tactical decision making.

Despite these advancements, traditional DSS and BI systems remained largely descriptive in nature. They were effective at answering questions such as "What happened?" and "Why did it happen?", but they were less capable of predicting future outcomes or recommending optimal actions. As organizations began to generate larger volumes of data through digital technologies, the limitations of traditional DSS became increasingly apparent.

To address these limitations, organizations began integrating advanced analytics techniques into decision support frameworks. Modern business analytics systems are often categorized into four levels of analytical capability: descriptive analytics, diagnostic analytics, predictive analytics, and prescriptive analytics (Choi et al., 2018).

Descriptive analytics focuses on summarizing historical data to provide insights into past performance. Diagnostic analytics attempts to identify the underlying causes of observed trends or events. Predictive analytics uses statistical models and machine learning algorithms to forecast future outcomes based on historical patterns. Prescriptive analytics extends predictive analysis by recommending actions that organizations can take to achieve desired outcomes.

We argue that the transition from descriptive analytics to predictive and prescriptive analytics represents a fundamental shift in how organizations approach decision making. Rather than relying solely on historical data analysis, modern decision support systems are increasingly designed to generate forward-looking insights that guide strategic planning and operational decision making.

Artificial intelligence plays a central role in enabling this transformation. AI technologies allow organizations to process large volumes of structured and unstructured data and identify patterns that would be difficult to detect using traditional analytical techniques (Davenport & Ronanki, 2018). Machine learning models can continuously learn from new data and improve their predictive capabilities over time, making them particularly valuable for dynamic business environments.

Within supply chain management, the adoption of AI-driven decision support systems has been particularly significant. Supply chains involve complex networks of suppliers, manufacturers, distributors, and customers, all of which generate large volumes of operational data. Managing these networks requires accurate forecasting, efficient resource allocation, and effective risk management strategies.

Traditional decision support tools often struggle to address the complexity of modern supply chains because they rely heavily on static analytical models. AI-driven DSS platforms, by contrast, enable organizations to analyze real-time operational data and generate predictive insights that support more adaptive decision-making processes.

Recent research has highlighted the growing importance of AI technologies in supply chain analytics. For example, Ivanov and Dolgui (2020) demonstrate that advanced analytics and digital technologies can significantly improve supply chain resilience by enabling organizations to anticipate disruptions and respond more effectively to operational uncertainties. Similarly, Baryannis et al. (2019) show that artificial intelligence techniques can enhance supply chain risk management by identifying potential disruptions and recommending mitigation strategies.

We emphasize that AI-driven decision support systems should not be viewed as replacements for human decision makers. Instead, these systems function as collaborative tools that augment managerial decision-making capabilities. By combining computational intelligence with human expertise, organizations can achieve more informed and effective decision outcomes.

In this chapter, we build on this perspective by examining how artificial intelligence technologies enhance decision support capabilities within supply chain and logistics operations. Specifically, we explore how machine learning, predictive analytics, and optimization algorithms can be integrated into decision support frameworks to improve business optimization and operational performance.

To illustrate the relationship between artificial intelligence technologies and supply chain decision systems, Figure 1 presents a conceptual framework of AI-driven decision support.

Figure 1. AI-driven decision support framework for supply chain management.

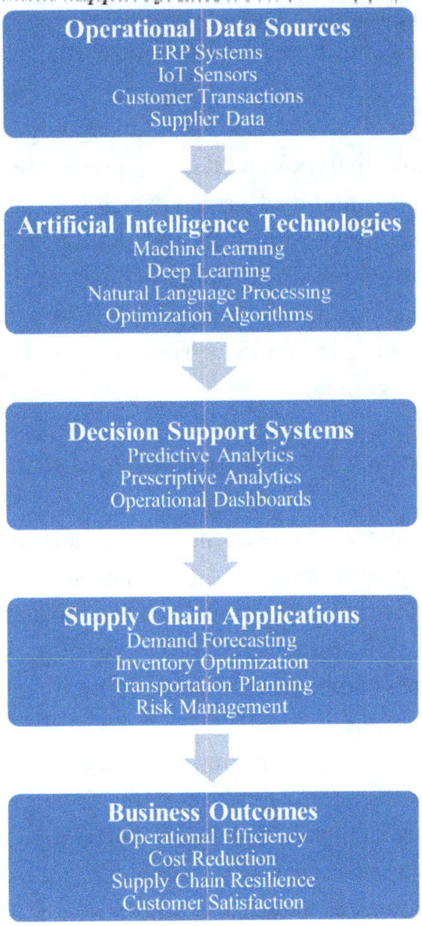

As shown in Figure 1, AI technologies transform operational data into actionable insights that support managerial decision-making.

3. ARTIFICIAL INTELLIGENCE TECHNOLOGIES FOR DECISION SUPPORT SYSTEMS

Artificial intelligence (AI) has become a central component of modern decision support systems by enabling organizations to process large datasets, identify complex relationships, and generate predictive insights. While traditional decision support tools relied primarily on statistical models and rule-based systems, recent advances in artificial intelligence have significantly expanded the analytical capabilities available to decision makers.

In this chapter, we argue that the integration of artificial intelligence technologies into decision support systems fundamentally changes how organizations approach operational and strategic decision making. AI technologies allow organizations to move beyond descriptive analytics and develop predictive and prescriptive models that support more adaptive and data-driven decision processes.

This section examines the primary artificial intelligence technologies that enable modern decision support systems, including machine learning, deep learning, natural language processing, and optimization algorithms. These technologies collectively form the analytical foundation of AI-driven decision support systems used in supply chain and logistics management.

3.1 Machine Learning for Predictive Decision Making

Machine learning represents one of the most widely used artificial intelligence techniques in modern business analytics. Machine learning algorithms analyze historical data in order to identify patterns and relationships that can be used to predict future outcomes. Unlike traditional statistical models, machine learning algorithms can process large volumes of data and continuously improve their predictive accuracy as new information becomes available.

Supervised learning is one of the most commonly applied machine learning approaches in business decision support systems. In supervised learning models, algorithms are trained using historical datasets that contain labeled outcomes. These models learn relationships between input variables and target outcomes, allowing them to generate predictions for new data observations. Common supervised learning algorithms include regression models, decision trees, support vector machines, and neural networks. Machine learning models such as logistic regression, random forests, and gradient boosting algorithms have demonstrated strong predictive capabilities in supply chain forecasting applications (Sheikh, Goodrich, & Sajja, 2025).

Within supply chain management, supervised learning models are widely used for demand forecasting, inventory optimization, and customer behavior prediction. For example, machine learning algorithms can analyze historical sales data alongside external variables such as promotional campaigns, economic indicators, and weather patterns to generate more accurate demand forecasts (Choi et al., 2018).

Unsupervised learning techniques also play an important role in decision support systems. Unlike supervised learning models, unsupervised learning algorithms analyze unlabeled datasets to identify hidden structures and patterns within the data. Clustering algorithms such as k-means and hierarchical clustering are commonly used to segment customers, identify product relationships, and detect anomalies within operational datasets.

We emphasize that machine learning enhances decision support systems by enabling organizations to identify patterns that may not be visible through traditional analytical approaches. By analyzing large and complex datasets, machine learning models provide decision makers with deeper insights into operational dynamics and emerging trends.

3.2 Deep Learning and Advanced Data Analysis

Deep learning represents a specialized subset of machine learning that utilizes multi-layer neural networks to analyze complex data structures. Deep learning models have demonstrated strong performance in tasks involving unstructured data such as images, text, and sensor signals.

One of the most important contributions of deep learning lies in its ability to automatically extract relevant features from large datasets. Traditional machine learning models often require manual feature engineering, where analysts must identify and construct relevant variables before building predictive models. Deep learning algorithms, by contrast, can automatically learn hierarchical feature representations from raw data (LeCun et al., 2015).

Deep learning technologies have several applications within supply chain and logistics operations. Convolutional neural networks (CNNs) are widely used in computer vision applications such as warehouse monitoring, product inspection, and automated quality control. These systems can analyze visual data captured from cameras and detect damaged goods, incorrect packaging, or operational safety violations.

Recurrent neural networks (RNNs) and long short-term memory (LSTM) models are commonly used to analyze sequential data. In supply chain contexts, these models are particularly useful for analyzing time-series data such as demand fluctuations, shipment tracking information, and equipment sensor data. By capturing temporal patterns within datasets, deep learning models can significantly improve forecasting accuracy and operational planning.

We argue that deep learning technologies extend the analytical capabilities of decision support systems by enabling organizations to process previously inaccessible forms of data, including visual and textual information. This capability significantly enhances the ability of organizations to monitor operational processes and identify potential issues before they escalate into major disruptions.

3.3 Natural Language Processing for Supply Chain Intelligence

Natural language processing (NLP) is another important artificial intelligence technology that contributes to modern decision support systems. NLP enables computer systems to analyze and interpret human language, allowing organizations to extract valuable insights from textual data sources.

Supply chains generate large volumes of textual data through documents such as supplier contracts, shipment records, customer feedback reports, and industry news articles. Traditionally, analyzing such data required significant manual effort. NLP technologies automate this process by enabling algorithms to extract relevant information from large collections of text.

One important application of NLP in supply chain management involves sentiment analysis. Organizations can analyze customer feedback, online reviews, and social media discussions to identify emerging trends and customer preferences. These insights can inform product development strategies, inventory planning decisions, and marketing initiatives.

NLP technologies can also be used to monitor supply chain risks. For example, AI systems can analyze global news sources, regulatory reports, and economic data to identify events that may disrupt supply chains, such as geopolitical tensions, trade restrictions, or natural disasters. Early identification of these risks enables organizations to implement mitigation strategies and reduce the potential impact of disruptions.

We emphasize that natural language processing significantly expands the range of information that decision support systems can analyze. By incorporating textual data sources into analytical frameworks, organizations gain access to a richer and more comprehensive set of insights that can inform strategic decision making.

3.4 Optimization Algorithms and Prescriptive Analytics

While predictive analytics helps organizations forecast future outcomes, prescriptive analytics focuses on identifying optimal decisions that maximize performance under specific constraints. Optimization algorithms play a critical role in enabling prescriptive decision support systems.

Optimization techniques are widely used in logistics and supply chain planning problems, where decision makers must allocate resources efficiently across complex operational networks. These problems often involve numerous constraints, including transportation capacity limits, delivery deadlines, production schedules, and cost considerations.

Linear programming and mixed-integer programming are commonly used optimization methods in supply chain management. These models enable organizations to determine optimal production quantities, transportation routes, and inventory allocation strategies.

More recently, metaheuristic optimization algorithms such as genetic algorithms and simulated annealing have been applied to complex logistics problems where traditional optimization models may be computationally expensive. These algorithms search for near-optimal solutions by exploring multiple possible configurations of operational decisions.

We argue that the integration of predictive analytics and optimization algorithms represents one of the most significant advancements in modern decision support systems. Predictive models generate forecasts and identify potential scenarios, while optimization algorithms recommend the most effective actions for achieving organizational objectives.

This combination of predictive and prescriptive capabilities enables organizations to transition from reactive decision making toward proactive operational management.

3.5 Human–AI Collaboration in Decision Support

Despite the increasing sophistication of artificial intelligence technologies, human expertise remains essential for effective decision making. AI-driven decision support systems are most effective when they operate as collaborative tools that augment managerial judgment rather than replacing it.

Managers provide contextual knowledge, ethical judgment, and strategic perspective that cannot easily be captured by computational models. AI systems, on the other hand, excel at processing large datasets and identifying patterns that may not be immediately visible to human analysts.

We argue that successful decision support systems combine the strengths of both human and artificial intelligence. By integrating computational insights with managerial expertise, organizations can achieve more balanced and effective decision outcomes.

This collaborative approach also helps address concerns related to algorithmic transparency and accountability. Human oversight ensures that AI-generated recommendations are evaluated critically and aligned with organizational goals and ethical standards.

Figure 2. Conceptual architecture of AI-driven decision support systems in supply chain management.

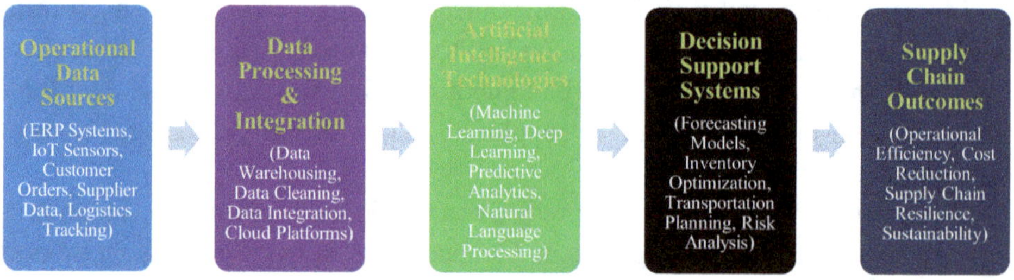

This framework illustrates how operational data from supply chain activities are integrated through data infrastructure and analyzed using artificial intelligence technologies to support managerial decision-making and improve supply chain performance.

Having examined the core artificial intelligence technologies that enable decision support systems, the next section explores how these technologies are applied in real-world supply chain and logistics operations. Understanding these applications is essential for evaluating the practical value of AI-driven decision systems.

4. APPLICATIONS OF ARTIFICIAL INTELLIGENCE IN SUPPLY CHAIN AND LOGISTICS

Artificial intelligence has increasingly become a central technological driver of innovation in supply chain and logistics operations. Modern supply chains generate vast quantities of data from sources such as enterprise resource planning systems, transportation management systems, warehouse management platforms, and Internet of Things (IoT) devices. Extracting actionable insights from these datasets requires analytical capabilities that extend beyond traditional business intelligence tools. Artificial intelligence technologies enable organizations to process complex datasets, identify hidden relationships, and generate predictive insights that support more effective operational decisions.

In this chapter, we argue that AI-driven decision support systems enhance supply chain performance by enabling organizations to optimize key operational processes such as demand forecasting, inventory management, transportation planning, and risk management. By integrating machine learning models with operational decision frameworks, firms can improve forecasting accuracy, reduce operational costs, and enhance supply chain resilience.

This section examines the major application areas in which artificial intelligence contributes to business optimization within supply chain and logistics operations.

Table 1. Major applications of artificial intelligence in supply chain management.

Supply Chain Area	AI Technology	Operational Impact
Demand Forecasting	Machine Learning	Improved forecast accuracy
Inventory Management	Predictive Analytics	Reduced stockouts and inventory cost
Warehouse Operations	Robotics & Computer Vision	Faster order processing
Transportation Planning	Routing Algorithms	Reduced delivery time and fuel consumption
Risk Management	Predictive Modeling	Early disruption detection

The figure summarizes how different artificial intelligence technologies support decision-making across supply chain activities.

4.1 Demand Forecasting and Predictive Planning

Demand forecasting represents one of the most critical activities in supply chain management. Accurate demand forecasts enable organizations to plan production schedules, allocate inventory efficiently, and coordinate transportation resources. However, forecasting demand in modern markets has become increasingly challenging due to volatile consumer preferences, seasonal fluctuations, and external economic factors.

Traditional forecasting models often rely on statistical techniques such as time-series analysis and regression models. While these approaches provide useful insights, they often struggle to capture complex nonlinear relationships within large datasets. Machine learning algorithms address these limitations by identifying patterns in historical data that may not be detectable through conventional analytical methods. Hybrid machine learning frameworks that combine historical sales data with market intelligence have also been proposed to improve forecasting accuracy in complex supply chain environments (Sheikh, Rinvee, & Sheikh, 2025).

Machine learning models such as random forests, gradient boosting algorithms, and neural networks have demonstrated strong performance in demand forecasting applications. These models can incorporate multiple variables simultaneously, including promotional activities, weather conditions, regional economic indicators, and consumer behavior data (Choi et al., 2018).

We argue that AI-driven forecasting systems significantly improve decision support by enabling organizations to generate more accurate and adaptive demand predictions. These systems can continuously update forecasts as new data becomes available, allowing managers to respond more effectively to market changes. Improved forecasting accuracy reduces the risk of both inventory shortages and excess stock, thereby improving operational efficiency and financial performance.

4.2 Inventory Optimization and Smart Replenishment

Inventory management is another area where artificial intelligence technologies have demonstrated substantial value. Organizations must maintain sufficient inventory levels to meet customer demand while minimizing holding costs and storage constraints. Achieving this balance requires accurate forecasting, efficient replenishment strategies, and real-time monitoring of inventory conditions.

AI-driven inventory optimization systems use predictive analytics to estimate future demand patterns and determine optimal stock levels across multiple locations. These systems analyze historical demand data, supplier lead times, seasonal variations, and logistical constraints to generate recommendations for inventory replenishment.

Advanced inventory optimization models can also incorporate probabilistic forecasting techniques that account for demand uncertainty. By modeling variability in demand patterns, AI systems enable organizations to determine appropriate safety stock levels that minimize the risk of stockouts.

Research suggests that organizations implementing AI-driven inventory systems can significantly improve supply chain efficiency. For example, predictive analytics can reduce inventory holding costs while maintaining high service levels by ensuring that products are available where and when they are needed (Min, 2019).

We emphasize that AI-enabled inventory optimization contributes not only to cost reduction but also to improved supply chain responsiveness. By continuously monitoring inventory levels and demand patterns, decision support systems can automatically trigger replenishment decisions and adjust distribution strategies.

4.3 Transportation and Logistics Optimization

Transportation operations represent one of the most significant cost drivers in supply chain management. Efficient route planning and fleet management are essential for minimizing transportation costs while ensuring timely deliveries.

AI-driven logistics systems use optimization algorithms and real-time data analysis to improve transportation planning. These systems analyze variables such as delivery schedules, traffic conditions, fuel consumption, vehicle capacity, and driver availability in order to generate optimal routing strategies.

Route optimization algorithms are particularly valuable in last-mile delivery operations, where transportation networks often involve numerous delivery destinations and tight time constraints. AI systems can dynamically adjust routes in response to real-time conditions such as traffic congestion, weather disruptions, or unexpected delays. Artificial intelligence technologies are also transforming transportation systems by improving routing efficiency, vehicle utilization, and traffic management capabilities (Sheikh, Sheikh, & Rinvee, 2025).

We argue that AI-enabled transportation planning significantly enhances logistics efficiency by reducing delivery times and improving asset utilization. In addition to cost savings, these systems contribute to environmental sustainability by reducing fuel consumption and greenhouse gas emissions associated with transportation activities.

4.4 Warehouse Automation and Intelligent Operations

Warehousing plays a critical role in supply chain operations by serving as a central hub for inventory storage, order fulfillment, and distribution activities. Traditionally, many warehouse processes relied heavily on manual labor and static operational procedures. However, advances in artificial intelligence and robotics have significantly transformed warehouse management practices.

AI-driven warehouse management systems enable organizations to automate key operational tasks such as order picking, product sorting, and storage allocation. Intelligent slotting algorithms analyze product demand patterns and determine optimal storage locations within warehouse facilities. By placing frequently ordered items closer to picking stations, these systems reduce travel time and improve operational efficiency.

Robotic systems guided by AI algorithms are increasingly used to perform repetitive tasks such as picking and packing products. These systems operate with high levels of accuracy and speed, reducing the likelihood of human errors while improving productivity.

Computer vision technologies further enhance warehouse operations by enabling automated inspection of goods and packages. Cameras and AI-based image recognition systems can detect damaged items, verify product labels, and ensure that orders are correctly assembled.

We emphasize that warehouse automation not only improves operational efficiency but also enhances workplace safety by reducing the need for workers to perform physically demanding tasks. As labor shortages continue to affect logistics operations in many regions, AI-enabled automation provides a scalable solution for maintaining operational performance.

4.5 Supply Chain Risk Management

Supply chains are vulnerable to a wide range of risks, including supplier disruptions, transportation delays, geopolitical instability, and natural disasters. These disruptions can significantly impact production schedules and customer service levels.

Artificial intelligence technologies enable organizations to implement proactive supply chain risk management strategies by analyzing large volumes of data from multiple sources. Machine learning models can identify patterns that indicate potential disruptions, such as abnormal supplier performance or emerging geopolitical risks.

AI systems can also simulate various disruption scenarios and evaluate their potential impact on supply chain performance. By analyzing alternative sourcing strategies and transportation routes, decision support systems can recommend mitigation strategies that reduce operational risk.

Research indicates that AI-enabled risk management systems significantly enhance supply chain resilience by enabling organizations to respond quickly to emerging disruptions (Baryannis et al., 2019). We argue that proactive risk detection and scenario analysis represent critical capabilities for organizations operating in volatile global markets.

4.6 Customer Experience and Last-Mile Delivery

The rapid growth of e-commerce has increased the importance of efficient last-mile delivery operations. Customers increasingly expect fast, reliable, and transparent delivery services. Meeting these expectations requires sophisticated logistics coordination and real-time decision making.

AI technologies support last-mile delivery optimization by integrating predictive analytics with real-time routing algorithms. These systems can forecast delivery demand patterns, allocate delivery resources efficiently, and provide accurate delivery time estimates to customers.

Furthermore, AI-driven logistics platforms enable organizations to track shipments in real time and communicate delivery updates to customers through digital interfaces. These capabilities improve transparency and enhance customer satisfaction.

We argue that AI-enabled last-mile delivery optimization plays a critical role in enhancing customer experience while maintaining operational efficiency. By improving delivery reliability and reducing delays, organizations can strengthen customer trust and competitive advantage.

4.7 Integrated Supply Chain Visibility

One of the most significant advantages of AI-driven decision support systems is their ability to provide integrated visibility across supply chain networks. Traditional supply chain systems often operate in isolated silos, making it difficult for organizations to obtain a comprehensive view of their operations.

AI technologies enable the integration of data from multiple sources, including suppliers, transportation providers, warehouses, and customers. By aggregating and analyzing these datasets, decision support systems provide managers with real-time insights into supply chain performance.

We emphasize that integrated supply chain visibility enhances coordination across organizational units and enables more informed decision making. When managers have access to comprehensive operational data, they can identify bottlenecks, evaluate performance metrics, and implement corrective actions more effectively.

5. INDUSTRY CASE STUDY: AI IN LARGE-SCALE E-COMMERCE LOGISTICS OPERATIONS

The rapid expansion of e-commerce has fundamentally transformed supply chain and logistics operations worldwide. Organizations operating large-scale digital marketplaces must coordinate complex logistics networks involving suppliers, fulfillment centers, transportation providers, and customers across multiple geographic regions. Managing these networks efficiently requires advanced analytical tools capable of processing large volumes of operational data in real time.

Case Example Box

Case Illustration: Artificial Intelligence in E-Commerce Logistics

Large-scale e-commerce logistics networks rely heavily on artificial intelligence to manage complex operational activities such as demand forecasting, inventory placement, and transportation routing. For example, modern fulfillment networks analyze large volumes of customer transaction data to predict product demand across geographic regions. Machine learning models process historical order data, seasonal patterns, and promotional activity to forecast demand with higher accuracy than traditional statistical methods.

AI-driven forecasting systems enable organizations to position inventory closer to anticipated customer demand. By distributing products strategically across fulfillment centers, firms can reduce delivery times while minimizing transportation costs. In addition, intelligent routing algorithms analyze real-time traffic conditions, delivery time windows, and vehicle capacity constraints to determine optimal delivery routes.

From a managerial perspective, these AI-enabled logistics systems provide significant advantages. They allow supply chain managers to respond quickly to fluctuations in demand, improve operational efficiency, and enhance customer service performance. At the same time, managers must ensure that AI recommendations are interpreted carefully and integrated with human judgment to support effective decision-making.

Artificial intelligence has emerged as a critical technology for enabling data-driven decision making in these environments. Many leading e-commerce organizations have integrated AI technologies into their logistics infrastructure to improve forecasting accuracy, optimize inventory placement, and enhance delivery efficiency. In this section, we examine how AI-driven decision support systems are applied within large-scale e-commerce logistics operations and analyze the managerial implications of these technologies.

We argue that AI technologies enable organizations to transform logistics networks into intelligent systems capable of adapting dynamically to demand fluctuations and operational disruptions.

5.1 AI-Driven Demand Forecasting in E-Commerce

E-commerce platforms generate massive volumes of customer transaction data, including purchase histories, browsing patterns, and product search behaviors. These datasets provide valuable insights into consumer demand patterns, but extracting actionable information from such large datasets requires advanced analytical techniques.

Machine learning models have been widely adopted in e-commerce logistics to improve demand forecasting accuracy. These models analyze historical sales data alongside external variables such as seasonal demand patterns, promotional campaigns, and regional purchasing behavior. By identifying complex relationships between these variables, AI models can generate more accurate demand forecasts than traditional statistical methods.

Improved forecasting accuracy has significant operational implications. Accurate demand forecasts allow organizations to allocate inventory more effectively across fulfillment centers, reducing the likelihood of stockouts while minimizing excess inventory. In addition, accurate forecasts enable better coordination between procurement, production, and distribution processes.

Research suggests that AI-driven demand forecasting systems can significantly improve forecasting accuracy compared with traditional analytical approaches (Choi et al., 2018). We emphasize that these improvements directly contribute to better operational planning and improved supply chain performance.

5.2 Intelligent Inventory Allocation Across Distribution Networks

Another critical challenge for e-commerce organizations involves determining how products should be distributed across fulfillment centers. In large logistics networks, products may be stored in multiple warehouses across different regions in order to minimize delivery times.

AI-driven inventory allocation systems analyze historical demand data, shipping costs, and delivery time constraints to determine the optimal distribution of inventory across warehouses. These systems continuously evaluate inventory levels and demand patterns to ensure that products are positioned as close as possible to expected customer demand.

We argue that intelligent inventory allocation significantly improves supply chain efficiency by reducing transportation distances and enabling faster delivery times. Additionally, these systems help organizations maintain balanced inventory levels across their logistics networks, reducing the need for costly emergency replenishment shipments.

Advanced machine learning models can also incorporate real-time operational data such as inventory availability, warehouse capacity, and transportation constraints. By analyzing these variables simultaneously, AI systems generate dynamic inventory placement decisions that adapt to changing market conditions.

5.3 AI-Enabled Transportation Optimization

Transportation coordination represents one of the most complex operational challenges in e-commerce logistics. Large logistics networks must coordinate thousands of daily shipments across multiple transportation modes, including trucks, air cargo, and last-mile delivery vehicles.

AI-enabled transportation management systems utilize optimization algorithms and real-time data analysis to determine efficient shipping routes and delivery schedules. These systems analyze traffic conditions, delivery time windows, vehicle capacity constraints, and driver availability in order to generate optimized transportation plans.

One important application of AI in transportation management involves dynamic route optimization. Unlike traditional routing models that rely on static route plans, AI-driven routing systems continuously update delivery routes based on real-time information such as traffic congestion, weather disruptions, and unexpected delays.

We emphasize that dynamic routing capabilities significantly enhance logistics efficiency by reducing delivery times and improving vehicle utilization. These improvements contribute to lower operational costs while maintaining high service levels for customers.

5.4 Warehouse Automation and Robotics in E-Commerce Fulfillment

Warehouse operations represent another critical component of e-commerce logistics. Large fulfillment centers must process thousands of customer orders each day while maintaining high levels of accuracy and efficiency.

AI technologies play a key role in enabling warehouse automation. Robotic systems guided by artificial intelligence algorithms are increasingly used to perform tasks such as product picking, order sorting, and package transportation within warehouse facilities. These systems operate continuously and with high levels of precision, significantly improving productivity compared with manual processes.

AI-powered warehouse management systems also analyze order patterns and product demand trends to determine optimal storage locations for inventory. Products with high demand frequencies are typically stored closer to picking stations, reducing travel distances for warehouse workers and robotic systems.

Computer vision technologies further enhance warehouse operations by enabling automated inspection processes. AI-based image recognition systems can detect damaged goods, verify product labels, and monitor warehouse safety conditions.

We argue that warehouse automation driven by artificial intelligence significantly enhances operational efficiency and scalability. As e-commerce demand continues to grow, these technologies enable organizations to expand fulfillment capacity without proportional increases in labor costs.

5.5 Predictive Maintenance in Logistics Infrastructure

Large logistics networks rely heavily on physical assets such as delivery vehicles, conveyor systems, and automated warehouse equipment. Equipment failures can disrupt operations and lead to significant financial losses.

Predictive maintenance systems powered by artificial intelligence analyze sensor data from equipment to detect early signs of mechanical failure. Machine learning algorithms identify abnormal operating patterns that may indicate potential breakdowns.

By detecting equipment issues before they escalate into major failures, predictive maintenance systems allow organizations to schedule repairs proactively. This approach reduces downtime and ensures that logistics operations continue without interruption.

Research has shown that predictive maintenance strategies can significantly improve asset reliability and reduce maintenance costs (Ivanov & Dolgui, 2020). We emphasize that predictive maintenance represents an important component of AI-driven decision support systems in logistics environments.

5.6 Managerial Implications of AI-Driven Logistics Systems

The implementation of AI technologies in e-commerce logistics has important implications for managerial decision making. First, AI-driven decision support systems enable managers to make decisions based on real-time data rather than relying solely on historical analysis.

Second, these systems enhance operational transparency by providing managers with comprehensive visibility across supply chain networks. This visibility enables organizations to identify inefficiencies, monitor performance metrics, and implement corrective actions more effectively.

Third, AI technologies enable organizations to build more resilient supply chains capable of responding to disruptions. By analyzing multiple operational scenarios and predicting potential risks, AI-driven systems allow managers to implement proactive mitigation strategies.

We argue that the adoption of AI-enabled decision support systems requires organizations to develop new managerial capabilities. Managers must understand how to interpret AI-generated insights and integrate them into strategic decision-making processes.

Ultimately, AI technologies should be viewed as tools that augment managerial expertise rather than replacing human judgment. The most effective supply chain decision systems combine computational intelligence with human experience and strategic insight.

6. IMPLEMENTATION CHALLENGES OF AI-DRIVEN DECISION SUPPORT SYSTEMS

While artificial intelligence technologies offer substantial opportunities for improving supply chain performance, organizations often encounter significant challenges when attempting to implement AI-driven decision support systems. The adoption of AI requires not only technological capabilities but also organizational readiness, data infrastructure, and managerial expertise. Without addressing these factors, organizations may struggle to fully realize the potential benefits of AI-enabled decision systems. AI-driven analytics also play a critical role in supply chain risk mitigation by enabling organizations to identify potential disruptions and develop resilient operational strategies (Sheikh & Sajja, 2026).

From a managerial perspective, organizations must also evaluate the financial and operational impact of AI-driven decision support systems. Performance evaluation metrics such as return on investment (ROI), forecasting accuracy improvement, inventory turnover rates, transportation cost reduction, and service level improvements can help qudantify the value generated by AI adoption. Establishing clear key performance indicators (KPIs) enables managers to assess whether AI-based decision systems produce measurable operational benefits.

In this chapter, we argue that successful implementation of AI in supply chain management requires careful consideration of several critical challenges, including data quality issues, technological integration barriers, organizational resistance, and ethical considerations. Understanding these challenges is essential for organizations seeking to develop effective AI-driven decision support systems.

6.1 Data Quality and Data Integration Challenges

Artificial intelligence systems rely heavily on large datasets for training predictive models and generating insights. Consequently, the quality of data used in AI systems plays a critical role in determining the accuracy and reliability of decision support outputs.

However, many organizations face significant challenges related to data quality and data integration. Supply chain data is often distributed across multiple information systems, including enterprise resource planning (ERP) systems, transportation management platforms, warehouse management systems, and supplier databases. These systems may store data in different formats and structures, making integration difficult.

Incomplete or inconsistent data can significantly reduce the accuracy of machine learning models. For example, missing shipment records or inaccurate inventory information can distort predictive analytics and lead to incorrect operational decisions. As Nguyen et al. (2018) note, data preprocessing and data cleaning represent some of the most time-consuming steps in developing effective machine learning models for supply chain analytics.

We emphasize that organizations must invest in robust data governance frameworks to ensure data accuracy, consistency, and accessibility. Effective data management practices, including data standardization and real-time data synchronization, are essential for supporting AI-driven decision support systems.

6.2 Technological Infrastructure and System Integration

Another major challenge in implementing AI-driven supply chain systems involves technological infrastructure. AI applications require substantial computing resources and advanced analytics platforms capable of processing large datasets and performing complex calculations.

Many organizations still rely on legacy information systems that were not designed to support advanced analytics or machine learning algorithms. Integrating AI technologies into these systems can be technically complex and costly. Organizations may need to upgrade their IT infrastructure or migrate data to cloud-based platforms that provide scalable computing capabilities.

Furthermore, AI-driven decision support systems often require integration with multiple operational platforms. For example, predictive forecasting models must communicate with inventory management systems, procurement platforms, and logistics coordination systems in order to support effective decision making.

We argue that successful AI implementation requires a well-designed digital infrastructure that allows seamless data exchange between different operational systems. Cloud computing technologies and modern data architecture frameworks play a crucial role in enabling this integration.

6.3 Organizational Resistance and Change Management

Beyond technical challenges, organizations must also address human and organizational factors when implementing AI technologies. The introduction of AI-driven decision systems often changes traditional decision-making processes and organizational workflows.

Employees may initially resist the adoption of AI technologies due to concerns about job displacement or reduced managerial autonomy. Managers who are accustomed to relying on personal experience and intuition may also be hesitant to trust algorithmic recommendations.

We emphasize that successful AI adoption requires effective change management strategies. Organizations must clearly communicate the role of AI as a decision support tool rather than a replacement for human expertise. Training programs can help employees develop the skills needed to interpret AI-generated insights and integrate them into operational decision making.

Research suggests that organizations that emphasize collaboration between human expertise and artificial intelligence are more likely to achieve successful technology adoption (Davenport & Ronanki, 2018). By fostering a culture that encourages data-driven decision making, organizations can overcome resistance and fully leverage the benefits of AI technologies.

6.4 Talent and Skills Shortage

Another significant challenge associated with AI implementation is the shortage of skilled professionals capable of developing and managing advanced analytics systems. AI-driven decision support systems require expertise in areas such as data science, machine learning engineering, supply chain analytics, and information systems management.

Many organizations struggle to recruit and retain professionals with the interdisciplinary skill sets required to develop AI solutions. Data scientists must not only understand machine learning algorithms but also possess domain knowledge related to supply chain operations.

We argue that organizations must invest in workforce development initiatives that support the development of AI-related skills. Universities and training institutions also play an important role in preparing future professionals for careers in data-driven supply chain management.

Additionally, organizations can address talent shortages by forming partnerships with technology providers and research institutions. Collaborative initiatives can help organizations access specialized expertise and accelerate the development of AI-driven decision support capabilities.

6.5 Ethical and Governance Considerations

The adoption of artificial intelligence technologies raises important ethical and governance concerns. AI models may unintentionally introduce biases into decision-making processes if the training data reflects historical inequalities or operational inefficiencies.

For example, machine learning models used in supplier selection or logistics planning could unintentionally favor certain suppliers or geographic regions if historical data contains systematic biases. Such outcomes could lead to unfair decision-making practices or unintended discrimination.

Transparency is therefore an essential component of responsible AI implementation. Organizations must ensure that decision support models are interpretable and that managers understand how algorithmic recommendations are generated.

Data privacy is another important consideration. Supply chain systems often process sensitive operational data, including customer information and supplier records. Organizations must implement strong cybersecurity measures and comply with relevant data protection regulations when deploying AI-driven systems.

We emphasize that effective governance frameworks are necessary to ensure responsible AI adoption. These frameworks should include guidelines for model validation, monitoring, and accountability to ensure that AI technologies are used ethically and transparently.

6.6 Financial and Strategic Considerations

Implementing AI-driven decision support systems also requires significant financial investment. Organizations must allocate resources for data infrastructure development, software acquisition, system integration, and workforce training.

While AI technologies can generate substantial long-term benefits, organizations must carefully evaluate the return on investment associated with these initiatives. Not all supply chain processes may benefit equally from AI implementation, and organizations must prioritize use cases that offer the greatest potential impact.

We argue that organizations should adopt a phased implementation strategy when introducing AI technologies. Rather than attempting to automate all supply chain processes simultaneously, firms should begin with high-impact applications such as demand forecasting or transportation optimization. Successful implementation in these areas can demonstrate the value of AI and support broader adoption across the organization.

7. ETHICAL AND GOVERNANCE CONSIDERATIONS IN AI-DRIVEN SUPPLY CHAINS

While artificial intelligence technologies offer substantial operational benefits, their adoption also introduces new ethical, regulatory, and governance challenges. AI-driven decision systems increasingly influence important operational decisions within supply chain networks, including supplier selection, inventory allocation, and transportation planning. As these systems become more autonomous and data-driven, organizations must ensure that they operate responsibly and transparently.

In this chapter, we argue that ethical governance should be considered a fundamental component of AI-driven decision support systems. Without appropriate governance structures, organizations risk creating systems that reinforce bias, compromise data privacy, or generate decisions that lack transparency and accountability.

7.1 Algorithmic Transparency and Explainability

One of the primary concerns associated with artificial intelligence systems is the lack of transparency in complex machine learning models. Many AI models, particularly deep learning algorithms, operate as "black box" systems whose internal decision processes are difficult to interpret.

In supply chain contexts, this lack of transparency can create challenges for managers who must justify operational decisions to stakeholders. For example, if an AI-driven forecasting system recommends major adjustments to inventory allocation or transportation routing, managers must understand the reasoning behind these recommendations before implementing them.

Explainable artificial intelligence (XAI) has emerged as an important research area aimed at improving transparency in machine learning systems. XAI techniques help identify the variables and relationships that influence model predictions, allowing managers to better understand how decisions are generated.

We emphasize that improving algorithmic transparency is essential for building trust in AI-driven decision support systems. Managers are more likely to adopt AI recommendations when they understand the reasoning behind them and can evaluate their validity.

7.2 Bias and Fairness in AI Models

Another significant ethical concern involves the potential for artificial intelligence models to reproduce or amplify biases present in historical datasets. Machine learning algorithms learn patterns from training data, which may contain embedded biases related to past operational decisions.

For example, if historical procurement data disproportionately favored certain suppliers due to geographic or economic factors, an AI-driven supplier evaluation model may replicate these patterns when generating recommendations. Similarly, logistics planning algorithms may unintentionally prioritize certain regions if historical transportation patterns reflect uneven infrastructure or market access.

These biases can lead to unfair outcomes and potentially undermine the credibility of AI-driven decision systems. Organizations must therefore carefully evaluate the datasets used to train machine learning models and implement mechanisms for detecting and correcting biased predictions.

We argue that fairness assessments should be integrated into the development and deployment of AI models in supply chain management. Regular auditing of model outputs can help identify potential biases and ensure that decision systems operate in a fair and balanced manner.

7.3 Data Privacy and Cybersecurity

AI-driven supply chain systems often rely on large volumes of operational data collected from various sources, including customer transactions, supplier records, logistics tracking systems, and sensor-enabled infrastructure. While these datasets enable powerful analytical capabilities, they also raise significant data privacy and cybersecurity concerns.

Supply chain networks frequently involve multiple organizations that share operational data to coordinate logistics activities. Ensuring that this data is protected from unauthorized access or cyber threats is therefore essential for maintaining trust among supply chain partners.

Cybersecurity risks are particularly important in AI-enabled logistics environments where automated systems control critical infrastructure such as warehouse robotics, transportation routing platforms, and inventory management systems. A cybersecurity breach could potentially disrupt operations and lead to significant financial losses.

Organizations must therefore implement strong cybersecurity protocols and data protection strategies when deploying AI-driven decision systems. Encryption technologies, access control mechanisms, and continuous monitoring of system activity can help mitigate these risks.

7.4 Governance Frameworks for AI Adoption

Effective governance frameworks play a critical role in ensuring that artificial intelligence technologies are implemented responsibly within supply chain organizations. Governance structures help define roles, responsibilities, and accountability mechanisms related to the development and use of AI systems.

Organizations should establish formal policies that guide the design, validation, and monitoring of AI-driven decision support systems. These policies should include procedures for model evaluation, performance monitoring, and periodic review of algorithmic outcomes.

In addition, governance frameworks should ensure that human oversight remains central to high-impact operational decisions. While AI technologies can generate valuable insights, final decision-making authority should remain with experienced managers who can consider broader strategic and ethical implications.

We argue that responsible AI governance requires collaboration between technical experts, supply chain managers, and organizational leadership. By combining technological expertise with managerial judgment, organizations can ensure that AI technologies are implemented in ways that support both operational efficiency and ethical responsibility.

7.5 Regulatory Considerations and Industry Standards

As artificial intelligence technologies continue to expand across industries, governments and regulatory institutions are increasingly developing guidelines to govern their use. These regulations often focus on issues such as data privacy, algorithmic transparency, and accountability in automated decision systems.

Supply chain organizations operating across international markets must therefore navigate complex regulatory environments when deploying AI technologies. Compliance with regional data protection laws and industry standards is essential to avoid legal risks and maintain stakeholder trust.

We emphasize that organizations should proactively monitor emerging regulatory developments related to artificial intelligence. Establishing compliance mechanisms early in the implementation process can help organizations avoid costly adjustments later.

8. FUTURE RESEARCH DIRECTIONS IN AI-DRIVEN SUPPLY CHAIN DECISION SYSTEMS

Artificial intelligence technologies continue to evolve rapidly, creating new opportunities for innovation in supply chain and logistics management. While significant progress has already been made in applying machine learning and predictive analytics to supply chain decision-making, many important research questions remain unresolved. Scholars and practitioners increasingly recognize that AI-driven supply chains represent an interdisciplinary research area that combines operations management, data science, information systems, and organizational strategy.

In this chapter, we argue that future research should focus on improving the integration, transparency, and adaptability of AI-driven decision support systems. Emerging technologies such as digital twins, Internet of Things (IoT) networks, and autonomous logistics systems are expected to reshape supply chain management in the coming years. Understanding how these technologies interact with artificial intelligence will be essential for developing more resilient and efficient supply chain networks.

8.1 Integration of Artificial Intelligence with Internet of Things (IoT)

One of the most promising areas for future research involves the integration of artificial intelligence with Internet of Things technologies. IoT devices enable continuous monitoring of physical assets and operational environments through sensor-based data collection. In logistics networks, sensors embedded in vehicles, warehouses, and shipment containers can provide real-time information about location, temperature, equipment performance, and inventory conditions.

When combined with artificial intelligence analytics, IoT-generated data can significantly enhance supply chain visibility and responsiveness. Machine learning models can analyze real-time sensor data to detect anomalies, predict disruptions, and optimize operational decisions. For example, predictive algorithms can monitor shipment conditions to detect potential product damage or environmental risks during transportation.

Despite the potential advantages of AI–IoT integration, several research challenges remain. Future studies should examine how organizations can manage the massive volumes of data generated by IoT devices and develop scalable analytical models capable of processing these datasets efficiently.

8.2 Digital Twin Technology in Supply Chain Simulation

Another promising research direction involves the development of digital twin technologies for supply chain simulation and decision support. A digital twin is a virtual representation of a physical system that continuously updates based on real-world operational data.

In supply chain contexts, digital twins can replicate logistics networks, warehouse operations, and transportation systems. These models allow managers to simulate different operational scenarios and evaluate potential strategies before implementing them in real-world environments. Recent studies highlight the role of digital twins in supply chain stress testing and resilience analysis (Ivanov, 2023).

Artificial intelligence plays an important role in enhancing the predictive capabilities of digital twins. Machine learning algorithms can analyze historical operational data to simulate demand fluctuations, supply disruptions, and transportation delays. These simulations enable organizations to evaluate the resilience of supply chain networks under different conditions.

Future research should investigate how digital twin systems can be integrated with AI-driven decision support systems to enable real-time scenario analysis and dynamic optimization of supply chain operations.

8.3 Autonomous Logistics Systems

The development of autonomous logistics technologies represents another emerging research area. Autonomous vehicles, delivery drones, and robotic warehouse systems are increasingly being explored as solutions for improving logistics efficiency and reducing operational costs.

Artificial intelligence technologies play a central role in enabling these autonomous systems. Machine learning algorithms support navigation, obstacle detection, and real-time decision-making in autonomous transportation systems. In warehouse environments, robotic systems use computer vision and AI-based planning algorithms to coordinate picking and sorting operations.

However, the large-scale deployment of autonomous logistics systems raises several research challenges. Questions remain regarding safety, regulatory compliance, and coordination between human workers and autonomous technologies. Future research should explore how organizations can integrate autonomous systems into existing logistics infrastructure while maintaining operational safety and efficiency.

8.4 Sustainability and Green Supply Chains

Sustainability considerations are becoming increasingly important in supply chain management. Organizations are under growing pressure from regulators, investors, and consumers to reduce the environmental impact of their operations.

Artificial intelligence technologies can play a significant role in supporting sustainable supply chain practices. AI-driven optimization models can help reduce transportation emissions by identifying fuel-efficient routes and improving vehicle utilization. Predictive analytics can also support energy-efficient warehouse operations by optimizing equipment usage and facility management.

Future research should explore how AI technologies can support broader sustainability objectives within supply chain networks. Scholars should investigate the potential for AI-driven decision support systems to balance economic performance with environmental and social sustainability goals.

8.5 Human–AI Collaboration in Supply Chain Decision-Making

Although artificial intelligence technologies provide powerful analytical capabilities, human expertise remains essential for effective decision-making in complex supply chain environments. Future research should therefore examine how human managers and AI systems can collaborate effectively.

Human–AI collaboration involves combining computational intelligence with managerial judgment and domain expertise. AI systems can analyze large datasets and generate predictive insights, while managers interpret these insights within the broader strategic and organizational context.

Research in this area should explore how organizations can design decision support systems that facilitate collaboration between human decision-makers and

AI technologies. User interface design, explainable AI methods, and organizational training programs may all play important roles in improving human–AI collaboration.

9. MANAGERIAL IMPLICATIONS OF AI-DRIVEN DECISION SUPPORT SYSTEMS

The increasing integration of artificial intelligence within supply chain management has significant implications for managers responsible for logistics planning, operational coordination, and strategic decision-making. AI-driven decision support systems enable organizations to process large volumes of operational data, generate predictive insights, and optimize complex supply chain processes. However, the successful implementation of these systems requires thoughtful managerial strategies and organizational readiness.

In this chapter, we argue that managers must move beyond viewing artificial intelligence as merely a technological innovation. Instead, AI should be considered a strategic capability that can reshape how organizations design, coordinate, and manage supply chain networks. Managers who understand how to integrate AI technologies into operational decision processes are more likely to achieve improvements in efficiency, resilience, and competitiveness.

9.1 Building Data-Driven Supply Chain Capabilities

One of the most important managerial implications of AI adoption involves the development of data-driven decision-making capabilities. Traditional supply chain management often relied heavily on managerial intuition and historical experience. While these approaches remain valuable, the complexity of modern logistics networks requires more systematic analysis supported by advanced analytics tools.

Managers must therefore prioritize the development of robust data infrastructures capable of supporting AI-driven decision support systems. This includes ensuring that operational data from different supply chain activities—such as procurement, transportation, and warehouse management—can be integrated into centralized analytical platforms.

We emphasize that managers should encourage a culture of data-driven decision-making within their organizations. Employees should be trained to interpret analytical outputs and incorporate these insights into operational planning processes. By fostering analytical literacy across the organization, managers can ensure that AI technologies enhance rather than replace human expertise.

9.2 Strategic Implementation of AI Technologies

Another important managerial consideration involves the strategic implementation of AI technologies within supply chain operations. While artificial intelligence offers many potential applications, organizations should avoid attempting to automate all processes simultaneously.

Instead, managers should begin with high-impact use cases where AI technologies can generate measurable improvements in operational performance. Examples include demand forecasting, inventory optimization, and transportation routing. These applications often produce immediate efficiency gains and demonstrate the value of AI-driven decision support systems.

We argue that adopting a phased implementation strategy allows organizations to build internal expertise and gradually expand their AI capabilities. Early successes can help generate organizational support for further investments in AI technologies and reduce resistance to change.

9.3 Enhancing Supply Chain Visibility and Coordination

Supply chain networks often involve numerous stakeholders, including suppliers, logistics providers, and distribution partners. Coordinating activities across these stakeholders requires accurate and timely information sharing.

AI-driven decision support systems can significantly enhance supply chain visibility by integrating data from multiple sources and presenting managers with real-time operational insights. For example, predictive analytics can identify potential delays in transportation routes or detect inventory shortages before they disrupt production schedules.

Managers should leverage these capabilities to improve coordination across supply chain partners. Enhanced visibility allows organizations to respond more effectively to operational disruptions and maintain service levels even during periods of uncertainty.

9.4 Developing Organizational Skills and Talent

The adoption of artificial intelligence technologies also has important implications for workforce development. AI-driven supply chain systems require employees who possess both analytical skills and domain expertise in logistics operations.

Managers must therefore invest in training programs that help employees develop competencies in data analytics, machine learning applications, and digital supply chain management. These training initiatives can improve employees' ability to interpret AI-generated insights and contribute to data-driven decision-making processes.

Additionally, organizations may need to recruit professionals with specialized expertise in data science and supply chain analytics. Collaboration between technical experts and supply chain managers is essential for designing effective AI-driven decision support systems.

9.5 Strengthening Supply Chain Resilience

Recent global disruptions, including pandemics, geopolitical conflicts, and natural disasters—have highlighted the importance of resilient supply chain networks. Managers must be prepared to respond quickly to unexpected disruptions while maintaining operational continuity.

Artificial intelligence technologies provide valuable tools for improving supply chain resilience. Predictive analytics can identify potential risks within supply networks, while simulation models can evaluate alternative operational strategies under different disruption scenarios.

Managers should incorporate AI-driven risk assessment tools into their strategic planning processes. By analyzing multiple potential disruption scenarios, organizations can develop contingency plans that enhance supply chain resilience and minimize operational disruptions.

9.6 Balancing Human Judgment and Algorithmic Decision-Making

Although artificial intelligence technologies provide powerful analytical capabilities, human judgment remains essential in complex supply chain environments. Managers must carefully balance the use of algorithmic decision support with managerial experience and strategic insight.

AI models generate recommendations based on historical data patterns, but these models may not fully capture unique organizational contexts or emerging market dynamics. Managers should therefore treat AI outputs as decision support tools rather than automated decision-making mechanisms.

We emphasize that the most effective supply chain decision systems combine computational intelligence with human expertise. Managers play a critical role in interpreting AI-generated insights and ensuring that operational decisions align with broader organizational objectives.

10. CONCLUSION

Artificial intelligence has emerged as one of the most transformative technologies shaping modern supply chain and logistics management. As global supply networks become increasingly complex and data-intensive, organizations must adopt advanced analytical tools capable of supporting efficient and responsive decision-making processes.

This chapter examined how artificial intelligence technologies enhance decision support systems within supply chain management. We discussed the evolution of decision support systems, explored key AI technologies such as machine learning and predictive analytics, and analyzed their applications across supply chain functions including demand forecasting, inventory optimization, warehouse automation, and transportation planning.

The chapter also presented an industry case study illustrating how AI-driven decision systems improve logistics operations in large-scale e-commerce networks. These systems enable organizations to analyze large datasets, generate predictive insights, and optimize operational decisions in real time.

Despite these benefits, organizations must address several challenges when implementing AI-driven decision support systems. Issues related to data quality, technological infrastructure, organizational resistance, and ethical governance must be carefully managed to ensure successful adoption.

Future research will continue to explore emerging technologies such as IoT-enabled logistics systems, digital twins, and autonomous transportation platforms. These innovations are expected to further enhance the capabilities of AI-driven supply chain decision systems.

In conclusion, artificial intelligence offers powerful opportunities for transforming supply chain management. Organizations that effectively integrate AI technologies with strong managerial practices and responsible governance frameworks will be better positioned to operate efficient, resilient, and sustainable supply chain networks in the digital economy.

Discussion Questions

1. What are the most significant barriers to AI adoption in supply chain management, and how can organizations overcome them?
2. How might small and medium-sized enterprises implement AI-driven logistics without the resources of large corporations?
3. What ethical considerations should guide the use of AI in workforce scheduling and warehouse automation?

4. How can organizations balance the efficiency gains of AI with the need for human judgment in decision-making?

REFERENCES

Baryannis, G., Validi, S., Dani, S., & Antoniou, G. (2019). Supply chain risk management and artificial intelligence: State of the art and future research directions. *Computers in Industry, 113*, 103131.

Choi, T. M., Wallace, S. W., & Wang, Y. (2018). Big data analytics in operations management. *Production and Operations Management, 27*(10), 1868–1883. DOI: 10.1111/poms.12838

Data Analytics and Artificial Intelligence in Smart Healthcare Logistics: Building Resilient and Sustainable Systems. (2025*American Journal of Data Science and Artificial Intelligence1*22630DOI: 10.54536/ajdsai.v1i2.6024

Davenport, T. H., & Ronanki, R. (2018). Artificial intelligence for the real world. *Harvard Business Review, 96*(1), 108–116.

Ivanov, D. (2023). Intelligent digital twins for supply chain stress testing and resilience. *International Journal of Production Economics, 263*, 108938. DOI: 10.1016/j.ijpe.2023.108938

Ivanov, D., & Dolgui, A. (2020). Viability of intertwined supply networks. *International Journal of Production Research, 58*(10), 2904–2915. DOI: 10.1080/00207543.2020.1750727

Ivanov, D., Sokolov, B., & Dolgui, A. (2014). The ripple effect in supply chains. *International Journal of Production Research, 52*(7), 215–222. DOI: 10.1080/00207543.2013.858836

Kache, F., & Seuring, S. (2017). Challenges and opportunities of big data in supply chain management. *International Journal of Operations & Production Management, 37*(1), 10–36. DOI: 10.1108/IJOPM-02-2015-0078

LeCun, Y., Bengio, Y., & Hinton, G. (2015). Deep learning. *Nature, 521*(7553), 436–444. DOI: 10.1038/nature14539

Min, H. (2019). Artificial intelligence in supply chain management. *International Journal of Logistics Research and Applications, 22*(4), 361–375.

Nguyen, T., Zhou, L., Spiegler, V., Ieromonachou, P., & Lin, Y. (2018). Big data analytics in supply chain management. *Computers & Operations Research, 98*, 254–264. DOI: 10.1016/j.cor.2017.07.004

Sheikh, A. (2025). AI-Powered Leadership in Supply Chain Management: Balancing Efficiency and Human Decision-Making. Journal of Global Economics. *Management and Business Research, 17*(3), 476–485. DOI: 10.56557/jgembr/2025/v17i39998

Sheikh, A., Goodrich, K., & Sajja, S. (2025). AI-Powered Forecasting for Supply Chain Resilience: Applications of Logistic Regression, Random Forest, and XGBoost in the U.S. Context. *American Journal of Innovation in Science and Engineering, 4*(3), 105–117. DOI: 10.54536/ajise.v4i3.6065

Sheikh, A., Rinvee, T. M., & Sheikh, Md. S. (2025). A Hybrid Machine Learning Framework for Supply Chain Demand Forecasting: Integrating Historical Data and Market Intelligence. DOI: 10.2139/ssrn.5621332

Sheikh, A., & Sajja, S. (2026). AI-Driven Risk Mitigation in Global Supply Chains to Build Resilience for U.S. Competitiveness: A Conceptual Review and Framework-Based Study. Journal of Global Economics. *Management and Business Research, 18*(1), 198–206. DOI: 10.56557/jgembr/2026/v18i110190

Sheikh, A., Sheikh, M., & Rinvee, T. M. (2025). Smart Transportation Systems with Artificial Intelligence: Enhancing Efficiency, Safety, and Sustainability. *American Journal of Smart Technology and Solutions, 4*(2), 87–90. DOI: 10.54536/ajsts.v4i2.6022

Waller, M. A., & Fawcett, S. E. (2013). Data science and predictive analytics in supply chain management. *Journal of Business Logistics, 34*(2), 77–84. DOI: 10.1111/jbl.12010

KEY TERMS AND DEFINITIONS

Artificial Intelligence (AI): Computer systems that perform tasks requiring human intelligence.

Deep Learning: ML using multi-layer neural networks for complex pattern recognition.

Digital Twin: Virtual replica of physical systems for simulation and analysis.

Machine Learning (ML): AI subset where systems learn from data without explicit programming.

Natural Language Processing (NLP): AI that understands and generates human language.

Optimization Algorithm: Mathematical method to find the best solution under constraints.

Predictive Maintenance: Using AI to forecast equipment failures before they occur.

Chapter 8
Artificial Intelligence as an Enabler of Integrated Brand Communication:
Strategic, Managerial, and Ethical Perspectives

Waziha Islam
http://orcid.org/0009-0004-6016-1778
Noakhali Science and Technology University, Bangladesh

S. M. Nafiz Rayun
http://orcid.org/0009-0002-2505-6265
University of Science and Technology, Chittagong, Bangladesh

Sadiul Alam Chowdhury
http://orcid.org/0009-0008-4864-2500
Noakhali Science and Technology University, Bangladesh

Md Rasel Mia
http://orcid.org/0009-0004-9484-2547
ISCTE, University Institute of Lisbon, Portugal

Raji Adewumi Ismaheel
UBD School of Business and Economics, Brunei

ABSTRACT

The rapid development of artificial intelligence (AI) is reshaping modern brand communication, particularly in digital and data-driven environments. Integrated Brand Communication (IBC) provides a strategic framework for delivering consistent brand

DOI: 10.4018/979-8-3373-9325-4.ch008

messages across multiple platforms and stakeholder groups. This study examines AI as a strategic enabler of IBC by enhancing data integration, personalization, and real-time communication management. Drawing on literature from marketing, brand management, and AI - it explains how technologies such as machine learning, natural language processing, and generative AI support automated content creation, predictive analytics, and adaptive communication strategies. It further highlights challenges related to AI adoption, including over-automation, algorithmic bias, and privacy concerns. It also emphasizes responsible AI governance and human-AI collaboration to strengthen integrated brand communication in the digital age.

1. INTRODUCTION

The rapid advancement of digital technologies has fundamentally reshaped the landscape of marketing and brand communication. The advancement of internet connectivity, mobile phones, social networks, and digital ecosystems has changed the paradigm of marketing to become dynamic, interactive and customer oriented. (Bharti et al., 2024). The current organizations communicate with consumers via multiple types of digital media, which allows them to engage in direct communication with consumers, feedback, and the joint creation of brand value (Kartajaya, 2021). This change has augmented the importance of offering regular, concerned, and customized brand communication via media in an effort to enhance customer experience and to broaden the long-lasting relationship. Connected devices, websites, social media, mobile apps, CRM systems, and other systems produce enormous structured and unstructured data (Odionu et al., 2024). This data helps the companies in making choices, preferences and behavior of consumers in a better way. Using sophisticated analytics and predictive modeling, marketers will first divide up audiences, make predictions of customer requirements, and craft more specific communication plans that engage and convert more (Al Rafi, 2023).

Marketing is changing through automation and information-driven insights (Kumari et al., 2024). Programmatic advertising, recommendation systems, chatbots and automated email marketing increases brand performance and communication with the consumer. In the recent past, with the emergence of AI-driven virtual influencers, the field of marketing and consumer engagement opportunities is transforming and is obliterating the lines between reality and digital creation (Salam et al., 2026). These solutions save the manual labor and enhance the relevancy and timeliness of messages, which are critical in brand associations in competitive web space. Multichannel and experience based brand communication has become a reality due to digitalization, big data and automation (Hoyer et al., 2020). Customers desire a similar brand message and uninterrupted interactions in and through the social media, internet, mobile applications, stores and support channels. The Artificial Intelligence cannot be considered a technological tool, but a decision-support system, and automation, capable of supplementing the human abilities (Gupta et al., 2022; Matsatsinis & Siskos, 2012). Brand communication is a key component in the design and management of a brand and interaction between the brand and the customers (Azize et al., 2012). Brand communication links the consumers and the producers and determines the consumption behavior (Martin & Schouten, 2014). Brand communication is an activity that aims at building awareness, trust and influencing the consumer to make the purchase with integrated communications. The AI will supplement the Integrated Brand Communication through complexity management, constancy, and adaptability within a real-time environment via intelligent integration (Wang et al., 2025). In addition to enhancing the functional side of the business and processes such as information processing and interaction with consumers, AI also forms the theoretical innovations in communication, interaction, and relationship establishment in digital space (Pires & Brandão, 2025).

The area of Integrated Brand Communication (IBC) is one of the directions where AI is beginning to alter the working routine (Gissi & Savelli, 2025). With increased digital platforms and touchpoints, IBC focuses on providing convergent and consistent messages through channels in an effort to build a unified brand experience to enhance brand meaning and brand equity over the long term (Keller, 2013; Schultz et al., 2014). The ability of consumers to expand, faster and more diverse information, has confronted the old brand communication models that were managed manually (Arthur, 2013). AI can solve this discrepancy through real-time, data-driven learning, pattern recognition, and decision-making that will be used to effectively handle complex brand communication (Russell & Norvig, 2021). AI-driven technologies allow organizations to analyze large volumes of consumer data, generate actionable insights, and deliver personalized, coordinated cross-channel communication that supports consistency, coherence, and customer-centricity (Davenport et al., 2020). In a strategic manner, AI can bring the boundaries of the IBC even beyond the message coordination and continue to continuously optimize the brand-consumer relationship (Raut et al., 2025). Although ML-based segmentation, predictive analytics, and dynamism in content assist brands in correcting communication to adjusting customer preferences, conceptual, managerial and ethical issues regarding over-automation, less creativity, privacy unfairness, and bias in the algorithms are also raised in IBC. Therefore, it is essential to ensure that not only scholars but also practitioners would be educated to use AI as a strategic enabler within an integrated brand communication system rather than a technological means of action (Dulloo et al., 2025).

This chapter constitutes an all-round, integrative perspective on the role of artificial intelligence (AI) in Integrated Brand Communication (IBC) in terms of conceptual, technological, managerial, and ethical aspects. Section 2 creates the theoretical scope of IBC by presenting its development that originated in the evolution of Integrated Marketing Communication and major IBC constructs like brand identity, brand meaning, and appointment of a stakeholder. Section 3 analyzes AI in brand communication by defining its fundamental dimensions, analyzing the existing technologies, and combining them into operating abilities. Deepening on this theme, Section 4 examines how AI allows IBC via customer centric integration, message consistency and real time adaptive communication and Section 5 will discuss practical uses in form of personalization, AI assisted content creation and social listening. The managerial and organizational implications discussed in sections 6 and 7 are strategic integration, human-AI collaboration, capability development, and performance evaluation. Section 8 measures the shortcomings and dangers of AI use critically, and Section 9 talks about the ethical, legal, and governance issues. Lastly, Section 10 concludes the strategic insights of the paper with AI being a strategic enabler of IBC and the necessity of using technology as a driver of innovation alongside human feedback, moral accountability, and long-term brand value creation.

2. CONCEPTUAL FOUNDATIONS OF INTEGRATED BRAND COMMUNICATION

The growing adoption of digital and artificial intelligence (AI)-driven technologies is fundamentally reshaping the structure of modern business ecosystems and consumer interactions (Corsaro et al., 2022; Rayun et al., 2025; Salam et al., 2024; Secundo et al., 2025). More and more companies are using these technologies to bring about more connectedness, better use of data to make decisions and develop more dynamic and personalized communication spaces. Research on mobile payment systems, virtual influencers, and AI-mediated communication points to a more fundamental change toward more integrated models of engagement that mediate real-time interaction, accessibility, and personalization in marketing cases (Rayun et al., 2025; Salam et al., 2026; Salam et al., 2024). In this shifting environment, the idea of an Integrated Brand Communication (IBC) has become popular as a strategic model of organizing brand messages that can be provided through various touchpoints and be consistent and customer-centric. Thus, it is necessary to comprehend the theoretical premises of IBC to place the role of AI in changing the current brand communication practices within a context.

2.1 Evolution from Integrated Marketing Communication (IMC) to Integrated Brand Communication (IBC)

The history of the integrated marketing communications (IMC) is the change of tactical coordination of tools to a strategic managerial philosophy (Blakeman, 2023; Zhang, 2026). The original definition of IMC is largely attributed to Schultz (1992), whose contribution is widely believed to have given the concept a holistic approach as opposed to the earlier approach toward individual aspects like advertising, public relations, sales promotion, procurement and inner communications. With the proliferation of the media channels, four stages of development were proposed by the scholars, which include tactical coordination, redefinition of the communications domain, application of information technology, and lastly, financial and strategic integration (Madhavaram et al., 2005). Such premises are significant to the achievement of the role of new technologies like AI in enhancing integration and cohesion especially in response to the despairing promotional activities that led to the development of IMC during the late 1900s (Duncan & Caywood, 2013). Another aspect that IMC paid attention to was the integration of these tools to deliver them the same voice message to the consumers, thereby increasing the efficiency and effectiveness of the communication (Schultz et al., 2014). Since brands were courting consumers, employees, shareholders, neighborhoods and online visitors, it became clear that a more comprehensive strategy based on the brand was required (Fournier & Avery, 2011). The specified change has led to the idea of an Integrated Brand Communication where the brand takes the central stage of integration and not the individual communication tools (Keller, 2013). Integrated Brand Communication (IBC) is a more sophisticated strategy of controlling messages related to the brand in a growing complicated communication context (Luxton et al., 2015). Compared to promotional tools integration, IBC is more holistic since it is preoccupied with the creation and reinforcement of brand meaning at every stakeholder touchpoint. IBC is an outside-in approach, beginning with the customer data in order to determine the best approach to communicate with their needs (Paramadina & Info, 2024). Unlike traditional IMC's mostly one-way communication, IBC emphasizes two-way interaction, value co-creation, and long-term relationship building. This evolution from IMC to IBC reflects a shift from tactical coordination to strategic brand management, highlighting the need for integrated, data-driven communication systems capable of managing complex stakeholder interactions.

2.2 Role of Brand Identity, Brand Meaning, and Stakeholder Alignment

The central theme of Integrated Brand Communication is brand identity as the results of association that an organization is interested in developing and upholding in the minds of stakeholders (Keller, 2013). Brand identity gives the strategic backbone to the entire communication operations in which a brand runs itself as expressed in its values, personality, symbols, and messages (Wheeler, 2017). A well-defined identity also helps organizations to stand alone in terms of consistency in all the channels of communication thus increasing brand recognition, credibility, and long term positioning (Nandan, 2005). The notion that is closely linked to brand identity is brand meaning, which is currently perceived as a process of co-creation between the organization and the stakeholder (Merrilees et al., 2016). Brand meaning is not conceived by just the firms, but rather formed through ongoing interactions as a result of multi-touchpoints through digital platforms, social media, and customer experiences. It is a dynamic process whereby communication should be managed as a message delivery mechanism and at the same time, as a dialogue which creates a perception among the stakeholders.

Another important component of IBC is stakeholder alignment because it expands the communication range since it shifts the interest beyond consumers and adds employees, partners and broader populations. The contemporary setting has several stakeholders and is likely to affect brand perception, but it is important to ensure that the internal communications do not undermine the external one (Gregory, 2007). These models are Kliatchko (2008) four-pillar model (stakeholders, content, channels, and results) where the key focus is on the cyclical processes where communication coordination is necessary. It has become more challenging to find a ground with the stakeholders in digital worlds where different channels, real-time communication and decentralization of communication channels are common. The disintegrated communications of various departments or touchpoints can undermine brand credibility and trust (Umoren et al., 2022). As a result, IBC ought to be structured at the organization-wide level because the players of the structure ought to perform in line with general branding principles and shared communication principles. The organizations can possibly provide a unified brand voice with alignment; this prelude to greater brand relations, increased engagement and brand loyalty (Kitchen & Schultz, 2003). However, the growing complexity of the communication situation also brings out the limitations of traditional methods of integrating. Manual systems have no capacity to handle large volumes of information, synchronize inter-channel communication, and respond in real time (Olayinka, 2021). There is also an opportunity to use artificial intelligence to make the integration easier by introducing innovative opportunities aimed at building knowledge-driven insights, automate coordination, and respond to the communication strategies. Thus, to analyze the opportunities of AI as a strategic provider of integrated and customer-oriented brand communication, one will need to understand the conceptual grounds of IBC.

3. UNDERSTANDING AI IN BRAND COMMUNICATION

3.1 Definition and Key Dimensions of Artificial Intelligence

Generally, the Artificial Intelligence (AI) is described as the ability of a machine to behave intelligently like a person or a subdivision of computer science that is concerned with the simulation of intelligent human behavior in computers (Grewal, 2014). Artificial Intelligence (AI) is a new technology that has been seen to transform the marketing and brand communication landscape by the way brands engage with consumers, manage knowledge, and generate value (Chintalapati, 2022). In modern digital ecosystems, AI does not only do what technologies can do but it provided strategic capabilities to personalize, automate, co-create, and make decisions based on data. According to Camilleri (2024), AI consists of expert systems that are able to simulate human intelligence, usually with the help of machine learning, natural language processing, and computer vision technologies. The primary aspects of the AI application in the business today are automation to streamline routine operations, personalization to suit the needs of different stakeholders, and data-driven insights to predict demands of different stakeholders. AI is becoming a part of strategic procedures in marketing environments. According to Chintalapati (2022), AI-based marketing is data-driven, automated, and intelligent to help companies improve content marketing, experiences marketing, and marketing activities. Equally, Marvi et al., (2026) place AI in the knowledge management (KM) perspective, which highlights the use of AI in decision making based on data and its ability to enhance business communication. A number of essential dimensions of AI appear: Learning and Adaptation (Chintalapati, 2022), Automation and Efficiency (Camilleri, 2024), Personalization and Customer-Centricity (Senyapar, 2024), Predictive and Analytical Capability, Ethical and Governance Considerations (Hassaan et al., 2023). Collectively, these dimensions illustrate that AI in brand communication is not limited to technical automation but encompasses strategic, relational, and ethical aspects.

3.2 Types of AI Relevant to Brand Communication

Several subfields of AI are currently transforming how brands communicate and engage with their audiences:

Machine Learning (ML)

Machine learning is one of the branches of AI, which allows systems to learn the patterns based on the data and enhance predictions without any explicit programs (Sarker, 2021). It forms the basis of customer analytics, behavioral segmentation, and recommendation engines. It increases interaction between the brand and its customers through the analysis of buying behavior, clickstream information and sentiment trends. In brand management, the engagement and loyalty of customers are enhanced by ML-based service integration (e.g., chatbots, voice assistants) (Begum, 2025). It is a sub-field that is concerned with the production of programmes that use unprocessed data to construct predictive models and generate decisions given some new data (Arias, 2022). ML is vital in brand communication, where the recommender systems implemented by platforms such as Spotify, Netflix, and Amazon are applicable in recommending the content to the user following the previous user behavior.

Natural Language Processing (NLP)

NLP also allows computers to read, comprehend and create human language. The technology underlines AI-based chatbots employed by companies such as H&M and Sephora to address regular queries of customers and offer 24/7 service (Haider, 2024). Sentiment analysis is another NLP practice that enables brands to filter a large volume of social media posts and feedbacks to get a real-time understanding of what the rest of the world thinks and how their customers feel.

Computer Vision

This field deals with image mathematical representation and processing to be recognized and analyzed. Brands apply computer vision to visual search (e.g., eBay or Pinterest), with the customers able to locate the products uploading photos (Nanne et al., 2020). It can also be applied in facial recognition when authenticating a customer as well as in emotion recognition which recognizes facial features to determine how an individual expresses themselves with regard to a product or an advertisement.

Generative AI (GenAI)

GenAI is a machine learning model to generate new original content - text, images, or video based on user prompts. It has also come up with a new paradigm of consumer-generated advertising (CGA), brands such as Coca-Cola or Heinz are engaging consumers to co-create brand stories and digital artwork using GenAI tools.

Although GenAI helps to increase the speed of content creation, it also brings up the issue of anthropocentrism to the forefront because GenAI uses an alternative method to express creativity as a human-specific ability (Feng & Sun, 2025). Although there is a variety of technical functions of these AI technologies, they all allow tackling the data processing, interaction, and content generation opportunities, which are at the center of current brand communication. They are strategically important not because of individual functionalities, but rather because of overall integration as an embedded portion of a much larger capability system that promotes personalization, automation, and real-time sensitivity.

3.3 Functional Capabilities of AI in Brand Communication

Artificial intelligence technologies discussed in the preceding sections—such as machine learning, natural language processing, computer vision, and generative AI—should not be viewed as isolated tools. Rather, the available literature reconciles on the postulation that these technologies come together to provide a list of functional capabilities which reverse the way organizations design, administer and appraise brand communication. Instead of addressing specific technologies, the recent findings view AI as a system of capabilities that facilitate personalization, automation, predictive decision-making, and real-time communication in an integrated marketing setting (Chintalapati, 2022; Davenport et al., 2020). Data-driven personalization is one of the most widely studied features because it enables companies to customize their communication according to the personal consumer profiles, which hinge on the behavioral and transactional data (V. Kumar et al., 2019; Navarro, 2024). Backing this is the ability to make messages relevant and engaging on the digital touchpoints. Nevertheless, there is also a paradoxical contradiction in the literature: on the one hand, the personalization will bring value, and, on the other, it will also introduce the problem of privacy, security of its data, and consumer trust (Milano et al., 2020). It implies that personalization should be perceived as a technical operation alongside a strategic compromise between an act of value creation and moral responsibility. The second core capability is automation and scalability of operation which allows organizations to handle large flows of communication effectively through numerous channels. Continuous interaction and constant message delivery are achieved by the AI-driven systems, including the chatbots and programmatic advertising platforms (Camilleri, 2024)

Strategically, automation will contribute to efficiency and coordination, but overdependence on any automated mechanism can result in standardized and less differentiated communication, which could undermine brand identity and emotional appeal (Makosa, 2024). Intimately connected is the predictive analytics and decision support ability, where AI is used to extrapolate patterns in data and predict consumer behavior and communication strategies (Okeleke et al., 2024; Sarker, 2021). Predictive models can enhance campaign effectiveness and targeting, but at the same time, they are less dependent on historical data, and they can promote the presence of existing errors, which requires constant supervision and human control (B. D. Mittelstadt et al., 2016). The other capability is the real-time interaction and responsiveness, which is facilitated by natural language processing and conversational AI. Brands using these technologies can also communicate with consumers in real-time and adjust their communication depending on real-time feedback (Haider, 2024). Nevertheless, ambiguity in context interpretation, e.g., sarcasm or cultural interpretation, can lead to an incorrect reaction, which is why the role of human judgment cannot be underestimated in communication (Joshi et al., 2017).

Finally, there is the capability to produce contents and innovatively refine them, with the use of generative AI, to produce marketing contents in extensive amounts and into dissimilar formats (Amini & Amini, 2024). This contributes to the effectiveness of the work, but it also evokes the question of the originality, authenticity, and homogenization of brand narratives (Feng & Sun, 2025; Rezwana & Maher, 2023). Remarkably, such skills do not operate without human judgments. Rather, AI will supplement the current system to augment the managerial judgment with data-oriented information and automation, and strategic direction, innovativeness, and human consideration will be assigned to the humans. These capabilities together as an integrated set of capabilities like personalization, automation, predictive analytics, real time responsiveness and content generation transform brand communication, a process previously conducted as infrequent and campaign based, into a dynamic, responsive system (Islam et al., 2024; Senyapar, 2024). More than that, they also bring the Integrated Brand Communication the working infrastructure of being consistent, coherent, and customer-concentrated on multiple touchpoints (Keller, 2013; Schultz et al., 2014). Their success however would later be based on their strategic integration and control under the organizational and ethical constraints.

4. AI AS AN ENABLER OF INTEGRATED BRAND COMMUNICATION

The role of artificial intelligence (AI) in enabling Integrated Brand Communication (IBC) is to coordinate, make consistent, and customer-focused brand messages in more and more complex digital environments. Whereas the old model of communication had challenges in terms of disjointed media channels and slow feedback systems, AI allows organizations to streamline information, streamline messages, and amend strategies in communication in real time. Notably, the usefulness of AI in the discussed context is not only in its technological functions, but in the strategic use of such functions in order to advance the key principles of IBC, i.e., coherence, consistency, and stakeholder alignment (Keller, 2013; Schultz et al., 2014).

The proposed framework depicts in Figure 1 that the concept of artificial intelligence (AI) facilitates Integrated Brand Communication (IBC) as a multi-layered process. The customer interaction ecosystem (including digital and physical touchpoints, social media, websites, CRM systems, mobile and IoT) at the base level produces pressurizing data streams. This information is computed in the AI intelligence layer that comprises machine learning, natural language processing, and generative AI technologies. Such technologies lead to the emergence of the most important AI features, which are data integration, personalization, predictive analytics, content automation, real-time decision-making, and social listening. These capabilities, together, serve core IBC dimensions, that is, customer-centricity, message consistency, cross-channel coordination, and stakeholder alignment. The successful application of such dimensions will result in better strategic achievements, including the quality of customer engagement, brand equity, quality decisions, and communicative approaches, which can be scaled. It is also based on the continuous learning and optimization cycle, which recommends the dynamic and iterative nature of AI-driven communication, where the insights gained through the results are recapitulated into the system to enhance its performance in the future. Moreover, governance and human control, such as ethical issues, data privacy, and human-AI cooperation, are applied at all levels to make the implementation responsible and effective. In general, the framework conceptualizes AI as a key enabler, which turns fragmented communication into a coordinated, adaptive and data-driven IBC system.

Figure 1. AI-Driven Integrated Brand Communication Ecosystem Framework

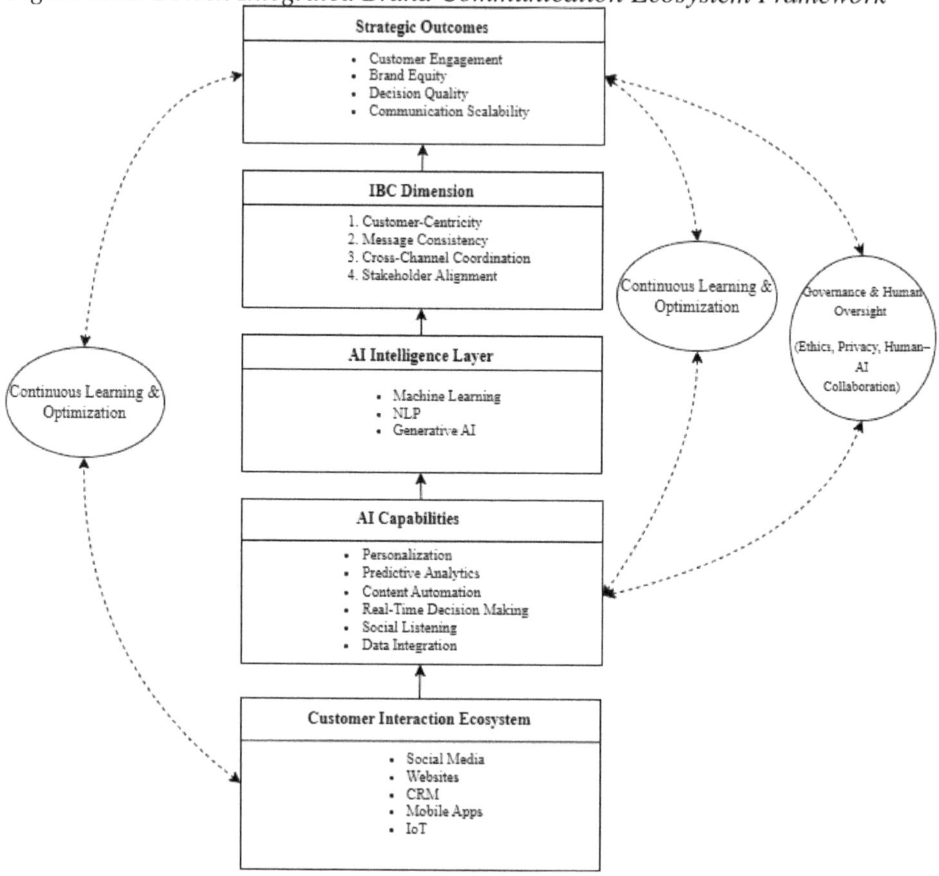

4.1 AI and Customer-Centric Integration Across Touchpoints

One of the most significant contributions of artificial intelligence (AI) to Integrated Brand Communication (IBC) is its ability to establish a unified and customer-centric view of the consumer journey. Consumers today have a diverse variety of touchpoints with the brand in the digital world, including social media, websites, mobile applications, email, and even in-store retail settings. Historically these interactions have been handled within the organizational silos and have led to disjointed communication and uncoordinated brand experiences. AI can overcome it by facilitating cross-platform integration of data, which will in turn help organizations build a holistic and continuous view of the consumer behavior within the channels (Bonetti et al., 2023; Kumari et al., 2024). As has been argued in Section 3.3, AI-driven capabilities, especially data integration and predictive analytics, allow firms to bring together structured and unstructured data sets, where a first-party (e.g., CRM systems) and second-party, as well as third-party data have been considered first and second. The implementation of AI-based solutions like customer data platforms (CDPs) will help organizations chart the customer journey in order to determine the most important points of contact and provide contextually relevant messages at every step of interaction. This multifaceted strategy will increase the customer-centricity of IBC because the communication will not only be personalized but also channel-integrated so that the coherence and consistency of brand experiences can be improved (Chintalapati, 2022; Davenport et al., 2020). Empirical studies indicate that this type of AI-based integration can make customer engagement and conversion rates much more effective (Davenport et al., 2020). Moreover, the AI will enable high-quality cross-channel coordination through the insights obtained on predictive consumer behaviour. Comparing real-time and historical data, AI systems could foresee the needs of customers, streamline the time when messages are delivered, and provide the appropriate communication approach (Okeleke et al., 2024). This has allowed organizations to migrate not only in the paradigm of communication that is reactive, but in proactive and anticipatory paradigms of engagement, which are essential in the extremely competitive digital arenas.

Still, in addition to all these positive aspects, the literature also tells about the fact that there are several mean problems concerning AI-powered integration. Being a universal tool of consumer data use, raises concerns that are related to privacy, security of data, and their ethical governance. The augmented threat of exploitation and potential violation of customer trust is the growing volume of personal data aggregation among sites (Milano et al., 2020). The regulatory systems, in addition, make the organizations transparent and require informed consent in gathering and processing information. Those battles imply that the customer-focused integration must demand more than a technological ability and that it needs to have the robust governance arms and ethics oversight. On the managerial front, firms ought to invest in data integration facilities and at the same time, they ought to abide by the data protection legislations and ethics. There is therefore a need to strike a balance between the notion of personalization and privacy issue so as to uphold trust and guarantee the effectiveness of AI-driven Integrated Brand Communication in the long-term.

An accessible and highly visible real-life case of an AI-oriented customer-centered integration is Amazon, which uses maintained complex systems of machine learning and data integration to coordinate the customer interactions in different departments, including its web site, mobile application, and email communications channels. Amazon recommendation engine offers highly tailored products guided by a browsing behavior, buying experience, search results, and immediate interactions and refresh the content of the communications. Such an integrated nature of the approach allows the firm to have a consistent and contextually pertinent brand interaction across the customer journey. In terms of Integrated Brand Communication, these capabilities contribute to the customer-centricity and coherence of communication by creating the alignment of messages with personal preferences between channels. There is empirical evidence that the recommendation system of Amazon has a positive impact on its sales figures, which proves the strategic importance of AI-based data integration in enhancing the results of engagement and conversion (Davenport et al., 2020; V. Kumar et al., 2019).

4.2 AI and Brand Consistency and Message Coherence

One of the key goals of the Integrated Brand Communication (IBC) is consistency of the brand image and coherence in brand communications across communication channels. When brands appeal to consumers across many different media, i.e. social media, mobile applications, websites and even physical touch points, the attainment of such consistency is now a complicated management issue. Different channels demand different formats, tones and types of interaction that may result in inconsistency in the message and consequently undermine brand name. The artificial intelligence (AI) is central to overcoming this difficulty as it provides the opportunity to standardize, coordinate, and constantly monitor brand communication at a variety of touchpoints (Huang & Rust, 2021; Keller, 2013). As will be outlined in Section 3.3, AI-powered innovation, especially automation and the creation of content, enable organizations to coordinate the output of the communication process with the pre-established brand principles, such as tone of voice, visual identity, and structure of a narrative. AI systems can be trained to produce and verify content that is held to these standards, and it will be consistent across the channels. As an illustration, the generative AI technology has the potential to create marketing messages, advertisements, social media content based on the predefined brand parameters, and validation systems evaluate the results of communication output against the brand identity. The ability increases the message repetition and narrative fluidity, which are core to the success of IBC (Davenport et al., 2020; Schultz et al., 2014). It is empirically indicated that brand messages that are continually repeated would lead to better brand recognition and customer trust (V. Kumar et al., 2019). Also, AI provides the coordination of cross-channels to make sure that brand messages do not lose alignment despite adapting them to the specifics of the platform. Organizational use of automated content optimization and real-time feedback systems can ensure that the organizations have a cohesive brand voice and tailor-fit the communication format in various contexts when using different media. Such a balanced approach to standardization and adaptation is a key to retaining brand equity and strengthening consumer confidence in the online space.

Nonetheless, the literature puts a serious conflict between consistency and creativity. Although AI-based standardization should make content more consistent and efficient, overdependence on automated tools can lead to homogenous and formulaic messages that do not appeal to the reader at an emotional level (Holt, 2004; Rezwana & Maher, 2023). This weakness is especially pertinent as far as brand communication is concerned because differentiation and cultural relevance form major sources of long-term brand equity. Moreover, AI bias in forms of algorithms can represent bias in architecture that unwillingly contributes to a specific representation of brand identity and, as a result, sends out-of-contextual or culturally inappropriate messages (Mittelstadt, 2019; Mittelstadt et al., 2016). Regarding the managerial approach, the organizations have to take the hybrid strategy that AI will help to create consistency, scalability and efficiency, human creativity will guarantee authenticity, cultural relevance and strategic differentiation. The balance is essential in order to be able to cohere and differentiate in brand communication. It is in this context that AI can be interpreted not as an alternative to a creative decision, but as an additional tool that should be applied to the integrity and integrity of Integrated Brand Communication.

4.3 AI and Adaptive, Real-Time Communication Systems

The other relevant contribution of artificial intelligence (AI) to Integrated Brand Communication (IBC) is that it produces adaptive and real-time communication. The past marketing systems have been based on slow feedback, which is collection of insights on consumer reaction only after execution of a marketing campaign, which does not enable dynamic response. Conversely, AI-based technologies facilitate businesses to choose and analyze customer information on the fly, and accordingly, interactive communication plans can be adjusted promptly (Alantari et al., 2022; D. Kumar et al., 2023). This attitude towards communication being more proactive, rather than reactive, boosts brand interactions largely in the responsiveness and agility. As described in Section 3.3, AI-enhanced features, especially real-time analytics and natural language processing, allow tracking consumer attitude, behaviour and engagement trends in online mediums all the time. Social listening systems, social media sentiments analysis tools, and other technologies offer organizations a chance to deal with a vast amount of user-generated content, including online communication, social media posts, and reviews. In such a way, AI systems are able to recognize new trends, determine changes in consumer feelings, and provide actionable insights (Alfreihat et al., 2024; Haider, 2024). This allows brands to tighten messaging planning, mitigate the possible reputational risk, as well as take advantage of emerging opportunities as quickly as possible. The empirical observation indicates that real-time analytics may greatly enhance responsiveness to a campaign and customer interaction (Alantari et al., 2022; Davenport et al., 2020). According to the IBC approach, in-time flexibility enhances the alignment and continuity of the stakeholders through consistent communication by maintaining brand messages to keep with the changes in consumer expectations at all touch points. This lifecycle competence helps to change the episodic and campaign-based communication patterns to the ongoing and dialogical ones and solidify the relationships brand over time (Keller, 2013).

Nevertheless, significant shortcomings related to AI-based real-time systems are also outlined in the literature. Although technology is improving, AI systems tend to be incapable of decoding certain languages and cultural peculiarities, including sarcasm, irony, and context-separated meaning (Joshi et al., 2017). The wrong interpretation of such messages may result in wrong or untimely reactions, which may tarnish the company image. Moreover, excessive dependence on automated decision-making can decrease the control and strategy of managers, creating unplanned outcomes of communication (Mittelstadt et al., 2016). In a managerial view, the organizations have to implement a hybrid strategy that involves using AI to be responsive, yet but humanly supervised. Speeding up and facilitating flexibility, the human judgment is still critical to guarantee contextual accuracy, ethical appropriateness, and strategic consistency. It is thus important to strike a balance between automation and supervision to ensure the real time communication is utilized towards the and upholding of trust and the brand name.

4.4 Integrative Perspective: AI as a Strategic Enabler of IBC

All those capabilities do not operate alone because, in a more complex and disintegrating media environment, brand communication is relying upon them, creating a network of capabilities, which as seen in Sections 4.1 to 4.3, are all more cohesive, harmonized, and customer centric (Keller, 2013; Schultz et al., 2014). The strategic value of AI is that it brings IBC nearer to conceptual framework and transforms it into working and operating systems that can be scaled. As such, AI can help facilitate the effective organization of brand touchpoints in the entire customer experience by enabling businesses to bridge the communication through data across touchpoints, apply the same brand message and dynamically change the communication in real-time. The specified partnership approach will strengthen the number of customer interactions, brand loyalty, and streamline the marketing decisions (Davenport et al., 2020). Empirical data also indicate that AI-driven speech engines can enhance responsiveness, targeting accuracy and general campaigner performance. Besides, AI may help to transition to a permanently present and constantly updated data-driven process of communication, which enables it to be more adaptable and interactive with stakeholders.

There are no challenges with integration of AI into the brand communication, though. The intensive use of consumer data also causes serious issues associated with privacy, security, and ethical management, especially with the accelerating level of regulatory attention (Milano et al., 2020). Besides that, algorithmic bias can contribute to an unfair or inaccurate representation of consumer groups, which can negatively affect trust and inclusivity (Mittelstadt et al., 2016; Obermeyer et al., 2019). Moreover, excessive reliance on AI and the inevitable onslaught of over-automation threaten the creative process and authenticity because the heavy reliance on AI-generated content can lead to standardized and fewer differentiated brand messages (Holt, 2004; Rezwana & Maher, 2023). All these issues speak of the necessity of a strategic and responsible attitude towards AI adoption in IBC. However, rather than taking the place of human judgment, AI can be considered a complement to the system, as it complements the decision-making procedure, helps with the process of creativity and also enables the communication that is scalable. This emphasizes the importance of the collaboration of human and AI, whereby the AI provides an analytical and operational capacity whilst the human players provide the strategic orientation, functional responsiveness, and moral accountability. Being a managerial aspect, it should be duly adopted by integration of technological skills and governing models, cross-disciplinarity, and continual controls. In this case, AI is not merely a tool of technology, but a source of strategy that will assist organizations to achieve the main targets of Integrated Brand Communications in dynamic digital environments. The true beauty of it lies in the fact that it will facilitate individuals to supplement their functionality and capabilities, allow the alignment of various systems, and deliver coherent, applicable, and meaningful experiences with the brand.

5. APPLICATIONS OF AI IN INTEGRATED BRAND COMMUNICATION

5.1 Personalization and Dynamic Brand Messaging

One of the most vivid illustrations of AI applications as far as Integrated Brand Communication is concerned is the assisted sophisticated personalization and dynamic communications on brand. The formation of customer profiles (built on a large scale of consumer information: browsing history, transaction history, real-time interactions, and so on) is the foundation of AI systems that are continuously being updated (Zaman, 2022). These profiles allow the organizations to project the consumer-taste anticipation and present stated messages in a highly narrow and context-based manner. On the personal level, regarding IBC, such personalization will raise brand centricity due to matching the different touchpoints against customer requirements. Investigations in the discipline of AI-mediated platforms, such as those that are engaged in the provision of personalised content by streaming and e-commerce platforms, demonstrate the potential of the personalisation of content dispensation to improve the engagement and foster loyalty to the customer in the long run (Hassan et al., 2025; Vashishth et al., 2024). Moreover, predictive analytics incorporated in customer relationship management (CRM) systems helps organizations to develop high-probability conversion identities and instigate customized communication, including customized offers or advice.

Automated systems of bidding and content optimisation enables companies to tailor the format, timing and delivery of messages based on the behaviour of user and hints in the context. This is helpful in replacing the low responsiveness communication with the responsive strategies of interaction. However, despite the fact that personalization can be useful to make the presentation more relevant and effective, it is also associated with serious issues. Extreme degrees of personalization may lead to the effects of intrusion, which may bring problems in terms of privacy, data security, and consumer trust. Therefore, to become a long term relationship organization organizations must achieve the balance between personalization on one side against transparency and ethical data practices on the other hand.

One of the most documented examples of AI-based personalization is Netflix, which, based on the advanced machine learning algorithms, will treat user behavior, viewing history, and interaction pattern data to present very personalized pieces of content suggestions. It is estimated that from these recommendation systems a large percentage of user interaction and retention is affected by matching the content to their preferences. In terms of the Integrated Brand Communication, such strategy empowers customer-centricity by making sure that the brand transactions are customized and unified across the digital touchpoints. Nevertheless, in addition to better user experience and loyalty, this kind of personalization brings certain issues of data privacy and transparency of algorithms, which contributes to the importance of responsible data governance (Davenport et al., 2020).

5.2 AI-Assisted Content Creation and Management

The content is still one of the principal elements of brand communication that needs to be constantly created on the level of the owned, earned, and paid media. Historically, the process of content creation was labor-intensive, with major investments into creative and production capabilities (Prakash & Sabharwal, 2024). AI is changing this process to automatize major steps in the processes of creating, curating, and distributing content, which increases efficiency and scales (Davenport et al.,

2020). AI-based solutions such as generative AI systems can help organisations to write, draw, and create multimedia materials on the large scales without losing brand consistency. This helps to maintain message consistency and coherence which is critical to IBC. Moreover, AI can be used to optimize content by utilizing the data on the level of audience interactions and suggest changes in the simplicity of tone of voice, the format, and delivery mode.

A growing use is the place of consumers in creating the content via AI-facilitated platforms commonly known as consumer-generated advertisement. Users become more and more engaged in the creation of content by the brands, which contributes to more significant involvement and the feeling of ownership (Feng & Sun, 2025). Nonetheless, studies suggest that overusing AI-generated creativity can make brand perceived authenticity lower as well as disconnect with the brand on an emotional level (Chui et al., 2023). This underscores a key managerial implication, namely that successful content strategies will need a human-AI synergistic approach with AI being used to facilitate efficiency and scale, and human actors being used to create originality, authenticity and the correct fit to brand personality. The absence of such balance would lead to the development of standardized content by organizations which will result in a lack of brand difference.

A good example of using AI in the creation of content is in the marketing campaign created by Coca-Cola using generative AI, the company has allowed consumers to co-create branded digital artwork and advertisements using AI tools. This is a hybrid between automation and consumer involvement which improves the involvement whilst preserving the brand consistency. In terms of IBC, this type of initiatives will influence message coherence as well as interaction with stakeholders by expanding to incorporate user-created content in a single brand story. Nonetheless, studies indicate that overdependence on AI-enhanced creativity can diminish subjective authenticity and affective bonding, as well as emphasize the need to balance the capabilities of AI application with the human input in the creativity (Chui et al., 2023; Feng & Sun, 2025).

5.3 Social Listening and Brand Sentiment Analysis

Another important application in the Integrated Brand Communication due to the AI-based social listening and sentiment analysis is that it allows organizations to be able to monitor and decipher the stakeholder perceptions in real-time. Using the methods of natural language processing and machine learning, AI systems can process large amounts of user-generated data, such as social media interactions, reviews, and online discussions, to determine and detect habits in consumer sentiment and trends (Alfreihat et al., 2024). Considering the IBC view, social listening helps in the alignment of the stakeholders and responsiveness to communication by making sure that brand messages are based on the current consumer attitudes and expectations. Maintaining a specific brand reputation is perhaps a major area where this real-time intelligence can be applied since AI systems can discern early warning signs of any possible crisis and allow organizations to take the initiative. Secondly, competitor analysis is another field where sentiment analysis can help firms conduct competitive benchmarking, analyze their brand image against competitors in the industry to determine strategic opportunities and gaps (Samal et al., 2025). Nevertheless, AI-based sentiment analysis has significant limitations despite the above benefits. The interpretation of the linguistic subtleties like sarcasm, irony, and culture is also a major challenge to tackle (Joshi et al., 2017). The wrong understanding of such signals can lead to improper reaction or wrong strategy. In addition, excessive dependence on automatized insights might decrease crucial managerial decision-making and situational cognition. Thus, social listening can make companies more responsive and more data-driven in their decision-making, but it should be combined with the power of AI and human control to guarantee a high level of accuracy, relevance, and alignment with the strategies.

5.4 Integrative Perspective on AI Applications in IBC

All these applications evoke the idea of how AI puts into practice the main tenets of Integrated Brand Communication. Customer-centricity is improved through personalization, consistency and coherence are ensured by automating content, and the responsiveness and alignment with the stakeholders is possible in real time with the help of social listening. Combined, these applications will bring brand communication out of a disjointed and reactive process, and create a coordinated, adaptive, and data-driven system. The success of these applications however depends on how they are strategically incorporated into organizational processes. The issues with privacy, ethical governance, creativity, and over-automatization highlight the necessity to take a sensible approach. The organizations should consequently embrace systems that have integrated technological skills alongside human talent, integrity, and inter-functional integration. In that regard, the concept of AI applications can be interpreted not only as tools of operation but rather as strategic tools that can help organizations to pursue the aims of the Integrated Brand Communication in dynamic and multifaceted digital spaces.

6 STRATEGIC BENEFITS OF AI-DRIVEN INTEGRATED BRAND COMMUNICATION

The conceptual requirements of integrated brand communication - coherence, consistency, and consumer-centricity have been long and clearly expressed in the marketing and communication literature (Kliatchko, 2008; Schultz et al., 1993). The actualisation of these imperatives by magnitude and complexities of contemporary media environments had, however, been curtailed by most of the twentieth century. Artificial intelligence has totally changed this calculus. Artificial Intelligence has transformed integration into a new theoretical and a viable option as it automatizes very analytical and innovative operations. In this section, three fundamental applications are debated where AI offers materialization through the integrated brand communication customizing brand communications, robots and manages content creation and implements social listening on brand sentiments analysis. It is the combination of such applications that will create a complete architecture of an AI agile brand communication, which will be data-driven, creatively agile and strategically oriented.

6.1 Strategic Implications for Organizations

Implementation of artificial intelligence in Integrated Brand Communication (IBC) demands organizations to stop taking artificial intelligence as a separate technological tool but treat AI as a strategic resource integrated in the context of the entire marketing and communication ecosystem. The fundamental change of the way organizations design, coordinate and evaluate brand communication is that by implementing data-driven decision making, integration of cross-channel communication, and adaptable strategies of engagement, organizations can radically change their approaches to brand communication. In that sense, it is important that firms tune AI competencies to the wider brand goals to make sure that technology implementation enhances brand equity and not operational efficiency in the short term. Strategically, AI implementation will require the movement towards the more integrated organizational structure. IBC also depends on the alignment of numerous functions, such as marketing, data analytics, customer relationship management, and IT, which should be coordinated to use AI-driven insights. This necessitates the dismantling of the traditional functional silo and the development of cross functional coordination to make sure that communication strategies are consistent and aligned throughout all of the touchpoints. Companies should also invest in their data infrastructure such as customer data programs and analytics to allow them to smoothly integrate and access real time consumer insights.

Moreover, AI improves the capability of companies to address intricate customer journeys by offering a piece of all information regarding the communication with consumers. This will allow the companies to shift away to continuous engagement strategies, replacing campaign aimed communication whereby there are adjustments in brand interactions based on the fluctuations in behavior of the consumer. However, there is also a strategic implication of this change, namely, balancing automation and brand authenticity. The excessive use of AI-based systems may result in the development of the so-called standardized communication that is not coupled with emotions and differentiation. Therefore, the concept of technology skill, as well as brand orientation mind, should be combined in the organization to be strategized. This will entail the creation of a simple governance structure, harmonization of AI projects and branding positioning besides ensuring that the communications provisions are not losing balance with the primary core brand value. In fact, it cannot be claimed that the strategic power of AI in IBC is confined to efficiency improvement only; instead, it can be regarded in the ability to ensure alignment of communication of brands and make it adaptive, flexible, and customer oriented at the same time.

6.2 Human–AI Collaboration in Brand Communication

Among the key implications of introducing AI into the sphere of Integrated Brand Communication, it should be mentioned that the frameworks of successful human-AI partnership should be created. Even though AI systems are associated with tremendous advantages in regards to data processing, automation, and predictive analytics, they are innately frail in relation to creative faculties, situational comprehending and moral decision making of human beings. Consequently, AI needs to be viewed as a supplementary mechanism rather than as substitutionary to human competencies in brand communication. In practice, AI is efficient in dealing with data-intensive and repetitive processes, including audience segmentation, analysis of performance, content optimization, and real-time tracking of consumer behavior. These functions can help organizations to scale communication initiatives and enhance work processes. Nevertheless, such human-centered aspects of strategic decision-making as setting brand positioning, building narratives, and cultural relevance are inherently human-based. Brand communication is both technical process and symbolic as well as emotional activity, which must be interpreted and seen creatively.

Success of human-AI collaboration lies in the fact that roles and responsibilities are clearly stated in the organization. Managers need to identify the activities that would be best done automatically and those that need the involvement of human beings. As an illustration, using AI, it is possible to create the first writing drafts or suggestions; however, it is worth noting that these recommendations should be corrected and checked by the human professional prior to adhering to the brand reputation and communication strategies. This human-in-the-loop methodology helps to improve efficiency and quality besides mitigating the risks of over-automation. Besides, cooperation between humans and AI is applied to ethical decision-making. The output of the AI systems can be technically correct but ethically dubious or unsuitable to the culture. Human control is, thus, necessary in order to evaluate the bigger message of AI-generated communication and make sure that it does not go against organizational values and expectations of the society. As a manager, to be able to promote the successful human-AI cooperation, one should invest in the development of skills and organizational culture. Staff should be educated to collaborate with AI and learn to use data-based insights and implement them in the strategies. Meanwhile, a culture of technological innovation and human creativity needs to be instilled in the organization. Through this balance, companies will be able to use AI to improve efficiency and still maintain the authenticity and emotional nuances, which are core principles of effective brand communication.

6.3 Ethical and Governance Considerations

The rising trend of artificial intelligence use in Integrated Brand Communication poses serious ethical and governance issues that institutions need to overcome on their own. Since the operation of AI systems rooted much in gathering, processing and analyzing high amounts of consumer information, the issues of privacy, security and transparency have become the core of the discussion of the AI adoption. These are some of the issues that, if they are not addressed, may destroy the brand logo and compromise the efficiency of communication strategies, as they may erode consumer trust. Data privacy is among the major ethical issues. The personalization and targeting based on AI needs access to comprehensive consumer data, some of which can be sensitive behavioral and demographic data. Companies should make sure that their data gathering procedures are set in accordance with the regulatory standards and consumers are well-informed about their data utilization. Data practice transparency is fundamental to building of trust and long-term relationships with the stakeholders.

Algorithms bias is another problem of major concern. AI systems are handled using historic data which might be subject to some systematic errors that might result to discrimination or unjust results. Biased algorithms can lead to the exclusion or misrepresentation of some groups of consumers in the context of brand communication, which can be harmful to brand inclusivity and equity. Companies should therefore put in place auditing and monitoring measures of the AI systems so that the bias can be detected and alleviated. Another key measure is accountability. The more the AI systems are autonomized, the harder it will be to determine who will be responsible in terms of what they produce. Companies will have to come up with certain governance mechanisms that will standardize roles and responsibilities and accountability settings of AI-led decisions. This will be through implementation of supervision measures, ethics, and risk handling measures to ensure that it is responsible in its use of AI technologies. Strategically, the use of a AI to put into effect strategic governance processes rather than being an after-thought, must be a matter of concern to managers. This translates to the availability of ethics that are critical when designing systems, conducting audits on a regular basis, and instilling in the organization, a culture of responsibility. Concentrating on ethical aspects, the organizations will be able to mitigate the risks and in an increasingly data-driven world, will enhance the brand name and trust.

6.4 Performance Measurement and Evaluation of AI-Driven Communication

Efficient integration of artificial intelligence in the Integrated Brand Communication needs well-developed performance measurement and evaluation mechanisms. Despite the opportunity to use AI in order to offer new possibilities in the field of personalization, automation, and real-time interaction, the companies should establish certain measures and assessments to determine the effectiveness of these possibilities and ensure that they align with the strategic priorities. The primary performance indicator (KPIs) can be viewed as the frontline in the measurement of communication that is AI backed. The question of the effectiveness of AI-based communication strategies to the consumer behavior can be resolved with the help of intelligence indicators (such as the engagement rate, conversion rate, customer retention, customer lifetime value, etc.). In addition to that, the measures of the long-term impact of communication activities will also need brand perception indicators (sentiment analysis and brand equity metrics).

The fact that AI is available will make it easier in terms of performance measurement since it will enable having real-time group analytics and continuous monitoring of performance in campaigns. Conversely, complex analytics systems can track the duties of exchange amongst the user on different touchpoints and provide an overall customer experience presence. This allows the organizations to know the most effective communication strategies and be able to react to the changes in real time with the assistance of the data to make amendments. Attribution models also widen the available evaluation by assigning the proportion of the contributions of various channels and touchpoints to the total results. Nevertheless, there are also difficulties in the use of AI in performance measurement. The dependency on numerical measures can make organisations focus on short-term performance measures of an organization, sacrificing long-term brand building. Also, advanced AI models can be not transparent enough, and results can hardly be interpreted by managers and used to make appropriate decisions. It shows the significance of using managerial judgment and quantitative analysis together. Strategically, the organizations need to maintain a balanced approach to performance assessment by combining factual knowledge with attitudinal measurements of brand impact. These involve the alignment of KPIs with larger business goals, transparency in the measurement process, and incessant improvements in the evaluation framework with the development of AI technologies. In this way, organizations will be able to receive the maximum of AI in Integrated Brand Communication without losing its overall perspective on the success of the brand in the long term.

7. ORGANIZATIONAL TRANSFORMATION AND CAPABILITY DEVELOPMENT

While Section 6 outlined the strategic and ethical implications of artificial intelligence (AI) in Integrated Brand Communication (IBC), this section focuses on the organizational and human dimensions of AI adoption. Specifically, it examines how AI is reshaping managerial roles, professional responsibilities, and the capabilities required to effectively implement AI-enabled communication strategies.

7.1 Changing Roles of Brand Managers and Communication Professionals

The process of incorporating artificial intelligence in the Integrated Brand Communication is permanently redefining brand managerial functions and communication practitioners. Historically, these functions were strongly oriented on the performance of the operational and repetitive functions, namely the content scheduling, the optimization of keywords, the monitoring of the campaigns, and the interactions with the customers. Nonetheless, AI-related systems are getting more automated in performing such functions, which are allowing organizations to shift human resource to more strategic tasks of high value. As an example, AI-based chatbots will be capable of processing a significant percentage of repetitive customer queries in real-time engagement without being staffed accordingly (Vashishth et al., 2024). On the same note, AI-driven analytics systems have the capacity to handle and analyze large amounts of data in speeds that are way faster than human processing and this saves a lot of time in producing actionable insights (Kumar et al., 2019). These efficiencies enable organizations to be more responsive besides minimizing operational costs and eliminating human error. Consequently, the role of communication professionals is least changing the execution-related tasks in favor of strategic decision-making, development of creative activities, and performance management. The tasks of brand managers become more and more to recognize AI-generated insights, construct comprehensive communication plans, and adjust them to the brand identity on various touchpoints. This change is indicative of a wider change of the manual management of campaigns to data-enabled adjustive systems of communication.

Besides, AI improves scalability through digital advertising and content creation, which allow organizations to coordinate communication with a great number of channels at the same time. Programmatic advertising and automation of media plan enable extremely accurate targeting and optimization of communication activities so that the message reaches the right audience at the right moment. But with such high dependency on automation, managers must also keep a control, to ensure that communication does not deviate during brand values and strategic goals.

Because of this change, on the organizational level, new managerial skills and workflow redesign would be needed to incorporate AI into the workflow. Finally, AI does not forget about the work of communication professionals but transforms it, focusing on strategic thinking, coordination between functionalities, and the capacity to control the AI-based systems within the framework of a more general brand communication.

7.2 Skills and Capabilities Required for AI-Enabled IBC

To achieve the success of AI-facilitated Integrated Brand Communication, the marketing and communication practitioners need to acquire new skills and abilities. Due to the increased integration of AI in communication processes, the outdated marketing competencies are insufficient. Rather, organizations need to develop a staff that is data literate, offers technological knowledge, is creative, and ethically aware. One of the most important competencies in the AI-driven communication settings is data literacy. It requires professionals to be able to interpret sophisticated datasets, which will be the result of the numerous digital touchpoints, such as analytics of customer behavior and sentiment analysis, as well as predictive modeling results (Baptista et al., 2025; Rehman et al., 2022). Being able to transform the data-driven insights into the actionable communication strategies is a key element to successful audience segmentation, personalization, and campaign optimization.

Besides data literacy, there is a rise in the importance of a basic knowledge of the AI technologies. Though communication professionals need not be technically advanced, they should be conversant with the concepts of the fundamentals of machine learning, natural language processing, and marketing automation systems. Knowing allows successfully cooperating with data scientists, engineers, and technology teams that work to implement AI solutions (Davenport et al., 2020). It also increases the capacity of managers to critically assess the AI-generated outputs and make sure that they correspond to the communication goals. Although technical skills have been on the increase, creativity and strategic thinking have remained the key elements of effective brand communications. AI is capable of helping in creating and optimization of content, but not in its capacity to be more authentic and replicate human creativity, emotional intelligence, and cultural sensitivity. Thus, specialists should have the capability to incorporate AI-generated data in conjunction with creative decision-making to create significant and distinguished brand narratives (Pappas et al., 2023).

The other critical capability is ethical awareness. Since AI-mediated communication generates issues around the concept of privacy, bias, and transparency, practitioners need to be empowered in order to unearth and mitigate these problems in practice. This involves making sure of the responsible data use, assessing the output of the algorithms, and trusting brand communication. Lastly, flexibility and lifelong learning is essential in an organization where the technological change is very rapid. Organizations are compelled to invest in capacity building and developing training on the updated AI tools and practices so that the employee can be in tandem with the changing tools and practices. This process continues to aid the establishment of a workforce that is engaged in providing human intuition and machine-based precision.

8. CHALLENGES AND LIMITATIONS OF AI IN INTEGRATED BRAND COMMUNICATION

The operational and strategic potential of artificial intelligence in unified brand communication is immense and much-read. However, a critical evaluation of the role of AI in brand communication should not be indifferent to its flaws, threats, and unresolved issues as well. Knowledge of these issues is not just a game of managing risks; it is a condition to the responsible, effective and sustainable implementation of AI in the brand communication strategy (Floridi et al., 2018).

8.1 Risk of over-automation and loss of human creativity

The possible threat against the integration of AI in brand communication is the risk of over-automation and the loss of human creativity in its turn. AI content is often shallow and lacking in contrast to human-created work because it consists of existing datasets and not original and distinct thinking. Excessive dependence on such systems may reduce key human judgment, critical thinking, and emotional intelligence in an organization, which may hurt the perceived authenticity of the brand. More so, studies show that there is a threshold effect, where consumers feel empowered by the use of AI augmentation, but can become threatened or alienated by coping with the idea that the technology has a level of creative challenge to the anthropocentric concept of creativity as a uniquely human quality (Rezwana & Maher, 2023). Since AI does not have the ability to make moral decisions, human control is therefore still necessary to make sure that automated messages do not sound socially inappropriate and completely un-strategic.

Over-automation, whereby the human creativity in marketing communication is substituted with algorithmic optimization is one of the biggest risks of deep AI integration in marketing communication. AI is proficient at recognizing patterns, optimizing iteratively, and executing clearly spelled out communicative tasks with efficiency, but it does not match the original, culturally appealing, and emotionally authentic creativity that makes a successful brand communication and a well-performing and generic content. The strategic value of brand communication has been the most important in creating and maintaining cultural meaning and positioning brands as participants in the symbolic lives of consumers (Holt, 2004). Current AI systems, no matter how brilliant, cannot intuitively grasp the significance of cultural context, emotional complexity, narrative structure and social signification in meaning-making.

In over-automation brand communication is formulaic and less creative. This conformity filter is detracting to all of these when it comes to creativity, cultural risk-taking and creating a unique brand voice that creates long-term equity. Educated intelligent systems that are learned through information on prior interaction prefer to learn what has succeeded them before. As Makosa (2024) points out, creative workers fear that AI optimization is standardizing brand communication and lowering brand cultural salience and memorability. Therefore, brand managers should employ AI to enhance creativity, but not eliminate it and retain the human cultural intelligence that equips brand communication with its perennial effect (Davenport et al., 2020).

8.2 Data Quality, Bias, and Algorithmic Limitations

Algorithms Bias and data quality are additional obstacles to effective communication with AI. The quality of AI-based insights fully relies on the quality of the input data; therefore, poor or incorrect data results in wrong business strategies and ineffective strategic choices. Most of the AI models are black-boxed, and the untransparency of the principles of decision-making undermines consumer and employee trust (B. D. Mittelstadt et al., 2016). One of the large issues of morality and finances is algorithmic bias. This is referred to as bias amplification when AI outputs are intentionally altered in such a way as to display and, in other cases, exacerbate the biases already present in the training data. Machine learning algorithms make use of past information by searching in the information to identify patterns. This implies that such factors as culture, behavior, and demographics might have an impact on them. According to Obermeyer et al., (2019), this may occur when the brands address people who belong to minority groups and fail to include them or represent them in a manner that is not accurate. It can also be observed in the way individuals retain their concept of what kind of items various categories of individuals like and how they use their money in a vital manner. Companies whose messages are perceived as restrictive, stereotyped, or cultural insensitive face immense reputation and financial problems in the modern world of more discriminating buyers. This means that such type of prejudices do not merely make sense, but they have a negative impact on your tactic.

The modern AI systems have numerous challenges that render them of less use in marketing brands. These weaknesses, in some cases, include bias and mere technological problems. The use of large language models in brand communication is risky as it may create plausible-sounding and yet false information, and this is the so-called hallucination (Wang et al., 2025). Some of the most specifics of modern digital culture are irony, sarcasm, cultural idioms, and situation-dependent meanings. Nevertheless, these nuances cannot be easily perceived and properly interpreted by sentiment analysis systems (Joshi et al., 2017). In cases of strategic communicative adaptation, prediction models based on previous consumer behaviour might fail to detect a shift in the cultural norms, consumer habits, or the competitive environment that did not anticipate (Lemon & Verhoef, 2016). In order to address these challenges, we must invest money in better data and models, and effective human supervision systems capable of closely examining AI output prior to it altering the way people discuss a brand.

9. ETHICAL, LEGAL, AND GOVERNANCE CONSIDERATIONS

9.1 Data Privacy and Consumer Consent

One of the essential issues of AI-enabled brand communication is data privacy since AI models need enormous amounts of data to train algorithms and yield predictive knowledge (Hermann & Hermann, 2022). Social media status updates to the grocery shopping habits of users are becoming terms of service that platforms are progressively updating to gather user-created content to feed their generative models such as ChatGPT and Bard. Such a data-driven approach establishes a conflict between privacy and personalization, sometimes known as the privacy-personalization paradox (Bychkov et al., 2024; Floridi, Cowls, Beltrametti, Chatila, et al., 2018).

Consumers are sensitive to the collection and use of their personal, financial, and health data, even though they are willing to have more customized experiences (Milano et al., 2020). Privacy by design has been declared a required operational principle by legal frameworks, predominantly the European Union's General Data Protection Regulation (GDPR). This demands that the brands must consider data protection during the design process of the AI tools and the process must require informed consent of consumers with regard to data collection (Rodriguez-Fernandez, 2025). Nevertheless, under these regulations, a lot of brands have incorporated ambiguous information in their terms of service, passing the responsibility of privacy protection onto the consumer. Moreover, brands who employ anonymous identity to safeguard identity can still be identified by AI as high stakes decisions like the denial of credit, which may still be in violation of individual interests.

9.2 Responsible AI and Brand Trust

The core of AI-based strategies is trust since the effectiveness of the systems is solely reliant on the data flow amid consumers (Boehm et al., 2022). When a brand becomes untrustworthy or unethical, it will mean that consumers will share less data, and hence reduce the capability of the brand to offer them custom solutions. Fairness, transparency, accountability, and safety are considered as the principles of responsible AI (Hosseini Tabaghdehi & Ayaz, 2025). Ethical considerations are frequently considered by managers as the most important theme in the adoption of AI, and even the performance measurement is less important than these considerations.

One obstacle to trust in the brand is algorithmic bias, in which systematic errors in AI models either promote or discriminate certain groups of people based on biased training inputs (V. Kumar et al., 2019). As an example, face recognition software has revealed enormous issues in categorizing individuals in terms of race and gender particularly women and those with dark skin. Similarly, the use of advertising algorithms that allow ethnically affinity to filter out individuals in the housing advertisements violates the law and damages the ethical trust within the community. In an attempt to reduce such risks, an increasing number of companies are adopting such governance frameworks as the EU AI Act. According to this law, human beings must monitor high-prone AI applications to ensure machines do not assume the moral reasoning. To date, strategic governance involves the establishment of AI Ethics Boards and algorithmic checks to detect and address bias (Bahangulu & Owusu-Berko, 2025). Ultimately, brand trust is strengthened when AI is applied in an evidently beneficial specific customer way such as through the prompt resolution of issues with clearly defined bots rather than through surreptitious or annoying surveillance.

10. CONCLUSION

The implementation of the Artificial Intelligence (AI) into the sphere of the Integrated Brand Communication (IBC) is no longer a mere theoretical notion, but a tangible concept that alters the manner in which organizations engage with their audiences. AI has become a strategic facilitator in order to facilitate brand consistency and message alignment in an increasing number of complicated digital environments and is the means to effect a transition to a more customer-focused interaction than mass communication by a firm. The principle of AI strengthened the IBC core objectives to be consistent, coherent, and customer-focused through allowing the massive data integration, real-time analytics, and responsive communication plans. Examples of technologies that help organizations customize messages and messages, automatize content creation, measure brand sentiments, and respond quickly to consumer wants on different channels include machine learning, natural language processing, and generative AI. This aspect can be used in transforming the previous trend of outdated method of communication through traditional campaigns to continuous, data-based communication that may enhance the brand equity and customer relations. In the meantime, AI as a concept is a major cause of concern, including the problem of over-automation, loss of human creativity, the algorithm bias, and the problem of data privacy and ethical management. AI, therefore, is not a replacement of human creativity and strategic judgment but an enabling tool, and it can be more efficient when it is applied in an integrated brand communication and in a responsible and strategic way.

REFERENCES

Al Rafi, M. (2023). Machine learning–enhanced predictive marketing analytics for optimizing customer engagement and sales forecasting. *International Journal of Research and Applied Innovations*, *6*(4), 9203–9213.

Alantari, H. J., Currim, I. S., Deng, Y., & Singh, S. (2022). An empirical comparison of machine learning methods for text-based sentiment analysis of online consumer reviews. *International Journal of Research in Marketing*, *39*(1), 1–19. DOI: 10.1016/j.ijresmar.2021.10.011

Alfreihat, M., Almousa, O. S., Tashtoush, Y., AlSobeh, A., Mansour, K., & Migdady, H. (2024). Emo-SL framework: Emoji sentiment lexicon using text-based features and machine learning for sentiment analysis. *IEEE Access : Practical Innovations, Open Solutions*, *12*, 81793–81812. DOI: 10.1109/ACCESS.2024.3382836

Amini, R., & Amini, A. (2024). An overview of artificial intelligence and its application in marketing with focus on large language models. *International Journal of Science and Research Archive*, *12*(2), 455–465. DOI: 10.30574/ijsra.2024.12.2.1223

Arias, C. R. (2022). *An Introduction to Artificial Intelligence*.

Arthur, L. (2013). *Big data marketing: engage your customers more effectively and drive value*. John Wiley & Sons.

Azize, Ş., Cemal, Z., & Hakan, K. (2012). Does brand communication increase brand trust? The empirical research on global mobile phone brands. *Procedia: Social and Behavioral Sciences*, *58*, 1361–1369. DOI: 10.1016/j.sbspro.2012.09.1120

Bahangulu, J. K., & Owusu-Berko, L. (2025). Algorithmic bias, data ethics, and governance: Ensuring fairness, transparency and compliance in AI-powered business analytics applications. *World Journal of Advanced Research and Reviews*, *25*(2), 1746–1763. DOI: 10.30574/wjarr.2025.25.2.0571

Baptista, R., de Almeida, C. V., & Belim, C. (2025). Intelligent Connections: AI-Driven Communication and the Path to Enhanced Literacies. In *Rethinking Literacy in the Era of Sustainability and Artificial Intelligence* (pp. 99–132). IGI Global Scientific Publishing.

Begum, N. (2025). *Beyond Automation : How AI Service Integration is Shaping the Future of Brand Management Beyond Automation : How AI Service Integration is Shaping the Future of Brand. 25*(1).

Bharti, R., Khatri, U., & Duralia, O. A. (2024). Examining the role of digital marketing in shaping consumer communication and behavior. *Feedback International Journal of Communication, 1*(4), 192–201. DOI: 10.62569/fijc.v1i4.76

Blakeman, R. (2023). *Integrated marketing communication: creative strategy from idea to implementation*. Bloomsbury Publishing PLC.

Boehm, J., Grennan, L., Singla, A., & Smaje, K. (2022). Why digital trust truly matters. *McKinsey & Company, 12*.

Bonetti, F., Montecchi, M., Plangger, K., & Schau, H. J. (2023). Practice co-evolution: Collaboratively embedding artificial intelligence in retail practices. *Journal of the Academy of Marketing Science, 51*(4), 867–888. DOI: 10.1007/s11747-022-00896-1 PMID: 36035334

Bychkov, N., Maximovich, I., & Pateyuk, D. (2024). *Negative aspects of the use of artificial intelligence (AI) in marketing*.

Camilleri, M. A. (2024). *Artificial intelligence governance : Ethical considerations and implications for social responsibility. June 2023*, 1–15. DOI: 10.1111/exsy.13406

Chintalapati, S. (2022). *Artificial intelligence in marketing : A systematic literature review*. DOI: 10.1177/14707853211018428

Chui, M., Hazan, E., Roberts, R., Singla, A., & Smaje, K. (2023). *The economic potential of generative AI*.

Corsaro, D., Vargo, S. L., Hofacker, C., & Massara, F. (2022). Artificial intelligence and the shaping of the business context. *Journal of Business Research, 145*, 145. DOI: 10.1016/j.jbusres.2022.02.072

Davenport, T., Guha, A., Grewal, D., & Bressgott, T. (2020). How artificial intelligence will change the future of marketing. *Journal of the Academy of Marketing Science, 48*(1), 24–42. DOI: 10.1007/s11747-019-00696-0

Dulloo, R., Appolloni, A., & Mathiyazhagan, K. (2025). AI-Powered Communication: Strategic Framework for Technological Innovation, Brand Perception, and Sustainable Marketing. In *Strategic Blueprints for AI-Driven Marketing in the Digital Era* (pp. 1–40). IGI Global Scientific Publishing.

Duncan, T., & Caywood, C. (2013). The concept, process, and evolution of integrated marketing communication. In *Integrated Communication* (pp. 13–34). Psychology Press.

Feng, Y., & Sun, Y. (2025). Consumer empowerment through generative artificial intelligence : Enhancing brand narrative with collaboration, creation, and communication. *International Journal of Advertising*, *0*(0), 1–33. DOI: 10.1080/02650487.2025.2547545

Floridi, L., Cowls, J., Beltrametti, M., Chatila, R., Chazerand, P., Dignum, V., Luetge, C., Madelin, R., Pagallo, U., Rossi, F., Schafer, B., Valcke, P., & Vayena, E. (2018). AI4People—An ethical framework for a good AI society: Opportunities, risks, principles, and recommendations. *Minds and Machines*, *28*(4), 689–707. DOI: 10.1007/s11023-018-9482-5 PMID: 30930541

Fournier, S., & Avery, J. (2011). The uninvited brand. *Business Horizons*, *54*(3), 193–207. DOI: 10.1016/j.bushor.2011.01.001

Gissi, V., & Savelli, E. (2025). Integrating Artificial Intelligence into Internal Brand Communication. *Micro & Macro Marketing*, *34*(3), 557–590.

Gregory, A. (2007). Involving stakeholders in developing corporate brands: The communication dimension. *Journal of Marketing Management*, *23*(1–2), 59–73. DOI: 10.1362/026725707X178558

Grewal, D. S. (2014). A critical conceptual analysis of definitions of artificial intelligence as applicable to computer engineering. *IOSR Journal of Computer Engineering*, *16*(2), 9–13. DOI: 10.9790/0661-16210913

Gupta, S., Modgil, S., Bhattacharyya, S., & Bose, I. (2022). Artificial intelligence for decision support systems in the field of operations research: Review and future scope of research. *Annals of Operations Research*, *308*(1), 215–274. DOI: 10.1007/s10479-020-03856-6

Haider, K. (2024). Natural language processing in AI-powered systems: Techniques and future prospects. *Journal of Ai Range*, *1*(1), 40–53.

Hassaan, A., Jamshaid, M. M., Siddique, M. N., Akbar, Z., & Niaz, S. (2023). Ethical Analytics & Digital Transformation In The Age Of Ai: Embedding Privacy, Fairness, And Transparency To Drive Innovation And Stakeholder Trust. *Contemporary Journal of Social Science Review*, *1*(04), 1–18.

Hassan, N., Abdelraouf, M., & El-Shihy, D. (2025). The moderating role of personalized recommendations in the trust–satisfaction–loyalty relationship: An empirical study of AI-driven e-commerce. *Future Business Journal*, *11*(1), 66. DOI: 10.1186/s43093-025-00476-z

Hermann, E., & Hermann, E. (2022). Leveraging Artificial Intelligence in Marketing for Social Good — An Ethical Perspective. *Journal of Business Ethics, 179*(1), 43–61. DOI: 10.1007/s10551-021-04843-y PMID: 34054170

Holt, D. B. (2004). *How brands become icons: The principles of cultural branding*. harvard business press.

Hosseini Tabaghdehi, S. A., & Ayaz, Ö. (2025). AI ethics in action: A circular model for transparency, accountability and inclusivity. *Journal of Managerial Psychology*. Advance online publication. DOI: 10.1108/JMP-03-2024-0177

Hoyer, W. D., Kroschke, M., Schmitt, B., Kraume, K., & Shankar, V. (2020). Transforming the customer experience through new technologies. *Journal of Interactive Marketing, 51*(1), 57–71. DOI: 10.1016/j.intmar.2020.04.001

Huang, M., & Rust, R. T. (2021). *A strategic framework for artificial intelligence in marketing*. 30–50.

Islam, M. A., Fakir, S. I., Masud, S., Hossen, M. D., Islam, M. T., & Siddiky, M. R. (2024). Artificial intelligence in digital marketing automation: Enhancing personalization, predictive analytics, and ethical integration. *Edelweiss Applied Science and Technology, 8*(6), 6498–6516. DOI: 10.55214/25768484.v8i6.3404

Joshi, A., Bhattacharyya, P., & Carman, M. J. (2017). Automatic sarcasm detection: A survey. *ACM Computing Surveys, 50*(5), 1–22. DOI: 10.1145/3124420

Kartajaya, H. (2021). *Marketing 5.0: Technology for humanity*. Wiley.

Keller, K. L. (2013). *Keller: Strategic Brand Management eBook GE 4e*. Pearson Higher Ed.

Kitchen, P. J., & Schultz, D. E. (2003). Integrated corporate and product brand communication (1). *Journal of Competitiveness Studies, 11*(1), 66.

Kliatchko, J. (2008). Revisiting the IMC construct: A revised definition and four pillars. *International Journal of Advertising, 27*(1), 133–160. DOI: 10.1080/02650487.2008.11073043

Kumar, D., Koul, S., & Siringoringo, H. (2023). Assessing antecedents of behavioral intention to use e-LMS: A case from a private institution in the northern region of India. *IEEE Transactions on Learning Technologies, 16*(5), 861–872. DOI: 10.1109/TLT.2023.3265016

Kumar, V., Rajan, B., Venkatesan, R., & Lecinski, J. (2019). Understanding the role of artificial intelligence in personalized engagement marketing. *California Management Review, 61*(4), 135–155. DOI: 10.1177/0008125619859317

Kumari, M., Sinha, R., Chakrabarty, P., Hasnain, M. G., Qamar, N., & Gupta, S. (2024). Exploring machine learning's impact on digital marketing. *2024 15th International Conference on Computing Communication and Networking Technologies (ICCCNT)*, 1–5.

Lemon, K. N., & Verhoef, P. C. (2016). Understanding customer experience throughout the customer journey. *Journal of Marketing*, *80*(6), 69–96. DOI: 10.1509/jm.15.0420

Luxton, S., Reid, M., & Mavondo, F. (2015). Integrated marketing communication capability and brand performance. *Journal of Advertising*, *44*(1), 37–46. DOI: 10.1080/00913367.2014.934938

Madhavaram, S., Badrinarayanan, V., & McDonald, R. E. (2005). Integrated marketing communication (IMC) and brand identity as critical components of brand equity strategy: A conceptual framework and research propositions. *Journal of Advertising*, *34*(4), 69–80. DOI: 10.1080/00913367.2005.10639213

Makosa, S. (2024). *Brand Management Driven by Artificial Intelligence*.

Martin, D. M., & Schouten, J. W. (2014). Sustainable marketing through the natural step. In *Humanistic marketing* (pp. 231–243). Springer. DOI: 10.1057/9781137353290_18

Marvi, R., Foroudi, P., & Cuomo, M. T. (2026). *Past, present and future of AI in marketing and knowledge management*. *29*(11), 1–31. DOI: 10.1108/JKM-07-2023-0634

Matsatsinis, N. F., & Siskos, Y. (2012). *Intelligent support systems for marketing decisions* (Vol. 54). Springer Science & Business Media.

Merrilees, B., Miller, D., & Halliday, S. (2016). *Brand-meaning co-creation by stakeholders: an interactive city brand*.

Milano, S., Taddeo, M., & Floridi, L. (2020). Recommender systems and their ethical challenges. *AI & Society*, *35*(4), 957–967. DOI: 10.1007/s00146-020-00950-y

Mittelstadt, B. (2019). Principles alone cannot guarantee ethical AI. *Nature Machine Intelligence*, *1*(11), 501–507. DOI: 10.1038/s42256-019-0114-4

Mittelstadt, B. D., Allo, P., Taddeo, M., Wachter, S., & Floridi, L. (2016). The ethics of algorithms: Mapping the debate. *Big Data & Society*, *3*(2), 2053951716679679. DOI: 10.1177/2053951716679679

Nandan, S. (2005). An exploration of the brand identity–brand image linkage: A communications perspective. *Journal of Brand Management*, *12*(4), 264–278. DOI: 10.1057/palgrave.bm.2540222

Nanne, A. J., Antheunis, M. L., Van Der Lee, C. G., Postma, E. O., Wubben, S., & Van Noort, G. (2020). The use of computer vision to analyze brand-related user generated image content. *Journal of Interactive Marketing*, *50*(1), 156–167. DOI: 10.1016/j.intmar.2019.09.003

Navarro, L. F. M. (2024). Machine Learning and Customer Behavior Insights: Exploring the Depth of Predictive Analytics in Enhancing Consumer Interaction and Engagement. *Journal of Empirical Social Science Studies*, *8*(2), 51–62.

Obermeyer, Z., Powers, B., Vogeli, C., & Mullainathan, S. (2019). Dissecting racial bias in an algorithm used to manage the health of populations. *Science*, *366*(6464), 447–453. DOI: 10.1126/science.aax2342 PMID: 31649194

Odionu, C. S., Bristol-Alagbariya, B., & Okon, R. (2024). Big data analytics for customer relationship management: Enhancing engagement and retention strategies. *International Journal of Scientific Research in Science and Technology*, *5*(2), 50–67.

Okeleke, P. A., Ajiga, D., Folorunsho, S. O., & Ezeigweneme, C. (2024). Predictive analytics for market trends using AI: A study in consumer behavior. *International Journal of Engineering Research Updates*, *7*(1), 36–49. DOI: 10.53430/ijeru.2024.7.1.0032

Olayinka, O. H.Olalekan Hamed Olayinka. (2021). Big data integration and real-time analytics for enhancing operational efficiency and market responsiveness. *Int J Sci Res Arch*, *4*(1), 280–296. DOI: 10.30574/ijsra.2021.4.1.0179

Pappas, A., Fumagalli, E., Rouziou, M., & Bolander, W. (2023). More than machines: The role of the future retail salesperson in enhancing the customer experience. *Journal of Retailing*, *99*(4), 518–531. DOI: 10.1016/j.jretai.2023.10.004

Paramadina, U., & Info, A. (2024). *Integrated marketing communication: a literature review*. 511–519.

Pires, A., & Brandão, A. (2025). *Evolutionary Scenario of Brand Management and Communication, Through the Integration of AI: A Bibliometric Analysis BT - Marketing and Smart Technologies* (J. L. Reis, L. M. Gomes, Z. Bogdanović, & J. P. M. dos Santos (eds.); pp. 145–172). Springer Nature Singapore.

Prakash, G., & Sabharwal, D. (2024). AI revolution in online media: Transforming content creation, distribution, and consumption. *Media and Al: Navigating, 179.*

Raut, S., Chandel, A., & Mittal, S. (2025). Enhancing marketing and brand communication with AI-driven content creation. In *AI, corporate social responsibility, and marketing in modern organizations* (pp. 139–172). IGI Global Scientific Publishing.

Rayun, S. M. N., Salam, M. A., Islam, W., Firmansyah, E. A., & Kalinaki, K. (2025). Unraveling the dynamics of mobile wallets in promoting cashless tourism in Bangladesh: Implementation of UTAUT2 model. *Journal of Hospitality and Tourism Technology*, *16*(5), 1046–1065. DOI: 10.1108/JHTT-04-2024-0222

Rayun, S. M. N., Salam, M. A., Islam, W., & Leong, V. S. (2025). Green FinTech Innovations: Empowering Inclusive Development and Advancing Towards the Sustainable Economy. Https://Www.Igi-Global.Com/Doi=10.4018/979-8-3373-1112-8.Ch009, 245–278. DOI: 10.4018/979-8-3373-1112-8.ch009

Rehman, S., Gulzar, R., & Aslam, W. (2022). *Developing the Integrated Marketing Communication (IMC) through Social Media (SM)*. The Modern Marketing Communication Approach., DOI: 10.1177/21582440221099936

Rezwana, J., & Maher, M. (2023). Designing creative AI partners with COFI: A framework for modeling interaction in human-AI co-creative systems. *ACM Transactions on Computer-Human Interaction*, *30*(5), 1–28. DOI: 10.1145/3519026

Rodriguez-Fernandez, F. (2025). Artificial intelligence and economic psychology: Toward a theory of algorithmic cognitive influence. *AI & Society*, •••, 1–12.

Russell, S. J., & Norvig, P. (2021). *Artificial Intelligence: A Modern Approach* (Global Edition 4e).

Salam, M. A., Leong, V. S., & Muhamad, N. (2026). The Transformative Prospects of AI-Powered Virtual Influencers in Digital Consumer Engagement and Marketing Strategies. In *Cases on Social Media Marketing Engagement Tactics* (pp. 251–290). IGI Global Scientific Publishing., DOI: 10.4018/979-8-3373-2357-2.ch009

Salam, M. A., Rayun, S. M. N., Islam, W., Hasan, R., Firmansyah, E. A., & Kalinaki, K. (2024). Consumer Engagement: Exploring Deepfake Applications in Consumer Marketing Communication. In *Navigating the World of Deepfake Technology* (pp. 397–421). IGI Global.

Salam, M. A., Rayun, S. M. N., & Leong, V. S. (2024). Examining Critical Factors Influencing Generation Z's Acceptance of Mobile Payment Systems in Bangladesh: A UTAUT Model Analysis. *Journal of Business and Economic Analysis*.

Samal, A., Bhargav, J., Selvakumar, P., Sharma, M., & TC, M. (2025). Measuring brand performance with AI tools. In *Strategic Brand Management in the Age of AI and Disruption* (pp. 279–302). IGI Global Scientific Publishing.

Sarker, I. H. (2021). Machine learning: Algorithms, real-world applications and research directions. *SN Computer Science*, *2*(3), 1–21. DOI: 10.1007/s42979-021-00592-x PMID: 33778771

Schultz, D. E. (1992). Integrated marketing communications. *Journal of Promotion Management, 1*(1), 99–104. DOI: 10.1300/J057v01n01_07

Schultz, D. E., Kim, I., & Kang, K. (2014). Integrated marketing communication research: its limited past and huge potential. *The Handbook of International Advertising Research*, 455–483.

Schultz, D. E., Tannenbaum, S., & Lauterborn, R. (1993). *Integrated Marketing Communications*. NTC Business Book.

Secundo, G., Spilotro, C., Gast, J., & Corvello, V. (2025). The transformative power of artificial intelligence within innovation ecosystems: A review and a conceptual framework. *Review of Managerial Science, 19*(9), 2697–2728. DOI: 10.1007/s11846-024-00828-z

Senyapar, H. N. D. (2024). Artificial intelligence in marketing communication: A comprehensive exploration of the integration and impact of AI. *Technium Soc. Sci. J., 55*, 64.

Umoren, O., Didi, P. U., Balogun, O., Abass, O. S., & Akinrinoye, O. V. (2022). Synchronized content delivery framework for consistent cross-platform brand messaging in regulated and consumer-focused sectors. *International Scientific Refereed Research Journal, 5*(5), 345–354.

Vashishth, T. K., Sharma, K. K., Kumar, B., Chaudhary, S., & Panwar, R. (2024). Enhancing customer experience through AI-enabled content personalization in e-commerce marketing. *Advances in Digital Marketing in the Era of Artificial Intelligence*, 7–32.

Wang, W., Chen, Z., & Kuang, J. (2025). Artificial Intelligence-Driven Recommendations and Functional Food Purchases: Understanding Consumer Decision-Making. *Foods, 14*(6), 976. DOI: 10.3390/foods14060976 PMID: 40231979

Wheeler, A. (2017). *Designing brand identity: an essential guide for the whole branding team*. John Wiley & Sons.

Zaman, K. (2022). Transformation of marketing decisions through artificial intelligence and digital marketing. *Journal of Marketing Strategies, 4*(2), 353–364. DOI: 10.52633/jms.v4i2.210

Zhang, Q. (2026). *The Theoretical Evolution of Integrated Marketing Communications Over Three Decades : From Communication Integration to Brand Integration Origins and Early Theories of Integrated Marketing Communications* (Issue Icedbc 2025). Atlantis Press International BV. DOI: 10.2991/978-94-6239-604-3

Chapter 9
Technology Transfer and Strategic Applications for Commercial Human–AI Interaction:
The Role of Virtual and Augmented Reality

Md. Mominul Islam
http://orcid.org/0009-0006-4694-9379
Begum Rokeya University, Rangpur, Bangladesh

Sabbir Ahmed
http://orcid.org/0009-0007-0301-7632
Begum Rokeya University, Rangpur, Bangladesh

Rafia Islam
Begum Rokeya University, Rangpur, Bangladesh

Israt Jahan
http://orcid.org/0009-0003-5375-8085
Begum Rokeya University, Rangpur, Bangladesh

Md Zainal Abedin
University of Ottawa, Canada

Badsha Mia
Noakhali Science and Technology University, Bangladesh

ABSTRACT

Augmented reality and virtual reality are changing the way consumers experience things by making them more interactive, personalized, and engaging across different industries, especially in e-commerce. Even though these technologies have great potential, their widespread use is limited by complex technology and high investment costs. This study reviews, in a structured way, the effect of AR/VR on shopping online with emphasis on virtual trying out products, immersive showrooms, and AI-based

DOI: 10.4018/979-8-3373-9325-4.ch009

personalization. Qualitative analysis along with panel data models will be used for this research to see how AR/VR helps overcome limitations of traditional e-commerce. Results will show the importance of AR/VR in retail, healthcare, tourism as well as education while discussing challenges regarding adoption. The paper will finally present insights into future opportunities for businesses, researchers, and developers who are looking to integrate AR/VR into digital commerce.

1.0 INTRODUCTION

AR and VR have the potential to revolutionize areas such as online retail; however, their adoption in these areas has been limited due to the technical complexity and investment required (Har et al., 2022). As e-commerce continues to grow, it is important to investigate how AR/VR technologies can be utilized to improve the online shopping experience (Shepherd et al., 2020). This paper investigates how AR/VR can be used as a solution for the limitations of e-commerce platforms. The two primary motivations for this study are the rapid growth of online retail and the relatively stagnant development of shopping platform features compared to other technologies (Singh et al., 2023).

The proposal investigates AR/VR mechanisms, their effects on the shopping experience, and challenges to adoption. It reviews AR/VR applications, traces the development of e-commerce, and discusses consumer behaviour models. A systematic review methodology is used to integrate research findings on AR/VR in e-commerce (Guthrie et al., 2021). The results are mapped onto existing online shopping models to assess AR/VR's contributions. The study concludes with recommendations for future research, encouraging further exploration of AR/VR's role in transforming digital commerce (Al-Sharafi et al., 2024). Although existing literature is very abundant regarding the practical advantages of AR and VR in retail, there is still a major gap as far as the theoretical framework that facilitates or obstructs consumer adoption is concerned. In particular, past research does not often relate immersive technology trends with such critical user constraints as the data privacy vulnerabilities and the hardware limitations in the framework of the existing leading models of behavior such as TAM and UTAUT. This is the gap that will be filled in this chapter, as it will be offering a balanced and analysis of the commercial uses as well as the complicated consumer issues that lie within these technologies.

1.1 Background

AR and VR more or less influence consumer behaviour by improving engagement, satisfaction, and decision-making (Ulusoy, 2024). Virtual try-ons and interactive displays are examples of AR applications that enhance shopping experiences, which in turn increase conversion rates and brand loyalty. In tourism, AR/VR improves the experience for visitors who explore the area; in education, it helps students engage with material and understand better. Financial services and hospitality industries use AR/VR for customized experiences (Lyu, 2024). These technologies redefine retail marketing through immersive and personalized interactions despite adoption challenges such as cost and usability. Future studies must prioritize technological barriers to realize the full potential of AR/VR in consumer engagement and business transformation.

1.2 Significant of the Book Chapter

This chapter examines an important moment in the history of digital commerce: the line is beginning to blur between the physical world and the virtual. To help companies break through the limitations of traditional screen-based (static) interfaces, this chapter serves as a foundational framework for understanding how businesses can incorporate Augmented Reality (AR) and Virtual Reality (VR) into their consumer engagement strategies (Bhuiyan et al., 2024). By methodically synthesizing results from 95 high-impact studies, the chapter goes beyond a theoretical overview of the effects of AR and VR on consumer behaviour - it provides concrete examples that can be utilized to develop and implement immersive technologies into consumer engagement strategies (e.g., improved retail decision-making through virtual try-ons, democratization of travel through immersive). Additionally, this chapter closes a critical void in the current literature by conducting a thorough analysis of the obstacles to implementation (e.g., cost, technological complexity) and proposing viable solutions for experimentation and long-term sustainability. This work also provides retailers, researchers, and policymakers with a vital resource for utilizing spatial computing in developing inclusive, customer-centric, and emotionally engaging consumer experiences in a post-pandemic world (Rayun et al., 2025).

1.3 The Rationale of the Book Chapter

Virtual reality and augmented reality are among the most transformative technologies that have gained significant attention for their ability to fundamentally alter the ways in which individuals' access and experience cultural sites (Rauschnabel et al., 2019). While AR adds digital features over the actual world to improve the user's experience of reality, VR allows users to fully immerse themselves in computer-generated landscapes that mimic real-world places (Salam et al., 2024). This book chapter's justification stems from the rising need for accessible, eco-friendly, and technologically advanced travel options. Following issues like growing travel expenses, environmental damage, and worldwide emergencies like the COVID-19 epidemic; virtual tourism has become an effective solution that enables people to see the globe without having to relocate physically (Usembayeva et al., 2024). Additionally, the use of VR and AR in tourism creates new opportunities for creative marketing, destination promotion, and consumer interaction (Dey et al., 2021). Virtual tours, immersive storytelling, and interactive experiences are being used more and more by tourism organisations to draw in tourists in the future and influence their choices (Caboni & Hagberg, 2019)

This chapter aims to investigate how these technologies contribute to enhancing user satisfaction, emotional connection, and behavioural intention toward virtual tourism. Additionally, it explores the psychological and experiential factors that drive tourists to engage with virtual platforms as substitutes or complements to physical travel. The tourism sector may create strategies to maximise tourist experiences and guarantee inclusivity for individuals who are unable to travel physically because of financial, health, or mobility constraints by understanding the mechanisms via which VR and AR boost participation (Jha et al., 2025).

1.4 Research Gaps

Although the literature on the subject has largely recognized the positive impact of AR and VR in the improvement of consumer engagement, most of the studies assess the technologies independently without solid theoretical bases (Ulusoy, 2024). Past studies usually point to the utilitarianism of AR or the hedonicity of VR but seldom combines the two as they coexist in various e-commerce ecosystems (Lyu, 2024). More so, the recent research has failed to sufficiently respond to the question of how companies can break significant obstacles to adoption such as cognitive load and cost of hardware (Lastrucci et al., 2024). This chapter fills this important research gap, as it bases its analysis on the Technology Acceptance Model (TAM), offering a critical comparison of recent findings that can serve to offer a broad framework of integrating immersive technologies.

1.5 Research Objectives

The objectives of this book chapter are:

RO1:To systematically review and analyze how AR and VR are reshaping consumer experiences across diverse sectors by shifting interactions from passive viewing to active engagement.
RO2: To investigate key adoption challenges, including cost and complexity, and propose strategic solutions for effective business integration.

RO3: To provide insights into the future convergence of AI and spatial computing, guiding the next generation of digital commerce experiences.

2.0 LITERATURE REVIEW

2.1 Overview of Virtual Reality and Augmented Reality

VR (Virtual Reality) and AR (Augmented Reality) are technologies changing how people experience travel by providing them with more options and information before they travel as well as during their trips. VR provides users with an immersive experience in a virtual environment through interactive 360° videos or models of places, accommodations, and things to do (Salam et al., 2024). It allows future travelers to preview what they can expect to experience which results in less uncertainty in making a booking (Hossain et al., 2024). AR adds another layer of information (digital information) to the real world by using a smartphone or AR glasses and enhances the experience of being present in the world by providing context-based information (contextual), history (historical), and a way to find your way (navigational) (Kumbhani & Kant, 2024).

VR along with AR create a bridge between the imagination and reality by connecting users emotionally, adding accessibility to all types of tourists, and promoting sustainable tourism through virtual tours of sensitive or remote locations (Dey et al., 2021). Not only do these technologies provide improved experience for tourists, but they also generate substantial business value through improved brand differentiation, efficiency in training and customer service (Lastrucci et al., 2024). In the case of tourism organizations, these technologies are used as virtual concierges to support and assist guests in multiple languages around the clock; provide augmented reality guided tours across museums; and use immersive destination marketing campaigns (Bhuiyan et al., 2024). With the continued evolution of immersive technologies, the way that travellers plan, experience and remember their travels will continue to evolve resulting in new forms of experiential, data-driven and inclusive tourism (Abid et al., 2025).

2.2 Immersive Simulations and AR-Enhanced Consumer Experiences

However, virtual Reality (VR) and Augmented Reality (AR) are redefining the experience economy, providing unique yet complementary solutions to improve both pre-purchase engagement and real-time physical interaction (Bhattacharya & Sharma, 2025). Immersive simulations, which are VR-based, allow consumers to explore environments, service settings, or attractions remotely via immersive 360-degree videos, 3D simulations, or interactive models viewed through VR headsets (e.g., Meta Quest) or web-based viewers. These digital experiences enable users to "walk through" a lobby, evaluate spatial designs, or envision paths in a natural setting, minimising doubt in choice (Quintana Vargas, 2024). For example, Google Earth VR or Matter port provides photorealistic simulations of global landmarks, while premium service providers utilise VR to showcase cabins and on-board activities. Especially useful for marketing exclusive experiences (e.g., remote expeditions) or re-stimulating interest in recovered locations by replicating pristine settings, VR stimulates emotional connections to the offering, induces purchase decisions, and allows consumers to plan their journey based on personal interests (Masud et al., 2024). Alternatively, AR-enhanced on-site experiences overlay digital information on the real world through Smartphone's (e.g., AR apps) or wearable's (e.g., Microsoft HoloLens) to augment real-time discovery. At cultural venues like the Colosseum or Machu Picchu, AR applications such as Google Lens or dedicated interactive guides superimpose historical reconstructions, animations, or multilingual commentary over physical structures, bringing static exhibits to life(Hossain et al., 2024). In London, for example, the "Street Museum" application allows users to point their camera at modern buildings to unlock historic photos of the same site. Use augmented reality (AR) to help you navigate easily; Google Maps Live View provides directional arrows displayed over existing streets and menus that display content in real time (Salam et al. 2023). Gamified AR applications that have a scavenger hunt experience similar to Pokémon Go (in an urban environment) entertain users with the ability to both discover and participate in interactive experiences simultaneously, which provides an individualised consumer journey through real-time augmentation with contextually relevant information (Sankar 2024). This kind of contextual relevance maximises the ability to learn, have access to what you need to know, and be able to accomplish your objectives conveniently.

Table 1. Differences between VR and AR in consumer experience

Aspect	VR Travel	AR Travel
Purpose and Timing	VR is a pre-trip tool focused on planning and inspiration, helping users visualise destinations before committing.	AR operates during the trip, enhancing on-ground experiences with real-time information.
Interaction with Reality	VR creates fully immersive, self-contained digital environments, isolating users from their physical surroundings.	AR enhances reality by adding digital layers (text, images, animations) to the real world, requiring users to engage with their actual environment.
Technology Requirements	VR often demands specialised hardware (headsets, controllers) and high bandwidth for rendering detailed simulations.	AR relies on everyday devices like smartphones or lightweight AR glasses, leveraging GPS, cameras, and sensors for context-aware overlays.
Content Type	VR delivers static, pre-designed environments (e.g., virtual hotel tours), prioritising visual fidelity and immersion.	AR provides dynamic, contextual information (e.g., real-time translations, historical facts), adapting to user location and behaviour.
User Engagement	VR prioritises emotional immersion—ideal for sparking wanderlust or showcasing luxury resorts.	AR emphasises practical utility, such as solving language barriers or enhancing educational value during tours.

2.3 Smart Business Case for AR and VR in Transforming Consumer Experiences

Consequently, imagine turning a standard visit into a time travel adventure or letting people experience a service environment from thousands of miles away! Augmented Reality (AR) and Virtual Reality (VR) make these interactions possible, and they offer incredible benefits for businesses focused on enhancing engagement (Bhuiyan et al., 2024). The essence of the experience economy is all about creating exciting and memorable moments for consumers. AR and VR revolutionize this process! Early adopters those among the first to use these technologies will gain a significant advantage (Salam et al., 2023). Virtual engagement can be broadly described as the totality of consumers' affective, cognitive, and sensorial responses before, during, and after interaction with the virtual environment. Applications of transforming consumer experience in research include exploring digital environments, service spaces, attractions, and artifacts that make it possible to examine and interact with them. Immersive explorations of historic sites and attractions were especially common during the pandemic with ancient Egyptian sites, Petra, the British Museum, the Louvre Museum, Freda Kahlo's house, the White House, and others (Hossain et al., 2024). Ancient sites that no longer exist (e.g., ancient Roman spaces and traditions) and extant or extinct exhibits (e.g., the world's first photographic exhibit) can be recreated with these technologies.

Table 2. Comparative Analysis: AR vs. VR transformation in consumer experience

Aspect	Augmented Reality (AR)	Virtual Reality (VR)
Technology	Overlays digital content onto the real world.	Creates a fully immersive, computer-generated environment.
Environment	Enhances real settings with digital layers (e.g., museum AR guides).	Replaces the real world entirely (e.g., virtual destination tours).
Devices	Smartphones, tablets, AR glasses (e.g., Snapchat, Apple Vision Pro).	VR headsets (e.g., Meta Quest, HTC Vive).
Use Cases	AR city maps, interactive exhibits, hotel previews.	Full destination simulations, immersive cultural experiences.
Cost	Lower setup costs; easier mobile integration.	Higher costs; requires specialized equipment.
Customer Interaction	Blends real and digital interaction in real time.	Deep emotional engagement through total immersion.
Primary Business Benefit	Enhances convenience and enriches real-world exploration.	Drives strong emotional connection and storytelling impact.

2.4 Virtual Reality (VR) in Customer Service

In addition, VR-powered virtual assistants enhance customer support with AI-driven avatars that simulate face-to-face interactions, reducing wait times while offering multi-language support for real-time translations, and improving accessibility (Salam et al., 2024). Product demonstrations become more immersive through virtual showrooms, where brands like Audi let customers explore car features and test-drive models, while training simulations provide risk-free environments for industries like healthcare and manufacturing. Remote collaboration further bridges gaps with shared virtual spaces, enabling technicians to guide repairs via VR headsets, cutting operational costs, and allowing real-time feedback, ensuring better service quality and customer satisfaction (Dey et al., 2021).

Figure 1. Virtual Reality in Customer Service

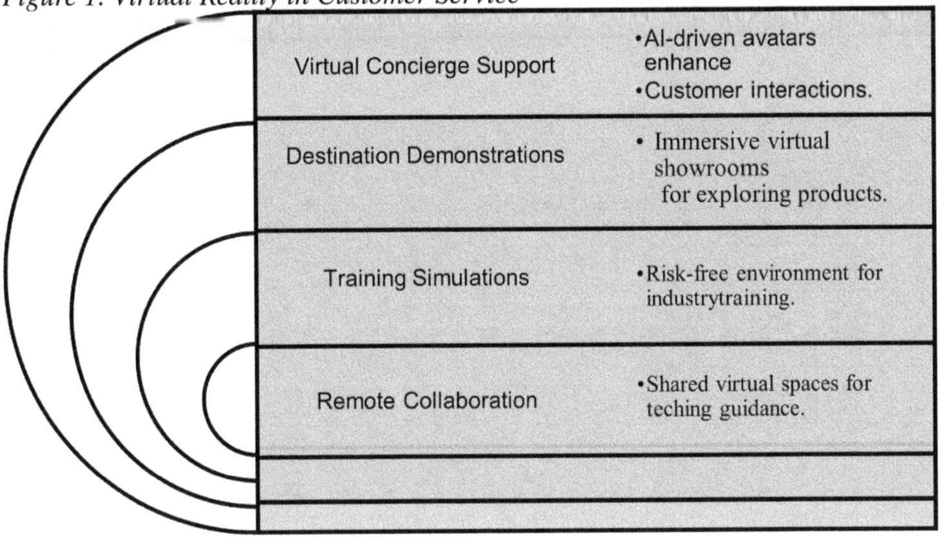

Source: Author's work

2.5 Theoretical Framework

The chapter uses a conceptual framework that combines the Technology Acceptance Model (TAM) with the Unified Theory of Acceptance and Use of Technology (UTAUT) to provide a strong theoretical premise (Kaya, 2026). The model displays the way the behavioral intention of the customers to adopt AR and VR technology depends directly on Performance Expectancy, Effort Expectancy, Social Influence, and Facilitating Conditions. Moreover, it considers the perceived threats and newness of immersive commerce with the help of the Perceived Trust and Personal Innovativeness as critical elements (Al-Adwan et al., 2025). The framework is a systematic way of analyzing consumer involvement and adoption challenges because it maps such characteristics and systematically presents how cognitive and environmental variables are translated into actual Use Behavior.

In order to be perfectly aware of the adoption of AR and VR, it is crucial to go beyond the functional utility of the simplest use and examine the cognitive, emotional, and behavioral processes involved. Although TAM mostly focuses on the cognitive assessment such as perceived usefulness, immersive technologies are extensive in creating a response of emotion such as enjoyment, telepresence, and hedonic motivation. This sensory stimulation eases the burden of cognition and increases the emotional involvement of the user when they virtually interact with a product. The ultimate result of this cognitive clarity and positive emotional affect is the ultimate behavioral mechanism which directly leads to increase in purchase intentions.

Figure 2. Conceptual Framework

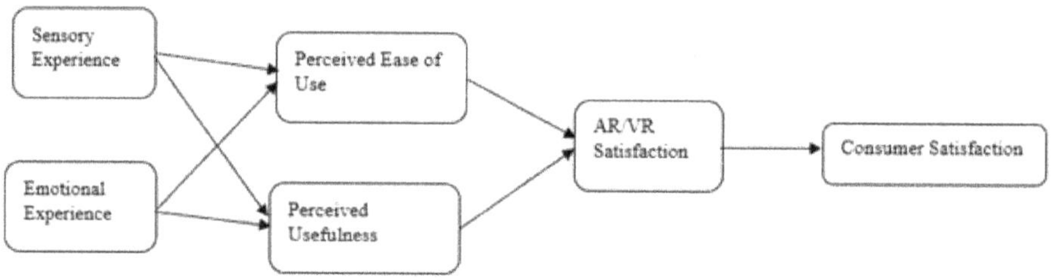

Source: Author's work

3.0 METHODOLOGY OF THE STUDY

3.1 Research Design

The authors used the qualitative data analysis software Atlantis to transcribe and code the interviews and identified key stakeholders for interviews through a snowball sampling technique (Kumbhani & Kant, 2024). The research methodology employed in this study follows a systematic review approach to analyse the role of augmented reality (AR) and virtual reality (VR) transforming online consumer experiences. This method involves collecting, evaluating and synthesizing existing literature to develop a comprehensive understanding of AR/VR integration in e-commerce (Chatzopoulos et al., 2017). The study examines peer-reviewed journal articles, conference papers, academic journals, research papers, news broadcasts, and internet sites to identify key themes, trends, and challenges associated with AR/VR adoption.

Table 3. The Steps of Research Process

Phase	Techniques	Description
Searching Technique	• Identify databases (Google Scholar, Emerald, Taylor & Francis) • Select keywords of topics • Apply search queries • Compile results	Initial stage to gather relevant literature sources.
Selection Technique	• Determine selection criteria • Apply inclusion & exclusion criteria • Remove duplicate papers	Filtering relevant and high-quality articles for review.
Analysis Technique	• Analyze literature found • Full-text reading • Extract models and frameworks • Generate relevant methods • Review and synthesize	Final analysis of selected papers to identify gaps, models, and insights.

3.2 Searching Technique

To find all relevant evidence, authors searched various academic databases, including Google Scholar, Emerald, Science Direct, Taylor & Francis, and IEEE Xplore. Authors developed a systematic search strategy with keywords like "Virtual Reality," "Augmented Reality," "Consumer Experiences," and "sustainability." Using Boolean operators (AND/OR) helped us combine these terms. Along with reviewing peer-reviewed journals, researcher also looked at practitioner-based publications, such as LinkedIn Pulse and industry white papers. This gave us more insights into the practical uses of virtual and augmented reality. Authors identified about 215 relevant articles while completing this section.

3.3 Selection Technique

The body of literature included in this review was developed through a four-stage process. First, criteria were created surrounding the direct relation to Virtual Reality (VR) and Augmented Reality (AR) base concepts, user engagement, and Consumer Experiences. Second, inclusion criteria consisted of peer-reviewed journals, articles, studies, and landmark conference proceedings between the years 2015 (when consumer-grade VR began to surge in production) and 2025. Third, exclusion criteria were applied to eliminate papers that were hardware technical reviews or studies that did not have consumer experiences as their primary focus and articles that discussed engagement in real-life environments. Last, duplicates between all databases were searched for and removed.

With these strict criteria applied, we were able to filter through and chose 95 quality articles. The purpose of this study is to qualitatively analyze prior research by way of review to combine and discover current themes. An initial search produced around 215 pertinent articles; after title and abstract screening, 162 were determined eligible for further assessment out of which the final set of 95 was picked to draw conclusions for the review. It described frameworks transforming consumer experience through an exploratory synthesis involving a systematic literature review alongside thematic analysis as detailed in Table 3.

3.4 Analysis Technique

Extracted data was mapped to existing online shopping behaviour models. This allowed for the structured evaluation of how AR/VR could potentially contribute to that type of behaviour. Although Lastrucci et al. (2024) show the data sources used in their analysis and the methods to measure the variables used, this chapter of the book involves authors who utilised multiple panel data models through STATA 14.0 software with a significant amount of practical insight for both businesses and researchers, plus concluding recommendations for future studies related to bridging knowledge gaps and developing AR/VR application(s) within e-commerce and other industries.

4.0 DISCUSSION

Both Augmented Reality (AR) and Virtual Reality (VR) are technologies that have revolutionised the way users have an enhanced user experience by creating interactive and immersive digital environments. (Pramanik, 2024). The application of these technologies has also expanded into fields such as Education, Vocational Training and Healthcare with experiential learning, simulations and other similar practices having had substantial success. For online shopping, AR/VR has been a revolutionary force by changing the way people interact with goods and services(Singh et al., 2023). These technologies power major aspects of the shopping process, such as convenience, interactivity, and subjective service quality. For instance, through virtual showrooms and interactive 3D product visualisation, consumers can browse, examine, and even "try on" products, leading to more-quality purchase decisions and reduced return rates (Usembayeva et al., 2024).

Further, AR/VR-enabled capabilities like AI-based personal avatars, spatial product placement, and personalised recommendation systems significantly enhance customer satisfaction and loyalty (Sankar, 2024). Unlike conventional 2D web shopping interfaces, AR/VR shatters the limitations of screen-based shopping by creating more immersive and touch-based experiences(Rayun et al., 2025).Retail giants such as Alibaba have already integrated mixed- reality technologies to merge online and offline shopping spaces, providing dynamic, real-time shopping assistance and gamified experiences (Lastrucci et al., 2024). Where technical issues persist, such as hardware costs, content scaling, and end-user accessibility, ongoing technological growth and consumer behaviour indicate high chances of widespread take-up. With ongoing development improving the solutions at lower costs, AR/VR is set to become the framework for future generations of e-commerce platforms (Quintana Vargas, 2024).

4.1transforming Retail With AR and VR: From Virtual Try-Ons to Immersive Showrooms

Furthermore, Augmented Reality (AR) and Virtual Reality (VR) are transforming the retail sector by increasing customer engagement; making shopping experiences more personal, and eliminating operational inefficiencies (Bhattacharya & Sharma, 2025). AR solutions enable customers to view products in their actual environment or on their person prior to purchase, thereby closing the gap between online and offline shopping. For instance, IKEA Place enables users to superimpose true- scale 3D models of furniture into their homes via smartphone cameras, ensuring the right size, style, and colour match (Dethe & Joy, 2023). Similarly, beauty companies like Sephora and L'Oréal utilise AR for virtual try-ons, where customers can apply makeup shades or hairstyles in real-time based on facial recognition and AI-powered simulations. They reduce the risk of online purchasing, which means fewer returns and higher satisfaction (Jha et al., 2025). By overlaying digital information onto the physical world, AR enhances decision-making via contextual interactivity—customers can rotate, resize, or customise products while seeing how they fit into their lives. This creates confidence in purchasing, particularly for high-involvement categories like home decor, fashion, and electronics (Kumar et al., 2025).

Figure 3. AR and VR in Retail

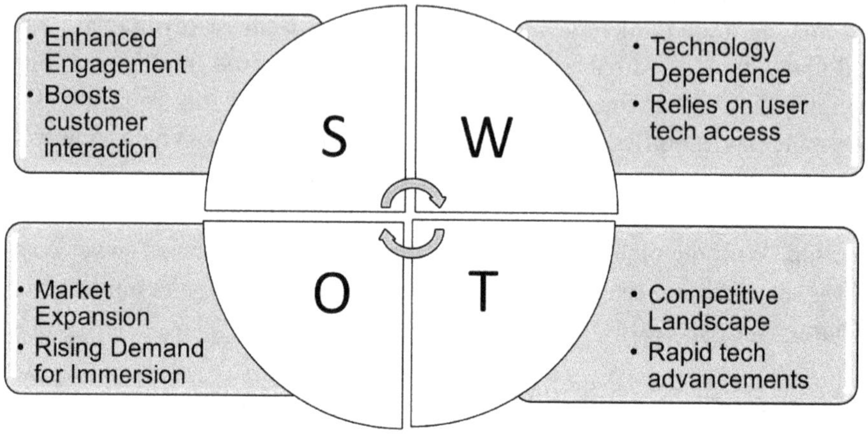

Source: Author's work

VR, on the other hand, places users in entirely virtual environments, offering experiential shopping without physical limitations. Retailers create 3D virtual showrooms that customers experience through VR headsets as they see products in real-life settings (Sankar, 2024) . Car manufacturers like Audi and Volvo use VR to simulate test drives or offer car customisation, while luxury fashion retailers like Tommy Hilfiger host virtual runway shows. These interactive spaces enable user engagement with products in ways impossible via online interfaces like testing textures, evaluating functionalities, or imagining products within dynamic settings (e.g., a sofa set in a digitally recreated living room) (Al-Saigh & Mahmoud, 2023). In addition, virtual reality allows virtual store browsing, where consumers walk down aisles, receive detailed product information via artificial intelligence avatars, and experience social interactions with other users, thus replicating the social aspect inherent in brick-and-mortar shopping (Billewar et al., 2022). Both technologies solve key retail problems. AR's availability through Smartphone's—positions it as a viable solution for mass adoption, especially for younger, tech-comfortable audiences. VR, while needing specialised hardware, provides richer engagement for higher-value purchases, like automobiles or high-end products (Stecuła et al., 2024). They work together by providing better ways for customers to understand the product and fit correctly, which leads to lower returns (one of the greatest challenges faced by e-commerce). As an example, ASOS experienced a 25% reduction in their return rate after offering AR try-on capability. Retailers also use data and analytics from AR/VR to give them insight into consumer preferences so that they can develop hyper-personalised marketing plans (Caboni and Hagberg, 2019).

Figure 4. Balancing AR and VR in Retail Solutions.

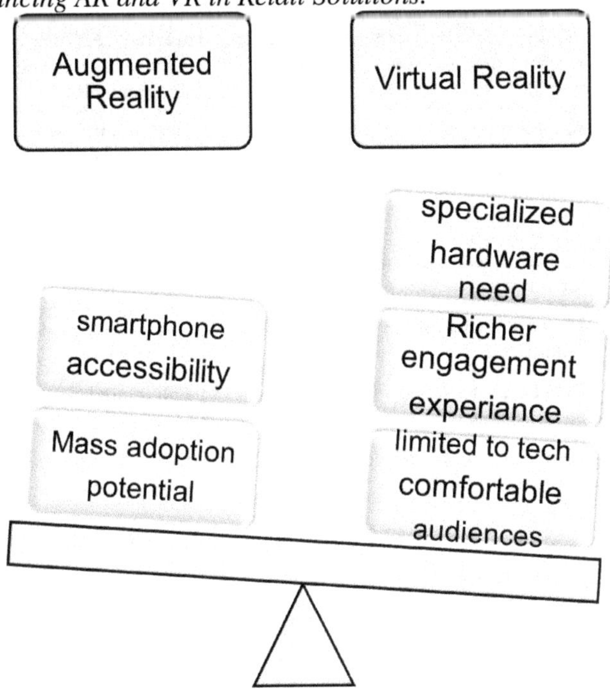

Source: Author's Contribution

AI-enabled IoT devices will further augment the current use cases described above in the future; for example, augmented reality (AR) applications could suggest clothing based on real-time weather conditions and virtual reality (VR) showrooms will alter their layouts depending on customer foot-traffic patterns (Dey et al., 2021). Augmented reality will provide customers with enhanced convenience and increased functionality; on the other hand, virtual reality will give brands the opportunity to tell stories about their products and create experiences for their consumers, redefining retail as a hybrid business model (or "dual" model) that allows for the simultaneous existence of both digital and physical spaces.

Table 4. Differences between AR and VR in Retail

Aspect	Augmented Reality (AR)	Virtual Reality (VR)
Technology	Overlays digital content onto the real world.	Creates a fully immersive virtual environment.
Environment	Enhances real-world settings with digital elements.	Replaces the physical world with a simulated one.
Devices	Smartphones, tablets, AR glasses (e.g., Snap chat).	VR headsets (e.g., Oculus Rift, HTC Vive).
Use Cases	Virtual try-ons (makeup, clothing), furniture previews.	Virtual showrooms, immersive product demos.
Cost	Lower implementation (app-based solutions).	Higher (VR hardware/software development).
Customer Interaction	Real-time interaction with physical and digital elements.	Full immersion in a controlled virtual space.
Primary Benefit	Enhances convenience and reduces purchase hesitation.	Delivers deep engagement and brand storytelling.

4.2 How AR and VR Are Creating Next-Level Media Experiences

In addition, augmented reality (AR) and virtual reality (VR) are transforming media since they merge digital innovation and user experience, but they implement and impact in different ways (Abid et al., 2025). VR creates 360-degree immersive experiences, enabling users to consume content as if present. In gaming, VR headsets like the Meta Quest 3 increase user engagement by 40% from traditional platforms, with a 25-minute average session due to hyper-realistic simulations. Immersive events like Travis Scott's Fortnite VR concert (26.7 million attendees) demonstrate VR's ability to merge entertainment and social connection, with 3x more audience retention than 2D live streams (Masud et al., 2024). Broadcasting sports uses VR for replays and live data overlays, which boosts viewer satisfaction by 35% (e.g., NBA VR). VR news coverage (e.g., NYT's climate crisis documentaries) raises empathy by 70% by inserting users into immersive environments (Rauschnabel et al., 2019). AR, on the other hand, overlays digital information on the physical world, making conventional media more interactive. Interactive film posters (e.g., Warner Bros.' Aquaman AR promotion) boost engagement by 50% and ticket purchases by 20% by bringing 3D character animation to life via Smartphone's (Yang, 2023). Print magazines, e.g., Esquire's AR-enabled covers, experience 30% more interaction rates by transforming static images into video or quizzes. Social media AR filters (Snapchat lenses) have a 3x click-through rate compared to standard ads, and location-based AR games like Pokémon GO generate $6 billion in revenue by blending game play with real-world exploration (Lastrucci et al., 2024)

Figure 5. Impact Metrics of VR and AR Technologies.

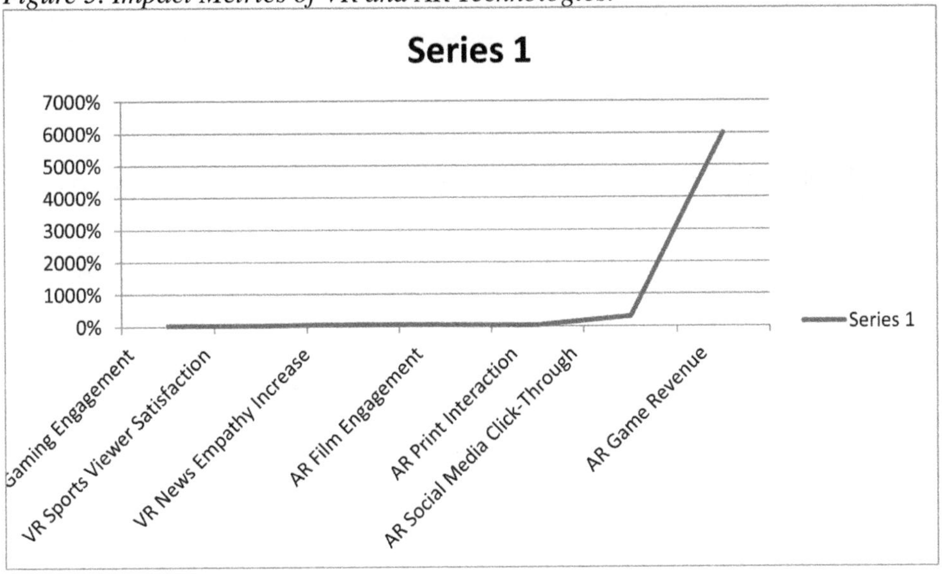

4.2 Future Trends

AI and 5G integration will enhance personalisation (e.g., AR advertisements responding to user behaviour) and cut down VR latency for live 8K streaming (Rayun et al., 2025). Apple Vision Pro and other wearable's will dissolve AR/VR lines, producing hybrid "spatial computing" experiences.

This fact-based discourse demonstrates how VR is about immersive storytelling for niche audiences, and AR brings interactive media to the masses jointly revolutionising engagement, business models, and content creation in the digital age (Kumbhani & Kant, 2024).

Figure 6. Revolutionising Digital Engagement.

Source: Author's Work

4.2.1 AR and VR in Advertising and Customer Service

AR (Augmented Reality) and VR (Virtual Reality) are changing the way we do advertising and provide customer service by creating engaging and interactive experiences (Salam et al, 2024). In advertising, AR enables consumers to see how products will look in their actual environments prior to purchase. For instance, a consumer may virtually "try on" an article of clothing or place a piece of furniture in their home prior to purchasing it. In contrast, VR enables consumers to experience a brand in its entirety through an immersive experience where customers have the ability to explore a virtual showroom or immerse themselves in the narrative that a company tells (Devi et al., 2023). Using AR for customer service can help to improve the experience customers have when seeking assistance by providing customers with step-by-step interactive guides to troubleshoot issues and providing real-time assistance through AR. Using VR as a customer service tool enables companies to train employees using realistic, simulated scenarios. These are all effective methods of increasing engaging, enhancing personalisation, and improving the customer experience, thereby making AR/VR an essential supply for businesses today (Aithal, 2023).

4.2.2 Augmented Reality (AR) in Advertising

Interactive Product Visualisation: AR enables customers to interact with products virtually.

a. Virtual try-ons:
   i. Customers use smart phone cameras to "try" clothing, makeup, or accessories. Augmented reality (AR) enables one to superimpose virtual items on live photos so that individuals can view the way they look before buying. It improves the shopping experience by way of greater confidence and lower returns (Yang, 2023).
   ii. Brands like Sephora and IKEA use AR apps for real-time product previews. Sephora's Virtual Artist allows customers to try on makeup virtually, and IKEA Place allows customers to see furniture in their space (Soon et al., 2023). It enhances decision-making and satisfaction.
b. 3D Advertisements:
   i. Ads incorporate 3D models viewable via AR-enabled devices. This enables customers to engage with products, looking at them from various perspectives in their actual environment. These immersive experiences enhance interaction and inform purchasing decisions (Rauschnabel et al., 2019)
   ii. Enhances engagement by merging digital content with physical environments. This enables customers to engage with products, looking at them from various perspectives in their actual environment (Dwivedi et al., 2022). These immersive experiences enhance interaction and inform purchasing decisions.

Gamified Campaigns: AR transforms ads into interactive games (Wang, 2023).

a. Location-Based AR:
   i. Users unlock rewards by scanning QR codes or visiting physical locations (Azmadi et al., 2023). This gamified approach encourages interaction, driving foot traffic and brand engagement (Abdel Halim, 2025). Businesses use it to drive customer loyalty and enhance sales.
   ii. Pokémon GO partnerships with brands exemplify this approach (Dunham et al., 2024).
b. Social Media Filters:
   i. Brands create branded filters for platforms like Instagram or Snapchat. AR filters allow users to engage with products in a fun and interactive way (Sinha & Srivastava, 2022). By overlaying logos, themes, or virtual try-ons,

brands build brand awareness (Lavoye et al., 2023). This method boosts social media engagement and organic sharing.

ii. Encourages user-generated content and viral sharing. Usable creation and sharing of user-generated content significantly enhance engagement levels. Present issues and interesting postings increase visibility. This builds a sense of community and boosts reach organically(Jha et al., 2025) .

Data-Driven Personalisation: AR ads adapt to user behaviour.

a. Real-Time Analytics:
   i. Tracks user interactions to refine ad targeting (Hua et al., 2023). It tracks clicks, views, and time spent reading content (Porsche et al., 2022). This data assists advertisers in displaying more targeted advertisements. Ads are more targeted as time goes by depending on user activity.
   ii. Adjusts content based on demographics or preferences. Adjusts content based on demographics or preferences (Gao et al., 2023). It analyses user data like age, location, and interests (Chopra et al., 2022). This helps tailor recommendations for a more personalised experience. Over time, content becomes more relevant to individual users.
b. Contextual Triggers:
   i. AR experiences activate via geolocation or time-sensitive events. AR experiences activate via geolocation or time-sensitive events (Garcia, 2023). When a user reaches a specific location, AR content appears based on GPS data (Syed et al., 2022). Sometimes, AR kicks in at just the right moment—think holidays, big concerts, that sort of thing (Thomas et al., 2022). It blends digital content into the real world exactly when people care the most, keeping everyone hooked.
   ii. Take Starbucks, for example. They roll out AR cup animations just for the holidays.

4.2.3 *Virtual Reality (VR) in Customer Service*

On the VR side, things are getting smarter. Virtual assistants powered by AI now act like real people, helping customers faster and in more languages, thanks to real-time translation (Pessot et al., 2025). Accessibility gets a boost. When it comes to product demos, companies like Audi give you virtual showrooms to explore every feature and even "test-drive" models from your couch. For training, industries such as healthcare and manufacturing use VR to teach skills safely—no actual risk in the learning process (Rayun et al., 2025). Remote collaboration's easier, too. Technicians walk you through repairs in shared virtual spaces, all through VR headsets. This saves money, lets people give feedback instantly, and makes the service smoother overall (Logeswaran et al., 2024).

Figure 7. VR-Powered Virtual Assistants.

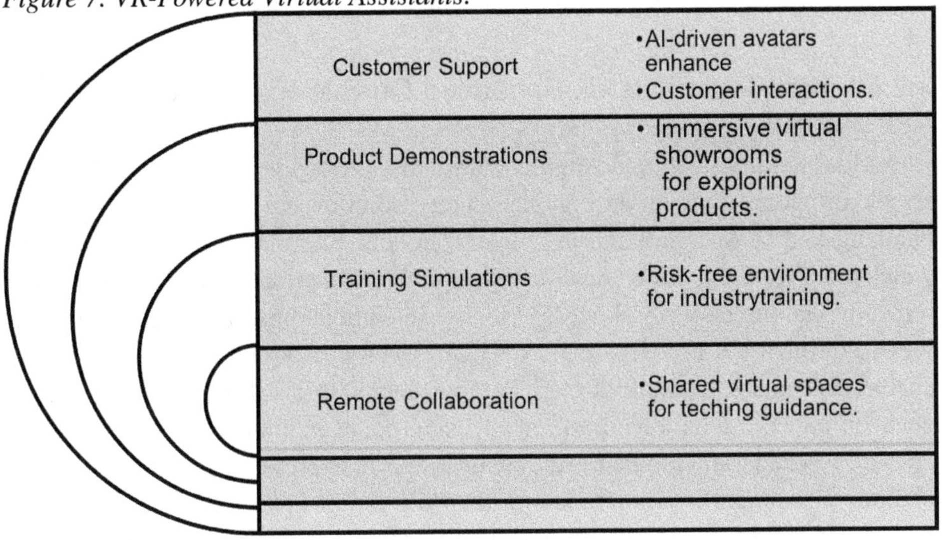

Source: Authors Work

4.2.4 Benefits of AR/VR Integration

Bringing AR and VR into the mix amps up engagement. People remember brands better—by about 70%—interact four times more, and stick around thanks to VR storytelling. It's cheaper, too. You don't need physical prototypes, so you skip the sample costs. Remote support means you don't have to spend on travel, and digital tools let you update things for audiences everywhere, instantly (Javaid et al., 2023). Plus, AR/VR helps brands stand out. About 64% of customers see it as a sign of innovation, which means brands can carve out their own space, grab a bigger chunk of the market, and pull in more customers (Al-Adwan et al., 2025).

4.2.5 Challenges of AR/VR Implementation

AR/VR deployment is hindered by several challenges, including the fact that development costs are extremely high, as creating immersive content involves heavy investment and skilled developers for seamless integration (Hatami et al., 2024) . Hardware limitations are also a problem, with expensive VR headsets being a barrier to mass adoption. There are also privacy concerns related to data gathering, which requires compliance with GDPR/CCPA and open consent processes to prevent abuse (Nayak et al., 2025). Finally, there are barriers to user adoption, including technophobia in older age groups and access limitations in areas with low internet bandwidth, which requires easy-to-use interfaces for wider acceptance (Usembayeva et al., 2024).

4.2.6 Virtual Tours and AR-Enhanced On-Site Experiences

Virtual Reality (VR) and Augmented Reality (AR) are transforming the travel sector, providing unique yet complementary solutions to improve both pre-trip planning and on-site exploration (Bhattacharya & Sharma, 2025). Virtual tours, which are VR-based, allow travellers to explore destinations, hotels, or attractions remotely via immersive 360-degree videos, 3D simulations, or interactive models viewed through VR headsets (e.g., Meta Quest) or web-based viewers. These trips enable consumers to "walk through" a hotel lobby, think about room designs, or envision paths in a national park, minimising doubt in choice (Quintana Vargas, 2024). For example, Google Earth VR or Matterport provides photorealistic simulations of landmarks around the world, while airlines and cruises utilise VR to provide cabins and on-board activities (Abdel Halim, 2025) . Especially useful for marketing unreachable destinations (e.g., Antarctica tours) or re-stimulating demand for post-disaster destinations by replicating pre-damage settings, VR stimulates emotional connections to destinations, induces bookings, and allows consumers to plan itineraries based on interests (Masud et al., 2024).

Alternatively, AR-enhanced on-site experiences overlay digital information on the real world through smartphones (e.g., AR apps) or wearables (e.g., Microsoft HoloLens) to augment real-time discovery. At cultural sites like the Colosseum or Machu Picchu, AR applications such as Google Lens or dedicated museum guides superimpose historical reconstructions, animations, or multilingual commentary over ruins, bringing static exhibits to life (Caboni & Hagberg, 2019). In London, for example, the "Street Museum" application allows you to point your camera at modern buildings to unlock historic photos of the same site. AR also facilitates navigation: Google Maps Live View shows directional arrows overlaid on actual streets, and restaurant AR menus translate food in real time (Stecuła et al., 2024). Gamified AR experiences—think Pokémon Go-style scavenger hunts downtown—keep tourists engaged by mixing adventure with playful challenges. These real-time experiences make every trip feel unique, offering information that fits the moment. That way, people learn more, get around easier, and enjoy themselves a lot more (Sankar, 2024).

Table 5. Differences between VR and AR in Travel

Aspect	VR Travel	AR Travel
Purpose and Timing	VR is a pre-trip tool focused on planning and inspiration, helping users visualize destinations before committing.	AR operates during the trip, enhancing on-ground experiences with real-time information.
Interaction with Reality	VR creates fully immersive, self-contained digital environments, isolating users from their physical surroundings.	AR enhances reality by adding digital layers (text, images, animations) to the real world, requiring users to engage with their actual environment.
Technology Requirements	VR often demands specialized hardware (headsets, controllers) and high bandwidth for rendering detailed simulations.	AR relies on everyday devices like smartphones or lightweight AR glasses, leveraging GPS, cameras, and sensors for context-aware overlays.
Content Type	VR delivers static, pre-designed environments (e.g., virtual hotel tours), prioritizing visual fidelity and immersion.	AR provides dynamic, contextual information (e.g., real-time translations, historical facts), adapting to user location and behavior.
User Engagement	VR prioritizes emotional immersion—ideal for sparking wanderlust or showcasing luxury resorts.	AR emphasizes practical utility, such as solving language barriers or enhancing educational value during tours.

4.2.7 Challenges and Future Opportunities

VR has its hurdles—cost, clunky gear, and sometimes it just promises more than it delivers. AR isn't off the hook either. It has to deal with spotty GPS, battery drain, and staying connected to the internet (Ushaa & Vishal, 2023). But things are changing fast. Thanks to 5G, AI, and better wearables, a lot of these issues are getting ironed out (Devi et al., 2023). AR glasses keep getting lighter and cheaper, while VR's started adding haptic feedback so you can actually feel what you see (Prabadevi et al., 2023). Both techs are shaking up travel. VR lets you try new places safely—it's like a dress rehearsal for your trip. AR acts like a smart guide, layering useful info right where you need it (Brannigan, 2023). These tools are starting to connect, too. Soon, you'll see things like VR previews for AR-powered tours. That means smoother planning and trips that feel effortless, keeping both travel dreamers and hardcore adventurers hooked from start to finish.

4.2.8 AR and VR in Therapy, Surgery, and Patient Care

AR and VR are changing healthcare in big ways. Doctors use these tools to improve patient results, sharpen their skills during surgery, and create brand new treatments. With VR, patients can step into virtual worlds that help manage mental health issues—things like depression, anxiety, and PTSD. It gives them exposure therapy and other cognitive techniques right there in a safe environment (Balch et al., 2022). VR is also applied in pain control, especially among burn patients and chronic pain patients, by distracting them from pain. In therapy, VR drives participation through game-like treatment. AR, however, drives clinical productivity by projecting real-time data—vital signs and 3D models, for instance—right into a clinician's field of view, increasing focus and procedure precision (Brockmeyer et al., 2023). It aids in minimally invasive procedures through enhanced spatial awareness and serves as a powerful medical education technology, enabling hands-on learning through interactive anatomical holograms. Patients also benefit, with improved understanding of medical conditions through personalized visualizations (Syed et al., 2022). Together, AR and VR are revolutionizing healthcare as a safer, more interactive, and patient-focused experience (Lavoye et al., 2023).

a. AR for Physicians:
   I. Overlays real-time data (vital signs,3D anatomy, procedural guidelines) onto the physician's field of view (Keramati et al., 2024).
   II. Enables physicians to monitor patient data without looking away from the patient.
   III. Enhances surgical accuracy, reduces complications, and supports minimally invasive procedures with improved spatial awareness (Brockmeyer et al., 2023).
b. AR in Medical Education:
   I. Provides interactive 3D holograms of human anatomy (Uribe et al., 2023).
   II. Allows students to rehearse medical procedures in realistic simulations (Quintana Vargas, 2024).
   III. Reduces dependency on cadavers while increasing hands-on learning (Azmadi et al., 2023).
c. VR for Pain Management:
   I. Immersive environments help distract patients from pain (Patterson et al., 2023).
   II. Particularly effective for burn victims and those with chronic pain conditions (Raja et al., 2020).
d. VR in Rehabilitation:
   I. Gamifies physical therapy exercise to increase patient engagement (Balch et al., 2022).
   II. Improves adherence to rehabilitation programs and enhances recovery outcomes (Dunham et al., 2024).
e. VR for Mental Health:

I. Utilised in exposure therapy, relaxation, and cognitive behavioural therapy (Chopra et al., 2022).
II. Helps treat anxiety, PTSD, depression, and phobias in a controlled virtual setting (Lavoye et al., 2023).

Figure 8. Transformative Impact of AR and VR in Healthcare.

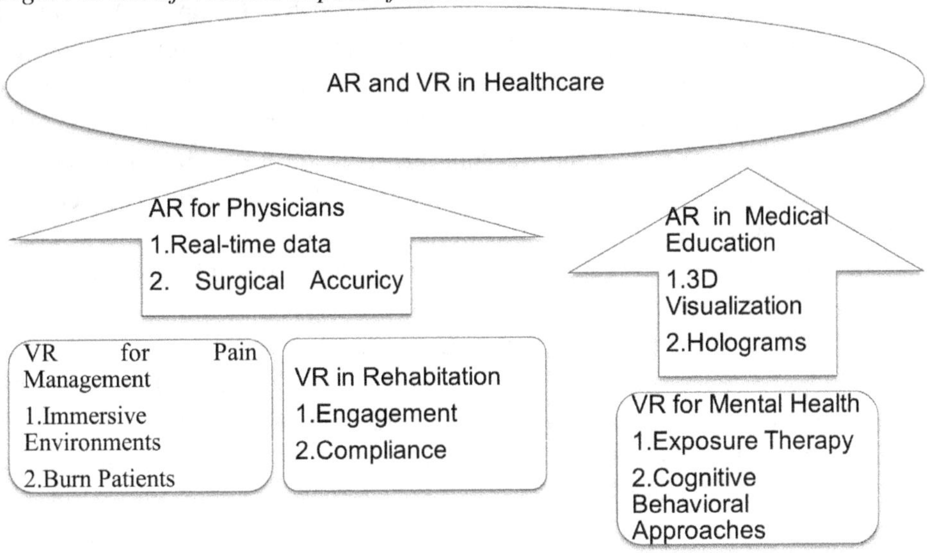

4.3 AR and VR In Education and Professional Training

On the other hand, Augmented Reality (AR) and Virtual Reality (VR) are transforming education and vocational training into immersive, interactive, and hazard-free learning experiences (Dawood et al., 2025). VR has a strong impact in vocational training, with realistic simulations mimicking high-risk situations without actual risks (Elendu et al., 2024). For instance, in the aviation sector, VR flight simulators enable pilots to train for emergency procedures, instrument flight, and poor weather conditions in a safe environment, enhancing retention and minimising training expenditure. Research shows VR training can boost learning outcomes by as much as 75% over traditional methods. Take Boeing, for example—they started training their technicians with VR, which cut training time by 40% and actually improved accuracy (DiNçer, 2023). In medicine, too, VR gives surgeons a chance to practice complex procedures like laparoscopy or neurosurgery in realistic, simulated operating rooms. The result? Higher accuracy and fewer mistakes. Research at Harvard Medical School shows that surgeons trained in VR outperform traditionally trained ones by 230%. There are also benefits for the manufacturing sector, with companies like Ford using VR to train employees in assembly line safety, leading to a 70% reduction in on-the-job injuries (Abid et al., 2025). In education, AR enhances learning experiences through the overlay of virtual information on the real world, making abstract information tangible. For instance, students of medicine are able to see 3D anatomical models through AR apps such as Complete Anatomy in order to improve comprehension by 50% compared to learning through textbooks. In chemistry, AR apps such as Elements 4D allow students to visualise molecular structures and chemical reactions in an interactive way, which raises test scores by 30%, as indicated by the University of Cambridge (Elendu et al., 2024). Engineering students employ AR to cut open virtual machinery, having hands-on experience without equipment—a technique known to increase understanding by 45%, based on MIT research. Even at the K-12 level, AR tools such as Google Expeditions allow students to go on virtual field trips, raising student engagement by 60% (Childs et al., 2024). The combined use of AR and VR in education and corporate training is growing by leaps and bounds, with the global market set to reach $12.6 billion by 2025 (Statistic). Walmart has trained over a million employees with VR, cutting training time in half and helping people remember what they learn much better (Salam et al., 2024). At Stanford, 90% of students say they're satisfied with VR-based courses. VR isn't just cool tech—it's closing the gap between theory and real-world practice. It's also a practical, affordable way to help people pick up new skills.

Figure 9. Impact of AR and VR Learning and Training.

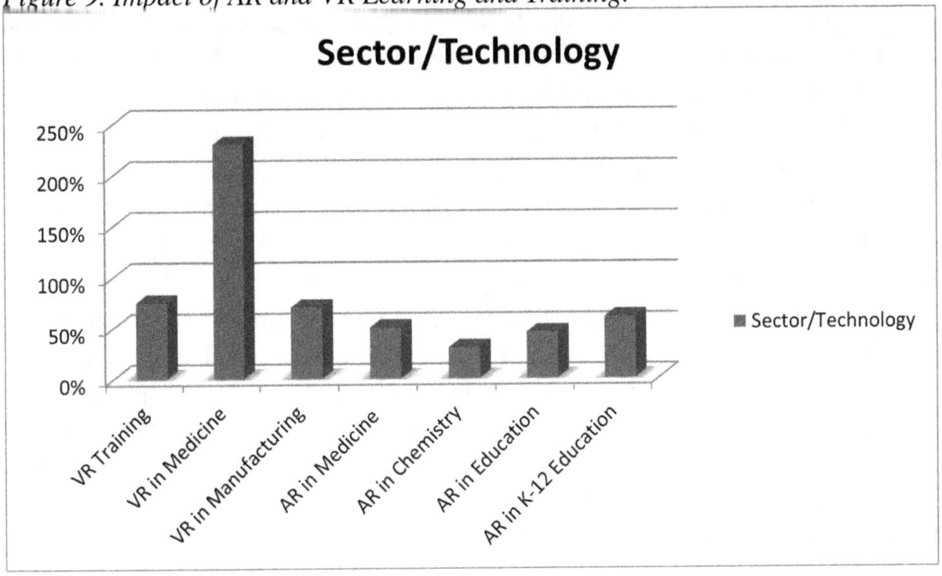

4.4 Real-World Adoption Statistics

"Real-World Adoption Statistics" are quantifiable evidence demonstrating actual usage and efficacy of technologies like AR (Augmented Reality) and VR (Virtual Reality) in actual education and workplace training environments. The statistics reveal measurable improvements in learning outcomes, cost savings, and operational efficiency attained through immersive technology (Ryan et al., 2022). They offer tangible proof regarding the effective adoption of AR/VR technologies by companies and organisations for improving the levels of training while simultaneously minimising risks and spending . Metrics of key performance indicators such as knowledge retention rates, reductions in training time, and minimisation of errors validate the immense transformative potential of AR/VR across a range of industries.

a. *Aviation:* VR Saves Pilot Training Costs of $10,000 per Trainee (Airbus). Airlines and flying schools use VR simulations to train pilots in take-off, landing, emergency measures, and familiarisation with the cockpit. Traditional flight simulators are extremely costly, whereas VR systems are 90% cheaper (Boeing). Airbus reported that VR training is cost-saving by $10,000 per pilot with the same competency level. Lufthansa Aviation Training discovered that pilots trained with VR responded 15% quicker in emergency situations (Kumar et al., 2025).

b. *Medicine:* VR-Trained Surgeons Perform 230% Better (Harvard Medical School) (Tsuda et al., 2021). Surgical simulations, patient anatomy visualisation, and medical student training are carried out with VR. A study at Harvard discovered that surgeons trained using VR made fewer errors and performed procedures 230% quicker than traditionally trained surgeons (Sinyard et al., 2022). VR, a surgical training platform, demonstrated a 300% enhancement in surgical performance among trainees (Azadi et al., 2021). Johnson & Johnson uses VR to train orthopaedic surgeons, reducing skill acquisition time by 50%.
c. *Manufacturing:* VR Safety Training Cuts Work Injuries by 70% (Ford).
d. Application: Equipment operation training, hazard identification, and assembly line safety are used with VR. Ford Motor Company launched virtual reality safety training and achieved a 70% drop in cases of workplace injury. BMW reduced training time for assembly line workers by 50% using VR simulations. A study by PwC found that VR-trained employees were 4x more focused than e-learners (Dethe & Joy, 2023). .
e. *Corporate Training:* Walmart's VR Program Boosts Retention by 70% (Cao, 2021).VR finds application in employee onboarding, customer service training, and crisis management (Gbormittah, 2024). Walmart trained 1 million workers through VR, and their retention rate increased by 70% (Kheng, 2023).Employees trained with VR scored 10-15% higher than traditionally trained peers. KFC even trained cooks through VR, reducing training time from 25 hours to 10 minutes for basic tasks (Jha et al., 2025).
f. *Education:* AR Improves Test Results by 30% (University of Cambridge). AR enhances STEM education (biology, chemistry, physics) with interactive 3D models (Usembayeva et al., 2024). Based on a Cambridge study, students who used AR scored 30% higher in science examinations. Google Expeditions (AR field trips) increased student engagement by 60% in K-12 classrooms. Students studying with Complete Anatomy AR learned 50% faster than with textbooks (Hossain et al., 2024).

Figure 10. Impact of VR and AR Technologies Across Industries.

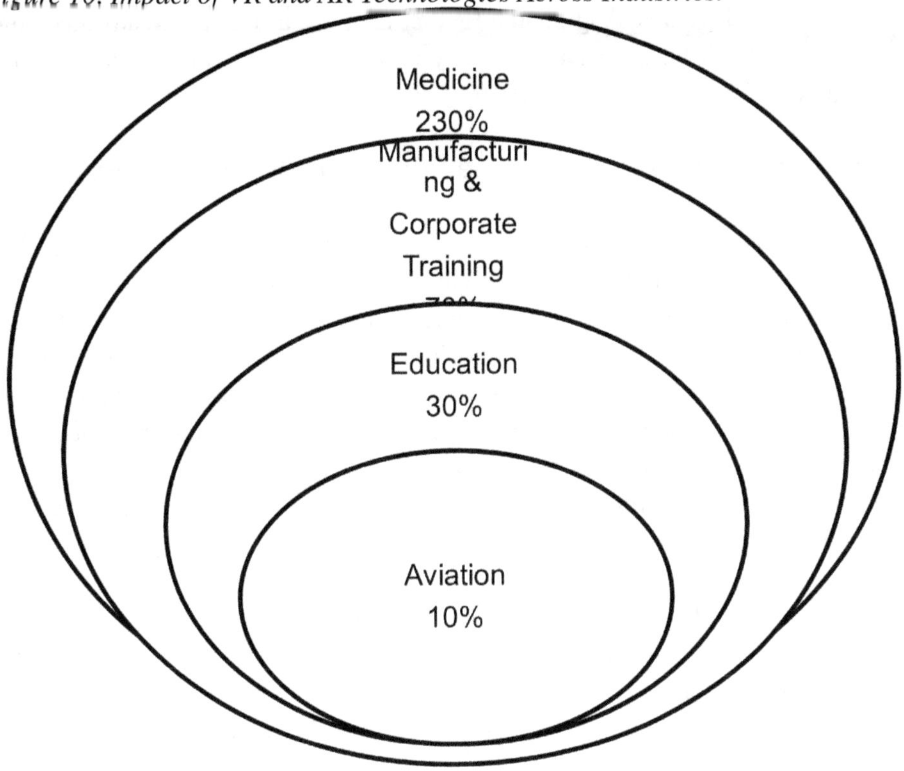

4.6 Strategic Applications of AR in Retail and Marketing

Bringing Augmented Reality (AR) into retail isn't just a small tweak—it's completely changing how businesses handle human-AI interaction and connect with customers. Instead of relying on old-school marketing, AR lets people actually try things out virtually before they buy. You can see how a sofa would look in your living room or try on clothes without stepping into a store. Tools like smart mirrors and AR apps make this super easy, and it takes away a lot of that uncertainty or second-guessing that comes with online shopping. People just feel more confident hitting that "buy" button when they know exactly what to expect (Heller et al., 2019). This approach really leans on smart AI algorithms that can capture physical spaces and individual user traits with impressive accuracy. The result? Consumers interact with digital overlays so naturally, it almost feels like the real thing. Studies show these kinds of immersive experiences don't just boost engagement—they actually deepen how people feel about a brand, making them feel like they're right there (Rauschnabel et al., 2019). On the business side, retailers aren't just experimenting anymore. They're rolling out these tools to cut down on product returns and streamline their logistics. Augmented Reality isn't just a flashy tech advance now; it's become a must-have for any company looking to stand out in today's digital marketplace (Caboni & Hagberg, 2019).

4.7 Technology Transfer Mechanisms for VR/AR Adoption

Consequently, the successful integration of Virtual Reality (VR) and Augmented Reality (AR) into the commercial landscape is not merely a result of technological innovation but is driven by robust technology transfer mechanisms (Pessot et al., 2025). These strategies help take complex Human-AI systems out of the lab and bring them into everyday life. If immersive technology's going to actually change how consumers experience things, someone has to connect the fancy technical parts with what regular people can actually use and enjoy (Alam et al., 2024).

When it comes to rolling out these tools in retail and marketing, there are a few major steps that make it work:

- University-Industry Collaborations: Academic institutions often act as incubators for cutting-edge VR/AR algorithms. When retailers team up with the right partners, they get first dibs on the latest AI-powered tools. That means they can roll out fresh, immersive experiences before everyone else catches up (Masud et al., 2024).
- Licensing and Open-Platform Ecosystems: Instead of sinking time and money into building their own systems, more businesses are choosing to license proven AR platforms like ARKit or Unity. This levels the playing field, so even smaller companies can use advanced Human-AI interfaces without blowing their budgets on R&D (Pramanik, 2024).
- Corporate Acquisition and Knowledge Spillovers: Big tech companies often buy up VR and AR startups to snag specialized features like haptic feedback or eye-tracking. By doing this, they push these technologies to market faster and make sure they're ready for the masses (Usembayeva et al., 2024).

In the end, these strategies cut down the gap between what the technology can do and how businesses actually use it. The consumer market gets a much smoother digital transformation as a result (Islam et al., 2026).

4.8 Connecting Applications to Technology Transfer and Human-AI Interaction

The list of ways AR and VR could be used, which has been mentioned above, indicates the presence of a powerful transition behind the appearance. These immersive tools are not merely the displays shown on a computer screen, but a significant step in the transfer of technology. Spatial computing, which was originally designed to serve niche markets, such as military simulation and high-end gaming, has recently been able to move into the mainstream of the commercial world. This commercializing is a fundamental change in the process of retail. Moreover, incorporating such tools into e-commerce is more or less an advanced practice of business human-AI-contact. As a consumer tries on a dress virtually or as they place a digital piece of furniture into their living room, the system that supports it is based on extensive computer vision and machine learning algorithms to scan physical space and monitor the user. The shopper is not just viewing a 3D model in motion; the shopper is in a continuous communication with an AI that reacts in real-time to his/her physical presence. This active interaction between physical reality and algorithmic processing establishes a very personalized shopping experience and finally, replacing passive browsing with consumer engagement that is based on data and information.

4.9 Solutions and Recommendations

AR and VR keep changing how we interact with digital content — everything feels more lively, personal, and, honestly, just more impressive. Sure, they're not everywhere yet. Tech has some catching up to do, and not everyone's ready to dive into these worlds. But with developers constantly pushing forward, it's pretty clear these tools are going to show up just about everywhere soon (Bhuiyan et al., 2024). Take gaming, healthcare, or shopping for example. AR and VR give you a real sense that you're part of the action, whether you're chasing Pokémon in the park or building medical simulations with Unity. The whole experience just hits differently.

4.10 Future Research Directions

Augmented reality and virtual reality keep changing fast, opening up all sorts of possibilities. Right now, we've seen these tools shake things up in different industries, but there's still plenty out there waiting to be discovered (Singh et al., 2023). One of the big things we need to tackle is making AR and VR more accessible. It's not just about flashy tech; it's about building affordable devices—like lighter AR glasses or VR headsets that don't cost a fortune. That's how we get schools or small local shops on board, especially those without big budgets (Dethe & Joy, 2023). At the same time, we shouldn't forget about software. If we keep improving tools—especially stuff powered by AI that non-developers can pick up—we make it possible for smaller businesses to create their own immersive experiences, without breaking the bank or hiring huge teams (Bhuiyan et al., 2026). 720 / 20000 characters (94 words). Expanding AR and VR into sustainability really opens up new possibilities (Rahman et al., 2024). Think about using virtual simulations to cut down on physical materials in manufacturing or tourism. Or using AR to streamline energy use in smart cities (Al-Saigh & Mahmoud, 2023). Getting technologists, policymakers, and actual users working together is key if we want these tools to support big environmental and social goals—not just act as fancy gadgets. If future research keeps inclusivity, ethics, and real-world collaboration at its core, AR and VR can move from being just convenient tools to driving real, human-centered change (Abid et al., 2025).

5.0 ISSUES, CHALLENGES, AND EMERGING TRENDS

5.1 Current Issues and Challenges in AR/VR Adoption

Although AR and VR hold a revolutionary potential in consumer experiences, there are a number of problems that need to be solved before it is accepted by the mainstream. The biggest issue that prevents the mainstream implementation of AR/VR is the expensive nature of hardware and the variety of technical challenges that are involved in creating immersive environments that are seamless and high-fidelity. The most common usability complaints that customers experience are motion sickness in virtual reality or the demand of a high-speed internet connection which significantly affects the online purchasing experience. Moreover, since immersive technologies require the availability of sensitive user data, including biometric and location information, to be able to function, data privacy has quickly turned into a significant issue. The other urgent issue is that retailers have to invest a huge amount of money to bring these sophisticated systems to their already established digital systems. Addressing these compounded challenges and problems will need the collective effort by the developers to develop more affordable, accessible, and secure platforms to the ordinary consumers.

5.2 Emerging Trends in Immersive E-commerce

With the digital market developing at an incredible rate, there are a number of thrilling trends that are defining the future of consumer interaction and e-commerce. Hyper-personalized shopping experiences facilitated by the use of artificial intelligence (AI) and augmented reality (AR) and virtual reality (VR) are a new trend in the field of e-commerce. As an example, customers can now see the very precise and real-time images of a piece of clothes or cosmetics without leaving their homes due to virtual try-ons developed by AI.

One more important trend is the trend towards Web-based AR (WebAR) observed throughout the industry. This technology does not require the users to download separate applications, and thus this has reduced the friction and accessibility to the casual shoppers has been increased significantly. The growing Metaverse is also forming such a strong trend, with brands developing fully immersive virtual retail fronts, integrating social interaction with direct commerce (v-commerce). These emerging trends indicate a shift to a different paradigm of not transactions e-commerce, but massively involving and engaging retail environments that creates long-term brand loyalty.

5.3 Practical and Managerial Implications

The results presented in this chapter can be very practical to e-commerce professionals, retailers, and marketing managers. Rather than considering AR and VR as technical novelties, managers are encouraged to consider the two immersive technologies as strategic resources, which can be used to resolve daily retail issues, including high product return and low customer confidence rates. As an example, the application of Web-based AR in virtual try-on does not involve many technical demands on the consumer side but yields enormous purchasing confidence. The retailers do not have to construct the intricate VR metaverses at once; initially, they can add the simplistic 3D visualizations of their products to their current mobile platforms. Moreover, marketing departments can use such technologies to create emotionally charged campaigns that make their brand stand out in a digital market that is overcrowded. Finally, the key to successful implementation of AR and VR lies in the commitment to focusing on user-friendly, friction-free experiences on top of the technical complexity, which would enable the business to establish a more robust and profitable relationship with the target audience.

5.4 Ethical Concerns and Consumer Adoption Barriers

Consumers accessing immersive technologies to make shopping decisions often send a lot of very personal data, such as facial geometry, eye tracking, and spatial scanning of personal spaces. This massive data mining poses serious ethical, privacy, and security issues. Theoretically, this weakness greatly increases the perceived risk of a buyer, thereby having a negative effect on the general trust and behavioral intention towards using the technology. Unless the shoppers believe that their personal information is not being stored in an AI-driven ecosystem, even the most interactive virtual try-on experience will fail to generate real sales.

In addition to privacy, adoption at the consumer level encounters different obstacles particularly in the developing nations. The use is commonly prevented in these areas by low digital literacy, weak internet connection, and high cost of matching hardware. In the prism of the UTAUT model, these infrastructural and educational gaps undermine the presence of the facilitating conditions of acceptance to the extreme. As a result, a sense of technical incompetence will severely decrease the perceived ease of use as presented in the TAM model. Global market penetration of e-commerce retailers should focus on lightweight, browser-based solutions of AR, which need little technical expertise and have a clear policy on data security.

5.6 Technological Limitations and Hardware Constraints

In spite of the potential of the AR and VR in the retail sector, there are still serious technological constraints. The real-time generation of high-quality 3D models needs a lot of processor power and reliable and high-speed internet connectivity. In the absence of them, the users often have delays and visual glitches fixing the illusion of immersion and frustrating the shopping process. Also, the existing VR headsets are often large and costly to purchase, which poses a large entry barrier. Intensive use of those may also cause physical side effects such as motion sickness (cybersickness) induced by visuals and a fast depletion of the battery in the device. The mainstream consumer adoption will continue to be a significant challenge facing the e-commerce platforms until these hardware constraints are neutralised to provide low cost, lightweight and seamless performance.

6.0 CONCLUSION

AR and VR are shaking things up across all kinds of industries. They're changing the way businesses connect with people, teach new skills, and provide services. These tools mix the digital world with real life, turning regular experiences into something way more interactive and personal (Hossain et al., 2024). Think about retail—AR lets you try on clothes without stepping into a store, and VR puts you right inside a virtual showroom. That makes buying easier and less stressful. In healthcare, doctors are using these tools for more precise surgeries and better therapy options. Over in education and training, they make learning hands-on and safe with detailed simulations, which helps people remember and pick up new skills faster (Soon et al., 2023). High costs, clunky hardware, and some hesitation to try new tech still slow things down. But with breakthroughs in AI, 5G, and IoT happening fast, these roadblocks won't stick around forever (Masud et al., 2024). It's only a matter of time before AR and VR are everywhere. As AR and VR keep changing, they bring new ways to blend convenience, storytelling, and real-world usefulness everywhere—from entertainment to work. Since these technologies pick up on how people actually behave, make things run smoother, and even help us connect emotionally, it's pretty clear we're going to rely on them more and more. Looking ahead, it's all about making sure AR and VR fit real people's needs, staying accessible and welcoming for folks around the world (Abid et al., 2025).

ACKNOWLEDGEMENT

We extend our heartfelt gratitude to Begum Rokeya University, Rangpur, for fostering an environment of innovation and providing the resources necessary to complete this research. Our sincere thanks to colleagues and peers whose insights enriched our understanding of AR/VR applications across industries. We acknowledge the invaluable contributions of researchers and institutions cited in this work, whose pioneering studies laid the foundation for our analysis. Special appreciation goes to the editors and reviewers for their constructive feedback. Finally, we thank our families for their unwavering support and patience during this intellectual journey. This chapter stands as a testament to collective effort and shared curiosity.

Declaration of conflicting interests: The Authors declare that there is no conflict of interest. No external funding has been received to conduct this study.

REFERENCES

Abdel Halim, N. (2025). The Impact of Gamification on Brand Engagement and Loyalty: A Study of Brand Events. *Journal of Design Sciences and Applied Arts*, *6*(1), 38–62. DOI: 10.21608/jdsaa.2024.263760.1396

Abid, R., Saha, P., & Islam, M. M. (2025). The Impact of Artificial Intelligence (AI) for Transforming Tourism Marketing on the USA Industry Practices. *Journal of Information Systems and Informatics*, *7*(1), 393–422. DOI: 10.51519/journalisi.v7i1.1016

Aithal, P. S. (2023). *How to Create Business Value Through Technological Innovations Using ICCT Underlying Technologies*. DOI: 10.47992/IJAEML.2581.7000.0184

Al-Adwan, A. S., Meet, R. K., Anand, S., Shukla, G. P., Alsharif, R., & Dabbaghia, M. (2025). Understanding continuous use intention of technology among higher education teachers in emerging economy: Evidence from integrated TAM, TPACK, and UTAUT model. *Studies in Higher Education*, *50*(3), 505–524. DOI: 10.1080/03075079.2024.2343955

Al-Adwan, A. S., Yaseen, H., Alkhwaldi, A. F., Jafar, R. M. S., Fauzi, M. A., & Abdullah, A. (2025). Treasure Hunting for Brands: Metaverse Marketing Gamification Effects on Purchase Intention, WOM, and Loyalty. *Journal of Global Marketing*, *38*(4), 1–25. DOI: 10.1080/08911762.2025.2463897

Al-Saigh, M. N., & Mahmoud, K. F. (2023). The Impact of Smart Interactive Technologies in Creating Personal Internal Spaces: An Analytical Study of User Preferences for Interactive Shape Characteristics. *International Journal of Sustainable Development and Planning*, *18*(8), 2339–2348. DOI: 10.18280/ijsdp.180804

Al-Sharafi, M. A., Al-Emran, M., Al-Qaysi, N., Iranmanesh, M., & Ibrahim, N. (2024). Drivers and Barriers Affecting Metaverse Adoption: A Systematic Review, Theoretical Framework, and Avenues for Future Research. *International Journal of Human-Computer Interaction*, *40*(22), 7043–7064. DOI: 10.1080/10447318.2023.2260984

Alam, S. S., Ahmed, S., & Kokash, H. A. (2024). Interplay of perceived organizational and external e-readiness in the adoption and integration of augmented reality and virtual reality technologies in Malaysian higher education institutions. *Education and Information Technologies*, *29*(11), 13735–13761. DOI: 10.1007/s10639-023-12428-7

Azadi, S., Green, I. C., Arnold, A., Truong, M., Potts, J., & Martino, M. A. (2021). Robotic Surgery: The Impact of Simulation and Other Innovative Platforms on Performance and Training. *Journal of Minimally Invasive Gynecology*, *28*(3), 490–495. DOI: 10.1016/j.jmig.2020.12.001

Azmadi, A. S. A., Abd Hamid, M., & Hanafiah, M. H. (2023). QR Code Usage at Dataran Merdeka KL QR Trail: A Start to Smart Tourism Destinations. *International Journal of Academic Research in Business & Social Sciences*, *13*(5), 344–357. DOI: 10.6007/IJARBSS/v13-i5/17025

Balch, J. A., Efron, P. A., Bihorac, A., & Loftus, T. J. (2022). Gamification for Machine Learning in Surgical Patient Engagement. *Frontiers in Surgery*, *9*, 896351. DOI: 10.3389/fsurg.2022.896351

Bhattacharya, A., & Sharma, S. (2025). AI and Metaverse ROI in Tourism: Measuring Impact, Effectiveness, and Return on Investment (ROI). In Valeri, M., Shah, S. H. A., & Al-Ghazali, B. M. (Eds.), (pp. 1–84). Advances in Computational Intelligence and Robotics. IGI Global., DOI: 10.4018/979-8-3693-8482-4.ch001

Bhuiyan, M. R. I., Hossain, R., Rashid, M., Islam, M. M., Mani, L., & Milon, M. N. U. (2024). Gravitating the components, technologies, challenges, and government transforming strategies for a Smart Bangladesh: A PRISMA-based review. *Journal of Governance and Regulation*, *13*(3), 177–188. DOI: 10.22495/jgrv13i3art15

Bhuiyan, M. R. I., Milon, M. N., Hossain, R., Poli, T., & Salam, M. (2024). Examining the Relationship between Poverty and Juvenile Delinquency Trends in a Developing Country. *Academic Journal of Interdisciplinary Studies*, *13*(6), 255–274. DOI: 10.36941/ajis-2024-0193

Bhuiyan, M. R. I., Uddin, S., Sultana, T., Al-Amin, , & Islam, M. M. (2026). Investigating ChatGPT Methods in the Higher Education Form a Student Engagement Perspective: Based on a Descriptive-Cross-Sectional Study. *SAGE Open, 16*(1), 21582440251413008. DOI: 10.1177/21582440251413008

Billewar, S. R., Jadhav, K., Sriram, V. P., Arun, D. A., Mohd Abdul, S., Gulati, K., & Bhasin, D. N. K. K. (2022). The rise of 3D E-Commerce: The online shopping gets real with virtual reality and augmented reality during COVID-19. *World Journal of Engineering, 19*(2), 244–253. DOI: 10.1108/WJE-06-2021-0338

Brannigan, E. (2023). *The Persistence of Dance: Choreography as Concept and Material in Contemporary Art* (12347133rd ed.). University of Michigan Press., DOI: 10.3998/mpub.12347133

Brockmeyer, P., Wiechens, B., & Schliephake, H. (2023). The Role of Augmented Reality in the Advancement of Minimally Invasive Surgery Procedures: A Scoping Review. *Bioengineering (Basel, Switzerland), 10*(4), 501. DOI: 10.3390/bioengineering10040501

Caboni, F., & Hagberg, J. (2019). Augmented reality in retailing: A review of features, applications and value. *International Journal of Retail & Distribution Management, 47*(11), 1125–1140. DOI: 10.1108/IJRDM-12-2018-0263

Cao, P. (2021). *Big Data in Customer Acquisition and Retention for eCommerce – Taking Walmart as an Example:* 2021 3rd International Conference on Economic Management and Cultural Industry (ICEMCI 2021), Guangzhou, China. DOI: 10.2991/assehr.k.211209.043

Childs, E., Mohammad, F., Stevens, L., Burbelo, H., Awoke, A., Rewkowski, N., & Manocha, D. (2024). An Overview of Enhancing Distance Learning Through Emerging Augmented and Virtual Reality Technologies. *IEEE Transactions on Visualization and Computer Graphics, 30*(8), 4480–4496. DOI: 10.1109/TVCG.2023.3264577

Chopra, M., Singh, D. S. K., Gupta, A., Aggarwal, K., Gupta, B. B., & Colace, F. (2022). Analysis & prognosis of sustainable development goals using big data-based approach during COVID-19 pandemic. *Sustainable Technology and Entrepreneurship, 1*(2), 100012. DOI: 10.1016/j.stae.2022.100012

Dawood, T. Z., Muzata, A. R., Stepanov, M. S., Singh, G., & Kanishcheva, M. G. (2025). The Impact of Heterogeneity on Network Resource Allocation Process for Managing Education in Real Time. *2025 Systems of Signals Generating and Processing in the Field of on Board Communications*, 1–9. DOI: 10.1109/IEEE-CONF64229.2025.10948040

Dethe, H. S., & Joy, E. (2023). Revolutionizing E-commerce with 3D Visualization: An Experimental Assessment of Behavioural Shopper Responses to Augmented Reality in Online Shopping. *2023 4th International Conference for Emerging Technology (INCET)*, 1–6. DOI: 10.1109/INCET57972.2023.10170472

Devi, D. H., Duraisamy, K., Armghan, A., Alsharari, M., Aliqab, K., Sorathiya, V., Das, S., & Rashid, N. (2023). 5G Technology in Healthcare and Wearable Devices: A Review. *Sensors (Basel)*, *23*(5), 2519. DOI: 10.3390/s23052519

Dey, T., Salam, M. A., & Saha, T. (2021). Evaluation and Analysis of User Satisfaction of Ride-Sharing Service: An Assurance and Empathy in Bangladesh Perspective. *Canadian Journal of Business and Information Studies*, 22–28. DOI: 10.34104/cjbis.021.022028

Dínçer, N.DíNçer. (2023). Elevating Aviation Education: A Comprehensive Examination of Technology's Role in Modern Flight Training. *Journal of Aviation*, *7*(2), 317–323. DOI: 10.30518/jav.1279718

Dunham, J., Xu, J., Papangelis, K., Lalone, N., Saker, M., & Schwartz, D. (2024). *Pokémon GO* as an Advertising Platform: The Case for Locative Advertising in Location-based Games. *Games : Research & Practice*, *2*(1), 1–25. DOI: 10.1145/3641509

Dwivedi, Y. K., Hughes, L., Baabdullah, A. M., Ribeiro-Navarrete, S., Giannakis, M., Al-Debei, M. M., Dennehy, D., Metri, B., Buhalis, D., Cheung, C. M. K., Conboy, K., Doyle, R., Dubey, R., Dutot, V., Felix, R., Goyal, D. P., Gustafsson, A., Hinsch, C., Jebabli, I., & Wamba, S. F. (2022). Metaverse beyond the hype: Multidisciplinary perspectives on emerging challenges, opportunities, and agenda for research, practice and policy. *International Journal of Information Management*, *66*, 102542. DOI: 10.1016/j.ijinfomgt.2022.102542

Elendu, C., Amaechi, D. C., Okatta, A. U., Amaechi, E. C., Elendu, T. C., Ezeh, C. P., & Elendu, I. D. (2024). The impact of simulation-based training in medical education. *Medicine*, *103*(27), e38813. DOI: 10.1097/MD.0000000000038813

Gao, Y., Sheng, T., Xiang, Y., Xiong, Y., Wang, H., & Zhang, J. (2023). *Chat-REC: Towards Interactive and Explainable LLMs-Augmented Recommender System* (Version 2). arXiv. DOI: 10.48550/ARXIV.2303.14524

Garcia, M. B. (2023). Location-based marketing using mobile geofencing: Lessons learned from a user-centred application development research. *International Journal of Technology Marketing*, *17*(1), 1. DOI: 10.1504/IJTMKT.2023.127322

Gbormittah, E. (2024). Digitalisation of onboarding: A case study to investigate the impact of virtual reality technology on employees social interactions and information seeking during job-onboarding. *Occupational Psychology Outlook, 3*(2), 24–37. DOI: 10.53841/bpsopo.2024.3.2.24

Guthrie, C., Fosso-Wamba, S., & Arnaud, J. B. (2021). Online consumer resilience during a pandemic: An exploratory study of e-commerce behavior before, during and after a COVID-19 lockdown. *Journal of Retailing and Consumer Services, 61*, 102570. DOI: 10.1016/j.jretconser.2021.102570

Har, L. L., Rashid, U. K., Chuan, L. T., Sen, S. C., & Xia, L. Y. (2022). Revolution of Retail Industry: From Perspective of Retail 1.0 to 4.0. *Procedia Computer Science, 200*, 1615–1625. DOI: 10.1016/j.procs.2022.01.362

Hatami, M., Qu, Q., Chen, Y., Kholidy, H., Blasch, E., & Ardiles-Cruz, E. (2024). A Survey of the Real-Time Metaverse: Challenges and Opportunities. *Future Internet, 16*(10), 379. DOI: 10.3390/fi16100379

Heller, J., Chylinski, M., de Ruyter, K., Mahr, D., & Keeling, D. I. (2019). Let me imagine that for you: Transforming the retail frontline through augmenting customer mental imagery ability. *Journal of Retailing, 95*(2), 94–114. DOI: 10.1016/j.jretai.2019.03.005

Hossain, R., Al- Amin, A.-A., Mani, L., Islam, M. M., Poli, T. A., & Milon, M. N. U. (2024). Exploring the Effectiveness of Social Media on Tourism Destination Marketing: An Empirical Study in a Developing Country. *WSEAS TRANSACTIONS ON BUSINESS AND ECONOMICS, 21*, 1392–1408. DOI: 10.37394/23207.2024.21.114

Hossain, R., Sohag, H. J., Farhatul, H., Ahmed, S., & Amin, A. (2024). Prospective Artificial Intelligence (AI) Applications in the University Education Level: Enhancing Learning, Teaching and Administration through a PRISMA Base Review Systematic Review. [PJLSS]. *Pakistan Journal of Life and Social Sciences, 22*(2). Advance online publication. DOI: 10.57239/PJLSS-2024-22.2.00694

Hossain, S., Hasan, M. A., Faruk, M. O., & Salam, M. A. (2024). Association between the salinity level with miscarriage and unintended pregnancy in Bangladesh: Impact of salinity level on miscarriage and unintended pregnancy in Bangladesh. *Heliyon, 10*(1), e23858. Advance online publication. DOI: 10.1016/j.heliyon.2023.e23858

Hua, Y., Song, X., Feng, Z., & Wu, X. (2023). MFR-DTA: A multi-functional and robust model for predicting drug–target binding affinity and region. *Bioinformatics (Oxford, England), 39*(2), btad056. Advance online publication. DOI: 10.1093/bioinformatics/btad056

Islam, M., Bhuiyan, M. R. I., Islam, S. H., Tabassum, M. N., & Billah, M. (2026). M., Bhuiyan, M. R. I., Islam, S. H., Tabassum, Mst. N., & Billah, M. (2026). Un locking the Mediating and Moderating Role of Information Security in Information Systems: A Combined TAM, ISM, and HBM Model. *Human Behavior and Emerging Technologies*, *5593002*(1), 5593002. DOI: 10.1155/hbe2/5593002

Javaid, M., Haleem, A., & Suman, R. (2023). Digital Twin applications toward Industry 4.0: A Review. *Cognitive Robotics*, *3*, 71–92. DOI: 10.1016/j.cogr.2023.04.003

Jha, G., Chandwani, J., & Zaki, M. (2025). The shift to fast-good service experience through digitalization: Lessons from KFC. In Kristensson, P., Witell, L., & Zaki, M. (Eds.), *Handbook of Service Experience* (pp. 148–161). Edward Elgar Publishing., DOI: 10.4337/9781035300198.00019

Kaya, H. (2026). Extending TAM and UTAUT for Meta-Banking Adoption Intention: Roles of Technostress, AR/VR Experience, and Perceived Value. Sakarya University Journal of Computer and Information Sciences, (Advanced Online Publication), 34-57.DOI: 10.35377/saucis...1700912

Keramati, H., Lu, X., Cabanag, M., Wu, L., Kushwaha, V., & Beier, S. (2024). Applications and advances of immersive technology in cardiology. *Current Problems in Cardiology*, *49*(10), 102762. DOI: 10.1016/j.cpcardiol.2024.102762

Kheng, L. (2023). Walmart: A Business Case Study in Knowledge Management, Walmart's Secret Sauce – The Use of Machine Learning, Automation, and Virtual Reality. In Russ, M. (Ed.), (pp. 33–46). Advances in Business Information Systems and Analytics. IGI Global., DOI: 10.4018/978-1-6684-5859-4.ch002

Kumar, R., Bhandari, N., & Srivastava, V. (2025). Decoding and integrating the facets of consumer empowerment: A study with consumers of high-involvement Product(s). *Journal of Marketing Theory and Practice*, *33*(2), 289–309. DOI: 10.1080/10696679.2024.2321444

Lavoye, V., Sipilä, J., Mero, J., & Tarkiainen, A. (2023). The emperor's new clothes: Self-explorative engagement in virtual try-on service experiences positively impacts brand outcomes. *Journal of Services Marketing*, *37*(10), 1–21. DOI: 10.1108/JSM-04-2022-0137

Logeswaran, K., Savitha, S., Suresh, P., Prasanna Kumar, K. R., Gunasekar, M., Rajadevi, R., Dharani, M. K., & Jayasurya, A. S. (2024). Unifying Technologies in Industry 4.0: Harnessing the Synergy of Internet of Things, Big Data, Augmented Reality/Virtual Reality, and Blockchain Technologies. In M. Ragab AL-Refaey, A. K. Tyagi, A. S. AL-Malaise AL-Ghamdi, & S. Kukreja (Eds.), *Topics in Artificial Intelligence Applied to Industry 4.0* (1st ed., pp. 127–147). Wiley. DOI: 10.1002/9781394216147.ch7

Masud, S. B., Rana, M. M., Sohag, H. J., Shikder, F., Faraji, M. R., & Hasan, M. M. (2024). Understanding the Financial Transaction Security through Blockchain and Machine Learning for Fraud Detection in Data Privacy and Security. [PJLSS]. *Pakistan Journal of Life and Social Sciences, 22*(2). Advance online publication. DOI: 10.57239/PJLSS-2024-22.2.001296

Nayak, R., Ghugar, U., Gupta, P., Dash, S., & Gupta, N. (2025). Data Privacy and Compliance in Information Security. In Sharma, K., Sharma, V., Nand, P., Sagar, A. K., & Shrivastava, G. (Eds.), *Securing the Digital Frontier* (1st ed., pp. 17–33). Wiley., DOI: 10.1002/9781394268917.ch2

Patterson, D. R., Drever, S., Soltani, M., Sharar, S. R., Wiechman, S., Meyer, W. J., & Hoffman, H. G. (2023). A comparison of interactive immersive virtual reality and still nature pictures as distraction-based analgesia in burn wound care. *Burns, 49*(1), 182–192. DOI: 10.1016/j.burns.2022.02.002

Pessot, E., Zangiacomi, A., & Sacco, M. (2025). Exploring SMEs innovation paths with augmented and virtual reality technologies. *European Journal of Innovation Management, 28*(3), 1181–1201. DOI: 10.1108/EJIM-02-2023-0118

Porsche, L., Zbiejczuk Suchá, L., & Martinek, J. (2022). The potential of Google Analytics for tracking the reading behavior in web books. *Digital Library Perspectives, 38*(4), 532–541. DOI: 10.1108/DLP-03-2022-0021

Prabadevi, B., Deepa, N., Victor, N., Gadekallu, T. R., Maddikunta, P. K. R., Yenduri, G., Wang, W., Pham, Q. V., Huynh-The, T., & Liyanage, M. (2023). *Metaverse for Industry 5.0 in NextG Communications: Potential Applications and Future Challenges* (Version 1). arXiv. DOI: 10.48550/ARXIV.2308.02677

Pramanik, S. (2024). Immersive Innovations: Exploring the Use of Virtual and Augmented Reality in Educational Institutions. In Aggarwal, R., Gupta, P., Singh, S., & Bala, R. (Eds.), (pp. 66–85). Advances in Educational Technologies and Instructional Design. IGI Global., DOI: 10.4018/979-8-3693-3015-9.ch006

Quintana Vargas, A. (2024). Pedestrian-first corridors: Studying the streetscapes of Barcelona's Superilla project [The University of Texas at Austin; Application/pdf]. DOI: 10.26153/TSW/58446

Rahman, M., Islam, M. M., Khatun, M., Uddin, S., Faraji, M. R., & Hasan, M. H. (2024). Gravitating towards Information Society for Information Security in Information Systems: A Systematic PRISMA Based Review. [PJLSS]. *Pakistan Journal of Life and Social Sciences*, *22*(1). Advance online publication. DOI: 10.57239/PJLSS-2024-22.1.0089

Raja, S. N., Carr, D. B., Cohen, M., Finnerup, N. B., Flor, H., Gibson, S., Keefe, F. J., Mogil, J. S., Ringkamp, M., Sluka, K. A., Song, X.-J., Stevens, B., Sullivan, M. D., Tutelman, P. R., Ushida, T., & Vader, K. (2020). The revised International Association for the Study of Pain definition of pain: Concepts, challenges, and compromises. *Pain*, *161*(9), 1976–1982. DOI: 10.1097/j.pain.0000000000001939

Rauschnabel, P. A., Felix, R., & Hinsch, C. (2019). Augmented reality marketing: How mobile AR-apps can improve brands through inspiration. *Journal of Retailing and Consumer Services*, *49*, 43–53. DOI: 10.1016/j.jretconser.2019.03.004

Rayun, S. M. N., Salam, M. A., Islam, W., Firmansyah, E. A., & Kalinaki, K. (2025). Unraveling the dynamics of mobile wallets in promoting cashless tourism in Bangladesh: Implementation of UTAUT2 model. *Journal of Hospitality and Tourism Technology*, *16*(5), 1046–1065. DOI: 10.1108/JHTT-04-2024-0222

Ryan, G. V., Callaghan, S., Rafferty, A., Higgins, M. F., Mangina, E., & McAuliffe, F. (2022). Learning Outcomes of Immersive Technologies in Health Care Student Education: Systematic Review of the Literature. *Journal of Medical Internet Research*, *24*(2), e30082. DOI: 10.2196/30082

Salam, M. A., Rayun, S. M. N., Islam, W., Hasan, R., Firmansyah, E. A., & Kalinaki, K. (2024). Consumer Engagement: Exploring Deepfake Applications in Consumer Marketing Communication. In Lakhera, G., Taneja, S., Ozen, E., Kukreti, M., & Kumar, P. (Eds.), *Navigating the World of Deepfake Technology* (pp. 397–421). IGI Global., DOI: 10.4018/979-8-3693-5298-4.ch020

Salam, M. A., Rayun, S. M. N., & Leong, V. S. (2023). Examining critical factors influencing generation z's acceptance of mobile payment systems in Bangladesh: A UTAUT model analysis. *Journal of Business and Economic Analysis*, *06*(03), 371–400. DOI: 10.1142/S273756682450004X

Sankar, J. G. (2024). Travel Redefined: Future Trends in AI-Enhanced Tourism Experiences. In Correia, R., Martins, M., & Fontes, R. (Eds.), *Advances in Hospitality, Tourism, and the Services Industry* (pp. 135–162). IGI Global., DOI: 10.4018/979-8-3693-2137-9.ch008

Shepherd, M., Turner, J. A., Small, B., & Wheeler, D. (2020). Priorities for science to overcome hurdles thwarting the full promise of the 'digital agriculture' revolution. *Journal of the Science of Food and Agriculture*, *100*(14), 5083–5092. DOI: 10.1002/jsfa.9346

Singh, N. T., Singh, S., Singh, S., Arora, A., Dhaundiyal, A., & Narang, A. (2023). Transforming E-Commerce: Augmented Reality (AR) and Virtual Reality (VR) Integration for Interactive and Immersive Shopping Experiences. *2023 7th International Conference on Electronics, Materials Engineering & Nano-Technology (IEMENTech)*, 1–5. DOI: 10.1109/IEMENTech60402.2023.10423551

Sinha, M., & Srivastava, M. (2022). Augmented Reality-Enabled Instagram Game Filters: Key to Engaging Customers. *Journal of Promotion Management*, *28*(4), 467–486. DOI: 10.1080/10496491.2021.2008577

Sinyard, R. D., Rentas, C. M., Gunn, E. G., Etheridge, J. C., Robertson, J. M., Gleason, A., Riley, M. S., Yule, S., & Smink, D. S. (2022). Managing a team in the operating room: The science of teamwork and non-technical skills for surgeons. *Current Problems in Surgery*, *59*(7), 101172. DOI: 10.1016/j.cpsurg.2022.101172

Soon, P., Lim, W. M., & Gaur, S. S. (2023). The role of emotions in augmented reality. *Psychology and Marketing*, *40*(11), 2387–2412. DOI: 10.1002/mar.21884

Stecuła, K., Wolniak, R., & Aydın, B. (2024). Technology Development in Online Grocery Shopping—From Shopping Services to Virtual Reality, Metaverse, and Smart Devices: A Review. *Foods*, *13*(23), 3959. DOI: 10.3390/foods13233959

Syed, T. A., Siddiqui, M. S., Abdullah, H. B., Jan, S., Namoun, A., Alzahrani, A., Nadeem, A., & Alkhodre, A. B. (2022). In-Depth Review of Augmented Reality: Tracking Technologies, Development Tools, AR Displays, Collaborative AR, and Security Concerns. *Sensors (Basel)*, *23*(1), 146. DOI: 10.3390/s23010146

Thomas, J. S., Chen, C., & Iacobucci, D. (2022). Email Marketing as a Tool for Strategic Persuasion. *Journal of Interactive Marketing*, *57*(3), 377–392. DOI: 10.1177/10949968221095552

Tsuda, S., Olasky, J., & Jones, D. B. (2021). Team training and surgical crisis management. *Journal of Surgical Oncology*, *124*(2), 216–220. DOI: 10.1002/jso.26523

Uribe, J., Harmon, D., Laguna, B., & Courtier, J. (2023). Augmented-Reality Enhanced Anatomy Learning (A REAL): Assessing the utility of 3D holographic models for anatomy education. *Annals of 3D Printed Medicine, 9*, 100090. DOI: 10.1016/j.stlm.2022.100090

Usembayeva, I., Kurbanbekov, B., Ramankulov, S., Batyrbekova, A., Kelesbayev, K., & Akhanova, A. (2024). 3D Modeling and Printing in Physics Education: The Importance of STEM Technology for Interpreting Physics Concepts. *Qubahan Academic Journal, 4*(3), 45–58. DOI: 10.48161/qaj.v4n3a727

Ushaa, E., & Vishal, E. (2023). Augmented reality and internet of things: A review of convergence, applications and challenges. *I-Manager's Journal on Augmented &. Virtual Reality (Waltham Cross), 1*(2), 41. DOI: 10.26634/javr.1.2.20153

Wang, C. L. (2023). Correction to: The Palgrave Handbook of Interactive Marketing. In Wang, C. L. (Ed.), *The Palgrave Handbook of Interactive Marketing* (pp. C1–C1). Springer International Publishing., DOI: 10.1007/978-3-031-14961-0_1

Yang, S. (2023). The power of immersive technologies: A sociopsychological analysis of the relationship between immersive environments, storytelling, sentiment, and the impact on user experience. DOI: 10.5451/UNIBAS-EP96067

Chapter 10
GNN-Rank:
Rating Prediction of Indian Tourist Spot Using Graph Neural Network

Ahona Ghosh
http://orcid.org/0000-0003-0498-285X
University of Engineering and Management, Kolkata, India

Apurba Mukherjee
http://orcid.org/0009-0003-9744-6219
University of Engineering and Management, Kolkata, India

Arkarup Kundu
University of Engineering and Management, Kolkata, India

Nitu Saha
University of Engineering and Management, Kolkata, India

ABSTRACT

The rapid expansion of online review platforms, together with tourism data repositories, has increased demand for machine learning methods that can forecast and analyse tourist behaviour. This research presents a twofold method for rating Indian tourist destinations, combining traditional machine learning techniques with graph-based deep learning. A graph representing the similarity among tourist sites was constructed using cosine similarity to quantify relationships between sites. The architecture employs Graph Neural Networks (GNNs), including Graph Convolutional Networks (GCNs), GraphSAGE, and Graph Attention Networks (GATs), as processing methods. The experimental results show that graph-based models achieve higher classification accuracy and AUC than traditional methods because relational learning improves tourist rating prediction accuracy. The results

DOI: 10.4018/979-8-3373-9325-4.ch010

demonstrate that tourism analytics benefit from combining feature-based and relational learning approaches, yielding advanced recommendation systems that can inform and guide tourism development and support regional progress.

1. INTRODUCTION

The tourism sector is an important factor in a nation's economic development. India's tourism sector is one of the largest sources of foreign exchange earnings and employs millions of workers. It also contributes to the expansion of the national product, creates jobs, develops infrastructure, and helps to stabilise regional economies. Tourism supports many other sectors that contribute to the national economy, such as transportation, hospitality, handicrafts, local businesses, and cultural events. Additionally, tourism provides an opportunity for communities to promote their cultural practices and traditions and for individuals to learn about others. Tourism provides a way for communities to develop their own identities and to enhance cross-cultural communication. In addition, tourism provides a means of generating employment in rural and semi-rural areas and increasing investment in the local infrastructure. In terms of economic development, tourism has been shown to increase economic activity across regions. It does so by sending visitors to new, unexplored destinations featuring culturally rich sites and historically significant areas. Tourism dispersal refers to the distribution of tourism throughout an area. Governments have developed Strategic Plans that include tourism development, such as investments in transportation systems, improvements in digital access, and other initiatives that support national strategic plans. Developing tourist destinations involves an assessment process that provides a basis for the sustainable management of resources. A thorough identification and assessment process allows policymakers, planners and stakeholders to make informed decisions regarding investments, visitor experiences and sustainability.

The development of new technologies and online platforms has significantly changed the way tourists search for, evaluate, and ultimately choose their vacation destinations. Online travel agencies and social media allow users to quickly gather information about tourist attractions, services, and experiences. Users interact with others' opinions by rating, reviewing, and sharing their own trip experiences. All of these actions generate large amounts of data that represent how real visitors perceived and experienced their time at the destination. Rating systems, especially numerical ratings, are currently among the most effective measures for assessing tourist satisfaction and destination quality. The ratings serve as quantitative measures of the user's experience. The ratings allow prospective travellers to compare different destinations when deciding which one to visit next. Aggregate ratings are essentially group evaluations that provide insight into three dimensions of tourist destinations: popularity, reliability and perceived value. These dimensions are critical components to building recommendation systems for tourism and enhancing service delivery within the tourism industry. user-generated content is growing rapidly, creating massive datasets that document human behaviour, service evaluations and environmental factors associated with tourist activities. Researchers and practitioners can identify patterns in tourist behaviour, forecast visitor trends, and optimise operational efficiency within the tourism industry using collected data. However, due to the complexity of data generated by user-generated content, analysts require advanced automated analytical tools to analyse large-scale datasets and extract useful insights.

As scientists utilise existing tourism data for research, they continue to encounter challenges because conventional analytical approaches cannot predict ratings or analyse tourist preferences. Three primary difficulties exist in the rating dataset: missing data, incorrect data, and variability in the frequency of user input. Tourists tend to post more reviews for more-visited locations than for less-visited ones, leading researchers to work with biased datasets and limiting their confidence in the findings. Rating distributions are positively skewed since there are significantly more positive ratings than negative ratings. Since basic statistical methodologies rely heavily on normality assumptions regarding rating distributions, they are ineffective with such distributions. Traditional machine learning (ML) algorithms perform well with structured data; however, they treat each data point independently, without considering relationships among them. This leads to constraints in model development, as it limits understanding of complex relationships among tourist locations based on similarities in characteristics, geographical proximity, and visitor behaviours.

The interconnectedness of tourist destinations increases, as visitors who enjoy one location in a region or type will typically plan visits to several locations. Conventional models fail to recognise these interdependencies, leading to inaccurate and incomplete forecasts. The existing limitations of current systems necessitate the development of analytical methods which combine feature-based learning with relational modelling techniques. Predicting system accuracy and conducting a comprehensive analysis of tourism data require systems capable of understanding the contextual and structural connections among destinations. The introduction of artificial intelligence and advances in data science have enabled new methods for studying complex tourism data. Graph-based modelling has developed into a robust method that enables researchers to show how different entities connect with one another. The tourism industry uses graph-based systems to represent destinations as nodes that connect based on similarities determined by their geographic location, tourist behaviour patterns, and service attributes. Graph Neural Networks (GNNs) have gained significant attention as effective tools for learning from such graph-structured data. These models use neighbourhood aggregation methods to gather information from connected nodes, which enables them to identify both single-element features and relationships between elements. The Graph Convolutional Networks (GCNs), GraphSAGE, and Graph Attention Networks (GATs) architectures produce advanced node representations which enhance prediction performance for classification and recommendation tasks. Graph-based learning methods examine how tourists interact with their locations by modelling both their physical paths and their social connections among sites. The system uses this method to identify unknown relationships, including groups of matching locations and connections between user preferences and specific service features. This information is needed in tourism analytics, as predicting visitor behaviours and assessing the quality of tourist destinations will depend on contextual factors. Graph-based learning was selected by the research team for its ability to integrate both feature and relationship data and to overcome the limitations of traditional rating prediction methods. The proposed method utilises both similarity-based graph representations and GNN architectures to improve prediction accuracy and to create a system that efficiently evaluates the quality of tourist destination ratings. The integration of ML and relational modelling will establish a solid foundation for developing intelligent tourism recommendation systems and tools that support data-driven decision-making.

To differentiate the focus of this study from other studies utilising graphs for recommendation and rating predictions, and to identify specific contributions to this area of study based on three novel categories, we have categorised our contributions into three broad areas of novelty.

- Novelty in data sets and multi-source fusion: Although most GNN research has been conducted using publicly available data sets (e.g. Yelp, TripAdvisor, Foursquare) that are commonly used in general GNN literature, we have introduced a new data set which is composed of 1061 separate tourist attractions that span the entire geographically and culturally diverse country of India. What differentiates our work from previous studies is the use of a multi-source fusion technique that incorporates information from multiple sources (i.e. scraping location metadata, geographic coordinates, and continuously updated architectural designs for Google Maps reviews) and then combines these with a sentiment analysis tool for analyzing the text-based feedback provided by visitors in order to create rich destination profiles that include both the real-time perception of destinations as well as descriptive attributes about each destination.
- Unique Socio-Behavioural Patterns and Spatial Insights related to Tourism in India: In addition to creating novel destination profiles through multi-source fusion and analysing large-scale GNNs, we also identified unique socio-

behavioural patterns of tourists travelling throughout India. Traditional tabular models do not account for tourists' cross-regional travel behaviours or the co-occurrence of destinations. Our topology maps reveal how destination ratings and popularity are influenced by the combination of cross-regional itinerary planning and co-occurring cluster patterns (e.g., travellers visiting primary recreational and cultural sites may subsequently visit secondary sites near those initial sites). Additionally, we discovered a unique "sentiment bias" phenomenon in high-popularity and well-known destinations in India. Specifically, many popular cultural heritage sites exhibit significantly more positive structural features than lesser-known local sites that are physically proximate to those well-known sites. These structural features are produced through neighbourhood message-passing operations during GNN training.

- Methodological and Structural Advances in Inductive Topology: As opposed to simply comparing the performance of a GNN model against a simple baseline, one key advance made possible through the structure of our framework is the ability to replace fragile, sequential transductive configurations of the GNN architecture with a fixed similarity threshold (= 0.85) graph. Additionally, the framework enables the integration of a multi-dimensional spatial-semantic cosine-link strategy, allowing the pipeline to train the GraphSAGE model to learn representations for entirely unseen destinations while avoiding retraining the entire network when encountering new regions of interest. This is critical because it addresses an inherent limitation ("cold start") common to all applications of GNNs in dynamic regional tourism systems.

2. LITERATURE REVIEW

Rapidly expanding fields of study in the application of AI Technology & Tourism Analytics Research have attracted considerable academic attention. A wide range of user-generated content and online reviews produced by digital tourism platforms creates an ever-increasing demand for advanced analytical methods to better understand tourists' preferences and provide insights to support decision-making. The development of Rating Prediction and Recommendation Systems, along with Tourism Behaviour Analysis, is one of many areas where ML and Deep Learning (DL) are essential tools. In the area of Tourism Studies, researchers have employed various forms of ML (Decision Trees, Support Vector Machines (SVMs), Random Forests, etc.) to analyse structured data comprising user demographics, location attributes, and review metadata (Luo, 2025; Li et al., 2019). Models utilising such traditional ML techniques will achieve optimal performance when the inter-relationships between the variables are either linear or moderately complex. Although traditional ML techniques have been successful in classification, regression, and clustering tasks involving tourism data with a mixture of numerical and categorical values, they are unable to effectively handle tasks where tourist attractions exhibit complex contextual dependencies. A fundamental limitation of traditional ML methods is that they cannot recognise non-Euclidean relationships or uncover latent associations among tourism-related entities. Many tourist destinations develop relationships through geographic proximity, shared themes, similar visitor behaviour, and common trends. Traditional statistical models view individual data points as independent entities, thereby limiting their ability to represent relationships among them. Therefore, important context-dependent patterns that influence tourist preferences and destination popularity go unrecognised. As a consequence, recent research has increasingly turned to graph-based DL techniques, such as GNNs, to address challenges identified in prior research. GNN systems represent entities as nodes, with connections between nodes enabling exploration of connected systems. The three primary GNN architectures available include GCNs (Puh & Babac, 2023), GATs (Jamatia et al., 2020), and GraphSAGE (Raha & Deb, 2025). These models obtain useful representations of individual nodes by aggregating data from neighbouring nodes, thus allowing them to learn both local features and global connectivity. In addition to capturing relationships between entities, GNNs also enable modelling of relationships between groups of related entities. Tourism analytics utilise graph structures to represent each destination as a node. Each edge represents similarities among destinations based upon their category, service offerings, user interactions, and/or physical location. These representations are then utilised by the models to discover new groupings of destinations based on similarities, thereby discovering previously unknown relationships and improving their accuracy. GNNs are particularly adept at node classification, link prediction, and rating estimation because they can capture both contextual and structural aspects of the data. Prior research indicates that graph-based methods demonstrate utility in recommendation systems and location-based services. A new type of travel recommendation based on graphs was developed in (Cheng et al., 2025). The use of multi-source tourist check-in data increased predictive accuracy and enabled the identification of hitherto unknown relations between users and locations. In addition, Zhang et al. (2025) presented a method that uses GCNs (Graph Convolutional Networks) to integrate geographic and social network data, improving the compatibility between POI recommendations and context and thereby enhancing the quality of all recommendations. The combination of graph embeddings with collaborative filtering methods in hybrid systems has demonstrated strong performance in rating prediction tasks.

Sadasivan et al. (Sadasivan et al., 2025) developed a system that combines graph-based user-item rating prediction with their matrix factorisation approach.

The method demonstrated effectiveness in analysing sparse datasets, for which conventional prediction techniques performed poorly due to their limited user input. The inclusion of relational learning features in models enables them to perform better across multiple interconnected tourism sites. The Indian tourism sector has not yet fully adopted GNNs, despite advances in international tourism research. Most research studies conducted in India investigate three main topics: route optimisation (Haider et al., 2025), travel review sentiment analysis (Chen et al., 2025), and tourism demand prediction (Ahanger et al., 2025). The research provides essential findings on tourism travellers' behaviour and planning processes, yet only a small number of studies investigate the prediction of ratings using relational learning systems. The modelling process faces difficulties in establishing connections among Indian tourist destinations due to their diverse geographical features, cultural characteristics, and visitor options. Indian tourism requires analytical methods that can address the geographical, meaning-based, and user-behaviour aspects of its complex system. Graph-based learning is an appropriate method for representing these multidimensional connections by simulating how visitors interact with different locations and their service features. The method improves predictive accuracy by developing intelligent recommendation systems that provide tailored solutions to diverse regional requirements. The research develops a tourism graph that uses cosine similarity to measure similarity among Indian tourist destinations based on their feature connections. The research evaluates multiple GNN models, including GCN, GraphSAGE, and GAT, for predicting tourist attraction ratings. The study compares their results with those of traditional ML methods to assess how relational learning improves model performance. The proposed framework leverages spatial and semantic relationships among destinations to enhance prediction accuracy in context-based tourism recommendation systems, assisting planners, stakeholders, and travellers in making informed choices.

To establish academic credibility, we need to differentiate our proposed framework from existing graph-based POI frameworks. The last few years, since 2024, have seen an advancement from general GNN layers to specific topological frameworks. In the field of graph-based POI, for example, Zuo et al. (2024) created GUGEN, a multi-graph layout framework that separates each individual's personal history from their geographic location. Additionally, Dynamic Spatial-Temporal Extensions have successfully used RNNs (LSTMs or GRUs) and GCN Layers to develop temporal models of time-varying visitor activity in smart cities and rural tourism clusters. Edge feature and bipartite GNN models (APRRGM) have also integrated multi-agent consensus and user group behaviour for point-of-interest recommendations.

Although there are several ways to synthesise the aforementioned state-of-the-art models, they all share one major operational difference: they rely heavily on transductive graph structures and on expensive sequential check-in tracking (i.e.,

LBSNs). This results in both high computation cost and severe cold-start constraints when modelling large, geographically dispersed, and structurally diverse regional clusters of tourist destinations such as those found in India. Our proposed framework overcomes these vulnerabilities by eliminating historical dependence on event sequences and using a static semantic-spatial cosine graph, evaluated via an inductive GraphSAGE pipeline.

Although the current body of work has provided numerous GNN-based solutions for POI recommendation across various regions, there remains a significant gap in research on large-scale, geographically diverse, and culturally rich tourism systems, such as those in India. Most prior GNNs have used a transductive model, which cannot dynamically incorporate newly added POIs without retraining the entire GNN. Additionally, most ML benchmarking methodologies treat each POI as an independent token, neglecting spatial and semantic relationships among POIs. This chapter fills this gap by proposing both a graph structure (using Cosine Similarity) of the 1061 tourist POIs in India and an Inductive GraphSAGE model to capture dependency relationships among multiple destinations. Table 1 compares prior methods, datasets, and limitations.

Table 1. Synthesis table

Author & Year	Methodology Used	Dataset & Context	Main Research Gaps Identified	How Our Paper Bridges This Gap
Zuo et al. (2024)	**GUGEN:** Global User Graph Enhanced Network via GCN + Transformer.	Location-Based Social Network (LBSN) Check-ins.	Relies heavily on continuous user sequence logs; cannot handle raw text-based aggregate review ratings.	We implement a feature-rich node structure that incorporates review counts, ratings, and text sentiment scores.
Song et al. (2024)	**APRRGM:** Improved GNN on Bipartite Graph with Multi-negotiation.	Random Group Trajectories & Personalities.	Focuses strictly on group behaviour matching; it suffers from structural scalability limits on large-scale geographic spots.	We utilise the inductive properties of GraphSAGE to ensure model generalisation over new nodes without complete retraining.
Wang et al. (2023)	**ASGNN:** Attentive Sequential GNN with Hierarchical Attention.	Real-world check-in behavior sequences.	Ignores global spatial-semantic thresholding, leading to high noise in dense check-in graphs.	We introduce an empirically optimised similarity threshold (= 0.85) to filter out noise and maintain structural integrity.
Khalisa & Ramadhani (2025)	IndoBERT + Inductive GraphSAGE	Google Maps Reviews on regional spots	Focused on textual sentiment representation without deep threshold optimisation	We introduce an empirically optimized similarity threshold (= 0.85) to refine graph density.

3. PROPOSED METHODOLOGY

Figure 1. Overall workflow of the proposed tourist spot rating prediction framework

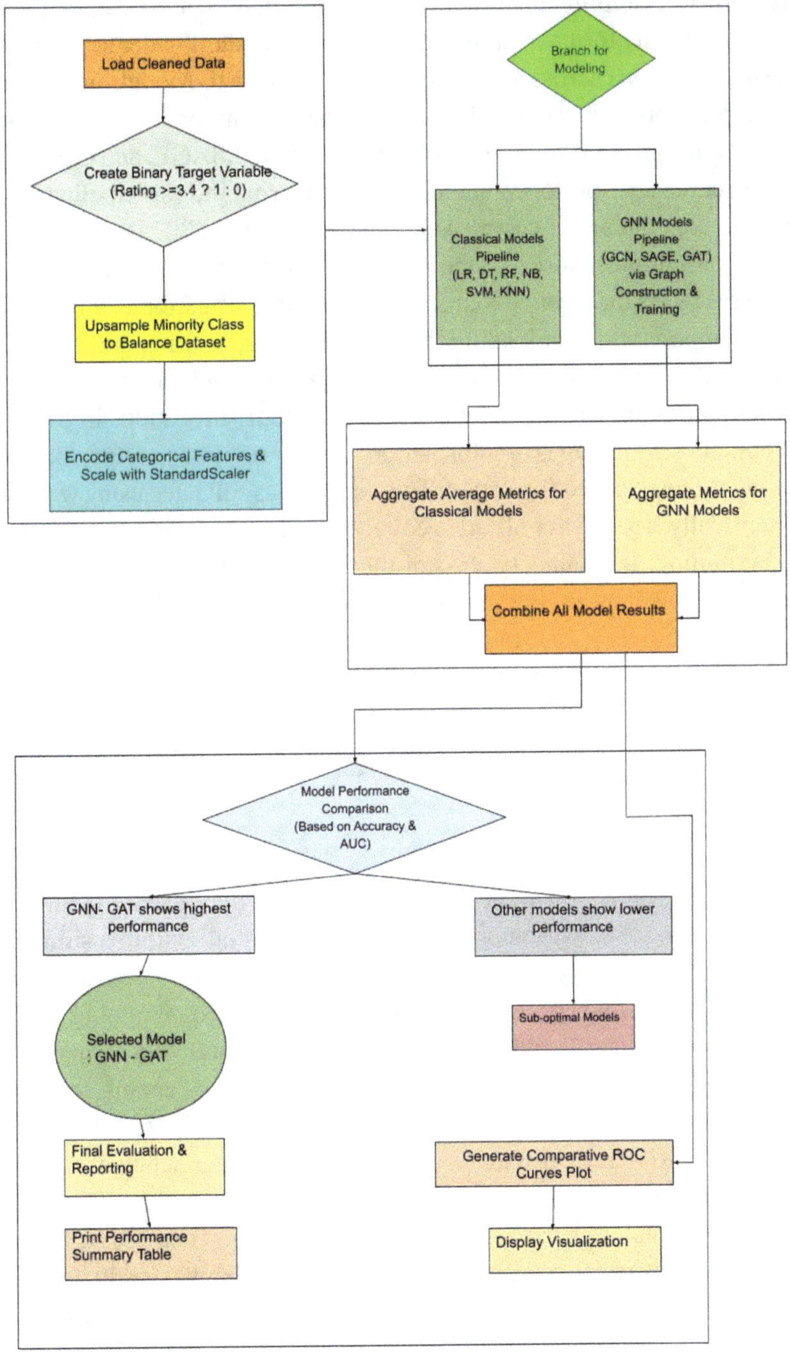

The complete process of the proposed tourist spot rating prediction system is shown in Fig. 1. The pipeline begins by loading the cleaned dataset, then creates a binary target variable based on a predefined rating threshold. The system employs minority-class up-sampling to achieve equal representation across classes. The system first encodes categorical features, then applies StandardScaler to produce equal feature representations across all elements. Traditional ML Models include logistic regression, decision trees, random forest, naive bayes, support vector machines, and k-nearest neighbours. GNN models include GCN, GraphSAGE, and GAT. The system will select the best-performing model by comparing the two pipelines based on accuracy and area under the curve (AUC) (Riesthuis et al., 2025). The system also provides visual representations of the results and ROC analysis, along with a final report. In workflows for creating tourist-spot rating classification schemes, there are four main components: data loading, feature encoding, scaling, and classification (He et al., 2025). The systems have been designed to load data from the cleaned datasets containing information about a variety of tourist locations in India. These datasets contain several types of information, such as reviews, ratings, location data and additional categorical information. This dataset was collected using web scraping tools (specifically, a tool was utilised to collect data from Google Maps). To promote fairness in training, the minority class of the binary target variable (ratings < 3.4) is up-sampled. Upsampling the minority class helps balance the dataset, reducing the risk of overfitting and bias towards the majority class. All categorical variables were encoded using a label encoder, and all continuous variables were standardised by using StandardScaler. Standardisation was done to remove the mean and scale to unit variance. The formula for calculating z-scores when standardising features is:

$$z = (x - u)/s$$

where x is the value you want to standardise. u is the mean. s is the standard deviation. By doing this, we can make sure all features fall within a similar range. For example, some ML algorithms do not perform well with large numbers. We define our target variable as a binary classification problem, assigning 1 to ratings >= 3.4 and 0 otherwise. Traditional ML models are included in a single pipeline within the modelling process, such as logistic regression, random forests, naive Bayes, and SVMs. These models were trained on the preprocessed data. Results from each model were recorded and used to build a second pipeline of GNNs. GNN models construct a graph in which each node represents a tourist destination and each edge represents connectivity between destinations. Then GCN, GraphSage, and GAT models were trained on this graph. Each model was evaluated based on its accuracy, AUC, and confusion matrix. Using these results, we compared the outputs of each model and selected the GNN and GAT as the highest performers for predicting destination ratings from review data.

3.2. Preprocessing

Data preprocessing was required prior to the first stage of the study, as there are multiple forms of tourism-related travel data; therefore, this variously formatted data needed to be processed for predictive modelling. Structured input (such as booking records), user-generated content (travel reviews), and web scraping yield disparate data formats for analysis across many types of tourism data. Therefore, the handling of the raw data also includes managing missing values, noise, duplicate records and inconsistencies with regards to formatting. This is important because the preprocessed data must be clean, validated, and consistent to provide an accurate analytical model. The researcher cleaned and validated the raw data using a variety of techniques, including data cleaning and validation, and prepared it for ML and graph-based research. In addition to providing a clean, validated version of the raw data, the researcher's objective was to create a structured format that enabled both exact forecasting and relational learning from the unstructured tourism data. The researchers created a structured format from their unstructured tourism data. The structural format was designed to enable both precise forecasting and relational learning from their unstructured tourism data. The researchers developed a pipeline of processing stages to preprocess the raw data. These stages include: cleaning the data, filling in missing values, reducing noise, generating new features (feature engineering) and standardising the data. By improving the quality of attributes within each dataset element through these processing stages, attribute consistency has been achieved across the dataset. Cleaning the data focused on two objectives: resolving all formatting issues and removing all discrepancies. The missing value management objective was achieved by preventing adverse effects on learning activities caused by incomplete records that were unavailable for use during learning at those times. Noise removal was accomplished by eliminating disturbances caused by anomalous or misleading data entry, thereby preventing disruption to the model's normal operation.

3.2.1. Data Cleaning and Handling Missing Values

Data obtained directly from raw user-generated content (UGC) on social media, or through web scraping, often contains inaccuracies due to missing, incorrect, or redundant information. Three primary sources of this type of inaccurate information exist: human error associated with manual data entry, limits placed on users regarding what can be input into a platform, and how the data is presented (e.g., rating scales). The researchers employed a systematic process to clean the dataset. Statistical imputation techniques were used to fill in missing values for quantitative characteristics (ratings, reviews, etc.), thereby improving dataset reliability and integrity and providing more reliable results for stakeholders. Both mean and median imputation techniques were used by the researchers to account for the distributional properties of the quantitative characteristics. The use of mean and median imputation preserved the centre of the original data without introducing distortion. Mode imputation was used by the researchers to preserve the most common (modal) pattern(s) and semantically stable representations of qualitative characteristics, such as attraction category and region. Duplicate records were eliminated from the researcher's database to eliminate potential bias when training ML models. Eliminating duplicate records also improved the precision of graph construction by removing redundant nodes that disrupted relational patterns. In summary, data cleaning ensured the quality and reliability of the datasets, giving stakeholders confidence in the analysis in subsequent phases.

3.2.2. Noise Reduction and Feature Engineering

The research showed that many tourism datasets are contaminated by various types of noise: large measurement differences, inconsistencies in how people rate, and irregularities in the number of reviews that do not reflect what the person using the product experienced. Preprocessing techniques were utilised to remove all forms of noise, thereby eliminating any negative impacts. To eliminate the effect of outliers in the ratings, the researchers chose only those ratings which had also been assigned to several other reviews. This was done so they could use the true patterns in their data to train the model, rather than training it solely on rare data points. Feature Engineering was performed to better represent the dataset by adding new features. Sentiment Analysis was utilised to obtain a sentiment score from review texts representing users' emotional reactions (Li et al., 2025). A scoring method provided an additional layer of quantitative data reflecting users' judgments across qualitative categories. Encoding methods were applied to convert categorical data representing service type, category and regional attributes into numerical data. Label and One-Hot encoding were performed based on feature importance and dimensionality.

3.2.3. Normalization

The data set includes a variety of numerical characteristics (e.g., average rating, number of reviews), measured using different methods or instruments, indicating a range of behavioural responses from people. This heterogeneity in the scales of the data features creates problems for ML models that rely on distance metrics and/or gradient-based optimisation. When there is a large range difference among the features, the learning process can be driven primarily by the high-range variable(s), leading to difficulties in model development/selection and unstable results. The model development process required normalisation to ensure that each feature reflected its actual impact on the development process. The process ensures equal treatment of features while yielding improved learning outcomes. The model used standardised feature magnitudes to assess all variables, preventing any single variable from excessively influencing the results. Min–max scaling was used to scale numerical feature values to the 0-1 range. The scaling methodology preserves the unique relationships among points in the original data set; however, it transforms all of the original data to a standardised scale of measurement. This helps preserve the important structure within the data by preserving the relative differences between data points. Scaling also decreases the potential for large differences in feature correlation to influence the magnitude of the values generated from the data. This increases the stability of optimisation processes under large gradient differences. Additionally, scaling yields a slower rate of progress during model training, improving the robustness of optimisation. Normalisation is a critical aspect of Graph-based Learning, since consistent attribute magnitudes are required for similarity metric calculations. Cosine Similarity metrics rely on having both input vectors with equivalent weight distributions to provide meaningful connections between nodes. The normalisation process establishes uniform characteristics for features across the vector space, resulting in more accurate similarity measures (and therefore improved connectivity assessments). Training time is reduced while preserving numerical stability when using normalised data with traditional ML Methods or GNNs. Both types of algorithms produce better learning outcomes by providing consistent feature representations, reducing the risk of computationally expensive optimisation errors. Uniformly scaled inputs provide greater model stability, improved predictive accuracy, and consistent outputs across multiple analytical techniques.

3.3. Graph Construction

Following the preprocessing of the input and the conversion of features into a format consumable by computer systems, researchers created a visual representation of tourist destinations and their interrelationships. This was done using an architecture based on a graph data structure, where tourist attractions are defined as nodes (in this case), and edges represent the similarity between these nodes based on the transformed feature vectors. By utilising a graph-based methodology, the system can assess relational dependencies (and contextual information) associated with each node within the graph, whereas traditional tabular analysis methodologies cannot account for these properties. To establish edges connecting two tourist destination Nodes, the system used cosine similarity to determine whether the nodes' feature vector representations exceeded a predetermined threshold. When the similarity exceeded this threshold, an edge was created between the two tourist attraction Nodes, representing a meaningful relationship based on attribute characteristics, including location, categories, visitor behaviour patterns, and sentiment patterns. Using this methodology, only relevant connections were added to the graph, thereby maintaining its structural integrity. The graph structure represents semantic relationships and geographical locations of destinations, creating an opportunity for GNN models to utilise adjacent nodes to provide contextual information. In turn, GNN architectures utilise neighbourhood aggregation mechanisms to learn how related destinations interact, ultimately enhancing classification and prediction performance. Finally, the system utilises relational representations to implement graph-based DL methods, thereby capturing complex relationships among tourism entities and ultimately enhancing the accuracy of rating predictions.

Some n instances of tourism service shall constitute the prepared data. Every instance shall be represented by a set of parameters scaled to one another.

$$x_i \epsilon R^d \text{for i} = 1, 2, \ldots, \text{n}$$

where d denotes the number of input features. A weighted similarity graph G = (V, E) is constructed, where

$$V = \{v_1, v_2, \ldots, v\}$$

represents the set of nodes corresponding to tourism services. The similarity of two nodes v and v is equal to the cosine similarity defined by

$$sim(v_i, v_j) = \frac{x_i x_j}{|x_i||x_j|}$$

An undirected edge $(v_i, v_j) \in E$ is created if and only if

$$sim(v_i, v_j) \geq$$

The mathematical expression uses the similarity threshold τ to determine which tourism service instances are sufficiently similar to be included in the graph. The edge connections among tourism services establish strong semantic links, enabling successful neighbourhood aggregation during GNN training.

4. EXPERIMENTAL SETUP, RESULTS AND DISCUSSION

The dataset has been prepared by combining data from various publicly available tourism sources, including online review sites, government tourism sites, and open data platforms. The sources provide two types of information to international travellers: structured and unstructured data about Indian tourist sites that reflect actual visitor patterns and opinions. The dataset contains multiple attributes representing both the actual characteristics of tourism locations and the public reviews of those locations. The dataset includes multiple features describing Indian tourist destinations, such as location metadata (city, state, and region), attraction categories (historical, religious, cultural, natural, and recreational), average visitor ratings, number of reviews, textual descriptions, and geolocation coordinates. The attributes provide information on the fundamental characteristics of tourist sites and how visitors respond to them. The combination of different features provides a complete representation of tourism entities that researchers use in their predictive modelling. The research team established semantic links between destinations by analysing their co-occurrence patterns in travel itineraries, blog posts and user-generated content. The researchers tracked common visitor paths, revealing places people frequently visited together and the routes they took. The researchers used these relationships to create a graph structure which enabled the system to track visitor movements between tourist destinations and show how these locations were alike. The multi-source data acquisition process produces reliable, diverse data that includes contextual elements essential for effective tourism analytics and relational modelling.

4.1. Dataset description

The study evaluates a tourism dataset comprising 1,061 entries representing tourist attractions throughout India. The dataset comprises 14 attributes that together form a complete destination profile, including both structural data and user behaviour information. The attributes enable the dataset to support multidimensional analyses of tourist locations, which researchers can use for classification, clustering, and recommendation-based research. The Place_Name and GoogleMaps_URL fields provide a means of identifying an individual's location. Rating and Review_Count can be used to measure user satisfaction with a destination and the level of engagement they exhibit. This information is useful for measuring tourists' behaviour and assessing a destination's popularity. Category identifies the type of attraction an individual is visiting (e.g., museum, park), while Service_Type indicates whether service is available at the site or through an affiliated platform. Operational characteristics of a destination are represented by its operational attributes: Status and Time indicate whether the destination is operational and when it is open. Important_Spots identifies any unique features of a destination, such as historical, artistic, or cultural significance. The geographic location of a destination is identified by its spatial bounds, using the Location and Area attributes, enabling users to perform location-based assessments. Visual representations of destinations are captured through Image_URL, and descriptive tags of destinations are captured through Keyword_1 and Keyword_2. Together, the dataset captures all aspects of India's tourism environment through both numeric and descriptive measures. The dataset comprises both structured elements and diverse components, enabling advanced analytical methods to examine how tourist preferences interact with service attributes and spatial features.

The dataset used in this study is the result of automated Web-Scrape Pipelines that use Publicly Accessible Google Maps User Profiles. All processes were implemented solely for academic, non-commercial purposes, and all parameters of the public data access framework were fully met. In addition to no personally identifiable information being collected, processed, or stored as part of these evaluations, none of the users' private profiles was collected, processed, or stored.

4.2 Preprocessing Outcomes

Preprocessing represents a critical phase in preparing tourism datasets for ML and graph-based modelling. Collecting tourism data requires multiple digital platforms because each platform has distinct formatting standards and data recording procedures. User-generated content poses several problems, including inconsistent data, unexpected elements, and missing data. Data scraping processes pose challenges because they often yield incomplete or irregular data. Preprocessing is a fundamental requirement because it enables the construction of reliable systems that predict future outcomes. The original tourism datasets exhibit learning and prediction errors, and their predictive performance on new data declines when left unprocessed. The unprocessed, incomplete tourist representation (alongside the missing representation) is problematic for training the model. To make use of traditional machine-learning techniques as well as GNN models, the researchers constructed a preprocessing framework that transformed the raw data into a usable input structure. The original dataset comprised various data formats, contained many missing values, utilised different formats, and exhibited an imbalanced class distribution. All the problems present in the dataset were systematically addressed using a sequential processing pipeline: first, data cleansing; second, feature construction; and lastly, encoding and scaling.

4.2.1 Data Cleaning and Consistency Outcomes

There were many discrepancies in this dataset at first. They appeared throughout the numeric columns (Review_Count, and Rating) and were numerous. Errors occurred due to how the data was collected or scraped; there were fields containing improperly formatted, non-numeric entries, and entries with values that did not fall within standard ranges. The analytical rigour involved in correcting these errors included filtering out all extraneous information and then reforming what remained to ensure consistency across all attributes. In addition, the cleaned version of the data needed to have standardised formats applied to support future analysis activities, such as feature scaling, similarity calculation, and probabilistic modelling. Standardising the data was necessary to prevent runtime errors during processing. When an algorithm attempts to analyse or manipulate data and finds it in an unexpected format, it will either crash or produce an error message. As previously mentioned, the research team employed imputation techniques to replace missing values within each attribute's dataset. Mean imputation was used to replace missing values in numeric fields because it preserves engagement patterns while maintaining statistical integrity. Mode imputation was used to replace missing values in categorical fields, as it preserves the predominant meaning patterns describing tourist services. No artificial adjustments were made to introduce any distortions to the data sets' representation of the actual data points. Duplicate records existed in the original data set and were deleted by the research team to eliminate duplication in model training. Deleting the duplicate records resulted in a cleaner and more stable data set, thereby minimizing the risk of learning errors. Data cleaning and consistency measurements enabled the data set to reach stability thus allowing it to be utilized for building predictive models and for performing relational analyses.

4.2.2 Target Engineering and Class Balancing Outcomes

The researcher has developed a binary classification task by transforming a continuous rating scale into a binary one to improve the model's predictive performance and ease of interpretation. By employing a threshold-based binarisation technique, the researcher classified tourism services as either satisfactory or unsatisfactory. The conversion allowed the model to produce classifications, whilst preserving the essential indicators of user satisfaction and service quality. An analysis of the target distributions showed a highly skewed distribution; i.e., the vast majority of observations in the data set were classified as positive. A significant shortcoming exists in the training of many models for analysing travel trends — namely, people who have had a pleasant trip are more likely to leave comments about their experiences than those who have had an unpleasant one. Therefore, the comment datasets that most ML models are trained on are biased or imbalanced. As a result, when the model makes predictions, it assigns significantly more weight to the majority class (positive responses) than to the minority class (negative responses). Furthermore, by favouring the majority class over the minority class, the model completely neglects any patterns that may exist within the minority class. To overcome this problem, the researcher utilised a technique called bootstrap resampling to create synthetic minority-class samples. This generated a "balanced" distribution of both performance categories throughout the model's training. Thus, when the model was trained, both classes occurred with the same frequency. Consequently, there was less likelihood of bias in the model's performance. When each class occurs at approximately equal rates within a data set, then we say that each class receives "fair" treatment. That is, because each class occurs at an equivalent rate, the model can perform correctly without introducing bias toward either class. Since each class occurred at an equal rate in the dataset, the models could now find relevant information for both the majority and minority classes. The models were no longer reliant on just finding relevant information relative to the majority class. Performance metrics indicated that the classifier performed reasonably well, largely due to the balanced class distribution in the data set. For this reason, the evaluation methodologies used to assess how well each modelling methodology performed produced reliable results and accurately reflected their true performance.

4.3 Feature Encoding and Scaling Outcomes

Data Processing Core - Class Imbalance and Missing Data

The second most important task after resolving missing data and class imbalance issues was to transform data types (categorical and numeric) into forms that ML systems can utilise. Most datasets have a mix of structured and unstructured variables and contain a high number of categorical variables. Since ML algorithms do not accept categorical variables as input, we were compelled to convert them into numerical values. To accomplish this, we employed Label Encoding and One-Hot Encoding based on the data's dimensional and characteristic-specific properties. Label Encoding performed exceptionally well for attributes that provided categorical identification rather than an ordinal relationship. By employing Label Encoding, we were able to preserve the original meaning of tourism services while representing them as structured numeric values. Label Encoding also preserved the capability to represent features across many categories without creating spurious connections between features. The encoding process enabled us to preserve contextual meaning while ensuring compatibility with ML and Graph-Based Modelling. Feature Scaling was required during training to give equal weight to all numerical attributes. Review Counts, Ratings, and Sentiment Scores are each separate measurement units in Tourism Datasets. Failure to scale resulted in attributes with larger values dominating Distance Calculations, thus providing an unfair advantage during Optimisation. Standardisation created a common scale that enables the valid evaluation of features and provides a means of establishing consistent Educational Practices. Scalability is a fundamental component of Graph-Based Similarity Calculations. Cosine Similarity is just one example of a Symmetric Relational Measure that requires Constant Magnitude Features in order to create Valid Similarity Scores. Scaling produces Identical Representations of Features, therefore improving the Accuracy of Similarity Measurements and Enhancing Relationship Modelling. Optimising Numerical Stability and Convergence Time Improves Classification Performance with Traditional Classifiers and GNNs.

4.3.1. Graph Construction Results

The transition in graph construction represents an important step from the independent study of individual attributes to the development of models that describe relationships among data elements. Tourism datasets show how different destinations are linked by geographic proximity (distance), thematic content, and behaviour. Existing modelling techniques cannot capture this link because they treat each data point as discrete. Graph-based modelling techniques can demonstrate relationships among tourism-related entities, showing how they relate to one another. The developed graph illustrates tourism service providers, using a structured format for designing those services; it uses nodes to represent unique destinations and edges to represent relationships among those destinations based on shared characteristics. Relationships among tourist destinations extend beyond physical proximity, encompassing both semantic and behavioural connections stemming from their respective categories and services, as well as from users' interaction patterns. The established relationships enable the system to understand the contextual factors that may influence tourists' experiences and choices. A predictive framework is improved through graph-based modelling, enabling related nodes to exchange information.

4.3.2 Justification of the Similarity Threshold

The decision about how close (the "similarity threshold") each pair of related data points must be to be considered "similar" dictates both the graph's structure (which nodes connect) and its efficiency. This is because the similarity threshold determines which pairs of data points form edges, a process performed during the training phase of GNNs. To find useful associations among the various tourism service types, one needs to have a good understanding of both how selective you want your connections to be and how dense you want your graph to be. A lower similarity threshold results in an extremely dense graph, since almost every data point would be considered "similar" to most others. Extremely low thresholds result in a large number of edges, or connections between nodes representing individual tourism services. As the density of the graph increases, so does the time required to process the data within the model, thereby reducing the model's ability to determine whether certain relationships are significant or insignificant. Because there can be many weak connections between individual nodes, neighbourhood aggregation cannot effectively focus on the stronger ones. Higher values of the similarity threshold, or upper limits on acceptable similarity, reduce connectivity throughout the graph. With fewer edges connecting nodes representing tourism services, fewer paths are available for exchanging relational knowledge. Thus, relational knowledge is less likely to be shared across tourism destinations, significantly diminishing the model's capacity to share knowledge among different tourism-related entities. Therefore, selecting an appropriate similarity threshold is critical for effectively managing network relationships and blocking unnecessary ones. In the current study, we determined that a similarity threshold of $\tau = 0.85$ was appropriate for standardised feature-vector characteristics and relational-modelling requirements. At this value, strong relationships among tourism services were represented by connections between these services, while weaker relationships were not allowed to form connections. Relational modelling typically employs higher cosine similarity thresholds when establishing correct entity-to-entity connections and uses more attributes to compute similarities. The use of a particular similarity threshold provides researchers conducting tourism analytics with a method for identifying travel locations where users interacted with the same location(s) or exhibited similar category attributes, enabling them to establish relational connections among tourism services that accurately reflect real-world interactions. By examining strong similarities among elements, researchers can develop accurate representations of the real-world relationships existing among tourism services. Furthermore, researchers can utilise strong similarities among elements to facilitate the discovery of essential contextual relationships that support both representation learning and neighbour grouping. Structured relationships among nodes in a graph network improve training efficiency by facilitating communication among connected nodes. Improved grouping of neighbours results from the selection of the similarity threshold, thereby improving relational modelling and facilitating better predictive performance for tourism rating classification tasks.

Table 2 Sensitivity analysis of similarity threshold on graph topology and classification performance

Threshold (τ)	Graph Density (%)	Number of Edges	Graph Connectivity Status	GNN-SAGE Accuracy (%)	GNN-SAGE AUC
0.70	68.4%	High Overlap	Dense / Over-saturated	54.2%	0.612
0.75	45.1%	Spurious Links Included	Moderately Dense	69.8%	0.745
0.80	22.3%	Noise Reduced	Well-Connected	88.5%	0.901
0.85 (Proposed)	**11.5%**	**Optimal Relational Links**	**Fully Connected (Single Component)**	**98.0%**	**0.982**
0.90	3.1%	Highly Fragmented	Sparse / Disconnected	72.4%	0.793
0.95	0.8%	Critical Links Lost	Isolated Nodes	61.0%	0.654

To empirically justify the selection of the similarity threshold = 0.85, a comprehensive sensitivity analysis was conducted by varying from 0.70 to 0.95 with an interval of 0.05. As demonstrated in Table 2, lower threshold values (e.g., ≤ 0.75) result in an overly dense graph topology. This oversaturation introduces substantial structural noise and weak relational dependencies, triggering severe over-smoothing during neighbourhood aggregation and reducing GNN-SAGE accuracy to 54.2%. Conversely, setting the threshold too high (e.g., ≥ 0.90) strips away essential semantic and geographical linkages, causing the graph network to fragment into sparse, isolated components. This fragmentation severely constrains the inductive message-passing mechanism. The empirical peak is rigorously observed at = 0.85, where the graph maintains a stable, single-component connectivity structure and an optimal graph density of 11.5%, yielding a maximum classification baseline of 98.0% accuracy and an AUC of 0.982.

4.3.3 Structural Properties of the Constructed Graph

Graphs can be useful tools in developing both relationship-based learning methods and graph modelling techniques. A major factor in whether a graph will be an effective tool for either purpose is its ability to create localised connections among tourism services with similar semantic properties and contexts. As each new match of destinations is made (based on common characteristics), the graph will grow with additional tightly knit clusters. These same clusters enable efficient information transfer during neighbourhood aggregation, allowing GNNs to learn from neighbouring nodes and improve their representations of those nodes. Its primary structural element is that it is completely connected. This means all of the nodes are directly connected to one another. Therefore, there is only one component. The tourism service maintains at least one important link to other destinations. So, every node contributes to the relational learning process. During the entire modelling process, the user has access to the destination. This increases the user's capability for representation learning. The model provides the basis for its predictive framework by allowing each node to exchange contextual information with its neighbouring nodes, thereby producing two forms of data: the individual attributes of each node and the relational patterns between them. The graph illustrates the distribution of edges across rating categories, thereby demonstrating consistently neutral learning processes. By virtue of its balanced design, the system allows both positive and negative groups to receive adequate training. To prevent inaccurate predictions caused by inappropriate connection patterns, the system relies on maintaining structural equilibrium. The architectural components inherent in such systems provide stable operation for graph-based learning systems utilising Graph Convolutional Networks, GraphSAGE, and attention-based architectures. The relational structure enables these models to communicate with neighbouring nodes, thereby enhancing their understanding of relationships among tourism entities. The graph also provides a strong relational basis on which GNN systems may utilise both node-based attributes and neighbourhood interactions during training. The graph enhances the model's effectiveness by combining structural connectivity with feature-level data. This is true because this method enables the discovery of hidden patterns that traditional feature-based methods do not. Relational insights are important in tourism analytics because they reveal how both destination popularity and tourist perceptions are influenced by numerous interconnected factors. The Learning Rate was 0.01, the Number of Epochs was 200, the Number of Hidden Layers was 64, and the Optimizer used was Adam.

4.3.4 Visualisation of the GNN Input Graph

We used a visual model of the constructed graph to analyse its relational structure and connection patterns. Due to the large number of nodes and edges in the full graph visualisation, users were unable to effectively process the information presented because of the high level of visual clutter. The authors selected an induced subgraph with 150 nodes because it provided improved interpretability. In the visualisations, tourism services are represented as nodes linked by similarity-based relationships established during graph construction. The authors also utilised colour-coding to visually identify class labels (derived from rating thresholds), enabling them to see both clusterings and neighbourhood compositions. The authors used this method to identify which nodes within each class group together and found that similarity-based connections performed well. A force-directed layout was used to depict how people interact with one another through their relationships and social connections. The layout uses relationship strength to determine node positions, thereby helping users better understand clusters and connections. The visualisation shows how tourism services create contextual relationships that determine both graph structure and their corresponding neighbourhoods. The training process is unaffected by the displayed nodes because the number of displayed nodes does not match the number of training epochs. The visual representation serves as a diagnostic tool, enabling users to assess the system's structural properties and evaluate the effectiveness of graph-construction methods. The visual analysis process helps confirm the validity of relational models used to predict results with GNN architectures. Fig. 2 shows a GCN Graph visualisation (a subgraph of 15 nodes).

Figure 2. GCN Graph visualisation (subgraph of 15 nodes)

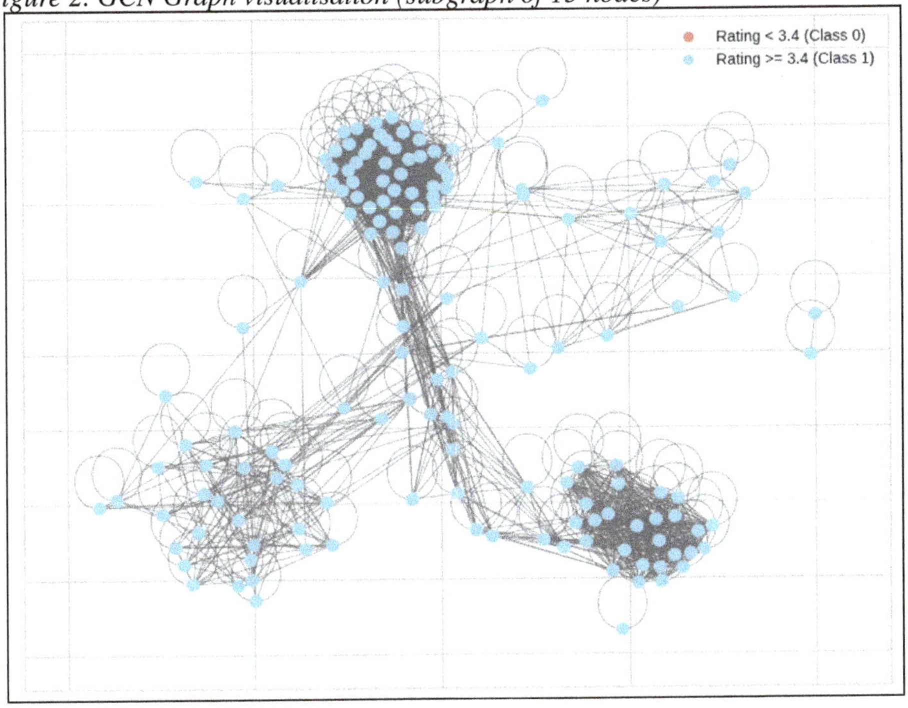

4.3.5 Sensitivity Analysis of Topological and Feature Engineering Choices

To assess the graph construction methodology for architectural resilience, a sensitivity analysis was conducted on two fundamental design variables: Edge filtering threshold limits and Node Feature Attribute Combinations. Next, to assess the impact of choosing which features to use for a given cosine similarity space, we compared the performance of GNN-SAGE against three different configurations using varying sets of node features:

Configuration A (only Spatial Metadata - City, State, Geolocation) – An accuracy of 64.2% and an AUC of .695 were achieved. The spatial metadata alone does not provide sufficient information about qualitative attractions in remote locations, so the GNN forms only close-proximity connections.

Configuration B (only Semantic-Categorical Features - Category, Service Type, Sentiment) – An accuracy of 78.5% and an AUC of .812 were achieved. However, this configuration does not allow modelling localised constraints based on visitor density.

Configuration C (fully integrated Spatial-Semantic Feature Vector - Proposed) – The highest performance level of 98.0% accuracy and an AUC of .982 were achieved when all the dimensions were used together to create a unified vector representation that allows for accurate computation of true relational similarity.

4.4 Classification Results and Performance Assessment

The purpose of this chapter was to show how each model performed, as well as the performance metrics for all models in the different evaluation settings. We are trying to build a classification framework that can classify accurately and consistently across different types of analyses. Any predictive framework has to perform in the realities of a working environment with diverse datasets, varied behaviours, and dynamic service systems. A practitioner wants more than just good results; they want the models to demonstrate performance, use entire datasets (including new or unknown items), and adapt to the increasing complexity of the tourism environment. The tourism business environment includes numerous components such as geographic areas, consumer behaviour, operating parameters, existing resources and other variables specific to each sector. Therefore, the classification models we develop should move beyond merely assessing features and instead incorporate additional domain knowledge to aid learning. Because the tourism business involves a number of interdependent variables, we require classification models that capture these dependencies while remaining easy for consumers to understand and scalable to address the demands of a rapidly growing ecosystem. An important factor in developing dependable classification models is that they provide understandable decision-making pathways and can process continually growing volumes of data from emerging tourism ecosystems. As planners and managers make decisions based on predictive information, it is crucial that scalable models produce interpretable results. This investigation attempts to determine which modelling methodology is best suited to building smart tourism systems. Examples of potential uses for these systems include recommendation systems, destination ranking systems, and decision-aid systems used by tourism authorities, policymakers, and service operators to assist them with planning, resource allocation, and service enhancements. By enabling data-driven decision-making, reliable classification models also enhance the predictive capability of tourism analytics through their core functions. Intelligent tourism systems, such as modern recommendation systems and decision-aid platforms, heavily rely on classification models that deliver consistent, accurate and contextually aware results over a broad range of operational conditions.

4.4.1 Evaluation Metrics and Experimental Setup

The experimental research design was utilised by the research team in order to test the effectiveness of several possible models; however, they also developed the testing environment to be as free of influence as possible. Stratified cross-validation maintained the original class distributions present throughout the entire experiment. It has been shown to reduce sampling bias and assist in assessing model performance, especially when the data being tested are highly imbalanced. In this research, two methods were used to measure each model's classification performance: Classification Accuracy and the Area Under the Receiver Operating Characteristic Curve (AUC). The accuracy metric measures the proportion of correct classifications across all tourism service classifications, allowing users to assess each model's performance. However, accuracy alone may not provide sufficient information about model reliability in imbalanced classification problems; these problems typically require different thresholds. The AUC method assesses a model's performance by measuring its ability to distinguish between positive and negative results across various threshold levels. Unlike accuracy, AUC does not rely on a particular threshold for assessment. Given the variety of uses of travel rating predictions and the potential need for different decision boundaries, using both accuracy and AUC will enable researchers to evaluate predictive systems' performance in an unbiased manner.

4.4.2 Exclusion of Overfitting-Prone Models

In the test phase, evidence emerged that both the Decision Tree and Random Forest algorithmic approaches achieved optimal classification results, given the balance of the pre-processed dataset. The preliminary indications were encouraging, indicating that the system was capable of making fairly accurate predictions. The study noted two particular applications for evaluation, as the researchers used resampling techniques to address class imbalances in their original dataset. Resampling is intended to improve class representation; however, it also generates synthetic patterns that are irrelevant to the real-world distributions of the observed data. The learning process establishes three separate conditions under which tree-based models are more prone to error: they attempt to store all available training data, resulting in highly accurate (but narrow) decisional boundaries. The model demonstrates perfect accuracy on the training data generated through resampling, yet it is unable to produce correct predictions on unobserved data. In addition to achieving high levels of accuracy on training and validation datasets, this result does not accurately reflect the model's ability to generate predictive values in a realistic application context. In other words, the system generates higher quality results by preserving patterns in the resampled data, which may produce spurious increases in performance. The extensive use of resampled data yields models that prioritise specific details over general concepts, leading to accurate training predictions that fail to perform when new tourism data are introduced. The problem worsens because tourism analytics rely on datasets that continually evolve as visitor behaviour shifts, seasonal patterns change, and new tourist destinations emerge. The final evaluation requires these models because their presence introduces errors that lead to misjudgments of their actual performance in real-world settings. The apparent performance advantage of these systems does not guarantee reliable decision-making when implemented in real-world business operations. Overfitting poses two problems for the model: it reduces system robustness and prevents it from learning from new tourism data, thereby impairing the trustworthiness of the prediction system. The final assessment excluded tree-based models to preserve our research methods, whereas the performance comparison was conducted to demonstrate the real-world knowledge-assessment capability. A valid research process requires comparative analysis and the use of models that develop skills that remain effective across different types of data. Dynamic tourism environments require this ability because their services, destinations, and user functions are continually transforming.

Table 3. Performance Comparison of Machine Learning and Graph Neural Network Models

Model	Accuracy (%)	AUC
Logistic Regression	52±0.3	0.871
Naïve Bayes	79±0.5	0.892
SVM	85.3±0.1	0.915
KNN	94.7±1.8	0.996
GNN-GCN	50±0.7	0.940
GNN-SAGE	**98±0.4**	**0.982**
GNN-GAT	85.5±0.8	0.946

4.4.3 Performance of Traditional Machine Learning Models

Traditional ML models have been compared with GNN models, revealing differences in performance on the tourism rating prediction task. The findings show that both feature-based models and relational learning models have distinct strengths across the three main aspects: forecasting, system scalability, and learning from the environment. Linear logistic regression is the worst-performing classifier in terms of predictive accuracy amongst the traditional classification algorithms. This poor performance results from the fact that linear decision boundaries cannot represent or account for all non-linear interactions present in a tourism data set. Traditional linear modelling techniques suffer from their inability to capture the interdependent relationship among multiple variables that influence the development of tourist destinations. KNN achieved higher predictive accuracy than many traditional classification algorithms and a better area under the ROC curve (AUC), primarily because it leverages local similarities within a dataset of tourism services. Through instance-based learning, KNN learns how to predict by identifying nearby patterns in the feature space. The primary advantages of using KNN include its ability to use instance-based learning and identify local patterns, but these advantages come at the expense of limited scalability. The reason KNN can be so limited in scale is that each prediction must compare against all available data points. For example, if we wanted to perform some form of analysis across a very large number of tourism-related data sets, there would be no way for us to make meaningful comparisons without being overwhelmed by the time required. As a result, our system does not currently have sufficient processing power to handle a large volume of tourism-related data, such as that found in tourism analytics work. Graph-based learning models delivered superior performance compared with most other classification methods, simply because they could recognise relationships among tourist locations. Traditional feature-based models failed to see these relationships, while graph-based models used connection between nodes to create context around relationships that may otherwise go unseen. GNN-SAGE achieved the best possible accuracy of 98% and an AUC of 0.982, as shown in Figure 3. GNN-SAGE's ability to combine node-level data with data from neighbouring nodes allowed it to create a much larger and more accurate representation of the world than traditional models. Using contextual information about similar tourist attractions allowed GNN-SAGE to discover patterns that other models had missed. As illustrated by our experimental results, GNNs can classify tourism ratings significantly better than traditional ML methods. Classifiers for the tourism service system must address both components in an integrated manner. Unlike traditional classifiers, traditional classifiers consider features individually rather than together.

Figure 3. ROC curves generated by applying traditional ML and GNN classifiers

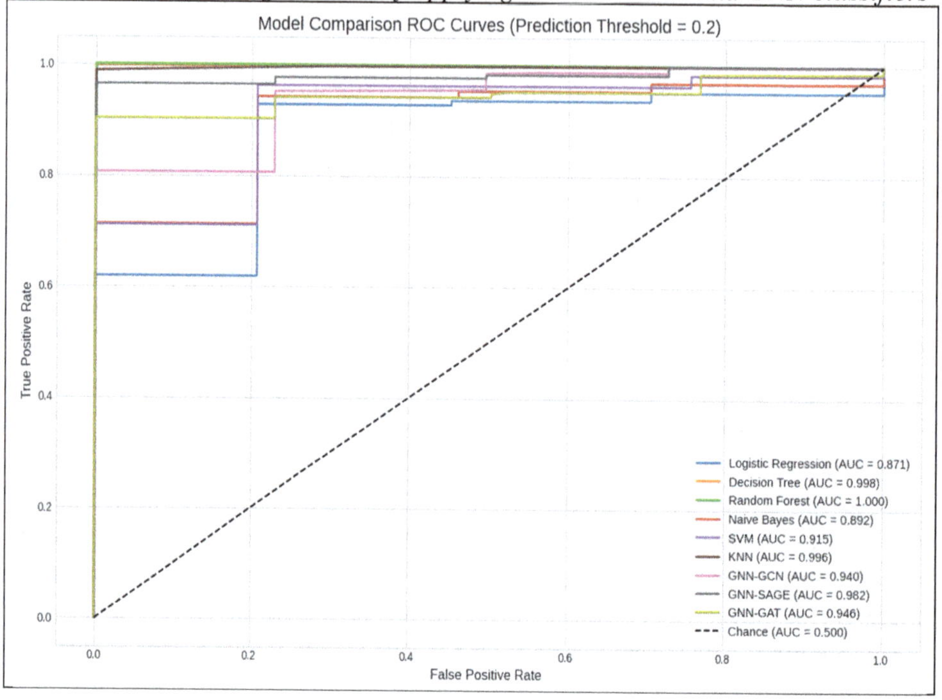

Naïve Bayes yielded moderate results, but its performance was limited by its assumption of feature independence. Tourists face challenges in predicting service outcomes because they must consider multiple tourism service attributes, including location category and visitor engagement, as reported in reference 3. The Support Vector Machine achieved improved performance because margin-based optimisation techniques are effective in standardised feature spaces and can, to some extent, capture nonlinear boundaries. The K-Nearest Neighbours algorithm achieved high AUC values by leveraging local similarity patterns among tourism entities. The algorithm produced different outcomes because the system depended on two components: distance measures and neighbourhood size. The system requires more computational power to handle larger datasets, thereby reducing its ability to perform effective tourism analytics, according to research. The results of the study demonstrate that relational modelling is an essential approach for forecasting tourism ratings, whereas traditional feature-based learning approaches fail to capture contextual dependencies.

4.4.4 Performance of Graph Neural Network Models

The system evaluated GNN models on a graph with standardised similarity-based features, as this configuration enabled it to identify individual attribute patterns and their relationships with various tourism services. GNNs use local data to assess connected nodes, enabling them to capture both specific attributes and the interrelationships that bind different nodes, setting them apart from conventional ML approaches. This feature is an important resource for tourism analysis because it enables researchers to examine human behaviour alongside service perceptions, derived from proximity to various sites and from similarities among sites based on their themes and corresponding behavioural patterns. The core building blocks of advanced graph-based tourism recommendation systems and decision-support platforms are interlinked representations of interconnected graph structures. Different implementations of GNN architectures showed variability in performance due to differences in design components and learning methodologies. Specifically, the GNN-GCN architecture yielded relatively low accuracy compared to other graph-based methods. This is because the propagation of information across the layers of the graph ultimately leads to extreme over-smoothing, rendering the resulting node representations nearly indistinguishable from one another. In contrast, the use of an attention mechanism in the GNN-GAT architecture significantly improved predictive performance by allowing the model to assign varying importance to adjacent nodes. By utilising this method, the model focuses on key relationships and excludes non-relevant ones. Both aspects -- namely, graph density and edge distribution patterns -- influence the system's performance. Previous research has demonstrated that changes in how individual components interact affect the determination of attention weights, thereby influencing both model reliability and accuracy. The GNN-SAGE architecture exhibited the best classification performance (i.e., 98 per cent accuracy with an area under the curve of 0.982) among all tested models, thereby demonstrating superior predictive capability for evaluating tourism services. GNN-SAGE operates efficiently by applying an inductive neighbourhood aggregation methodology. The model aggregates multiple types of information for each node (while preserving each's distinctiveness), thereby enabling the generation of higher-quality representations of tourism destinations. As such, the model is effective at processing unstructured data and adapting to environmental changes (e.g., the emergence of new destinations and evolving visitor preferences) within tourism ecosystems. Because the tourism ecosystem continues to evolve due to the emergence of new destinations, shifting preferences, and the availability of additional services, GraphSAGE's inductive capabilities enable it to generalise beyond previously trained nodes and utilise newly available data without necessitating full retraining. As such, it appears that GraphSAGE demonstrates adaptability to projectable needs, as evidenced by prior empirical research in real-world tourism settings.

4.4.5 Comparative Analysis and Model Selection

Graph-based learning has been shown to be better at predicting tourism ratings than traditional ML approaches. The main difference lies in the type of learning used in the traditional approach. Traditional approaches use feature-level learning, in which all features related to a particular service must be analysed separately. Each service may have unique features; therefore, each would require individual analysis based on its features. The primary disadvantage of using a feature-level learning approach is that it does not capture complex relationships among destinations or visitor behaviour. Examples of such relationships include travel behaviours, geographic location, and visitor preferences.

GNNs represent these relationships between tourism destinations via connection(s) between these entities. Connections exist for several reasons, including geographic proximity, thematic similarities, and similar interests/attributes among visitors. These types of relationships provide context to help identify patterns hidden in traditional feature-based models. GNNs can improve the model's prediction accuracy while also offering insights into patterns of tourist behaviour.

Of the three GNN models studied, GraphSAGE was the most effective. One reason for this effectiveness is that GraphSAGE is scalable and adaptable across many environments while retaining its ability to utilise contextual information to make predictions. In addition to being able to scale well, GraphSAGE creates a representation of a destination by combining node-specific data with its neighbours. Therefore, GraphSAGE can extract patterns associated with similarity (e.g., what makes one destination similar to another) and interaction (e.g., how do visitors interact with different services). These patterns are very valuable for analysing tourism trends because they highlight how different contextual factors influence both visitors' perceptions and experiences.

4.4.6 Explanation of Accuracy and AUC Results

Table 3 illustrates the outcome of all classifiers' evaluations. Accuracy and AUC were chosen as the primary indicators for evaluating each classifier's performance. Accuracy represents the number of samples correctly classified by the model. Area Under the Curve (AUC) represents the average time it takes the model to classify an example. Both accuracy and AUC values were reported with their respective standard deviations to provide quantitative information on the variance in classification accuracy. The non-parametric model showed a relatively stable level of precision (highest standard deviation) compared to the other models; however, its precision was very low (approximately 52.0% ± 0.3%) due to extreme underfitting caused by the linear nature of its decision boundaries. On the other hand, traditional instance-based classifiers like kNN relied heavily on the neighbourhood of features around each training example and therefore exhibited high accuracy variance (94.7% ± 1.8%). Therefore, the three metrics together provide two distinct views of model performance: overall predictive power and the ability to accurately distinguish between performance levels. The accuracy of classification of tourism services represents the proportion of correctly classified tourism services out of the total number of tourism services, while AUC represents the model's ability to differentiate among classes at many decision points. Each ML classifier type produced multiple test results because it was assessed across various testing scenarios. Since tourism datasets involve complex interactions among variables, logistic regression, which assumes linear relationships, yields poor accuracy. Although naïve Bayes can be more accurate than logistic regression, it still suffers from the same limitations because it assumes feature independence. Because SVM constructs optimal decision boundaries in high-dimensional feature spaces, it performs better than other types of ML. SVM used margin-based optimisation techniques to better capture non-linear relationships among variables and produce better accuracy and AUC. k-NN achieves a good AUC because it captures local similarity patterns in the dataset. However, both neighbourhood size and distance metrics need to be specified in order to use k-nn effectively. These metrics can pose problems when dealing with large volumes of tourism data. The system maintained its operational capacity because the graph's design and node arrangement determined how attention was distributed and results were produced. GraphSAGE achieved the highest accuracy (98%) and AUC (0.982), making it the top-performing model among the approaches evaluated. The model's inductive neighbourhood aggregation mechanism enables learning from node-level features and contextual relationships while preserving each destination's distinct characteristics. The combination of relational learning and feature representation enables GraphSAGE to produce consistent predictions across different threshold values. The GraphSAGE algorithm achieved better results because it used relational modelling together with tourism data analysis. The model achieves excellent generalisation and prediction accuracy by capturing contextual relationships while preserving individual node attributes. The research results demonstrate that graph-based learning methods are effective for predicting tourism ratings, which should be used in recommendation systems and intelligent decision support systems.

4.4.7 Error Case Analysis and Limitations

The inductive GNN-SAGE approach achieved a state-of-the-art classification accuracy for tourist destinations (98.0%); however, a full diagnostic assessment was conducted to investigate the reasons for the 2.0% errors observed in 21 samples (out of 1061 tourist destination samples). There are only two possible types of failures:

Failure Type I: High Popularity/Structural Bias (false positives): Several lesser-known areas with low service and structural ratings (< 3.4; Class 0) were incorrectly classified as highly rated (Class 1). These errors resulted from the fact that the area surrounding these smaller sites has numerous other well-reviewed tourist attractions that have many reviews. Thus, the GNN's message-passing mechanism propagated the most frequently occurring positive structural information from these larger areas to their neighbouring weaker areas. As a result, excessive smoothing throughout the area causes the lower-rated neighbour's rating to be "over-smoothed" away, so it no longer reflects its original low rating. Failure Type II: Multi-thematic ambiguity (false negatives): Areas with higher-than-average ratings (>= 3.4; Class 1) that also contain very atypical, multi-use operational attributes (for example, a resort that serves as both a historical site, spiritual site, recreation site and ecological preservation site) had too many diluted semantically similar features. Since these locations do not provide strong evidence of belonging to a particular category, their cosine similarity values with all neighbouring locations were below the chosen threshold (τ=0.85). Therefore, when computing the aggregated vector representation of each location within the hierarchical layers of this model, it received insufficient contextual support and was identified as a relatively isolated node within the network layer.

For both tourism planners and travel platform developers, this GNN-based rating prediction model provides a tool to mitigate popularity bias in travel destination ratings. By enabling the evaluation of unobserved (spatial-semantic) characteristics of links between users or locations, the model can support a recommendation engine's proactive presentation of lesser-known but potentially appealing travel options aligned with a given user's preferences. As such, it will help balance economic growth at the regional level and alleviate problems associated with excessive tourist traffic.

4.4.8 Data Biases and Representative Limitations

Data quality can be compromised by the inherent biases and representative limitations of the curated crowdsourced dataset used in the proposed analytics framework. Thus, for empirical transparency and ethical considerations in the proposed analytics framework, it will be essential to identify and critically examine the inherent data biases and representational limitations within the dataset.

Popularity Biases and Structural Skewness: A large amount of User-Generated Content (UGC) collected using Web Scraping techniques is likely to have a strong popularity bias because globally recognised, tier-1 heritage destinations and urban tourist hubs (i.e. historical sites in larger metropolitan areas) are going to generate an order-of-magnitude greater number of reviews than smaller, less populated areas or ecotourism destinations. This population disparity introduces structural skewness when constructing a graph-based learning environment, as high-population hubs act as highly connected "super-nodes," and neighbourhood message-passing layers may excessively smooth features from these super-nodes onto adjacent, less-connected peripheral regions, possibly obscuring local service characteristics that are not evident at lesser-known tourism venues.

Positivity Bias in Digital Feedback Cycles: The binary classification target distribution exhibited significant positivity bias, i.e., a documented psychological phenomenon in Hospitality Analytics, where positive traveller experiences are much more likely to generate formal online feedback than those that were neither positive nor significantly negative. Although our framework employed minority-class bootstrap up-sampling to create an equal-probability space of target-label experience types, the baseline data still exhibits demographics associated with digitally active consumers (i.e., vocal customers) and thus does not reflect the full range of passively engaged tourists.

Socio-Demographics Representation Limits: The use of Google Maps Review Data creates an inherent demographic sampling bias. Specifically, there is a sampling bias toward tech-literate smartphone users, both domestically and internationally, who access location-based services while travelling. As such, the behaviours of other tourist segments, including but not limited to: older pilgrim travellers, lower-income rural travellers, and/or off-grid leisure travellers who do not use online travel marketplaces, will remain underrepresented in this framework. Future versions of the framework should integrate diverse non-platform-based offline metadata, government foot-traffic registers, and physical surveys to mitigate the aforementioned platform-related representation limits.

5. CONCLUSION

This chapter develops a unified analytical framework integrating ML methods and GNN architectures to build an all-encompassing system for tourism service classification and rating prediction. The research shows that user-generated evaluation indicators become effective tools for measuring tourism service quality when researchers apply structured preprocessing and relational modelling techniques to their assessment process. The proposed method improves tourism data analysis by capturing features and contextual relationships that traditional analytical methods cannot. The framework transforms diverse tourism data into graph-compatible formats, enabling researchers to apply relational learning methods to improve model evaluation and prediction accuracy. The method of building similarity-based graphs is one of the most important ways to reveal hidden relationships among tourism entities, thereby enabling the detection of interrelationships between environmental conditions (such as locations) and the ways these are experienced by users. In addition, the graph structure shows large amounts of connections between neighbourhoods. This enables GNNs to perform neighbour aggregation and propagate information within each neighbourhood. Therefore, it improves predictive power. The research demonstrated that traditional ML classifiers perform well with preprocessing methods and class-balancing techniques; however, there are limits to their ability to capture the complex relationships among tourism destinations. The classifiers can only represent features at a level of individual locations. Because the models use graph-based methods to learn both node attributes and relationships between nodes, they can achieve higher predictive performance. As mentioned above, Tree-based Models were not considered in the final assessment because they exhibited excessive overfitting on resampled training sets. Thus, they were used to consider all possible methods and to assess whether the other methods could adequately evaluate their performance. GraphSAGE achieved the highest predictive accuracy among the tested methods. It does so by utilising the inductive learning paradigm to combine node feature representations and neighbourhood information. The system has developed the capability to derive new knowledge from existing knowledge and to develop new tourism destinations, services, and user interactions. Users need the ability to analyse results from multiple data sources to create flexible solutions that meet the varying requirements of their operational environments. The results of the research indicate that graph-based relational learning methods are effective in predicting tourist ratings and developing recommendation systems. However, additional development of the framework is needed in subsequent studies to include temporal elements. Temporal elements would allow researchers to examine seasonal tourism trends or changes in visitor preferences. Additionally, integration of user behavioural data, social interaction data, and a variety of tourism-related data sources (including multimedia materials and real-time user feedback) will enhance the system's predictive capabilities. Furthermore, expanding the framework to develop an adaptive, real-time recommendation system will create sophisticated decision-making tools that support tourism planning and management, promote sustainable tourism development, and improve the user experience.

REFERENCES

Ahanger, A. S., Khan, S. M., Masoodi, F., & Salau, A. O. (2025). Advanced intrusion detection in internet of things using graph attention networks. *Scientific Reports*, *15*(1), Article 9831. DOI: 10.1038/s41598-025-09831-x

Chen, J., Luo, X., Yuan, Y., & Wang, Z. (2025). Enhancing graph convolutional networks with an efficient k-hop neighborhood approach. *Information Fusion*, *124*. *Information Fusion, 103297*, 103297. Advance online publication. DOI: 10.1016/j.inffus.2025.103297

Cheng, D., Zou, Y., Xiang, S., & Jiang, C. (2025). Graph neural networks for financial fraud detection: A review. *Frontiers of Computer Science*, *19*(9), Article 199609. DOI: 10.1007/s11704-025-199609-x

Haider Rizvi, S. M., Imran, R., & Mahmood, A. (2025). Text classification using graph convolutional networks: A comprehensive survey. *ACM Computing Surveys*, *57*(8), 1–38. DOI: 10.1145/3698123

He, Z., Zhang, Q., Song, M., Tan, X., & Wang, W. (2025). Four overlooked errors in ROC analysis: How to prevent and avoid. *BMJ Evidence-Based Medicine*, *30*(3), 208–211. DOI: 10.1136/bmjebm-2024-112000

Jamatia, A., Baidya, U., & Paul, S. DebBarma, S., & Dey, S. (2020). Rating prediction of tourist destinations based on supervised machine learning algorithms. In *Advances in Intelligent Systems and Computing* (Vol. 990, pp. 453–465). Springer. DOI: 10.1007/978-981-13-8406-6_41

Khalisa, T. N., & Ramadhani, D. P. (2025, January). *Exploring tourist perceptions of Greater Bandung tourism destinations: An IndoBERT-based big data analytics study on Google Maps reviews* [Paper presentation]. *2025 International Conference on Computer Sciences, Engineering, and Technology Innovation (ICoCSETI)*, IEEE. DOI: 10.1109/ICoCSETI63724.2025.11020554

Li, B., Li, R., Wang, J., & Song, A. (2025). Tourism sentiment chain representation model and construction from tourist reviews. *Future Internet*, *17*(7), Article 276. DOI: 10.3390/fi17070276

Li, G., Chen, X., & Wang, Y. (2019). A novel recommendation system for tourist spots based on hierarchical sampling and matrix factorization. *Mathematical Problems in Engineering*, *2019*. *Article, 8170293*. Advance online publication. DOI: 10.1155/2019/8170293

Luo, L. (2025). RARE: Right Algorithm for the Right Errand – A graph-based multi-model approach for tourism route and spot recommendation. *PeerJ Computer Science*, *11*, Article e2412. DOI: 10.7717/peerj-cs.2412

Puh, K., & Bagić Babac, M. (2023). Predicting sentiment and ratings of tourist reviews using machine learning techniques. *Journal of Hospitality and Tourism Insights*, *6*(4), 1542–1563. DOI: 10.1108/JHTI-04-2022-0143

Raha, S., & Deb, S. (2025). Tourism potential zone mapping using multi-criteria decision making and machine learning models. *GeoPlanning: Journal of Geomatics and Planning*, *12*(1), 45–60. DOI: 10.14710/geoplanning.12.1.45-60

Riesthuis, P., Otgaar, H., & Bücken, C. (2025). Ready to ROC? A tutorial on simulation-based power analyses for null hypothesis significance, minimum-effect, and equivalence testing for ROC curve analyses. *Behavior Research Methods*, *57*(4), Article 120. DOI: 10.3758/s13428-025-0120-x

Sadasivan, A., Gananathan, K., Pal Nesamony Rose Mary, J. D., & Balasubramanian, S. (2025). A systematic survey of graph convolutional networks for artificial intelligence applications. *Wiley Interdisciplinary Reviews: Data Mining and Knowledge Discovery*, *15*(2), Article e70012. DOI: 10.1002/widm.70012

Song, B., Li, R., Wang, J., & Song, A. (2024, August). *APRRGM: Accurate point-of-interest recommendation for random groups via attentive bipartite graph neural networks*. In *Proceedings of the 30th ACM SIGKDD International Conference on Knowledge Discovery and Data Mining (KDD '24)* (pp. 1102–1111). Association for Computing Machinery. DOI: 10.1145/3637528.3671890

Wang, H., Li, Y., Santos, T., & Khan, A. (2023). Attentive sequential graph neural networks for next POI and rating prediction in tourism analytics. *ACM Transactions on Information Systems*, *40*(2), 45–67. DOI: 10.1145/3543612

Zhang, O., Lin, H., Zhang, X., Wang, X., Wu, Z., Ye, Q., Zhao, W., Wang, J., Ying, K., Kang, Y., & Hsieh, C. Y. (2025). Graph neural networks in modern AI-aided drug discovery. *Chemical Reviews*, *125*(20), 10001–10103. DOI: 10.1021/acs.chemrev.4c00213

Zuo, Y., Wu, M., & Shen, L. (2024). GUGEN: Global user graph enhanced network for spatio-temporal point-of-interest recommendation. *IEEE Transactions on Knowledge and Data Engineering*, *36*(4), 1845–1858. DOI: 10.1109/TKDE.2023.3314561

Chapter 11
AI-Based User Experience Improvement of Online Book Retail Platforms:
A Case Study of MyBookOne

Xianting Ma
http://orcid.org/0009-0003-3812-1211
The University of Hong Kong, Hong Kong

Apple Hiu Ching Lam
http://orcid.org/0000-0002-2587-6979
The University of Hong Kong, Hong Kong

Dickson K. W. Chiu
http://orcid.org/0000-0002-7926-9568
The University of Hong Kong, Hong Kong

ABSTRACT

This chapter investigates the systematic improvement of the comprehensive user experience of online book retail platforms by integrating artificial intelligence technologies, proposing a set of improvements for the platform MyBookOne as a case study. We analyzed the MyBookOne platform using the literature, guided by the DeLone & McLean Information System Success (D&M) model and the 5Es usability model. Problems with system quality, information quality, and service quality were revealed. To address these problems, we propose a systematic AI-based approach that includes measures such as intelligent semantic search, personalized recommendation and screening, AIGC content enhancement, interactive guidance, intelligent customer service, and improvements in information depth and transparency. This study contributes to the field by innovatively integrating the D&M and

DOI: 10.4018/979-8-3373-9325-4.ch011

5Es models, providing an integrated framework for user experience evaluation and digital platform enhancements, as well as a systematic AI-based scheme to improve similar cultural e-commerce platforms.

1 INTRODUCTION

With the rapid development of the digital economy, the retail industry is undergoing great changes. Online retail has become an important channel. Users can complete browsing, ordering, after-sales, and other processes on the online platform (Kumar, 2025). Competition in e-commerce is intensifying, and user experience has become a focus of online retail (Tiutiu & Dabija, 2023). The emergence of artificial intelligence has created unprecedented opportunities for developing retail platforms. AI can be used for personalized recommendations, intelligent customer service, and related applications, thereby improving the platform's operational efficiency and altering users' purchasing behavior and experience (Mustafa Ayobami Raji et al., 2024). In the shopping process, users not only consider the cost-effectiveness of goods but also the overall shopping experience (Chen et al., 2021).

As an important part of retail, book retail has gradually shifted from traditional physical bookstores to a comprehensive online platform. However, due to the wide variety of books and users' diverse interests, traditional online bookstores face challenges such as retrieval difficulties and limited recommendations. Users not only seek transaction convenience but also value services such as discovering personalized content and in-depth decision-making support. The services provided by the online platform do not fully meet users' needs.

Against this background, this study takes MyBookOne, Hong Kong's largest online book shopping platform, as a case. The platform aggregates the resources of many well-known publishing houses such as “Hong Kong Business Printing House”, “Hong Kong Sanlian”, and “Zhonghe Publishing”, provides rich, genuine books through the “store-in-store” model, and sets up special columns such as “Theme Bookstore” and “Book Review”, with a good content foundation and brand credibility. However, when using the platform, it is found that its service model still follows traditional e-commerce logic, providing only basic functions such as search, classification, and purchase. There is still significant room to increase attractiveness, improve decision-making efficiency, and lower the operating threshold.

This study aims to provide a systematic solution to the platform's existing problems and improve the user experience. The core goal is to build an AI-driven plan to improve users’ experience on online book retail platforms and to analyze it across three levels: system quality, information quality, and service quality. Among them, system quality is analyzed across five dimensions: effectiveness, efficiency, engagement, error tolerance, and ease of learning. This study provides detailed application design and path-planning for the MyBookOne platform.

At the theoretical level, this research integrates the success model of information systems with the IS success model and the 5Es model, systematically designing a user experience analysis framework that incorporates AI into the design of e-commerce platform user experience. At the practical level, this study outlines a clear path for AI technology adoption on e-commerce platforms, such as MyBookOne, which is complete and operational. In terms of social values, the research results can improve users' experience and efficiency in knowledge acquisition, promote the effective dissemination of knowledge and the development of in-depth reading habits, and indirectly contribute to achieving the goal of quality education (SDG 4) under the United Nations Sustainable Development Goals.

This research employs the case study method and adheres to academic ethics. All analysis is based on the public observation of the MyBookOne website and relevant industry reports and academic literature. The structure of the chapter is as follows. The second part conducts a literature review; the third part conducts an in-depth analysis of the current situation and pain points of the MyBookOne platform; the fourth part elaborates on AI-driven solutions; the fifth part discusses the mechanism, challenges, and implementation strategies; finally, it summarizes the full text, analyzes the shortcomings, and suggests future research directions.

2 LITERATURE REVIEW

The Digital Transformation of the Book Retail Industry

The rise of e-books and audiobooks has driven the digital transformation of book retail, and paper books have gradually shifted to two sales channels: traditional physical bookstores and online platforms (Jiang & Katsamakas, 2010). The emergence of digital platforms has weakened traditional physical retail's control over users, and users' decision-making has shifted from in-store shelves to mobile devices (Reinartz et al., 2018). In traditional retail, books rely on physical attributes such as covers and paper to create product advantages. However, in the digital environment, these advantages are weakened, and users pay more attention to non-physical attributes such as content depth, breadth of subject matter, IP operations, etc. (Miller & Wang, 2024). Driven by digital, the retail business model is following a similar path of innovation. Integrate from a single channel to a multi-channel, provide high-quality services and user experience while selling products, and drive business decision-making and automation processes with advanced technologies such as AI and big data (Mostaghel et al., 2022).

User Experience Evaluation of Digital Platforms

The evaluation and optimization of user experience are important focuses of digital platform design. Among many evaluation models, the 5Es model proposed by Whitney Quesenbery has become a widely recognized evaluation framework in both academia and industry due to its comprehensiveness, structure, and strong operability. It transforms the abstract concept of "user experience" into specific and measurable research questions.

Quesenbery (2004) proposed the 5Es usability model to evaluate software platforms, systematically breaking down user experience into five distinct dimensions: Effective, Efficient, Engaging, Error-tolerant, and Easy to learn, which laid the theoretical groundwork for subsequent e-learning evaluations. Adi et al. (2024) analyzed the user experience of the teacher development platform, using the 5Es model as a framework to summarize the experience and to form a systematic list of problems and suggestions for improvement.

Matraf et al. (2025) developed an e-book platform for visually impaired patients, used the 5Es model to identify their needs, and ensured those needs were met. The 5Es model is also used to evaluate user experience across multiple scenarios. Huang & Li (2019) used the 5Es model to evaluate user experience for computer input devices and combined it with the AHP method to obtain quantitative weights. Baj-Rogowska & Sikorski (2023) combined 5Es with text mining to analyze user comments on social media applications and identify pain points in the experience. The above analysis shows that the 5Es model provides a multidimensional, structured theoretical framework for user experience analysis and demonstrates strong adaptability across various application scenarios, especially in software platforms.

The DeLone & McLean Information System Success model (also known as the D&M model) is also used in a large number of studies. In the early days, Lin (2007) applied the D&M model to the online learning system and found that system quality, information quality, and service quality significantly affect actual use through satisfaction and intention to use.

Later, research on e-learning systems revealed that system quality significantly affects the use and satisfaction. Both use and satisfaction positively influence system success (Efiloğlu Kurt, 2019). Some scholars use the D&M model to analyze user experience on different online platforms, such as travel voucher booking platforms (Viriando, 2021) and real estate platforms (Ullah et al., 2021). And in digital services, examine how information, functions, systems, and services affect the overall experience through perceptions of satisfaction, cost, and processes (Mustafa et al., 2020). The above analysis shows that the D&M model can be used to analyze the system architecture and user experience of the online platform, has strong interpretive power, and provides a stable theoretical framework.

Application of Artificial Intelligence in User Experience

There has been extensive research on applying artificial intelligence to improve the platform's user experience, and remarkable results have been achieved. AI-driven personalized recommendations and dynamic pricing can reduce decision-making fatigue and input errors, and improve user satisfaction and process efficiency, such as hotel reservations (Ibirinoye-Abdulkareem et al., 2025) and the government e-Permitting System (Sneha Deepika Kalagarla, 2025).

Existing relevant artificial intelligence technologies can automatically adjust layout, components, and interaction processes in real time through behavior analysis and generative models to optimize user participation and satisfaction (Alti & Lakehal, 2025). Machine learning algorithms can guide UI optimization by analyzing user behavior data, such as page views and dwell time (Liu et al., 2024). And platforms can use algorithms, such as deep neural networks in AI, to personalize content recommendations and interface layouts, thereby increasing indicators such as session duration and retention rate (Kalathot, 2025).

Research Gap and Research Questions

Although existing studies have widely applied the D&M and 5Es models across various digital platforms, few have explored their integration. Most D&M model applications in e-commerce focus on overall system success but do not provide a detailed diagnosis of the user experience. Meanwhile, most 5Es model applications focus solely on usability without linking to business outcomes. This study addresses this gap by integrating the two models to provide a more comprehensive evaluation framework. Moreover, research on improving user experience on comprehensive cultural e-commerce platforms is insufficient. In particular, a traditional online book platform like MyBookOne has a solid content foundation, but has encountered obvious user experience bottlenecks. At present, there is no in-depth case study to formulate a systematic AI-driven optimization strategy for it. Therefore, this study focuses on the following research questions:

RQ1: How to build an integrated theoretical analysis framework to connect the macro-success dimension of the digital platform with the micro-user experience dimension?

RQ2: How to use this integrated framework to reveal the shortcomings and pain points of online book retail platforms like MyBookOne in terms of user experience?

RQ3: How to design a systematic solution driven by AI technology to effectively improve the overall user experience of the MyBookOne platform and promote its overall success?

3 THEORETICAL FRAMEWORK

DeLone & McLean Information System Success Model

Since its introduction, the DeLone & McLean Information System Success model (D&M model) has become one of the most influential theories for evaluating the value of information technology investment. The model holds that the success of an information system is a multidimensional, dynamic process. The 2003 version clearly stated that system quality, information quality, and service quality are three key dimensions that together affect users' willingness and satisfaction, and that these behaviors and attitudes ultimately lead to net benefits for individuals and organizations, fostering continued system use. The online book retail platform is regarded as a complex information system, and the model can be analyzed from the following dimensions (Prasetyo et al., 2021; Widyaningrum et al., 2024):

- System quality: the technical performance, functional availability, and interaction fluency of the platform itself.
- Information quality: the accuracy, completeness, and timeliness of the book metadata (title, author), description, book review, and other contents provided by the platform.
- Service quality refers to the support the platform provides to users, including customer service and after-sales support.
- Net income: For users, it is the efficient acquisition of favorite books and the pleasure of knowledge; for the platform, it is the growth of sales, user loyalty, and market share.

5Es Usability Model

To make a concrete and measurable evaluation of the abstract "system quality", this study introduces the 5Es usability model proposed by Whitney Quesenbery as its operational definition. The 5Es model analyzes the user's experience when using the system from five core dimensions (Quesenbery, 2003):

- Effectiveness: Whether users can achieve the goal accurately and completely.
- Efficiency: the time, steps, and cognitive load required for users to complete the task.
- Engagement: Whether the interface and interaction process can arouse users' interest, pleasure, and emotional input.
- Error tolerance: whether the system can prevent users from making mistakes and provide a clear recovery path after the error occurs.

- Ease of learning: Whether new users can quickly understand the system logic and master the basic operation.

These five dimensions capture the core experience of user interaction with the system and can be used to assess the platform's "system quality."

Theoretical Integration

In summary, this study takes the D&M model as the top-level logic, the 5Es model as a specific tool for diagnosing "system quality", and plans AI technology as the core means of improvement, ultimately promoting the evolution of the whole system to a more successful state. Table 1 summarizes user experience problems and their AI-based solutions.

Table 1. Limitations and AI-Driven Solutions for MyBookOne Platform

Dimensions	Limitations	AI-Driven Solutions
System quality	Effectiveness: Search only supports literal keyword matching and cannot understand natural-language intent; cannot handle pinyin input or typos; classification and recommendations are static and cannot understand user intent.	Semantic search and intention understanding: Based on the large language model, build a book semantic retrieval system, which supports natural language queries, pinyin error correction, typo correction, etc.
	Efficiency: The decision-making path is long, requiring users to click through books and compare them manually; the information display is lengthy and unstructured; and there is a lack of multidimensional screening and comparison tools.	Intelligent decision-making assistance: AI generates summary cards, readability labels, and similar book comparison tables; dynamically generates professional screening dimensions; and provides intelligent comparison tools.
	Engagement: the interface is static and homogeneous, lacking personalized and emotional design; user participation is weak.	AIGC content enhancement and personalized experience: generate multimedia content (audio, pictures, video), immersive viewing audition, personalized reading experience.
	Error Tolerance: There is no fault tolerance mechanism for input errors or out-of-stock conditions, and the task is interrupted.	Intelligent fault tolerance and guidance: search for error correction and intention speculation; recommend similar books when there are no accurate matching results, and provide arrival reminders.
	Ease of Learning: The entrance to the characteristic function is hidden and lacks guidance for novices; there is no explanation of technical terms.	Situational guidance and AI assistant: bubble prompts for new functions; AI dialogue assistant; automatic term identification and interpretation.

continued on following page

Table 1. Continued

Dimensions	Limitations	AI-Driven Solutions
Information Quality	Information accuracy: UGC (such as book reviews) may contain subjective biases and promotional content, which can affect its credibility.	Content quality control: an intelligent audit system to identify spam comments; a user credibility scoring mechanism.
	Information integrity: lack of in-depth content (such as book reviews, trial readings, comparative analyses); users need to jump to external platforms.	AIGC in-depth content generation: automatically generates a summary of core views, reader portraits, the author's background, and interpretation of key concepts.
	Information timeliness: book pages are static and disconnected from external hotspots and academic dynamics.	Dynamic information association: access external news and academic databases to update book-related hotspots, awards, and quoted information in real time.
	Information relevance: the recommended content is homogeneous, lacks personalization, and pushes information that is not related to users' interests.	Personalized recommendation system: build user portraits, build a recommendation system based on deep learning, and serve thousands of people.
	Information structure: Books are described as unstructured text, which is difficult to use efficiently.	Knowledge atlas and structured extraction: entity identification, relationship extraction, label system construction, and forming a queryable knowledge network.
Service quality	Service response: only email or message support; no real-time communication, leading to a poor experience in emergency scenarios.	Intelligent customer service robot: 7×24-hour response, handling high-frequency problems, seamless transfer of complex problems to manual.
	Privacy protection: black box of recommendation algorithms; users do not understand the recommendation logic; lack of data-use instructions.	Explainable AI and transparent communication: explain the rationale for the recommendation; ensure transparency in data use; allow users to adjust the intensity of the recommendation.
	Personalized service: the relationship ends after the transaction, lack of continuous care, and service standardization.	User life cycle management: post-purchase care emails, personalized activity push notifications, and high-value user identification and exclusive services.

Research Methodology

This study adopts a single-case design to systematically examine the user experience problems of a specific online book retail platform and to formulate targeted AI solutions. We select MyBookOne as the research object, which is the largest online book shopping platform in Hong Kong. The platform offers a comprehensive range of books and a large user base, which better represent a regional cultural e-commerce platform. At the same time, this bookstore still follows the traditional e-commerce logic. Although the functions are basically complete, there is significant room for AI-driven improvement.

To ensure the reliability of the research, we use the triangular verification method to cross-check data from multiple sources (platform observations, industry reports, academic literature). To effectively identify problems, this study first uses the DeLone & McLean information system success model to evaluate system quality, information quality, and service quality; then, the 5Es usability model is used to further decompose system quality into five micro-experience dimensions.

The D&M model provides a comprehensive macro-level framework for evaluating information system success, but it lacks granularity in diagnosing micro-level user interaction experiences. Conversely, the 5Es usability model focuses on assessing system usability but overlooks the system's overall impact. This study integrates the two models and bridges the gap between macro-level information systems success theory and micro-level user experience research. Table 2 compares the characteristics of the two models and the integrated framework proposed in this study.

Table 2. Comparison of the D&M IS Success Model, 5Es Usability Model, and Integrated Framework

Model	Analysis Level	Coverage Dimensions	Key Strengths	Key Limitations
D&M IS Success Model	Macro	System quality, information quality, service quality	Comprehensive evaluation of the overall information system success	Lacks granularity in diagnosing micro-level user interaction experiences
5Es Usability Model	Micro	Effectiveness, efficiency, engagement, error tolerance, ease of learning	User-centric and operationally measurable. Detailed assessment of system usability	Does not cover information quality or service quality dimensions
Integrated Framework	Macro + Micro	All dimensions from both the D&M and 5Es models	Combines comprehensive system-level evaluation with detailed user interaction diagnosis. Creates a unified framework for AI-driven UX improvement and business impact assessment	Requires more complex multi-level analysis

4 PLATFORM ANALYSIS BASED ON THE INTEGRATED FRAMEWORK

Based on the DeLone & McLean Information System Success Model (Delone & McLean, 2003), this chapter systematically analyzes MyBookOne across three dimensions: "system quality", "information quality", and "service quality". In the context of system quality, this study introduces the 5Es model as an evaluation tool to analyze the platform's problems in greater depth. Through this theoretical framework, we aim to go beyond the description of superficial phenomena and reveal the user experience on the platform.

"System Quality" Dimensional Evaluation

"System quality" refers to the "desirable characteristics of an information system" (Petter et al., 2008) and directly affects user interactions with the platform. Using the 5Es model, the MyBookOne platform was carefully evaluated. The problems in system quality were identified in five dimensions.

Effectiveness

The core functions of the MyBookOne platform are complete. Users can complete the core tasks of "searching-browsing-understanding-buying," but these functions do not fully meet the user's intentions.

The platform's search function only supports literal keyword matching and cannot understand natural language semantics. When the user enters "19th-century romantic novel " in the search box, their original intention is to find a novel written in the 19th century with a romantic theme. The system cannot understand the meaning of the phrase and can only mechanically match the book with the words "19th century", "romanticism", and "novel" in its title, returning unrelated search results. In addition, for the novel The Three-Body Problem, if the user uses the Chinese Pinyin "san ti" to input, the system lacks error correction and associative capabilities, and will give irrelevant results or simply no results, forming a dead end, resulting in the interruption of the search path.

Users' discovery behaviors rely on their own active search and static classification. The recommendation modules on the platform's homepage (such as "Recommends" and "Store-In-Store Recommendations") have limited coverage and do not dynamically adjust based on user behavior data. This means that if users do not have a clear book title or author, it is difficult to actively and accurately find potentially interesting books through the platform.

Effectiveness in the 5Es model is used to evaluate "whether the software is useful and helps users achieve their goals accurately" (Quesenbery, 2004), and MyBookOne failed to support users in completing the purpose of retrieving and discovering books. Tsagkias et al. (2020) noted that platform search and recommendation are key mechanisms for understanding user behavior and driving user participation. Yaswanth Jeganathan (2025) noted that search ability is a fundamental factor affecting purchasing decisions, conversion rates, and customer satisfaction. Platforms need to optimize search, classification, and personalization to maintain competitiveness in the dynamic digital market. Therefore, MyBookOne's shortcomings in this dimension will lead to a poor user experience, even as online consumer expectations continue to rise. A negative online experience will weaken user loyalty and prompt them to switch to other platforms and websites to buy goods (El-Manstrly et al., 2024).

Efficiency

When making purchase decisions on the platform, users need to click through books one by one, read large amounts of homogeneous basic information (such as authors and publishers), and compare multiple pages of content separately before making a decision. This involves unnecessary time, steps, and cognitive effort, increasing the cost of completing the transaction.

The book details page for MyBookOne includes the title, price, author, publisher, publication date, and ISBN. This information can only meet users' basic information needs. Useful information is always mixed up. For example, core content, writing style, and other details are arranged in the introduction without structure, making it lengthy and complicated. Users must scan the text, locate the information, and understand the content, which increases users' cognitive burden. There is a lack of comparison tools between two similar products on the platform. For instance, if users want to buy a book on the ancient history of Hong Kong, they need to switch tabs repeatedly to choose between the two books, "Concise Ancient History of Hong Kong" and "New Edition of Ancient History of Hong Kong". They need to compare the author's background and book content with their own memories, which makes the decision-making process more cumbersome.

The product categorization on MyBookOne is relatively broad and cannot meet users' deep filtering needs. For example, under the history category, there are historical theory, Chinese history, world history, biography, and other categories. Users cannot filter content by historical period or region. The system transfers the task of information classification and aggregation to users. Given many mixed books, users can only browse page by page and perform manual filtering, resulting in low decision-making efficiency.

In the 5Es model, Efficiency is the speed (with accuracy) for work execution (Quesenbery, 2004). The existing interaction design of MyBookOne contradicts the 5Es model's pursuit of efficiency. Complex information and uncertainty may increase excessive cognitive load, triggering negative emotions and leading customers to abandon their shopping carts (Mittal, 2023; Patharia & Jain, 2024). Xu & Huang (2015) found that users' continuous product organization, research, and cross-site comparison during the shopping cart stage directly and significantly affect cart abandonment. MyBookOne's current navigation path is single, and the classification dimension is coarse, which increases the user's decision-making burden and time cost, and reduces the user's willingness to complete the transaction.

Engagement

After the user completes actions like purchasing or writing a book review, the platform provides incentive feedback, such as digital stamp cards, badges, and points. However, the overall platform interface and interactive design can deliver only relevant functions, failing to create a user experience that attracts users, stimulates exploration, and establishes emotional connections.

The platform's interface is unified, but it primarily consists of static images and text. All users face the same home page layout and marketing content, and lack personalized surprises and emotional design. The platform fails to leverage the interface to convey a sense of uniqueness and interaction to users, which is not conducive to cultivating user stickiness and user expectations.

Engagement in the 5Es model "is how pleasant, satisfying, or interesting an interface is to use" (Quesenbery, 2004). Kim et al. (2016) noted that the degree of personalization is the strongest predictor of the application's usefulness and stickiness, thereby promoting continued use and word-of-mouth dissemination by enhancing pleasant participation. Benlian (2015) noted that content and design personalization cues affect website stickiness and willingness through "preference matching" and "perceived enjoyment," and that content personalization has a particularly strong effect on stickiness. The experience MyBookOne currently provides is only a basic book-purchase tool, which puts it at a disadvantage in cultivating long-term, loyal users.

Error Tolerance

Users will inevitably make mistakes during platform use, which may interrupt the entire task process and degrade the user experience.

If the user types a typo or an unused expression in the search box, the platform will search for the misspelled word and display irrelevant products or return "no products". However, shopping platforms such as Amazon will provide error-correction suggestions and approximate result recommendations to prevent errors that could completely disrupt the task. For example, if you enter the misspelled word "physiss" in a search, MyBookOne will indicate that no product is available. But if you search for "physiss" on Amazon, it will automatically correct the spelling to "physics" and retrieve the relevant content.

When users search for an out-of-stock book, the platform only shows "out of stock" without offering any constructive alternatives, such as recommending similar items on sale or offering arrival notification subscriptions. This approach directly ends the user's current task flow.

Error Tolerance refers to how well the software handles errors (Quesenbery, 2004). Strong error tolerance ensures that users can easily recover from errors, reduces users' learning anxiety and operational pressure, and encourages exploration. Mustafa et al. (2020) note that integrating Tan's failure model and D&M model indicates that failures in digital services significantly affect user satisfaction and usage outcomes, and emphasize that platforms should actively reduce failures to improve user experience. Studying online services reveals that the compensation recovery strategies significantly affect customers' repurchase intention and retention (Ozuem et al., 2021). MyBookOne's limited fault tolerance makes its user experience highly fragile, leading to user loss.

Ease of Learning

The design of some platform functions does not account for new users' cognitive thresholds. The lack of effective guidance will prevent users from recognizing and using the platform's characteristic functions.

For example, the "store in store" and "book review community" entrances on the MyBookOne platform are hidden, and the system does not provide scenario-based guidance for novices. Many users are unaware of these sections and cannot appreciate their value.

In particular, "store in store" is a special section of MyBookOne, which aggregates brand resources such as "China Book Bureau" and "Business Printing House". However, its entrance is a link on the sidebar. New users cannot learn from other places in advance. Without guidance from the platform, it is difficult for new users to understand the functions and specific operations of this section.

In academic monographs and professional tool books, introductions often contain industry jargon. The platform provides no explanation or hints. Non-professional users cannot quickly understand the goods' content, which invisibly raises the transaction's knowledge barrier.

Ease of learning concerns how well the product supports both initial orientation and deeper learning (Quesenbery, 2004). Clear instructional design can reduce the initial use threshold. Clear guidance design can improve usability and learning efficiency, and promote the continuous use of the platform (Ghai & Tandon, 2023). MyBookOne failed to deliver the services it was designed to provide, so the commercial investment in its specialized functions could not be translated into effective user-perceived value, resulting in idleness and wasted functional resources.

"Information Quality" Dimensional Evaluation

Information quality refers to the inherent characteristics of the content provided by the platform. Based on the D&M model and related research, this section evaluates the information ecology of the MyBookOne platform from five sub-dimensions: accuracy, integrity, timeliness, relevance, and structure (Arabia & Elsdaig, 2019; Delone & McLean, 2003; Ghalavand et al., 2024). Although the platform meets the basic data accuracy standard, there is a significant gap in building a knowledge service system that supports in-depth decision-making, dynamic association, and personalized distribution.

Information accuracy

The core transaction metadata (book title, author, publisher, ISBN, price) provided by the platform is highly accurate and serves as the basis for the transaction. However, the introduction of user-generated content increases the risk of information accuracy. The platform lacks clear signals, such as "high-quality book reviews," to guide users toward high-quality evaluations. But UGC content, such as book reviews, may contain subjective bias, marketing-speak, and other problems, which can easily pollute the information environment, undermine the overall credibility and authority of platform content, and affect information quality.

Information integrity

The platform provides basic information about books, but there is a serious lack of in-depth value information to motivate users to make high-quality purchasing decisions. The information available on the platform is often not enough to support users in completing the cognitive process from "interested" to "deciding to buy".

The details page of the vast majority of books only contains the introduction and table of contents provided by the publisher. They lack multidimensional value-added content, such as professional book reviews from authoritative media or KOLs, trial readings of representative chapters, and comparative analysis with similar books.

If users want to understand a book's value deeply, they must leave the platform and turn to professional book review websites or general search engines to integrate cross-platform information. Users cannot complete in-depth purchase research on the platform, and the user experience is disrupted, further increasing transaction uncertainty.

Complete and rich information is an important factor in improving user satisfaction (Lutfi et al., 2022). Incomplete information means the platform fails to reduce the uncertainty in user decision-making. From the perspective of consumers, this prolongs the decision-making cycle, forcing users to incur additional costs for information search and verification (Kivetz & Simonson, 2000). It weakens the platform's one-stop service value and increases transaction resistance.

Information timeliness

The platform reliably ensures real-time updates to transactional information, such as product prices and inventory levels. But the cultural attributes and knowledge content related to books are static and lack updates. MyBookOne lacks timely associations. When a book sparks social discussion because it is adapted into a popular film or TV series, or when an author wins important awards, the platform page cannot associate this dynamic information with static book listings. For example, the TV series adapted from the book "The Three-Body Problem" sparked online discussions. But on the MyBookOne page, users cannot learn about relevant news or social discussions. The book's details page is like an isolated information island that fails to keep pace with the flow of knowledge in the outside world. Timely information association can create "freshness" and "community vitality", which is an important means to attract users to return (Li et al., 2022). The current static information presentation makes the platform's content feel lifeless, reduces user appeal, and misses the opportunity to increase value and traffic through associated hotspots. When a book resonates with current social discussion, its value to readers is often much higher than its isolated text.

Information relevance

The platform has certain shortcomings in the relevance of its information. The book recommendations and promotional information displayed to all users are highly homogeneous and cannot be dynamically adjusted based on users' browsing history, purchase records, and real-time interests. For specific users, much of the information displayed is an irrelevant "noise". For example, a parent who focuses on buying children's books; the most conspicuous banner on their home page is a recommendation for ancient books. This kind of information is not related to user habits and wastes valuable screen space. The inefficiency of finding valuable information will also affect user satisfaction and stickiness.

The recommendation section of the book details page, titled “Users who have read this book have also read it”, is recommended only based on simple tags. It fails to explore the deep connections among books’ themes, ideological veins, methodologies, and even emotional tones, limiting the breadth and depth of the discovery path. For example, on the purchase page for “Homo Deus: A Brief History of Tomorrow,” MyBookOne recommended children's books and romance novels instead of macro-history books like Guns, Germs, and Steel or cognition-related books like Thinking, Fast and Slow, thereby missing the opportunity to encourage users to explore purchases.

In the D&M model, information relevance is an important attribute in evaluating information quality. High information quality can significantly improve user satisfaction and perceived benefits, thereby affecting the intention and behavior of continuous use (Salim et al., 2021). In digital services, pushing unrelated information directly leads to negative perceptions of the system among users (Lv & Liu, 2022). For MyBookOne, low relevance reduces users’ efficiency in finding books. The path users take to find their favorite books is longer and cannot provide a unique information flow that suits their personal interests, which falls short of the experience standards of modern personalized e-commerce platforms.

Information structure

The books on the platform are structured with only six pieces of information: title, price, author, publisher, date of publication, and ISBN. Other descriptive aspects of the books are presented in unstructured natural language. For users, unstructured text means higher reading costs. Users need to extract key information, such as the core views and expression logic, from the content introduction. In essence, the platform transfers the burden of information processing to users. For the platform, unstructured data hinders knowledge association. For example, the introduction to The Second Sex states that the book is “a masterpiece of modern feminist thought”. The system should extract “feminism” as a label and structure the information. After that, a knowledge graph can be built based on these conceptual entities, establishing clear associations with “feminism”, “gender research”, and other nodes. If the information is not structured, building knowledge associations requires significant manual annotation and natural language processing.

The higher the degree of information structure on a digital platform, the greater the potential of data computability, reusability, and intelligent utilization (Pandurangan, 2025). MyBookOne has rich content resources, but cannot convert them into machine-understandable, usable data assets. It not only increases the burden on user information processing but also represents a fundamental infrastructure weakness for the platform's data-driven, intelligent upgrade.

"Service Quality" Dimensional Evaluation

Service quality primarily refers to the platform's ability to provide support, assistance, and guarantee to users. Based on the D&M model, this section systematically evaluates MyBookOne's service system from three dimensions: service response, privacy protection, and personalized services (Daghouri et al., 2018; Nugroho & Prasetyo, 2018; Salisu et al., 2025).

Service response

The platform primarily relies on email and messaging, and lacks real-time communication channels. This service model cannot meet users' expectations for instant feedback. Imagine a scenario: when the user places an order late at night, they encounter the abnormality of "payment has been successful but the order has not been generated". They need to confirm the status of the funds and order immediately, but they can only submit an email form or leave an online message. During the few hours of waiting for the reply, the user could not be sure whether the money was safe, and the anxiety continued to accumulate. This approach is not consistent with the instant response characteristics of digital services.

Even for non-emergency routine consultations, the disadvantages of asynchronous communication are equally obvious. A complete consultation often requires many back-and-forths: the user sends a question, waits several hours for a reply. And the user adds information, and the customer service replies again. This repetition not only lengthens the problem-solving cycle but also wears down users' patience. In contrast, platforms that can provide real-time chat support can complete the same consultation process in a few minutes.

For routine inquiries such as "change the delivery address", users might accept a wait of several hours. However, when encountering payment failures, order abnormalities, or other issues involving transaction security and capital risks, users need an immediate response. Asynchronous communication provided by MyBookOne cannot provide the necessary sense of security and support to users in this scenario.

Instant response ability is a key factor for e-commerce platforms to build user trust and alleviate transaction anxiety. Real-time interaction can significantly improve trust and impulse purchase (Peng et al., 2024). Chatbots can answer questions in real time and solve problems quickly, a key design feature that improves service quality and customer relations (Chen et al., 2021). On the other hand, MyBookOne's lagging response time cannot support users at critical moments, which not only constitutes a shortcoming of the current experience but is also likely to erode users' long-term trust.

Privacy protection

The platform provides basic terms of service and privacy policies, but there is still room for improvement in terms of operational transparency and data security. At a time when people are paying increasing attention to privacy issues, this problem has become a potential obstacle to building user trust.

When the platform introduces recommendation algorithms in the future and uses AI to provide users with personalized book suggestions, the problem will become even more pronounced. Users don't know why they recommend this book to me. There are no explanatory labels next to the recommendation results, such as "based on the history books you have recently browsed" and "similar to the style of social science books you often buy". This kind of "black box" recommendation can make users feel manipulated by algorithms.

Data privacy is increasingly a concern. The strength of privacy protection will strongly affect users' willingness, especially among consumers who are not sensitive to price and service quality (Van Hoboken & Fathaigh, 2021). The website lacks relevant security certification identifiers and fails to explain in understandable terms how the platform protects data. For consumers who value service and privacy, such ambiguity will raise certain suspicions (Wylde et al., 2022). When users can't understand the system's operating logic, they often remain vigilant and suspicious. Conversely, when users understand the rationale for the recommendation and how the data is used, they are more likely to lower their guard and accept the system's suggestions.

MyBookOne's passivity and silence in privacy protection not only degrade the current service quality, but also create a potential trust barrier to its future introduction of AI technology. When users have doubts about the recommendation algorithm and lack confidence in data security, even if the algorithm itself is accurate, it is difficult to translate that into actual adoption and continuous use.

Personalized service

The platform's services exhibit a high level of standardization and lack personalized care that accounts for user differences. After the transaction, the relationship between the user and the platform is basically over. Imagine a scenario in which the user purchases an introductory Python book on the platform. After the book is delivered, its relationship with the platform falls silent. The platform will not send follow-up emails later to ask about progress in learning, nor will it take this opportunity to recommend advanced readings. When there is a relevant online technology-sharing meeting, the author's live broadcast, or a new book release, the platform will not push accurate notifications. Imagine another example. When scholars who frequently buy sociological works visit the platform, it lacks personalized recommendations or new-book reminders in the field, and different users see the same homepage.

The platform lacks personalized services and regards users as single traders rather than long-term interactive partners. But the user's lifetime value is much higher than the amount of a single transaction. Users who receive continuous care and personalized services on the platform are more likely to become active users and then become brand supporters (Tyrväinen et al., 2020).

Personalized service is not only a means to improve user experience, but also a strategic choice to build a differentiated competitive advantage. For goods such as books, they are highly dependent on the depth of content and cultural identity. Users are looking not only for books but also for cultural partners who can understand the interest in reading and accompany the growth of knowledge (Vlieghe et al., 2016). MyBookOne's current standardized service misses the opportunity to turn single-transaction customers into long-term brand partners, which has great potential in building user emotional connections.

5 AI-DRIVEN ENHANCEMENT SOLUTIONS

Based on the analysis of the MyBookOne platform in the previous chapter, this chapter will use artificial intelligence technology to improve user experience in three aspects: system quality, information quality, and service quality.

Reshape the System Quality

Improving system quality directly affects the speed and satisfaction of users completing transactions, which, in turn, affects the conversion rate and user retention. This section proposes AI-driven solutions for the system deficiencies identified through the 5Es model.

Improve effectiveness and understand user intentions

As noted earlier, the platform's search function only supports keyword literal matching, which cannot understand the user's natural-language query intent, making it difficult for users to find their favorite books.

The Web-scale BERT semantic retrieval model proposed by Amazon has improved the relevance index by up to 23%, and the online A/B test has improved accurate matching and alternative recall (Muhamed et al., 2023). Alibaba's ReprBERT distilled the interactive BERT and deployed it on Taobao, achieving an AUC that was more than 10% higher than that of the previous optimal representation model (Yao et al., 2022). This shows that the pre-trained language model has achieved significant results in browsers, e-commerce platforms, and other scenarios. MyBookOne can fine-tune the AI model and use book metadata and user behavior data accumulated by the platform to train the book semantic retrieval model. By building a semantic retrieval model for the MyBookOne platform, the user's natural language queries and the system's search results can be accurately matched, thereby improving the "effectiveness" dimension in the 5Es model.

Improving search success rates can reduce user abandonment rates. Understanding intentions can uncover users' hidden needs, increasing sales opportunities for similar books. During technical implementation, it is necessary to control calculation costs, protect data privacy, and ensure user information is anonymized. At the same time, it is necessary to avoid algorithmic bias and ensure that the recommended results are not affected by it. Thus, we propose the following approaches:

Vague intent query: the user enters "Find me an English novel similar to The Grapes of Wrath, depicting ordinary people struggling through hardship but with a sense of humanity and warmth." Traditional searches in MyBookOne may only match "The Grapes of Wrath" and "English novel". And the semantic search engine can analyze the key elements: social realism/historical novels; warmth of humanity; John Steinbeck; the life of ordinary people during the Great Depression or economic difficulties to recommend accurately works like "Of Mice and Men," and "The Pearl," which are similar in theme and style.

Conceptual phrase query: Suppose a user inputs "Introductory books on the ethics of artificial intelligence". The system identifies the core concept of "artificial intelligence ethics" and the demand type "introductory book". It not only retrieves books with these words in their titles, but also extracts relevant content from book introductions, catalogs, and even book reviews. It recommends works such as Algorithms of Oppression and others highly related to user intentions.

Input wording tolerance: In Chinese, if the user enters "san ti" (Pinyin) or makes a typo, the system should automatically convert and correct the pinyin, and give tips like "Are you looking for: The Three-Body Problem?" Meanwhile, the platform displays relevant science fiction to offer users alternative choices. For English, it automatically corrects spelling errors. When the user inputs "physiss", the system automatically corrects the error, prompts "Are you looking for: physics?", and displays the search results for physics.

Improve efficiency and assist intelligent decision-making

As noted earlier, users face challenges with information extraction and cumbersome comparisons during the decision-making process. To deal with the above problems, multimodal content understanding and knowledge graphs can be considered. Entity recognition, relationship extraction, and topic modeling can be applied to book texts to build rich metadata for each book.

Through AI-assisted decision-making, the platform can effectively shorten the user's decision path, thereby reducing shopping cart abandonment. In addition, intelligent filters can also guide users to discover high-value goods and increase average order value. From the perspective of the 5Es model, this move directly optimizes the "efficiency" dimension and frees users from tedious information comparison tasks. When constructing filters, it is necessary to ensure the screening mechanism is fair to avoid systematic neglect of certain book categories caused by flaws in the labeling system. Thus, we propose the following approaches:

AI-generated summary card: On each book detail page, in addition to the original description, add structured information cards generated by AI, such as "summary of core views", "readable people label", and "comparison table of similar books". An LLM generates such content based on the introduction, table of contents, and book reviews.

Dynamic personalized filter: based on the deep analysis of book content, it dynamically generates professional filtering dimensions for different categories. For example, under the classification of "psychology", add filters like "genre" (behavioralism, humanism), "applicable questions" (anxiety, depression, children's education), "content type" (academic monographs, self-help books. Under the classification of "sociology", add "research method" (qualitative, quantitative), "research theme" (urbanization, social stratification), etc. These tags are automatically generated and annotated by AI based on the book's content.

Intelligent comparison tool: allows users to select 2-3 candidate books, and the system automatically generates a comparison table that displays dimensions such as the author's background, core point of view, reader score, price, and more.

Enhance engagement and immersive interaction

As noted earlier, the platform interface is static and uniform, lacks personalized surprises and emotional feedback, and makes it difficult for users to build an emotional connection and stickiness. To address such problems, AIGC technology can be used to generate customized copywriting, images, audio, and videos based on users' historical behavior and current instructions, thereby improving the quality and subjective experience of recommendations (Zhan et al., 2024). Integrating emotional design in personalized recommendations helps to improve emotional trajectory and continuous participation (Yang et al., 2021). From the perspective of the 5Es model, these designs directly enhance the "participation" dimension and transform reading from an isolated behavior into an experience with emotional rewards. During implementation, it is necessary to ensure the copyright and accuracy of AIGC content. The generated infographics and abstracts need to be manually reviewed or have the source marked. Thus, we propose the following approaches:

AIGC Content Enhancement: Use generative AI to create more attractive multimedia content for each book. For example, generate a "three-minute immersive audition" for novels (synthesize audio with TTS technology and background music); automatically generate "core knowledge infographics" and "key data visualization" for popular science books; generate "character relationship maps" or "timeline" for history books.

Personalized reading journey: generate an exclusive "reading map" based on the user's book purchase and browsing history. For example, if users have purchased From the Soil and Peasant Life in China, the system can present a knowledge tree for "Chinese Social Research" to mark the fields they have explored and the directions for further exploration.

Strengthen error tolerance

As noted earlier, the platform lacks tolerance and guidance for input errors and abnormal states. Small mistakes lead to process interruption and a vulnerable user experience. To address this problem, AI will be used to correct errors and recommend similar books. Service failure will significantly reduce satisfaction, but timely and adequate recovery will significantly affect passenger satisfaction and relationship quality (Ali et al., 2020). From the 5Es model perspective, this design significantly strengthens "error tolerance", frees users from the state of "fearing mistakes," and encourages more free exploration. Thus, we propose the following approaches:

Search error correction and intention guessing: The system can integrate AI error-correction algorithms into the search box. When a possible spelling error or pinyin input is detected, the system will automatically correct the error and prompt at the top of the result display area: "Are you looking for ___?". At the same time, even if there is no accurate matching result, the system does not directly display the empty page, but recommends content-related books based on the valid word elements entered by the user, and the accompanying instructions: "No fully matching books were found. The following are recommendations related to the theme of ___."

Intelligent guidance for abnormal states: When users encounter "Item out of stock" or "link invalid", the page does not simply display an error message; instead, it actively provides alternatives. For example: "This book is out of stock, but the following similar books are still in stock for your reference", and a list of similar books calculated by AI is displayed. At the same time, provide a one-click subscription option for "Notify when back in stock." For instance, if the book Guns, Germs, and Steel is out of stock, the page could redirect to recommendations for similar macro-history works like Sapiens and Collapse, with brief reasons: These books are similar to the theme of the books you are looking for, both exploring the driving force of civilization evolution.

Provide intuitive situational guidance

As noted earlier, the platform's characteristic functions (such as store-in-store and review communities) are not transparent to new users, and there is also a cognitive threshold for professional content. To solve this problem, contextual guidance and AI assistants are helpful. Contextual guidance can use the rule engine, while AI assistants need to build a knowledge base and access the LLM API. In studies of mental health platforms, researchers found that optimized UI and clear operating instructions can significantly increase users' behavioral participation (Hentati et al., 2021). A variety of onboarding methods, such as step-by-step guidance, examples, scrollytelling, and instructional videos, can help users understand complex interfaces (Stoiber et al., 2022). From the 5Es model perspective, these designs directly lower the threshold of "ease of learning", enabling new users to quickly appreciate the platform's core value and improving the functional utilization rate. Thus, we propose the following approaches:

Contextual user guidance: The system analyzes user behavior to determine whether this is the first time a user has visited a specific functional area. When the user enters the "store-in-store" for the first time, a non-invasive bubble prompt is triggered to explain the value and usage of the function briefly. For example, when new registered users visit the platform, they are confused by the concept of "store in the store" icon. After they click, the system pops up a bubble: "This is the exclusive space of renowned publishers like The Commercial Press and SDX Joint Publishing Company. Click to enter and find more quality books." After understanding, users begin browsing their favorite publishing house. Thus, we propose the following approaches:

Embedded AI assistant: Set up a wake-up AI conversation assistant in the lower right corner of the page. Users can ask questions in natural language at any time, such as "How to use the coupon of 'store in the store'?" "Help me find some introductory philosophy books suitable for high school students". The assistant not only answers questions but can also directly guide users to the corresponding page or actively recommend books based on the content of the dialogue.

Explanation of technical terms: On the book's details page, the system automatically identifies and underlines terms that may be beyond the comprehension of ordinary readers (such as "deconstructivism" and "rooted theory"). Users can hover to display a concise, easy-to-understand explanation, and click to view more relevant content.

Improve Information Quality

The above analyzes the platform's systematic shortcomings in integrity, timeliness, relevance, and structure from the perspective of information quality. Information quality is of great value to knowledge platforms. This section proposes AI-driven solutions to transform existing static data into valuable information assets.

Control the accuracy of information

As noted earlier, with the introduction of UGC, the risk of information accuracy gradually emerges. We propose a text quality evaluation technology based on deep learning that is relatively mature, enabling the quality control of UGC content and improving information accuracy by screening, identifying, and evaluating user credibility.

Content quality screening: Introduce an intelligent review system to identify obvious spam comments. Identify batch scoring, malicious low scoring, and other behaviors using abnormal-detection algorithms.

User credibility evaluation: Establish a dynamic credibility score for each user; comprehensively consider the quality of historical content, community recognition, and behavioral norms; and manually review the content published by low-reputation users.

Enhance information integrity

As noted earlier, the platform's information is insufficiently rich and complete, making it difficult to support the user's comprehensive decision-making process and requiring the user to search for external information themselves. In the face of this problem, the MyBookOne platform can leverage a large language model to generate in-depth content in batches of many books. AI-driven personalized content and recommendations can significantly improve user participation, satisfaction, and conversion (Bag et al., 2022). From the D&M model, this move directly improves "information integrity" and provides users with a more adequate basis for decision-making.

Traditional content production relies on manual writing, which is expensive and inefficient. Through AIGC, the platform can generate in-depth content at scale with low marginal cost. It can not only improve the efficiency of users' decision-making, but also increase the density of page content and attract users' attention. Strategically, automated content production enables the platform to differentiate from competitors at a lower cost and create unique advantages. Thus, we propose the following approaches:

Automatically generate a "core views summary": For each book, the AI reads the book's introduction, table of contents, and key reviews to distill the core views and present them as key points.

Generate "readable population portraits": based on the difficulty of the content, theme, and writing style, automatically judge and generate a description of "who is suitable for reading this book" (such as "suitable for sociology undergraduates to understand quantitative research methods").

Automatically compile "In-depth Interpretation of the Author's Background": Combine the author's other works, academic background, and social influence to craft an introduction that highlights his ideological context and academic contributions.

Build the "Explanation of Key Concepts" module: extract key terms from the book, provide concise explanations, and build a small glossary inside the book.

Enhance information timeliness

As noted earlier, the book page is frozen and disconnected from the external knowledge world. To solve this problem, the system can access external information sources such as news APIs, academic databases, and social media, continuously monitor dynamic information related to each book, and automatically update it on the book page. Deep learning and Transformer-based models have enabled information extraction and the construction of knowledge atlases across diverse fields (Al-Moslmi et al., 2020; Nasar et al., 2022). From the D&M model, this significantly improves the "timeliness of information", makes books become nodes embedded in dynamic knowledge networks, and enhances the vitality and attractiveness of the platform.

Besides, the platform can link books to hot events. When users search for relevant news, the platform page may appear in search results, helping the platform drive more traffic. At the same time, dynamic updates increase users' motivation to return, and they may regularly check the latest developments in books. From a strategic point of view, this enables the platform to build a knowledge dynamic center to improve user stickiness and brand authority. Thus, we propose the following approaches:

Establish a dynamic association system for books and hot events: The system accesses external information sources, continuously monitors dynamic information for each book, and automatically updates the book page.

Hot topic association: When a book wins an important award, the author publishes new views, the book is adapted into a film and television drama, and the views in the book trigger social discussion, the system adds the "Hot News" module on the book page to present relevant news reports, comment article links, or user discussion essence.

Academic citation tracking: For academic works, the latest citations in academic papers are systematically tracked, and the label "this book is cited by recent research" is displayed on the page to reflect its academic influence.

Enhance information relevance

As noted earlier, the platform information push is seriously homogenized and lacks personalization, and users are disturbed by a large amount of irrelevant information. Product recommendation is among the most mature AI applications in e-commerce. The platform can build a personalized information recommendation system based on deep learning to deal with the above problems. Mainstream platforms (such as Alibaba and Amazon) widely adopt sorting models based on deep learning, such as DeepFM, DIN, etc., to build a personalized recommendation system and a homepage push of "thousands of people and thousands of faces" (Shen et al., 2022). From the D&M model, this directly optimizes the "information relevance", frees users from information noise, and makes them feel the value of the platform, "understanding me".

For MyBookOne, improving the homepage's personalization can increase user click rates. By optimizing recommendations on the detail page, the cross-sales ratio can be improved, and the customer unit price can be increased. The personalized feature elevates the platform from a shelf to a shopping guide, thereby giving it a core competitive advantage. Thus, we propose the following approaches:

Multi-source user portrait: integrate users' browsing history, purchase records, search words, page dwell time, book reviews, likes, and other behaviors to build dynamically updated user interest vectors. For example, after a parent who often buys children's picture books logs in, the home page's first screen is no longer an ancient book promotion, but "Guess you like it: (new emotional management picture books)."

Recommended system integration: Adopt the mainstream two-stage "Retrieval-Ranking" architecture in the recommended system field. In the recall stage, hundreds of candidates are screened from a large number of books through collaborative filtering, vector retrieval, and other methods. The sorting stage uses deep neural networks to personalize recommendations and predict user click probabilities.

Contextual recommendation: Make situational recommendations based on the user's current context (e.g., category, time of day, and season).

Enhance information structure

As noted earlier, the platform's textual data is mostly unstructured, which not only affects the user experience but also hinders in-depth AI use.

To improve the information structure, a Large Language Model will be used to understand and extract information, and unstructured content will be automatically converted into a standardized structural representation. The structured knowledge base is the data foundation for all subsequent intelligent applications, enabling the release of the potential value of platform data and paving the way for the expansion of AI applications in the future (Razniewski & Das, 2020; Zhuang et al., 2017). From the D&M model, structured information is the basic premise for improving all information quality dimensions. Large-scale and high-quality structured data is a necessary prerequisite for the effectiveness of AI systems (Gong et al., 2023; Mohammed et al., 2025). Thus, we propose the following approaches:

Entity identification: Identify people's names, place names, concepts, theories, genres, events, and other entities from the text.

Relationship extraction: identify relationships between entities, such as "author-creation-book", "book-adoption-theory", and "theory-origin-school".

Label system construction: generate multidimensional label vectors for each book, covering the theme, difficulty, style, readability, etc.

Knowledge atlas storage: The extracted entities and relationships are stored in a graph database to form a queryable, inferable knowledge network.

Improve Service Quality

The evaluation of service quality indicates that the platform has significant shortcomings in response speed, transparency, and personalized care. This section will design an AI-driven service enhancement scheme, upgrade the platform from passive response to active service, and build user trust and emotional connection.

Improve the response speed

As noted earlier, the platform relies on asynchronous customer service channels and cannot provide instant support in emergencies. To improve response speed, a large-language-model-driven dialogue system can be introduced, combined with intention recognition, entity extraction, and task-based dialogue management. Intelligent customer service robots improve response speed and shorten user wait times through instant replies and 24/7 online service. Conversational AI has been shown to alleviate anxiety, stress, and other negative emotions across a variety of applications (Gaffney et al., 2019; Zhong et al., 2024). In the medical consulting service scenario, intelligent dialogue systems are often comparable to, if not superior to, manual services in terms of information quality and problem-solving rates (Ayers et al., 2023), thereby improving problem-solving efficiency and user satisfaction. From the D&M model, this directly improves the responsiveness of "service quality", provides users with a sense of security at critical moments, promotes the establishment of a "reliable platform" reputation, and promotes repurchase. Thus, we propose a solution that combines intelligent customer service robots with seamless manual connections.

Deploy an intelligent customer service engine based on the large language model to achieve 7×24-hour instant response. The robot can handle high-frequency standardized consultations, including order inquiry, logistics tracking, return and exchange policy, coupon use, etc. When the robot identifies that the problem is complex and requires manual intervention, it will automatically transfer the case to manual customer service and attach the conversation history and preliminary analysis to improve manual processing efficiency.

For example, when paying late at night, users encounter an anomaly: the payment is successful, but the order is not generated, and they anxiously contact online customer service. The robot responded immediately: "Hello, I understand that you have encountered a payment problem. Please wait a moment while I check your order status." The robot calls the background interface to check; it finds that the payment was successful, but the system was delayed. It informed the user: "Your order has been generated and is being processed, likely ready in 10 minutes." It helps relieve users' anxiety and improve the platform's goodwill.

Improve the transparency of AI

As noted earlier, the platform lacks transparency into its algorithms and data use, which risks eroding trust. Transparency is the basic cloud of data processing and the ethical premise for AI systems to be accepted by users (Felzmann et al., 2019). From the perspective of service quality, explainable AI decision-making will improve users' trust and reliability evaluation of the system (Wanner et al., 2022). When the recommendation system provides a reasonable explanation, the user's trust, perceived fairness, satisfaction, and system acceptability are all significantly improved (Shin, 2021). Therefore, transparency and privacy protection are not only compliance requirements but also competitive differentiators that help gain user trust. By leveraging explainable AI and transparent communication, the platform can reduce users' resistance to algorithms and increase the acceptance of recommendations. Strategically, this helps attract high-value users who prioritize privacy. Thus, we propose the following approaches.

Show recommendation reasons: Next to each book recommended by AI, add a "reason for recommendation" link, and click to display a personalized explanation. For example: "I recommend this book because: 1. You have recently browsed 'Cognitive Science' books; 2. Users who have purchased this book also like the "Thinking, Fast and Slow" you bought before.

Transparency of data use: Set up the "AI and Privacy" column in a prominent position of the platform (such as the bottom of the home page and the account setting page), explain how the platform uses user data to improve the experience in a popular language and diagrams, and clearly commit to data security measures. Display the security certification logo, such as ISO 27001.

Enhanced user control: A "Recommended intensity adjustment slider" is available in personalized settings, allowing users to choose the level of personalization independently and even turn off personalized recommendations. This kind of control is itself an important way to build trust.

Enhance personalized care

As noted earlier, the platform service is highly standardized, and the relationship will end after the transaction. To improve the user experience, user lifecycle management is helpful, and LLMs can be used to generate personalized care emails. Personalized post-purchase care is a key strategy to improve user loyalty and lifetime value. The "net benefit" dimension in the D&M model includes not only income from a single transaction but also the improvement in users' long-term value. Through these measures, the platform can turn single-transaction users into long-term brand supporters. Thus, we propose the following approaches:

Post-purchase care and advanced recommendation: The system predicts the user's likely completion time for the purchased book and automatically sends a personalized care email. For example: "Hello, it has been a month since you purchased Introduction to Data Science. We recommend the advanced book Python for Data Analysis to you and have attached the author's latest online lecture link.

High-value user identification and exclusive service: Identify high-value users using the RFM model (most recent purchase date, purchase frequency, purchase amount), and provide them with exclusive service access. When such users enter online customer service, the system automatically assigns priority to senior customer service and provides more flexible solutions, such as exclusive discounts and priority delivery.

Personalized notifications and invitations to activities: Based on users' interests, push notifications for new book releases, author signings, online book clubs, etc., so users feel the platform's continuous attention and companionship.

Phased Implementation Roadmap

To ensure the program's practicality and maximize return on investment, the Institute's proposed AI solution can be divided into three implementation stages.

Short-term (0-12 months): Quickly hit the core pain point

The key goal is to solve the most urgent user experience problems and quickly show the value.

Specific measures include:

1. Deploy a BERT-based semantic search system, support natural language queries, and have spelling and pinyin correction functions.
2. Launched an intelligent customer service robot driven by a large language model to handle high-frequency consultation;
3. Introduce the basic dynamic filtering dimension for different book categories.
4. Add search error correction and alternative recommendations when books are out of stock.

Medium-term (12-24 months): Build core competitiveness

The key goal is to establish differentiated advantages through personalized service and content enhancement.

Specific measures include:

1. Deploy a personalized recommendation system.
2. Launch the AIGC content generation function, including core view summaries, suitable reader labels, and author background introductions. core view summaries, suitable reader labels, and author background introductions.
3. Launch the construction of knowledge graphs, and initially cover the core entities and their relationships.
4. Implement the basic explainable AI recommendation and clearly explain the reason for the recommendation to users.

Long-term (24-36 months): Establish a sustainable leading position

The key goal is to transform the platform from book sales to comprehensive knowledge services.

Specific measures include:

1. Improve the book knowledge graph, and have the ability of cross-book knowledge association and reasoning.
2. Launch immersive multimedia content, such as audio previews, knowledge graph visualizations, and character relationship maps.
3. Implement personalized services covering the whole life cycle (pre-purchase, during-purchase, post-purchase).
4. Establish a comprehensive AI governance and privacy protection system.

6 DISCUSSION AND OUTLOOK

The above AI solutions have optimized system, information, and service quality in an all-around way. Each solution addresses the pain points of Chapter 4 diagnosis individually and provides practical solutions based on the latest AI technical literature.

AI empowers improving the "quality" of the system, information, and services, thereby enhancing "user satisfaction" and "willingness to use", and ultimately transforming it into the "net income" of the platform (including higher conversion rates, repurchase rates, and user loyalty). At the same time, users also get more efficient knowledge acquisition and a more pleasant reading experience. The current platform and users are a win-win.

Ethical Considerations and Mitigation Strategies

Although the AI-driven solution has the potential to improve the user experience, its deployment also poses ethical, operational, and technical risks.

Data privacy in personalized services

Personalized recommendations, intelligent customer service, and user life cycle management rely on the collection of user behavior data (e.g., browsing history, purchase history, and time spent). Without appropriate safeguards, these practices may infringe on user privacy, damage trust, or violate local laws and regulations.

To mitigate this risk, the platform needs to provide a clear, easy-to-understand explanation of what data is collected and how it is used. Before enabling the personalized function, the user's explicit consent must be obtained. Meanwhile, users have control over their data. They can view their own data, delete history, adjust the intensity of personalization, including the "non-personalization" mode. Before model training, the platform collects only data necessary for the expected artificial intelligence function and establishes anonymization procedures to remove personally identifiable information (PII).

Algorithm bias and fairness

Semantic search and recommendation models are trained based on historical user interaction data, which may amplify existing biases. Bestsellers may dominate search results, while niche books or older books (such as academic monographs and books published by small publishers) are systematically ignored. This will reduce content diversity and may adversely affect some publishers or authors.

To manage this situation, the platform should include diversity indicators in its ranking process, ensuring that less popular, niche books also have a fair chance to be shown. Regular bias audits should be conducted to evaluate whether search and recommendation results exhibit systematic deviations due to factors such as type, author background, or publisher size. In addition, the platform needs to allow users to choose exploration mode, such as "discovering niche books" or "adventurous discovery mode". Finally, editors participate in reviewing the recommendations of labels and high-risk categories (such as academic books) generated by artificial intelligence.

Technical maturity and implementation cost

Some artificial intelligence solutions, such as knowledge graph construction, require significant engineering investment, high-quality structured data, and continuous maintenance. For regional platforms like MyBookOne, these costs may be too high.

To respond to these challenges, the platform should adopt a phased implementation strategy, prioritizing low-risk, high-impact functions, such as semantic search. And use commercial or open-source APIs and perform fine-tuning with platform-specific book metadata, rather than developing in-house models from scratch. Knowledge representation starts with a lightweight, rule-based labeling system combined with a small-scale graph database and gradually adds relational extraction as data volume grows. At the same time, the platform needs to track the operating costs and business benefits of each artificial intelligence function and reduce or redesign those functions with poor returns.

User trust and the interpretability of AI

Recommended algorithms usually run in a "black box" way. If users don't understand why some books are recommended, they may feel manipulated or distrust the platform. This is especially important for knowledge platforms that readers value independent thinking.

To build user trust, the platform should adopt a set of mitigation measures. It should provide explainable recommendations by offering a brief, personalized reason for each suggested book. It should also maintain a transparent interface, including an easy-to-understand page that clearly explains data usage and how recommendations work. Furthermore, the platform should incorporate a feedback mechanism that allows users to rate the usefulness of recommendations and explicitly reject certain categories, using this input to improve the model continuously. Finally, the platform should conduct regular trust audits through surveys or interviews to gauge users' perceptions of fairness, transparency, and satisfaction with AI-driven features.

Research Limitations

This study integrates the D&M model with the 5Es model, taking the D&M model as the macro-success dimension and the 5Es as the micro-analysis tool of system quality. Although this integration addresses some of the shortcomings of a single model, the theoretical connection between the two still needs further development.

This study adopts a single-case study method and uses MyBookOne, an online book retail platform in Hong Kong, as the research object. This choice helps to deeply analyze the real problems of a specific platform and ensure the relevance and operability of the research, but it also brings limitations to the scope of application of the conclusion. As a regional platform, MyBookOne's user group, market environment, and technical foundation are significantly different from those of large platforms such as Amazon. MyBookOne users are more concentrated in Hong Kong and have a strong preference for traditional Chinese and Cantonese culture, whereas large platforms need to serve a wider range of users. Therefore, whether the AI solution proposed in this study is suitable for platforms in other cultural contexts, at different scales, or with different business models still needs to be verified through cross-case comparison.

The AI enhancement scheme proposed in this study spans many technical fields, including semantic search, personalized recommendation, AIGC content generation, intelligent customer service, and interpretable AI. These technologies have varying degrees of maturity in academia and industry. However, this study has conducted a preliminary analysis of the technical feasibility, implementation costs, and risks of these schemes in the specific environment of MyBookOne, but failed to conduct a systematic technical maturity assessment and a quantitative cost-effectiveness analysis. This study only makes qualitative discussions and lacks measurements based on actual data.

This study argues for the potential impact of various AI schemes on business indicators at the theoretical level, but these arguments are mainly based on qualitative reasoning and lack quantitative verification using actual MyBookOne platform data. The exact data needs to be obtained through A/B testing or quasi-experimental research. The scheme design of this study provides a basis for subsequent empirical verification, but this verification link itself has not been completed.

Future Research Prospects

As ongoing research, we can continue to explore the cross-integration of the D&M and 5Es models in the dimensions of information quality and service quality, and refine the three quality dimensions with the five experience dimensions of 5Es, respectively, to achieve a more refined diagnosis of the platform experience. At the same time, other models are integrated into the existing framework to better explain the user experience and the effects of AI functions on the platform.

Future research can select multiple types of online retail platforms for cross-case comparison, such as large-scale comprehensive platforms and social e-commerce platforms, to test the applicability and adjustment needs of the AI scheme proposed in this study across different scenarios. Through comparative analysis, more universal technology transfer strategies and strategic application models can be distilled.

The effectiveness of the various AI functions proposed in this study plan can be quantitatively verified through on-site experiments or a quasi-experimental design in the future. A/B tests can be carried out on the MyBookOne platform or other cooperation platforms for semantic search, personalized recommendations, AIGC content enhancement, and other functions, and compare the differences between the experimental group and the control group in key indicators such as search success rate, click rate, conversion rate, customer unit price, repurchase rate, user stay time, etc. Different. By collecting actual user behavior data, the marginal contribution of each AI function can be accurately evaluated, and the platform's resource investment decision-making can be provided.

7 CONCLUSION

This research has made certain contributions to theoretical integration, problem diagnosis, and program design, providing a systematic reference framework and implementation blueprint for the AI empowerment of online book retail platforms such as MyBookOne. However, the research is limited to a single case, the depth of theoretical framework integration is insufficient, and the technical feasibility assessment is cursory. Future research should continue to deepen in these directions and constantly improve and expand the results of this research. Realize the effective transfer of AI technology from laboratory to business scenarios, maximize its strategic value, and finally build a people-oriented, reliable, and secure business human-computer interaction paradigm.

REFERENCES

Adi, H. P., Wardoyo, A. E., & Azizah, H. (2024). An In-Depth Analysis of SIMPKB: Revealing Performance Tests and Efficiency from a User Experience. *Sinkron, 8*(2), 911–918. DOI: 10.33395/sinkron.v8i2.13574

Al-Moslmi, T., Gallofre Ocana, M., & Opdahl, L., A., & Veres, C. (. (2020). Named Entity Extraction for Knowledge Graphs: A Literature Overview. *IEEE Access : Practical Innovations, Open Solutions, 8*, 32862–32881. DOI: 10.1109/ACCESS.2020.2973928

Ali, S. R. O., Said, N. S. M., Jislan, F., Mat, K. A., & Aznan, W. N. M. W. (2020). The Relationship between Service Failure and Service Recovery with Airline Passenger Satisfaction. *Journal of Physics: Conference Series, 1529*(2), 022062. DOI: 10.1088/1742-6596/1529/2/022062

Alti, A., & Lakehal, A. (2025). AI-MDD-UX: Revolutionizing E-Commerce User Experience with Generative AI and Model-Driven Development. *Future Internet, 17*(4), 180. DOI: 10.3390/fi17040180

Arabia, S., & Elsdaig, M. (2019). Evaluation of Healthcare Information System Using Delone and McLean Quality Model, Case study KSA. *International Journal of Advanced Trends in Computer Science and Engineering, 8*(1.4), 522–527. DOI: 10.30534/ijatcse/2019/8181.42019

Bag, S., Srivastava, G., Bashir, M. M. A., Kumari, S., Giannakis, M., & Chowdhury, A. H. (2022). Journey of customers in this digital era: Understanding the role of artificial intelligence technologies in user engagement and conversion. *Benchmarking, 29*(7), 2074–2098. DOI: 10.1108/BIJ-07-2021-0415

Baj-Rogowska, A., & Sikorski, M. (2023). Exploring the usability and user experience of social media apps through a text mining approach. *Engineering Management in Production and Services, 15*(1), 86–105. DOI: 10.2478/emj-2023-0007

Benlian, A. (2015). Web Personalization Cues and Their Differential Effects on User Assessments of Website Value. *Journal of Management Information Systems, 32*(1), 225–260. DOI: 10.1080/07421222.2015.1029394

Chen, J.-S., Le, T.-T.-Y., & Florence, D. (2021). Usability and responsiveness of artificial intelligence chatbot on online customer experience in e-retailing. *International Journal of Retail & Distribution Management, 49*(11), 1512–1531. DOI: 10.1108/IJRDM-08-2020-0312

Daghouri, A., Mansouri, K., & Qbadou, M. (2018). Enhanced Model For Evaluating Information System Success: Determining Critical Criteria. *Engineering, Technology &. Applied Scientific Research, 8*(4), 3194–3198. DOI: 10.48084/etasr.2148

Delone, W. H., & McLean, E. R. (2003). The DeLone and McLean Model of Information Systems Success: A Ten-Year Update. *Journal of Management Information Systems, 19*(4), 9–30. DOI: 10.1080/07421222.2003.11045748

Efiloğlu Kurt, Ö. (2019). Examining an e-learning system through the lens of the information systems success model: Empirical evidence from Italy. *Education and Information Technologies, 24*(2), 1173–1184. DOI: 10.1007/s10639-018-9821-4

El-Manstrly, D., Herhausen, D., Guha, A., Blut, M., & Grewal, D. (2024). Should online retailers emphasize efficiency or experience? First insights on the evolution and heterogeneity of website attributes. *Journal of Retailing, 100*(2), 274–292. DOI: 10.1016/j.jretai.2024.03.002

Ghai, A., & Tandon, U. (2023). Integrating gamification and instructional design to enhance usability of online learning. *Education and Information Technologies, 28*(2), 2187–2206. DOI: 10.1007/s10639-022-11202-5

Ghalavand, H., Shirshahi, S., Rahimi, A., Zarrinabadi, Z., & Amani, F. (2024). Common data quality elements for health information systems: A systematic review. *BMC Medical Informatics and Decision Making, 24*(1), 243. DOI: 10.1186/s12911-024-02644-7

Gong, Y., Liu, G., Xue, Y., Li, R., & Meng, L. (2023). A survey on dataset quality in machine learning. *Information and Software Technology, 162*, 107268. DOI: 10.1016/j.infsof.2023.107268

Hentati, A., Forsell, E., Ljótsson, B., Kaldo, V., Lindefors, N., & Kraepelien, M. (2021). The effect of user interface on treatment engagement in a self-guided digital problem-solving intervention: A randomized controlled trial. *Internet Interventions : The Application of Information Technology in Mental and Behavioural Health, 26*, 100448. DOI: 10.1016/j.invent.2021.100448

Huang, Z., & Li, H. (2019). Research on UX Evaluation Model of Computer Input Devices (Keyboard and Mouse) Based on AHP. *IOP Conference Series. Materials Science and Engineering, 686*(1), 012005. DOI: 10.1088/1757-899X/686/1/012005

Ibirinoye-Abdulkareem, B. S., Adedotun, K. J., Adekunle, J. O., & Raji, A. K. (2025). Enhancing Guest Satisfaction in Hotel Booking Websites through AI-Driven Personalization and Adaptive User Interfaces. *Nigerian Journal of Technical Education, 24*(2), 83–93. DOI: 10.63996/njte.v24i2.32

Jeganathan, Y. (2025). Improving searchability of products in E-commerce platforms. *International Journal of Science and Research Archive, 16*(3), 666–672. DOI: 10.30574/ijsra.2025.16.3.2594

Jiang, Y., & Katsamakas, E. (2010). The Impact of e-Book Technology on Book Retailing. *2010 43rd Hawaii International Conference on System Sciences*, 1–8. DOI: 10.1109/HICSS.2010.383

Kalagarla, S. D.Sneha Deepika Kalagarla. (2025). Enhancing User Experience in ePermitting Systems Through AI-Driven Personalization. *International Journal of Science & Technoledge, 16*(1), 2923. DOI: 10.71097/IJSAT.v16.i1.2923

Kalathot, R. (2025). Artificial Intelligence for Dynamic User Experience Personalization in SaaS. *Journal of Data Analysis and Critical Management, 1*(03), 1–8. DOI: 10.64235/20rneq83

Kim, S., Baek, T. H., Kim, Y.-K., & Yoo, K. (2016). Factors affecting stickiness and word of mouth in mobile applications. *Journal of Research in Interactive Marketing, 10*(3), 177–192. DOI: 10.1108/JRIM-06-2015-0046

Kivetz, R., & Simonson, I. (2000). The Effects of Incomplete Information on Consumer Choice. *JMR, Journal of Marketing Research, 37*(4), 427–448. DOI: 10.1509/jmkr.37.4.427.18796

Kumar, A. (2025). AI-Powered Personalization for Enhancing Customer Retention in Online Retailing. *International Journal of Research and Analytical Reviews, 12*(2). Advance online publication. DOI: 10.56975/ijrar.v12i2.314472

Li, K., Zhou, C., Luo, X., Benitez, J., & Liao, Q. (2022). Impact of information timeliness and richness on public engagement on social media during COVID-19 pandemic: An empirical investigation based on NLP and machine learning. *Decision Support Systems, 162*, 113752. DOI: 10.1016/j.dss.2022.113752

Lin, H.-F. (2007). Measuring Online Learning Systems Success: Applying the Updated DeLone and McLean Model. *Cyberpsychology & Behavior, 10*(6), 817–820. DOI: 10.1089/cpb.2007.9948

Liu, Y., Xu, Y., & Zhou, S. (2024). Enhancing User Experience through Machine Learning-Based Personalized Recommendation Systems: Behavior Data-Driven UI Design. *Applied and Computational Engineering, 112*(1), 42–46. DOI: 10.54254/2755-2721/2024.17905

Lutfi, A., Al-Okaily, M., Alsyouf, A., & Alrawad, M. (2022). Evaluating the D&M IS Success Model in the Context of Accounting Information System and Sustainable Decision Making. *Sustainability (Basel), 14*(13), 8120. DOI: 10.3390/su14138120

Lv, L., & Liu, X. (2022). The Impact of Information Overload of E-Commerce Platform on Consumer Return Intention: Considering the Moderating Role of Perceived Environmental Effectiveness. *International Journal of Environmental Research and Public Health*, *19*(13), 8060. DOI: 10.3390/ijerph19138060

Matraf, M. S. B., Hashim, N. L., Hussain, A., Habbal, A., Hamouda, H., & Ghazali, O. (2025). Enhancing mobile e-book usability for the visually impaired: A novel model validated via the fuzzy delphi method. *Journal of King Saud University. Computer and Information Sciences*, *37*(7), 179. DOI: 10.1007/s44443-025-00180-6

Miller, C. D., & Wang, R. D. (2024). Product digitization and differentiation strategy change: Evidence from the book publishing industry. *Strategic Management Journal*, *45*(7), 1241–1272. DOI: 10.1002/smj.3586

Mittal, B. (2023). The Abandoned E-Tailer Shopping Cart: Factors and Business Strategies to Reverse the Barriers. *Journal of Global Strategic Management*, *15*(2), 45–63. DOI: 10.20460/JGSM.2022.302

Mohammed, S., Budach, L., Feuerpfeil, M., Ihde, N., Nathansen, A., Noack, N., Patzlaff, H., Naumann, F., & Harmouch, H. (2025). The effects of data quality on machine learning performance on tabular data. *Information Systems*, *132*, 102549. DOI: 10.1016/j.is.2025.102549

Mostaghel, R., Oghazi, P., Parida, V., & Sohrabpour, V. (2022). Digitalization driven retail business model innovation: Evaluation of past and avenues for future research trends. *Journal of Business Research*, *146*, 134–145. DOI: 10.1016/j.jbusres.2022.03.072

Muhamed, A., Srinivasan, S., Teo, C.-H., Cui, Q., Zeng, B., Chilimbi, T., & Vishwanathan, S. V. N. (2023). Web-Scale Semantic Product Search with Large Language Models. In Kashima, H., Ide, T., & Peng, W.-C. (Eds.), *Advances in Knowledge Discovery and Data Mining* (Vol. 13937, pp. 73–85). Springer Nature Switzerland., DOI: 10.1007/978-3-031-33380-4_6

Mustafa, S. Z., Kar, A. K., & Janssen, M. F. W. H. A. (2020). Understanding the impact of digital service failure on users: Integrating Tan's failure and DeLone and McLean's success model. *International Journal of Information Management*, *53*, 102119. DOI: 10.1016/j.ijinfomgt.2020.102119

Nasar, Z., Jaffry, S. W., & Malik, M. K. (2022). Named Entity Recognition and Relation Extraction: State-of-the-Art. *ACM Computing Surveys*, *54*(1), 1–39. DOI: 10.1145/3445965

Nugroho, Y., & Prasetyo, A. (2018). Assessing information systems success: A respecification of the DeLone and McLean model to integrating the perceived quality. *Problems and Perspectives in Management, 16*(1), 348–360. DOI: 10.21511/ppm.16(1).2018.34

Ozuem, W., Ranfagni, S., Willis, M., Rovai, S., & Howell, K. (2021). Exploring customers' responses to online service failure and recovery strategies during Covid-19 pandemic: An actor–network theory perspective. *Psychology and Marketing, 38*(9), 1440–1459. DOI: 10.1002/mar.21527

Pandurangan, S. K.Sathish Kuppan Pandurangan. (2025). Data Platform Engineering: Revolutionizing Societal Infrastructure through Intelligent Systems. *Journal of Information Systems Engineering & Management, 10*(58s), 997–1009. DOI: 10.52783/jisem.v10i58s.12754

Patharia, I., & Jain, T. (2024). Antecedents of Electronic Shopping Cart Abandonment during Online Purchase Process. *Business Perspectives and Research, 12*(3), 400–418. DOI: 10.1177/22785337221148810

Peng, Y., Wang, Y., Li, J., & Yang, Q. (2024). Impact of AI-Oriented Live-Streaming E-Commerce Service Failures on Consumer Disengagement—Empirical Evidence from China. *Journal of Theoretical and Applied Electronic Commerce Research, 19*(2), 1580–1598. DOI: 10.3390/jtaer19020077

Petter, S., DeLone, W., & McLean, E. (2008). Measuring information systems success: Models, dimensions, measures, and interrelationships. *European Journal of Information Systems, 17*(3), 236–263. DOI: 10.1057/ejis.2008.15

Prasetyo, Y. T., Ong, A. K. S., Concepcion, G. K. F., Navata, F. M. B., Robles, R. A. V., Tomagos, I. J. T., Young, M. N., Diaz, J. F. T., Nadlifatin, R., & Redi, A. A. N. P. (2021). Determining Factors Affecting Acceptance of E-Learning Platforms during the COVID-19 Pandemic: Integrating Extended Technology Acceptance Model and DeLone & McLean IS Success Model. *Sustainability (Basel), 13*(15), 8365. DOI: 10.3390/su13158365

Quesenbery, W. (2003). The Five Dimensions of Usability. In *Content and Complexity*. Routledge.

Quesenbery, W. (2004). Balancing the 5Es: Usability. *Cutter IT Journal, 17*, 4–11.

Mustafa Ayobami Raji, Hameedat Bukola Olodo, Timothy Tolulope Oke, Wilhelmina Afua Addy, Onyeka Chrisanctus Ofodile, & Adedoyin Tolulope Oyewole. (2024) E-commerce and consumer behavior: A review of AI-powered personalization and market trends. *GSC Advanced Research and Reviews, 18*(3), 066–077. DOI: 10.30574/gscarr.2024.18.3.0090

Razniewski, S., & Das, P. (2020). Structured Knowledge: Have we made progress? An extrinsic study of KB coverage over 19 years. *Proceedings of the 29th ACM International Conference on Information & Knowledge Management*, 3317–3320. DOI: 10.1145/3340531.3417447

Reinartz, W. J., Wiegand, N., & Imschloss, M. (2018). The Impact of Digital Transformation on the Retailing Value Chain. SSRN *Electronic Journal*. DOI: 10.2139/ssrn.3299669

Salim, M., Alfansi, L., Anggarawati, S., Saputra, F. E., & Afandy, C. (2021). The role of perceived usefulness in moderating the relationship between the DeLone and McLean model and user satisfaction. *Uncertain Supply Chain Management, 9*(3), 755–766. DOI: 10.5267/j.uscm.2021.4.002

Salisu, I., Sappri, M. M., Omar, M. F., Nasir, A., Ejaz, S., & Hossain, M. B. (2025). Social media applications through the lens of DeLone and McLean's information system success model: Does perceived privacy matter? *Humanities & Social Sciences Communications, 12*(1), 1028. DOI: 10.1057/s41599-025-05010-8

Shen, Q., Wen, H., Tao, W., Zhang, J., Lv, F., Chen, Z., & Li, Z. (2022). Deep Interest Highlight Network for Click-Through Rate Prediction in Trigger-Induced Recommendation. *Proceedings of the ACM Web Conference 2022*, 422–430. DOI: 10.1145/3485447.3511970

Stoiber, C., Ceneda, D., Wagner, M., Schetinger, V., Gschwandtner, T., Streit, M., Miksch, S., & Aigner, W. (2022). Perspectives of visualization onboarding and guidance in VA. *Visual Informatics, 6*(1), 68–83. DOI: 10.1016/j.visinf.2022.02.005

Tiutiu, M., & Dabija, D.-C. (2023). Improving Customer Experience Using Artificial Intelligence in Online Retail. *Proceedings of the International Conference on Business Excellence, 17*(1), 1139–1147. DOI: 10.2478/picbe-2023-0102

Tsagkias, M., King, T. H., Kallumadi, S., Murdock, V., & De Rijke, M. (2020). Challenges and research opportunities in eCommerce search and recommendations. *ACM SIGIR Forum, 54*(1), 1–23. DOI: 10.1145/3451964.3451966

Tyrväinen, O., Karjaluoto, H., & Saarijärvi, H. (2020). Personalization and hedonic motivation in creating customer experiences and loyalty in omnichannel retail. *Journal of Retailing and Consumer Services*, *57*, 102233. DOI: 10.1016/j.jretconser.2020.102233

Ullah, F., Sepasgozar, S. M. E., Jamaluddin Thaheem, M., Cynthia Wang, C., & Imran, M. (2021). It's all about perceptions: A DEMATEL approach to exploring user perceptions of real estate online platforms. *Ain Shams Engineering Journal*, *12*(4), 4297–4317. DOI: 10.1016/j.asej.2021.04.023

Van Hoboken, J., & Fathaigh, R. Ó. (2021). Smartphone platforms as privacy regulators. *Computer Law & Security Review*, *41*, 105557. DOI: 10.1016/j.clsr.2021.105557

Viriando, Y. F. (2021). Using Delone & McLean Information System Success Model to Evaluate the Success of Online Platform. *Journal of System and Management Sciences*, *11*(2), 182–198. DOI: 10.33168/JSMS.2021.0212

Vlieghe, J., Muls, J., & Rutten, K. (2016). Everybody reads: Reader engagement with literature in social media environments. *Poetics*, *54*, 25–37. DOI: 10.1016/j.poetic.2015.09.001

Widyaningrum, T., Sholihah, Q., & Haryono, B. S. (2024). The Delone and McLean Information System Success Model: Investigating User Satisfaction in Learning Management System. *Journal of Education Technology*, *8*(1), 86–94. DOI: 10.23887/jet.v8i1.71080

Wylde, V., Rawindaran, N., Lawrence, J., Balasubramanian, R., Prakash, E., Jayal, A., Khan, I., Hewage, C., & Platts, J. (2022). Cybersecurity, Data Privacy and Blockchain: A Review. *SN Computer Science*, *3*(2), 127. DOI: 10.1007/s42979-022-01020-4

Xu, Y., & Huang, J.-S. (2015). Factors Influencing Cart Abandonment in the Online Shopping Process. *Social Behavior and Personality*, *43*(10), 1617–1627. DOI: 10.2224/sbp.2015.43.10.1617

Yang, C., Chen, X., Liu, L., & Sweetser, P. (2021). Leveraging semantic features for recommendation: Sentence-level emotion analysis. *Information Processing & Management*, *58*(3), 102543. DOI: 10.1016/j.ipm.2021.102543

Yao, S., Tan, J., Chen, X., Zhang, J., Zeng, X., & Yang, K. (2022). ReprBERT: Distilling BERT to an Efficient Representation-Based Relevance Model for E-Commerce. *Proceedings of the 28th ACM SIGKDD Conference on Knowledge Discovery and Data Mining*, 4363–4371. DOI: 10.1145/3534678.3539090

Zhan, X., Xu, Y., & Liu, Y. (2024). Personalized UI Layout Generation using Deep Learning: An Adaptive Interface Design Approach for Enhanced User Experience. *Journal of Artificial Intelligence General Science (JAIGS) ISSN:3006-4023, 6*(1), 463–478. DOI: 10.60087/jaigs.v6i1.270

Zhuang, Y., Wu, F., Chen, C., & Pan, Y. (2017). Challenges and opportunities: From big data to knowledge in AI 2.0. *Frontiers of Information Technology & Electronic Engineering, 18*(1), 3–14. DOI: 10.1631/FITEE.1601883

Chapter 12 Transforming Digital Marketing Communication Through Generative Engine Optimization: A Strategic Framework for the AI Era

Hasanuzzaman Hasanuzzaman
http://orcid.org/0009-0004-0676-4199
International Islamic University Malaysia (IIUM), Malaysia

Md. Soleman Mollik
http://orcid.org/0009-0003-5703-0606
Bangladesh University of Professionals, Bangladesh

Md. Mominul Islam
http://orcid.org/0009-0008-6566-623X
International University of Business Agriculture and Technology (IUBAT), Bangladesh

ABSTRACT

This chapter examines Generative Engine Optimization (GEO) as an emerging strategic capability in digital marketing communication shaped by generative AI and large language models (LLMs). Using a PRISMA-guided systematic literature review (2021-2025), it synthesizes key themes related to AI-driven content, semantic

DOI: 10.4018/979-8-3373-9325-4.ch012

visibility, trust, and ethical considerations within generative search environments. The analysis highlights a gap in existing research, which largely frames GEO as a strategic tactic rather than a strategic resource. To address this, the chapter proposes a capability-based framework that positions GEO as a mechanism for enhancing visibility, relevance, and engagement in AI-mediated ecosystems, and outlines the implications for theory, practice, and future research.

1. INTRODUCTION

1.1 Background and Context

Generative artificial intelligence has commenced a paradigm shift in digital marketing. This transition takes marketing from a search-centric space into a solution-driven sphere. For nearly two decades, Search Engine Optimization (SEO) dominated commercial engagement. SEO depended on keyword indexing and backlink authority to rank the infamous "ten blue links" (Dwivedi et al., 2023). These traditional link-based experiences are losing dominance as LLMs (Large Language Models) and generative search experiences rise. But customers are increasingly interacting with AI agents that synthesize information rather than retrieve it (Google, 2024; Mollik, 2024). This synthesis rewrites the rules of how visibility operates online. Generative engine optimization (GEO) is needed for visibility now, no longer relying on basic indexing but rather on AI-generated citations, semantic frameworks, and contextual authority. So, organizations need to reimagine digital strategies—the place of GEO in strategy today. The definition of GEO holds that it should not be thought of merely as a technical niche but rather as a strategic necessity for sustaining market relevance within human–AI ecosystems (Grewal et al., 2024), and indeed this is how one must approach GEO from the standpoint of contemporary strategy.

Market relevance is also being shaped by the acceleration of artificial intelligence, particularly generative artificial intelligence (GenAI). GenAI has transformed how an organization approaches content creation, distribution, and consumption across digital channels. The creation of content is not entirely in human hands. Now, large language models, generative search engines such as ChatGPT and Gemini, and conversational agents co-create marketing messages for them and guide consumer decision-making (Dwivedi et al., 2023; Mollik et al., 2024). Real-time influence creates additional optimization challenges. In a recent scholarly preprint, we discuss Generative Engine Optimization (GEO), a framework for AI-driven search environments, as well as parallels with the historical evolution of SEO (Chen et al., 2025a). The framework outlines how more traditional forms of search visibility differ from AI visibility and provides tips for optimizing content to perform well on generative systems. Organizations need to reconsider their marketing communication strategies due to these changes. Strategies will need to evolve away from traditional SEO models toward approaches based on semantic relevance, contextual authority, and human–AI interaction. As such, GEO works as a strategic capability in constant motion as opposed to being an exclusively technical tactic (Paschen et al., 2019).

GEO research has not yet completely developed a strategic capability. Existing research indicates growing interest in industry, but the theoretical grounding of academic literature is weak and fragmented. This gap is the impetus for this chapter. The chapter performs a Systematic Literature Review based on the PRISMA framework to summarize recent scholarship related to Generative AI and Generative Engine Optimization. GEO is, as hoped, positioned in this review as a strategic capability that rewrites digital marketing communication for the AI era.

1.2 Problem Statement

Current research on Generative Engine Optimization (GEO) lacks Strategic capability. While generative AI technologies are revolutionizing digital marketing contexts at an unprecedented pace, there remains a limited, conceptually diffuse, and ineffectual theoretical academic comprehension of GEO precisely. Most of the existing research focuses on technical and operational roles of AI, including automation, content generation, and personalization. Nevertheless, these studies focus less on how GEO modifies strategic digital marketing communication (Huang & Rust, 2021a), organizational capabilities (Dwivedi et al., 2023), and value-creation processes.

As organizations scale their use of AI tools, strategic comprehension of these factors becomes even more consequential (Mollik et al., 2026a). As a field, most previous studies perceive AI more as an operational asset than as a component of a communication strategy (Hossain & Mollik, 2022). The narrow view results in a considerable gap by falling short in communicating how organizations may systematically leverage GEO to achieve brand communication, improve consumer engagement, and ensure sustainable competitive advantage under an AI-laden setting (Huang & Rust, 2021a).

Strong theoretical integration is also crucial to sustaining competitive advantage. This lack of a theory-driven and integrative overview of GEO-relevant research, in turn, hampers conceptual development and diminishes the generation of actionable insights for practitioners working within such AI-mediated ecosystems. Without a clear structure comparing GEO to other concepts, scholars and practitioners find it difficult to see how GEO informs communication strategy and organizational transformation. Accordingly, a systematic as well as conceptually grounded review of literature is required to cluster existing knowledge and frame GEO as an umbrella framework in the digital marketing communication research arena.

This calls for the construction of a structured framework and indicates some research gaps in existing studies. Most research around generative artificial intelligence centers on content creation, automation, and efficiency gains. Much of this content portrays GenAI as a technological tool, not a strategic communication capability. Consequently, little is known about how Generative Engine Optimization (GEO) significantly alters digital marketing communication at the strategic level.

Transformation requires more than optimizing operations. However, despite academic discussions regarding search visibility and AI-driven marketing practices, there is a limited conceptual framework offered for GEO from the perspective of marketing communication research. Current discourse is still divided between technical, managerial, and consumer dynamics. This fragmentation inhibits scholars from devising a coherent framework for understanding GEO´s influence on semantic visibility, personalization, and communication strategy.

A more robust theoretical underpinning is also needed for the communication strategy. The prevailing literature does not often observe an integration of GEO with a strategic capability or dynamic capability perspectives. If this integration does not occur, the role of GEO in organizational adaptation and long-term competitive positioning is uncertain. Hence, there is an urgent need for a synthesis that addresses this gap, elucidates GEO's strategic role, and facilitates the development of a capability-based framework for digital marketing communication.

1.3 Significance of the Study

This capability-based framework contributes significantly not only to research but also to practice. Theoretically, this study contributes to the digital marketing communication and human–AI interaction literature by providing one of the first systematic syntheses of GEO. It reframes GEO as more of a strategic capability than just a technical tool. In this way, positioning enhances interdisciplinary links between marketing communication, strategic management, and artificial intelligence studies.

If used for practical understanding, interdisciplinary integration can also improve conceptual comprehension. From a managerial standpoint, the findings provide insights with actionable implications for marketers, brand managers, and digital strategists who operate under AI-mediated conditions. It also explains different organizational capabilities to collaborate on GEO, enabling companies to maintain visibility and relevance while engaging with consumers. It also aligns responsible use of AI, strategic adaptation, and governance in communications as the main priorities. The study further advances technology adoption and capability development with consideration for the larger purpose of the IGI Global volume by clarifying GEO's strategic role.

1.4 Chapter's Objectives, Questions, and Structure

Objectives

The specific objectives of this chapter are:

1. To examine how GEO is conceptualized and applied within digital marketing communication contexts.
2. To develop a strategic framework that explains how GEO transforms digital marketing communication.
3. To propose a future research agenda to guide scholars and marketers in advancing GEO research and application.

Questions

To achieve these objectives, the chapter addresses the following questions:

1. How is GEO conceptualized and applied in existing digital marketing communication literature?
2. In what ways does GEO transform digital marketing communication, and how can these transformations be synthesized into a strategic framework?
3. What future research directions emerge from existing literature to guide scholars and practitioners in advancing GEO research and application in digital marketing communication?

1.5 Chapter Structure

The chapter is organized according to the research questions. Following a hierarchical structure, one informs the other until we reach a clear definition of Generative Engine Optimization (GEO) as an operational capability. A theoretical background of the following section. It examines fundamental concepts on generative artificial intelligence (GenAI), SEO and GEO evolvement, perspectives on strategic capabilities, and human–AI interaction in digital marketing communication.

The chapter outlines the research methodology after this theoretical discussion. This section outlines the qualitative Systematic Literature Review prediction approach, especially its PRISMA framework, data collection procedures, and thematic analysis methods. The findings section then provides descriptive and thematic analysis of the selected studies. Then, the discussion develops a strategic framework that illustrates how GEO reconfigures the allocation of digital marketing communication. The chapter ends with a future research agenda, managerial and theoretical implications, as well as key contributions.

2. SCOPE OF THE REVIEW

2.1 Generative AI in Digital Marketing Communication

In marketing scholarship, generative AI is likely a disruptive force. This force transforms how marketers engage customers and create content for cross-channel communication (Grewal et al., 2025). This transformation is more than rapid drafting or rudimentary automation. Rather, it transforms creative work, decision support, and customer-facing conversational tools in ways that impact strategy and execution (Dwivedi et al., 2023; Peres et al., 2023).

And strategy also depends on how marketers read signals from consumers. AI and machine learning amplify that potential through improved prediction, higher-quality decision support, and scalable personalization. This increased capacity brings new responsibilities (Mustak et al., 2021), which means marketers need better governance, stricter quality control and clearer ethical safeguards. These safeguards matter as GenAI outputs become more humanlike, multimodal and real-time. These outputs directly influence consumers' evaluation of credibility and the perception of brand intent (Hermann & Puntoni, 2024; Kshetri et al., 2024).

Brand intent also relies on the context in which AI navigates. Marketing communication research reveals that AI operates within an ecosystem rather than in a vacuum. The ecosystem perspective, therefore, views AI-driven marketing communication as interplaying components (Malthouse & Copulsky, 2023), such as data/models and digital environments/content assets. Why does this ecosystem lens matter for GEO? GEO does not rely solely on the quality of content. GEO is also contingent on how brands design content, substantiate claims with evidence, link information across sources, and communicate contextual authority via AI-mediation (Aggarwal et al., 2024; Zhu et al., 2025).

2.2 From SEO to GEO: Evolution of Digital Visibility

SEO has influenced the way brands get found online for a long time now. The visibility model used was based on ranked retrieval. Brands focused on optimizing keywords, deepening relevance signals, and building link-based authority to move up the rankings. This ranking process is also a major part of competition in search markets. It affected consumer welfare, organic result quality, and the trade-off between organic and paid results (Berman & Katona, 2013).

In generative search environments, ranking positions now matter much less. In such environments, the unit of visibility shifts. Brands no longer just compete for a clickable link in a ranked list. Instead, brands are competing for inclusion within a synthesized response. This inclusion might manifest itself through direct citation and attribution. This inclusion might also be through content absorption, where the device borrows ideas without explicit credit. That shift is part of a larger change in how we retrieve information. Researchers call this shift a transition from "matching" to "generation." Matching retrieves and ranks documents. Generation gives answers using LLM-assisted retrieval and synthesis pipelines (Li et al., 2025; Zhu et al., 2025).

The production of answers generates a new logic of visibility. GEO addresses the same logic by emphasizing visibility in generative engine outputs. Aggarwal et al. (2024) describe GEO as a paradigm that enhances content visibility in generative outputs. They also demonstrate measurable visibility under experimental conditions (Aggarwal et al., 2024). This frame matters from the perspective of marketing communication because it diverts attention away from ranking signals and toward that generative mediation. Generative mediation refers to a model that aggregates, recomposes, and displays information under mostly black-box conditions. This black-box aspect amplifies uncertainty for marketers. It also adds dependence on grounding and retrieval quality. To better understand this, information retrieval scholars argue that while generative AI circumvents more familiar types of searches, it should complement (rather than replace) search; they emphasize that issues of reliability and evidence remain indelibly core concerns in searching for information.

Reliability also determines the overall shift from SEO to GEO. This move is not just a semantic shift. Instead, it suggests a structural change in the way brand messages travel through digital ecosystems. SEO emphasized link-centric discovery. GEO emphasizes answer-centric mediation. This transformation modifies what marketers measure and what marketers have in their hands. It is relevant to the inclusion rate, citation share, message framing, and trust calibration (Aggarwal et al., 2024; Stahl & Eke, 2024).

2.3 Theoretical Foundation: Strategic Capability and Dynamic Capability Lens

Generative engine optimization (GEO) should not be treated as a short-term technical tactic. That narrow view overlooks the organizational work that supports visibility in generative environments. In answer-based systems, brands gain exposure when their knowledge is easy to retrieve, easy to verify, and easy to summarize. That condition depends on resource quality, knowledge structure, editorial discipline, and governance, not only on keywords or backlinks (Aggarwal et al., 2024).

The resource-based view helps explain this shift. Barney (1991) argued that firms sustain an advantage when they control resources that are valuable, rare, difficult to imitate, and supported by the organization. GEO fits this logic when a firm builds proprietary knowledge assets, trusted documentation, expert content, and cross-functional routines for maintaining factual consistency. These assets improve AI-facing visibility, but competitors cannot quickly copy the underlying evidence base, source credibility, and domain knowledge that make those assets effective (Barney, 1991).

Dynamic capability theory extends this argument. Teece (2007) showed that firms perform well in turbulent markets when they can sense change, seize opportunities, and reconfigure resources. Generative search is such a turbulent setting. Firms must sense changes in answer behaviour, seize new visibility opportunities, and reconfigure content, data, analytics, and governance processes for AI-mediated discovery. GEO, therefore, is not one isolated action. It is a repeatable capability that links environmental sensing, content design, technical readiness, and organizational learning (Teece, 2007; Aggarwal et al., 2024).

This capability also has a user-side logic. Pirolli and Card's (1999) information foraging theory explains that users seek the highest information value at the lowest search cost. Generative engines reduce that cost by producing direct answers instead of ranked lists of links. That reduction changes consumer behavior. Users often stop at the answer layer rather than visit several webpages. The unit of competition then shifts from click-through rank to answer inclusion, citation presence, and message fidelity (Pirolli & Card, 1999; Aggarwal et al., 2024).

Fidelity matters because generative systems do not only retrieve information; they also reframe it. Miller (2019) noted that people judge AI outputs through explanation, plausibility, and social expectations. In marketing settings, that judgment influences trust, engagement, and perceived authenticity (Hermann & Puntoni, 2024; Hollebeek et al., 2024). When consumers detect automation without clarity or human oversight, they may question the brand's authenticity and intent (Brüns & Meißner, 2024). GEO, therefore, belongs at the intersection of strategy, information behavior, and human–AI interaction. It manages not only whether a brand appears in an answer, but also how that brand is interpreted after the answer appears.

2.4 Technology Transfer in GEO: From Crawlers to Retrieval-Augmented Generation

The shift from SEO to GEO is not only a communication shift. It is also a technology transfer shift. Traditional SEO relies on crawling, indexing, and ranking.

Search engines collect webpages, index their terms, and rank links based on relevance and authority signals. Generative systems use a more layered process. They retrieve semantically relevant passages and then generate a synthesized response from that evidence. This change moves visibility from a page-ranking problem to a retrieval-and-summarisation problem (Karpukhin et al., 2020; Zhao et al., 2026).

This technical change explains why GEO needs a different strategic logic. In retrieval-augmented systems, content is often transformed into dense representations that support semantic matching rather than simple keyword overlap. A retriever identifies passages that are most relevant to the prompt. A generator then composes an answer from those retrieved passages and from the model's broader language capabilities. In this architecture, the quality of the final answer depends heavily on the quality, consistency, and retrievability of the source material (Karpukhin et al., 2020; Zhao et al., 2026).

That dependence clarifies the technology transfer problem for firms. Companies no longer optimize only webpages for ranking. They must also prepare knowledge assets for machine ingestion, retrieval, and synthesis. This preparation includes structuring factual content, separating evidence from promotional language, aligning product and policy information across channels, and maintaining stable terminology across documents. In practice, the firm converts commercial knowledge into retrievable evidence for generative systems (Aggarwal et al., 2024; Zhao et al., 2026).

Evidence now becomes the new unit of visibility. If a product page, help-centre article, policy statement, or FAQ contains clear facts, stable entities, and verifiable claims, a generative engine is more likely to retrieve and summarize it accurately. If the same knowledge is fragmented, inconsistent, or overly promotional, the system may ignore it, distort it, or replace it with a competitor's clearer evidence base (Aggarwal et al., 2024; Kshetri et al., 2024).

This pipeline changes managerial priorities. Managers need technical readiness before they pursue answer visibility. That readiness includes clean content architecture, structured metadata, consistent entity naming, controlled updates, and regular audits of AI-facing knowledge assets. These routines make GEO more than a communication tactic. They turn GEO into an organizational capability that links data, content, technology, and strategy in one workflow (Aggarwal et al., 2024; Zhao et al., 2026).

2.5 Human-AI Interaction, Trust, and Ethical Communication

Generative visibility shapes more than search outcomes. It also shapes how consumers interpret brands. In traditional search, users could compare many links and sources before making a judgment. In generative environments, users often receive one synthesized answer first. That answer reduces search effort, but it also increases the influence of the system that frames the response (Pirolli & Card, 1999; Hermann & Puntoni, 2024).

Framing matters because consumers do not judge information only by factual content. They also judge tone, source cues, explanation quality, and perceived neutrality. If a generative engine presents a brand in a clear, balanced, and well-supported way, users may see the answer as credible. If the answer appears vague, overly confident, or weakly sourced, trust may decline. This process can be described as trust calibration. Trust calibration refers to how users decide whether an AI-generated response is reliable enough to guide a belief, preference, or purchase decision (Miller, 2019; Glassberg et al., 2025).

This trust problem is especially important in marketing communication. Brands no longer control the full path from message creation to message reception. A third-party AI system may summarize, rephrase, reorder, or simplify the brand's content before the user sees it. This mediation can improve convenience, but it can also distort brand meaning. When distortion occurs, consumers may misunderstand product value, service terms, or brand identity. In such settings, GEO becomes a trust-management capability partly. It helps firms increase the chance that AI systems retrieve accurate content and present it in a form that preserves brand meaning (Hermann & Puntoni, 2024; Hollebeek et al., 2024).

Meaning also depends on authenticity. Recent research shows that consumers may react negatively when they believe brand communication is generated by AI without sufficient transparency or human oversight. This concern does not mean firms should avoid AI. Instead, it means firms need clear editorial standards, human review, and evidence-based content design. These practices help reduce the risk that generative communication appears artificial, manipulative, or detached from the brand's values (Brüns & Meißner, 2024).

Ethics, therefore, moves to the centre of GEO. Generative systems can amplify hallucination, bias, and information asymmetry. They may overrepresent some sources, underrepresent others, or summarize content in ways that flatten nuance. In commercial settings, these risks affect not only consumer welfare but also legal compliance, brand equity, and competitive fairness. Responsible GEO should therefore include transparency, source integrity, disclosure, update control, and factual verification as core principles rather than optional add-ons (Saura et al., 2024; Stahl & Eke, 2024).

This ethical issue also extends to privacy and data use. Firms may seek stronger personalization in AI-mediated communication, yet consumers often remain uneasy about how personal data is collected, inferred, and applied. This tension reinforces the need for privacy-aware knowledge design and governance. A firm that treats GEO as a strategic capability should therefore invest not only in visibility but also in accuracy, accountability, and trust. In this sense, effective GEO is not merely about appearing in AI-generated answers. It is about appearing responsibly.

3. RESEARCH METHODOLOGY

3.1 Research Design and Rationale

This chapter employs a qualitative systematic literature review (SLR). It summarizes research on Generative AI (GenAI) and Generative Engine Optimization (GEO) related to digital marketing communication. A qualitative SLR is a good fit when the subject is novel and accelerating in nature. And it fits when researchers use different theories and methods. In such contexts, an SLR assists the researcher with identifying studies transparently, comparing evidence systematically, and synthesising rather than loose statistical aggregation.

This synthesis is needed because GEO research spans multiple disciplines. Some are published in marketing journals and delve into strategy and engagement. Other studies are published in computer science venues and concern benchmarking and optimization. Other studies are published in interdisciplinary venues and examine AI applications in marketing. This dispersion creates conceptual fragmentation. Fragmentation reduces visibility on how the field conceptualizes GEO and how it connects GEO to outcomes of marketing communication. An SLR thus benefits in three ways. First, it provides a theory of how scholars conceptualize GEO. Second, it identifies common themes across research traditions. Third, it reinforces an integrative lens that positions GEO as a strategic capability rather than just a technical ploy (Grewal et al., 2025; Aggarwal et al., 2024).

3.2 PRISMA Protocol and Reporting Approach

This chapter uses a qualitative systematic literature review because GEO research is still fragmented across marketing, information systems, and computer science. A systematic review is appropriate in such a setting because it supports transparent study selection and structured thematic synthesis across diverse research traditions (Snyder, 2019). To improve reporting rigour, the review followed PRISMA 2020 and documented the stages of identification, screening, eligibility assessment, and final inclusion (Page et al., 2021).

The search covered the period from 2021 to 2025 and focused on studies relevant to generative AI, GEO, digital marketing communication, and AI-mediated visibility. The search process identified 430 records. After duplicate removal, 154 records remained for title and abstract screening. This stage excluded 66 records.

The review then sought 88 full-text records, retrieved 75, and retained 19 studies for final synthesis based on relevance, conceptual fit, and direct connection to the chapter's objectives.

The analysis used thematic synthesis rather than statistical aggregation. This choice suited the field because the literature differs widely in theory, method, and publication format. The final studies were coded around five recurring themes: strategic capability, technical readiness, semantic visibility, trust and consumer response, and governance. These themes later informed the capability gaps identified in the review and provided the basis for the proposed GEO framework (Snyder, 2019; Page et al., 2021).

Figure 1. PRISMA flow diagram adapted from Page et al., 2021

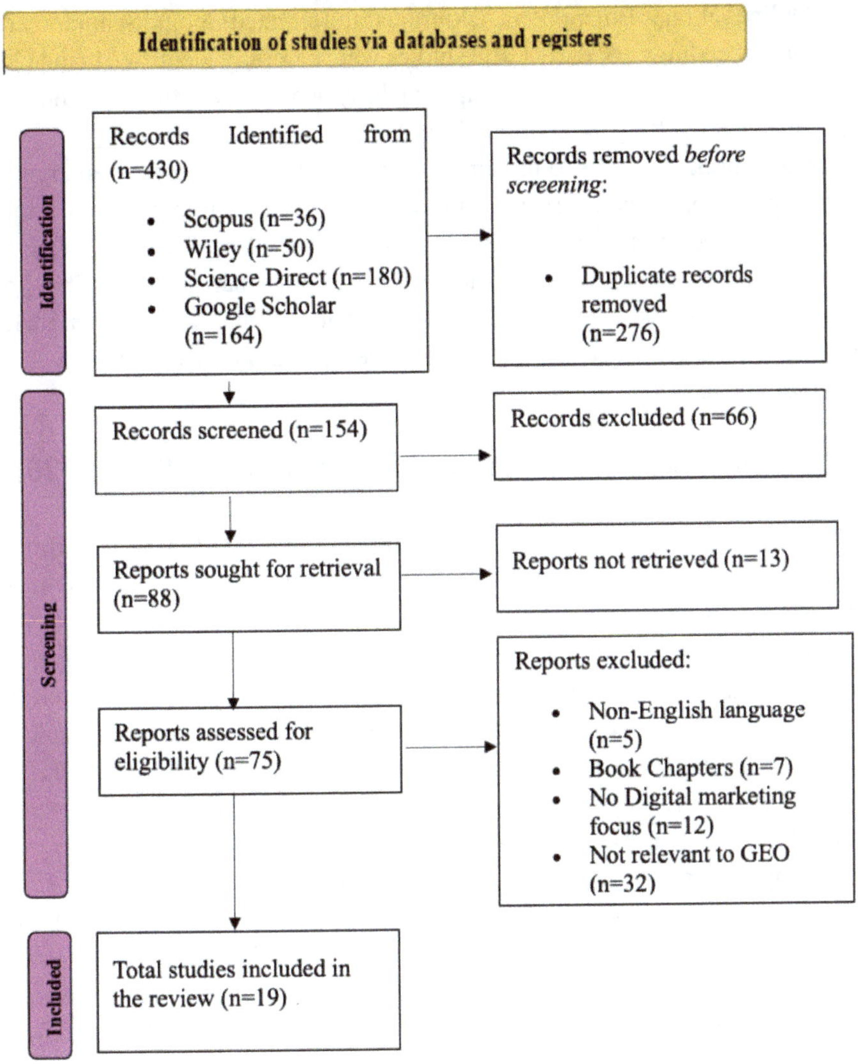

3.3 Data Sources/Databases and Justification

The database approach strikes a balance between quality control and interdisciplinary coverage. GEO is located between marketing communication, information retrieval and artificial intelligence. Thus, it is anchored in Scopus for the review as it covers both marketing outlets and computing outlets. The review then extends retrieval with extra resources to minimize database bias. These include (when available): Web of Science Core Collection; EBSCO Discovery Services; ScienceDirect; Wiley Online Library; Emerald; Sage Journals, and targeted Google Scholar searches. Relevant proceedings and early GEO studies were carefully identified using Google Scholar. This was a multi-database approach, which aligns with SLR guidance on topics that cross-cutting and publication formats Page et al., 2021).

Interdisciplinary coverage matters, too, as GEO research can be emergent and appear in places other than the usual journal pathways. Some important contributions start as conference papers or preprints indexed by discipline. Scopus also increased preprint visibility through SSRN integration and other partnerships. This growth means that benchmarking of early GEO work outside journal channels is more likely. Accordingly, the search strategy permitted method-explicit early evidence, which aided GEO benchmarking and optimization.

3.4 Search Strategy and Keywords (Timeframe: 2021–2025)

The search strategy covered the period between 2021 and 2025. The time span signifies when generative search and GEO emerged as observable ideas in the literature. Search terms were constructed with three concept blocks. Searching keywords encompass "Generative AI" OR "large language model" OR "LLM" OR "generative search" OR "generative engine optimization" OR GEO OR "generative search engine optimization" "digital marketing communication" OR "marketing communication" OR consumer engagement OR content marketing OR personalization OR "brand communication OR "digital marketing communication" OR "marketing communication" OR "consumer engagement".

To support conceptual completeness, there were two boundary rules. First, for the SEO-to-GEO comparison, we kept one of the foundational studies on baselines in SEO (Matta et al., 2020). Second, the review excluded a handful of "online first" studies published in the end-of-2025 publications but assigned to 2026 issues (e.g., Salih et al., 2026; Borimnejad & Borimnejad, 2026). The rules governed and helped provide continuity to the conceptual timeline.

3.5 Inclusion and Exclusion Criteria

Studies that met the following conditions were included:

Topic relevance: direct treatment of GenAI-impacted marketing communication and/or AI-mediated search visibility (SEO transformation, GEO, generative search optimization, citation/inclusion dynamics).

Publication quality and traceability: peer-reviewed journal articles and those indexed in major proceedings were prioritized (e.g., JAMS; Psychology & Marketing; ACM KDD; Springer proceedings). Preprints were included only where they presented methods-explicit, reproducible GEO benchmarks or optimization pipelines that are not currently well reflected across journals and were considered as early findings rather than definitive theory statements (Aggarwal et al., 2024; Chen et al., 2025a; Chen et al., 2025b; Chen et al., 2025c).

Language: English.

Context importance: implications for outcomes of digital marketing communication are clear (visibility, engagement, message creation, trust/governance, ethics, and organizational transformation).

Studies were excluded if they: (a) pertained to purely technical terms not relevant to marketing communication; (b) were opinions only without transparency of method; (c) were duplicates; or (d) did not have full text available for inclusion eligibility assessment (as per PRISMA 2020).

3.6 Study Selection Process

Study selection followed PRISMA logic. First, the review removed duplicates across databases. Second, the review screened titles and abstracts against inclusion criteria. This screening focused on GenAI and GEO relevance and clear marketing communication implications. Third, the review assessed full texts for eligibility and logged exclusion reasons. Finally, the review retained 19 papers for qualitative synthesis.

3.7 Data Extraction

Table 1 presents studies addressing GEO in recent research. Scholars find that GEO is replacing SEO and other platforms with advanced features. Some studies cement GEO with minimal focus and find that the recent platforms have some limitations. People are searching for and using GEO rather than SEO and related domains. They suggest that GEO could be treated as the most advanced digital platform for transforming digital marketing communications.

Table 1. Literature characteristics and GEO integration

Study Title	Affiliated authors & countries	Study type	Key findings	GEO integration
GEO: Generative Engine Optimization	Pranjal Aggarwal et al. (2024, India/USA)	Quantitative	Introduces a black-box GEO framework and GEO-bench; reports visibility improvements up to 40%. Tactics such as adding citations/quotes/statistics improve visibility; keyword stuffing is less effective.	Yes
Generative Engine Optimization: How to Dominate AI Search	Mahe Chen et al. (2025, Canada)	Quantitative	AI search tends to favor earned media over brand/social content; behavior differs by engine/region/ vertical. Recommends machine-scannable, evidence-backed content and engine/language-specific approaches.	Yes
Beyond Keywords: Driving Generative Search Engine Optimization with Content-Centric Agents	Qiyuan Chen et al. (2025, China)	Quantitative	Introduces CC-GSEO-Bench and a multi-dimensional influence evaluation beyond attribution. Proposes a multi-agent analyze-revise-evaluate workflow to refine content and improve influence in generative search answers.	Yes
The New Digital Compass: Navigating SEO's Evolution in the AI Era	Srinivas Reddy Kosna (2025)	Qualitative	Practitioner-oriented guidance for AI-era visibility (structured data, AI readability) and proposes metrics such as citation visibility/ share of voice/brand sentiment.	Yes
The Future of Search Engine Optimization: Exploring the Role of AI	Rajawat Manisha (2024, India)	Mixed Method	Survey of 200 SEO professionals plus literature synthesis: perceived efficiency and analytics benefits, alongside concerns about privacy/bias and need for human oversight.	Yes
Search Engine Optimization in Digital Marketing: Present Scenario and Future Scope	Himanshu Matta et al. (2020, India)	Qualitative	Secondary-data-based overview of SEO as a marketing tool; emphasizes mobile SEO and white-hat practices.	Yes
The End of the Search Engine Era and the Rise of Generative AI	Eslam Amer et al. (2024, UK)	Mixed	Argues a shift from link-based retrieval to generative answers; discusses limits of traditional search (including SEO manipulation) and ethical/ economic implications.	Yes
Generative AI and the future of marketing: a consumer protection perspective	Bram Duivenvoorde (2025, Netherlands)	Qualitative	Analyzes consumer risks (synthetic ads/deepfakes, exploitative personalization, deceptive chatbots) and argues EU law offers some protection but may be insufficient in practice.	No

continued on following page

Table 1. Continued

Study Title	Affiliated authors & countries	Study type	Key findings	GEO integration
Exploring Ethical Implications of AI-Powered Personalization in Digital Marketing	Amin Karami et al. (2024, UK)	Qualitative	Synthesizes issues (privacy, bias, manipulation, transparency/ accountability) and provides governance recommendations.	No
Generative AI in marketing & principles for ethical design/deployment	Erik Hermann et al. (2025, Germany/USA)	Qualitative	Maps GenAI applications across marketing and proposes ASSURANCE principles for responsible design/deployment; discusses policy implications.	No
How generative AI is shaping the future of marketing	Grewal et al. (2025, USA/UK/Mexico)	Qualitative	Presents a framework (inputs × human augmentation) to guide tool selection; highlights trade-offs (speed/cost vs accuracy/risk/ privacy).	No
Generative AI in innovation & marketing processes: roadmap	Paola Cillo et al. (2025, Italy)	Qualitative	Research roadmap across innovation phases; notes risks of repeated GenAI use for capabilities and consumer behavior; highlights privacy/ disinformation as future research areas.	No
Role of GenAI in shaping consumer–brand relationships	Zahy Ramadan et al. (2025, Lebanon)	Qualitative	Threads supports deeper engagement/loyalty (especially for non-GenAI brands). GenAI automation boosts awareness/ purchases on X but may feel transactional and reduce emotional depth.	No
Transforming Digital Marketing with Generative AI	Tasin Islam et al. (2024, UK)	Qualitative and Case studies	Proposes MARK-GEN steps for using GenAI in marketing content; demonstrates fashion use-cases and argues speed/cost benefits for SMEs.	No
AI applications for marketing: literature-based study	Abid Haleem et al. (2022, India)	Qualitative	Literature synthesis of AI for targeting/personalization, channel timing, and competitor analysis; emphasizes dependence on business context and data-driven decisioning.	No
A model for GAI in customer decision-making using social interaction	Hojatollah Hamidi (2025, Iran)	Quantitative	Survey-based model: information quality most influential and internet usage least. Satisfaction/ inertia affect engagement in GAI-based marketing; credibility of message source and social effects matter.	No

continued on following page

Table 1. Continued

Study Title	Affiliated authors & countries	Study type	Key findings	GEO integration
Exploring AI's role in shaping future marketing strategies	Bobro et al. (2024, Ukraine/Switzerland)	Qualitative	Narrative discussion of AI for personalization and decision-making; highlights opportunities and challenges of AI integration into marketing strategies.	No
Adoption of Generative AI in content creation: advertising industry case study	Nguyet et al. (2024)	Qualitative	Reports perceived efficiency gains (e.g., ideation time), and notes the role of industry competition and need for accessible support systems for successful integration.	No
The Cutting Edge of AI in E-Marketing: How the Use of Digital Tools Boosts Performance in Jordan	Al-Gasawneh et al. (2025, Jordan/Saudi Arabia/Iraq)	Quantitative	Survey of Jordanian e-commerce firms: AI dimensions (deep learning, chatbots, customization) are positively correlated with e-marketing performance; digital marketing tools (SMM/SEO/content marketing) moderate these relationships.	No

Source: Authors' creation

3.8 Data Analysis Method (Thematic Synthesis and ATLAS.ti Logic)

The synthesis was guided by a thematic analysis process that facilitates qualitative integration across diverse evidence. This involved four steps, including familiarizing with the findings of the study, conducting open coding, axial coding and refining themes via naming (Braun & Clarke, 2006). In ATLAS. The coding process went through iterative cycles in the TI terms.

The review initially employed open coding to examine organizational claims. They codified resonant themes like citation dynamics, semantic authority signals, hallucination risks, and machine scannability. Axial coding was employed after that to link these similar codes and combine them under higher-order categories. Such categories corresponded to the chapter's research questions. They spanned visibility transformation, content co-creation, engagement and personalization, and governance and trust. The review also developed a codebook and engaged in memoing. The codebook allowed for consistent decisions at each step of the coding process. Code implementation documented meaning; less drift across cycles.

3.9 Trustworthiness/Rigour (Qualitative Quality)

The review enhanced rigour by forming established trustworthiness criteria. PRISMA transparency, established clear inclusion and exclusion criteria, and outlet-type triangulation supported credibility. Reliability was enhanced by a documented protocol and decision trail throughout screening and coding. Confirmability was ensured with the use of codebook definitions and analytic memos. These materials aimed to minimize interpretive drift and enhance traceability from themes back to source studies. Explicit handling of boundaries also strengthened transparency. This encompassed "online first" articles and method-explicit preprints. The review treated those sources as preliminary evidence, not settled doctrine.

4. FINDINGS FROM DESCRIPTIVE ANALYSIS OF LITERATURE

This section summarizes publication, outlet, method, and focus patterns derived from your 21-study extraction table.

4.1 Concept Analysis

Figure 2 presents a conceptual overview of the key themes shaping Generative Engine Optimization (GEO) in the context of AI-driven digital marketing communication. The word cloud highlights *GEO*, *AI*, *marketing*, *consumer*, and *content* as the most prominent concepts, indicating that GEO operates at the intersection of artificial intelligence and marketing strategy. The prominence of terms such as *search*, *engine*, *intelligence*, and *model* reflects the technological foundations of GEO, where AI models process user queries and generate responses that influence information discovery and brand visibility.

Figure 2. Concept mapping (Source: Authors' creation)

In addition, several supporting concepts, such as *customer*, *brand*, *strategy*, *SEO*, *interaction*, and *decision,* demonstrate the marketing-oriented implications of GEO. These terms suggest that GEO is not only a technical optimization approach but also a strategic communication mechanism that shapes consumer engagement, information accessibility, and brand positioning within AI-mediated search environments. The presence of terms like *privacy*, *risk*, *bias*, and *framework* further indicates emerging research concerns related to ethical considerations, transparency, and governance in AI-driven marketing ecosystems. To achieve sustainability, digital communication requires a long-term plan and strategy (Dhar et al., 2026; Mollik et al., 2026b; Uddin et al., 2026).

4.2 Content Analysis

Figure 3 presents a tree map visualization illustrating the frequency distribution of keywords identified in the content analysis. The dominance of the term *GEO* indicates that Generative Engine Optimization serves as the central focus of the literature, followed by *AI*, *marketing*, and *opportunities*, which collectively highlight the transformative potential of AI-powered search environments for digital marketing communication. Other highly frequent terms, such as *consumer*, *content*, *model*, *research*, and *Gen AI*, further reinforce the importance of AI-driven content generation and consumer interaction in shaping contemporary marketing strategies.

Figure 3. Content mapping (Source: Authors' creation)

The tree map also reveals several supporting thematic clusters, including *search*, *engine*, *intelligence*, *strategy*, *SEO*, *interaction*, and *decision*. These terms reflect the operational and strategic dimensions of GEO, emphasizing how AI-generated responses influence search behaviour, customer engagement, and organizational decision-making. Additionally, the presence of terms such as *privacy*, *bias*, *risk*, and *platform* suggests that while GEO offers substantial opportunities for marketers, it also raises concerns related to ethical governance, transparency, and the reliability of AI-generated information within digital marketing ecosystems.

4.3 GEO performance Indicators and Measurement Logic

A strategic framework needs measurable outcomes. Measurement makes GEO actionable, comparable, and managerially useful. Traditional SEO indicators, such as keyword rank, impressions, and click-through rate, still matter, but they do not capture what happens when a generative engine answers the query itself. GEO therefore requires answer-level and trust-level indicators that reflect semantic visibility, message quality, and governance performance (Aggarwal et al., 2024).

The first indicator is citation frequency. This indicator measures how often a brand or brand-owned source appears in AI-generated answers across a defined set of target prompts. The second indicator is citation prominence. This indicator shows whether the brand appears as a primary source, a supporting source, or not at all. The third indicator is answer share. This indicator captures the proportion of relevant prompts in which the brand is included in the generated answer. Together, these measures assess semantic visibility rather than simple page position (Aggarwal et al., 2024).

Visibility alone is not enough. The fourth indicator is brand sentiment alignment. This indicator evaluates whether the AI summary preserves the intended brand meaning, tone, and value proposition. The fifth indicator is factual fidelity. This indicator checks whether prices, product features, service terms, or policy claims remain accurate after the system paraphrases them. The sixth indicator is trust signal integrity. This indicator assesses whether the answer includes credible cues such as source attribution, transparency, balanced framing, or clear explanation. These measures matter because consumers respond not only to presence but also to authenticity, clarity, and credibility (Hermann & Puntoni, 2024; Brüns & Meißner, 2024; Glassberg et al., 2025).

The seventh indicator is zero-click substitution risk. This indicator measures the gap between answer visibility and site visitation. A brand may appear often in generative answers yet lose traffic, first-party data, and direct relationship value. The eighth indicator is update latency. This indicator measures how quickly revised brand information appears in AI outputs after a source document changes. Slow update cycles increase operational, legal, and reputational risk. The ninth indicator is governance compliance. This indicator assesses whether AI-visible content follows internal standards for privacy, accuracy, disclosure, and responsible communication (Saura et al., 2024).

These indicators allow firms to evaluate GEO as a strategic capability rather than as a technical experiment. They track visibility, meaning, trust, and control at the same time. They also support cross-functional coordination because marketing, legal, analytics, and knowledge-management teams can use the same measurement logic to evaluate performance, identify risk, and guide future improvement.

4.4 GEO-Driven Communication Transformation Model

Capabilities Theory explains how organizations can adapt their digital marketing communication strategies within AI-driven ecosystems. The model begins with key organizational inputs, including knowledge assets, structured content architecture, data and measurement infrastructure, and governance mechanisms (Figure 4). These inputs enable firms to develop the capability to monitor AI-driven search environments, detect shifts in AI visibility, and identify semantic gaps in digital content. Through the sensing stage, organizations continuously observe changes in generative AI systems and evolving user information needs, allowing marketers to understand how AI platforms interpret, prioritize, and present brand-related information.

Figure 4. GEO-Driven Communication Transformation Model (Source: Authors' creation)

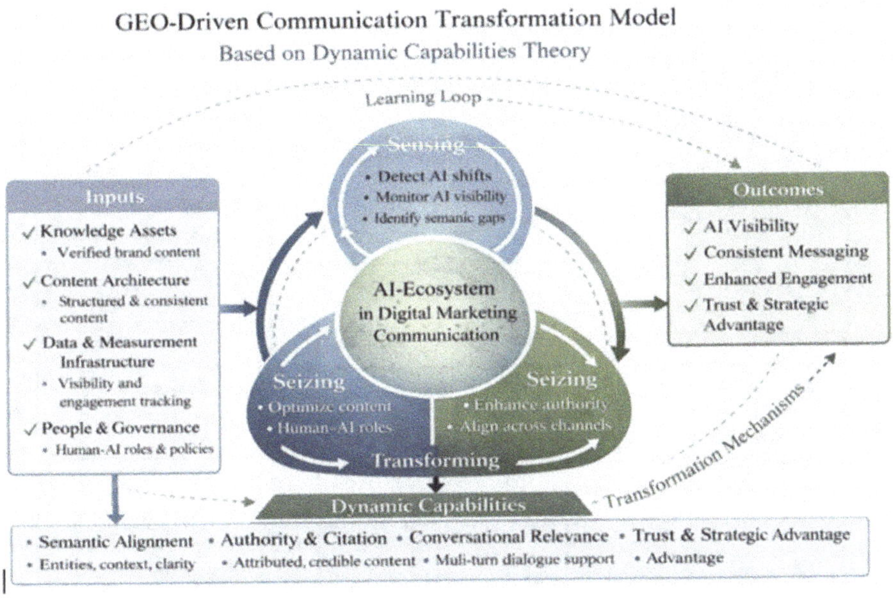

The model further emphasizes the seizing and transforming processes, where organizations actively optimize content, strengthen brand authority, and align communication across multiple channels. These actions occur within an AI-ecosystem in digital marketing communication and are supported by dynamic capabilities such as semantic alignment, credible citations, conversational relevance, and trust-building strategies. The model also highlights a continuous learning loop that allows organizations to refine their strategies based on performance feedback. As a result, firms can achieve outcomes including improved AI visibility, consistent messaging, stronger consumer engagement, and enhanced trust and strategic advantage in AI-mediated marketing environments.

Figure 5 presents Generative Engine Optimization (GEO) as a strategic capability that helps firms adapt their digital marketing communication to AI-mediated search and conversational environments. The model begins with the antecedents of GEO capability. These antecedents include contextual drivers, such as the growing use of AI search, the expansion of generative content, and stronger pressure to adapt. These pressures make visibility harder to manage through traditional SEO alone. Visibility therefore becomes a capability problem, not only a content problem. The model also highlights organizational enablers that support GEO, including leadership alignment, content and data infrastructure, and ethical governance policies. These enablers matter because GEO relies on repeatable routines that firms must build and coordinate over time, which fits the logic of capability-based advantage (Barney 1991).

Figure 5. Conceptual model (Source: Authors' creation)

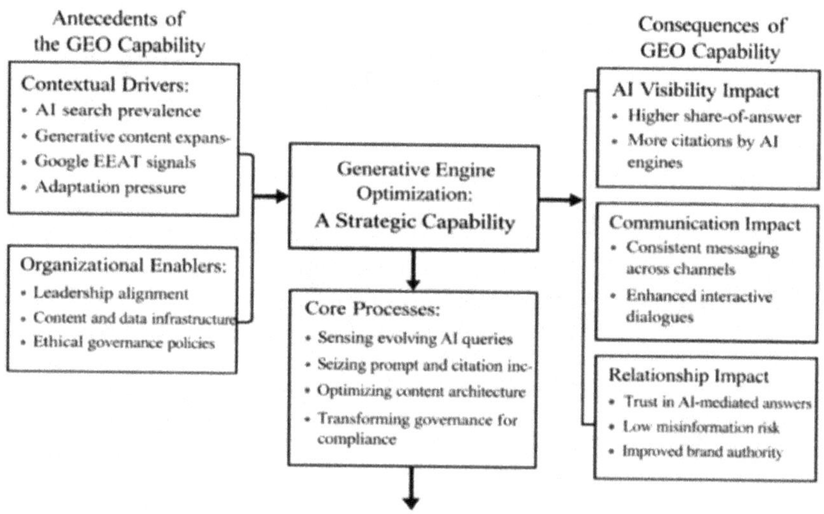

Dynamic Capabilities Theory connects directly to the model's core processes. These processes show how GEO functions through sensing, seizing, and transforming routines, which help firms respond to fast-changing environments (Teece, 2007; Eisenhardt & Martin, 2000). Sensing helps firms detect evolving AI queries and shifts in visibility patterns. Seizing helps firms act by optimizing content architecture and improving how generative engines cite or include brand content.

Transforming then stabilizes these gains by embedding governance and compliance into communication operations. These processes drive consequences across three areas. The model predicts stronger AI visibility through higher share-of-answer and more citations, improved communication through consistent messaging and better dialogues, and stronger relationships through trust, reduced misinformation risk, and higher brand authority. These outcomes align with emerging GEO research that frames visibility as inclusion within AI-generated responses rather than only ranking positions (Aggarwal et al., 2024).

5. IMPLICATIONS AND FUTURE RESEARCH AGENDA

This chapter offers several theoretical implications. First, it extends digital marketing communication research by positioning GEO as a strategic capability rather than as a narrow technical tactic. This move helps connect the GEO discussion with the resource-based view, dynamic capability theory, and human–AI interaction research. Second, it contributes to the emerging AI marketing literature by linking retrieval systems, answer generation, and consumer trust in one framework. Third, it adds to governance research by showing that ethical communication in generative environments is not a peripheral issue. It is a central design requirement.

The chapter also offers managerial implications. Managers should not treat GEO as a simple extension of SEO. Generative environments require different priorities. Firms need structured knowledge assets, consistent evidence, cross-functional coordination, and answer-level monitoring. They also need to shift from page-rank thinking to answer-quality thinking. This means managers should ask new questions: Is the brand cited? Is the answer accurate? Does the AI summary preserve the intended meaning? Does visibility improve trust, or does it create confusion?

These implications also affect measurement. Firms should combine traditional digital metrics with GEO-specific indicators. Citation frequency, answer share, factual fidelity, sentiment alignment, and zero-click substitution risk can help managers evaluate whether generative visibility produces strategic value. This broader measurement logic is especially important because direct traffic may decline even when AI visibility increases. Without answer-level metrics, managers may misread performance.

The framework also has implications for governance. Firms should build internal rules for source quality, disclosure, content updates, and risk review. These rules are especially important in sectors where AI-generated advice can influence sensitive decisions, such as health, education, finance, and public services. In such contexts, accuracy and accountability are not only communication goals. They are operational and ethical obligations.

Several future research directions emerge from this review. One direction is measurement research. Scholars should test and refine GEO-specific indicators across industries and platforms. Another direction is consumer research. Future studies should examine how users interpret attribution, explanation, and trust signals in AI-generated answers. A third direction is comparative sector research. GEO may operate differently in retail, healthcare, tourism, education, and B2B markets, and those differences deserve systematic attention.

A fourth direction is multilingual and regional research. Generative systems may perform unevenly across languages, markets, and cultural settings. This issue matters for firms operating in emerging economies or multilingual consumer environments. A fifth direction is governance research. Scholars should explore how firms can design responsible GEO routines that balance visibility goals with accuracy, fairness, privacy, and regulatory compliance. A sixth direction is longitudinal capability research. Future work should examine whether GEO capabilities become path-dependent and whether they create competitive advantage that rivals cannot easily imitate.

Together, these directions can move GEO research from early conceptual debate toward cumulative theory building and stronger managerial guidance.

6. CONCLUSION

Generative AI is changing digital marketing communication by changing how visibility is produced, how brand messages are mediated, and how consumers encounter information. In link-based search, firms competed for rank. In generative environments, firms compete for retrieval, citation, and accurate representation inside synthesized answers. That shift creates new strategic, technical, and ethical demands.

This chapter showed that GEO should not be viewed only as an optimization tactic. It should be understood as a capability that combines knowledge readiness, technical readiness, strategic orchestration, trust calibration, and governance. This capability-based view responds to a major gap in the current literature, which often treats GEO in fragmented ways across marketing, technology, and ethics. By integrating these dimensions, the chapter offers a more complete explanation of how firms can adapt to AI-mediated visibility.

The chapter also showed that effective GEO depends on more than appearing in AI-generated answers. Firms must also preserve factual accuracy, brand meaning, and consumer trust. Visibility without fidelity may create risk. Visibility without governance may damage credibility. Visibility without strategy may fail to produce long-term value. For these reasons, GEO should be managed as part of a broader communication and capability agenda.

In conclusion, GEO represents a structural shift in digital marketing communication for the AI era. It changes the unit of competition, the logic of discoverability, and the conditions under which brand authority is built. Firms that develop GEO as a strategic capability will be better positioned to remain visible, relevant, and trusted in increasingly generative digital ecosystems.

7. LIMITATIONS

The corpus reveals an emerging discipline wherein review research and benchmark/preprint work coexist. Certain entries in the submitted table refer to materials not associated with stable DOI metadata (and one seems to correspond with content uploaded by a practitioner), limiting index validation and repeatability. Moreover, due to the pace of changeableness of generative search platforms, there is a need for continuous updating of empirical findings via longitudinal designs and regular revisit refresh cycles (Page et al., 2021).

As generative search becomes a default discovery layer, GEO represents a strategic imperative for marketing communication: it determines whether organizational knowledge and brand meaning become visible, trusted, and actionable inside AI-generated answers—making capability building, not isolated optimization tactics, the central challenge of the AI era.

8. FUTURE RESEARCH DIRECTION

Future research should treat GEO as an organizational capability, not a checklist of tactics. Scholars need to explain how firms build repeatable routines that improve inclusion in AI-generated answers while keeping brand meaning consistent across channels. This work should also clarify how GEO changes the balance between message control and platform mediation, since generative engines can reframe, compress, or omit brand information during synthesis.

Future studies should strengthen empirical evidence. Researchers can run controlled experiments to test which content structures, evidence cues, and authority signals increase inclusion and citation in generative outputs. Researchers should also use longitudinal and mixed-method designs to trace how GEO practices evolve over time inside firms, including how teams coordinate content creation, verification, and updating cycles across marketing, SEO, analytics, and governance functions.

Future research should expand context and measurement. Scholars should compare regulated and non-regulated industries, SMEs and large firms, and English and non-English markets to test boundary conditions. Measurement work should develop standard indicators such as share-of-answer visibility, citation presence, message integrity, and trust-related outcomes, and link these indicators to engagement quality and long-term brand performance.

RFFERENCES

Aggarwal, P., Murahari, V., Rajpurohit, T., Kalyan, A., Narasimhan, K., & Deshpande, A. (2024). GEO: Generative engine optimization. In *Proceedings of the 30th ACM SIGKDD Conference on Knowledge Discovery and Data Mining (KDD '24)* (pp. 5–16). Association for Computing Machinery. DOI: 10.1145/3637528.3671900

Al-Gasawneh, J. A., AlSokkar, A. A. M., Alamro, A. S., Binkhamis, M., Khalaf, O. I., & AbdElminaam, D. S. (2025). The cutting edge of AI in e-marketing: How the use of digital tools boosts performance in Jordan. *SN Computer Science*, *6*(1), 82. DOI: 10.1007/s42979-024-03600-y

Barney, J. B. (1991). Firm resources and sustained competitive advantage. *Journal of Management*, *17*(1), 99–120. DOI: 10.1177/014920639101700108

Berman, R., & Katona, Z. (2013). The role of search engine optimization in search marketing. *Marketing Science*, *32*(4), 644–651. DOI: 10.1287/mksc.2013.0783

Borimnejad, H., & Borimnejad, V. (2026). Emerging trends, challenges and research opportunities in artificial intelligence applications in marketing. *Discover Artificial Intelligence*, *6*(1), 9. Advance online publication. DOI: 10.1007/s44163-025-00705-y

Braun, V., & Clarke, V. (2006). Using thematic analysis in psychology. *Qualitative Research in Psychology*, *3*(2), 77–101. DOI: 10.1191/1478088706qp063oa

Brüns, J. D., & Meißner, M. (2024). Do you create your content yourself? Using generative artificial intelligence for social media content creation diminishes perceived brand authenticity. *Journal of Retailing and Consumer Services*, *79*, 103790. DOI: 10.1016/j.jretconser.2024.103790

Chen, M., Wang, X., Chen, K., & Koudas, N. (2025a). *Generative engine optimization: How to dominate AI search*. arXiv. https://doi.org//arXiv.2509.08919DOI: 10.48550

Chen, Q., Chen, J., Huang, H., Shao, Q., Chen, J., Hua, R., Xu, H., Wu, R., Chuan, R., & Wu, J. (2025b). *Beyond keywords: Driving generative search engine optimization with content-centric agents*. arXiv. https://doi.org//arXiv.2509.05607DOI: 10.48550

Chen, X., Wu, H., Bao, J., Chen, Z., Liao, Y., & Huang, H. (2025c). *Role-augmented intent-driven generative search engine optimization*. arXiv. https://doi.org//arXiv .2508.11158DOI: 10.48550

Dhar, B. K., Karim, R., & Mollik, M. S. (2026). Stitching sustainability in fashion: Strengthening circular economy drivers in the textile industry. In *Strategic innovations for circular economy* (pp. 179–208). IGI Global Scientific Publishing., DOI: 10.4018/979-8-3373-2454-8.ch007

Dwivedi, Y. K., Kshetri, N., Hughes, L., Slade, E. L., Jeyaraj, A., & Kar, A. K.. (2023). So what if ChatGPT wrote it? Multidisciplinary perspectives on generative conversational AI. *International Journal of Information Management*, *71*, 102642. DOI: 10.1016/j.ijinfomgt.2023.102642

Eisenhardt, K. M., & Martin, J. A. (2000). Dynamic capabilities: What are they? *Strategic Management Journal*, *21*(10–11), 1105–1121. DOI: 10.1002/1097-0266 (200010/11)21:10/11<1105::AID-SMJ133>3.0.CO;2-E

Google. (2024). *Overview of SGE (Search Generative Experience)*. Google Search Central. https://developers.google.com/search

Grewal, D., Satornino, C. B., Davenport, T. H., & Guha, A. (2025). How generative AI is shaping the future of marketing. *Journal of the Academy of Marketing Science*, *53*(3), 702–722. DOI: 10.1007/s11747-024-01064-3

Haleem, A., Javaid, M., Qadri, M. A., Singh, R. P., & Suman, R. (2022). Artificial intelligence (AI) applications for marketing: A literature-based study. *International Journal of Intelligent Networks*, *3*, 119–132. DOI: 10.1016/j.ijin.2022.08.005

Hermann, E., & Puntoni, S. (2024). Artificial intelligence and consumer behavior: From predictive to generative AI. *Journal of Business Research*, *180*, 114720. DOI: 10.1016/j.jbusres.2024.114720

Hollebeek, L. D., Menidjel, C., Sarstedt, M., Jansson, J., & Urbonavicius, S. (2024). Engaging consumers through artificially intelligent technologies. *Psychology and Marketing*, *41*(4), 880–898. DOI: 10.1002/mar.21957

Hossain, M. K., & Mollik, M. S. (2022). Exploring the impact of social media platforms on instigating tourist's emotions and behavioral intentions to co-create and visit tourist spots: Bangladesh perspective. *Journal of Business Studies*, *3*(1), 217–236. DOI: 10.58753/jbspust.3.1.2022.13

Huang, M.-H., & Rust, R. T. (2021a). A strategic framework for artificial intelligence in marketing. *Journal of the Academy of Marketing Science*, *49*(1), 30–50. DOI: 10.1007/s11747-020-00749-9

Karpukhin, V., Oğuz, B., Min, S., Lewis, P., Wu, L., Edunov, S., Chen, D., & Yih, W.-t. (2020). Dense passage retrieval for open-domain question answering. In *Proceedings of the 2020 Conference on Empirical Methods in Natural Language Processing (EMNLP)* (pp. 6769–6781). Association for Computational Linguistics. DOI: 10.18653/v1/2020.emnlp-main.550

Kshetri, N., Dwivedi, Y. K., Davenport, T. H., & Panteli, N. (2024). Generative artificial intelligence in marketing: Applications, opportunities, challenges, and research agenda. *International Journal of Information Management, 75*, 102716. DOI: 10.1016/j.ijinfomgt.2023.102716

Li, X., Jin, J., Zhou, Y., Zhang, Y., Zhang, P., Zhu, Y., & Dou, Z. (2025). From matching to generation: A survey on generative information retrieval. *ACM Transactions on Information Systems, 43*(3), 83. Advance online publication. DOI: 10.1145/3722552

Malthouse, E. C., & Copulsky, J. R. (2023). Artificial intelligence ecosystems for marketing communications. *International Journal of Advertising, 42*(1), 128–140. DOI: 10.1080/02650487.2022.2122249

Mollik, M. S. (2024). Investigating tertiary students' perceptions about ChatGPT use in higher education: Bangladesh perspective. *BAUET Journal, 4*(2). Advance online publication. DOI: 10.59321/BAUETJ.V4I2.19

Mollik, M. S., Karim, R., & Mahmud, S. (2026). Identifying critical success factors for adopting sustainable tourism in emerging economies. In *EMIDWORLD 3rd International Congress on Economics, Public Finance, Business & Social Sciences*. Baku, Azerbaijan.

Mollik, M. S., Karim, R., Sahabuddin, M., & Eneizan, B. (2026a). Industry 5.0 and the circular economy: A transformative nexus. In *Industry 5.0 and sustainable development* (pp. 237–267). Routledge.

Mollik, M. S., Rahman, S. M., Rahat, M. R., Kulsum, C. U., & Sagir, S. M. (2024). Does trustworthiness influence travel service use intentions at an online travel agency? A study on the digitalization of the tourism sector in Bangladesh. *Geo Journal of Tourism and Geosites, 52*(1), 30–40. DOI: 10.30892/gtg.52103-1180

Mustak, M., Salminen, J., Plé, L., & Wirtz, J. (2021). Artificial intelligence in marketing: Topic modeling and scientometric analysis. *Journal of Business Research, 124*, 389–404. DOI: 10.1016/j.jbusres.2020.10.044

Page, M. J., McKenzie, J. E., Bossuyt, P. M., Boutron, I., Hoffmann, T. C., Mulrow, C. D., Shamseer, L., Tetzlaff, J. M., Akl, E. A., Brennan, S. E., Chou, R., Glanville, J., Grimshaw, J. M., Hróbjartsson, A., Lalu, M. M., Li, T., Loder, E. W., Mayo-Wilson, E., McDonald, S., & Moher, D. (2021). The PRISMA 2020 statement: An updated guideline for reporting systematic reviews. *BMJ (Clinical Research Ed.), 372*(71), n71. Advance online publication. DOI: 10.1136/bmj.n71 PMID: 33782057

Paschen, J., Kietzmann, J., & Kietzmann, T. C. (2019). Artificial intelligence (AI) and its implications for market knowledge in B2B marketing. *Journal of Business and Industrial Marketing, 34*(7), 1410–1419. DOI: 10.1108/JBIM-10-2018-0295

Peres, R., Schreier, M., Schweidel, D., & Sorescu, A. (2023). On ChatGPT and beyond. *International Journal of Research in Marketing, 40*(2), 269–275. DOI: 10.1016/j.ijresmar.2023.03.001

Saura, J. R., Škare, V., & Ozretić Došen, Đ. (2024). Is AI-based digital marketing ethical? Assessing a new data privacy paradox. *Journal of Innovation & Knowledge, 9*(4), 100597. DOI: 10.1016/j.jik.2024.100597

Stahl, B. C., & Eke, D. (2024). The ethics of ChatGPT: Exploring the ethical issues of an emerging technology. *International Journal of Information Management, 74*, 102700. DOI: 10.1016/j.ijinfomgt.2023.102700

Teece, D. J. (2007). Explicating dynamic capabilities: The nature and microfoundations of sustainable enterprise performance. *Strategic Management Journal, 28*(13), 1319–1350. DOI: 10.1002/smj.640

Uddin, M. S., Mollik, M. S., & Nasrullah, A. M. (2026). Integrating circular economy principles into responsible consumption and production. In *Strategic innovations for circular economy* (pp. 209–244). IGI Global Scientific Publishing., DOI: 10.4018/979-8-3373-2454-8.ch008

Zhu, Y., Yuan, H., Wang, S., Liu, J., Liu, W., Deng, C., Chen, H., Liu, Z., Dou, Z., & Wen, J.-R. (2025). Large language models for information retrieval: A survey. *ACM Transactions on Information Systems, 44*(1), 12. Advance online publication. DOI: 10.1145/3748304

Zierau, N., Hildebrand, C., Bergner, A., Busquet, F., Schmitt, A., & Leimeister, J. M. (2023). Voice bots on the frontline. *Journal of the Academy of Marketing Science, 51*(4), 823–842. DOI: 10.1007/s11747-022-00868-5

Compilation of References

Abd-Alrazaq, A. A., Alajlani, M., Alalwan, A. A., Bewick, B. M., Gardner, P., & Househ, M. (2019). An overview of the features of chatbots in mental health: A scoping review. *International Journal of Medical Informatics*, *132*, 103978. DOI: 10.1016/j.ijmedinf.2019.103978 PMID: 31622850

Abdel Halim, N. (2025). The Impact of Gamification on Brand Engagement and Loyalty: A Study of Brand Events. *Journal of Design Sciences and Applied Arts*, *6*(1), 38–62. DOI: 10.21608/jdsaa.2024.263760.1396

Abdul, A., Vermeulen, J., Wang, D., Lim, B. Y., & Kankanhalli, M. (2018) 'Trends and trajectories for explainable, accountable and intelligible systems: An hci research agenda', in *Proceedings of the 2018 CHI conference on human factors in computing systems*, pp. 1-18. Available at: DOI: 10.1145/3173574.3174156

Abid, R., Saha, P., & Islam, M. M. (2025). The Impact of Artificial Intelligence (AI) for Transforming Tourism Marketing on the USA Industry Practices. *Journal of Information Systems and Informatics*, *7*(1), 393–422. DOI: 10.51519/journalisi.v7i1.1016

Abrardi, L., Cambini, C., & Rondi, L. (2021). Artificial intelligence, firms and consumer behavior: A survey. *Journal of Economic Surveys*, *36*(4), 969–991. DOI: 10.1111/joes.12455

Acemoglu, D., & Restrepo, P. (2020). Robots and jobs: Evidence from US labor markets. *Journal of Political Economy*, *128*(6), 2188–2244. DOI: 10.1086/705716

Adi, H. P., Wardoyo, A. E., & Azizah, H. (2024). An In-Depth Analysis of SIMPKB: Revealing Performance Tests and Efficiency from a User Experience. *Sinkron*, *8*(2), 911–918. DOI: 10.33395/sinkron.v8i2.13574

Aggarwal, P., Murahari, V., Rajpurohit, T., Kalyan, A., Narasimhan, K., & Deshpande, A. (2024). GEO: Generative engine optimization. In *Proceedings of the 30th ACM SIGKDD Conference on Knowledge Discovery and Data Mining (KDD '24)* (pp. 5–16). Association for Computing Machinery. DOI: 10.1145/3637528.3671900

Agrawal, A., Gans, J. S., & Goldfarb, A. (2019). Artificial intelligence: The ambiguous labor market impact of automating prediction. *The Journal of Economic Perspectives*, *33*(2), 31–50. DOI: 10.1257/jep.33.2.31

Aguirre, E., Mahr, D., Grewal, D., De Ruyter, K., & Wetzels, M. (2015). Unraveling the personalization paradox: The effect of information collection and trust-building strategies on online advertisement effectiveness. *Journal of Retailing*, *91*(1), 34–49. DOI: 10.1016/j.jretai.2014.09.005

Ahanger, A. S., Khan, S. M., Masoodi, F., & Salau, A. O. (2025). Advanced intrusion detection in internet of things using graph attention networks. *Scientific Reports*, *15*(1), Article 9831. DOI: 10.1038/s41598-025-09831-x

Aithal, P. S. (2023). *How to Create Business Value Through Technological Innovations Using ICCT Underlying Technologies*. DOI: 10.47992/IJAEML.2581.7000.0184

Al Rafi, M. (2023). Machine learning–enhanced predictive marketing analytics for optimizing customer engagement and sales forecasting. *International Journal of Research and Applied Innovations*, *6*(4), 9203–9213.

Al-Adwan, A. S., Meet, R. K., Anand, S., Shukla, G. P., Alsharif, R., & Dabbaghia, M. (2025). Understanding continuous use intention of technology among higher education teachers in emerging economy: Evidence from integrated TAM, TPACK, and UTAUT model. *Studies in Higher Education*, *50*(3), 505–524. DOI: 10.1080/03075079.2024.2343955

Al-Adwan, A. S., Yaseen, H., Alkhwaldi, A. F., Jafar, R. M. S., Fauzi, M. A., & Abdullah, A. (2025). Treasure Hunting for Brands: Metaverse Marketing Gamification Effects on Purchase Intention, WOM, and Loyalty. *Journal of Global Marketing*, *38*(4), 1–25. DOI: 10.1080/08911762.2025.2463897

Alam, S. S., Ahmed, S., & Kokash, H. A. (2024). Interplay of perceived organizational and external e-readiness in the adoption and integration of augmented reality and virtual reality technologies in Malaysian higher education institutions. *Education and Information Technologies*, *29*(11), 13735–13761. DOI: 10.1007/s10639-023-12428-7

Alantari, H. J., Currim, I. S., Deng, Y., & Singh, S. (2022). An empirical comparison of machine learning methods for text-based sentiment analysis of online consumer reviews. *International Journal of Research in Marketing, 39*(1), 1–19. DOI: 10.1016/j.ijresmar.2021.10.011

Aldoseri, A., Khalifa, M., Al-Khalifa, N., & Hamouda, A. M. (2023). Re-thinking data strategy and integration for artificial intelligence: Concepts, opportunities, and challenges. *Applied Sciences (Basel, Switzerland), 13*(12), 7082. DOI: 10.3390/app13127082

Alfreihat, M., Almousa, O. S., Tashtoush, Y., AlSobeh, A., Mansour, K., & Migdady, H. (2024). Emo-SL framework: Emoji sentiment lexicon using text-based features and machine learning for sentiment analysis. *IEEE Access : Practical Innovations, Open Solutions, 12*, 81793–81812. DOI: 10.1109/ACCESS.2024.3382836

Al-Gasawneh, J. A., AlSokkar, A. A. M., Alamro, A. S., Binkhamis, M., Khalaf, O. I., & AbdElminaam, D. S. (2025). The cutting edge of AI in e-marketing: How the use of digital tools boosts performance in Jordan. *SN Computer Science, 6*(1), 82. DOI: 10.1007/s42979-024-03600-y

Ali, S. R. O., Said, N. S. M., Jislan, F., Mat, K. A., & Aznan, W. N. M. W. (2020). The Relationship between Service Failure and Service Recovery with Airline Passenger Satisfaction. *Journal of Physics: Conference Series, 1529*(2), 022062. DOI: 10.1088/1742-6596/1529/2/022062

Alkhazaleh, R., Mykoniatis, K., & Alahmer, A. (2022). The success of technology transfer in the industry 4.0 era: A systematic literature review. *Journal of Open Innovation, 8*(4), 202. DOI: 10.3390/joitmc8040202

Allal-Chérif, O., Simón-Moya, V., & Ballester, A. C. C. (2021). Intelligent purchasing: How artificial intelligence can redefine the purchasing function. *Journal of Business Research, 124*, 69–76. DOI: 10.1016/j.jbusres.2020.11.050

ALLAN, J., Ferreri, A., Grande, S., Giannantonio, R., & Matteucci, F. (2019). *Technology transfer in nanotechnology*. DOI: 10.2760/183529

Al-Moslmi, T., Gallofre Ocana, M., & Opdahl, L., A., & Veres, C. (. (2020). Named Entity Extraction for Knowledge Graphs: A Literature Overview. *IEEE Access : Practical Innovations, Open Solutions, 8*, 32862–32881. DOI: 10.1109/ACCESS.2020.2973928

Al-Saigh, M. N., & Mahmoud, K. F. (2023). The Impact of Smart Interactive Technologies in Creating Personal Internal Spaces: An Analytical Study of User Preferences for Interactive Shape Characteristics. *International Journal of Sustainable Development and Planning*, *18*(8), 2339–2348. DOI: 10.18280/ijsdp.180804

Al-Sharafi, M. A., Al-Emran, M., Al-Qaysi, N., Iranmanesh, M., & Ibrahim, N. (2024). Drivers and Barriers Affecting Metaverse Adoption: A Systematic Review, Theoretical Framework, and Avenues for Future Research. *International Journal of Human-Computer Interaction*, *40*(22), 7043–7064. DOI: 10.1080/10447318.2023.2260984

Alti, A., & Lakehal, A. (2025). AI-MDD-UX: Revolutionizing E-Commerce User Experience with Generative AI and Model-Driven Development. *Future Internet*, *17*(4), 180. DOI: 10.3390/fi17040180

Alt, R. (2021). Electronic Markets on digital platforms and AI. *Electronic Markets*, *31*(2), 233–241. DOI: 10.1007/s12525-021-00489-w

Amershi, S., Weld, D. S., Vorvoreanu, M., Fourney, A., Nushi, B., Collisson, P., Suh, J., Iqbal, S. T., Bennett, P. N., Quinn, K., Teevan, J., Kikin-Gil, R., & Horvitz, E. (2019). Guidelines for human-AI interaction. *International Conference on Human Factors in Computing Systems*. https://doi.org/DOI: 10.1145/3290605.3300233

Amini, R., & Amini, A. (2024). An overview of artificial intelligence and its application in marketing with focus on large language models. *International Journal of Science and Research Archive*, *12*(2), 455–465. DOI: 10.30574/ijsra.2024.12.2.1223

Anam, A. S. M. T., Bhuiyan, M. R. I., Islam, S., Ullah, M. N., & Rakib, M. A. A. (2026). *'Factors influencing university students' adoption of online education platforms in Bangladesh: an extended TAM-based analysis*. Educational and Developmental Psychologist., DOI: 10.1080/20590776.2026.2619742

Anayat, S., & Rasool, G. (2024). Artificial intelligence marketing (AIM): Connecting-the-dots using bibliometrics. *Journal of Marketing Theory and Practice*, *32*(1), 114–135. DOI: 10.1080/10696679.2022.2103435

Ancillai, C., Sabatini, A., Gatti, M., & Perna, A. (2023). Digital technology and business model innovation: A systematic literature review and future research agenda. *Technological Forecasting and Social Change*, *188*, 122307. DOI: 10.1016/j.techfore.2022.122307

Arabia, S., & Elsdaig, M. (2019). Evaluation of Healthcare Information System Using Delone and McLean Quality Model, Case study KSA. *International Journal of Advanced Trends in Computer Science and Engineering*, *8*(1.4), 522–527. DOI: 10.30534/ijatcse/2019/8181.42019

Arias, C. R. (2022). *An Introduction to Artificial Intelligence.*

Arora, N., Dreze, X., Ghose, A., Hess, J., Iyengar, R., Jing, B., & Zhang, Z. J. (2008). Putting one-to-one marketing to work: Personalization, customization, and choice. *Marketing Science*, *27*(3), 305–321. DOI: 10.1287/mksc.1070.0316

Arthur, L. (2013). *Big data marketing: engage your customers more effectively and drive value.* John Wiley & Sons.

Arunasalam, A. (2025) Advancing the security and privacy of sociotechnical systems: human-centered approaches to study threat actors and end-user trust. Doctoral dissertation. Purdue University Graduate School.

Arya, V., Saraf, A., Chichkanov, N., et al. (2025). AI-enhanced competency transfer hubs: A conceptual framework for university-industry engagement and knowledge sharing. The Journal of Technology Transfer, 51, 682–712. https://doi.org/10.1007/s10961-025-10233-7, DOI: 10.1007/s10961-025-10233-7

Auernhammer, J. (2020). Human-centered AI: The role of human-centered design research in the development of AI. In S. Boess, M. Cheung, & R. Cain (Eds.), *Synergy: Proceedings of the DRS International Conference 2020.*https://doi.org/DOI: 10.21606/drs.2020.282

Auerswald, P. E., & Branscomb, L. M. (2003). Valleys of death and Darwinian seas. *The Journal of Technology Transfer*, *28*(3–4), 227–239. DOI: 10.1023/A:1024980525678

Azadi, S., Green, I. C., Arnold, A., Truong, M., Potts, J., & Martino, M. A. (2021). Robotic Surgery: The Impact of Simulation and Other Innovative Platforms on Performance and Training. *Journal of Minimally Invasive Gynecology*, *28*(3), 490–495. DOI: 10.1016/j.jmig.2020.12.001

Azize, Ş., Cemal, Z., & Hakan, K. (2012). Does brand communication increase brand trust? The empirical research on global mobile phone brands. *Procedia: Social and Behavioral Sciences*, *58*, 1361–1369. DOI: 10.1016/j.sbspro.2012.09.1120

Azmadi, A. S. A., Abd Hamid, M., & Hanafiah, M. H. (2023). QR Code Usage at Dataran Merdeka KL QR Trail: A Start to Smart Tourism Destinations. *International Journal of Academic Research in Business & Social Sciences*, *13*(5), 344–357. DOI: 10.6007/IJARBSS/v13-i5/17025

Bag, S., Srivastava, G., Bashir, M. M. A., Kumari, S., Giannakis, M., & Chowdhury, A. H. (2022). Journey of customers in this digital era: Understanding the role of artificial intelligence technologies in user engagement and conversion. *Benchmarking*, *29*(7), 2074–2098. DOI: 10.1108/BIJ-07-2021-0415

Bahangulu, J. K., & Owusu-Berko, L. (2025). Algorithmic bias, data ethics, and governance: Ensuring fairness, transparency and compliance in AI-powered business analytics applications. *World Journal of Advanced Research and Reviews*, *25*(2), 1746–1763. DOI: 10.30574/wjarr.2025.25.2.0571

Bahmani, M., Morse, L., Carnevale, P., Nagpal, M., De Cremer, D., Van Hiel, A., & Woolley, A. W. (2024) 'Humans+ AI: organizational behavior research on human-machine interactions', in 84th Annual Meeting of the Academy of Management, AOM 2024, 2024(1). Available at: DOI: 10.5465/AMPROC.2024.20641symposium

Baj-Rogowska, A., & Sikorski, M. (2023). Exploring the usability and user experience of social media apps through a text mining approach. *Engineering Management in Production and Services*, *15*(1), 86–105. DOI: 10.2478/emj-2023-0007

Balakrishnan, J., & Dwivedi, Y. K. (2021). Role of cognitive absorption in building user trust and experience. *Psychology and Marketing*, *38*(4), 643–668. Advance online publication. DOI: 10.1002/mar.21462

Balakrishnan, J., & Dwivedi, Y. K. (2024). Conversational commerce: Entering the next stage of AI-powered digital assistants. *Annals of Operations Research*, *333*(2), 653–687. DOI: 10.1007/s10479-021-04049-5

Balakrishnan, J., Dwivedi, Y. K., Hughes, L., & Boy, F. (2024). Enablers and inhibitors of AI-powered voice assistants: A dual-factor approach by integrating the status quo bias and technology acceptance model. *Information Systems Frontiers*, *26*(3), 921–942. DOI: 10.1007/s10796-021-10203-y

Balch, J. A., Efron, P. A., Bihorac, A., & Loftus, T. J. (2022). Gamification for Machine Learning in Surgical Patient Engagement. *Frontiers in Surgery*, *9*, 896351. DOI: 10.3389/fsurg.2022.896351

Banh, L., & Strobel, G. (2023). Generative artificial intelligence. *Electronic Markets*, *33*(1), 63. Advance online publication. DOI: 10.1007/s12525-023-00680-1

Bankins, S., Ocampo, A. C., Marrone, M., Restubog, S. L. D., & Woo, S. E. (2024). A multilevel review of artificial intelligence in organizations: Implications for organizational behavior research and practice. *Journal of Organizational Behavior*, *45*(2), 159–182. DOI: 10.1002/job.2735

Baptista, R., de Almeida, C. V., & Belim, C. (2025). Intelligent Connections: AI-Driven Communication and the Path to Enhanced Literacies. In *Rethinking Literacy in the Era of Sustainability and Artificial Intelligence* (pp. 99–132). IGI Global Scientific Publishing.

Barney, J. (1991). Firm resources and sustained competitive advantage. *Journal of Management*, *17*(1), 99–120. DOI: 10.1177/014920639101700108

Baryannis, G., Validi, S., Dani, S., & Antoniou, G. (2019). Supply chain risk management and artificial intelligence: State of the art and future research directions. *Computers in Industry*, *113*, 103131.

Bawack, R. E., Wamba, S. F., Carillo, K. D. A., & Akter, S. (2022). Artificial intelligence in E-Commerce: A bibliometric study and literature review. *Electronic Markets*, *32*(1), 297–338. DOI: 10.1007/s12525-022-00537-z PMID: 35600916

Bawa, P. (2016). How value congruence affects customer focus and survival of business. *International Journal of Applied Business and Economic Research*, *14*(7), 5085–5096.

Bawa, P. (2017). Evidence based classroom management practices: An analysis through kano's model. *Indian Journal of Marketing*, *47*(6), 35–49. DOI: 10.17010/ijom/2017/v47/i6/115368

Bawa, P., & Bathurutheen, F. (2016). Effect of extrinsic cues on perception of private label quality and customer satisfaction. *Indian Journal of Marketing*, *46*(7), 55–66. DOI: 10.17010/ijom/2016/v46/i7/97127

Bednar, P. M., & Welch, C. (2020). Socio-technical perspectives on smart working: Creating meaningful and sustainable systems. *Information Systems Frontiers*, *22*(2), 281–298. DOI: 10.1007/s10796-019-09921-1

Begum, N. (2025). *Beyond Automation : How AI Service Integration is Shaping the Future of Brand Management Beyond Automation : How AI Service Integration is Shaping the Future of Brand. 25*(1).

Benlian, A. (2015). Web Personalization Cues and Their Differential Effects on User Assessments of Website Value. *Journal of Management Information Systems*, *32*(1), 225–260. DOI: 10.1080/07421222.2015.1029394

Benotsmane, R., Kovács, G., & Dudás, L. (2019). Economic, social impacts and operation of smart factories in Industry 4.0 focusing on simulation and artificial intelligence of collaborating robots. *Social Sciences (Basel, Switzerland)*, *8*(5), 143. DOI: 10.3390/socsci8050143

Bergner, A. S., Hildebrand, C., & Häubl, G. (2023). Machine talk: How verbal embodiment in conversational AI shapes consumer-brand relationships. *The Journal of Consumer Research*, *50*(4), 742–764. DOI: 10.1093/jcr/ucad014

Berman, R., & Katona, Z. (2013). The role of search engine optimization in search marketing. *Marketing Science*, *32*(4), 644–651. DOI: 10.1287/mksc.2013.0783

Berretta, S., Tausch, A., Peifer, C., & Kluge, A. (2023). The Job Perception Inventory: Considering human factors and needs in the design of human–AI work. *Frontiers in Psychology*, *14*, 1128945. DOI: 10.3389/fpsyg.2023.1128945 PMID: 37287772

Bharadiya, J. P. (2023). A comparative study of business intelligence and artificial intelligence with big data analytics. *American Journal of Artificial Intelligence*, *7*(1), 24. DOI: 10.11648/j.ajai.20230701.14

Bharti, R., Khatri, U., & Duralia, O. A. (2024). Examining the role of digital marketing in shaping consumer communication and behavior. *Feedback International Journal of Communication*, *1*(4), 192–201. DOI: 10.62569/fijc.v1i4.76

Bhattacharya, A., & Sharma, S. (2025). AI and Metaverse ROI in Tourism: Measuring Impact, Effectiveness, and Return on Investment (ROI). In Valeri, M., Shah, S. H. A., & Al-Ghazali, B. M. (Eds.), (pp. 1–84). Advances in Computational Intelligence and Robotics. IGI Global., DOI: 10.4018/979-8-3693-8482-4.ch001

Bhimavarapu, U. (2025). AI in Technology Transfer Developing Sustainable Models Through University-Industry Collaboration. In *Bridging Technology and Development for Sustainable Innovation and Geopolitical Dynamics* (pp. 67–86). IGI Global Scientific Publishing., DOI: 10.4018/979-8-3693-9072-6.ch004

Bhuiyan, M. R. I., Akter, M. S., Amin, A., & Hossain, R. (2025). The mediating effect of innovation capabilities, information quality and supply chain resilience in the relationship between big data analytics capability (BDAC) and healthcare performance. *SAGE Open*, *15*(3), 21582440251362262. Advance online publication. DOI: 10.1177/21582440251362262

Bhuiyan, M. R. I., Faraji, M. R., Tabassum, M. N., Ghose, P., Sarbabidya, S., & Akter, R. (2024). Leveraging machine learning for cybersecurity: Techniques, challenges, and future directions. *Edelweiss Applied Science and Technology*, *8*(6), 4291–4307. DOI: 10.55214/25768484.v8i6.2930

Bhuiyan, M. R. I., Hossain, R., Rashid, M., Islam, M. M., Mani, L., & Milon, M. N. U. (2024). Gravitating the components, technologies, challenges, and government transforming strategies for a Smart Bangladesh: A PRISMA-based review. *Journal of Governance and Regulation*, *13*(3), 177–188. DOI: 10.22495/jgrv13i3art15

Bhuiyan, M. R. I., Husain, T., Islam, S., & Amin, A. (2025b). Exploring the prospective influence of artificial intelligence on the health sector in Bangladesh. A study on awareness, perception and adoption. *Health Education*, *125*(3), 279–297. DOI: 10.1108/HE-10-2024-0125

Bhuiyan, M. R. I., Milon, M. N., Hossain, R., Poli, T., & Salam, M. (2024). Examining the Relationship between Poverty and Juvenile Delinquency Trends in a Developing Country. *Academic Journal of Interdisciplinary Studies*, *13*(6), 255–274. DOI: 10.36941/ajis-2024-0193

Bhuiyan, M. R. I., Uddin, S., Sultana, T., Al-Amin, , & Islam, M. M. (2026). Investigating ChatGPT Methods in the Higher Education Form a Student Engagement Perspective: Based on a Descriptive-Cross-Sectional Study. *SAGE Open*, *16*(1), 21582440251413008. Advance online publication. DOI: 10.1177/21582440251413008

Billewar, S. R., Jadhav, K., Sriram, V. P., Arun, D. A., Mohd Abdul, S., Gulati, K., & Bhasin, D. N. K. K. (2022). The rise of 3D E-Commerce: The online shopping gets real with virtual reality and augmented reality during COVID-19. *World Journal of Engineering*, *19*(2), 244–253. DOI: 10.1108/WJE-06-2021-0338

Blakeman, R. (2023). *Integrated marketing communication: creative strategy from idea to implementation*. Bloomsbury Publishing PLC.

Bock, D. E., Wolter, J. S., & Ferrell, O. C. (2020). Artificial intelligence: Disrupting what we know about services. *Journal of Services Marketing*, *34*(3), 317–334. DOI: 10.1108/JSM-01-2019-0047

Boehm, J., Grennan, L., Singla, A., & Smaje, K. (2022). Why digital trust truly matters. *McKinsey & Company, 12*.

Böhmer, N., & Schinnenburg, H. (2023). Critical exploration of AI-driven HRM to build up organizational capabilities. *Employee Relations*, *45*(5), 1057–1082. DOI: 10.1108/ER-04-2022-0202

Bolton, C., Machová, V., Kovacova, M., & Valaskova, K. (2018). The power of human–machine collaboration: Artificial intelligence, business automation, and the smart economy. *Economics, Management, and Financial Markets*, *13*(4), 51–56.

Bonetti, F., Montecchi, M., Plangger, K., & Schau, H. J. (2023). Practice co-evolution: Collaboratively embedding artificial intelligence in retail practices. *Journal of the Academy of Marketing Science*, *51*(4), 867–888. DOI: 10.1007/s11747-022-00896-1 PMID: 36035334

Borimnejad, H., & Borimnejad, V. (2026). Emerging trends, challenges and research opportunities in artificial intelligence applications in marketing. *Discover Artificial Intelligence*, *6*(1), 9. Advance online publication. DOI: 10.1007/s44163-025-00705-y

Bormane, S., & Blaus, E. (2024). Artificial intelligence in the context of digital marketing communication. *Frontiers in Communication*, *9*, 1411226. Advance online publication. DOI: 10.3389/fcomm.2024.1411226

Bositkhanova, N., & Dadaboyev, S. M. U. (2025). Revolutionizing workforce planning: The strategic role of AI in HR strategy. *Discover Global Society*, *3*(1), 100. DOI: 10.1007/s44282-025-00252-y

Bradford, A. (2020). *The Brussels effect: How the European Union rules the world.* Oxford University Press. DOI: 10.1093/oso/9780190088583.001.0001

Brannigan, E. (2023). *The Persistence of Dance: Choreography as Concept and Material in Contemporary Art* (12347133rd ed.). University of Michigan Press., DOI: 10.3998/mpub.12347133

Braun, V., & Clarke, V. (2006). Using thematic analysis in psychology. *Qualitative Research in Psychology*, *3*(2), 77–101. DOI: 10.1191/1478088706qp063oa

Brockmeyer, P., Wiechens, B., & Schliephake, H. (2023). The Role of Augmented Reality in the Advancement of Minimally Invasive Surgery Procedures: A Scoping Review. *Bioengineering (Basel, Switzerland)*, *10*(4), 501. DOI: 10.3390/bioengineering10040501

Brüns, J. D., & Meißner, M. (2024). Do you create your content yourself? Using generative artificial intelligence for social media content creation diminishes perceived brand authenticity. *Journal of Retailing and Consumer Services*, *79*, 103790. DOI: 10.1016/j.jretconser.2024.103790

Burton, J. W., Stein, M. K., & Jensen, T. B. (2020). A systematic review of algorithm aversion in augmented decision making. *Journal of Behavioral Decision Making*, *33*(2), 220–239. DOI: 10.1002/bdm.2155

Bychkov, N., Maximovich, I., & Pateyuk, D. (2024). *Negative aspects of the use of artificial intelligence (AI) in marketing.*

Caboni, F., & Hagberg, J. (2019). Augmented reality in retailing: A review of features, applications and value. *International Journal of Retail & Distribution Management*, *47*(11), 1125–1140. DOI: 10.1108/IJRDM-12-2018-0263

Callari, T. C., & Puppione, L. (2025). Can generative artificial intelligence productivity tools support workplace learning? A qualitative study on employee perceptions in a multinational corporation. *Journal of Workplace Learning, 37*(3), 266–283. DOI: 10.1108/JWL-11-2024-0258

Camilleri, M. A. (2024). *Artificial intelligence governance : Ethical considerations and implications for social responsibility. June 2023*, 1–15. DOI: 10.1111/exsy.13406

Cao, P. (2021). *Big Data in Customer Acquisition and Retention for eCommerce – Taking Walmart as an Example:* 2021 3rd International Conference on Economic Management and Cultural Industry (ICEMCI 2021), Guangzhou, China. DOI: 10.2991/assehr.k.211209.043

Cavanagh, J., Pariona-Cabrera, P., & Halvorsen, B. (2023). In what ways are HR analytics and artificial intelligence transforming the healthcare sector? *Asia Pacific Journal of Human Resources, 61*(4), 785–793. DOI: 10.1111/1744-7941.12392

Celestin, P. (2024). *How E-Commerce Law Is Evolving To Address Consumer Protection And Digital Marketplace Regulations*. Brainae Journal of Business, Sciences and Technology.

Cetindamar, D., Lammers, T., & Zhang, Y. (2020). Exploring the knowledge spillovers of a technology in an entrepreneurial ecosystem—The case of artificial intelligence in Sydney. *Thunderbird International Business Review, 62*(5), 457–474. DOI: 10.1002/tie.22158

Charisi, V. (2025) 'How does AI Impact Human Behaviour? The Interplay among Research, Design, and Policy Perspectives', in Proceedings of the 3rd International Conference of the ACM Greek SIGCHI Chapter, September, pp. 1-2. DOI: 10.1145/3749012.3759274

Cheng, D., Zou, Y., Xiang, S., & Jiang, C. (2025). Graph neural networks for financial fraud detection: A review. *Frontiers of Computer Science*, *19*(9), Article 199609. DOI: 10.1007/s11704-025-199609-x

Chen, J., Luo, X., Yuan, Y., & Wang, Z. (2025). Enhancing graph convolutional networks with an efficient k-hop neighborhood approach. *Information Fusion*, *124*. *Information Fusion, 103297*, 103297. Advance online publication. DOI: 10.1016/j.inffus.2025.103297

Chen, J.-S., Le, T.-T.-Y., & Florence, D. (2021). Usability and responsiveness of artificial intelligence chatbot on online customer experience in e-retailing. *International Journal of Retail & Distribution Management, 49*(11), 1512–1531. DOI: 10.1108/IJRDM-08-2020-0312

Chen, L., Jiang, M., Jia, F., & Liu, G. (2022). Artificial intelligence adoption in business-to-business marketing: Toward a conceptual framework. *Journal of Business and Industrial Marketing*, *37*(5), 1025–1044. DOI: 10.1108/JBIM-09-2020-0448

Chesbrough, H. (2003). *Open innovation*. Harvard Business School Press.

Childs, E., Mohammad, F., Stevens, L., Burbelo, H., Awoke, A., Rewkowski, N., & Manocha, D. (2024). An Overview of Enhancing Distance Learning Through Emerging Augmented and Virtual Reality Technologies. *IEEE Transactions on Visualization and Computer Graphics*, *30*(8), 4480–4496. DOI: 10.1109/TVCG.2023.3264577

Chintalapati, S., & Pandey, S. K. (2022). Artificial intelligence in marketing: A systematic literature review. *International Journal of Market Research*, *64*(1), 38–68. DOI: 10.1177/14707853211018428

Choi, T. M., Wallace, S. W., & Wang, Y. (2018). Big data analytics in operations management. *Production and Operations Management*, *27*(10), 1868–1883. DOI: 10.1111/poms.12838

Chopra, M., Singh, D. S. K., Gupta, A., Aggarwal, K., Gupta, B. B., & Colace, F. (2022). Analysis & prognosis of sustainable development goals using big data-based approach during COVID-19 pandemic. *Sustainable Technology and Entrepreneurship*, *1*(2), 100012. DOI: 10.1016/j.stae.2022.100012

Chuang, S., Shahhosseini, M., Javaid, M., & Wang, G. G. (2024). Machine learning and AI technology-induced skill gaps and opportunities for continuous development of middle-skilled employees. *Journal of Work-Applied Management*. Advance online publication. DOI: 10.1108/JWAM-08-2024-0111

Chui, M., Hazan, E., Roberts, R., Singla, A., & Smaje, K. (2023). *The economic potential of generative AI*.

Cloarec, J. (2020). The personalization–privacy paradox in the attention economy. *Technological Forecasting and Social Change*, *161*, 120299. DOI: 10.1016/j.techfore.2020.120299

Corsaro, D., Vargo, S. L., Hofacker, C., & Massara, F. (2022). Artificial intelligence and the shaping of the business context. *Journal of Business Research*, *145*, 145. DOI: 10.1016/j.jbusres.2022.02.072

Costa, A. F., & Marques, R. P. (2025). Research trends in artificial intelligence in education and the ethics of privacy. In *2025 IEEE International Conference on Advances in Data-Driven Analytics and Intelligent Systems (ADACIS)* (pp. 1–6). IEEE. https://doi.org/DOI: 10.1109/ADACIS65663.2025.11436431

Cukurova, M. (2025). The interplay of learning, analytics and artificial intelligence in education: A vision for hybrid intelligence. *British Journal of Educational Technology*, *56*(2), 469–488. DOI: 10.1111/bjet.13514

Dadaboyev, S. M. U., Abdullayeva, J., Abbosova, N., Suleymenova, A., & Mamadjanova, K. (2025). Role of artificial intelligence in employee recruitment: Systematic review and future research directions. *Discover Global Society*, *3*(1), 99. DOI: 10.1007/s44282-025-00246-w

Dadaboyev, S. M. U., Baxtiyorova, F., & Akbarova, Y. (2025). AI and the Future of Work: How Can We Design Jobs That Benefit Both Organizations and Employees. In *Proceedings of the AAAI Symposium Series* (Vol. 6, No. 1, p. 59). DOI: 10.1609/aaaiss.v6i1.36025

Dadaboyev, S., Hojimurodova, S., & Gulomova, G. (2025). AI in HR analytics: A synthesis of current research and future directions. In *Proceedings of the AAAI Symposium Series* (Vol. 6, No. 1, p. 60). DOI: 10.1609/aaaiss.v6i1.36026

Daghouri, A., Mansouri, K., & Qbadou, M. (2018). Enhanced Model For Evaluating Information System Success: Determining Critical Criteria. *Engineering, Technology &. Applied Scientific Research*, *8*(4), 3194–3198. DOI: 10.48084/etasr.2148

Data Analytics and Artificial Intelligence in Smart Healthcare Logistics: Building Resilient and Sustainable Systems. (2025*American Journal of Data Science and Artificial Intelligence1*22630DOI: 10.54536/ajdsai.v1i2.6024

Davenport, T. H., & Ronanki, R. (2018). Artificial intelligence for the real world. *Harvard Business Review*, *96*(1), 108–116.

Davenport, T., Guha, A., Grewal, D., & Breßgott, T. (2020). How artificial intelligence will change the future of marketing—. *Journal of the Academy of Marketing Science*, *48*(1), 24–42. Advance online publication. DOI: 10.1007/s11747-019-00696-0

Davis, F. D. (1989). Perceived usefulness, perceived ease of use, and user acceptance of information technology. *Management Information Systems Quarterly*, *13*(3), 319–340. DOI: 10.2307/249008

Dawood, T. Z., Muzata, A. R., Stepanov, M. S., Singh, G., & Kanishcheva, M. G. (2025). The Impact of Heterogeneity on Network Resource Allocation Process for Managing Education in Real Time. *2025 Systems of Signals Generating and Processing in the Field of on Board Communications*, 1–9. DOI: 10.1109/IEEE-CONF64229.2025.10948040

De Bruyn, A., Viswanathan, V., Beh, Y. S., Brock, J. K. U., & Von Wangenheim, F. (2020). Artificial intelligence and marketing: Pitfalls and opportunities. *Journal of Interactive Marketing*, *51*(1), 91–105. DOI: 10.1016/j.intmar.2020.04.007

Dean, S. O. (1988). Commercial objectives, technology transfer, and systems analysis for fusion power development. *Journal of Fusion Energy*, *7*(1), 25–47. DOI: 10.1007/BF01108257

Delone, W. H., & McLean, E. R. (2003). The DeLone and McLean Model of Information Systems Success: A Ten-Year Update. *Journal of Management Information Systems*, *19*(4), 9–30. DOI: 10.1080/07421222.2003.11045748

Dethe, H. S., & Joy, E. (2023). Revolutionizing E-commerce with 3D Visualization: An Experimental Assessment of Behavioural Shopper Responses to Augmented Reality in Online Shopping. *2023 4th International Conference for Emerging Technology (INCET)*, 1–6. DOI: 10.1109/INCET57972.2023.10170472

Devi, D. H., Duraisamy, K., Armghan, A., Alsharari, M., Aliqab, K., Sorathiya, V., Das, S., & Rashid, N. (2023). 5G Technology in Healthcare and Wearable Devices: A Review. *Sensors (Basel)*, *23*(5), 2519. DOI: 10.3390/s23052519

Dey, T., Salam, M. A., & Saha, T. (2021). Evaluation and Analysis of User Satisfaction of Ride-Sharing Service: An Assurance and Empathy in Bangladesh Perspective. *Canadian Journal of Business and Information Studies*, 22–28. DOI: 10.34104/cjbis.021.022028

Dhar, B. K., Karim, R., & Mollik, M. S. (2026). Stitching sustainability in fashion: Strengthening circular economy drivers in the textile industry. In *Strategic innovations for circular economy* (pp. 179–208). IGI Global Scientific Publishing., DOI: 10.4018/979-8-3373-2454-8.ch007

Di Guardo, A., Trovato, F., Cantisani, C., Dattola, A., Nisticò, S. P., Pellacani, G., & Paganelli, A. (2025). Artificial Intelligence in Cosmetic Formulation: Predictive Modeling for Safety, Tolerability, and Regulatory Perspectives. *Cosmetics*, *12*(4), 157. DOI: 10.3390/cosmetics12040157

Di Vaio, A., Boccia, F., Landriani, L., & Palladino, R. (2020). Artificial intelligence in the agri-food system: Rethinking sustainable business models in the COVID-19 scenario. *Sustainability (Basel)*, *12*(12), 4851. DOI: 10.3390/su12124851

Dietvorst, B. J., Simmons, J. P., & Massey, C. (2015). Algorithm aversion. *Journal of Experimental Psychology. General*, *144*(1), 114–126. DOI: 10.1037/xge0000033 PMID: 25401381

Dignum, V. (2019). *Responsible artificial intelligence*. Springer., DOI: 10.1007/978-3-030-30371-6

Dînçer, N.DîNçer. (2023). Elevating Aviation Education: A Comprehensive Examination of Technology's Role in Modern Flight Training. *Journal of Aviation, 7*(2), 317–323. DOI: 10.30518/jav.1279718

Dosi, G. (1982). Technological paradigms and technological trajectories. *Research Policy, 11*(3), 147–162. DOI: 10.1016/0048-7333(82)90016-6

Dulloo, R., Appolloni, A., & Mathiyazhagan, K. (2025). AI-Powered Communication: Strategic Framework for Technological Innovation, Brand Perception, and Sustainable Marketing. In *Strategic Blueprints for AI-Driven Marketing in the Digital Era* (pp. 1–40). IGI Global Scientific Publishing.

Duncan, T., & Caywood, C. (2013). The concept, process, and evolution of integrated marketing communication. In *Integrated Communication* (pp. 13–34). Psychology Press.

Dunham, J., Xu, J., Papangelis, K., Lalone, N., Saker, M., & Schwartz, D. (2024). *Pokémon GO* as an Advertising Platform: The Case for Locative Advertising in Location-based Games. *Games : Research & Practice, 2*(1), 1–25. DOI: 10.1145/3641509

Du, S., & Xie, C. (2020). Paradoxes of artificial intelligence in consumer markets: Ethical challenges and opportunities. *Journal of Business Research, 129*, 961–974. DOI: 10.1016/j.jbusres.2020.08.024

Dwivedi, Y. K., Hughes, L., Baabdullah, A. M., Ribeiro-Navarrete, S., Giannakis, M., Al-Debei, M. M., Dennehy, D., Metri, B., Buhalis, D., Cheung, C. M. K., Conboy, K., Doyle, R., Dubey, R., Dutot, V., Felix, R., Goyal, D. P., Gustafsson, A., Hinsch, C., Jebabli, I., & Wamba, S. F. (2022). Metaverse beyond the hype: Multidisciplinary perspectives on emerging challenges, opportunities, and agenda for research, practice and policy. *International Journal of Information Management, 66*, 102542. DOI: 10.1016/j.ijinfomgt.2022.102542

Dwivedi, Y. K., Kshetri, N., Hughes, L., Slade, E. L., Jeyaraj, A., Kar, A. K., Baabdullah, A. M., Koohang, A., Raghavan, V., Ahuja, M., Albanna, H., Albashrawi, M. A., Al-Busaidi, A. S., Balakrishnan, J., Barlette, Y., Basu, S., Bose, I., Brooks, L., Buhalis, D., & Wright, R. (2023). Opinion Paper: "So what if ChatGPT wrote it?" Multidisciplinary perspectives on opportunities, challenges and implications of generative conversational AI for research, practice and policy. *International Journal of Information Management, 71*, 102642. DOI: 10.1016/j.ijinfomgt.2023.102642

Ebers, M. (2021). 'Liability for artificial intelligence and EU consumer law', Journal of Intellectual Property. *Information Technology and E-Commerce Law, 12*, 204.

Efiloğlu Kurt, Ö. (2019). Examining an e-learning system through the lens of the information systems success model: Empirical evidence from Italy. *Education and Information Technologies, 24*(2), 1173–1184. DOI: 10.1007/s10639-018-9821-4

Eisenhardt, K. M., & Martin, J. A. (2000). Dynamic capabilities: What are they? *Strategic Management Journal, 21*(10–11), 1105–1121. DOI: 10.1002/1097-0266(200010/11)21:10/11<1105::AID-SMJ133>3.0.CO;2-E

El Arab, R. A., Al Moosa, O. A., & Sagbakken, M. (2025). Economic, ethical, and regulatory dimensions of artificial intelligence in healthcare: An integrative review. *Frontiers in Public Health, 13*, 1617138. DOI: 10.3389/fpubh.2025.1617138 PMID: 40951387

Elendu, C., Amaechi, D. C., Okatta, A. U., Amaechi, E. C., Elendu, T. C., Ezeh, C. P., & Elendu, I. D. (2024). The impact of simulation-based training in medical education. *Medicine, 103*(27), e38813. DOI: 10.1097/MD.0000000000038813

El-Manstrly, D., Herhausen, D., Guha, A., Blut, M., & Grewal, D. (2024). Should online retailers emphasize efficiency or experience? First insights on the evolution and heterogeneity of website attributes. *Journal of Retailing, 100*(2), 274–292. DOI: 10.1016/j.jretai.2024.03.002

Eriksson, T., Bigi, A., & Bonera, M. (2020). Think with me, or think for me? On the future role of artificial intelligence in marketing strategy formulation. *The TQM Journal, 32*(4), 795–814. DOI: 10.1108/TQM-12-2019-0303

Erol, B. A., Majumdar, A., Benavidez, P., Rad, P., Choo, K. K. R., & Jamshidi, M. (2019). Toward artificial emotional intelligence for cooperative social human–machine interaction. *IEEE Transactions on Computational Social Systems, 7*(1), 234–246. DOI: 10.1109/TCSS.2019.2922593

Esmark Jones, C. L., Hancock, T., Kazandjian, B., & Voorhees, C. M. (2022). Engaging the avatar: The effects of authenticity signals during chat-based service recoveries. *Journal of Business Research, 144*, 703–716. DOI: 10.1016/j.jbusres.2022.01.012

Etzkorn, M., Römer, Y., Tavakoligargari, M., Lumiere, M. M., Lamdaghri, N., & von Korflesch, H. (2025). The Interface Between Technology Transfer and Artificial Intelligence: A Systematic Literature Review. In *International Scientific-Practical Conference* (pp. 476-489). Springer, Cham. https://doi.org/DOI: 10.1007/978-3-031-88052-0_38

Etzkowitz, H., & Leydesdorff, L. (2000). The dynamics of innovation. *Research Policy, 29*(2), 109–123. DOI: 10.1016/S0048-7333(99)00055-4

European Commission. (2021). *Proposal for a regulation laying down harmonised rules on artificial intelligence (Artificial Intelligence Act)*. European Commission.

European Commission. (2022). *The Digital Markets Act and the Digital Services Act explained*. European Commission.

European Union (2023) Regulation (EU) 2023/2854 on harmonised rules on fair access to and use of data (Data Act). Official Journal of the European Union.

Faisal-E-Alam, M., Bhuiyan, M. R. I., Mimi, A., & Miah, M. T. (2025). The role of the three zero framework in advancing global sustainable development through bibliometric and text mining analysis. *Discover Sustainability, 6*(1), 1128. DOI: 10.1007/s43621-025-01919-x

Fangyu, G., Di, C., Shuai, Y., Zhenghu, H., Qiong, W., & Xu, Z. (2024, October). Research on Enhancing Technology Transfer Efficiency through Artificial Intelligence and Recommendation Algorithms. In *2024 3rd International Conference on Data Analytics, Computing and Artificial Intelligence (ICDACAI)* (pp. 770-773). IEEE. https://doi.org/DOI: 10.1109/ICDACAI65086.2024.00145

Fassiaux, S. (2023). Preserving consumer autonomy through European Union regulation of artificial intelligence: A long-term approach. *European Journal of Risk Regulation, 14*(4), 710–730. DOI: 10.1017/err.2023.58

Feng, Y., & Sun, Y. (2025). Consumer empowerment through generative artificial intelligence : Enhancing brand narrative with collaboration, creation, and communication. *International Journal of Advertising, 0*(0), 1–33. DOI: 10.1080/02650487.2025.2547545

Flew, T. (2024). Mediated trust, the internet and artificial intelligence: Ideas, interests, institutions and futures. *Policy and Internet, 16*(2), 443–457. DOI: 10.1002/poi3.390

Floridi, L., Cowls, J., Beltrametti, M., Chatila, R., Chazerand, P., Dignum, V., Luetge, C., Madelin, R., Pagallo, U., Rossi, F., Schafer, B., Valcke, P., & Vayena, E. (2018). AI4People—An ethical framework. *Minds and Machines, 28*(4), 689–707. DOI: 10.1007/s11023-018-9482-5 PMID: 30930541

Følstad, A., Araujo, T., & Law, E. L.-C.. (2021). Future directions for chatbot research. *Computers in Human Behavior, 123*, 106843. DOI: 10.1016/j.chb.2021.106843

Fournier, S., & Avery, J. (2011). The uninvited brand. *Business Horizons, 54*(3), 193–207. DOI: 10.1016/j.bushor.2011.01.001

Frenkenberg, A., & Hochman, G. (2025). *It's scary to use it, it's scary to refuse it: The psychological dimensions of AI adoption - anxiety, motives, and dependency*. Syst., DOI: 10.3390/systems13020082

Gachayeva, S., Morozova, D., Moser, C., & Tursunbayeva, A. (2025) 'Charting the Ethical and Moral Landscapes of Human-AI Interactions', in *Academy of Management Annual Meeting Proceedings*. DOI: 10.5465/AMPROC.2025.12338symposium

Gaczek, P., Leszczyński, G., Kot, M., & Pozharliev, R. (2025). How locus of causality shapes human-AI decision-making. *Management Decision*, *63*(13), 522–544. Advance online publication. DOI: 10.1108/MD-07-2024-1635

Gao, Y., Sheng, T., Xiang, Y., Xiong, Y., Wang, H., & Zhang, J. (2023). *Chat-REC: Towards Interactive and Explainable LLMs-Augmented Recommender System* (Version 2). arXiv. DOI: 10.48550/ARXIV.2303.14524

Gao, Y., & Liu, H. (2023). Artificial intelligence-enabled personalization in interactive marketing: A customer journey perspective. *Journal of Research in Interactive Marketing*, *17*(5), 663–680. DOI: 10.1108/JRIM-01-2022-0023

Gao, Z., Hua, M., Jia, Z., Li, L., & Hao, Y. (2025). Intelligent Pathway: Artificial Intelligence and the Path to Energy Sustainability. *Growth and Change*, *56*(4), e70050. DOI: 10.1111/grow.70050

Garcia, M. B. (2023). Location-based marketing using mobile geofencing: Lessons learned from a user-centred application development research. *International Journal of Technology Marketing*, *17*(1), 1. DOI: 10.1504/IJTMKT.2023.127322

Gbormittah, E. (2024). Digitalisation of onboarding: A case study to investigate the impact of virtual reality technology on employees social interactions and information seeking during job-onboarding. *Occupational Psychology Outlook*, *3*(2), 24–37. DOI: 10.53841/bpsopo.2024.3.2.24

Gentile, A., Santangelo, A., Sorce, S., & Vitabile, S. (2011). Human-to-human interfaces: Emerging trends and challenges. *International Journal of Space-Based and Situated Computing*, *1*(1), 3–17. DOI: 10.1504/IJSSC.2011.039103

Ghai, A., & Tandon, U. (2023). Integrating gamification and instructional design to enhance usability of online learning. *Education and Information Technologies*, *28*(2), 2187–2206. DOI: 10.1007/s10639-022-11202-5

Ghalavand, H., Shirshahi, S., Rahimi, A., Zarrinabadi, Z., & Amani, F. (2024). Common data quality elements for health information systems: A systematic review. *BMC Medical Informatics and Decision Making*, *24*(1), 243. DOI: 10.1186/s12911-024-02644-7

Ghasemaghaei, M., & Calic, G. (2023). Artificial intelligence adoption and firm performance. *Journal of Business Research, 155*, 113391. DOI: 10.1016/j.jbusres.2022.113391

Gissi, V., & Savelli, E. (2025). Integrating Artificial Intelligence into Internal Brand Communication. *Micro & Macro Marketing, 34*(3), 557–590.

Glikson, E., & Woolley, A. W. (2020). Human trust in artificial intelligence. *Academy of Management Review, 45*(3), 627–660. DOI: 10.5465/amr.2018.0196

Gołąb-Andrzejak, E. (2023). AI-powered digital transformation: Tools, benefits and challenges for marketers-Case study of LPP. *Procedia Computer Science, 219*, 397–404. DOI: 10.1016/j.procs.2023.01.305

Gong, Y., Liu, G., Xue, Y., Li, R., & Meng, L. (2023). A survey on dataset quality in machine learning. *Information and Software Technology, 162*, 107268. DOI: 10.1016/j.infsof.2023.107268

Google. (2024). *Overview of SGE (Search Generative Experience)*. Google Search Central. https://developers.google.com/search

Grebe, M., Franke, M. R., & Heinzl, A. (2023). Artificial intelligence: How leading companies define use cases, scale-up utilization, and realize value. *Informatik Spektrum., 46*(4), 197–209. DOI: 10.1007/s00287-023-01548-6

Gregory, A. (2007). Involving stakeholders in developing corporate brands: The communication dimension. *Journal of Marketing Management, 23*(1–2), 59–73. DOI: 10.1362/026725707X178558

Grewal, D. S. (2014). A critical conceptual analysis of definitions of artificial intelligence as applicable to computer engineering. *IOSR Journal of Computer Engineering, 16*(2), 9–13. DOI: 10.9790/0661-16210913

Grewal, D., Satornino, C. B., Davenport, T. H., & Guha, A. (2025). How generative AI is shaping the future of marketing. *Journal of the Academy of Marketing Science, 53*(3), 702–722. DOI: 10.1007/s11747-024-01064-3

Grundner, L., & Neuhofer, B. (2021). The bright and dark sides of artificial intelligence: A futures perspective on tourist destination experiences. *Journal of Destination Marketing & Management, 19*, 100511. DOI: 10.1016/j.jdmm.2020.100511

Güner Gültekin, D., Pinarbasi, F., Yazici, M., & Adiguzel, Z. (2025). Commercialisation of artificial intelligence: A research on entrepreneurial companies with challenges and opportunities. *Business Process Management Journal, 31*(2), 605–630. DOI: 10.1108/BPMJ-10-2023-0836

Gupta, A. S., & Mukherjee, J. (2025). Framework for adoption of generative AI for information search of retail products and services. *International Journal of Retail & Distribution Management*, *53*(2), 165–181. DOI: 10.1108/IJRDM-05-2024-0203

Gupta, S., Modgil, S., Bhattacharyya, S., & Bose, I. (2022). Artificial intelligence for decision support systems in the field of operations research: Review and future scope of research. *Annals of Operations Research*, *308*(1), 215–274. DOI: 10.1007/s10479-020-03856-6

Guthrie, C., Fosso-Wamba, S., & Arnaud, J. B. (2021). Online consumer resilience during a pandemic: An exploratory study of e-commerce behavior before, during and after a COVID-19 lockdown. *Journal of Retailing and Consumer Services*, *61*, 102570. DOI: 10.1016/j.jretconser.2021.102570

Guzman, A. L., & Lewis, S. C. (2020). Artificial intelligence and communication: A human–machine communication research agenda. *New Media & Society*, *22*(1), 70–86. DOI: 10.1177/1461444819858691

Hacker, P., Cordes, J., & Rochon, J. (2024). Regulating gatekeeper artificial intelligence and data: Transparency, access and fairness under the digital markets act, the general data protection regulation and beyond. *European Journal of Risk Regulation*, *15*(1), 49–86. DOI: 10.1017/err.2023.81

Haider Rizvi, S. M., Imran, R., & Mahmood, A. (2025). Text classification using graph convolutional networks: A comprehensive survey. *ACM Computing Surveys*, *57*(8), 1–38. DOI: 10.1145/3698123

Haider, K. (2024). Natural language processing in AI-powered systems: Techniques and future prospects. *Journal of Ai Range*, *1*(1), 40–53.

Hajiyeva, H., Carillo, K., & Bayraktar, S. (2026). Navigating Across Realities: A User-Informed Theoretical Framework for Extended Reality in Information Systems. *Communications of the Association for Information Systems*, *55*(1), 50. https://aisel.aisnet.org/cais/vol55/iss1/50

Haleem, A., Javaid, M., Qadri, M. A., Singh, R. P., & Suman, R. (2022). Artificial intelligence (AI) applications for marketing: A literature-based study. *International Journal of Intelligent Networks*, *3*, 119–132. DOI: 10.1016/j.ijin.2022.08.005

Hamilton, R. H., & Davison, H. K. (2022). Legal and ethical challenges for HR in machine learning. *Employee Responsibilities and Rights Journal*, *34*(1), 19–39. DOI: 10.1007/s10672-021-09377-z

Hancock, J. T., Naaman, M., & Levy, K. (2020). AI-mediated communication: Definition, research agenda, and ethical considerations. *Journal of Computer-Mediated Communication*, *25*(1), 89–100. DOI: 10.1093/jcmc/zmz022

Har, L. L., Rashid, U. K., Chuan, L. T., Sen, S. C., & Xia, L. Y. (2022). Revolution of Retail Industry: From Perspective of Retail 1.0 to 4.0. *Procedia Computer Science*, *200*, 1615–1625. DOI: 10.1016/j.procs.2022.01.362

Hartley, K., & Aldag, A. (2024). Public trust and support for government technology: Survey insights about Singapore's smart city policies. *Cities (London, England)*, *154*, 105368. DOI: 10.1016/j.cities.2024.105368

Hassaan, A., Jamshaid, M. M., Siddique, M. N., Akbar, Z., & Niaz, S. (2023). Ethical Analytics & Digital Transformation In The Age Of Ai: Embedding Privacy, Fairness, And Transparency To Drive Innovation And Stakeholder Trust. *Contemporary Journal of Social Science Review*, *1*(04), 1–18.

Hassan, N., Abdelraouf, M., & El-Shihy, D. (2025). The moderating role of personalized recommendations in the trust–satisfaction–loyalty relationship: An empirical study of AI-driven e-commerce. *Future Business Journal*, *11*(1), 66. DOI: 10.1186/s43093-025-00476-z

Hatami, M., Qu, Q., Chen, Y., Kholidy, H., Blasch, E., & Ardiles-Cruz, E. (2024). A Survey of the Real-Time Metaverse: Challenges and Opportunities. *Future Internet*, *16*(10), 379. DOI: 10.3390/fi16100379

Haupt, M., Freidank, J., & Haas, A. (2024). Consumer responses to human-AI collaboration at organizational frontlines: Strategies to escape algorithm aversion in content creation. *Review of Managerial Science*, *19*(2), 377–413. https://hdl.handle.net/10419/318868. DOI: 10.1007/s11846-024-00748-y

He, Z., Zhang, Q., Song, M., Tan, X., & Wang, W. (2025). Four overlooked errors in ROC analysis: How to prevent and avoid. *BMJ Evidence-Based Medicine*, *30*(3), 208–211. DOI: 10.1136/bmjebm-2024-112000

Heaven, D. (2020). Why faces don't always tell the truth about feelings. *Nature*, *578*(7796), 502–505. DOI: 10.1038/d41586-020-00507-5 PMID: 32103200

Helberger, N., Zuiderveen Borgesius, F., & Reyna, A. (2020). The perfect match? Consumer manipulation in the age of AI. *European Law Journal*, *26*(1–2), 38–60.

Heller, J., Chylinski, M., de Ruyter, K., Mahr, D., & Keeling, D. I. (2019). Let me imagine that for you: Transforming the retail frontline through augmenting customer mental imagery ability. *Journal of Retailing*, *95*(2), 94–114. DOI: 10.1016/j.jretai.2019.03.005

Hentati, A., Forsell, E., Ljótsson, B., Kaldo, V., Lindefors, N., & Kraepelien, M. (2021). The effect of user interface on treatment engagement in a self-guided digital problem-solving intervention: A randomized controlled trial. *Internet Interventions : The Application of Information Technology in Mental and Behavioural Health, 26*, 100448. DOI: 10.1016/j.invent.2021.100448

Hermann, E., & Hermann, E. (2022). Leveraging Artificial Intelligence in Marketing for Social Good — An Ethical Perspective. *Journal of Business Ethics, 179*(1), 43–61. DOI: 10.1007/s10551-021-04843-y PMID: 34054170

Hermann, E., & Puntoni, S. (2024). Artificial intelligence and consumer behavior: From predictive to generative AI. *Journal of Business Research, 180*, 114720. DOI: 10.1016/j.jbusres.2024.114720

Hesel, N., Buder, F., & Unfried, M. (2022). *The next frontier in intelligent augmentation: Human-machine collaboration in strategic marketing decision-making*. NIM Marketing Intelligence Review., DOI: 10.2478/nimmir-2022-0017

Hofmann, P., Urbach, N., Lanzl, J., & Desouza, K. C. (2024). AI-enabled information systems: Teaming up with intelligent agents in networked business. *Electronic Markets, 34*(1), 52. Advance online publication. DOI: 10.1007/s12525-024-00734-y

Hollebeek, L. D., Menidjel, C., Sarstedt, M., Jansson, J., & Urbonavicius, S. (2024). Engaging consumers through artificially intelligent technologies. *Psychology and Marketing, 41*(4), 880–898. DOI: 10.1002/mar.21957

Holt, D. B. (2004). *How brands become icons: The principles of cultural branding*. harvard business press.

Hongladarom, S., & Bandasak, J. (2024). Non-western AI ethics guidelines: Implications for intercultural ethics of technology. *AI & Society, 39*(4), 2019–2032. DOI: 10.1007/s00146-023-01665-6

Hossain, R., Al- Amin, A.-A., Mani, L., Islam, M. M., Poli, T. A., & Milon, M. N. U. (2024). Exploring the Effectiveness of Social Media on Tourism Destination Marketing: An Empirical Study in a Developing Country. *WSEAS TRANSACTIONS ON BUSINESS AND ECONOMICS, 21*, 1392–1408. DOI: 10.37394/23207.2024.21.114

Hossain, M. K., & Mollik, M. S. (2022). Exploring the impact of social media platforms on instigating tourist's emotions and behavioral intentions to co-create and visit tourist spots: Bangladesh perspective. *Journal of Business Studies, 3*(1), 217–236. DOI: 10.58753/jbspust.3.1.2022.13

Hossain, R., Sohag, H. J., Farhatul, H., Ahmed, S., & Amin, A. (2024). Prospective Artificial Intelligence (AI) Applications in the University Education Level: En hancing Learning, Teaching and Administration through a PRISMA Base Review Systematic Review. [PJLSS]. *Pakistan Journal of Life and Social Sciences, 22*(2). Advance online publication. DOI: 10.57239/PJLSS-2024-22.2.00694

Hossain, S., Hasan, M. A., Faruk, M. O., & Salam, M. A. (2024). Association between the salinity level with miscarriage and unintended pregnancy in Bangladesh: Impact of salinity level on miscarriage and unintended pregnancy in Bangladesh. *Heliyon, 10*(1), e23858. Advance online publication. DOI: 10.1016/j.heliyon.2023.e23858

Hosseini Tabaghdehi, S. A., & Ayaz, Ö. (2025). AI ethics in action: A circular model for transparency, accountability and inclusivity. *Journal of Managerial Psychology*. Advance online publication. DOI: 10.1108/JMP-03-2024-0177

Hoyer, W. D., Kroschke, M., Schmitt, B., Kraume, K., & Shankar, V. (2020). Transforming the customer experience through new technologies. *Journal of Interactive Marketing, 51*(1), 57–71. DOI: 10.1016/j.intmar.2020.04.001

Huang, M., & Rust, R. T. (2021). *A strategic framework for artificial intelligence in marketing*. 30–50.

Huang, M. H., & Rust, R. T. (2018). Artificial intelligence in service. *Journal of Service Research, 21*(2), 155–172. DOI: 10.1177/1094670517752459

Huang, M. H., & Rust, R. T. (2021). A strategic framework for artificial intelligence in marketing. *Journal of the Academy of Marketing Science, 49*(1), 30–50. DOI: 10.1007/s11747-020-00749-9

Huang, M. H., & Rust, R. T. (2022). A framework for collaborative artificial intelligence in marketing. *Journal of Retailing, 98*(2), 209–223. DOI: 10.1016/j.jretai.2021.03.001

Huang, M.-H., & Rust, R. (2023). The caring machine: Feeling AI for customer care. *Journal of Marketing*. Advance online publication. DOI: 10.1177/00222429231224748

Huang, X., Yang, F., Zheng, J., Feng, C., & Zhang, L. (2023). Personalized human resource management via HR analytics and artificial intelligence: Theory and implications. *Asia Pacific Management Review, 28*(4), 598–610. DOI: 10.1016/j.apmrv.2023.04.004

Huang, Z., & Li, H. (2019). Research on UX Evaluation Model of Computer Input Devices (Keyboard and Mouse) Based on AHP. *IOP Conference Series. Materials Science and Engineering, 686*(1), 012005. DOI: 10.1088/1757-899X/686/1/012005

Hua, Y., Song, X., Feng, Z., & Wu, X. (2023). MFR-DTA: A multi-functional and robust model for predicting drug–target binding affinity and region. *Bioinformatics (Oxford, England), 39*(2), btad056. Advance online publication. DOI: 10.1093/bioinformatics/btad056

Huh, J., Kim, H.-Y., & Lee, G. (2023). "Oh, happy day!" Examining the role of AI-powered voice assistants as a positive technology in the formation of brand loyalty. *Journal of Research in Interactive Marketing, 17*(5), 794–812. Advance online publication. DOI: 10.1108/JRIM-10-2022-0328

Hurmuzlu, O. (2024). Ethical implications of the commercialization of artificial intelligence (AI). In *Innovative and Intelligent Digital Technologies; Towards an Increased Efficiency* (Vol. 1, pp. 321–333). Springer Nature Switzerland. DOI: 10.1007/978-3-031-70399-7_23

Ibirinoye-Abdulkareem, B. S., Adedotun, K. J., Adekunle, J. O., & Raji, A. K. (2025). Enhancing Guest Satisfaction in Hotel Booking Websites through AI-Driven Personalization and Adaptive User Interfaces. *Nigerian Journal of Technical Education, 24*(2), 83–93. DOI: 10.63996/njte.v24i2.32

Ienca, M. (2023). On artificial intelligence and manipulation. *Topoi, 42*(3), 833–842. DOI: 10.1007/s11245-023-09940-3

International Labour Organization (ILO). (2024). *Generative AI and jobs: A global analysis of potential effects on job quantity and quality*. ILO Publishing.

Islam, M.M., Bhuiyan, M.R.I., Islam, S.H., Tabassum, M.N. and Billah, M. (2026) 'Unlocking the Mediating and Moderating Role of Information Security in Information Systems: A Combined TAM, ISM, and HBM Model', Human Behavior and Emerging Technologies, 2026(1). Available at:_.DOI: 10.1155/hbe2/5593002

Islam, M. A., Fakir, S. I., Masud, S., Hossen, M. D., Islam, M. T., & Siddiky, M. R. (2024). Artificial intelligence in digital marketing automation: Enhancing personalization, predictive analytics, and ethical integration. *Edelweiss Applied Science and Technology, 8*(6), 6498–6516. DOI: 10.55214/25768484.v8i6.3404

Ivanov, D. (2023). Intelligent digital twins for supply chain stress testing and resilience. *International Journal of Production Economics, 263*, 108938. DOI: 10.1016/j.ijpe.2023.108938

Ivanov, D., & Dolgui, A. (2020). Viability of intertwined supply networks. *International Journal of Production Research, 58*(10), 2904–2915. DOI: 10.1080/00207543.2020.1750727

Ivanov, D., Sokolov, B., & Dolgui, A. (2014). The ripple effect in supply chains. *International Journal of Production Research*, *52*(7), 215–222. DOI: 10.1080/00207543.2013.858836

Jalilvand, M. R., & Ataei, J. (2026). Using artificial intelligence in digital branding: A two-phase qualitative approach. *EuroMed Journal of Business*, 1–52. DOI: 10.1108/EMJB-12-2024-0353

Jamatia, A., Baidya, U., & Paul, S. DebBarma, S., & Dey, S. (2020). Rating prediction of tourist destinations based on supervised machine learning algorithms. In *Advances in Intelligent Systems and Computing* (Vol. 990, pp. 453–465). Springer. DOI: 10.1007/978-981-13-8406-6_41

Janiesch, C., Zschech, P., & Heinrich, K. (2021). Machine learning and deep learning. *Electronic Markets*, *31*(3), 685–695. DOI: 10.1007/s12525-021-00475-2

Jankovic, S. D., & Curovic, D. M. (2023). Strategic integration of artificial intelligence for sustainable businesses: Implications for data management and human user engagement in the digital era. *Sustainability (Basel)*, *15*(21), 15208. DOI: 10.3390/su152115208

Jarrahi, M. H., Kenyon, S., Brown, A., Donahue, C., & Wicher, C. (2023). Artificial intelligence: A strategy to harness its power through organizational learning. *The Journal of Business Strategy*, *44*(2), 126–135. DOI: 10.1108/JBS-11-2021-0182

Javaid, M., Haleem, A., & Suman, R. (2023). Digital Twin applications toward Industry 4.0: A Review. *Cognitive Robotics*, *3*, 71–92. DOI: 10.1016/j.cogr.2023.04.003

Jeganathan, Y. (2025). Improving searchability of products in E-commerce platforms. *International Journal of Science and Research Archive*, *16*(3), 666–672. DOI: 10.30574/ijsra.2025.16.3.2594

Jha, G., Chandwani, J., & Zaki, M. (2025). The shift to fast-good service experience through digitalization: Lessons from KFC. In Kristensson, P., Witell, L., & Zaki, M. (Eds.), *Handbook of Service Experience* (pp. 148–161). Edward Elgar Publishing., DOI: 10.4337/9781035300198.00019

Jianchun, Y. (2024). Enhancing employee job satisfaction through organizational climate and employee happiness at work: A mediated–moderated model. *BMC Psychology*, *12*(744), 744. Advance online publication. DOI: 10.1186/s40359-024-02269-5 PMID: 39696658

Jiang, Y., & Katsamakas, E. (2010). The Impact of e-Book Technology on Book Retailing. *2010 43rd Hawaii International Conference on System Sciences*, 1–8. DOI: 10.1109/HICSS.2010.383

Jiang, T., Sun, Z., Fu, S., & Lv, Y. (2024). Human-AI interaction research agenda: A user-centered perspective. *Data and Information Management*, *8*(4), 100078. DOI: 10.1016/j.dim.2024.100078

Jiang, Y., Li, X., Luo, H., Yin, S., & Kaynak, O. (2022). Quo vadis artificial intelligence? *Discover Artificial Intelligence*, *2*(1), 4. DOI: 10.1007/s44163-022-00022-8

Jiménez-Luna, J., Grisoni, F., Weskamp, N., & Schneider, G. (2021). Artificial intelligence in drug discovery: Recent advances and future perspectives. *Expert Opinion on Drug Discovery*, *16*(9), 949–959. DOI: 10.1080/17460441.2021.1909567 PMID: 33779453

Jin, E., & Eastin, M. (2022). Birds of a feather flock together: Matched personality effects of product recommendation chatbots and users. *Journal of Research in Interactive Marketing*. Advance online publication. DOI: 10.1108/JRIM-03-2022-0089

Jin, S. V., & Youn, S. (2022). Social presence and imagery processing as predictors of chatbot continuance intention in human-AI-interaction. *International Journal of Human-Computer Interaction*. Advance online publication. DOI: 10.1080/10447318.2022.2129277

Jiyoung, P., Woo, S. E., & Kim, J. J. (2024). Attitudes towards artificial intelligence at work: Scale development and validation. *Journal of Occupational and Organizational Psychology*, *97*(3), 920–951. DOI: 10.1111/joop.12502

Joshi, A., Bhattacharyya, P., & Carman, M. J. (2017). Automatic sarcasm detection: A survey. *ACM Computing Surveys*, *50*(5), 1–22. DOI: 10.1145/3124420

Kache, F., & Seuring, S. (2017). Challenges and opportunities of big data in supply chain management. *International Journal of Operations & Production Management*, *37*(1), 10–36. DOI: 10.1108/IJOPM-02-2015-0078

Kalagarla, S. D.Sneha Deepika Kalagarla. (2025). Enhancing User Experience in ePermitting Systems Through AI-Driven Personalization. *International Journal of Science & Technoledge*, *16*(1), 2923. DOI: 10.71097/IJSAT.v16.i1.2923

Kalathot, R. (2025). Artificial Intelligence for Dynamic User Experience Personalization in SaaS. *Journal of Data Analysis and Critical Management*, *1*(03), 1–8. DOI: 10.64235/20rneq83

Karkošková, S. (2023). Data governance model to enhance data quality in financial institutions. *Information Systems Management*, *40*(1), 90–110. DOI: 10.1080/10580530.2022.2042628

Karpukhin, V., Oğuz, B., Min, S., Lewis, P., Wu, L., Edunov, S., Chen, D., & Yih, W.-t. (2020). Dense passage retrieval for open-domain question answering. In *Proceedings of the 2020 Conference on Empirical Methods in Natural Language Processing (EMNLP)* (pp. 6769–6781). Association for Computational Linguistics. DOI: 10.18653/v1/2020.emnlp-main.550

Kartajaya, H. (2021). *Marketing 5.0: Technology for humanity*. Wiley.

Karunakaran, A., Lebovitz, S., Narayanan, D., & Rahman, H. A. (2025). Artificial Intelligence at Work: An Integrative Perspective on the Impact of AI on Workplace Inequality. *Academy of Management Annals*, (ja), annals-2023. https://doi.org/DOI: 10.5465/annals.2023.0230

Kaya, H. (2026). Extending TAM and UTAUT for Meta-Banking Adoption Intention: Roles of Technostress, AR/VR Experience, and Perceived Value. Sakarya University Journal of Computer and Information Sciences, (Advanced Online Publication), 34-57.DOI: 10.35377/saucis...1700912

Keegan, B., Dennehy, D., & Naudé, P. (2022). Implementing artificial intelligence in traditional B2B marketing practices: An activity theory perspective. *Information Systems Frontiers*. Advance online publication. DOI: 10.1007/s10796-022-10294-1 PMID: 35637917

Keller, K. L. (2013). *Keller: Strategic Brand Management eBook GE 4e*. Pearson Higher Ed.

Keramati, H., Lu, X., Cabanag, M., Wu, L., Kushwaha, V., & Beier, S. (2024). Applications and advances of immersive technology in cardiology. *Current Problems in Cardiology*, *49*(10), 102762. DOI: 10.1016/j.cpcardiol.2024.102762

Khalisa, T. N., & Ramadhani, D. P. (2025, January). *Exploring tourist perceptions of Greater Bandung tourism destinations: An IndoBERT-based big data analytics study on Google Maps reviews* [Paper presentation]. *2025 International Conference on Computer Sciences, Engineering, and Technology Innovation (ICoCSETI)*, IEEE. DOI: 10.1109/ICoCSETI63724.2025.11020554

Khanal, S., Zhang, H., & Taeihagh, A. (2024). Building an AI ecosystem in a small nation: Lessons from Singapore's journey to the forefront of AI. *Humanities & Social Sciences Communications*, *11*(1), 1–12. DOI: 10.1057/s41599-024-03289-7

Khanal, S., Zhang, H., & Taeihagh, A. (2025). Why and how is the power of Big Tech increasing in the policy process? The case of generative AI. *Policy and Society*, *44*(1), 52–69. DOI: 10.1093/polsoc/puae012

Khan, M. S., Umer, H., & Faruqe, F. (2024). Artificial intelligence for low income countries. *Humanities & Social Sciences Communications*, *11*(1), 1–13. DOI: 10.1057/s41599-024-03947-w

Khanom, M. T. (2023). Business strategies in the age of digital transformation. *The Journal of Business*, *8*, 28–35.

Khatun, M., Bhuiyan, M. R. I., Amin, M. A., Hossen, M., & Mia, M. A. H. (2026). Evaluating E-Commerce Satisfaction: The Impact of Trust, Information Quality, Usability, and Perceived-to-Actual Performance. *SAGE Open*, *16*(1), 21582440261423039. Advance online publication. DOI: 10.1177/21582440261423039

Khatun, M., Hossain, R., Bhuiyan, M. R., Tabassum, M. N., & Riaj, M. A. (2025). Green Entrepreneurship and Digital Transformation for Sustainable Development: A Systematic Review. In Mouloudj, K., & Bouarar, A. (Eds.), *Digitizing Green Entrepreneurship* (pp. 153–180). IGI Global Scientific Publishing., DOI: 10.4018/979-8-3693-7442-9.ch006

Kheng, L. (2023). Walmart: A Business Case Study in Knowledge Management, Walmart's Secret Sauce – The Use of Machine Learning, Automation, and Virtual Reality. In Russ, M. (Ed.), (pp. 33–46). Advances in Business Information Systems and Analytics. IGI Global., DOI: 10.4018/978-1-6684-5859-4.ch002

Khrais, L. T. (2020). Role of artificial intelligence in shaping consumer demand in E-commerce. *Future Internet*, *12*(12), 226. DOI: 10.3390/fi12120226

Kim, S., Baek, T. H., Kim, Y.-K., & Yoo, K. (2016). Factors affecting stickiness and word of mouth in mobile applications. *Journal of Research in Interactive Marketing*, *10*(3), 177–192. DOI: 10.1108/JRIM-06-2015-0046

Kingsley, G., Bozeman, B., & Coker, K. (1996). Technology transfer and absorption: An 'R & D value-mapping' approach to evaluation. *Research Policy*, *25*(6), 967–995. DOI: 10.1016/0048-7333(96)00890-6

Kitchenham, B., Budgen, D., Brereton, P., Turner, M., Charters, S., & Linkman, S. (2007). Large-scale software engineering questions–expert opinion or empirical evidence? *IET Software*, *1*(5), 161–171. DOI: 10.1049/iet-sen:20060052

Kitchen, P. J., & Schultz, D. E. (2003). Integrated corporate and product brand communication (1). *Journal of Competitiveness Studies*, *11*(1), 66.

Kivetz, R., & Simonson, I. (2000). The Effects of Incomplete Information on Consumer Choice. *JMR, Journal of Marketing Research*, *37*(4), 427–448. DOI: 10.1509/jmkr.37.4.427.18796

Kliatchko, J. (2008). Revisiting the IMC construct: A revised definition and four pillars. *International Journal of Advertising*, *27*(1), 133–160. DOI: 10.1080/02650487.2008.11073043

Klumpp, M. (2018). Automation and artificial intelligence in business logistics systems: Human reactions and collaboration requirements. *International Journal of Logistics*, *21*(3), 224–242. DOI: 10.1080/13675567.2017.1384451

Kotha, S. (2024). *The convergence of artificial intelligence and human marketing: A framework for enhanced customer insights and personalization.* International Journal For Multidisciplinary Research., DOI: 10.36948/ijfmr.2024.v06i06.30266

Kowert, W. (2017). The foreseeability of human-artificial intelligence interactions. *Texas Law Review*, *96*, 181.

Krakowski, S., Haftor, D., Luger, J., Pashkevich, N., & Raisch, S. (2026). Human-centered artificial intelligence: A field experiment. *Management Science*, *72*(1), 57–72. DOI: 10.1287/mnsc.2022.03849

Krarup, T., & Horst, M. (2023). European artificial intelligence policy as digital single market making. *Big Data & Society*, *10*(1), 20539517231153811. Advance online publication. DOI: 10.1177/20539517231153811

Kronemann, B., Kizgin, H., Rana, N. P., & Dwivedi, Y. K. (2023). How AI encourages consumers to share their secrets? The role of anthropomorphism, personalisation, and privacy concerns, and avenues for future research. *Spanish Journal of Marketing - ESIC*, *27*(1), 3–19. DOI: 10.1108/SJME-10-2022-0213

Kshetri, N., Dwivedi, Y. K., Davenport, T. H., & Panteli, N. (2024). Generative artificial intelligence in marketing: Applications, opportunities, challenges, and research agenda. *International Journal of Information Management*, *75*, 102716. DOI: 10.1016/j.ijinfomgt.2023.102716

Kulshrestha, C., & Kapoor, A. (2025). Conversational AI and Consumer Decision Pathways: A Comparative Analysis of Impulsive versus Deliberate Buying in Voice Commerce. *Advances in Consumer Research. Association for Consumer Research (U. S.)*, *2*(5).

Kumar, A., & Kumari, N. (2025). The future of tourism: the metaverse as a tool for promoting sustainable tourism. Asia Pacific Journal of Tourism Research, 0(0), Article 2574038. https://doi.org/10.1080/10941665.2025.2574038, DOI: 10.1080/10941665.2025.2574038

Kumar, A. (2025). AI-Powered Personalization for Enhancing Customer Retention in Online Retailing. *International Journal of Research and Analytical Reviews*, *12*(2). Advance online publication. DOI: 10.56975/ijrar.v12i2.314472

Kumar, D., Koul, S., & Siringoringo, H. (2023). Assessing antecedents of behavioral intention to use e-LMS: A case from a private institution in the northern region of India. *IEEE Transactions on Learning Technologies*, *16*(5), 861–872. DOI: 10.1109/TLT.2023.3265016

Kumari, M., Sinha, R., Chakrabarty, P., Hasnain, M. G., Qamar, N., & Gupta, S. (2024). Exploring machine learning's impact on digital marketing. *2024 15th International Conference on Computing Communication and Networking Technologies (ICCCNT)*, 1–5.

Kumar, R., Bhandari, N., & Srivastava, V. (2025). Decoding and integrating the facets of consumer empowerment: A study with consumers of high-involvement Product(s). *Journal of Marketing Theory and Practice*, *33*(2), 289–309. DOI: 10.1080/10696679.2024.2321444

Kumar, V., Rajan, B., Venkatesan, R., & Lecinski, J. (2019). Understanding the role of artificial intelligence in personalized engagement marketing. *California Management Review*, *61*(4), 135–155. DOI: 10.1177/0008125619859317

Lankton, N. K., McKnight, D. H., & Tripp, J. F. (2015). Technology, humanness, and trust. *Journal of Management Information Systems*, *32*(4), 116–151.

Laux, J., Wachter, S., & Mittelstadt, B. (2024). Trustworthy artificial intelligence and the European Union AI Act: On the conflation of trustworthiness and acceptability of risk. *Regulation & Governance*, *18*(1), 3–32. DOI: 10.1111/rego.12512 PMID: 38435808

Lavoye, V., Sipilä, J., Mero, J., & Tarkiainen, A. (2023). The emperor's new clothes: Self-explorative engagement in virtual try-on service experiences positively impacts brand outcomes. *Journal of Services Marketing*, *37*(10), 1–21. DOI: 10.1108/JSM-04-2022-0137

Lazaroiu, G., Gedeon, T., Rogalska, E., Valaskova, K., Nagy, M., Musa, H., Zvarikova, K., Poliak, M., Horak, J., Cre oiu, R. I., Krulicky, T., Ionescu, L., Popa, C., Hurloiu, L. R., Nistor, F., Avram, L. G., & Braga, V. (2024). Digital twin-based cyber-physical manufacturing systems, extended reality metaverse enterprise and production management algorithms, and Internet of Things financial and labor market technologies in generative artificial intelligence economics. *Oeconomia Copernicana*, *15*(3), 837–870. DOI: 10.24136/oc.3183

LeCun, Y., Bengio, Y., & Hinton, G. (2015). Deep learning. *Nature*, *521*(7553), 436–444. DOI: 10.1038/nature14539

Ledro, C., Nosella, A., & Vinelli, A. (2022). Artificial intelligence in customer relationship management: Literature review and future research directions. *Journal of Business and Industrial Marketing*, *37*(13), 48–63. DOI: 10.1108/JBIM-07-2021-0332

Lee, J. C., & Chen, X. (2022). Exploring users' adoption intentions in the evolution of artificial intelligence mobile banking applications: The intelligent and anthropomorphic perspectives. *International Journal of Bank Marketing*, *40*(4), 631–658. DOI: 10.1108/IJBM-08-2021-0394

Lemon, K. N., & Verhoef, P. C. (2016). Understanding customer experience throughout the customer journey. *Journal of Marketing*, *80*(6), 69–96. DOI: 10.1509/jm.15.0420

Li, B., Li, R., Wang, J., & Song, A. (2025). Tourism sentiment chain representation model and construction from tourist reviews. *Future Internet*, *17*(7), Article 276. DOI: 10.3390/fi17070276

Li, B., Qi, P., Liu, B., Di, S., Liu, J., Pei, J., Yi, J., & Zhou, B. (2023). Trustworthy AI: From principles to practices. *arXiv*. https://doi.org//arXiv.2110.01167DOI: 10.48550

Liang, Z., Zhang, F., & Zhou, T. (2025). Generative AI in LEGO education: Opportunities and ethical challenges in digital learning development. In *2025 5th International Conference on Artificial Intelligence and Education (ICAIE)* (pp. 779–784). IEEE. https://doi.org/DOI: 10.1109/ICAIE64856.2025.11158547

Lichtenthaler, U. (2018). Substitute or synthesis: The interplay between human and artificial intelligence. *Research Technology Management*, *61*(5), 12–14. DOI: 10.1080/08956308.2018.1495962

Li, G., Chen, X., & Wang, Y. (2019). A novel recommendation system for tourist spots based on hierarchical sampling and matrix factorization. *Mathematical Problems in Engineering*, *2019*. *Article*, *8170293*. Advance online publication. DOI: 10.1155/2019/8170293

Li, J., Qu, L., Cai, T., Zhao, Z., Haldar, N. A. H., Krishna, A., Kong, X., Macau, F., Chakraborty, T., Deroy, A., Lin, B., Blackmore, K., Noman, N., Cheng, J., Cui, N., & Xu, J. (2025). AI-generated content in cross-domain applications: Research trends, challenges, and propositions. *Knowledge-Based Systems*, *330*, 114634. Advance online publication. DOI: 10.1016/j.knosys.2025.114634

Li, J., Zhu, Z., Zhang, R., & Lee, Y. C. (2025). Exploring the effects of chatbot anthropomorphism and human empathy on human prosocial behavior toward chatbots. *Proceedings of the ACM on Human-Computer Interaction, 9*(7), 1–29. DOI: 10.1145/3757596

Li, K., Zhou, C., Luo, X., Benitez, J., & Liao, Q. (2022). Impact of information timeliness and richness on public engagement on social media during COVID-19 pandemic: An empirical investigation based on NLP and machine learning. *Decision Support Systems, 162*, 113752. DOI: 10.1016/j.dss.2022.113752

Lin, H.-F. (2007). Measuring Online Learning Systems Success: Applying the Updated DeLone and McLean Model. *Cyberpsychology & Behavior, 10*(6), 817–820. DOI: 10.1089/cpb.2007.9948

Liu, R., Hao, J.-X., Yu, Y., & Shan, W. (2025). Helpful or harmful? A curvilinear perspective on AI agent anthropomorphism in service failure tolerance. *Journal of Retailing and Consumer Services, 85*, 104299. DOI: 10.1016/j.jretconser.2025.104299

Liu-Thompkins, Y., Okazaki, S., & Li, H. (2022). Artificial empathy in marketing interactions: Bridging the human-AI gap in affective and social customer experience. *Journal of the Academy of Marketing Science, 50*(6), 1198–1218. DOI: 10.1007/s11747-022-00892-5

Liu, Y., Xu, Y., & Zhou, S. (2024). Enhancing User Experience through Machine Learning-Based Personalized Recommendation Systems: Behavior Data-Driven UI Design. *Applied and Computational Engineering, 112*(1), 42–46. DOI: 10.54254/2755-2721/2024.17905

Liu, Z., Wang, X., Luo, X. R., Song, X., Liu, N., & Zhang, Y. (2023). Be together, run more: Enhancing group participation in fitness technology. *Journal of the Association for Information Systems, 24*(2), 530–554. DOI: 10.17705/1jais.00779

Li, X., Jin, J., Zhou, Y., Zhang, Y., Zhang, P., Zhu, Y., & Dou, Z. (2025). From matching to generation: A survey on generative information retrieval. *ACM Transactions on Information Systems, 43*(3), 83. Advance online publication. DOI: 10.1145/3722552

Lockey, S., & Gillespie, N. (2024). Understanding trust in artificial intelligence: A research agenda. In Mayer, R. C., & Mayer, B. M. (Eds.), *A research agenda for trust: Interdisciplinary perspectives* (pp. 11–24). Edward Elgar Publishing., DOI: 10.4337/9781802200942.00009

Logeswaran, K., Savitha, S., Suresh, P., Prasanna Kumar, K. R., Gunasekar, M., Rajadevi, R., Dharani, M. K., & Jayasurya, A. S. (2024). Unifying Technologies in Industry 4.0: Harnessing the Synergy of Internet of Things, Big Data, Augmented Reality/Virtual Reality, and Blockchain Technologies. In M. Ragab AL-Refaey, A. K. Tyagi, A. S. AL-Malaise AL-Ghamdi, & S. Kukreja (Eds.), *Topics in Artificial Intelligence Applied to Industry 4.0* (1st ed., pp. 127–147). Wiley. DOI: 10.1002/9781394216147.ch7

Lopes da Costa, R., Dias, Á., Pereira, L., António, N., & Capelo, A. (2019). The impact of artificial intelligence on commercial management. *The Impact of Artificial Intelligence on Commercial Management*, (4), 441–452.

Loureiro, S. M. C., Guerreiro, J., & Tussyadiah, I. (2021). Artificial intelligence in business: State of the art and future research agenda. *Journal of Business Research*, *129*, 911–926. DOI: 10.1016/j.jbusres.2020.11.001

Luo, L. (2025). RARE: Right Algorithm for the Right Errand – A graph-based multi-model approach for tourism route and spot recommendation. *PeerJ Computer Science*, *11*, Article e2412. DOI: 10.7717/peerj-cs.2412

Luo, X., Tong, S., Fang, Z., & Qu, Z. (2019). Frontiers: Machines vs. Humans: The impact of artificial intelligence chatbot disclosure on customer purchases. *Marketing Science*, mksc.2019.1192. Advance online publication. DOI: 10.1287/mksc.2019.1192

Lutfi, A., Al-Okaily, M., Alsyouf, A., & Alrawad, M. (2022). Evaluating the D&M IS Success Model in the Context of Accounting Information System and Sustainable Decision Making. *Sustainability (Basel)*, *14*(13), 8120. DOI: 10.3390/su14138120

Luxton, S., Reid, M., & Mavondo, F. (2015). Integrated marketing communication capability and brand performance. *Journal of Advertising*, *44*(1), 37–46. DOI: 10.1080/00913367.2014.934938

Lv, J., & Liu, X. (2022). The Impact of Information Overload of E-Commerce Platform on Consumer Return Intention: Considering the Moderating Role of Perceived Environmental Effectiveness. *International Journal of Environmental Research and Public Health*, *19*(13), 8060. DOI: 10.3390/ijerph19138060

Madancian, M., & Taherdoost, H. (2023, October). The impact of artificial intelligence on human resource management: opportunities and challenges. In *International Conference on Interdisciplinarity in Engineering* (pp. 406-424). Cham: Springer Nature Switzerland.

Madhavaram, S., Badrinarayanan, V., & McDonald, R. E. (2005). Integrated marketing communication (IMC) and brand identity as critical components of brand equity strategy: A conceptual framework and research propositions. *Journal of Advertising, 34*(4), 69–80. DOI: 10.1080/00913367.2005.10639213

Maedche, A., Legner, C., Benlian, A., Berger, B., Gimpel, H., Hess, T., Hinz, O., Morana, S., & Söllner, M. (2019). AI-Based Digital Assistants. *Business & Information Systems Engineering, 61*(4), 535–544. DOI: 10.1007/s12599-019-00600-8

Mahboub, R., & Ghanem, M. G. (2024). The mediating role of knowledge management practices and balanced scorecard in the association between artificial intelligence and organization performance: Evidence from MENA region commercial banks. *Cogent Business & Management, 11*(1), 2404484. DOI: 10.1080/23311975.2024.2404484

Makosa, S. (2024). *Brand Management Driven by Artificial Intelligence.*

Malthouse, E., & Copulsky, J. (2023). Artificial intelligence ecosystems for marketing communications. *International Journal of Advertising, 42*(1), 128–140. DOI: 10.1080/02650487.2022.2122249

Margetis, G., Ntoa, S., Antona, M., & Stephanidis, C. (2021). Human-centered design of artificial intelligence. *Handbook of human factors and ergonomics*, 1085-1106.

Markman, G. D., Siegel, D. S., & Wright, M. (2008). Research and technology commercialization. *Journal of Management Studies, 45*(8), 1401–1423. DOI: 10.1111/j.1467-6486.2008.00803.x

Martin, D. M., & Schouten, J. W. (2014). Sustainable marketing through the natural step. In *Humanistic marketing* (pp. 231–243). Springer. DOI: 10.1057/9781137353290_18

Marvi, R., Foroudi, P., & Cuomo, M. T. (2026). *Past, present and future of AI in marketing and knowledge management. 29*(11), 1–31. DOI: 10.1108/JKM-07-2023-0634

Masud, S. B., Rana, M. M., Sohag, H. J., Shikder, F., Faraji, M. R., & Hasan, M. M. (2024). Understanding the Financial Transaction Security through Blockchain and Machine Learning for Fraud Detection in Data Privacy and Security. [PJLSS]. *Pakistan Journal of Life and Social Sciences, 22*(2). Advance online publication. DOI: 10.57239/PJLSS-2024-22.2.001296

Mathur, A., ... (2021) 'Dark patterns at scale', Proceedings of the ACM on Human-Computer Interaction, 5(CSCW2), pp. 1–25.

Matraf, M. S. B., Hashim, N. L., Hussain, A., Habbal, A., Hamouda, H., & Ghazali, O. (2025). Enhancing mobile e-book usability for the visually impaired: A novel model validated via the fuzzy delphi method. *Journal of King Saud University. Computer and Information Sciences, 37*(7), 179. DOI: 10.1007/s44443-025-00180-6

Matsatsinis, N. F., & Siskos, Y. (2012). *Intelligent support systems for marketing decisions* (Vol. 54). Springer Science & Business Media.

Ma, X., & Wang, J. (2024). Simulation analysis of artificial intelligence technology diffusion under market competition and policy incentives based on complex network evolutionary game models. *Systems, 12*(7), 242. DOI: 10.3390/systems12070242

McDaniel, A. (2025). Integrating artificial intelligence in STEM education: Enhancing learning through smart technologies. *American Journal of STEM Education, 7*, 1–10. DOI: 10.32674/6s0qz548

Menzies, J., Sabert, B., Hassan, R., & Mensah, P. K. (2024). Artificial intelligence for international business: Its use, challenges, and suggestions for future research and practice. *Thunderbird International Business Review, 66*(2), 185–200. DOI: 10.1002/tie.22370

Merrilees, B., Miller, D., & Halliday, S. (2016). *Brand-meaning co-creation by stakeholders: an interactive city brand.*

Mihai, F., Aleca, O. E., & Gheorghe, M. (2023). Digital transformation based on AI technologies in European Union organizations. *Electronics (Basel), 12*(10), 2386. DOI: 10.3390/electronics12112386

Milano, S., Taddeo, M., & Floridi, L. (2020). Recommender systems and their ethical challenges. *AI & Society, 35*(4), 957–967. DOI: 10.1007/s00146-020-00950-y

Miller, C. D., & Wang, R. D. (2024). Product digitization and differentiation strategy change: Evidence from the book publishing industry. *Strategic Management Journal, 45*(7), 1241–1272. DOI: 10.1002/smj.3586

Min, H. (2019). Artificial intelligence in supply chain management. *International Journal of Logistics Research and Applications, 22*(4), 361–375.

Mittal, B. (2023). The Abandoned E-Tailer Shopping Cart: Factors and Business Strategies to Reverse the Barriers. *Journal of Global Strategic Management, 15*(2), 45–63. DOI: 10.20460/JGSM.2022.302

Mittelstadt, B. (2019). Principles alone cannot guarantee ethical AI. *Nature Machine Intelligence, 1*(11), 501–507. DOI: 10.1038/s42256-019-0114-4

Mittelstadt, B. D., Allo, P., Taddeo, M., Wachter, S., & Floridi, L. (2016). The ethics of algorithms. *Big Data & Society*, *3*(2), 2053951716679679. Advance online publication. DOI: 10.1177/2053951716679679

Mohammed, S., Budach, L., Feuerpfeil, M., Ihde, N., Nathansen, A., Noack, N., Patzlaff, H., Naumann, F., & Harmouch, H. (2025). The effects of data quality on machine learning performance on tabular data. *Information Systems*, *132*, 102549. DOI: 10.1016/j.is.2025.102549

Mohammed, T., Naas, S. A., Sigg, S., & Di Francesco, M. (2022). Knowledge sharing in ai services: A market-based approach. *IEEE Internet of Things Journal*, *10*(2), 1320–1331. DOI: 10.1109/JIOT.2022.3206585

Mohapatra, S. (2021). Human and computer interaction in information system design for managing business. *Information Systems and e-Business Management*, *19*(1), 1–11. DOI: 10.1007/s10257-020-00475-3

Moharrak, M., Nguyen, N. P., & Mogaji, E. (2024). Business environment and adoption of AI: Navigation for internationalization by new ventures in emerging markets. *Thunderbird International Business Review*, *66*(4), 355–372. DOI: 10.1002/tie.22384

Moin, M. F., & Zhang, J. (2025). Stemming the tide: Linking AI technology with worker retention. *International Journal of Managing Projects in Business*, *18*(4-5), 721–732. DOI: 10.1108/IJMPB-01-2024-0015

Molla, C., Bhuiyan, M. R. I., Islam, M. T., & Amin, A. (2026). Mediating role to banking performance for adopting digital bank using a technology organizational environment model. *Digital Finance*, *8*(1), 4. DOI: 10.1007/s42521-025-00168-x

Mollik, M. S., Karim, R., & Mahmud, S. (2026). Identifying critical success factors for adopting sustainable tourism in emerging economies. In *EMIDWORLD 3rd International Congress on Economics, Public Finance, Business & Social Sciences*. Baku, Azerbaijan.

Mollik, M. S., Karim, R., Sahabuddin, M., & Eneizan, B. (2026a). Industry 5.0 and the circular economy: A transformative nexus. In *Industry 5.0 and sustainable development* (pp. 237–267). Routledge.

Mollik, M. S. (2024). Investigating tertiary students' perceptions about ChatGPT use in higher education: Bangladesh perspective. *BAUET Journal*, *4*(2). Advance online publication. DOI: 10.59321/BAUETJ.V4I2.19

Mollik, M. S., Rahman, S. M., Rahat, M. R., Kulsum, C. U., & Sagir, S. M. (2024). Does trustworthiness influence travel service use intentions at an online travel agency? A study on the digitalization of the tourism sector in Bangladesh. *Geo Journal of Tourism and Geosites*, *52*(1), 30–40. DOI: 10.30892/gtg.52103-1180

Moro-Visconti, R. (2026). Natural and artificial intelligence interactions in digital networking: A multilayer network model for economic value creation. *Journal of Comprehensive Business Administration Research*, *3*(1), 1–9. DOI: 10.47852/bonviewJCBAR42024127

Morozovaite, V. (2023). Hypernudging in the changing European regulatory landscape for digital markets. *Policy and Internet*, *15*(1), 78–99. DOI: 10.1002/poi3.329

Mostaghel, R., Oghazi, P., Parida, V., & Sohrabpour, V. (2022). Digitalization driven retail business model innovation: Evaluation of past and avenues for future research trends. *Journal of Business Research*, *146*, 134–145. DOI: 10.1016/j.jbusres.2022.03.072

Muhamed, A., Srinivasan, S., Teo, C.-H., Cui, Q., Zeng, B., Chilimbi, T., & Vishwanathan, S. V. N. (2023). Web-Scale Semantic Product Search with Large Language Models. In Kashima, H., Ide, T., & Peng, W.-C. (Eds.), *Advances in Knowledge Discovery and Data Mining* (Vol. 13937, pp. 73–85). Springer Nature Switzerland., DOI: 10.1007/978-3-031-33380-4_6

Mustafa Ayobami Raji, Hameedat Bukola Olodo, Timothy Tolulope Oke, Wilhelmina Afua Addy, Onyeka Chrisanctus Ofodile, & Adedoyin Tolulope Oyewole. (2024). E-commerce and consumer behavior: A review of AI-powered personalization and market trends. *GSC Advanced Research and Reviews, 18*(3), 066–077. DOI: 10.30574/gscarr.2024.18.3.0090

Mustafa, S. Z., Kar, A. K., & Janssen, M. F. W. H. A. (2020). Understanding the impact of digital service failure on users: Integrating Tan's failure and DeLone and McLean's success model. *International Journal of Information Management*, *53*, 102119. DOI: 10.1016/j.ijinfomgt.2020.102119

Mustak, M., Salminen, J., Plé, L., & Wirtz, J. (2021). Artificial intelligence in marketing: Topic modeling and scientometric analysis. *Journal of Business Research*, *124*, 389–404. DOI: 10.1016/j.jbusres.2020.10.044

Nalbant, K. G., & Aydin, S. (2022). Development and Transformation in Digital Marketing and Branding with Artificial Intelligence and Digital Technologies Dynamics in the Metaverse Universe. *Journal of Metaverse*, *3*(1), 9–18. DOI: 10.57019/jmv.1148015

Nam, K., Dutt, C. S., Chathoth, P., Daghfous, A., & Khan, M. S. (2020). The adoption of artificial intelligence and robotics in the hotel industry: Prospects and challenges. *Electronic Markets, 31*(3), 553–574. DOI: 10.1007/s12525-020-00442-3

Nandan, S. (2005). An exploration of the brand identity–brand image linkage: A communications perspective. *Journal of Brand Management, 12*(4), 264–278. DOI: 10.1057/palgrave.bm.2540222

Nanne, A. J., Antheunis, M. L., Van Der Lee, C. G., Postma, E. O., Wubben, S., & Van Noort, G. (2020). The use of computer vision to analyze brand-related user generated image content. *Journal of Interactive Marketing, 50*(1), 156–167. DOI: 10.1016/j.intmar.2019.09.003

Nasar, Z., Jaffry, S. W., & Malik, M. K. (2022). Named Entity Recognition and Relation Extraction: State-of-the-Art. *ACM Computing Surveys, 54*(1), 1–39. DOI: 10.1145/3445965

National Academies of Sciences, Engineering, and Medicine. (2021). Technology Transfer Pathways for Digital Products. In *Advancing Commercialization of Digital Products from Federal Laboratories*. National Academies Press (US).https://doi.org/DOI: 10.17226/26006

Navarro, L. F. M. (2024). Machine Learning and Customer Behavior Insights: Exploring the Depth of Predictive Analytics in Enhancing Consumer Interaction and Engagement. *Journal of Empirical Social Science Studies, 8*(2), 51–62.

Nayak, R., Ghugar, U., Gupta, P., Dash, S., & Gupta, N. (2025). Data Privacy and Compliance in Information Security. In Sharma, K., Sharma, V., Nand, P., Sagar, A. K., & Shrivastava, G. (Eds.), *Securing the Digital Frontier* (1st ed., pp. 17–33). Wiley., DOI: 10.1002/9781394268917.ch2

Neumann, O., Guirguis, K., & Steiner, R. (2023). Exploring artificial intelligence adoption in public organizations: A comparative case study. *Public Management Review*. Advance online publication. DOI: 10.1080/14719037.2023.2182901

Nguyen, T., Zhou, L., Spiegler, V., Ieromonachou, P., & Lin, Y. (2018). Big data analytics in supply chain management. *Computers & Operations Research, 98*, 254–264. DOI: 10.1016/j.cor.2017.07.004

Nizioł, K. (2021). The challenges of consumer protection law connected with the development of artificial intelligence on the example of financial services (chosen legal aspects). *Procedia Computer Science, 192*, 4103–4111. DOI: 10.1016/j.procs.2021.09.185

Noranee, S., & Othman, A. K. B. (2023). Understanding consumer sentiments: Exploring the role of artificial intelligence in marketing. *JMM17: JurnalIlmuEkonomi dan Manajemen*. https://doi.org/DOI: 10.30996/jmm17.v10i1.8690

Norberg, P. A., Horne, D. R., & Horne, D. A. (2007). The privacy paradox. *The Journal of Consumer Affairs*, *41*(1), 100–126. DOI: 10.1111/j.1745-6606.2006.00070.x

Novozhilova, E., Mays, K., & Katz, J. E. (2024). Looking towards an automated future: U.S. attitudes towards future artificial intelligence instantiations and their effect. *Humanities & Social Sciences Communications*, *11*(1), 1–11. DOI: 10.1057/s41599-024-02625-1

Ntoutsi, E., Fafalios, P., Gadiraju, U., Iosifidis, V., Nejdl, W., Vidal, M. E., & Staab, S. (2020). Bias in data-driven artificial intelligence systems—An introductory survey. *Wiley Interdisciplinary Reviews. Data Mining and Knowledge Discovery*, *10*(3), e1356. DOI: 10.1002/widm.1356

Ntoutsi, E., Zliobaite, I., & Kizilcec, R. (2025). Why anti-discrimination laws are not enough for AI fairness. *Nature Machine Intelligence*, *7*(2), 98–105.

Nugroho, Y., & Prasetyo, A. (2018). Assessing information systems success: A respecification of the DeLone and McLean model to integrating the perceived quality. *Problems and Perspectives in Management*, *16*(1), 348–360. DOI: 10.21511/ppm.16(1).2018.34

O'Callaghan, M. (2023). Can decision intelligence help organizations retain employees? Serial multiple mediation of job characteristics and meaningful work. *Cogent Psychology*, *10*(1), 2258475. Advance online publication. DOI: 10.1080/23311908.2023.2258475

O'Neil, C. (2017). *Weapons of math destruction: How big data increases inequality and threatens democracy*. Crown Publishing Group.

Obermeyer, Z., Powers, B., Vogeli, C., & Mullainathan, S. (2019). Dissecting racial bias in an algorithm. *Science*, *366*(6464), 447–453. DOI: 10.1126/science.aax2342 PMID: 31649194

Obrenovic, B., Gu, X., Wang, G., Godinic, D., & Jakhongirov, I. (2025). Generative AI and human–robot interaction: Implications and future agenda for business, society and ethics. *AI & Society*, *40*(2), 677–690. DOI: 10.1007/s00146-024-01889-0

Odeibat, A. (2024). *The impacts of artificial intelligence on the future of marketing and customer behaviour*. Cross-Cultural Management Journal., DOI: 10.70147/c261934

Odionu, C. S., Bristol-Alagbariya, B., & Okon, R. (2024). Big data analytics for customer relationship management: Enhancing engagement and retention strategies. *International Journal of Scientific Research in Science and Technology*, *5*(2), 50–67.

OECD. (2022). *Consumer policy and artificial intelligence*. OECD Publishing.

Ojha, R., Dash, J., Satpathy, S. S., Ojha, P. C., & Pradhan, D. (2025). A brief review on factors affecting the performance of microbial fuel cell and integration of artificial intelligence. *Discover Sustainability*, *6*(1), 702. DOI: 10.1007/s43621-025-01619-6

Okeleke, P. A., Ajiga, D., Folorunsho, S. O., & Ezeigweneme, C. (2024). Predictive analytics for market trends using AI: A study in consumer behavior. *International Journal of Engineering Research Updates*, *7*(1), 36–49. DOI: 10.53430/ijeru.2024.7.1.0032

Olayinka, O. H.Olalekan Hamed Olayinka. (2021). Big data integration and real-time analytics for enhancing operational efficiency and market responsiveness. *Int J Sci Res Arch*, *4*(1), 280–296. DOI: 10.30574/ijsra.2021.4.1.0179

Oliveira, F. S. (2025). From commands to connections: how voice assistants shape and are shaped by consumer–brand relationships.

Oliveira, P., Carvalho, J. M., & Faria, S. (2025). AI integration in organisational workflows: A case study on job reconfiguration, efficiency, and workforce adaptation. *Information (Basel)*, *16*(9), 764. DOI: 10.3390/info16090764

Oshadi Karunanayaka, K. A. Y. R. O., Jahankhani, H., El-Deeb, S., Will Arachchige, I. S., & Amin Metwally Hussien, O. A. (2024). Artificial Intelligence in Digital Marketing: The Ethical Implications of Digital Influence on Markets and Consumer. In *Market Grooming: The Dark Side of AI Marketing* (pp. 173–197). Emerald Publishing Limited. DOI: 10.1108/978-1-83549-001-320241009

Oswald, F. L., Behrend, T. S., Putka, D. J., & Sinar, E. (2020). Big data in industrial-organizational psychology and human resource management: Forward progress for organizational research and practice. *Annual Review of Organizational Psychology and Organizational Behavior*, *7*(1), 505–533. DOI: 10.1146/annurev-orgpsych-032117-104553

Öztaş, Y. E., & Arda, B. (2025). Re-evaluating creative labor in the age of artificial intelligence: A qualitative case study of creative workers' perspectives on technological transformation in creative industries. *AI & Society*, *40*(5), 4119–4130. DOI: 10.1007/s00146-025-02180-6

Ozuem, W., Ranfagni, S., Willis, M., Rovai, S., & Howell, K. (2021). Exploring customers' responses to online service failure and recovery strategies during Covid 19 pandemic: An actor–network theory perspective. *Psychology and Marketing*, *38*(9), 1440–1459. DOI: 10.1002/mar.21527

Page, M. J., McKenzie, J. E., Bossuyt, P. M., Boutron, I., Hoffmann, T. C., Mulrow, C. D., Shamseer, L., Tetzlaff, J. M., Akl, E. A., Brennan, S. E., Chou, R., Glanville, J., Grimshaw, J. M., Hróbjartsson, A., Lalu, M. M., Li, T., Loder, E. W., Mayo-Wilson, E., McDonald, S., & Moher, D. (2021). The PRISMA 2020 statement: An updated guideline for reporting systematic reviews. *BMJ (Clinical Research Ed.)*, *372*(71), n71. Advance online publication. DOI: 10.1136/bmj.n71 PMID: 33782057

Pakuhinezhad, O., & Afsham, N. (2025). AI Regulation in Cross-Border E-Commerce: Legal Challenges and Global Remedies. *International Journal of Scientific Research*, *14*(6), 44–47. DOI: 10.36106/ijsr/1529990

Pande, D., Khanal, S., & Taeihagh, A. (2025). Conceptualising public trust in high-risk AI policymaking: A comparative analysis of three Asian cities. *Journal of Comparative Policy Analysis*, *27*(5–6), 578–602. DOI: 10.1080/13876988.2025.2543546

Pande, D., & Taeihagh, A. (2024). A governance perspective on user acceptance of autonomous systems in Singapore. *Technology in Society*, *77*, 102580. DOI: 10.1016/j.techsoc.2024.102580

Pandurangan, S. K.Sathish Kuppan Pandurangan. (2025). Data Platform Engineering: Revolutionizing Societal Infrastructure through Intelligent Systems. *Journal of Information Systems Engineering & Management*, *10*(58s), 997–1009. DOI: 10.52783/jisem.v10i58s.12754

Pappas, A., Fumagalli, E., Rouziou, M., & Bolander, W. (2023). More than machines: The role of the future retail salesperson in enhancing the customer experience. *Journal of Retailing*, *99*(4), 518–531. DOI: 10.1016/j.jretai.2023.10.004

Paramadina, U., & Info, A. (2024). *Integrated marketing communication: a literature review*. 511–519.

Paramesha, M., Rane, N., & Rane, J. (2024). Artificial intelligence, machine learning, deep learning, and blockchain in financial and banking services: A comprehensive review. DOI: 10.2139/ssrn.4855893

Paschen, J., Kietzmann, J., & Kietzmann, T. C. (2019). Artificial intelligence (AI) and its implications for market knowledge in B2B marketing. *Journal of Business and Industrial Marketing*, *34*(7), 1410–1419. DOI: 10.1108/JBIM-10-2018-0295

Paschen, J., Pitt, C., & Kietzmann, J. (2020). Artificial intelligence in marketing. *Journal of Business Research, 124*, 404–414. DOI: 10.1016/j.jbusres.2020.10.016

Pasch, S., & Ha, S.-Y. (2025). Human-AI interaction and user satisfaction: Empirical evidence from online reviews of AI products. *International Journal of Human-Computer Interaction*. Advance online publication. DOI: 10.1080/10447318.2025.2545463

Patharia, I., & Jain, T. (2024). Antecedents of Electronic Shopping Cart Abandonment during Online Purchase Process. *Business Perspectives and Research, 12*(3), 400–418. DOI: 10.1177/22785337221148810

Patil, D. (2024) 'Artificial intelligence in retail and e-commerce: Enhancing customer experience through personalization, predictive analytics, and real-time engagement', Social Science Research Network (SSRN), 26 November.

Patterson, D. R., Drever, S., Soltani, M., Sharar, S. R., Wiechman, S., Meyer, W. J., & Hoffman, H. G. (2023). A comparison of interactive immersive virtual reality and still nature pictures as distraction-based analgesia in burn wound care. *Burns, 49*(1), 182–192. DOI: 10.1016/j.burns.2022.02.002

Peltier, J. W., Dahl, A. J., & Schibrowsky, J. A. (2024). Artificial intelligence in interactive marketing: A conceptual framework and research agenda. *Journal of Research in Interactive Marketing, 18*(1), 54–90. DOI: 10.1108/JRIM-01-2023-0030

Peng, Y., Wang, Y., Li, J., & Yang, Q. (2024). Impact of AI-Oriented Live-Streaming E-Commerce Service Failures on Consumer Disengagement—Empirical Evidence from China. *Journal of Theoretical and Applied Electronic Commerce Research, 19*(2), 1580–1598. DOI: 10.3390/jtaer19020077

Peres, R., Schreier, M., Schweidel, D., & Sorescu, A. (2023). On ChatGPT and beyond. *International Journal of Research in Marketing, 40*(2), 269–275. DOI: 10.1016/j.ijresmar.2023.03.001

Perez, F., Conway, N., & Roques, O. (2022). The autonomy tussle: AI technology and employee job crafting responses. *Relations Industrielles. Relations Industrielles, 77*(3), 1–25. DOI: 10.7202/1094209ar

Perifanis, N.-A., & Kitsios, F. (2023). Investigating the influence of artificial intelligence on business value in the digital era of strategy: A literature review. *Information (Basel), 14*(2), 85. DOI: 10.3390/info14020085

Pessot, E., Zangiacomi, A., & Sacco, M. (2025). Exploring SMEs innovation paths with augmented and virtual reality technologies. *European Journal of Innovation Management, 28*(3), 1181–1201. DOI: 10.1108/EJIM-02-2023-0118

Petrescu, M., & Krishen, A. S. (2023). ' collaboration in marketing analytics'. *Journal of Marketing Analytics, 11*(3), 263–274. DOI: 10.1057/s41270-023-00245 3

Petropoulos, G. (2022). *The dark side of artificial intelligence: manipulation of human behaviour*. Bruegel-Blogs.

Petter, S., DeLone, W., & McLean, E. (2008). Measuring information systems success: Models, dimensions, measures, and interrelationships. *European Journal of Information Systems, 17*(3), 236–263. DOI: 10.1057/ejis.2008.15

Pires, A., & Brandão, A. (2025). *Evolutionary Scenario of Brand Management and Communication, Through the Integration of AI: A Bibliometric Analysis BT - Marketing and Smart Technologies* (J. L. Reis, L. M. Gomes, Z. Bogdanović, & J. P. M. dos Santos (eds.); pp. 145–172). Springer Nature Singapore.

Porsche, L., Zbiejczuk Suchá, L., & Martinek, J. (2022). The potential of Google Analytics for tracking the reading behavior in web books. *Digital Library Perspectives, 38*(4), 532–541. DOI: 10.1108/DLP-03-2022-0021

Prabadevi, B., Deepa, N., Victor, N., Gadekallu, T. R., Maddikunta, P. K. R., Yenduri, G., Wang, W., Pham, Q. V., Huynh-The, T., & Liyanage, M. (2023). *Metaverse for Industry 5.0 in NextG Communications: Potential Applications and Future Challenges* (Version 1). arXiv. DOI: 10.48550/ARXIV.2308.02677

Prakash, G., & Sabharwal, D. (2024). AI revolution in online media: Transforming content creation, distribution, and consumption. *Media and Al: Navigating, 179.*

Pramanik, S. (2024). Immersive Innovations: Exploring the Use of Virtual and Augmented Reality in Educational Institutions. In Aggarwal, R., Gupta, P., Singh, S., & Bala, R. (Eds.), (pp. 66–85). Advances in Educational Technologies and Instructional Design. IGI Global., DOI: 10.4018/979-8-3693-3015-9.ch006

Prasetyo, Y. T., Ong, A. K. S., Concepcion, G. K. F., Navata, F. M. B., Robles, R. A. V., Tomagos, I. J. T., Young, M. N., Diaz, J. F. T., Nadlifatin, R., & Redi, A. A. N. P. (2021). Determining Factors Affecting Acceptance of E-Learning Platforms during the COVID-19 Pandemic: Integrating Extended Technology Acceptance Model and DeLone & McLean IS Success Model. *Sustainability (Basel), 13*(15), 8365. DOI: 10.3390/su13158365

Puh, K., & Bagić Babac, M. (2023). Predicting sentiment and ratings of tourist reviews using machine learning techniques. *Journal of Hospitality and Tourism Insights*, *6*(4), 1542–1563. DOI: 10.1108/JHTI-04-2022-0143

Puntoni, S., Reczek, R. W., Giesler, M., & Botti, S. (2021). Consumers and artificial intelligence: An experiential perspective. *Journal of Marketing, 85*(1), 131–151. DOI: 10.1177/0022242920953847

Qiu, X., Wang, Y., Zeng, Y., & Cong, R. (2025). Artificial intelligence disclosure in cause-related marketing: A persuasion knowledge perspective. *Journal of Theoretical and Applied Electronic Commerce Research, 20*(3), 193. DOI: 10.3390/jtaer20030193

Quesenbery, W. (2003). The Five Dimensions of Usability. In *Content and Complexity*. Routledge.

Quesenbery, W. (2004). Balancing the 5Es: Usability. *Cutter IT Journal, 17*, 4–11.

Quintana Vargas, A. (2024). Pedestrian-first corridors: Studying the streetscapes of Barcelona's Superilla project [The University of Texas at Austin; Application/pdf]. DOI: 10.26153/TSW/58446

Ragu-Nathan, T. S., Tarafdar, M., Ragu-Nathan, B. S., & Tu, Q. (2008). The consequences of technostress for end users in organizations: Conceptual development and empirical validation. *Information Systems Research, 19*(4), 417–433. DOI: 10.1287/isre.1070.0165

Raha, S., & Deb, S. (2025). Tourism potential zone mapping using multi-criteria decision making and machine learning models. *GeoPlanning: Journal of Geomatics and Planning*, *12*(1), 45–60. DOI: 10.14710/geoplanning.12.1.45-60

Rahman, M. M., Islam, M., Islam, M. A., Saha, R., Hossain, D., & Rahman, M. M. (2025). Emerging Trends in Digital Transformation and Information Systems by Bibliometric Analysis in the United States. *Journal of Information Systems and Informatics, 7*(4), 3792–3825. DOI: 10.63158/journalisi.v7i4.1340

Rahman, M., Islam, M. M., Khatun, M., Uddin, S., Faraji, M. R., & Hasan, M. H. (2024). Gravitating towards Information Society for Information Security in Information Systems: A Systematic PRISMA Based Review. [PJLSS]. *Pakistan Journal of Life and Social Sciences, 22*(1). Advance online publication. DOI: 10.57239/PJLSS-2024-22.1.0089

Rai, A. (2020). Explainable AI. *Journal of the Academy of Marketing Science, 48*(1), 137–141. DOI: 10.1007/s11747-019-00710-5

Rai, A.. (2021). Explainable AI: From black box to glass box. *Journal of the Academy of Marketing Science, 49*(3), 1–22.

Rai, A., Constantinides, P., & Sarker, S. (2019). Editor's comments: Next-generation digital platforms: Toward human–AI hybrids. *Management Information Systems Quarterly*, *43*(1), iii–ix. DOI: 10.25300/MISQ/2019/431E0

Raisch, S., & Krakowski, S. (2021). Artificial intelligence and management: The automation–augmentation paradox. *Academy of Management Review*, *46*(1), 192–210. DOI: 10.5465/amr.2018.0072

Rajagopal, N. K., Qureshi, N. I., Durga, S., Ramirez Asis, E. H., Huerta Soto, R. M., Gupta, S. K., & Deepak, S. (2022). Future of business culture: An artificial intelligence-driven digital framework for organization decision-making process. *Complexity*, *2022*(1), 7796507. DOI: 10.1155/2022/7796507

Raja, S. N., Carr, D. B., Cohen, M., Finnerup, N. B., Flor, H., Gibson, S., Keefe, F. J., Mogil, J. S., Ringkamp, M., Sluka, K. A., Song, X.-J., Stevens, B., Sullivan, M. D., Tutelman, P. R., Ushida, T., & Vader, K. (2020). The revised International Association for the Study of Pain definition of pain: Concepts, challenges, and compromises. *Pain*, *161*(9), 1976–1982. DOI: 10.1097/j.pain.0000000000001939

Raji, I. A., Ismail, A. I., & Salam, M. A. (2026). High-performance work systems, organizational identification, trust in leader, perceived organizational support and healthcare professionals' turnover intention. Journal of Health Organization and Management, 40(4), 785-810. https://doi.org/10.1108/JHOM-06-2025-0366, PMID: 41171870

Raji, M.A., Olodo, H.B., Oke, T.T., Addy, W.A., Ofodile, O.C. and Oyewole, A.T. (2024) 'E-commerce and consumer behavior: A review of AI-powered personalization and market trends', GSC Advanced Research and Reviews, 18(3), pp. 066-077.

Raman, R., Gandhi, A., Banerjee, U., & Banerjee, S. (2026). Agentic AI and Flexible Management: Multidisciplinary and Behavioural Perspectives on Evolving Practices, Strategic Opportunities, and Policy Implications. *Global Journal of Flexible Systems Management*, 1-23. DOI: 10.1007/s40171-026-00483-1

Rauschnabel, P. A., Felix, R., & Hinsch, C. (2019). Augmented reality marketing: How mobile AR-apps can improve brands through inspiration. *Journal of Retailing and Consumer Services*, *49*, 43–53. DOI: 10.1016/j.jretconser.2019.03.004

Raut, S., Chandel, A., & Mittal, S. (2025). Enhancing marketing and brand communication with AI-driven content creation. In *AI, corporate social responsibility, and marketing in modern organizations* (pp. 139–172). IGI Global Scientific Publishing.

Rawashdeh, A. (2023). The consequences of artificial intelligence: An investigation into the impact of AI on job displacement in accounting. *Journal of Science and Technology Policy Management*. DOI: 10.1108/JSTPM-02-2023-0030

Rayun, S. M. N., Salam, M. A., Islam, W., & Leong, V. S. (2025). Green FinTech Innovations: Empowering Inclusive Development and Advancing Towards the Sustainable Economy. Https://Www.Igi-Global.Com/Doi=10.4018/979-8-3373-1112-8.Ch009, 245–278. DOI: 10.4018/979-8-3373-1112-8.ch009

Rayun, S. N., Salam, M. A., Islam, W., & Leong, V. S. (2026). Green FinTech Innovations: Empowering Inclusive Development and Advancing Towards the Sustainable Economy. In *Promoting Inclusivity and Accessibility With FinTech* (pp. 245-278). IGI Global Scientific Publishing.

Rayun, S. N., Salam, M. A., Islam, W., Firmansyah, E. A., & Kalinaki, K. (2025). Unraveling the dynamics of mobile wallets in promoting cashless tourism in Bangladesh: Implementation of UTAUT2 model. *Journal of Hospitality and Tourism Technology*, *16*(5), 1046–1065. DOI: 10.1108/JHTT-04-2024-0222

Razniewski, S., & Das, P. (2020). Structured Knowledge: Have we made progress? An extrinsic study of KB coverage over 19 years. *Proceedings of the 29th ACM International Conference on Information & Knowledge Management*, 3317–3320. DOI: 10.1145/3340531.3417447

Rehman, S., Gulzar, R., & Aslam, W. (2022). *Developing the Integrated Marketing Communication (IMC) through Social Media (SM)*. The Modern Marketing Communication Approach., DOI: 10.1177/21582440221099936

Reinartz, W. J., Wiegand, N., & Imschloss, M. (2018). The Impact of Digital Transformation on the Retailing Value Chain. SSRN *Electronic Journal*. DOI: 10.2139/ssrn.3299669

Renz, A., & Hilbig, R. (2020). Prerequisites for artificial intelligence in further education: Identification of drivers, barriers, and business models of educational technology companies. *International Journal of Educational Technology in Higher Education*, *17*(1), 14. DOI: 10.1186/s41239-020-00193-3

Rezwana, J., & Maher, M. (2023). Designing creative AI partners with COFI: A framework for modeling interaction in human-AI co-creative systems. *ACM Transactions on Computer-Human Interaction*, *30*(5), 1–28. DOI: 10.1145/3519026

Ribeiro, M. T., Singh, S., & Guestrin, C. (2016). "Why should I trust you?" Explaining the predictions of any classifier. *Proceedings of the ACM SIGKDD*, 1135–1144. https://doi.org/DOI: 10.1145/2939672.2939778

Riesthuis, P., Otgaar, H., & Bücken, C. (2025). Ready to ROC? A tutorial on simulation-based power analyses for null hypothesis significance, minimum-effect, and equivalence testing for ROC curve analyses. *Behavior Research Methods*, *57*(4), Article 120. DOI: 10.3758/s13428-025-0120-x

Rodgers, W., & Nguyen, T. (2022). Advertising benefits from ethical artificial intelligence algorithmic purchase decision pathways. *Journal of Business Ethics, 178*(4), 1043–1061. DOI: 10.1007/s10551-022-05048-7

Rodriguez-Fernandez, F. (2025). Artificial intelligence and economic psychology: Toward a theory of algorithmic cognitive influence. *AI & Society*, •••, 1–12.

Romanchuk, L. A., Shchytov, D. M., & Mormul, M. F. (2025). Artificial Intelligence in E-Commerce: Main Directions, Benefits, and Potential Risks. *Ukrainian Economic Journal*, (8), 108–115.

Romanchuk, O., Petrenko, Y., & Koval, V. (2025). Balancing automation and human judgment in commercial human–AI interaction systems. *Journal of Innovation & Knowledge*, *10*(1), 100482.

Rowe, F., Jeanneret Medina, M., Journé, B., Coëtard, E., & Myers, M. (2024). Understanding responsibility under uncertainty: A critical and scoping review of autonomous driving systems. *Journal of Information Technology*, *39*(3), 587–615. DOI: 10.1177/02683962231207108

Rožman, M., Oreški, D., & Tominc, P. (2023). Artificial intelligence-supported reduction of employees' workload to increase company performance in today's VUCA environment. *Sustainability (Basel)*, *15*(6), 5019. DOI: 10.3390/su15065019

Russell, S. J., & Norvig, P. (2021). *Artificial Intelligence: A Modern Approach* (Global Edition 4e).

Ryan, G. V., Callaghan, S., Rafferty, A., Higgins, M. F., Mangina, E., & McAuliffe, F. (2022). Learning Outcomes of Immersive Technologies in Health Care Student Education: Systematic Review of the Literature. *Journal of Medical Internet Research*, *24*(2), e30082. DOI: 10.2196/30082

Sadasivan, A., Gananathan, K., Pal Nesamony Rose Mary, J. D., & Balasubramanian, S. (2025). A systematic survey of graph convolutional networks for artificial intelligence applications. *Wiley Interdisciplinary Reviews: Data Mining and Knowledge Discovery*, *15*(2), Article e70012. DOI: 10.1002/widm.70012

Sahut, J. M., & Laroche, M. (2025). Using artificial intelligence (AI) to enhance customer experience and to develop strategic marketing: An integrative synthesis. *Computers in Human Behavior*, *170*, 108684. DOI: 10.1016/j.chb.2025.108684

Salam, M. A., Rayun, S. M. N., & Leong, V. S. (2024). Examining Critical Factors Influencing Generation Z's Acceptance of Mobile Payment Systems in Bangladesh: A UTAUT Model Analysis. *Journal of Business and Economic Analysis.*

Salam, M. A., Rayun, S. M. N., Islam, W., Hasan, R., Firmansyah, E. A., & Kalinaki, K. (2024). Consumer Engagement: Exploring Deepfake Applications in Consumer Marketing Communication. In *Navigating the World of Deepfake Technology* (pp. 397–421). IGI Global.

Salam, M. A., Leong, V. S., & Muhamad, N. (2026). The Transformative Prospects of AI-Powered Virtual Influencers in Digital Consumer Engagement and Marketing Strategies. In *Cases on Social Media Marketing Engagement Tactics* (pp. 251–290). IGI Global Scientific Publishing.

Salam, M. A., Rayun, S. M. N., & Leong, V. S. (2023). Examining critical factors influencing generation z's acceptance of mobile payment systems in Bangladesh: A UTAUT model analysis. *Journal of Business and Economic Analysis, 06*(03), 371–400. DOI: 10.1142/S273756682450004X

Salam, M. A., Rayun, S. N., Islam, W., Hasan, R., Firmansyah, E. A., & Kalinaki, K. (2024). Consumer engagement: exploring deepfake applications in consumer marketing communication. In *Navigating the World of Deepfake Technology* (pp. 397–421). IGI Global. DOI: 10.4018/979-8-3693-5298-4.ch020

Salim, M., Alfansi, L., Anggarawati, S., Saputra, F. E., & Afandy, C. (2021). The role of perceived usefulness in moderating the relationship between the DeLone and McLean model and user satisfaction. *Uncertain Supply Chain Management, 9*(3), 755–766. DOI: 10.5267/j.uscm.2021.4.002

Salisu, I., Sappri, M. M., Omar, M. F., Nasir, A., Ejaz, S., & Hossain, M. B. (2025). Social media applications through the lens of DeLone and McLean's information system success model: Does perceived privacy matter? *Humanities & Social Sciences Communications, 12*(1), 1028. DOI: 10.1057/s41599-025-05010-8

Samal, A., Bhargav, J., Selvakumar, P., Sharma, M., & TC, M. (2025). Measuring brand performance with AI tools. In *Strategic Brand Management in the Age of AI and Disruption* (pp. 279–302). IGI Global Scientific Publishing.

Samara, D., Magnisalis, I., & Peristeras, V. (2020). Artificial intelligence and big data in tourism: A systematic literature review. *Journal of Hospitality and Tourism Technology, 11*(2), 343–367. DOI: 10.1108/JHTT-12-2018-0118

Samtani, S., Kantarcioglu, M., & Chen, H. (2021). A multi-disciplinary perspective for conducting artificial intelligence-enabled privacy analytics: Connecting data, algorithms, and systems. [TMIS]. *ACM Transactions on Management Information Systems*, *12*(1), 1–18. DOI: 10.1145/3447507

Sankar, J. G. (2024). Travel Redefined: Future Trends in AI-Enhanced Tourism Experiences. In Correia, R., Martins, M., & Fontes, R. (Eds.), *Advances in Hospitality, Tourism, and the Services Industry* (pp. 135–162). IGI Global., DOI: 10.4018/979-8-3693-2137-9.ch008

Sarker, I. H. (2021). Machine learning: Algorithms, real-world applications and research directions. *SN Computer Science*, *2*(3), 1–21. DOI: 10.1007/s42979-021-00592-x PMID: 33778771

Satornino, C. B., Du, S., & Grewal, D. (2024). Using artificial intelligence to advance sustainable development in industrial markets: A complex adaptive systems perspective. *Industrial Marketing Management*, *116*, 145–157. DOI: 10.1016/j.indmarman.2023.11.011

Saura, J. R., Škare, V., & Ozretić Došen, Đ. (2024). Is AI-based digital marketing ethical? Assessing a new data privacy paradox. *Journal of Innovation & Knowledge*, *9*(4), 100597. DOI: 10.1016/j.jik.2024.100597

Scantamburlo, T., Cortés, A., Foffano, F., Barrué, C., Distefano, V., Pham, L., & Fabris, A. (2025). Artificial intelligence across Europe: A study on awareness, attitude and trust. *IEEE Transactions on Artificial Intelligence*, *6*(2), 477–490. DOI: 10.1109/TAI.2024.3461633

Schultz, D. E., Kim, I., & Kang, K. (2014). Integrated marketing communication research: its limited past and huge potential. *The Handbook of International Advertising Research*, 455–483.

Schultz, D. E. (1992). Integrated marketing communications. *Journal of Promotion Management*, *1*(1), 99–104. DOI: 10.1300/J057v01n01_07

Schultz, D. E., Tannenbaum, S., & Lauterborn, R. (1993). *Integrated Marketing Communications*. NTC Business Book.

Secundo, G., Spilotro, C., Gast, J., & Corvello, V. (2025). The transformative power of artificial intelligence within innovation ecosystems: A review and a conceptual framework. *Review of Managerial Science*, *19*(9), 2697–2728. DOI: 10.1007/s11846-024-00828-z

Seenivasan, D. (2023). ETL (extract, transform, load) best practices. *International Journal of Computer Trends and Technology*, *71*(1), 40–44. DOI: 10.14445/22312803/IJCTT-V71I1P106

Senyapar, H. N. D. (2024). Artificial intelligence in marketing communication: A comprehensive exploration of the integration and impact of AI. *Technium Soc. Sci. J.*, *55*, 64.

Shabankareh, M., Khamoushi Sahne, S. S., Nazarian, A., & Foroudi, P. (2025). The impact of AI perceived transparency on trust in AI recommendations in healthcare applications. *Asia-Pacific Journal of Business Administration*. Advance online publication. DOI: 10.1108/APJBA-12-2024-0690

Sharma, P. B., & Kumar, A. (2024). Interventions of organizational identification and job satisfaction on person-environment perceptions and work engagement: Insights for K12 school administrators in India. *International Journal of Public Administration*, *47*(10), 690–703. DOI: 10.1080/01900692.2023.2175852

Sharma, P., Bhattacharya, S., & Bhattacharya, S. (2025). HR analytics and AI adoption in IT sector: Reflections from practitioners. *Journal of Work-Applied Management*. Advance online publication. DOI: 10.1108/JWAM-12-2024-0179

Sharma, P., Kaur, G., & Pathak, R. (2025). The effect of COVID-19 induced work stressors on life satisfaction of university teachers in India: An empirical study. *International Journal of Business and Globalisation*, *40*(1), 130–150. DOI: 10.1504/IJBG.2025.146219

Sharma, P., & Sarmah, R. (2020). Perception and awareness of youth towards digital India campaign [IJM]. *International Journal of Management (Kolkata)*, *11*(6), 1381–1393.

Sharma, S., Islam, N., Singh, G., & Dhir, A. (2022). Why do retail customers adopt artificial intelligence (AI) based autonomous decision-making systems? *IEEE Transactions on Engineering Management*, *71*, 1846–1861. DOI: 10.1109/TEM.2022.3157976

Sheikh, A., Rinvee, T. M., & Sheikh, Md. S. (2025). A Hybrid Machine Learning Framework for Supply Chain Demand Forecasting: Integrating Historical Data and Market Intelligence. DOI: 10.2139/ssrn.5621332

Sheikh, A. (2025). AI-Powered Leadership in Supply Chain Management: Balancing Efficiency and Human Decision-Making. Journal of Global Economics. *Management and Business Research*, *17*(3), 476–485. DOI: 10.56557/jgembr/2025/v17i39998

Sheikh, A., Goodrich, K., & Sajja, S. (2025). AI-Powered Forecasting for Supply Chain Resilience: Applications of Logistic Regression, Random Forest, and XGBoost in the U.S. Context. *American Journal of Innovation in Science and Engineering*, *4*(3), 105–117. DOI: 10.54536/ajise.v4i3.6065

Sheikh, A., & Sajja, S. (2026). AI-Driven Risk Mitigation in Global Supply Chains to Build Resilience for U.S. Competitiveness: A Conceptual Review and Framework-Based Study. Journal of Global Economics. *Management and Business Research*, *18*(1), 198–206. DOI: 10.56557/jgembr/2026/v18i110190

Sheikh, A., Sheikh, M., & Rinvee, T. M. (2025). Smart Transportation Systems with Artificial Intelligence: Enhancing Efficiency, Safety, and Sustainability. *American Journal of Smart Technology and Solutions*, *4*(2), 87–90. DOI: 10.54536/ajsts.v4i2.6022

Shen, Q., Wen, H., Tao, W., Zhang, J., Lv, F., Chen, Z., & Li, Z. (2022). Deep Interest Highlight Network for Click-Through Rate Prediction in Trigger-Induced Recommendation. *Proceedings of the ACM Web Conference 2022*, 422–430. DOI: 10.1145/3485447.3511970

Shepherd, M., Turner, J. A., Small, B., & Wheeler, D. (2020). Priorities for science to overcome hurdles thwarting the full promise of the 'digital agriculture' revolution. *Journal of the Science of Food and Agriculture*, *100*(14), 5083–5092. DOI: 10.1002/jsfa.9346

Shneiderman, B. (2022). Human-centered AI. *International Journal of Human-Computer Interaction*, *38*(16), 1472–1492. DOI: 10.1080/10447318.2022.2071257

Sidlauskiene, J., Joye, Y., & Auruskeviciene, V. (2023). AI-based chatbots in conversational commerce and their effects on product and price perceptions. *Electronic Markets*, *33*(1), 24. DOI: 10.1007/s12525-023-00633-8 PMID: 37252674

Singh, N. T., Singh, S., Singh, S., Arora, A., Dhaundiyal, A., & Narang, A. (2023). Transforming E-Commerce: Augmented Reality (AR) and Virtual Reality (VR) Integration for Interactive and Immersive Shopping Experiences. *2023 7th International Conference on Electronics, Materials Engineering & Nano-Technology (IEMENTech)*, 1–5. DOI: 10.1109/IEMENTech60402.2023.10423551

Singh, H., Arora, M., & Singh, A. (2024). ChatGPT in marketing: Innovative pathways, decision systems, and forward perspectives. *Journal of Decision Systems*, •••, 1–28. DOI: 10.1080/12460125.2024.2438615

Sinha, M., & Srivastava, M. (2022). Augmented Reality-Enabled Instagram Game Filters: Key to Engaging Customers. *Journal of Promotion Management, 28*(4), 467–486. DOI: 10.1080/10496491.2021.2008577

Sinyard, R. D., Rentas, C. M., Gunn, E. G., Etheridge, J. C., Robertson, J. M., Gleason, A., Riley, M. S., Yule, S., & Smink, D. S. (2022). Managing a team in the operating room: The science of teamwork and non-technical skills for surgeons. *Current Problems in Surgery, 59*(7), 101172. DOI: 10.1016/j.cpsurg.2022.101172

Soliman, M. M., Ahmed, E., Darwish, A., & Hassanien, A. E. (2024). Artificial intelligence powered Metaverse: Analysis, challenges and future perspectives. *Artificial Intelligence Review, 57*(2), 36. DOI: 10.1007/s10462-023-10641-x

Song, X., &BonaSidaoui, K., Jaakkola, M., & Burton, J. (2020). AI feel you: customer experience assessment via chatbot interviews. https://doi.org/DOI: 10.1108/JOSM-11-2019-0341

Song, B., Li, R., Wang, J., & Song, A. (2024, August). *APRRGM: Accurate point-of-interest recommendation for random groups via attentive bipartite graph neural networks*. In *Proceedings of the 30th ACM SIGKDD International Conference on Knowledge Discovery and Data Mining (KDD '24)* (pp. 1102–1111). Association for Computing Machinery. DOI: 10.1145/3637528.3671890

Soon, P., Lim, W. M., & Gaur, S. S. (2023). The role of emotions in augmented reality. *Psychology and Marketing, 40*(11), 2387–2412. DOI: 10.1002/mar.21884

Spulbar, L. F. (2025). Legal frameworks for AI-driven markets and their challenges and opportunities in the digital economy. *Revista de Ştiinţe Politice*, (86), 288–304.

Stahl, B. C., & Eke, D. (2024). The ethics of ChatGPT: Exploring the ethical issues of an emerging technology. *International Journal of Information Management, 74*, 102700. DOI: 10.1016/j.ijinfomgt.2023.102700

Stecuła, K., Wolniak, R., & Aydın, B. (2024). Technology Development in Online Grocery Shopping—From Shopping Services to Virtual Reality, Metaverse, and Smart Devices: A Review. *Foods, 13*(23), 3959. DOI: 10.3390/foods13233959

Stoiber, C., Ceneda, D., Wagner, M., Schetinger, V., Gschwandtner, T., Streit, M., Miksch, S., & Aigner, W. (2022). Perspectives of visualization onboarding and guidance in VA. *Visual Informatics, 6*(1), 68–83. DOI: 10.1016/j.visinf.2022.02.005

Strusani, D., & Houngbonon, G. V. (2019). *The role of artificial intelligence in supporting development in emerging markets.* International Finance Corporation. DOI: 10.1596/32365

Susser, D., Roessler, B., & Nissenbaum, H. (2019). Online manipulation. *Georgetown Law Technology Review*, *4*(1), 1–45.

Syed, T. A., Siddiqui, M. S., Abdullah, H. B., Jan, S., Namoun, A., Alzahrani, A., Nadeem, A., & Alkhodre, A. B. (2022). In-Depth Review of Augmented Reality: Tracking Technologies, Development Tools, AR Displays, Collaborative AR, and Security Concerns. *Sensors (Basel)*, *23*(1), 146. DOI: 10.3390/s23010146

Tapalova, O., & Zhiyenbayeva, N. (2022). Artificial intelligence in education: AIEd for personalised learning pathways. *Electronic Journal of e-Learning*, *20*(5), 639–653. https://eric.ed.gov/?id=EJ1373006. DOI: 10.34190/ejel.20.5.2597

Teece, D. J. (1986). Profiting from technological innovation. *Research Policy*, *15*(6), 285–305. DOI: 10.1016/0048-7333(86)90027-2

Teece, D. J. (2007). Explicating dynamic capabilities: The nature and microfoundations of sustainable enterprise performance. *Strategic Management Journal*, *28*(13), 1319–1350. DOI: 10.1002/smj.640

Thamik, H., & Wu, J. (2022). The impact of artificial intelligence on sustainable development in electronic markets. *Sustainability (Basel)*, *14*(6), 3568. DOI: 10.3390/su14063568

Thierer, A. D., Castillo O'Sullivan, A., & Russell, R. (2017) 'Artificial intelligence and public policy', Mercatus Research Paper.

Thomas, J. S., Chen, C., & Iacobucci, D. (2022). Email Marketing as a Tool for Strategic Persuasion. *Journal of Interactive Marketing*, *57*(3), 377–392. DOI: 10.1177/10949968221095552

Thomaz, F., Salge, C., Karahanna, E., & Hulland, J. (2019). Learning from the Dark Web: Leveraging conversational agents in the era of hyper-privacy to enhance marketing. *Journal of the Academy of Marketing Science*. Advance online publication. DOI: 10.1007/s11747-019-00704-3

Tiutiu, M., & Dabija, D.-C. (2023). Improving Customer Experience Using Artificial Intelligence in Online Retail. *Proceedings of the International Conference on Business Excellence, 17*(1), 1139–1147. DOI: 10.2478/picbe-2023-0102

Tong, S., Jia, N., Luo, X., & Fang, Z. (2021). The Janus face of artificial intelligence feedback: Deployment versus disclosure effects employee performance. *Strategic Management Journal*, *42*(9), 1600–1631. DOI: 10.1002/smj.3322

Trocin, C., Hovland, I. V., Mikalef, P., & Dremel, C. (2021). How artificial intelligence affords digital innovation: A cross-case analysis of Scandinavian companies. *Technological Forecasting and Social Change, 173*, 121081. Advance online publication. DOI: 10.1016/j.techfore.2021.121081

Tsagkias, M., King, T. H., Kallumadi, S., Murdock, V., & De Rijke, M. (2020). Challenges and research opportunities in eCommerce search and recommendations. *ACM SIGIR Forum, 54*(1), 1–23. DOI: 10.1145/3451964.3451966

Tsakalerou, M., Tynybayeva, N., & Abil, A. S. (2025). Bridging minds and machines: Emotional intelligence as intellectual capital for human-AI collaboration. *European Conference on Knowledge Management*. https://doi.org/DOI: 10.34190/eckm.26.2.4006

Tsamados, A., Floridi, L., & Taddeo, M. (2024). Human control of AI systems: From supervision to teaming. *AI and Ethics*. Advance online publication. DOI: 10.1007/s43681-024-00489-4 PMID: 40352578

Tschang, F. T., & Almirall, E. (2021). Artificial intelligence as augmenting automation: Implications for employment. *The Academy of Management Perspectives, 35*(4), 642–659. DOI: 10.5465/amp.2019.0062

Tsolakis, N., Schumacher, R., Dora, M., & Kumar, M. (2023). Artificial intelligence and blockchain implementation in supply chains: A pathway to sustainability and data monetisation? *Annals of Operations Research, 327*(1), 157–210. DOI: 10.1007/s10479-022-04785-2 PMID: 35755830

Tsuda, S., Olasky, J., & Jones, D. B. (2021). Team training and surgical crisis management. *Journal of Surgical Oncology, 124*(2), 216–220. DOI: 10.1002/jso.26523

Tsvetovatyy, M., Gini, M., Mobasher, B., Ski, Z. W., & Ski, W. (1997). Magma an agent based virtual market for electronic commerce. *Applied Artificial Intelligence, 11*(6), 501–523. DOI: 10.1080/088395197118046

Turki, H. (2025). AI-Powered Personalization in E-Commerce: Governance, Consumer Behavior, and Explanatory Insights from Big Data Analytics. *Technology in Society, 83*, 103033. DOI: 10.1016/j.techsoc.2025.103033

Tyrväinen, O., Karjaluoto, H., & Saarijärvi, H. (2020). Personalization and hedonic motivation in creating customer experiences and loyalty in omnichannel retail. *Journal of Retailing and Consumer Services, 57*, 102233. DOI: 10.1016/j.jretconser.2020.102233

Tyukin, I. Y., Gorban, A. N., Sofeykov, K. I., & Romanenko, I. (2018). Knowledge transfer between artificial intelligence systems. *Frontiers in Neurorobotics*, *12*, 49. DOI: 10.3389/fnbot.2018.00049 PMID: 30150929

Ullah, F., Sepasgozar, S. M. E., Jamaluddin Thaheem, M., Cynthia Wang, C., & Imran, M. (2021). It's all about perceptions: A DEMATEL approach to exploring user perceptions of real estate online platforms. *Ain Shams Engineering Journal*, *12*(4), 4297–4317. DOI: 10.1016/j.asej.2021.04.023

Umoren, O., Didi, P. U., Balogun, O., Abass, O. S., & Akinrinoye, O. V. (2022). Synchronized content delivery framework for consistent cross-platform brand messaging in regulated and consumer-focused sectors. *International Scientific Refereed Research Journal*, *5*(5), 345–354.

UNESCO. (2023). *Guidance on generative AI and education*. UNESCO Publishing.

Uribe, J., Harmon, D., Laguna, B., & Courtier, J. (2023). Augmented-Reality Enhanced Anatomy Learning (A-REAL): Assessing the utility of 3D holographic models for anatomy education. *Annals of 3D Printed Medicine, 9*, 100090. DOI: 10.1016/j.stlm.2022.100090

Usembayeva, I., Kurbanbekov, B., Ramankulov, S., Batyrbekova, A., Kelesbayev, K., & Akhanova, A. (2024). 3D Modeling and Printing in Physics Education: The Importance of STEM Technology for Interpreting Physics Concepts. *Qubahan Academic Journal*, *4*(3), 45–58. DOI: 10.48161/qaj.v4n3a727

Ushaa, E., & Vishal, E. (2023). Augmented reality and internet of things: A review of convergence, applications and challenges. *I-Manager's Journal on Augmented &. Virtual Reality (Waltham Cross)*, *1*(2), 41. DOI: 10.26634/javr.1.2.20153

Vallabhaneni, A. S., Perla, A., Regalla, R. R., & Kumari, N. (2024). The power of personalization: AI-driven recommendations. In *Minds Unveiled* (pp. 111–127). Productivity Press. DOI: 10.4324/9781032711089-9

Vallabhaneni, S., Prasad, R., & Kumar, A. (2024). AI-driven personalization and commercial performance: Evidence from digital recommendation systems. *Journal of Business Research*, *167*, 114–126.

Van Hoboken, J., & Fathaigh, R. Ó. (2021). Smartphone platforms as privacy regulators. *Computer Law & Security Review*, *41*, 105557. DOI: 10.1016/j.clsr.2021.105557

Van Veldhoven, Z., & Vanthienen, J. (2021). Digital transformation as an interaction-driven perspective between business, society, and technology. *Electronic Markets*, *32*(2), 629–644. DOI: 10.1007/s12525-021-00464-5

Vashishth, T. K., Sharma, K. K., Kumar, B., Chaudhary, S., & Panwar, R. (2024) 'Enhancing customer experience through AI-enabled content personalization in e-commerce marketing', in Advances in digital marketing in the era of artificial intelligence, pp. 7-32. DOI: 10.1201/9781003450443-2

Vashishth, T. K., Sharma, K. K., Kumar, B., Chaudhary, S., & Panwar, R. (2024). Enhancing customer experience through AI-enabled content personalization in e-commerce marketing. *Advances in Digital Marketing in the Era of Artificial Intelligence*, 7–32.

Veale, M., & Zuiderveen Borgesius, F. (2021). Demystifying the draft EU Artificial Intelligence Act. *Computer Law Review International, 22*(4), 97–112. DOI: 10.9785/cri-2021-220402

Venkatesh, V., Morris, M. G., Davis, G. B., & Davis, F. D. (2003). User acceptance of information technology. *Management Information Systems Quarterly, 27*(3), 425–478. DOI: 10.2307/30036540

Venugopal, M., Madhavan, V., Prasad, R., & Raman, R. (2024). Transformative AI in human resource management: Enhancing workforce planning with topic modeling. *Cogent Business & Management, 11*(1), 2432550. Advance online publication. DOI: 10.1080/23311975.2024.2432550

Viriando, Y. F. (2021). Using Delone & McLean Information System Success Model to Evaluate the Success of Online Platform. *Journal of System and Management Sciences, 11*(2), 182–198. DOI: 10.33168/JSMS.2021.0212

Virvou, M. (2022) 'The emerging era of human-AI interaction: Keynote address', in 2022 13th International Conference on Information, Intelligence, Systems & Applications (IISA), July, IEEE, pp. 1-10. Available at: DOI: 10.1109/IISA56318.2022.9904422

Vlieghe, J., Muls, J., & Rutten, K. (2016). Everybody reads: Reader engagement with literature in social media environments. *Poetics, 54*, 25–37. DOI: 10.1016/j.poetic.2015.09.001

Vuori, V., Helander, N., & Okkonen, J. (2019). Digitalization in knowledge work: The dream of enhanced performance. *Cognition Technology and Work, 21*(2), 237–252. DOI: 10.1007/s10111-018-0501-3

Waller, M. A., & Fawcett, S. E. (2013). Data science and predictive analytics in supply chain management. *Journal of Business Logistics, 34*(2), 77–84. DOI: 10.1111/jbl.12010

Wang, H., Li, Y., Santos, T., & Khan, A. (2023). Attentive sequential graph neural networks for next POI and rating prediction in tourism analytics. *ACM Transactions on Information Systems*, *40*(2), 45–67. DOI: 10.1145/3543612

Wang, C. L. (2023). Correction to: The Palgrave Handbook of Interactive Marketing. In Wang, C. L. (Ed.), *The Palgrave Handbook of Interactive Marketing* (pp. C1–C1). Springer International Publishing., DOI: 10.1007/978-3-031-14961-0_1

Wang, W., Chen, Z., & Kuang, J. (2025). Artificial Intelligence-Driven Recommendations and Functional Food Purchases: Understanding Consumer Decision-Making. *Foods*, *14*(6), 976. DOI: 10.3390/foods14060976 PMID: 40231979

Wang, Z. (2025). *The influence of AI on consumer behavior: Shaping choices and preferences in the digital marketplace*. Systems and Soft Computing.

Wani, N. U. H., Hamza, N., & Saboori, B. (2025). Legal and Ethical Frameworks for AI in Financial Services: Balancing the Innovation with Responsibility and Effective Protection. In *Green Horizons: Role of AI in Sustainable Finance* (pp. 177–196). Springer Nature Singapore. DOI: 10.1007/978-981-96-6495-5_10

Wan, Y., Tao, H., Zhao, Y., & Huang, L. (2025). The economic impact of artificial intelligence as a general purpose technology and its innovations in economic research. *International Journal of Computer Science and Information Technologies*, *5*(1), 22–34. DOI: 10.62051/ijcsit.v5n1.03

Wheeler, A. (2017). *Designing brand identity: an essential guide for the whole branding team*. John Wiley & Sons.

Widyaningrum, T., Sholihah, Q., & Haryono, B. S. (2024). The Delone and McLean Information System Success Model: Investigating User Satisfaction in Learning Management System. *Journal of Education Technology*, *8*(1), 86–94. DOI: 10.23887/jet.v8i1.71080

Williams, S. D. (2020). A textual analysis of racial considerations in human resource analytics vendors' marketing. *Management Research and Practice*, *12*(4), 49–63.

Wilson, A. V., & Bellezza, S. (2022). Consumer Minimalism. *The Journal of Consumer Research*, *48*(5), 796–816. DOI: 10.1093/jcr/ucab038

Wirtz, J., Patterson, P., Kunz, W., Gruber, T., Lu, V., Paluch, S., & Martins, A. (2018). Brave new world: Service robots in the frontline. *Journal of Service Management*, *29*(5), 907–931. Advance online publication. DOI: 10.1108/JOSM-04-2018-0119

Wylde, V., Rawindaran, N., Lawrence, J., Balasubramanian, R., Prakash, E., Jayal, A., Khan, I., Hewage, C., & Platts, J. (2022). Cybersecurity, Data Privacy and Blockchain: A Review. *SN Computer Science*, *3*(2), 127. DOI: 10.1007/s42979-022-01020-4

Xia, S., Zhou, Y., Wang, Z., He, Q., & Parry, G. (2026). Enhancing green innovation through university–industry collaboration and artificial intelligence: Insights from regional innovation systems in China. The Journal of technology transfer, 51(2), 653-681. https://doi.org/10.1007/s10961-025-10232-8, DOI: 10.1007/s10961-025-10232-8

Xiao, Q., Yan, J., & Bamber, G. J. (2025). How does AI-enabled HR analytics influence employee resilience: Job crafting as a mediator and HRM system strength as a moderator. *Personnel Review*, *54*(3), 824–843. DOI: 10.1108/PR-03-2023-0198

Xu, Y., & Huang, J.-S. (2015). Factors Influencing Cart Abandonment in the Online Shopping Process. *Social Behavior and Personality*, *43*(10), 1617–1627. DOI: 10.2224/sbp.2015.43.10.1617

Yang, C., Chen, X., Liu, L., & Sweetser, P. (2021). Leveraging semantic features for recommendation: Sentence-level emotion analysis. *Information Processing & Management*, *58*(3), 102543. DOI: 10.1016/j.ipm.2021.102543

Yang, S. (2023). The power of immersive technologies: A sociopsychological analysis of the relationship between immersive environments, storytelling, sentiment, and the impact on user experience. DOI: 10.5451/UNIBAS-EP96067

Yanxia, C., Shijia, Z., & Yuyang, X. (2024). A meta-analysis of the effect of chatbot anthropomorphism on the customer journey. *Marketing Intelligence & Planning*, *42*(1), 1–22. DOI: 10.1108/MIP-03-2023-0103

Yao, S., Tan, J., Chen, X., Zhang, J., Zeng, X., & Yang, K. (2022). ReprBERT: Distilling BERT to an Efficient Representation-Based Relevance Model for E-Commerce. *Proceedings of the 28th ACM SIGKDD Conference on Knowledge Discovery and Data Mining*, 4363–4371. DOI: 10.1145/3534678.3539090

Yau, K., Saad, N., & Chong, Y.-W. (2021). Artificial Intelligence Marketing (AIM) for enhancing customer relationships. *Applied Sciences (Basel, Switzerland)*, *11*(18), 8562. Advance online publication. DOI: 10.3390/app11188562

Yu, C., Zhang, Z., Lin, Y., & Wu, Y. (2025a). Trust–risk duality in AI-mediated purchase decisions: The role of content quality and platform accountability. *Journal of Retailing and Consumer Services*, *76*, 103608.

Yu, T., Pan, Y., & Jang, W. (2025b). Modeling Consumer Reactions to AI-Generated Content on E-Commerce Platforms: A Trust–Risk Dual Pathway Framework with Ethical and Platform Responsibility Moderators. *Journal of Theoretical and Applied Electronic Commerce Research*, *20*(4), 257. DOI: 10.3390/jtaer20040257

Yu, X., Xu, S., & Ashton, M. (2023). Antecedents and outcomes of artificial intelligence adoption and application in the workplace: The socio-technical system theory perspective. *Information Technology & People*, *36*(1), 454–474. DOI: 10.1108/ITP-04-2021-0254

Zaman, K. (2022). Transformation of marketing decisions through artificial intelligence and digital marketing. *Journal of Marketing Strategies*, *4*(2), 353–364. DOI: 10.52633/jms.v4i2.210

Zhan, X., Xu, Y., & Liu, Y. (2024). Personalized UI Layout Generation using Deep Learning: An Adaptive Interface Design Approach for Enhanced User Experience. *Journal of Artificial Intelligence General Science (JAIGS) ISSN:3006-4023*, *6*(1), 463–478. DOI: 10.60087/jaigs.v6i1.270

Zhang, O., Lin, H., Zhang, X., Wang, X., Wu, Z., Ye, Q., Zhao, W., Wang, J., Ying, K., Kang, Y., & Hsieh, C. Y. (2025). Graph neural networks in modern AI-aided drug discovery. *Chemical Reviews*, *125*(20), 10001–10103. DOI: 10.1021/acs.chemrev.4c00213

Zhang, Q. (2026). *The Theoretical Evolution of Integrated Marketing Communications Over Three Decades : From Communication Integration to Brand Integration Origins and Early Theories of Integrated Marketing Communications* (Issue Icedbc 2025). Atlantis Press International BV. DOI: 10.2991/978-94-6239-604-3

Zhang, Y., Ding, Z., Sun, J., Zhao, X., Hu, X., & Yang, Z. (2025). Optimizing AI strategies in e-commerce customer service: An agent-based simulation. *Electronic Markets*, *35*(1), 77. Advance online publication. DOI: 10.1007/s12525-025-00821-8

Zhou, Y., Wang, L. J., & Chen, W. S. (2023). The dark side of AI enabled HRM on employees based on AI algorithmic features. *Journal of Organizational Change Management*, *36*(7), 1222–1241. DOI: 10.1108/JOCM-10-2022-0308

Zhuang, Y., Wu, F., Chen, C., & Pan, Y. (2017). Challenges and opportunities: From big data to knowledge in AI 2.0. *Frontiers of Information Technology & Electronic Engineering*, *18*(1), 3–14. DOI: 10.1631/FITEE.1601883

Zhu, Y., Yuan, H., Wang, S., Liu, J., Liu, W., Deng, C., Chen, H., Liu, Z., Dou, Z., & Wen, J.-R. (2025). Large language models for information retrieval: A survey. *ACM Transactions on Information Systems*, *44*(1), 12. Advance online publication. DOI: 10.1145/3748304

Zierau, N., Hildebrand, C., Bergner, A., Busquet, F., Schmitt, A., & Leimeister, J. M. (2023). Voice bots on the frontline. *Journal of the Academy of Marketing Science*, *51*(4), 823–842. DOI: 10.1007/s11747-022-00868-5

Zuo, Y., Wu, M., & Shen, L. (2024). GUGEN: Global user graph enhanced network for spatio-temporal point-of-interest recommendation. *IEEE Transactions on Knowledge and Data Engineering*, *36*(4), 1845–1858. DOI: 10.1109/TKDE.2023.3314561

About the Contributors

Muhammad Abdus Salam, known professionally as Dr. Salam Shadhin, is an award-winning academic and researcher. He is an Assistant Professor of Management Information Systems (MIS) at Noakhali Science and Technology University (NSTU). His research interests encompass topics related to Artificial Intelligence; Digital Literacy; Technology Transformation; Human-Computer Interaction; Generative AI, Deepfake, and Emerging Technologies; AI Ethics, Trust, and Governance; Sustainability, Green AI, and Digital Responsibility; and Technology in Consumer Culture and Societal Change. His research advances understanding of artificial intelligence and emerging technologies from commercial, social, and ethical perspectives, emphasizing real-world industry needs, responsible governance, digital literacy, community engagement, and sustainable innovation. His work highlights how the strategic design and deployment of AI and emerging technologies can enhance human–technology interaction, foster consumer trust, and generate transformative value across markets and society. He was awarded the "Best Paper Award" at the 4th International Conference on Business, Economics, and Finance (ICBEF 2023) held at Universiti Brunei Darussalam, "Best Extended Abstract Award" at the 9th World Business Ethics Forum (WBEF 2025) hosted by City University of Macau, as well as the "PhD Colloquium Award 2025," and "Best PhD Colloquium Award 2026" organized by the UBD School of Business and Economics (UBDSBE). Dr. Muhammad Abdus Salam earned his PhD from the UBD School of Business and Economics, an AACSB-accredited business school at Universiti Brunei Darussalam. He has published widely in scholarly journals and proceedings and coauthored several books through broad international research collaborations. Additionally, he provides expert commentary on technology and development in interviews with television channels and newspapers, and authors articles for both newspapers and scholarly periodicals. He has held the role of Tutor for multiple academic modules at the UBDSBE. He completed his Bachelor of Business Administration (BBA) and Master of Business Administration (MBA) from the University of Dhaka. He has presented research insights at numerous national and international conferences, seminars, and symposia. Dr. Salam Shadhin has served as a moderator and chair for many international conferences, while also playing a vital role as a member of several conference committees. He serves as an expert reviewer for scholarly work, including journals such as Journal of Health Organization and Management, Journal of Advanced Transportation, Cogent Business & Management, Discover Global Society, and Discover Psychology, as well as for numerous books published by Springer, Wiley, Emerald, Elsevier, IGI Global, Sage, and Taylor & Francis.

Vai Shiem Leong is a Senior Assistant Professor at the UBD School of Business and Economics, Universiti Brunei Darussalam. She received her PhD in Marketing from the University of Nottingham, United Kingdom. Her primary research interests lie in marketing communication and service marketing. She has authored papers published in reputed journals, like Journal of Services Marketing, International Journal of Advertising, International Journal of Quality and Service Sciences, Journal of Consumer Behaviour, and more.

Nazlida Muhamad received her Phd in Marketing from The University of Western Australia in 1999. She has taught marketing modules in Malaysian, Saudi and Australian public universities, prior to working at UBD. Her research interests and publications are in the area of consumer behavior -with special interest on issues pertaining to Islam, and its role on Muslim consumer behaviors in the marketplace. Among others, her works are published in Psychology and Marketing, Journal of Islamic Marketing, Journal of Business and Policy Research, and Journal of computer-mediated communication.

***

Sadia Akter is a Master's student in Business Administration specializing in Management Information Systems at International American University, Los Angeles, California, USA. With a strong interest in Information Systems, Emerging Technologies, AI, Cybersecurity, and Machine Learning, she is dedicated to exploring the intersection of technology and business. Sadia is passionate about leveraging cutting-edge technologies to solve real-world challenges, particularly in the fields of data security and automation. Her work aims to contribute to advancements in these domains and drive innovation within the technology sector.

Md. Sobhan Ali is a Lecturer in Accounting and Information Systems at Begum Rokeya University, Rangpur, Bangladesh. He completed his BBA and

MBA from the University of Dhaka and has more than ten years of teaching experience, including service in private universities and the Bangladesh Civil Service (Education Cadre).His research interests include taxation, Environmental, Social, and Governance (ESG) issues, corporate governance, and gender diversity on boards and audit committees. He has published several research articles in indexed international journals, including Scopus-listed journals. In recognition of his scholarly contributions, he received the ICMAB Research Excellence Award 2025. He is actively engaged in teaching, research, academic writing, and scholarly discussion.

Kundan Sagar Bedmutha is an undergraduate student pursuing a Bachelor of Technology in Artificial Intelligence and Data Science at Vishwakarma University, India, and is expected to graduate in 2027. His academic interests focus on Artificial Intelligence, Machine Learning, Data Science, and Computer Science. He has actively worked on projects involving AI-driven decision support systems, intelligent web-based applications, predictive modeling, and data analytics. His areas of interest include AI commercialization frameworks, intelligent personalization systems, and applied machine learning for real-world problem solving. He is particularly interested in bridging theoretical AI concepts with practical system implementation and scalable software architectures.

Mohammad Rakibul Islam Bhuiyan is now working as Assistant Professor at Management Information Systems department in the Begum Rokeya University, Rangpur since September 2025. He completed his BBA and MBA from the University of Dhaka in Management Information Systems Department. He was working as Lecturer at Khaja Yunus Ali University in Sirajgonj for 1.5 years. He has also worked as Lecturer in MIS at School of Business at Uttara University in Bangladesh. He also worked as a research assistant, project research associate, teaching assistant and has many notable contributions in different research aspects. His research interest topic is including Digital Economy, Cashless Society, Cashless Economy, Digital Transformation, Emerging Technologies, E-wallet and so on. I have been reviewed more than 255 peer reviews and published more than 45 publications including article,conference paper, book chapter, technical paper, reports in national and international level.

Dickson K.W. Chiu is included in the Stanford's 2025 Top 2% Scientists List (Career-long and Single-year Impact). He received the B.Sc. (Hons.) degree in Computer Studies from the University of Hong Kong in 1987. He received the M.Sc. (1994) and Ph.D. (2000) degrees in Computer Science from the Hong Kong University of Science and Technology (HKUST). He started his own computer consulting company while studying part-time. He has also taught at several universities in Hong Kong. His teaching and research interests are in Library & Information Management, Service Computing, and E-learning, with a cross-disciplinary approach involving library and information management, e-learning, e-business, service sciences, and databases. The results have been widely published in over 400 international publications (most of them have been indexed by SCIE, SSCI, Scopus, and EI, such as top journals MIS Quarterly, Computer & Education, Government Information Quarterly, Decision Support Systems, Information Sciences, Knowledge-Based Systems, Expert Systems with Application, Information Systems Frontiers, IEEE Transactions, including many taught master and undergraduate project results and 20 edited books. He received a Best Paper Award at the 37th Hawaii International Conference on System Sciences in 2004. He served as an Editor(-in-chief) of Library Hi Tech, a prestigious journal. He is the founding Editor-in-Chief of Library, Information & Services, a Senior Editor of the Journal of Organizational Computing and Electronic Commerce (SCIE), and the Editor-in-Chief Emeritus of the International Journal on Systems and Service-Oriented Engineering (founding) and the International Journal of Organizational and Collective Intelligence. He serves on the editorial boards of several international journals. He co-founded several international workshops and co-edited many journal special issues. He also served as a program committee member for over 300 international conferences and workshops. Dr. Chiu is a Senior Member of both the ACM and the IEEE and a life member of the Hong Kong Computer Society. According to Google Scholar, he has over 11,000 citations, an h-index of 58, and an i-10 index over 220, ranking him worldwide first in the fields of "m-learning" and "e-services."

Tasfia Afrin Faria is working as a lecturer at Uttara University,Dhaka in Department of Business Administration. She completed her BBA and MBA from Jahangirnagar University in the Department of Marketing. She has experience in the teaching and research sector for more than 1 year. She has published a few articles and has conference papers. Her research interest topic is including digital marketing, tourism, consumer behavior, and sustainable marketing practices.

Jannatul Ferdousi is a researcher in artificial intelligence and business analytics, currently pursuing a Master of Science in Artificial Intelligence with a specialization in Data Analytics at Indiana Wesleyan University, United States. Her research focuses on AI-driven decision support systems, human–AI collaboration, and data-driven organizational performance. She has contributed to academic publications in areas including business analytics, financial decision-making, and marketing intelligence. Her work examines how artificial intelligence can enhance managerial decision-making, improve operational efficiency, and support sustainable competitive advantage in modern organizations. Her research interests also include AI ethics, data privacy, and intelligent systems, reflecting a multidisciplinary approach that integrates technology with business strategy. She aims to develop practical AI-driven solutions that support organizational resilience and informed decision-making in dynamic environments.

Hasanuzzaman is a PhD Candidate at the Department of Business Administration at the International Islamic University Malaysia. He is also the co-founder of The Halal Marketing School, bridging scholarly research with industry practice. Previously, he served as Assistant Manager at Amorino UK Gelato Ltd., in the UK, as Manager of Digital Marketing at Career Paths, and Senior Executive of Digital Marketing at LifeSpring in Bangladesh. He obtained his MSc in Marketing Management from the University of Chester, UK, as a recipient of the University of Chester with Merit Studentship. He also earned a Bachelor of Business Administration (BBA) in Marketing, with a second major in Economics, from United International University, Bangladesh, graduating with First-Class Honours and receiving a full scholarship for his outstanding academic performance. His research interests include Digital marketing, Halal Marketing, AI-driven digital marketing, Social media marketing, Branding and the integration of practical industry insights into marketing pedagogy. Email: hasanuzzaman.1712@gmail.com

Taha Husain excelled in his secondary education in 2011 and went on to earn his Bachelor's and Master's degrees in Social Science, specializing in Peace and Conflict Studies from Dhaka University. His dedication to research is evident through his publication of over 47 research papers across various social science disciplines. He is working as assistant professor at the Department of Gender and Development Studies at Begum Rokeya University, Rangpur, Taha Husain has been imparting knowledge and inspiring future generations with his expertise in human rights, war studies, international relations, political thought, and more. His research interest includes political ecology and women's rights in Bangladesh.

Md Mominul Islam is an Assistant Professor of Marketing at the School of Business, International University of Business Agriculture and Technology (IUBAT). Previously, he served as a faculty member at BGMEA University of Fashion & Technology (BUFT) and Darul Ihsan University. He also worked in the housekeeping services department at Scandic Hotels in Sweden. Notably, he collaborates closely with the Bangladesh-Malaysia Chamber of Commerce and Industry on fostering the halal economy and halal certification. He obtained his PhD from the School of Business and Economics, Universiti Brunei Darussalam, under the prestigious

Graduate Scholarship. He also earned an MSc in Business and Economics from the Swedish University of Agricultural Sciences under a Swedish government scholarship, as well as an MBA and BBA in Marketing from the University of Rajshahi. His research interests include Islamic marketing, Islamic entrepreneurship, halal certification, sustainable marketing, halal cosmetics, spiritual and halal tourism, halal supply chain management, and marketing pedagogies. His scholarly works have been published in the Journal of Islamic Marketing, International Journal of Islamic Accounting and Business Research, International Journal of Islamic Marketing and Branding, International Journal of Religious Tourism and Pilgrimage, International Journal of Internet Marketing and Advertising, International Journal of Hospitality and Event Management, as well as by Springer, IGI Global, Emerald and Edward Elgar Publishing, USA. Md Mominul Islam was also the recipient of The Bangladesh Education Leadership Awards 2017".]

Waziha Islam is a graduate student at Noakhali Science and Technology University, has dedicated four years to academic research, contributing to multiple projects. Her expertise was recognized with the Best Presenter Award at the International Conference on Embracing Industry 4.0 for Sustainable Business Growth in 2024. Her research interests include technology adoption, cashless tourism, technology adoption in tourism, and smart tourism.

Rajkumar Jagdale is an Assistant Professor and Head of the Department of Computer Science at the Faculty of Science and Technology, Vishwakarma University, Pune. He earned his Ph.D. in Computer Science and IT from Dr. Babasaheb Ambedkar Marathwada University, Chh. Sambhajinagar, Maharashtra, India.With over six years of teaching and research experience, complemented by two years in the industry as Data Scientist, Dr. Jagdale specializes in Sentiment Analysis, Opinion Mining, Text Mining, ML, Big Data Analytics, and RPA. He has made significant academic contributions, with 13 publications in reputable international journals and conferences, and holds one patent related to his research. Dr. Jagdale's work has received notable recognition, including prestigious scholarships such as the JASSO Scholarship to attend a Spring School on "Smart Materials and AI" at Tokushima University, Japan, and the DST Inspire Fellowship from the Department of Science and Technology, Government of India. Additionally, he was awarded a Gold Medal for his exemplary performance in the M.Sc. Computer Science program. He reviewed conference papers and journals and He is member of CSI, ISCA and IAENG.

Satish Kumar is currently working as a professor in the Department of Management Studies at G L Bajaj Institute of Technology and Management, Greater

Noida. Prior to this, he worked as Professor and Dean in school of commerce and management, IIMT university meerut for 6 years and 2 months. He has also worked as Director of the Dewan Institute of management studies,Meerut during the period (2014-18) and Director of the Viday School of Business (2010-14), and He has more than 25 years of experience in the fields of academics, research, and industry. He has also worked as the IQAC coordinator at the IIMT University. Recently, he has received an award from IIMT University for his exemplary contribution in conducting IIC activities effectively and securing the highest four-star rating in IIC 2021-22 for the university, as declared by MHRD, India. Recently, he was appointed as a member of the National Education Committee' set up by the PHD Chamber of Commerce and Industry, New Delhi, in January 2023. He is an alumnus of MJP Rohilkhand University, Bareilly, having a doctorate in business administration. He completed his Master in Business Administration from Dr. B. R. Ambedkar University, Agra, and qualified for the NET Management in June 1998. He played a key role in initiating the Vidya International Journal of Management Research and was the chief coordinator of the AICTE-sponsored Industry Institute Partnership Cell (IIPC). He is the recipient of the Best Teachers Award from the Confederation of Education Excellence, New Delhi (2014), the Best Teacher Award from the International Association of Lions Clubs, Lions Clubs of Meerut Industrial Estate, Meerut (2012), and the "Award of Excellence" from H.E. the Government of Haryana, Dr. A. R. Kidwai (2007). He has guided two doctoral candidates. He has published six patents, one copyright, six books, book chapters in various books, and more than 60 research papers in national and international journals of repute. He has attended various workshops on financial research at the IIM Kolkata, IIM, Bangalore, and IMT Ghaziabad. He is also a member of AIMA, AIMS, YJMA. He has resource persons in various faculty development programs across the country. He has organised 16 national seminars (3 AICTE-sponsored) and 12 faculty development programs in the past. Dr.Satish Kumar Professor, Department of Management Studies, G L Bajaj Institute of Technology and Management Greater Noida ORCID ID:0000-0001-6071-0109

Arkarup Kundu is a B.Tech student in Computer Science and Engineering at the Institute of Engineering and Management, Kolkata(School of University of Engineering and Management, Kolkata), India. His areas of interest include Data Analytics, Machine Learning, and Artificial Intelligence. He has developed projects in predictive analytics and is passionate about solving real-world problems using data-driven approaches.

Apple Hiu Ching LAM obtained her degree of Bachelor of Business Administration (Honors) in International Business from City University of Hong

Kong (2016) and her Master of Science in Library and Information Management with distinction from the University of Hong Kong (2020). She is a doctoral candidate in Education at the University of Hong Kong. Her current research interests are social media in libraries, user education, and the 5E Instructional Model.

Xianting Ma, a master student in Library and Information Management (Information Management stream), The University of Hong Kong. Her research interests center on human–AI interaction, user information behavior, and computational social science. She is interested in how analytical insights can inform the design and adoption of AI systems in commercial settings.

Golam Mehadi is a Bachelor of Business Administration (BBA) student majoring in Management Information Systems (MIS) at Begum Rokeya University, Rangpur, Bangladesh. His academic interests focus on the intersection of digital technologies, organizational systems, and workforce transformation, with particular emphasis on human–AI interaction, technology-enabled decision-making, and information systems strategy. He has engaged in academic writing and research-oriented coursework related to business analytics, information systems, and emerging technologies in service industries. His current work explores frameworks for integrating artificial intelligence into frontline operations to enhance productivity, efficiency, and human-centered service delivery.

Afsana Mimi is currently working as a lecturer in the Department of Management Information Systems (MIS) at Begum Rokeya University, Rangpur. She served as a former lecturer at the Business Administration department, Faculty of Business and Entrepreneurship, Daffodil International University (DIU). She has completed her BBA & MBA from department of Management Information Systems, University of Dhaka. Her teaching focuses on MIS and ICT, areas in which she specializes. Her primary research interests include information systems, information technology, e-commerce, and data analytics.

Md. Soleman Mollik is a lecturer at the Department of Business Administration in Marketing, Faculty of Business Studies, Bangladesh University of Professionals, Mirpur Cantonment, Dhaka-1216, Bangladesh. He completed his MBA and BBA in Marketing from the Department of Marketing, University of Rajshahi, Bangladesh. His research interests include the contemporary issues of marketing, service marketing, digital tourism and hospitality marketing, Islamic marketing, and sustainable marketing. He has published his research works in several journals including the Geojournal of Tourism and Geosites (Scopus indexed, Q3), the International Journal of Services and Operations Management, Interscience Publisher (Forthcoming), (Scopus indexed, Q3), the International Journal of Religious Tourism and Pilgrimage (Forthcoming), Technological University, Dublin, UK (Scopus indexed, Q1) the Global Journal of Management and Business Research, Journal of Business Studies (Pabna University of Science and Technology), and the Journal of integrated marketing communications and digital marketing. He received "Dean's Award" from the University of Rajshahi in the year of 2018 for his first position at MBA in the batch. His contact addresses include email ID solemanmollik1993@gmail.com and cell: +8801742643740.

Sakshi Narula has been working as an Assistant Professor at Chandigarh University, Mohali, Punjab (India) for more than 2 years. With 10.5 years of experience at Dav College, Phillaur, Jalandhar.

Md Ferdaus Ahmed Pranto is presently teaching in the Department of Tourism and Hospitality Management (THM) in The People's University of Bangladesh (PUB), Dhaka. He pursued his MBA and BBA from department of Tourism and Hospitality Management, Islamic University, Bangladesh. The area of his teaching is tourism, hospitality management, and sustainable tourism. The main areas of his studies are senior tourism development, sustainable tourism, digital transformation in the hospitality industry, and tourism policy and management.

Md. Rakibul Hafiz Khan Rakib is an Assistant Professor of Marketing at Begum Rokeya University, Rangpur-5404, Bangladesh. He has almost ten years of teaching experience at the University level. His areas of interest in teaching and research include Marketing, Tourism and Hospitality Marketing, Sustainable Tourism, and Sustainable Entrepreneurship Development. He authored more than 25 articles, book chapters and books published in top-tier journals, and edited books, and conference proceedings.

Promit Roy is a bachelor student in the Department of Tourism and Hospitality Management (THM) at Rangamati Science and Technology University (RMSTU). The area of interest in colonial tourism, digital transformation in tourism and hospitality, sustainable tourism development, and the emerging technology in the tourism industry.

Susmitha Sajja is a technology professional specializing in Data Center Automation at Amazon. Affiliated with the University of Missouri–Kansas City, her work spans the intersection of artificial intelligence, automation, and intelligent decision-making systems. She has contributed research to the areas of human-AI interaction and AI-driven supply chain and logistics optimization, with a focus on bridging theoretical advancements with practical, large-scale enterprise applications.

Abdullah Sheikh is a data analytics and supply chain operations professional based in the United States. He holds a Master's degree in Marketing Analytics and Insights from Wright State University. His research interests include artificial intelligence, predictive analytics, supply chain optimization, and data-driven decision support systems.

Index

Symbols

A

B

C

D

www.ingramcontent.com/pod-product-compliance
Lightning Source LLC
LaVergne TN
LVHW061531290926
849162LV00004B/748